Organizational and End-User Interactions:
New Explorations

Steve Clarke
Hull University Business School, UK

Ashish Dwivedi
Hull University Business School, UK

Information Science
REFERENCE

Senior Editorial Director:	Kristin Klinger
Director of Book Publications:	Julia Mosemann
Editorial Director:	Lindsay Johnston
Acquisitions Editor:	Erika Carter
Development Editor:	Mike Killian
Production Coordinator:	Jamie Snavely
Typesetters:	Jennifer Romanchak and Michael Brehm
Cover Design:	Nick Newcomer

Published in the United States of America by
Information Science Reference (an imprint of IGI Global)
701 E. Chocolate Avenue
Hershey PA 17033
Tel: 717-533-8845
Fax: 717-533-8661
E-mail: cust@igi-global.com
Web site: http://www.igi-global.com/reference

Library of Congress Cataloging-in-Publication Data

Organizational and end-user interactions : new explorations / Steve Clarke and Ashish Dwivedi, editors.
p. cm.
Includes bibliographical references and index.
Summary: "This book provides a comprehensive look at studies that show a significant contribution in EUC by relating organizational and end user computing to organizational and end user performance and productivity, strategic and competitive advantage, and electronic commerce"--Provided by publisher.
ISBN 978-1-60960-577-3 (hardcover) -- ISBN 978-1-60960-578-0 (ebook) 1. Electronic commerce. 2. End-user computing. I. Clarke, Steve, 1950- II. Dwivedi, Ashish N.
HF5548.32.O744 2011
381`.142--dc22

2011009955

British Cataloguing in Publication Data
A Cataloguing in Publication record for this book is available from the British Library.

Table of Contents

Detailed Table of Contents

access to in sourced data on applications level. An authentication to end-user proposed in this article is a simple three level ticket request model solution in an open distributed environment. We also develop an analytical password for the proposed mechanism and validate this approach through experiment. Furthermore, we explore this approach to end user authentication and demonstrate the conception of a textual password which in many cases improves the security. We analyze Deffie-Hellman exchange weakness and present how it can be made robust against attacks. Our approach is based on the use of the Kerberos authentication technique and the Diffie-Hellman Key exchange.

One important aspect of consumer relationships is trust. Conducting business on the Web is relatively new compared to traditional business and many of the factors related to consumer trust related to the Web remained unexplored. To increase our understanding about trust building on the Internet, this article studies trust with a focus on its relationship to Web design characteristics, specifically perceived quality of presentation, perceived ease of navigation, and several user attributes: prior internet experience, Web users' self efficacy, and gender differences. A research model is proposed that builds upon prior research on trust. A survey is developed based on the constructs and relationships in the model. The data analysis and results confirm five out of eight of the hypotheses associated with the model. Theoretical and practical implications are provided.

The behavioral and dynamic implications of an ERP deployment are, to say the least, not well understood. Getting the switches set to enable the ERP software to go live is tedious. But the difficult part is understanding all of the dynamic interactions that accrue as a consequence. Connectionist and causal models are proposed in this article to facilitate an understanding of the dynamics and to enable control of the information-enhanced processes to take place. The connectionist model facilitates the understanding of the dynamic behavioral implications of the larger ERP implementation installation per se. The underlying connectionist model will observe and detect information transfers and workflow. Once maps of the total infrastructure are determined by the models, an analyst can suggest improvements. The models become decision support aids for process analysts in situations where ideal process flows/information transfers are sought.

Studies of information technology (IT) use have focused on numerous antecedents to behavioral intent to use. Although some antecedents (such as subjective norms) reflect aspects of the organizational environment, most antecedents reflect beliefs or attitudes about the technology itself. Using TAM, social exchange theory, and social information processing theories as conceptual bases, we posit that general beliefs about the organizational environment influence IT use on the job. Specifically, we propose that affective commitment, autonomy, and team member trust will directly influence behavioral intent to use IT. However, TAM variables (perceived usefulness, subjective norm, and perceived ease of use) will mediate the effects of organizational variables on behavioral intent to use IT. The results provide initial evidence that organizational variables are related to behavioral intent to use IT, but only when IT is perceived to be useful, and subjective norms favor its use. We suggest that when introducing IT, managers need to pay attention not only to technology-related issues, but also to the broader organizational environment in which IT will be used. Implications for researchers and practitioners are offered.

While the number of employees who primarily use computers to complete their work increases, a significant subset of those employees simply do not enjoy computer work. This dislike has an influence on work-related outcomes like perceived technology overload and job satisfaction. It is important to examine how work-related support from either supervisors or coworkers can minimize/buffer the negative outcomes related to an individual's disliking computer work. Using a sample of 225 workers from a range of businesses and industries, we investigated the influence of facilitating conditions on liking computer work. The results show that liking computer work is positively related to job satisfaction, and supervisor support helps moderate the relationships between liking computer work and the outcomes of job satisfaction and technology work overload. Implications for research and practice and directions for future research are offered.

can info*m managers as they evaluate proposals for and implementation plans of new information systems in their organizations.

Preface

Welcome to the latest annual volume of Advances in End-User Computing (EUC). This will be my fourth volume as Editor-in-Chief, and I am delighted to be joined in this task by my colleague, Ashish Dwivedi.

Since my editorship began with contributions written in 2007, Ashish and I felt that it would be an opportune time to conduct a retrospective of the Advances Series over the past three plus years, and from that to look at the direction the domain of End-User Computing is taking, and some likely topics of interest for the future.

Perhaps the most striking fact stemming from an analysis of past issues is the sheer range of topics covered by the contributed chapters. Nevertheless, it is possible to draw some conclusions regarding trends in EUC, using this publication as a guide.

Topics consistently represented during the period include ethics, training and ease of use, the internet, and group dynamics related to computing. Perhaps none of this is particularly surprising, but it would seem that certain conclusions might be drawn from the *under representation* of certain topics, from which we have chosen two domains for further analysis in this section. User involvement is poorly represented (only one specific article in the period) for such a key subject, and it would be encouraging if this were to improve. Users are subject to actions which bring into conflict the needs / characteristics of human actors and the demands of technology, and the wealth of research in this area looks to be a fertile ground for future exploration in the EUC domain. Secondly, computer security is, curiously, not well represented. Our own suspicion is that many practitioners and researchers explicitly or implicitly dismiss this as a technical domain, to be addressed through virus checkers and firewalls. In our view this is an impoverished perception, and there is extensive scope for the investigation of human activity as it impacts EUC security.

On the flip side of this under representation, there are some topics which have been researched and reported extensively in these volumes. Issues related to Knowledge Management (KM), for which there were no chapters at all four years ago, have seen eight appear in the following three years. Design and development of end user systems have, perhaps unsurprisingly, consistently appeared, and a wide range of these issues has been covered. Technology acceptance has also been well reported, both from the perspective of technology acceptance models, and in the more general sense of user acceptance of end user systems.

Given this situation, we thought it would be interesting to look at possible future directions for some of the topics which we view as important for the future of OEUC. We stress that this is very much a personal view, informed from our own research interests, but we hope you will find these worthwhile, and we have attempted to adhere to the volume aim (as contained within the title) of providing "New Explorations" in "Organizational and End-User Interactions".

Figure 1. Descriptive model of user involvement

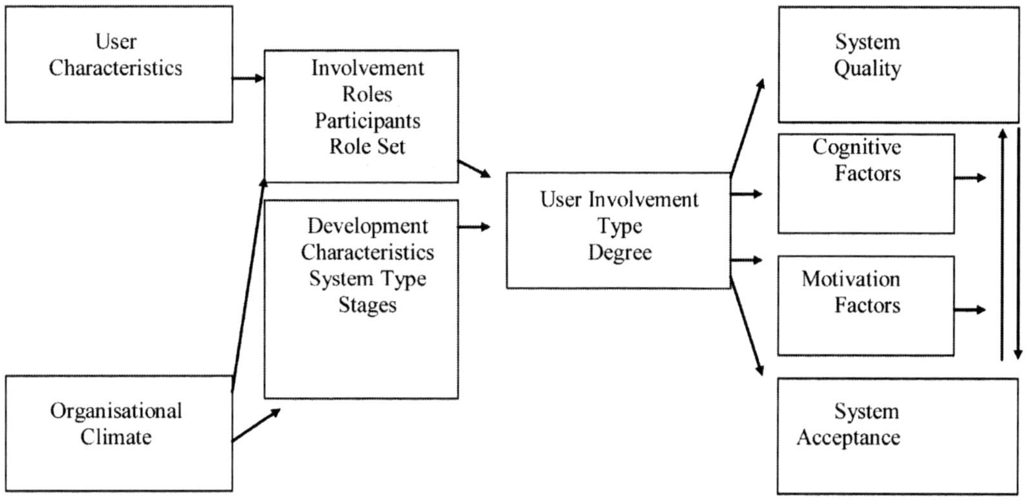

USER INVOLVEMENT AND INFORMATION SYSTEMS SUCCESS

To begin with, we want to look at some of the issues related to user involvement. It is common in studies of information systems (IS) success to see reference to the necessity for user involvement. Justification for this varies from the rights of end users to be involved in systems development, through a "common sense" notion that systems improvement must result, to "proof" of success resulting from the users' input to the development process. User involvement research focuses on two outcome variables: system quality and system acceptance. But underlying these are the more complex issues of cognitive and motivational factors which give rise to improved quality or improved acceptance.

As long ago as 1984, Ives and Olson suggested a model of user involvement (Figure 1) which illustrates the relevant issues. Their research, interestingly, did not support the belief that user involvement improves the success of computer based information systems. In their extensive review of user involvement studies, few show a strong correlation between involvement and success, and even where such a correlation appears, the link is too weak to be of statistical significance. Having said this, Ives and Olson believe there to be theoretical evidence to support the "common sense notion" of user involvement being important. Their view is that difficulties are caused by lack of rigor in research rather than in the evidence not being available.

This weakness in the empirical evidence is echoed by other researchers, leading to a possible conclusion that IS user involvement research suffers from the lack of a solid conceptual foundation. Interestingly a review of the involvement literature in psychology, marketing and organisational behaviour revealed that researchers in such disciplines have also gone through a period of struggle before achieving conceptual clarity.

Since publication of the Ives and Olsen research, there has been extensive *pragmatic* analysis of the user in IS, supported by the strong practical predilection towards the belief that user participation is essential to the success of systems, and utilising both quantitative and qualitative methods. There seems little doubt that *users* agree that in determining the success of the development project, user attitude toward system development is an important factor. Such an attitude can be seen in a willingness or otherwise to participate in development and implementation, and the factors that may cause the users to avoid participation need to be reviewed. These factors include senior management behaviour, from full support to unwillingness to spend, complaints about cost, corporate culture and organisational politics, and user background and personality.

Causes of user dissatisfaction with information systems are said to include autocratic management, lack of communication before implementation, lack of consultation with users in design and implementation, fear of job losses, lack of training and so on. The issue, however, is not whether user dissatisfaction exists, but what is the effect of such dissatisfaction on the success of the system.

For some, the view that improved system implementation will result from increased user involvement can be ultimately traced to behavioural theory, and in particular the theories of participative decision making and planned organisational change. Participative decision making (PDM) is expected to yield the benefits of increased job satisfaction, increased user acceptance, and improved productivity, by such factors as:

- Providing a more complete assessment of user requirements.
- Providing expertise about the organisation the system is to support.
- Avoiding the development of unacceptable or unnecessary features.
- Improving user understanding.
- Developing realistic expectations about system capabilities.
- Providing an arena for bargaining and conflict resolution about design issues.
- Improving system ownership by users.
- Decreasing user resistance to change.
- Committing users to the system.

So we have a number of suggestions as to how PDM is going to improve systems development and implementation. But two major factors are said to affect the success of participation. Firstly, who should be involved in the development: suggestions include affected parties; top level management; and the actual manager receiving the project. Secondly, the development conditions, in particular what type of system is being developed. For example, with highly technical systems involvement may be wholly inappropriate; and similarly, where systems are clearly defined and have set goals or objectives system quality may not be improved by user involvement.

The other important factor to consider in the development process is that user involvement may not be relevant at all stages, and it may be important to choose the stage at which involvement is applied. One idea is that we regard groups as either consultative, representative, or consensus. This can be taken further by looking at the degree of involvement of users, ranging from no involvement, through involvement by advice, to involvement by doing, where users are members of the design team, to involvement by strong control, where users pay directly for development from their own budgets.

On balance, the lack of confirmation from published studies should not be regarded as evidence that involvement has no effect on ultimate system success, rather it is suggested that the studies themselves are at fault. The need for involvement is stressed by many MIS practitioners, and in the absence of strong theoretical support the "common sense" view that involvement can lead to more acceptable or higher quality systems prevails. Care needs to be taken, however, in deciding who should be involved, at what stages of development, and how the involvement should be carried out - the type and degree. This decision is largely dependent on organisational climate and the type of system being developed.

Information Security

Computer security is, curiously, not well represented within recent Advances in EUC volumes. Our own suspicion, as mentioned earlier, is that many practitioners and researchers explicitly or implicitly dismiss this as a technical domain, to be addressed through virus checkers and firewalls. In our view this leaves extensive scope for the investigation of human activity as it impacts EUC security.

Currently, information security aims primarily to protect information and to ensure it is available to those authorised to access it. What we hope to make clear in this section is that such an approach has led to a practice which constrains rather than enables end users.

One well established definition of Information Security can be found in the US Department of Defense 'Orange Book' (DOD 1985:3)

In general, secure systems will control, through use of specific security features, access to information such that only properly authorised individuals, or processes operating on their behalf, will have access to read, write, create, or delete information.

Another, more widespread and perhaps broader definition can be found in UK Government publications, for example the Communications-Electronics Security Group, the British Standard for Information Security Management (ISO 2000; BSI 2002), and in the documentation and practice within a large number of organisations who have adopted information security practices. That definition concerns the *Confidentiality, Integrity and Availability* (CIA) of information.

In the United Kingdom, the source of this can be traced to the early 1990s, when a group of security professionals formed a committee under the auspices of the British Standards Institute, and with the support of the UK Government's Department of Trade and Industry, to document current 'best information security practice' based on the current experience, knowledge and practice of those contributing. The product of this effort was the Code of Practice for Information Security Management. The committee continued to work towards maintaining and improving the code of practice, and today it has developed into the British Standard for information security (ISO 2000; BSI 2002). The same committee continues to maintain and revise this Standard. During the various iterations, Part 1 of the Standard has been accepted by the International Organization for Standardization, commonly known as ISO, as an international standard, ISO-17799.

Part 1 of the Standard (ISO 2000) is a code of practice which contains around 130 controls to be considered and implemented. Part 2 (BSI 2002) contains the same number of controls but *specifies* their use and is therefore auditable. Both parts of the Standard provide guidance for the development and implementation of a risk-based management system that allows the continued assessment and management of risks. This is delivered through an Information Security Management System (ISMS) that incorporates a cycle which, in essence, compiles a list of the 130 controls and determines whether the absence, or inadequate implementation of these controls is likely to harm the organisation and if so, by how much. Proper management of risks and correct implementation of applicable controls can attract certification to the Standard and the right to use the British Standard kite mark to signify appropriate management of information security.

Whilst the British Standard is not the only approach to Information Security, all of the other key techniques have been reviewed during our research, and a comparison of the British Standard with other available models does nothing to alter the above picture.

Moving from the Standard to current information security literature, a similar pattern emerges of a domain that includes some broad risk-based theory and becomes progressively more specific and technically biased over time, although with some excursions into business and human centred domains. How successful these human centred excursions have been is unclear as they typically focus on superficial ethical issues such as data privacy, and how to get people to accept the required information security practice. Business-aligned literature tends towards the attainment of resources to maintain the security practice rather than a true attempt to align security with business objectives. In terms of quantity of literature there is a massive bias towards technical and operational controls within the domain. In fairness, as technology continues to evolve there is an almost continual need to update the technical security literature base to keep pace. However, this does not adequately explain the relative absence of social literature within what is essentially a domain that radically affects users and how they are expected to behave.

So, through a detailed examination of the British Standard and an extensive review of available information security literature a model has emerged which clearly shows a domain which is dominated by a set of practical controls which are seen as rigid, unclear and largely irrelevant to the business needs of most organisations. What has become clear, even within some recent developments that have sought to provide a more accessible model for managing information such as information assurance, is that all current practice is centric around the needs of the technology and of information rather than the needs of people in general and users in particular. Where human or end user issues are explored in this domain, it is to confer responsibilities and education on people to conform to the needs of the system and to regulate their behaviour.

What emerges then is a domain which is to all intents and purposes technological and operational, as proven by the absence of sufficient consideration for human issues; and a domain dominated by pragmatism as demonstrated by the way in which the principle models in the domain were constructed and are maintained.

But what are the user issues, and how might we best address them? Figure 2 gives some idea of the complexity here.

In terms of user involvement, it is clear that one outcome of an effective implementation of an information security system will be to either reinforce or modify the behaviours of people; to either bring about change or to resist change; and to determine whether external factors are desirable or undesirable. If the behaviours of a person or group of people is considered desirable then the information security system will seek to recognise and reinforce that behaviour, and if the behaviours are considered undesirable then the system will seek to modify those behaviours. Likewise, if a change is either proposed or taking place that is desirable then the system will embrace that change, if the change is undesirable then the system would resist it. If the environment is acceptable and there are no visible opportunities to improve security, then the system would seek to maintain the current position. If the environment is unacceptable then the system will seek to positively change the current position.

It has been argued that the current information security domain can be best represented as a technical practice, with scant regard to human (end user) or social needs. The comparison of social and technical and theoretical and practical issues in Figure 3 forms a link from the factors seen to be most relevant to Information Security to those relating to end users. Information Security is a domain which has hitherto been dominated by technologically–biased, operationally–focused, pragmatic controls. Deeper research

Figure 2. The complexity of information security

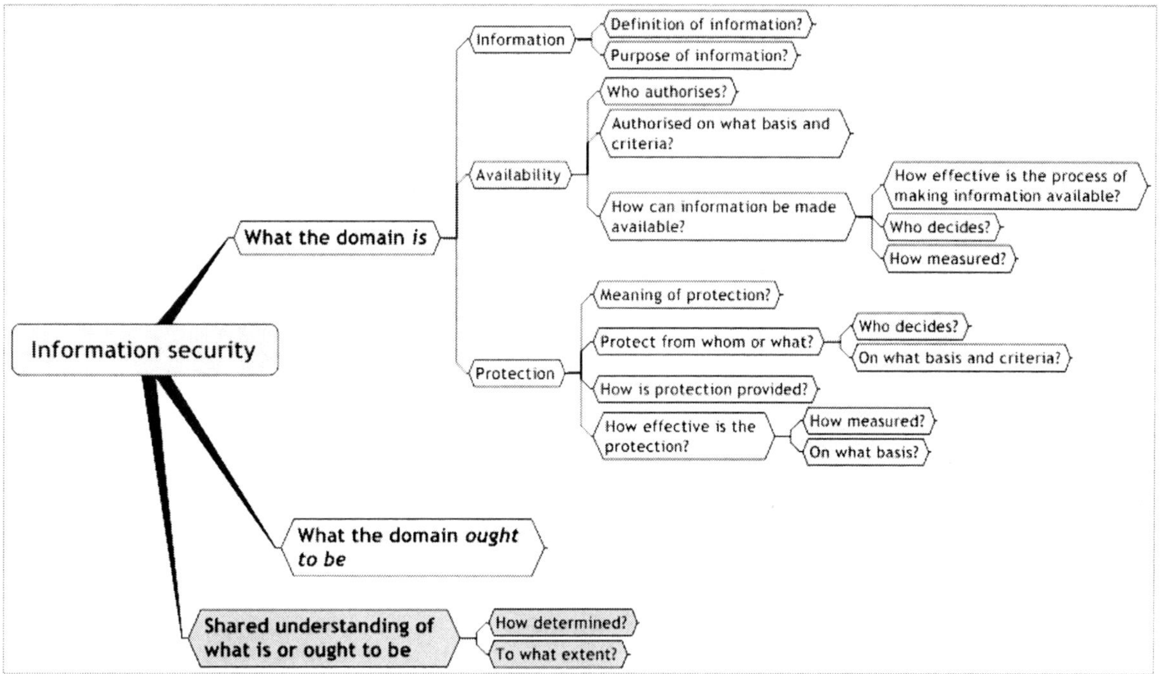

of the domain is revealing a set of largely ignored considerations, in respect of which more human-centred methods are proving of value.

The approach adopted in this section gains its credibility from an explicit basis in social theory. Shortcomings in one of the key standard approaches to Information Security, and in the application of Information Security within a large organisation, have further improved our understanding of how strategies can best be derived and managed to address user issues in this domain. Information Security emerges as a domain dominated by pragmatic, technology-based methods. By acceding to these methods, both the British Standard and industrial practice has favoured a short-term, operationalist approach, in which human factors are seen as largely external to the Information Security 'system'.

Knowledge Management Systems

As with other issues in this paper, knowledge management (KM) can be argued from a human-centred perspective. Figure 4 views KM and knowledge acquisition generally as a product of human activity, where people in interaction acquire and manage knowledge

All of this may be made sense of through systems theory, and Table 1 shows how the properties of a (human activity or knowledge) system are enabled by elements of organisational structure or technology.

Knowledge Management has been defined by some as the extraction and conversion of 'tacit' knowledge on an individual and organisational level into 'explicit' knowledge. Further, it is argued, this explicit knowledge often takes the form of specific electronic 'tools' or 'assets' which can be manipulated for competitive gain, examples being intranets, groupware and knowledge repositories. 'Tacit' knowl-

Figure 3. Theoretical vs. practical and social vs. technical comparison grid

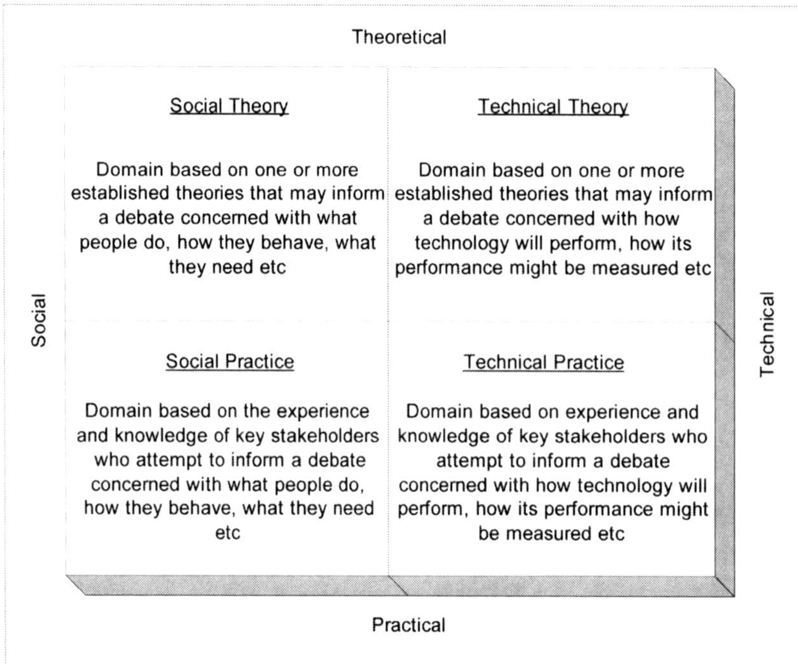

edge, by contrast, is often described as the 'hunches, intuition and know-how' of people, or their 'skills, routines and competencies'. The aim of KM as regards tacit knowledge might be seen as an attempt to make this often highly subjective knowledge explicit, thereby facilitating its management through such enabling media as technology.

Additionally, a number of studies have called for a more holistic, systemic approach to KM. One such example is the division into the 'know-why, know-what, know-who, know-how' questions of KM. Know-how might be seen as technologically focused, know-who as socially constructed and depending on processes of debate, whilst know-why and know-what relate to issues of power and coercion in societal structures.

Finally, there are numerous classifications which aim to demystify KM. We feel that two taxonomies of knowledge detailed below offer a systemic approach towards classification of knowledge, and consequently can aid in demystifying KM.

POLANYI'S TAXONOMY OF KNOWLEDGE

A number of leading management theorists have affirmed that the Hungarian chemist, economist and philosopher Michael Polanyi was among the earliest theorists to have popularised the concept of characterising knowledge as tacit or explicit. This is now recognised as the de-facto knowledge categorisation approach (Beijerse, 1999; Gupta, Iyer and Aronson, 2000; Hansen, Nohria, and Tierney, 1999; Nonaka, 1988; Nonaka and Konno, 1998; Zack, 1999). Explicit knowledge typically takes the form of company documents and is easily available whilst Tacit knowledge is subjective and cognitive. The cornerstone

Figure 4. The nature of knowledge management systems

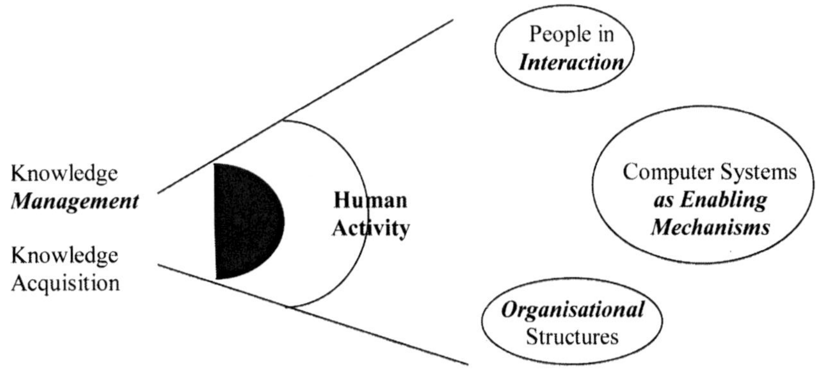

of any KM project is to transform tacit knowledge into explicit knowledge so as to allow its effective dissemination (Gupta, Iyer and Aronson, 2000).

Nonaka and Konno (1998) have also substantiated Polanyi's contention that there are two kinds of knowledge: explicit knowledge and tacit knowledge. They add that there are significant differences between the way these two kinds of knowledge are viewed in the western and the eastern-based management entities. Western management organisations lay more emphasis on explicit knowledge as it is more recognised and scientifically organised. Eastern management entities and in particular Japanese firms "view knowledge as being primarily tacit, something not easily visible and expressible" (Nonaka and Konno, 1998, pp.42). They also mention that whilst there are two dimensions of tacit knowledge: (1) technical, (2) cognitive, it is the cognitive dimension that moulds the manner in which we perceive the information available to us. This supports the notion raised earlier that creation of knowledge requires human insight.

Zack (1999) also affirms that tacit knowledge is not easily expressed, as we comprehend tacit knowledge at a subconscious level. Explicit knowledge, conversely is more precisely and formally articulated, although removed from the original context creation or use. This definition of explicit knowledge brings to light an important feature of explicit knowledge: that the knowledge passed on is not original.

An analogy can be drawn between explicit knowledge and secondary data. Explicit knowledge can never be like primary data: (i.e. based upon a new concept, which has not been validated). Explicit knowledge has to be based upon real life experiences, which have already taken place. Another distinguishing feature of tacit knowledge is that it is often based upon first hand experiences that others have gone through. The transfer component of tacit knowledge comes into effect when it is disseminated. When dissemination is carried out in written format (manuals etc), tacit knowledge becomes explicit knowledge.

According to Davenport and Prusak (1998) personal knowledge is the outcome of an intellectual process which includes an individuals' personal experiences, values and sagacity. Organisational knowledge refers to the codified knowledge that is present in organisational storage (document repositories etc) and communication mediums (organisational practices and norms).

Table 1. Systems of Knowledge Management

	Implications for Knowledge Management		
		Enabling Mechanisms: Designed Physical Systems	
System Property	**Human Activity Systems**	**Structure**	**Technology**
Boundary	The limits of that which can be known	The organisation, or relevant part of it	Bounded technological sub-systems which enable the whole system of Knowledge Management to function more effectively
Emergence	Emergent properties of a knowledge system: e.g. decision making	Structure and technology must be seen in terms of their contribution to the emergent properties of the whole KM system	
Holism	Encompasses technical, human (cognitive and social), and organisational factors	Must not be viewed in isolation, but only as part of the whole KM system	
Interdependence	Changes in part of the system (e.g. human knowledge acquisition) effect changes in other parts (e.g. the use of enabling technologies)	Technology, organisation, and human activity working together are the source of success in any KM system	
Hierarchy	As human beings we see structures in knowledge systems (hence the data structures in computerised systems)	Organisational structures help facilitate human knowledge acquisition and sharing	Technologies support the organisation and/or human actors
Transformation	The acquisition of knowledge always leads to changes, which may be perceived in organisational terms as transformation processes	The key in transformation achieved through Knowledge Management: technology and structure are enablers	
Communication and Control	These are fundamental to knowledge systems, and once more require understanding of the interactions between human, technical, and organisational issues	Used as aids to communication and control in the overall KM system	

Blackler Taxonomy of Knowledge

Blackler (1995, pp.1021) has reiterated that the concept of knowledge is complex and, in an organisational context, its relevance to organisation theory has as yet not been sufficiently understood and documented. He further argues that this is one of the fundamental reasons why KM does not have a widely accepted framework which can assist organisations in KM systems. He has identified five main categories of knowledge: embrained, embodied, encultured, embedded and encoded.

- *Embrained knowledge* refers to the knowledge that is dependent on conceptual skills and cognitive abilities. It is also normally associated with scientific knowledge. This kind of knowledge has commanded a high status in western cultures.
- *Embodied knowledge* is rooted in specific contexts and is generally acquired by doing. As such it often said to be action-oriented. It is also assumed to be "partly explicit" as its transmission requires "peoples' physical presence, on sentient and sensory information, physical cues and face-to-face discussions" (Blackler, 1995, pp.1024)
- *Encultured knowledge* is knowledge that is achieved through a process of socialisation or what Blackler calls "shared understandings". The author further mentions that encultured knowledge is strongly dependent on language and is "socially constructed and open to negotiations". As such it would be fair to reflect that encultured knowledge is embedded in the organisations cultural systems.
- *Embedded knowledge* is knowledge "which resides in systemic routines" and which is present in the form of explicit practices and is generally embedded in technology.
- *Encoded knowledge* refers to knowledge that is recorded via signs and symbols, such as books, manuals and codes of practice. In the modern IT age, encoded knowledge has also incorporated electronic forms of knowledge (Blackler, 1995, pp.1025).

Blackler (1995) has noted that the above approach of knowledge categorisation can be problematic. He further mentions that as the concept of knowledge is continuously evolving (as knowledge is continuously being constructed and transformed) it might be more advantageous to focus on the process of knowing. Blackler (1995) views the process of knowing as being mediated, situated, provisional, pragmatic, and contested:

- *Knowing as Mediated*: "New ICT are combining with other developments, such as new economic and organisational structures and new approaches to management to transform the contexts of action". Here the emphasis is on technologies that support an organisation to collaborate whilst ensuring that there is no fundamental loss of control.
- *Knowing as Situated*: Blackler (1995, pp.1041) points out that knowing as situated "emphasises the significance of peoples' interpretations of the contexts within which they act and the key role that 'communities of practitioners' play in the acquisition and development of skill". Herein, Blackler highlights the fact that knowledge is formed primarily through a process of practice and reflection, both of which are based upon group interactions and experiences.
- *Knowing as Provisional*: This refers to the fact that the process of knowledge is essentially continuous and implies that we are not able to develop a complete bank of knowledge (Blackler, 1995).

- *Knowing as Pragmatic*: Advances in ICT are likely to bring about a change in the way people learn and work at the workplace. Current organisational systems are becoming "interrelated and complex" resulting in the failure of traditional approaches in organising knowledge. It is fair to assume that the above would lead to a scenario whereby organisational employees would aim to acquire knowledge which would be driven by a pragmatic aim and purpose such as adjusting to the changes in "work methods and priorities" (Blackler, 1995, pp.1041).
- *Knowing as Contested*: Blackler's (1995, pp.1042) statement that "the concepts of knowledge and power are interrelated" implies that "conflicts are to be expected within and between the new generation of symbolic analysts and problem solvers, and established professionals and managers". Knowledge is formed primarily when we contest our understanding of what we perceive to be knowledge with others. The outcome of this process is that the contested knowledge finally emerges out of the process of knowing, which occurs through dialogue and interaction with others.

Blackler (1995) has reiterated that the concept of knowledge is complex and, in an organisational context, its relevance to organisation theory has not yet been sufficiently understood and documented. This is one of the fundamental reasons why we believe that KM does not have a widely accepted framework that enables organisations to: (a) create KM systems, and (b) a culture conducive to KM practices.

But what does 'managing knowledge' infer from the standpoints discussed in this section (see Figure 5)?

Figure 5. Early Lessons from Philosophy and Theory

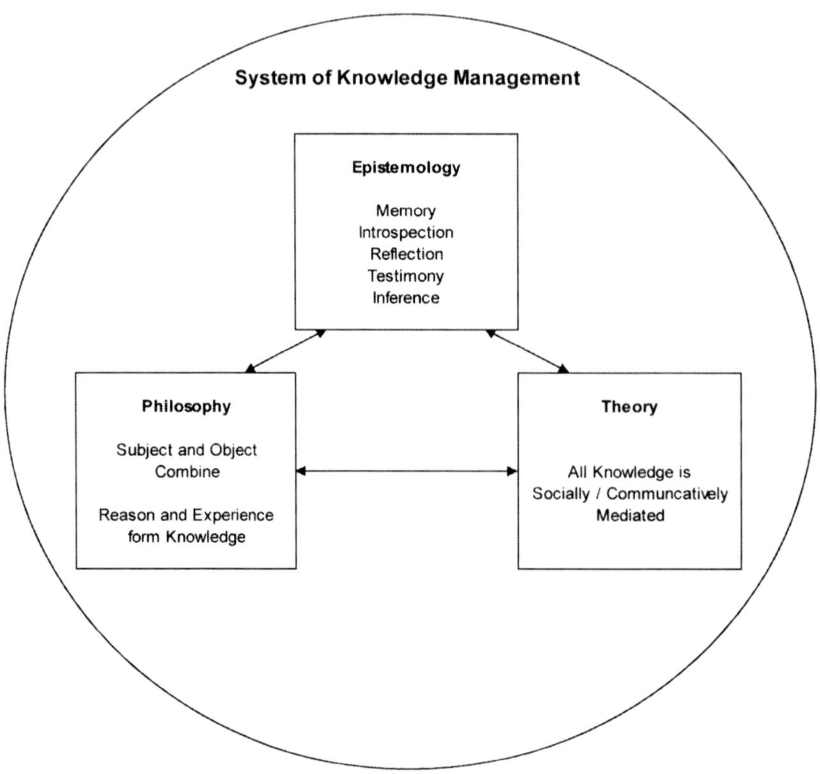

Epistemology, philosophy and theory all have a part to play in determining the elements of a system of Knowledge Management. Epistemology tells us that knowledge derives from perception, memory, introspection, reflection and testimony. It is subject to a priori concepts, and is extended by inference.

In philosophy, from the time of the Greeks, there have existed fundamental arguments regarding knowledge being a search for truth, or for normative agreement. Initially the argument raged between rationalism and empiricism, and one of Kant's unique contributions, through the 'Copernican revolution in philosophy', was to unite subject and object in knowledge production: subject and object, according to Kant, make each other possible.

Theoretically, following the thinking of Habermas, in which can be seen the echoes of Kant, science produces only one form of knowledge – believing all knowledge to be scientific is an 'objectivist illusion'. What Habermas does that is so helpful to us is he sites knowledge as mediated by social action, and subject to reflection, without which we end up with self-referential systems which are in danger of producing 'knowledge' based on disputable 'facts'.

One key element of human interaction is communication, and in so far as this may be oriented toward mutual understanding, it might be argued as the foundation of knowledge creation and sharing. In these terms, knowledge is not reducible (as is so often seen in scientific or pseudo-scientific study) to the properties of an objective world, but can be defined according to the a priori concepts that the knowing subject brings to the act of perception. This knowing subject, being social, mediates all knowledge through social action and experience: subject and object are linked in the acts of cognition and social interaction, and the so-called subjective and objective 'paradigms' may be represented as just a convenient tool for understanding, which has been accorded too much primacy as a form of reality.

Rather, then, than relying on the concept of paradigms, this concept, and particularly the idea of paradigm incommensurability, should be opened up to challenge. Consider the so-called subjective / objective dichotomy. According to the paradigm argument, viewed (say) from an epistemological perspective, one who sees a problem context as positivistic, and seeks, for example, a technological solution, will be unable to communicate and share knowledge with another who views the same problem context as existing in the views and opinions of those participants involved in and affected by the system of concern. There are at least two fundamental difficulties with this:

1. It contradicts common human practice, and, dare it be suggested, common sense. Human participants in social groups commonly combine technical ('positivistic') and interpretative ('anti-positivistic') activity, seemingly denying the paradigm incommensurability thesis from an epistemological standpoint.
2. Theoretically, the paradigm incommensurability view seems to have dubious support. At its most basic level, it derives from the idea that technical, scientific, functionalist activity cannot be conducted together with interpretivistic, subjective activity. But if, theoretically, subjective and objective are inseparable, paradigm incommensurability becomes much less compelling.

In essence, then, it is the argument of this section that these difficulties disappear once a scientific basis for our thinking is denied. For example, suppose science (as is suggested by Kant: 1724-1804; and Habermas: 1929-) is seen as just one form of knowledge, which in any case is simply a convenient human perception of how the world works. Now, all human endeavour becomes mediated through subjective understanding, and the paradigms as impenetrable barriers disappear. So, the problem of interest constitution theory being no longer defensible is resolved, since it is no longer being relied on. However, this problem has been replaced with another, which may be stated as follows:

1. Accepting all human actions as mediated through subjective understanding leads to the possibility of a basis for KM in the universal characteristics of language.
2. The dichotomy between subject and object has gone, and with it, paradigm incommensurability.
3. Organisational intervention is recast as an entirely communicative issue. For example, the so-called technical interest of knowledge constitution theory becomes instead a question of how technology may further enable human interaction, all within a framework of human intercommunication.
4. The difficulty which now arises is essentially a practical one, of how to incorporate these ideas into management practice.

The thinking of Habermas (1976; 1987) on communicative action presents a universal theory of language which suggests that all language is oriented toward three fundamental validity claims: truth, rightness and sincerity. What is most compelling about this theory, however, is that all three validity claims are communicatively mediated. This viewpoint is most radically seen in respect of the truth claim, where it is proposed that such a claim results not from the content of descriptive statements, but from the Wittgenstinian approach casting them as arising in language games which are linked to culture: truth claims are socially contextual.

'Truth', can therefore be assessed by reference to communication. Rightness is about norms of behaviour, which are culturally relevant, and are therefore to be determined by reference to that which is acceptable to those involved and affected in the system of concern as a cultural group. Finally, sincerity is about the speaker's internal world: his/her internal subjectivity.

These ideas can now be taken forward to provide a KM approach, or set of approaches, which are theoretically grounded, and closer to that which is experienced in action. The conclusions below begin this process through design of a critical action framework for KM interventions, based on critical theory.

OEUC and the Internet

This section seeks to offer insights into EUC and the Internet by applying learning from the fields of social theory and information systems to the specific context of the internet. Key to this understanding is the extent to which the *scope* of information systems (IS) analysis is often seen to be problematic: IS 'problems' are frequently 'solved' by redefining organisational and human issues in technical terms, and developing the necessary technical solution. Studies on which this section are based have raised significant questions regarding such approaches, exposing many IS developments as not susceptible to a technical solution, but exhibiting complexities stemming from high levels of human activity. Arguably, such findings are of particular importance in web development and management, depending as it does on the understanding and commitment of users who are often remote from and external to the organisation. A clue to how such complex, human-centered issues may be dealt with is to be found in the scoping of these studies which, in systems terms, implies a need to assess the *system boundary*. Within this section an approach to such boundary setting is described, together with the way in which this may be used to inform user-focused internet development.

Table 3 summarises the issues from social theory in relation to the world-wide web. A functionalist approach sees a set of problems to be solved: objective problems which can be determined indepen-

Table 2. A Critical Action Framework for Knowledge Management

Investigation Of	Investigation Through	Outcome – Knowledge to be Managed
Knowledge as:	Subject and Object investigated through Participative Analysis	"Manage" as a systemic process of participative inquiry
Memory	Tests of Communicative Rationality:	Outcomes in the form of:
Introspection	Truth	Systems Descriptions
Reflection	Rightness	Process
Testimony	Sincerity	Content
Inference		
	Involves Application Of	Leads to Understanding Of
	Methodologies for Problem Context Analysis	Context in which KM is to be Applied
	Methodologies for Participative Analysis	Processes for Knowledge Exchange to be embedded within the organisation
	Critical Method for Tests of Communicative Rationality	Knowledge Explicated to be Recorded for Shared Use
		Knowledge for which dissemination is to be Restricted

The review of KM undertaken in this section indicates the potential for approaches explicitly grounded in critical social theory, and points to a possible future direction through a Critical Action Framework for Knowledge Management (Table 2). Research and practice built on this foundation will, we would suggest, more adequately address issues of users in KM environments.

dently of any human viewpoint. In web design this describes a technological, expert-informed approach, where the views of users are seen to be secondary. Through interpretivism, the web is understood as a social, subjective phenomenon, in which the views and opinions of participants become fundamental to its understanding.

From a radical humanist, or critical social perspective, the view of IS as functionalist, 'hard', problem solving, is seen to be an impoverished one, over-focused on the use of computer technology. 'Soft' methodologies have been pursued as a solution to this problem, and have been to some extent successful. But recent thinking questions the ability of 'hard' and 'soft' approaches to achieve the agenda they apparently set out for themselves, and points to a need to combine approaches under the radical humanist umbrella. Issues of particular relevance in this respect to web management are determination of the scope, or boundaries, of the system, and, given the boundaries, choice of development, implementation, and management methodologies.

A typical approach to web design, implementation and management, is represented (Figure 6) by the primary boundary. The information to be included is often at best from an expert group, and most of the activity takes place between designers and managers, with system users cast in a passive role.

But such an approach largely ignores the wider user issues, under which users become an active part of the system.

Table 3. Social Theory and the World Wide Web

Radical Humanist	Interpretative	Functionalist
The web as a social construction, but now introducing a need to ensure inclusion of those involved and affected to challenge authoritative views.	Web management and usafe seen to be a social interpretation. Technical (functionalist) issues serve only to enable the social interaction.	Web management and usage as a technical problem to be solved by experts

Figure 6. Critique of the System Boundary

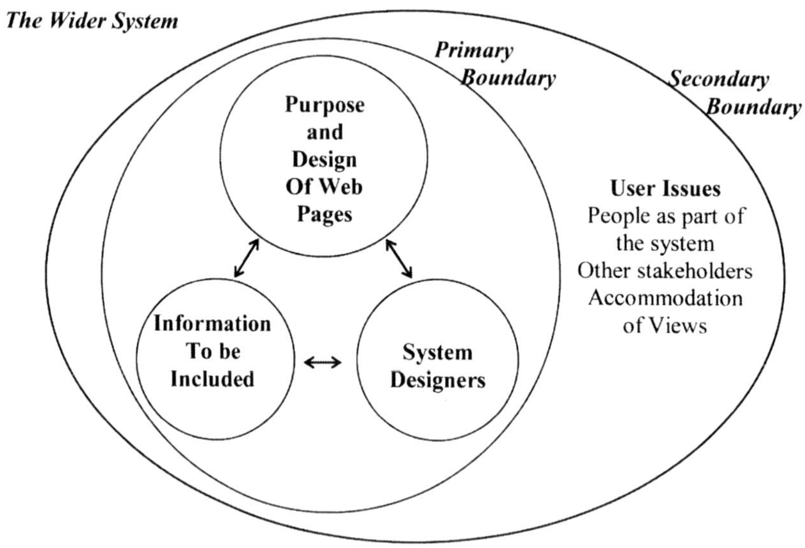

Critical boundary setting, focusing on the normative system definition, has further enhanced this study. Just as a structured approach tends to focus on technical issues, so a concentration on 'what is' tends to lead to a belief that there is only one accurate perception of the system of concern. A critical approach to boundary judgements has opened up a wider consideration of 'what ought to be' in web management, including those involved and affected as participants with whom expertise is seen to reside. The richness this has brought to 'user analysis' within the web systems domain contrasts with the simplicity with which this part of a web-based intervention is normally undertaken.

Our position in relation to the approach taken is embryonic, and it offers many challenges which have not as yet been addressed by me or other practitioners and theorists. To progress this, we feel concentration now needs to be on web developments in which users are actively involved in the whole process.

Arguments about whether to use a hard or soft methodology, and which hard or soft methodology to use, in web development, implementation and management, seem to offer only a limited perception of this problem. A critical social view gives a richer image. Web-based systems are not per se computer systems, but are systems of human activity, consequently, functionalist science or interpretative sociology appear an inadequate basis on which to study them, a wider critical social context seeming more relevant.

We hope that this brief review, and our ideas regarding some of the key domains in EUC, have proved interesting to you. If they inspire you to contribute in the future we will have our reward.

Finally, as always, we hope that you, as researchers, educators, and professionals in the domain, find something to enhance your understanding within the content of this volume, and, more particularly, that you enjoy reading about them.

Steve Clarke
Hull University Business School, UK

Ashish Dwivedi
Hull University Business School, UK

REFERENCES

Beijerse, P. R. (1999). Questions in knowledge management: defining and conceptualising a phenomenon. *Journal of Knowledge Management*, *3*(2), 94–109. doi:10.1108/13673279910275512

Blackler, F. (1995). Knowledge, knowledge work and organizations: An overview and interpretation. *Organization Studies*, *16*(6), 1021–1046. doi:10.1177/017084069501600605

BSI. (2002). *BS7799-2:2002. Information Security Management*. Specification With Guidance For Use, British Standards Institute.

CESG (1994). CESG Electronic Information Systems Security: System Security Policies. Memorandum No.5.

Davenport, T., & Prusak, L. (1998). *Working Knowledge: How organizations manage what they know*. Boston: Harvard Business School Press.

DOD. (1985). *DoD Trusted Computer System Evaluation Criteria (The Orange Book)*. DOD 5200.28-STD. United States Department of Defense.

Gupta, B., Iyer, L. S., & Aronson, J. E. (2000). Knowledge management: practices and challenges. *Industrial Management & Data Systems*, *100*(1), 17–21. doi:10.1108/02635570010273018

Habermas, J. (1976). On Systematically Distorted Communication. *Inquiry*, *13*, 205–218. doi:10.1080/00201747008601590

Habermas, J. (1987). *Lifeworld and System: A Critique of Functionalist Reason*. Boston, Mass: Beacon Press.

Hansen, M. T., Nohria, N., & Tierney, T. (1999). What's your strategy for managing knowledge? *Harvard Business Review*, *77*(2), 106–116.

ISO. (2000). *BS ISO/IEC 17799:2000, BS7799-1:2000. Information Technology*. Code of Practice For Information Security Management, International Standards Organisation.

Ives, B., & Olsen, M. (1984). User Involvement and MIS Success: A Review of Research. *Management Science*, *30*(5), 586–603. doi:10.1287/mnsc.30.5.586

Nonaka, I. (1988). *The Knowledge-Creating Company. Harvard Business Review on Knowledge Management* (pp. 21–45). Boston, MA: Harvard Business School Press.

Nonaka, I., & Konno, N. (1998). The concept of "ba":Building a foundation for knowledge creation. *California Management Review, 40*(3), pp - 40-54.

Zack, M. H. (1999). Managing codified knowledge. *Sloan Management Review*, *40*(4), 45–58.

Section 1

Chapter 1
The Impacts of Brand Equity, Security, and Personalization on Trust Processes in an E-Commerce Environment: An Updated Discussion

Catharina Stoecklin-Serino
Florida State University, USA

David Paradice
Florida State University, USA

Robert E. Hooker
Florida State University, USA

ABSTRACT

This research broadens the study of trust as it applies to developing stable relationships in electronic environments. Prior studies have investigated many aspects of trust, but few have looked at its incremental development. Previous empirical research identifies antecedents to initial perceptions of trust that may influence the progression of trust to deeper levels. More conceptual work identifies antecedents that swiftly cultivate trust, allowing for stable relationships to develop more quickly. The antecedents investigated in this study, using regression and structural equation modeling, are the use of security symbols, trustworthy brand names, and personalization techniques. The results of the study indicate that the use of security symbols and trustworthy brand names have a positive and lasting effect on trusting beliefs and that personalization has a decreasing and lasting effect on trusting beliefs. There was no support for the hypothesis that trust develops over time in electronic environments.

DOI: 10.4018/978-1-60960-577-3.ch001

INTRODUCTION

Electronic commerce is a notably difficult environment in which to display trustworthy behaviors. This environment offers limited personal interaction and minimal support to develop and maintain trusting relationships (Coursaris et al., 2003). Researchers have proposed that stable and trusting relationships are swiftly formed by parties (Meyerson et al., 1996) and factors have been identified that increase initial trust in electronic commerce environments (Gefen, 2000; McKnight et al., 2002). However, longitudinal studies to identify whether these factors are stable influences of trust and continue to increase trust after initial interactions are very limited in these areas.

When exploring previous research in electronic commerce and trust, several questions emerge. These questions are:

Do institutional structures, brand names, and personalization techniques influence calculus-based trust and the formation of knowledge-based and identification-based trusts?

Do individuals change their behavior as they develop deeper levels of trust?

Does trust develop in an electronic environment beginning with calculus-based trust, then progressing to knowledge-based trust, and finally to identification-based trust?

This study answers these questions.

Three methods are used to swiftly develop trust. These methods include the presence of security symbols, use of trustworthy brand names, and personalization techniques. We posit that using trustworthy brand names and security emblems enhances a consumer's initial trust and contributes (longitudinally) to the swift development of deeper types of trusts. This study also investigates whether brand names or institutional structures enhance trust more effectively. Additionally, we examine the use of personalization to encourage the swift formation of trust.

LITERATURE REVIEW

There are various definitions of trust proposed in the literature, all similar to the extent that they define trust as the willingness to act based on a state of confidence about another party's motives and the degree of risk involved with acting. This state of confidence is usually influenced through interactions with the other party that are reliable, predictable, and benevolent (Mayer et al., 1995).

The bases for confidence about another person's motives are different depending on the disciplinary field. Social psychologists theorize that trust is based on the person's perceived control over his/her environment (Rotter et al., 1968), and self-confidence factors (Lillibridge & Lundstedt, 1967). Sociologists indicate that the religious affiliation, ethnicity, birth order, and the economic level of a person influence his/her ability to trust (Rotter, 1971). Economic researchers believe trust is derived from a process of assessing the risks and rewards of entering into a transaction (Williamson, 1993). Marketing researchers have found that a supplier's reputation, support, and competence affect the supplier's trustworthiness (Anderson & Weitz, 1989). Management researchers indicate that repeated and honest interactions influence trustworthiness (Gulati, 1995). Researchers in management information systems have shown that familiarity and the presence of institutional structures are also antecedents of trust (Gefen, 2000; McKnight et al., 2002).

Integrative Model: Calculus, Knowledge, and Identification-Based Trust

Clearly, disciplines have unique perspectives on trust formation. However, two integrative studies by Shapiro et al. (1992) and Lewicki and Bunker

(1996) propose that there are three foundations for trust: calculation, knowledge, and identification.

Calculus-based trust originates from the theory of transaction cost economics (Williamson, 1993). According to this theory, any person will behave opportunistically whenever it is profitable and feasible. Examples of opportunistic behavior are withholding information, shirking, or failing to fulfill promises or obligations. Calculus-based trust is formed by evaluating the possibility that the other party will adopt these opportunistic behaviors (Shapiro et al., 1992; Williamson, 1993).

Knowledge-based (or cognition-based) trust is a process where people choose whom they trust based on evidence of trustworthiness (Lewis & Weigert, 1985). There are several nuances of knowledge-based trust (Shapiro et al., 1992). First, information influences one's ability to predict opportunistic behavior. Second, additional information improves one's knowledge, improving the accuracy of the prediction. Third, increasing the frequency or length of interactions between parties also fosters trust. Regular and frequent communications assists parties in identifying with one another and improves their ability to think alike. If parties are unable to identify with one another after frequent and regular communications, their ability to predict one another's behavior will dissolve, and trust between the parties will also deteriorate.

Identification-based trust is a process where trust is built through "genuine care and concern for the welfare of partners, belief in the intrinsic virtue of the relationship, and belief that these sentiments are reciprocated" (McAllister, 1995). With identification-based trust, parties understand one another and subsequently are able to anticipate one another's needs and wants. Over time, parties with identification-based trust develop a mutual understanding of one another and are able to act on each other's behalf. Since parties with identification-based trust act as agents or substitutes for one another in transactions, monitoring of the relationship is not required (Deutsch, 1958). This "acting for another," builds knowledge and identification of the other party, and thus enhances understanding and identification-based trust.

Disposition to Trust

Another antecedent to trust is a person's disposition to trust (Luhmann, 1979), which affects how he or she views humanity and perceives the likelihood of opportunistic behavior (Rotter, 1971). A disposition to trust is different from other bases of trust in that it is not specific to a party or environment. It is a more permanent characteristic, influenced by early childhood experiences as well as socialization factors (Fukuyama, 1995). Strong bonds with one's caregiver increase a person's disposition to trust. Other factors such as birth order, social economic level, and religious affiliation change a person's social structure and subsequently, their disposition to trust (Rotter, 1971).

A high or low disposition to trust limits a person's ability to assess the risk of interacting in an environment, determining his/her behaviors and subsequent rewards or costs (Luhmann, 1979). A person with a high disposition to trust typically under predicts the risk of interacting in an environment and subsequently exhibits vulnerable behavior. On the other hand, a person having a low disposition to trust is more likely to over predict the risk of interacting in an environment and circumvent a positive experience or opportunity.

Institutional-Based Trust and Familiarity

In the MIS literature, researchers have created two other bases of trust: institutional-based trust and familiarity (Gefen, 2000; McKnight et al., 2002). Institutional-based trust is a concept derived from sociology and is similar to the concepts of knowledge-based and calculus-based trusts. Institutional-based trust differs in that it is developed through the presence of legal structures or familiar formats. It has been shown to increase trust in an electronic commerce environment through the presence of structures such as encryption and familiar Web interfaces (McKnight et al., 1998; 2002). There are two categories of institutional-based trust: structural assurance and situational normality (Zucker, 1986). Structural assurance is the presence of legal protections such as guarantees (Zucker, 1986; Shapiro, 1987) as well as technological protections like data encryption (McKnight et al., 2002). Researchers indicate that the presence of these structures lower perceptions of risk. Situational normality reflects an environment that is structured in a customary way using common interface designs and functions (McKnight et al., 2002). Familiarity builds trust by creating structures of norms and meanings that help form expectations of anticipated behavior and explanations of what the behavior means (Weick, 1995).

Conceptual Studies of Variance Theories

Variance models of trust posit that one determines trustworthiness based on cognitive, affective, and behavioral factors (Mayer et al., 1995; McAllister, 1995; McKnight et al., 1998; 2002). There have been several conceptual studies that have presented variance models of trust.

Ring and Van de Ven (1994) produced one of the first conceptual models of trust in their study of inter-organizational relationships (IOR). They indicate that trust between individuals of different organizations is achieved when both perceive one another's interactions as efficient and equitable. When individuals of different organizations begin to trust one another, their need for legal structures to support the relationship is reduced. Likewise, monitoring costs and transaction costs are decreased for both organizations.

Mayer et al. (1995) created an integrative model of trust containing four factors from the fields of sociology, management, and psychology. Three of the factors, ability, benevolence, and integrity, relate to perceived trustworthiness. The fourth factor, disposition to trust, is based on socialization factors. McKnight et al. (1998) extended this model to assess the antecedents of initial trust in an electronic commerce environment. They theorize that both dispositional trust and institutional structures increase trust. They relate the theory of reasoned action (TRA) to the trusting process and posit that trusting beliefs lead to trusting intentions, which later develop into trusting behavior.

Empirical Studies of Variance Theories

McAllister (1995) empirically tested the relationships between potential antecedents of affect-based and cognitive-based trusts. He indicated but did not empirically test that cognitive-based trust must be established before affect-based trust can develop. Three factors, peer role performance, cultural similarity, and professional credentials were tested as predictors of cognitive-based trust with none of these factors producing significant relationships.

Zaheer et al. (1998) looked at 107 buyer-supplier relationships and found that interpersonal and organizational trusts are related but distinctly different constructs. They found support for Ring and Van de Ven's (1994) conceptual model, showing that institutional structures provide a mechanism for building trust and reducing transaction costs.

Cannon and Doney (1997), on the other hand, looked at how trust develops in a commercial exchange relationship. They tested five processes as antecedents for trust: calculation (Williamson, 1993; Dasgupta, 2000), prediction (Deutsch, 1958; Lewicki & Bunker, 1995), intentionality (Rempel & Holmes, 1986), capability (Barber, 1983; Butler & Cantrell, 1984), and transference (Granovetter, 1985). Surveying 210 members of the National Association of Purchasing Management, they found empirical support for their model.

Gefen (2000), using Luhmann's (1979) concept of familiarity, tested another conceptual model of trust. He found that both familiarity and dispositional factors influence trust in an electronic commerce environment. He also found that trust strongly influences a customer's behavior. The disposition to trust construct was a stronger predictor than familiarity in influencing trusting beliefs. However, familiarity more accurately predicted the customer's decision to inquire about and purchase books.

McKnight et al. (2002) found empirical support for an early conceptual model (McKnight et al., 1998). Using an electronic commerce environment, they found that both institutional structures (e.g., security icons) and dispositional factors were antecedents to trusting beliefs.

Conceptual Studies of Process Theories

Process models of trust posit that trust changes over time (Lewicki & Bunker, 1996). A relationship begins with calculus-based activities. If these activities develop in a manner that confirms the other party is consistent, deterrence is not necessary and the parties begin to collect information about one another's needs. Information seeking represents the foundation of knowledge-based trust. However, not all relationships are able to evolve past calculus-based trust. One reason is that the parties do not require more trust in their relationship. A second reason is their interdependence is already highly regulated. A third reason is that they already have enough information about one another. Lastly, one or more violations of calculus-based trust may have occurred.

The movement from knowledge-based to identification-based trust occurs as parties begin to know one another and begin to identify strongly with one another's needs, preferences, and priorities, leading them to see them as their own. Identification leads to a search for more information, which creates a foundation for identification-based trust and more dimensions where the parties can identify with one another. Identification-based trust requires a great deal of time and energy, and many successful relationships do not require identification-based trust in their interactions. If parties have a desire to learn more about one another and want a closer relationship, they will move from knowledge-based trust to identification-based trust.

Meyerson et al. (1996) posit that trust can be achieved quickly by changing factors in the environment, the nature of interactions, and behaviors of the parties. They suggest that trust evolves more swiftly when parties behave in a more personal manner and have a reputation for acting in a trustworthy way. Additionally, the swift development of trust is achieved when interactions between the parties do not increase one party's vulnerability.

Empirical Studies of Process Theories

Ba et al. (2003) tested Lewicki and Bunker's (1995) process model of trust using an electronic commerce environment. Taking a game theoretic approach, they showed support for Lewicki and Bunker's model. Although they limit their study to the development of calculus-based trust, their analytical results demonstrate that when online transactions take place with the assistance of digital certificates issued by a trusted third party, the most utilitarian course of action for a market participant is to behave honestly. This represents the only known empirical study validating a process model of trust.

Brand Equity

A consumer's trust for a product or service can be enhanced when the brand equity of the product or service is increased (Aaker, 1996; 2000; Aaker, 1997; Chaudhuri & Holbrook, 2001). Brand equity is defined as the assets and liabilities associated with a brand name (Aaker, 1996; 2000). These assets and liabilities can be grouped into four dimensions: brand awareness, perceived quality, brand associations, and brand loyalty.

Brand awareness is the strength of a brand's presence on the consumer's mind (Aaker, 2000). The ability for a person to recognize or recall the brand name or associate the brand as the only brand in a product category is indicative of how familiar it is. A brand's perceived quality, defined as how many consumers view the product as being reliable (Aaker, 1996; 2000), is the only factor that drives the financial performance of the brand. Brand associations are the relations that consumers associate with a brand. These associations may include a product's attributes, celebrity spokespersons, or symbols used in advertising. Brand loyalty is a measure of how many consumers generate predictable sales. Brand loyalty affects the marketing costs of the product. It is always more expensive to market to new consumers than to a loyal customer base.

Some of the dimensions of brand equity can be applied to new brands. For example, a brand name based on familiar and pleasant words increases brand awareness and associates the brand name with positive feelings (Peterson & Ross, 1972). A favorable brand name can even be used as a cue, helping consumers make product judgments (Maheswaranam et al., 1992) and recall the brand during advertising campaigns (Keller et al., 1998).

Dimensions of brand equity are closely associated with brand trust (Chaudhuri & Holbrook, 2001). Brand trust is the willingness of the average consumer to rely on the ability of the brand to perform its stated function. Brand trust affects purchase loyalty and attitudinal loyalty and determines the brand's market share.

Personalization

A consumer's trusting beliefs can also be enhanced through behaviors such as identifying with the consumer's needs and wants (Meyerson et al., 1996), something that personalization can accomplish. Personalization occurs when a business recommends products to a consumer based on the consumer's past purchases, demographics, and preferences (Nan Si & Murthy, 2003).

Within the context of electronic commerce applications, it is important to distinguish between "personalization" and "customization," as they are often mistakenly used interchangeably (Coner, 2003). The key distinction is that customization refers to configuring a product or service to a buyer's specifications; personalization refers to tailoring product or service offerings to a buyer's preferences. Personalization is often considered service-related because it often involves showing products to the customer based on the customer's preferences. Customization involves configuring a product to the customer's specifications, so it is often considered product-related.

One may also find terms such as "adaptive" and "adaptable" in the computer-human interaction (CHI) literature. According to Fan and Poole (2006), and "adaptive system" employs cognitive modeling of users to enable the system to distinguish among them. An "adaptable system" requires users to explicitly indicate how the user wants the system to be different. Fan and Poole suggest the different terminologies for similar concepts are due to the perspectives of the knowledge domains. The CHI research is system-oriented and thus focuses on the system capabilities. The business (i.e., e-commerce) literature tends to be more focused on the application.

A conceptual framework for personalization was developed by Vesanen (2007), who noted that marketers increasingly look to personalization for advantages. Vesanen describes a range of personalization types. Segment marketing is used to better match customer preferences compared to mass marketing approaches. Adaptive personalization allows users to choose from different options. Cosmetic personalization occurs when the organization changes the package of a standard good (e.g., when a google search changes the advertisements displayed with search results).

Transparent personalization, as used in this study, occurs when the content of good changes. Finally, collaborative customization occurs when a service provider and a service user work together to build a product.

Fan and Poole (2006) also provide a classification scheme for personalization systems. They focus on what is personalized, the target of the personalization, and the degree to which personalization is automated. The system in this study personalizes content, the target is an individual, and the degree is "implicit" due to the automation of the process. According to Wu et al. (2002) content is on e of the most important items that can be personalized.

The ability to personalize helps companies to mitigate the lack of interpersonal interactions in an online market that decrease a consumer's trust, and consequently, subsequent purchases. In a traditional face-to-face business environment, eye contact, a handshake, even chatting helps develop trust. These behaviors are not possible in an online environment. Using personalization, companies identify with consumers and better predict their needs. This practice has the potential to build a consumer's trust and increase the likelihood of future transactions (Cannon & Doney, 1997). Businesses that use the right technology and the correct algorithm are more likely to identify with a consumer and attain the consumer's trust (Cannon & Doney, 1997).

Self Disclosure

Many empirical studies in electronic commerce have determined a relationship between calculus- and knowledge-based trusts and intentions (Gefen & Straub, 2000; McKnight et al., 2002). These studies do not, however, measure behavior as an outcome of intentions. Other research indicates that when individuals attain deeper levels of trust for one another, they disclose more personal information over time (Altman & Taylor, 1973). The amount and the intimacy of communication measure the amount of trust that parties have for one another.

Communication is critical in developing and maintaining personal relationships. Open communication involves revealing personal feelings, interests, or tastes as part of developing an understanding of one another and identifying with one another's needs. Individuals who maintain open communication maintain healthier relationships and as a result have less emotional and physical problems (Jourard, 1973). More importantly, open communication helps individuals enjoy greater intimacy and enjoyment through their interactions. Self-disclosure is a central concept in social penetration theory (Altman & Taylor, 1973), which focuses on the development and growth of relationships. According to the theory, relationships develop systematically from superficial communication into more intimate levels of exchange over time.

Taylor and Altman (1987) suggest that there are four stages of relationship development. In the orientation stage, individuals display the most public parts of their personality, disclosing very little information about themselves. The second stage, the exploratory-affective exchange stage, is where individuals reveal aspects of their personality that were initially hidden. Although caution is taken with exchanges, the atmosphere is friendly and relaxed. Close friendships and romantic relationships are developed in the next stage, the affective-exchange stage. Interactions are described as free and casual. The final stage, the stable exchange stage, occurs when communication is continually more open and parties reveal more information across all layers of their personality. Parties know one another and can reliably and accurately predict one another's feelings and probable behavior.

Initially, the decision for parties to increase their levels of communication intimacy is somewhat based on norms of reciprocity (Altman, 1973) and the social rewards gained from the exchanges (Jones & Archer, 1976). However, as the relationship progresses, trust between the parties is a crucial element in determining the level of exchange intimacy (Altman, 1973; Dindia & Duck, 2000). Rubin and Shenker (1978) operationalized each of these four stages and found that individuals reveal only information concerning their tastes in the orientation stage. In more intimate stages, individuals reveal information about their attitudes, feelings, and sexuality.

Originally, research on self-disclosure occurred only in face-to-face (FtF) environments (Altman & Taylor, 1973). More recently, research has been extended into computer-mediated communication (CMC) environments (Parks & Floyd, 1996). As more CMC research has been performed, it has been established that people need more time to familiarize themselves with these environments and find adaptations for textual cues to meet their communication needs (Walther, 1992; 1993; Walther & Burgoon, 1992; Walther et al., 1994). The important point is not that CMC may be able to convey relational and personal information, if consumers are given sufficient time to do so.

RESEARCH MODEL

Conceptual Design

The conceptual design driving this research is presented in Figures 1, 2, and 3. The first model (Figure 1) is based on research from McKnight et al. (1998), Gefen (2000), Gefen and Straub (2003), Meyerson et al. (1996), and Cannon and Doney (1997). The model is a second order model containing two latent variables: trusting beliefs and self-disclosure. Trusting beliefs and self-disclosure are not directly measured from manifest variables but rather as composites of other latent variables and are assumed to be formative constructs.

In this model, we posit that there is a relationship between disposition to trust and trust. Gefen (2000) was first to empirically validate this relationship in an electronic commerce environment. An individual's disposition to trust represents a base line of trust that the individual possesses initially for any party. We theorize that individuals who have a low disposition to trust will find it difficult to move to higher forms of trust, regardless of what treatments are imposed on the individual in the experimental environment.

Three control variables are used to increase trusting beliefs: the presence of institutional structures, trustworthiness of the brand name, and personalization techniques. McKnight et al. (2002) was first to empirically validate a relationship between institutional structures and trust in an electronic commerce environment. Gefen (2000) empirically validated a relationship between a familiar vendor name (a similar construct to our trustworthy brand name) and trust. Cannon and Doney (1997) empirically validated a relationship between willingness to customize and trust (similar

Figure 1. Research model

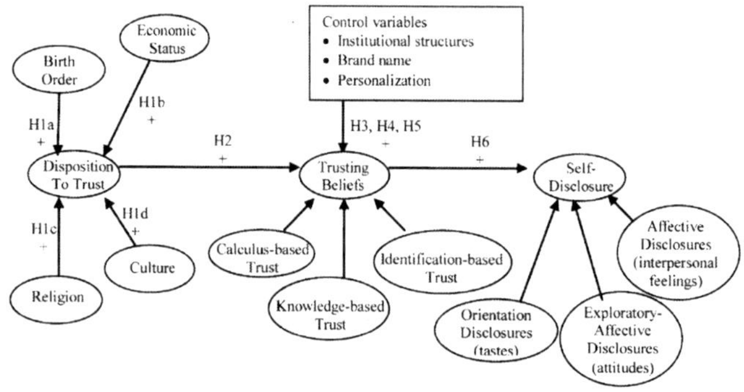

Figure 2. Lewicki and Bunker's trust model

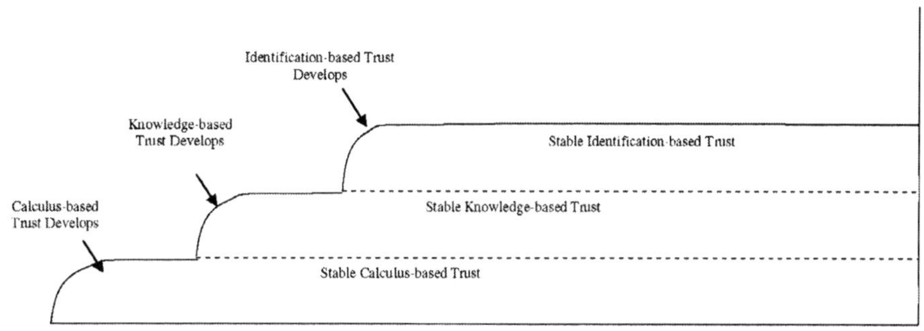

Figure 3. Process model of trust

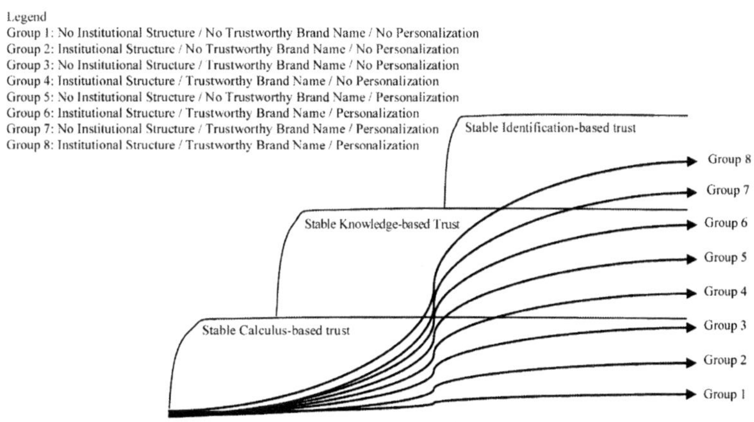

to our concept of personalization). Additionally, Meyerson et al. (1996) posited that personalization has the potential to swiftly develop trust.

Formative indicators of trusting beliefs are calculus-based, knowledge-based, and identification-based trusts. The model assumes that the presence of all formative indicators are needed to measure trusting beliefs and further asserts that trusting beliefs are measured on a continuum. A low level of trust corresponds to a high level of calculus-based trust and low levels of knowledge-based and identification-based trusts. A high level of knowledge-based trust and low levels of calculus-based and identification-based-trusts reflect an intermediate level of trust, where a high level of identification-based trust and low levels of calculus-based and knowledge-based trusts indicate a high level of trust. The absence of calculus-based trust in intermediate levels of trust reflects the individual has ceased using calculus-based processes to assess the trustworthiness of a party and has begun to use knowledge-based processes to determine the party's trustworthiness. Likewise, the absence of calculus-based and knowledge-based trusts in high levels of trust reflects that the individual has ceased using these processes to assess trustworthiness and has begun using identification-based processes.

Figure 1 also proposes that different categories of trusting beliefs influence behavior, affecting the intimacy of his/her exchanges (Guerin, 1993; Lewicki & Bunker, 1996; Kelly 2002; McKnight et al., 2002). The stages of self-disclosure are orientation, exploratory-affective, affective, and stable exchanges (Altman & Taylor, 1973). Stable exchanges are characterized by revealing information about sexuality, but because transactions between vendors and consumers do not typically require this level of intimacy, we did not explore such exchanges. The model proposes that levels of trusting beliefs influence behavior, which is measured as the individual's level of self-disclosure. Like trusting beliefs, the model assumes that the presence of all formative indicators is needed to measure disclosure, asserting that trusting beliefs are measured on a continuum. An individual reflecting low levels of self-disclosure reveals only taste information. An individual reflecting an intermediate level of self-disclosure reveals information about tastes and attitudes, but no more. An individual reflecting high levels of self-disclosure reveals information across the self-disclosure continuum, revealing tastes, attitudes, and interpersonal feelings. Unlike trusting beliefs, the movement from low to higher levels of self-disclosure does not necessarily exclude the presence of lower levels of disclosure.

The model depicted in Figure 1 can be integrated into a process model that explains the development of trust over time. Lewicki and Bunker's (1996) model, shown in Figure 2, is one such model. Their model reflects the belief that many individuals increase their trusting beliefs over time. Individuals in these relationships are represented on the solid line as moving from stable calculus-based trust to stable knowledge-based trust, and finally to stable identification-based trust. However, many relationships do not increase their trusting beliefs over time. These relationships may not progress past calculus-based or knowledge-based trusts. Individuals in these relationships are also represented in Figure 2 as progressing on or below the dotted lines labeled stable calculus-based trust or stable knowledge-based trust.

The model for this research is derived from Figures 1 and 2 and is shown in Figure 3. This model was developed from propositions posited by Meyerson et al. (1996), McKnight et al. (2002), Lewicki and Bunker (1996), and Cannon and Doney's research (1997). It predicts that individuals will develop calculus-based, knowledge-based, and identification-based trusts more swiftly in environments that display institutional structures, use trustworthy brand names, and employ personalization techniques (Group 8). This model further asserts that the use of institutional structures will reduce the consumer's perception of risk associated with interactions with the service provider and enable the swift development of stable calculus-based trust. Trustworthy brand names further the consumer's knowledge about the service provider and consumers are likely to develop stable knowledge-based trust for providers with trustworthy brand names. Because personalization techniques essentially identify with the consumer's needs and wants, the model also predicts service providers that utilize these techniques will increase a consumer's ability to develop stable identification-based trust. This model also predicts that knowledge-based trust can only be attained once calculus-based trust has been established and identification-based trust can only be created once knowledge-based trust has been developed. Thus, the swift development of stable calculus-based trust positively influences the swift development and stable knowledge-based and identification-based trusts. Likewise the swift development of stable knowledge-based trust positively influences the development of stable identification-based trust.

In Figure 3, it is posited that four time periods will be a sufficient amount of time to move some individuals from calculus-based trust to knowledge-based trust, and finally to identification-based trust. There is very limited data on how quickly consumers develop trust in a face-to-face environment, and even less data on how quickly consumers develop trust in an electronic environment. Most data collected on trust is either collected at the very beginning of a relationship or many years after a relationship has been established (Dindia & Duck, 2000; Gefen & Straub, 2000; McKnight et al., 2002). Four time periods were chosen as it is a well established time period necessary in longitudinal studies to demonstrate causality (Chidambaram et al., 1990; Hollingshead et al., 1993; Miranda & Bostrom, 1993).

Statement of Hypotheses

The first set of hypotheses investigates mechanisms to enhance calculus-based trust and swiftly develop knowledge-based and identification-based trusts. The controls do not use any mechanisms to enhance or swiftly develop trust.

Brand name, institutional structures, and dispositional factors can enhance calculus-based trust and influence the swift development of knowledge-based and identification-based trusts. Such mechanisms lower an individual's perception of risk when interacting with the party. Additionally, these factors provide knowledge that the party is trustworthy, and the party has the ability to identify with needs of the trusting individual.

Personalization techniques can also be used to enhance the swift development of trust. These techniques show that the party is knowledgeable of the needs of the individual and considers the individual's needs when recommending products. Knowledge and consideration factors have a strong likelihood of influencing the development of knowledge-based and identification-based trusts. Research question 1 was:

Do institutional factors, brand names, and personalization techniques and an individual's disposition to trust influence calculus-based trust and the formation of knowledge-based and identification-based trusts?

The following hypotheses investigate demographic factors related to this question.

H1: *An individual's demographic factors will correlate with an individual's disposition to trust.*

H1a: *Individuals of a higher birth order will have a higher disposition to trust than individuals of a lower birth order.*

H1b: *Individuals with a higher social economic status will have a higher disposition to trust than individuals of a lower economic status.*

H1c: *Individuals of the Jewish faith will have the highest disposition to trust, followed by Protestants, Catholics, and finally agonists and atheists.*

H1d: *Individuals of Chinese and Japanese ethnicity will have a higher disposition to trust than individuals of Caucasian, Hispanic, or African American ethnicity.*

These particular demographic variables were chosen because they have been cited in the literature as important factors in understanding trust or because the impact of their influence is mixed and we wanted to avoid omitting a potentially important factor. For example, Rotter (1971) alludes to faith as an important factor, but hedges that his results may reflect the socio-economic status of his subjects. Notably, these variables can be interesting in the context of online business as well. Many online businesses now incorporate recommendation algorithms and personal notifications of upcoming birthdays. An online business may want to structure the recommendation differently if suggesting a gift for an older sibling versus a younger one. Socio-economic status has clear implications for target market success. If Rotter's results hold for the faith variable, then businesses operating in religious niche areas may want to adopt more trustworthy approaches, as appropriate. The developing Asian market promises to be huge, but there is no guidance as yet regarding whether it should treated differently from a trust perspective, in spite of studies that indicate persons in collectivist societies exhibit less trusting behaviors (Huff & Kelley, 2003).

The following hypotheses further investigate the first question.

H2: *An individual's disposition to trust will positively influence trusting beliefs.*

H3: *The presence of institutional structures will increase trusting beliefs.*

H4: *A trustworthy brand name will increase trusting beliefs.*

H5: *The presence of personalization will increase trusting beliefs.*

The evolution of calculus-based trust to knowledge-based trust and then to identification-based trust influences the intimacy of interactions between parties. Individuals having only calculus-based trust disclose information about their tastes, but not information about the attitudes or interpersonal feelings (Rubin & Shenker, 1978). Individuals with knowledge-based trust are more demonstrative of intimacy and reveal attitudinal information but not interpersonal information. Finally, individuals possessing identification-based trust exhibit the most intimacy in their interactions, and also reveal their interpersonal feelings to other parties. Research question 2 addresses these issues. It asks:

Do individuals change their behavior as they develop deeper levels of trust?

The following hypothesis examines this question.

H6: *Increased trusting beliefs will result in higher self-disclosure.*

Research question 3 asks:

Does trust develop in an electronic environment beginning with calculus-based trust, then progressing to knowledge-based trust, and finally to identification-based trust?

The last set of hypotheses examine whether trust develops according to Lewicki and Bunker's (1996) trust model. These hypotheses determine whether trust is developed beginning with calculus-based trust, then progressing to knowledge-based trust, and finally to identification-based trust.

H7a: *The presence of calculus-based trust will occur before the presence of knowledge-based and identification-based trusts.*

H7b: *The presence of knowledge-based trust will occur after the presence of calculus-based trust and before the presence of identification-based trust.*

H7c: *The presence of identification-based trust will occur after the presence of calculus-based and knowledge-based trusts.*

RESEARCH METHODOLOGY

An experiment was conducted at a laboratory at a large university in the southeastern United States. A Web portal was designed containing Web sites for four service providers. Additionally, brand names, an institutional structure, and a computer program were created based on one of the commonly used strategies for recommending products. The effectiveness of the brand name, institutional structure, and personalization technique in influencing trust and trusting behaviors were determined in a pilot study. Study subjects were junior and senior undergraduate business majors. Only students that reported at least some experience with Internet technology were permitted to participate in the study. Because participation was voluntary, students were compensated academically for their participation.

Independent Variables

- **Disposition to Trust.** A measure of disposition to trust was adapted, with minor wording changes as related to an electronic commerce service provider, from Gefen (2000). The instrument consists of a six-item, seven-point Likert scale with anchors of 1 (strongly disagree) to 7 (strongly agree). Demographic variables were also collected to test the validity of this measure.
- **Disclosure Information.** The types of information revealed were identified using a measure adapted, with minor wording changes, from Rubin and Shenker (1978). The measure was changed from a numerical scale (1 to 10) to a type of person (i.e., trusted authority, friend, acquaintance, a familiar Web site, and unknown Web site). The scale consists of 24 items from three different topic areas (i.e., tastes, attitudes, and interpersonal feelings). Subjects were asked to express what types of information they would reveal to each type of person.
- **Institutional Structures.** The institutional structure was manipulated by displaying a familiar security symbol on the portal. This approach has been used in previous studies of trust (McKnight et al., 2002).
- **Brand Name.** Four hypothetical brand names (two trustworthy and two untrustworthy) were created for this study. The effectiveness of these names was tested in a pilot study. The results of the pilot study indicated the names "Direct Mobile" and "DiLink" were adequate at conveying trust and lack of trust, respectively, so they were selected for this study.
- **Personalization.** A program was implemented that created a personalized Web environment. The program recommended products to a user based on the user's personal characteristics and the product's attributes. The effectiveness of the recommendation strategy in enhancing a consumer's trust was also tested in a pilot study. The results of the pilot study indicated that personalization significantly reduced trusting beliefs. Though the results differed from the hypotheses, they were significant and hence the computer program was not altered.

Experimental Design

The experiment utilized a 2 x 2 x 2 longitudinal design, reflecting the presence of security (present/absent), trustworthiness of the brand (trustworthy/untrustworthy), and the presence of personalization (present/absent). There were five steps in this study. In the first step, participants completed an electronic survey ascertaining their nature to reveal different types of information to different types of people. This data was used with data collected later in the experiment to determine the presence of trusting behaviors. Background data was also collected along with the brand names of the products that the subject identified as his/her brand preferences. Brand preferences were used later in the experiment in operationalizing the personalization construct.

In the second step of the experiment, subjects were placed in one of eight research settings as needed to balance the demographic factors. The eight possible treatments were formed by combining the four security and personalization treatment combinations (secure and personalized, secure and un-personalized, insecure and personalized, and insecure and un-personalized) for each service provider (the trustworthy Direct Mobile and the untrustworthy DiLink). A large security emblem shown on each screen of the system alerted the subject that the setting was secure. The brand name was also displayed on each screen to operationalize either the trustworthy or untrustworthy brand name construct. Displaying products based on the subject's brand preferences operationalized the personalization construct.

The subjects launched the system after signing a consent waiver and listening to instructions. This action caused a new screen to appear displaying an introductory Web site for one of the two service providers. On this screen, the service provider offered the subject a gift certificate for 20% off on products identified as products that he or she would be interested in purchasing. Next, a screen appeared that collected the subject's unique ID and guided the subject through a tour of the service provider's Web site.

After the tour was completed, the system gathered the subject's levels of calculus based, knowledge-based, and identification-based trusting beliefs for the service provider. The system then displayed another screen offering the subject a $10 gift certificate from the provider for answering a set of personal questions. Each subject was required to read an information screen, instructing the subject to provide the service provider with only the amount of information that they subject felt comfortable in revealing. The subject electronically indicated that he or she understood these instructions before proceeding to answer the questions. Subjects could reveal information to the service provider by answering questions or press a "continue" button to essentially opt out. After this, subjects were dismissed from the research setting.

In steps three, four, and five each subject again entered the system, took a tour of the service provider's Web site, and answered questions to determine the subject's level of calculus-based, knowledge-based, and identification-based trusting beliefs for the service provider. One week elapsed between each of these steps. Subjects were placed in the same research setting throughout the study. Web sites for service providers were similar in functionality and appearance throughout the study. However, the product categories displayed to subjects were varied in each step according to their personalization preferences, if applicable. After all data were collected, the subjects were debriefed and thanked for their participation.

Dependent Variables

- **Calculus-based trust**, **knowledge-based trust**, and **identification-based trust** were measured using the only known measures available (with minor wording changes). All were measured on a seven-point Likert scale with anchors of 1 (strongly disagree) to 7 (strongly agree). Calculus-based trust was determined using a three-item measure adapted from Gefen and Straub (2003). Knowledge-based trust was determined using a six-item measure adapted from McAllister (1995). Identification-based trust was determined using a five-item measure adapted from McAllister (1995).
- **Trusting Beliefs.** Formative indicators of trusting beliefs include calculus-based, knowledge-based, and identification-based trust. These were measured as described in the section above where the conceptual design is described. If trust develops over time, then the mean scores of these formative indicators should be different in different time periods.
- **Self-Disclosure.** Formative indicators of self-disclosure include orientation, exploratory-affective, and affective disclosures. Measures for orientation, exploratory-affective, and affective disclosures were adapted with minor wording changes from measures taken from Rubin and Shenker (1978). Other measures of self-disclosure exist, but this is the only known instrument

where the breath and depth of communication are considered in determining the intimacy between parties. There are twelve measures for each indicator. Each measure consists of two items, asking the subject to reveal information about their tastes, attitudes, or interpersonal feelings reflecting that the subject had made an orientation, exploratory-affective, and affective disclosure, respectively.

FINDINGS

Preliminary Analysis

After resolving issues to remove bad data, 182 subject responses were coded into groups depending on their respective experimental treatment. In the statistical analysis, brand name, security, and personalization were coded as "1" indicating the presence of the factor and "0" indicating its absence. As part of the preliminary analysis, a wide range of analyses were performed. The analyses indicate there is little threat to statistical validity due to departures from normality and that the sample size satisfies requirements for PLS, the structural equation modeling technique employed, and ANOVA. Manipulation checks verified that no significant variation of experiences between experimental groups for prior retail or online purchases was found. Factor analysis was used to test this theoretical model. For the data used in this study, the factors explain a significant amount of the variance of each solution. The measurement model was assessed for convergent and discriminant validity and reliability (Barclay et al., 1995; Chin, 1998; Compeau et al., 1999). All test criteria were satisfied, therefore, convergent and divergent validity was assumed. Finally, the reliability for the seven constructs was determined using Cronbach's alpha and internal consistency reliability (ICR). Both ICR and Cronbach alpha were greater than 0.70, indicating high reliability.

Hypothesis Testing

Six out of 12 hypotheses were fully supported and 1 hypothesis was partially supported (Table 1).

Hypothesis 1: Antecedents to Disposition to Trust. In order to test H1a, responses were coded 0=first born, 1=middle child, 2= youngest child, and 4= only child. In order to test H1b, responses were coded 0=Less than $15,000/year, 1= 15,001/year - 25,000/year, 2=25,001/year - 35,000/year, 3=35,001/year -45,000/year, 4= 45,001/year-55,000/year, 5=55,001/year-75,000/year, 6=75,001/year -100,000/year, 7=100,001/year-150,000/year, and 8= greater than 150,000. In order to test H1c, responses were coded 0=Agnostic or Atheist, 1=Catholic, 2=Baptist, 2=Christian, 2=Nondenominational Christian, 2=Protestant, 3=Mormon, 4=Christian Scientist, 5=Jehovah Witness, 6=Buddhism, 6=Hindu, 7=Jewish, and 8=other. In order to test H1d, responses were coded 0=Caucasian, 1=Hispanic, 2=African American, 3=Indian, 4=European, 5=Caucasian/Hispanic, and 6=Asian.

Hypothesis 1 (H1) stated that demographic factors would be positively related to an individual's disposition to trust. PLS was used to test these hypotheses (see Figure 4). Findings provide support for hypothesis 1a, relating birth order to disposition to trust ($b = -0.247$, $p > 0.001$).

Table 1. Hypothesis results

Antecedents to Disposition to Trust			**Antecedents to Trusting Beliefs**		
1a	Birth Order	Supported	2	Disposition to Trust	Supported
1b	Economic Status	Supported	3	Institution Structures	Partially Supported
1c	Religion	Supported	4	Brand Name	Supported
1d	Culture	Not Supported	5	Personalization	Not Supported
Antecedents to Self-Disclosure			**Trust Development**		
6	Trusting Beliefs	Supported	7	Increase Over Time	Not Supported

Hypothesis 1b, that a positive relationship exists between economic status and disposition to trust, was supported ($b = 0.151$, $p < 0.05$). Hypothesis 1c (that individuals of certain faith will have a higher disposition to trust) was also significant ($b = 0.158$, $p < 0.05$). As for hypothesis 1d, culture was not significantly related to disposition to trust at the 0.10 level ($b = 0.075$, $p > 0.10$). The R^2 for the endogenous construct disposition to trust, which indicates the amount of variance explained in this model (Chin, 1998), was 0.112.

Hypothesis 2: Antecedents to Trusting Beliefs. Hypothesis 2 (H2) stated that a higher disposition to trust would lead to higher levels of trust. This relationship was tested in PLS four times, once in each trial (see Figure 5). Findings provided support for hypothesis 2 in the first ($b = 0.479$, $p < 0.001$), second ($b = 0.297$, $p < 0.10$), third ($b = 0.287$, $p < 0.05$), and fourth trial ($b = 0.275$, $p < 0.05$). The R^2 calculated for the endogenous construct, trusting beliefs, was 0.352, 0.287, 0.328, and 0.383 for trials one through four, respectively.

Hypothesis 3: Institutional Structures. Hypothesis 3 (H3) stated that a presence of institutional structures would lead to higher levels of trust. This relationship was tested in PLS four times, once for each trial (see Figure 6). Findings did not support hypothesis 3 in the first trial ($b = 0.061$, $p > 0.10$). However, the findings for the second ($b = 0.228$, $p < 0.01$), third ($b = 0.270$, $p < 0.05$), and fourth trial ($b = 0.384$, $p < 0.10$) were significant.

Hypothesis 4: Brand Name. Hypothesis 4 (H4) stated that a trustworthy brand name would lead to higher levels of trust. This relationship was tested in PLS four times, once for each trial (see Figure 7). Findings provided support for hypothesis 4 in trials one ($b = 0.331$, $p < 0.001$), two ($b = 0.394$, $p < 0.05$), three ($b = 0.406$, $p < 0.10$), and four ($b = 0.366$, $p < 0.05$).

Hypothesis 5: Personalization. Hypothesis 5 (H5) stated that personalization would lead to higher levels of trust. This relationship was also tested in PLS four times (see Figure 8). Findings were significant in the first ($b = -0.156$, $p < 0.05$), second ($b = -0.149$, $p < 0.10$), third ($b = -0.265$, $p < 0.05$), and fourth trial ($b = -0.109$, $p < 0.10$). However, all findings were in the direction opposite to that hypothesized. A discussion explaining these results is provided below.

Hypothesis 6: Disclosure. Hypothesis 6 (H6) stated that higher levels of trust are associated with more self-disclosure. PLS was used to test this relationship (see Figure 9). Findings were significant in trials one ($b = 0.369$, $p < 0.001$), two ($b = -0.295$, $p < 0.10$), three ($b = -0.149$, $p < 0.05$), and four ($b = 0.167$, $p < 0.05$). The R^2 calculated for the endogenous construct, self-disclosure, were 0.136, 0.121, 0.187, and 0.223 for trials one through four, respectively.

Hypothesis 7: Trust Development. Hypothesis 7 (H7) stated that trust changes over time. That is, that calculus-based trust will develop before the knowledge-based or identification-based trust and knowledge-based trust will develop before identification-based trust. H7 was analyzed using ANOVA to determine if the mean scores of subjects' levels of trust were statistically different over the four trials.

Results from the ANOVA indicate that the means were not significantly different for calculus-based ($F=0.81$, $p> 0.49$), knowledge-based ($F=1.17$, $p>0.32$), and identification-based trusts ($F=1.84$, $p>0.14$). Thus, there is not sufficient evidence to support H7 at the $p<0.10$ level. In other words, there is insufficient evidence to show that trust develops over time. These results are also discussed further in the next section.

DISCUSSION OF RESULTS

Antecedents of Disposition to Trust

Three of the four hypothesized constructs were found to be significant and in the direction as hypothesized. Culture was the only construct that was

Figure 4. Results of tests of hypotheses 1a, 1b, 1c, and 1d

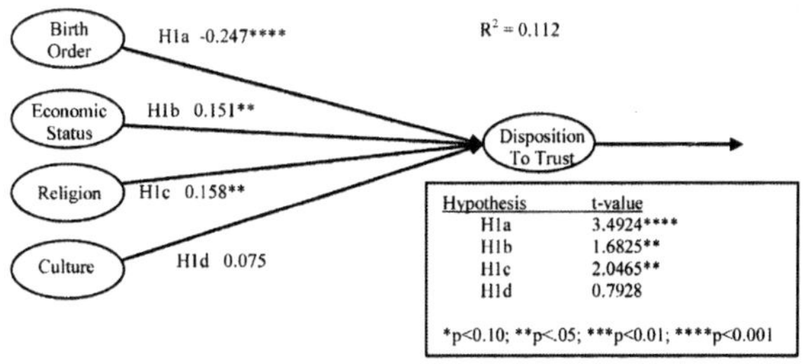

Figure 5. Results of tests of hypothesis 2

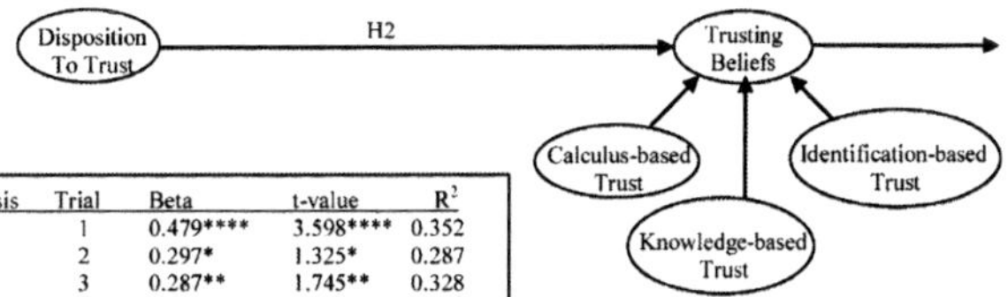

Hypothesis	Trial	Beta	t-value	R^2
H2	1	0.479****	3.598****	0.352
H2	2	0.297*	1.325*	0.287
H2	3	0.287**	1.745**	0.328
H2	4	0.275**	2.235**	0.383

*p<0.10; **p<.05; ***p<0.01; ****p<0.001

Figure 6. Results of tests of hypothesis 3

Hypothesis	Trial	Beta	t-value
H3	1	0.061	0.852
H3	2	0.228*	2.466*
H3	3	0.270**	1.856**
H3	4	0.384*	1.335*

*p<0.10; **p<.05; ***p<0.01; ****p<0.001

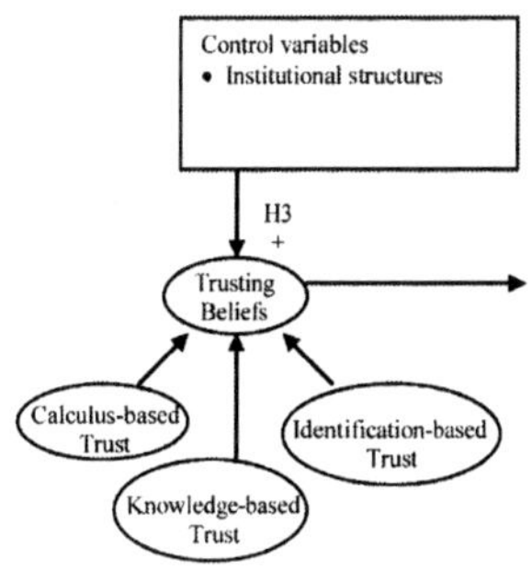

Figure 7. Results of tests of hypothesis 4

Hypothesis	Trial	Beta	t-value
H4	1	0.331****	4.248****
H4	2	0.394**	2.423**
H4	3	0.406*	1.567*
H4	4	0.366**	1.865**

*p<0.10; **p<.05; ***p<0.01; ****p<0.001

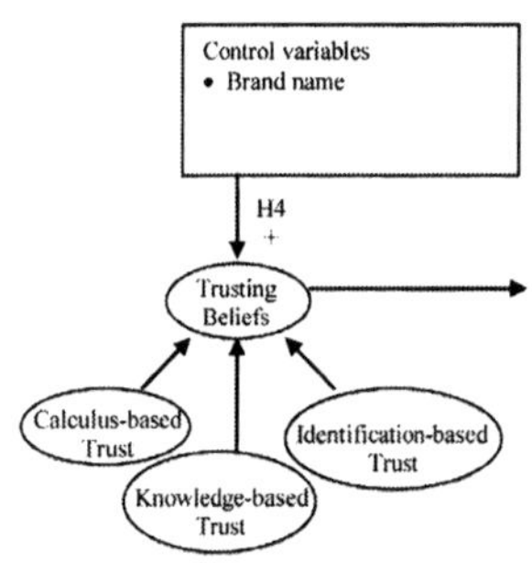

Figure 8. Results of tests of hypothesis 5

Hypothesis	Trial	Beta	t-value
H5	1	-0.156**	1.465**
H5	2	-0.149*	1.345*
H5	3	-0.265**	1.756**
H5	4	-0.109*	1.298*

*p<0.10; **p<.05; ***p<0.01; ****p<0.001

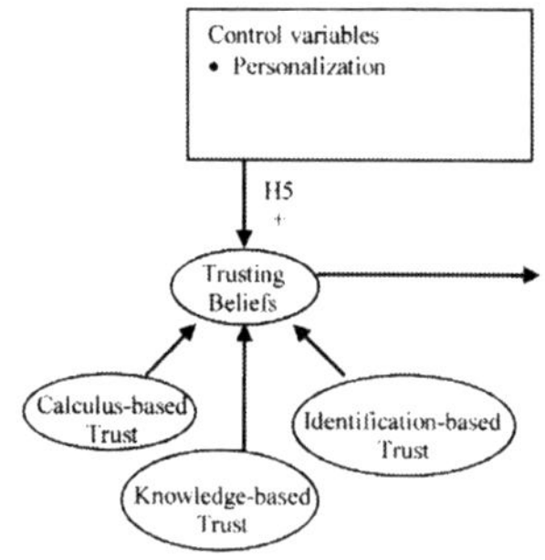

Figure 9. Results of tests of hypothesis 6

Hypothesis	Trial	Beta	t-value	R^2
H6	1	0.369****	4.325****	0.136
H6	2	0.295*	1.465*	0.121
H6	3	0.149**	2.236**	0.187
H6	4	0.167**	1.923**	0.223

*p<0.10; **p<.05; ***p<0.01; ****p<0.001

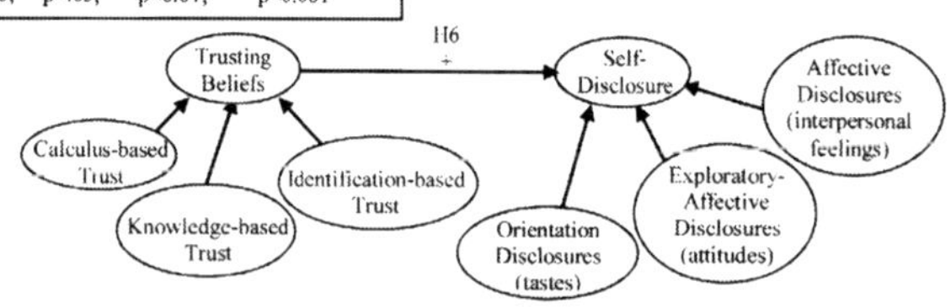

not found to significantly influence the disposition to trust construct. This finding is not surprising. Studies indicate that a subject's organizational culture and country of residence can have a confounding effect on an individual's disposition to trust (Huff & Kelley, 2003). All individuals that participated in this study lived in the southeastern United States and were students of the same university and college. Thus, the cultural values of the student's university and college as well as the cultural values of the southeastern United States could have had a confounding influence on each subject's disposition to trust. This confounding effect may have caused insignificance in the relationship between the culture and disposition to trust constructs.

In a similar study on culture and trust, Lohtia et al. (2009) discovered that cultural sensitivity, while important, is not necessary for trust formation. Meanwhile, Kim (2008) found that transference-based determinants of trust (i.e., the perception of a third-party seal or a positive referral) are more positively associated with consumer trust in e-vendors in collectivist (strong uncertainty avoidance, high long-term orientation, high context) cultures than individualistic cultures. Clearly, the relationship between culture and trust will continue to remain areas requiring the attention of researchers, as cultural barriers impact business models, particularly within the e-commerce context (Schuette, 2000; Oudan 2010).

Antecedents to Trusting Beliefs

- **Disposition to Trust.** As hypothesized, a higher disposition to trust led to higher trusting beliefs in all four trials. This finding is consistent with prior research indicating a relationship with a person's disposition to trust and trusting beliefs for a Web site vendor or other entity (Gefen, 2000; McKnight et al., 2002).

- **Institutional Structures.** Institutional structures were found to significantly influence trusting beliefs in all trials with the exception of the first trial. These results are consistent with similar studies examining institutional structures in e-commerce environments McKnight & Chervany, 2001; Kim & Benbasat, 2006; 2010). In the first trial, there was not a significant relationship between institutional structures and trusting beliefs. The results in the first trial contradict earlier studies. For example, McKnight et al. (2002) found that institutional structures increase initial trusting beliefs. However, it is important to note that they operationalized institutional structures by creating and validating an instrument to measure institutional trust. In this study, we believe the verisimilitude of a security emblem provides a better operationalization of the construct than the one used by McKnight et al. (2002). The security emblem used in this study was identical to the emblem used at most electronic commerce Web sites (e.g., Amazon.com, Target.com, and Walmart.com). One explanation for the lack of significance in trial one is that subjects did not notice the security emblem in the first trial. Although the security emblem was placed prominently on each screen of the electronic environment, many subjects could have ignored the emblem, paying more attention to experimental task. Over the course of the four trials, subjects may have noticed the security emblem and as a result increased their trusting beliefs for the electronic vendor. Familiarity with a trustworthy e-vendor should increase consumer trust, because more familiarity implies an increasing amount of accumulated knowledge derived from experience from previous successful interactions through the Web site (Gefen 2000, Gefen, Karahanna, & Straub 2003, Kim & Benbasat 2006).
- **Brand Name.** Brand name had a significant impact on trusting beliefs in all four trials. This finding is consistent with prior research looking at the influence of familiarity and brand equity on trusting beliefs (Gefen, 2000; Chaudhuri & Holbrook, 2001). However, this study is one of the first studies to look at the impact of a new brand name on trusting beliefs. This finding provides significant evidence that a new brand name that connotes trustworthiness can have a significant and lasting impact on trusting beliefs. Since this study, however, it has been suggested that consumers in emerging economies may lack sufficient knowledge of a foreign brands' heritage (Millan & Mittal, 2010). As a result, they tend place their trust in the product and not the brand (Crain, 2006; Keller & Moorthi, 2003; Millan & Mittal, 2010). Thus, the applicability of our results may be limited in an international setting.
- **Personalization.** Personalization was shown to have a significant and negative impact on trusting beliefs in all four trials. The use of personalization to increase trusting beliefs was supported by earlier conceptual studies (Meyerson et al., 1996). The findings in this study contradict earlier theories and are supported by anecdotal evidence from practitioners who indicate that persons feel that personalization violates their privacy and trust (Alpert et al., 2003). However, at least one other study (Dwyer, 2010) has found similar results.

A decrease in trusting beliefs may be related to a sense of loss of control by users over how a system is performing. Jameson and Schwartzkopf (2002) also note that users may become disenchanted with a system that automatically makes recommendations that are inaccurate with respect to the user's preferences. In this case, the system is providing little value and may be seen as annoying. Jameson and Schwartzkopf describe another potentially negative aspect of automatic recommendation systems is that they may generate more recommendations than a user can adequately process. In this situation, the user may become frustrated.

Montgomery and Smith (2008) observe that there are design problems that still need to be resolved. Taking the computer science perspective, they note that "adaptive interfaces" must balance the costs of user errors with the potential gains of the system performance. They note that the problems that occur in personalization occur in many online contexts. Since research on "adaptive choice" is scattered across many fields, they suggest integrating the many diverse research streams.

Self-Disclosure

As seen in Figure 9, there is a significant and positive relationship between trusting beliefs and self-disclosure. This finding supports earlier conceptual work that higher trusting beliefs for a person or entity will positively influence a person's willingness to disclose personal information (Altman & Taylor, 1973; Jourard, 1973; Walther et al., 1994; Dindia & Duck, 2000; Kelly, 2002). The relationship also provides some support that when individuals feel a deeper level of trust for a person or entity they will disclose more personal information to that person or entity. This finding also supports the conclusion that individuals will disclose more personal information to electronic vendors that display security emblems or use trustworthy brand names.

Trust Development

Much of the past research devoted to trust development examines it as a static, independent/dependent, or mediating variable, measuring it at a single point in time. Lewicki, Tomlinson, and Gillespie (2006) posit that trust can not only be measured with a unidimensional or two-demensional approach, but that trust is also transformational, changing over time. More recently, Gupta et al. (2010) indicate that trust task-facilitating tools provided by a vendor play an important role on the formation of trust. Such tools include those used for searching, attaining information about a product, simplifying the choice options, and buying guides, among others (Gupta et al., 2010).

There was no evidence that trust developed over time. Although, there was a slight increase of trusting beliefs between trials, a statistically significant increase of trusting beliefs was not observed. There are several explanations for this lack of significance. One explanation is that the study simply did not last long enough to create an effective test for trust development. Although a longitudinal design was used, the constraints of testing in an academic environment limited our ability to extend the study beyond the weeks when it was conducted. A longer study period might reveal a different outcome. Another explanation is that there is not enough variability in the experimental design between trials to expose the relationship. The experimental design emulated a typical electronic commerce environment in that subjects had a similar experience with the experimental environment in each trial. Barring any difficulties with shipping or technical difficulties with an Internet vendor, electronic commerce is described by its similarity in each experience. The quality of a website, as well as the richness of the website's privacy disclosure, play important roles in a user's experience and trust of a specific website (Lowry et al., 2008; Abbasi et al., 2010; Aljukhadar, 2010). That is, when a consumer visits an electronic commerce Web site, his/her experience is identical to the prior online shopping experience. Because there is no variability in the experiences, trusting beliefs are neither increased nor decreased.

On the other hand, brick and mortar establishments provide different experiences to consumers with every visit. For example, a consumer may be able to find a product quickly or have a salesperson provide exceptional service on one visit and on the next visit receive inconsiderate treatment by one of the salespersons. Experiences with the establishment vary and trusting beliefs in the vendor also vary (Young & Albaum, 2003).

In this experiment, there is no difference in a subject's experiences with the electronic environment between the four trials. Thus, there is little impetus for a subject to change his/her trusting beliefs in either of the treatment conditions.

CONCLUSION

This research provides many theoretical and practical benefits. For researchers, this study identifies and tests four antecedents of trusting beliefs: disposition to trust, the use of security symbols, brand names, and personalization techniques. This research also provides researchers with a framework in which to study trusting beliefs over time. This research provides a basis in which researchers can apply the concept of self-disclosure as a trusting behavior. This study is also beneficial to practitioners as it provides some guidelines for developers of electronic commerce environments.

REFERENCES

Aaker, D. (1996). *Building strong brands*. New York: Free Press.

Aaker, D. (2000). *Brand leadership*. New York: Free Press.

Aaker, J. (1997). Dimensions of brand personality. *JMR, Journal of Marketing Research, 34*(3), 347–357. doi:10.2307/3151897

Abbasi, A., Zhang, Z., Zimbra, D., Chen, H., & Nunamaker, J. F. (2010). Detecting fake websites: The contribution of statistical learning theory. *Management Information Systems Quarterly, 34*(3), 435–461.

Agarwal, R., & Karahanna, E. (2000). Time flies when you're having fun: Cognitive absorption and beliefs about information technology usage. *Management Information Systems Quarterly, 24*, 665–694. doi:10.2307/3250951

Aljukhadar, M. (2010). Can the media richness of a privacy disclosure enhance outcome? A multifaceted view of trust in rich media environments. *International Journal of Electronic Commerce, 14*(4), 103–126. doi:10.2753/JEC1086-4415140404

Alpert, S., Karat, J., Karat, C.-M., Brodie, C., & Vergo, J. (2003). User attitudes regarding a user-adaptive e-commerce Web site. *User Modeling and User-Adapted Interaction, 13*(4), 373–396. doi:10.1023/A:1026201108015

Altman, I., & Taylor, D. (1973). *The development of interpersonal relationships*. New York: Holt, Rinehart & Winston.

Anderson, E., & Weitz, B. (1989). Determinants of continuity in conventional industrial dyads. *Marketing Science, 8*(4), 310–323. doi:10.1287/mksc.8.4.310

Ba, S., Whinston, A., & Zhang, H. (2003). Building trust in online auction markets through an economic incentive mechanism. *Decision Support Systems, 35*(3), 273–286. doi:10.1016/S0167-9236(02)00074-X

Barber, B. (1983). *The logic and limits of trust*. New Brunswick, NJ: Rutgers University Press.

Barclay, D., Higgins, C., & Thompson, R. (1995). The partial least squares approach to causal modeling: Personal computer adoption and use as an illustration. *Technology Studies, 2*(2), 285–309.

Butler, J., & Cantrell, R. (1984). A behavioral decision theory approach to modeling dyadic trust in superiors and subordinates. *Psychological Reports*, *55*, 19–28.

Cannon, J., & Doney, P. (1997). An examination of the nature of trust in buyer-seller relationships. *Journal of Marketing*, *61*(2), 35–51. doi:10.2307/1251829

Chaudhuri, A., & Holbrook, M. (2001). The chain of effects from brand trust and brand affect to brand performance: The role of brand loyalty. *Journal of Marketing*, *65*(2), 81–93. doi:10.1509/jmkg.65.2.81.18255

Chidambaram, L., Bostrom, R., & Wynne, B. (1990). A longitudinal study of the impact of group decision support systems on group development. *Journal of Management Information Systems*, *7*(3), 7–25.

Chin, W. (1998). Issues and opinion on structural equation modeling. *Management Information Systems Quarterly*, *22*(1), vii–xvi.

Compeau, D., Higgins, C., & Huff, S. (1999). Social cognitive theory and individual reactions to computing technology: A longitudinal study. *Management Information Systems Quarterly*, *23*(2), 145–158. doi:10.2307/249749

Coner, A. (2003). Personalization and customization in financial portals. *Journal of American Academy of Business*, *2*(2), 498–504.

Coursaris, C., Hassanein, K., & Head, M. (2003). M-commerce in Canada: An interaction framework for wireless privacy. *Canadian Journal of Administrative Sciences*, *20*, 54–73. doi:10.1111/j.1936-4490.2003.tb00305.x

Crain, R. (2006). Czech advertising business lacks a footbridge to the future, *Advertising Age*, September 17, 14.

Dasgupta, P. (2000). Trust as a commodity, in Gambetta, Diego (ed.) *Trust: Making and Breaking Cooperative Relations*, electronic edition, Department of Sociology, University of Oxford, Chapter 4, <http://www.sociology.ox.ac.uk/papers/dasgupta49-72.pdf>: 49-72.

Deutsch, M. (1958). Trust and suspicion. *The Journal of Conflict Resolution*, *2*, 265–279. doi:10.1177/002200275800200401

Dindia, K., & Duck, S. (2000). *Communication and personal relationships*. Chichester, England: Wiley.

Dwyer, C. (2010) The effect of behavioral targeting on trust in e-commerce. Available at http://csis.pace.edu/~dwyer/research/

Fan, H., & Poole, M. S. (2006). What is personalization? Perspectives on the design and implementation of personalization in information systems. *Journal of Organizational Computing and Electronic Commerce*, *16*(3), 179–202. doi:10.1207/s15327744joce1603&4_2

Fornell, C., & Larcker, D. (1981). Evaluating structural equation models with unobservable variables and measurement error. *JMR, Journal of Marketing Research*, *18*, 39–50. doi:10.2307/3151312

Fukuyama, F. (1995). *Trust: The social virtues and the creation of prosperity*. New York: The Free Press.

Gefen, D. (2000). E-commerce: The role of familiarity and trust. *Omega: The International Journal of Management Science*, *28*, 725–737. doi:10.1016/S0305-0483(00)00021-9

Gefen, D., Karahanna, E., & Straub, D. W. (2003). Trust and TAM in online shopping: An integrated model. *Management Information Systems Quarterly*, *27*(1), 51.

Gefen, D., & Straub, D. (2000). The relative importance of perceived ease-of-use in IS adoption: A study of e-commerce adoption. *Journal of the Association for Information Systems*, *1*(8), 1–30.

Gefen, D., & Straub, D. (2003). Trust and TAM in online shopping: An integrated model. *Management Information Systems Quarterly*, *27*(1), 51–90.

Granovetter, M. (1985). Economic action and social structure: The problem of embeddedness. *American Journal of Sociology*, *91*, 481–510. doi:10.1086/228311

Guerin, B. (1993). *Social facilitation*. Cambridge, Great Britain: Cambridge University Press. doi:10.1017/CBO9780511628214

Gulati, R. (1995). Does familiarity breed trust? The implications of repeated ties for contractual choices in alliances. *Academy of Management Journal*, *38*(1), 85–112. doi:10.2307/256729

Gupta, P., Yadav, M. S., & Varadarajan, R. (2010). How task-facilitative interactive tools foster buyers' trust in online retailers: A process view of trust development in the electronic marketplace. *Journal of Retailing*, *85*(2), 159–176. doi:10.1016/j.jretai.2009.02.001

Hair, J., Anderson, R., Tatham, R., & Black, W. (1998). *Multivariate data analysis*. Upper Saddle River: Prentice Hall.

Hollingshead, A., McGrath, J., & O'Connor, K. (1993). Group task performance and communication technology: A longitudinal study of computer-mediated vs. face-to-face work groups. *Small Group Research*, *24*(3), 307–333. doi:10.1177/1046496493243003

Huff, L., & Kelley, L. (2003). Levels of organizational trust in individualist versus collectivist societies. *Organization Science*, *14*(1), 81–90. doi:10.1287/orsc.14.1.81.12807

Jameson, A., & Schwarzkopf, E. (2002). Pros and cons of controllability: an empirical study. Adaptive Hypermedia 2002. *Lecture Notes in Computer Science*, *2347*, 193–202. doi:10.1007/3-540-47952-X_21

Jones, E., & Archer, R. (1976). Are there special effects of personalistic self-disclosure? *Journal of Experimental Social Psychology*, *12*, 180–193. doi:10.1016/0022-1031(76)90069-X

Jourard, S. (1973). *Transparent self*. New York: Van Nostrand Reinhold Company.

Keller, K., Heckler, S., & Houston, M. (1998). The effects of brand name suggestiveness on advertising recall. *Journal of Marketing*, *62*, 48–57. doi:10.2307/1251802

Keller, K. L., & Moorthi, Y. L. R. (2003). Branding in developing markets. *Business Horizons*, *46*(3), 49–59. doi:10.1016/S0007-6813(03)00029-6

Kelly, A. (2002). *The psychology of secrets*. New York: Kluwer Academic Plenum Publishers.

Kim, D. (2008). Self-perception-based versus transference-based trust determinants in computer-mediated transactions: A cross-cultural comparison study. *Journal of Management Information Systems*, *24*(4), 13–45. doi:10.2753/MIS0742-1222240401

Kim, D., & Benbasat, I. (2006). The effects of Trust-assuring arguments on consumer trust in Internet stores: Application of Toulmin's model of argumentation. *Information Systems Research*, *17*(3), 286–300. doi:10.1287/isre.1060.0093

Kim, D., & Benbasat, I. (2009-10). Trust-assuring arguments in b2c e-commerce: Impact of content, source, and price on trust. *Journal of Management Information Systems*, *26*(3), 175–206. doi:10.2753/MIS0742-1222260306

Kirk, R. (1995). *Experimental design: Procedures for the behavioral sciences* (3rd ed.). Pacific Grove, CA: Brooks/Cole Publishing Company.

Lewicki, R., & Bunker, B. (1995). Trust in relationship. In Bunker, B., & Rubin, J. (Eds.), *Conflict, cooperation, and justice* (pp. 133–169). San Francisco, CA: Jossey-Bass Inc.

Lewicki, R., & Bunker, B. (1996). Developing and maintaining trust in work relationships. In Kramer, R., & Tyler, T. (Eds.), *Trust in organizations: Frontiers of theory and research* (pp. 114–139). Thousand Oaks, CA: Sage.

Lewis, J., & Weigert, A. (1985). Trust as a social reality. *Social Forces*, *63*, 967–985. doi:10.2307/2578601

Lillibridge, J., & Lundstedt, S. (1967). Some initial evidence for an interpersonal risk theory. *The Journal of Psychology*, *66*, 119–128.

Lohtia, R., Bello, D., & Porter, C. (2009). Building trust in US-Japanese business relationships: Mediating role of cultural sensitivity. *Industrial Marketing Management*, *38*(3), 239–252. doi:10.1016/j.indmarman.2007.06.016

Lowry, P. B., Vance, A., Moody, G., Beckman, B., & Read, A. (2008). Explaining and predicting the impacts of brand alliances and web site quality on initial consumer trust of e-commerce web sites. *Journal of Management Information Systems*, *24*(4), 199–224. doi:10.2753/MIS0742-1222240408

Luhmann, N. (1979). *Trust and power*. Chichester, UK: Wiley.

Maheswaranam, D., Mackie, D., & Chaiken, S. (1992). Brand name as a heuristic cue: The effects of task importance and expectancy confirmation on consumer judgments. *Journal of Consumer Psychology*, *1*(4), 317–336. doi:10.1016/S1057-7408(08)80058-7

Mayer, R., Davis, J., & Schoorman, F. (1995). An integration model of organizational trust. *Academy of Management Review*, *20*(3), 709–734. doi:10.2307/258792

McAllister, D. (1995). Affect- and cognition-based trust as foundations for interpersonal cooperation in organizations. *Academy of Management Journal*, *38*(1), 24–59. doi:10.2307/256727

McKnight, D., Choudhury, V., & Kacmar, C. (2002). The impact of initial consumer trust on intentions to transact with a Web site: a trust building model. *The Journal of Strategic Information Systems*, *11*(3-4), 297–323. doi:10.1016/S0963-8687(02)00020-3

McKnight, D., Cummings, L., & Chervany, N. (1998). Initial trust formation in new organizational relationships. *Academy of Management Review*, *23*(3), 473–490. doi:10.2307/259290

McKnight, D. H., & Chervany, N. L. (2001). What trust means in e-commerce customer relationships: An interdisciplinary conceptual typology. *International Journal of Electronic Commerce*, *6*(2), 35–59.

Meyerson, D., Weick, K., & Kramer, R. (1996). Swift trust in temporary groups. In Kramer, R., & Tyler, T. (Eds.), *Trust in organizations: Frontiers of theory and research* (pp. 114–139). Thousand Oaks, CA: Sage.

Millan, E., & Mittal, B. (2010). Advertising's new audiences: Consumer response in the new free market economies of central and eastern Europe-The case of the Czech republic. *Journal of Advertising*, *39*(3), 81–98. doi:10.2753/JOA0091-3367390300

Miranda, S., & Bostrom, R. (1993). The impact of group support systems on group conflict and conflict management. *Journal of Management Information Systems*, *10*(3), 63–95.

Montgomery, A., & Smith, M. D. (2008) Prospects for personalization on the internet. Available at SSRN: http://ssrn.com/abstract=1169874

Nan Si, S., & Murthy, V. (2003). *Architecture issues of Web-enabled electronic business*. Hershey, PA: Idea Group Publishing.

Oudan, R. (2010). Strategic decision-making in the emerging field of e-Commerce, International. *Journal of Management Information Systems*, *14*(2), 19–26.

Parks, M., & Floyd, K. (1996). Making friends in cyberspace. *The Journal of Communication*, *46*(1), 80–98. doi:10.1111/j.1460-2466.1996.tb01462.x

Peterson, R., & Ross, I. (1972). How to name new brands. *Journal of Advertising*, *12*(6), 29–34.

Ring, P., & Van de Ven, A. (1994). Developmental processes of cooperative interorganizational relationships. *Academy of Management Review*, *19*, 90–118. doi:10.2307/258836

Rotter, J. (1971). Generalized expectancies for interpersonal trust. *The American Psychologist*, *26*(5), 443–452. doi:10.1037/h0031464

Rotter, J. (1980). Interpersonal trust, trustworthiness, and gullibility. *The American Psychologist*, *35*(1), 1–7. doi:10.1037/0003-066X.35.1.1

Rotter, J., Hamsher, J., & Geller, J. (1968). Interpersonal trust, internal-external control, and the Warren commission report. *Journal of Personality and Social Psychology*, *9*, 210–215. doi:10.1037/h0025900

Rubin, Z., & Shenker, S. (1978). Friendship, proximity, and self-disclosure. *Journal of Personality*, *46*, 1–23. doi:10.1111/j.1467-6494.1978.tb00599.x

Schuette, D. (2000). Turning e-business barriers into strengths. *Information Systems Management*, *17*(4), 20–25. doi:10.1201/1078/43193.17.4.20000901/31248.4

Shapiro, D., Shepard, B., & Cheraskin, L. (1992). Business on a handshake. *Negotiation Journal*, *8*, 365–377. doi:10.1111/j.1571-9979.1992.tb00679.x

Shapiro, S. (1987). The social control of impersonal trust. *American Journal of Sociology*, *93*(3), 623–658. doi:10.1086/228791

Taylor, D., & Altman, I. (1987). Social penetration processes. In Roloff, M., & Miller, G. (Eds.), *Interpersonal processes: New directions in communication research* (*Vol. 14*). New York: Sage Publications.

Vesanen, J. (2007). What is personalization? A conceptual framework. *European Journal of Marketing*, *41*(5/6), 409–418. doi:10.1108/03090560710737534

Walther, J. (1992). Interpersonal effects in computer-mediated interaction: A relational perspective. *Communication Research*, *19*, 52–90. doi:10.1177/009365092019001003

Walther, J. (1993). Impression development in computer-mediated interaction. *Western Journal of Communication*, *57*, 381–398.

Walther, J., Anderson, J., & Park, D. (1994). Interpersonal effects in computer-mediated interaction: A meta-analysis of social and antisocial communication. *Communication Research*, *21*, 460–487. doi:10.1177/009365094021004002

Walther, J., & Burgoon, J. (1992). Relational communication in computer-mediated interaction. *Human Communication Research*, *19*, 50–88. doi:10.1111/j.1468-2958.1992.tb00295.x

Weick, K. (1995). *Sensemaking in organizations*. Thousand Oaks, CA: Sage Publications.

Williamson, O. (1993). Calculativeness, trust, and economic organization. *The Journal of Law & Economics*, *36*, 453–486. doi:10.1086/467284

Wu, D., Im, I., Tremaine, M., Instone, K., & Turoff, M. (2002). A framework for classifying personalization scheme used on e-commerce websites. *Proceedings of the 36th Hawaii International Conference on Systems Sciences*, 12 pp., doi: 10.1109/HICSS.2003.1174586; http://ieeexplore.ieee.org/stamp/stamp.jsp?tp=&arnumber=1174586&isnumber=26341.

Young, L., & Albaum, G. (2003). Measurement of trust in salesperson-customer relationships in direct selling. *Journal of Personal Selling & Sales Management*, *23*(3), 253–264.

Zaheer, A., McEvily, B., & Vincenzo, P. (1998). Does trust matter? Exploring the effects of interorganizational and interpersonal trust on performance. *Organization Science*, *9*(2), 141–159. doi:10.1287/orsc.9.2.141

Zucker, L.-G. (1986). Production of trust: Institutional sources of economic structure, 1840-1920. *Research in Organizational Behavior*, *8*, 53–111.

APPENDIX: INSTRUMENTS USED AND VALIDATION TECHNIQUES

Instruments Used

I. Background Information

1. What category best represents your current educational standing?
   Freshman
   Sophomore
   Junior
   Senior
   Graduate
2. What is your gender?
   Male
   Female
3. What year were you born? 19___
4. What is your e-mail address?
5. What is your marital status?
   Single, never married
   Married
   Divorced/Separated
   Widow/Widower
   Other
6. What is your birth order?
   Only
   First Born
   Middle child
   Youngest
7. How would you describe the social economic status of you family of origin?
   Below poverty
   Middle class
   Upper middle class
   Upper class
8. How would you best describe your race?
   African American
   Asian
   Caucasian
   French American
   Spanish American
   Other (please write in) _______________
9. How would you best describe your religion?
   Agnostic
   Atheist
   Catholic
   Jewish
   Protestant
   Other (please write in) _____________

II. Background Disclosure Information

Please indicate what types of information would you give to a ...?						
TA = priest, minister, or therapist	FR = Friend,	AC = Acquaintance,	TR = Trustworthy Brand Name (Direct Mobile)	UT = Untrustworthy Brand Name (DiLink Mobile)		

Interpersonal relationships	**TA**	**FR**	**AC**	**TR**	**UT**
1. Disappointments or bad experiences I have had with love affairs					
2. Times that I felt that I was in love					
3. The things that I worry most about					
4. My attitudes toward my closest friends					
5. The kinds of things that make me especially proud of myself					
6. My thoughts about how intelligent I am compared to other people					
7. The kinds of things that make me especially proud of myself					
8. Why some people like or dislike me					
Attitudes	**TA**	**FR**	**AC**	**TR**	**UT**
1. My religious views					
2. How important school grades are to me					
3. My feelings about the FSU student body					
4. The kind of work that I would like to do in the future					
5. My feeling about my teachers at FSU					
6. My feeling about the Iraq War					
7. My opinion of the American political system					
8. My view of the Bush administration					
Tastes	**TA**	**FR**	**AC**	**TR**	**UT**
1. How I feel about smoking cigarettes					
2. Hobbies that I would like to take up					
3. My taste in clothing					
4. My likes and dislikes in music					
5. How I would like to spend my summers					
6. My likes and dislikes in fiction					
7. Types of newspapers and magazines that I enjoy					
8. My preferences in food					

III. Disposition to Trust

Indicate your level of agreement or disagreement with each statement below.						
1 = Strongly Disagree	2 = Disagree	3 = Mildly Disagree	4 = Neutral	5 = Mildly Agree	6 = Agree	7 = Strongly Agree

	SD	**D**	**MD**	**N**	**MA**	**A**	**SA**
1. I generally trust other people							
2. I tend to count on other people							
3. I generally have faith in humanity							
4. I feel that people are generally reliable							
5. I generally trust other people unless they give me reason not to							

III. Calculus based Trust

Indicate your level of agreement or disagreement with each statement below.							
1 = Strongly Disagree	2 = Disagree	3 = Mildly Disagree	4 = Neutral	5 = Mildly Agree	6 = Agree	7 = Strongly Agree	
	SD	D	MD	N	MA	A	SA
1. This provider has nothing to gain by being dishonest in its interactions with me.							
2. This provider has nothing to gain by not caring about me.							
3. This provider has nothing to gain by being knowledgeable when helping me.							

III. Knowledge based

Indicate your level of agreement or disagreement with each statement below.							
1 = Strongly Disagree	2 = Disagree	3 = Mildly Disagree	4 = Neutral	5 = Mildly Agree	6 = Agree	7 = Strongly Agree	
	SD	D	MD	N	MA	A	SA
1. This vendor approaches me with professionalism.							
2. Given this vendor's track record, I see no reason to doubt the competence of this vendor.							
3. I can rely on this vendor not to make my life more difficult							
4. Most customers, even those who have not purchased from the vendor, trust and respect this vendor.							
5. Other customers must interact with the vendor, before considering the vendor trustworthy.							
6. If people knew more about the vendor's background, they would monitor this vendor's behavior more closely.							

III. Identification based Trust

Indicate your level of agreement or disagreement with each statement below.							
1 = Strongly Disagree	2 = Disagree	3 = Mildly Disagree	4 = Neutral	5 = Mildly Agree	6 = Agree	7 = Strongly Agree	
	SD	D	MD	N	MA	A	SA
1. I have a strong relationship with this vendor. The vendor's representatives and I share our ideas and feelings.							
2. I can express myself freely to the vendor's representatives about the difficulty that I am having with the vendor's products.							
3. The vendor and I both would have a sense of loss if I could no longer purchase from the vendor.							
4. If I express my problems about the vendors products, I know that the vendor would respond constructively and caringly.							
5. I would say that the vendor and I have made considerable emotional investments in our relationships.							

IV. Request for personal information (Tastes)

1. What types of restaurants to you like (check all that apply)?
   Chinese
   Fast food
   French
   Greek
   Indian
   Italian
   Japanese
   Pizza
   Subway
   Other ___________________________
2. What Brand of jeans do you like to wear the most (check all that apply)?
   Banana Republic
   Calvin Kline
   DKNY
   Diesel
   Forenza
   Gap
   Guess
   Lands' end
   Lee
   Levis
   Lucky
   Old Navy
   Ralph Lauren/Polo
   Roebuck
   Talbot's
   Tommy Hilfiger
   Timberland
   Other ___________________________
3. What types of newspapers do you like (check all that apply)?
   NY Times
   St Pete Times
   Tampa Tribune
   Times Union
   Tallahassee Democrat
   USA Today
   Wall Street Journal
   Other ___________________________
4. What types of books do you like to read (check all that apply)?
   Art

Computer
Biographies of Movie Start
Biographies of Political Figures
History
Humanities
Love Stories
Mystery
Poetry
Science
Science Fiction
Other ____________________________

5. What are your hobbies (check all that apply)?
Crafts
Boating
Fishing
Hunting
Reading
Running
Swimming
Other ____________________________

6. What movies do you like to watch (check all that apply)?
Action
Classics
Documentary
Drama
Horror
Musical
Western
Other ____________________________

IV. Request for personal information (Attitude)

1. How would you describe the FSU student body (check all that apply)?
Attractive
Attentive
Considerate
Intelligent
Lucky
Motivated
Punctual
Lazy
Lackadaisical
Inconsiderate

Unintelligent
Unlucky
Lazy
Always late
Other ______________________

2. How would you describe professors at FSU (check all that apply)?
Attractive
Attentive
Considerate
Intelligent
Lucky
Motivated
Punctual
Lazy
Lackadaisical
Inconsiderate
Unintelligent
Unlucky
Lazy
Always latc
Other ______________________

3. How would you describe the American Political System (check all that apply)?
Fair
Sometimes Fair
Unfair
Other ______________________

4. What are your opinions on smoking cigarettes (check all that apply)?
I like to smoke a great deal
I like to smoke occasionally
Its okay for others but not for me
I dislike the smell
I dislike seeing other smoke
It should be illegal
I would vote to make it illegal
Other ______________________

5. How would you describe your feeling on the Iraq war (check all that apply)?
I am strongly against the war
I am against the war
I have no feeling toward the war
I strongly support the war
I support the war
Other ______________________

6. How would you describe the Bush Administration (check all that apply)?

Honest
Dishonest
I have no feeling either way
Other ____________________________

IV. Request for personal information (Interpersonal)

1. Comparing yourself to others at FSU are you (check all that apply)?
   More intelligent
   Have about the same intelligence
   Not as intelligent
   Other ____________________________
2. What types of things make you proud of yourself (check all that apply)?
   A good test grade
   A job interview
   A romantic date
   Attending a religious function
   Voting
   Receiving an award
   Working with charities
   Finding money
   A job offer
   Helping another out
   Other ____________________________
3. Why do people like you (check all that apply)?
   I am attractive
   I am considerate
   I am nice
   I am funny
   I am smart
   I have money
   I have power
   Other ____________________________
4. What do you worry about the most (check all that apply)?
   Finding a spouse/companion
   Grades
   Getting a job
   Getting older
   Money
   My health
   My family's health
   My weight
   Retirement

Other ___________________________

5. How would you describe your closest friends (check all that apply)?
   Attractive
   Attentive
   Considerate
   Intelligent
   Lucky
   Motivated
   Punctual
   Lazy
   Lackadaisical
   Inconsiderate
   Unintelligent
   Unlucky
   Lazy
   Always late
   Other ______________________
6. What are your greatest disappointments (check all that apply)?
   Getting a bad grade
   Losing a friend
   Losing money (e.g. Stock market)
   Losing a football game
   Not getting a job
   Not getting an award
   Not getting a raise
   Other ___________________________

Data Supporting the Development of the Instruments Used in the Study

A total of 321 subjects participated in this study. Twenty-five of 321 subjects encountered technical difficulties during the study and their data was eliminated from the data set. Fifteen subjects were found to have entered erroneous data (e.g., birth date, race, or culture) and were also eliminated from the study. Ninety-nine of the remaining 317 subjects did not complete the entire survey. Attrition figures are summarized for each login in Table 2. The remaining 182 subjects' responses were coded into groups depending on their respective experimental condition. Experimental conditions are summarized in Table 3. In the statistical analysis, brand name, security, and personalization were dummy coded as "1" indicating the presence of a trustworthy brand name, security emblem, or personalization and "0" indicating the absence of these treatment conditions.

As part of the preliminary analysis, data explaining each variable were analyzed to determine if the distribution represented a departure from normality. Departures from normality are important because they violate assumptions of statistical procedures such as regression and ANOVA (Hair et al., 1998). Two main indicators of normality are skewness and kurtosis. Skewness is a measure of the lack of symmetry in the distribution of data points. For example, a distribution that is skewed to the right or left will

Table 2. Attrition Rates for Each Login

	Number of subjects that did not finish
Background	30
1st login	23
2nd login	18
3rd login	14
4th login	9
Total	99

Table 3. Experimental Conditions (Yes indicates presence of factor, No indicates absence)

Experimental Condition	Trustworthy Brand Name	Security	Personalization	Number of Subjects
A	Yes	No	No	24
B	No	No	No	23
AS	Yes	Yes	No	22
BS	No	Yes	No	22
AP	Yes	No	Yes	22
BP	No	Yes	Yes	24
ASP	Yes	Yes	Yes	21
BSP	No	Yes	Yes	24
Total				182

result in values of skewness of greater than two standard errors of skewness (SES). SES is measured as $2 * (6/N)^{1/2}$, where N is the number of subjects. For this data set, values of skewness above $(2 * (6/N)^{1/2}) = 2 * (6/182)^{1/2} = 2 * (0.18) = 0.36$ would represent a departure from normality. Kurtosis is a measure of whether the distribution is peaked or flat relative to a normal distribution. The amount of kurtosis that represents a departure from normality is measured as greater than 2 standard errors of kurtosis (SEK). SEK is measured as $2 * (24/N)^{1/2}$, where N is the number of subjects. For this data set, kurtosis above $2 * (24/182)^{1/2} = 2 * (0.36) = 0.73$) would represent a departure from normality. Results for means, standard deviations, and skewness, and kurtosis for constructs are presented in Table 4.

Departures from normality recognized in the constructs disposition to trust (BACK), calculus-based trust (CAL), identification-based trust (INDEN), and taste (TA), attitude (AT), and interpersonal (IN) disclosures do not impact the statistical analysis. The statistical method used to test hypotheses 1 through 6, structural equation modeling or SEM, does not require that constructs are normally distributed (Chin, 1998). The statistical method to test hypothesis 7, analysis of variance or ANOVA, does require each construct be normally distributed (Kirk, 1995). However, departures of normality are allowed for sample sizes greater than 12. For this study, the sample size was greater than 180 and subjects were evenly distributed within groups. Therefore, there is little threat to statistical validity due to departures from normality.

Table 4. Descriptive Statistics and Normality Estimates N=182

	Mean	S.D.	Skewness	Kurtosis
Birth Order	1.67	1.04	0.02	-1.29
Income	4.74	2.75	0.36	-0.70
Culture	2.06	1.09	0.19	0.41
Religion	4.10	2.97	0.31	**-1.54**
Disposition to Trust (BACK)	4.74	1.21	**-0.69**	-0.13
Calculus-based Trust (CAL)	4.79	1.58	**-0.37**	-0.59
Knowledge-based Trust (KNOW)	4.41	0.90	0.05	0.72
Identification-based Trust (INDEN)	3.30	1.18	**-0.39**	-0.43
Taste Disclosure (TA)	0.99	0.05	**-9.64**	**20.73**
Attitude Disclosure (AT)	0.93	0.21	**-3.24**	**10.52**
Interpersonal Disclosure (IN)	0.59	0.38	-0.31	**-1.34**

* Bolded items indicate departures from normality.

To test hypotheses 1 through 6, partial least squares (PLS) was used. PLS is a widely used technique to analyze structural models with formative and reflective constructs (Chin, 1998). PLS only requires sample sizes equal to ten times the most complex construct's number of indicators or the largest number of paths leading to a latent construct. The most complex construct of this model is disposition to trust (BACK). This construct has five indicators and four leading paths. Thus, (10 * 5) subjects are required to provide an adequate sample size to proceed with analysis (Chin, 1998). The theoretical model was estimated using PLS Graph 2.91.03.04.

Analysis of variance (ANOVA) was used to test hypothesis 7. ANOVA requires that there are at least 20 subjects per each group and that subjects are evenly distributed among groups.

To ensure that subjects' trusting beliefs were not influenced by outside shopping experiences, subjects were asked if they had made purchases either online or in brick and mortar establishments and to rate the quality of their experience. Responses for quality of experience were scored from 1 (Excellent) to 7 (Horrible). Results shown in Table 5 indicate that over 30% of the subjects made retail purchases at brick and mortar establishments between logins and on average rated their experience as good with a mean of 4.18 (S.D. = 1.53). Over 5% of the subjects made retail purchases online between logins and also rated their experience as good with a mean of 4.40 (S.D. = 1.68). There was no significant variation of experiences between experimental groups for either retail or online purchases.

Prior to testing the theoretical model using PLS, ANOVA, or any other statistical technique, the accuracy of the theoretical model is assessed. The goals of testing the theoretical model are to validate the accuracy of the measurement model and to demonstrate that the measures adequately explain the underlying constructs. Testing of the theoretical model was performed through factor analysis.

Factor analysis requires that measures have identical scales (Hair et al., 1998). Within this analysis two different scales were used. Of the seven constructs that used scale items, four of the constructs used a seven-point Likert scale with anchors of 1 (strongly disagree) to 7 (strongly agree) and three used a dichotomous scale of 0 (indicating they had disclosed information) or 1 (indicating that had not disclosed information). Disposition to trust (BACK), calculus-based trust (CAL), knowledge-based trust (KNOW), and identification-based trust (INDEN) used a seven-point scale; taste (TA), attitude

Table 5. Manipulation Check

	1st login	2nd login	3rd login	4th login	Sum or Weighted Average
Retail Purchases					Sum
Group A	9	10	7	6	33
Group AS	10	9	12	12	44
Group AP	4	7	8	4	23
Group ASP	7	7	7	7	28
Group B	5	2	6	4	18
Group BS	8	5	4	3	20
Group BP	11	11	7	9	38
Group BSP	11	5	8	5	30
Average	8.13	7.50	7.38	6.25	29.25
Rating					Weighted Average
Group A	3.56 (SD = 1.51)	4.00 (SD = 1.41)	3.14 (SD = 1.46)	4.00 (SD = 1.67)	3.73 (SD = 1.46)
Group AS	3.90 (SD = 1.20)	3.89 (SD = 1.45)	4.33 (SD = 1.78)	4.75 (SD = 1.71)	4.27 (SD = 1.55)
Group AP	4.25 (SD = 2.22)	4.43 (SD = 1.90)	4.00 (SD = 1.51)	4.00 (SD = 1.15)	4.17 (SD = 1.61)
Group ASP	4.71 (SD = 1.80)	4.00 (SD = 1.73)	4.84 (SD = 2.19)	4.71 (SD = 0.76)	4.57 (SD = 1.64)
Group B	3.00 (SD= 1.22)	3.00 (SD = 0.00)	3.33 (SD = 0.82)	4.50 (SD = 1.00)	3.56 (SD = 1.10)
Group BS	3.75 (SD = 1.04)	4.60 (SD = 1.67)	3.50 (SD = 1.00)	4.33 (SD = 1.15)	4.00 (SD = 1.21)
Group BP	4.18 (SD = 1.47)	5.09 (SD = 1.81)	5.86 (SD = 1.07)	5.00 (SD = 1.00)	4.95 (SD = 1.49)
Group BSP	3.64 (SD = 1.43)	4.20 (SD = 1.79)	3.50 (SD = 1.77)	3.80 (SD = 1.10)	3.70 (SD = 1.47)
Average	3.88 (SD = 1.40)	4.30 (SD = 1.59)	4.12 (SD = 1.70)	4.50 (SD = 1.28)	4.18 (SD = 1.53)
Online Purchases					Sum
Group A	2	7	2	3	14
Group AS	3	2	6	5	16
Group AP	3	2	3	1	9
Group ASP	6	1	3	3	13
Group B	5	1	4	2	12
Group BS	4	3	0	2	9
Group BP	4	2	3	2	11
Group BSP	3	4	3	4	14
Average	3.75	2.75	3.00	2.75	12.25
Rating					Weighted Average
Group A	5.00 (SD = 0.00)	3.33 (SD = 1.86)	3.00 (SD = 0.00)	5.33 (SD = 2.89)	3.73 (SD = 1.46)
Group AS	3.67 (SD = 1.15)	5.00 (SD = 2.83)	3.67 (SD = 1.15)	3.00 (SD = 1.63)	3.63 (SD = 1.41)
Group AP	3.67 (SD = 1.15)	5.00 (SD = 2.83)	5.00 (SD = 2.00)	3.00 (SD = 1.15)	4.17 (SD = 0.00)
Group ASP	3.33 (SD = 0.82)	5.00 (SD = 0.00)	5.00 (SD = 2.00)	4.33 (SD = 1.15)	4.08 (SD = 1.32)
Group B	3.00 (SD = 1.22)	7.00 (SD = 0.00)	4.00 (SD = 1.15)	4.00 (SD = 1.41)	4.83 (SD = 1.59)
Group BS	5.00 (SD = 1.63)	5.00 (SD = 2.00)	0.00 (SD = 0.00)	4.00 (SD = 1.41)	4.78 (SD = 1.56)
Group BP	4.75 (SD = 2.06)	6.00 (SD = 1.41)	5.67 (SD = 2.31)	5.00 (SD = 0.00)	5.27 (SD = 1.68)
Group BSP	3.67 (SD = 1.15)	4.75 (SD = 2.63)	5.00 (SD = 2.00)	5.50 (SD = 1.91)	4.79 (SD = 1.93)
Average	3.75 (SD = 1.47)	4.59 (SD = 2.04)	4.42 (SD = 1.61)	4.32 (SD = 1.73)	4.40 (SD = 1.68)

(AT), and interpersonal (IN) used a dichotomous scale. Sixteen factors were used in the entire theoretical model with the remaining nine independent, intermediate, and dependent variables operationalized using single measures.

There are several steps to performing factor analysis. The first step is to perform a pre-analysis check of whether the data sets are appropriate for factor analysis. Next, factors are extracted using principle component analysis (PCA) and rotated into a simple structure. After this, the solution is evaluated to determine whether it explains a sufficient amount of the variance. Finally, the solution is evaluated for convergent and divergent validity and reliability.

The appropriateness of using factor analysis with each data series was determined using the Kaiser-Meyer-Olkin (KMO) measure of sampling adequacy and Bartlett's test of sphericity. A KMO of equal or greater than 0.50 indicates partial correlations between variables are small. Bartlett's test of sphericity tests whether the correlation matrix is an identity matrix, indicating that a factor model is inappropriate (Hair et al., 1998). For the first data set, the KMO is 0.806 and the chi-square statistic is 1517.441 ($p<0.000$), thus factor analysis is appropriate for examining the factors BACK, CAL, KNOW, and INDEN. For the second data set, the KMO is 0.774 and the chi-square statistic is 1451.038 ($p<0.000$), thus factor analysis is appropriate for examining the factors TA, AT, and IN.

The next step in factor analysis is to perform principle components analysis (PCA). PCA examines the factor loading of each indicator, extracting items that do not significantly load on the construct of interest. An item is extracted if it does not load above 0.50 on its own construct or above 0.30 on another construct (Hair et al., 1998). In this solution, many of the items were closely correlated with each other. Thus, a large number of items were dropped yielding a solution that best explained the constructs of interest. For the construct calculus-based trust (CAL), one item was dropped. For the construct knowledge-based trust (KNOW), three items were dropped. For the construct identification-based trust (INDEN), two items were dropped. For the disclosure measures (taste (TA), attitude (AT), and interpersonal (IN)) three items were dropped from the constructs attitude (AT) and taste (TA) and two items were dropped from the interpersonal (IN) construct. The final solution contained a loading greater than 0.50 and no cross loadings greater than.30. Tables 6 and 7 show the respective factor loadings.

After determining the appropriate number of factors, the final factor matrix was rotated using an oblique rotation. Factor matrices are rotated to manipulate or adjust the factor axes to achieve a simpler and more meaningful factor solution (Hair et al., 1998). Varimax rotation was chosen over Oblique because it rotates the factors to an orthogonal angle (i.e., 90 degrees).

Next, the solution was subjected to the latent root criterion, or Kaiser Rule, to determine whether the factors explain a sufficient amount of the variance (Hair et al., 1998). The Kaiser Rule states that factors having eigenvalues greater than 1 are considered significant. For the first data set, as shown in Table 8, the solution contains four factors with eigenvalues greater than 1. Again for the second data set, shown in Table 9, factors one to three also all have eigenvalues greater one. Therefore, for both data sets, the factors explain a significant amount of the variance of each solution.

To further support the factor solution, the variance explained by each factor solution was analyzed. For the first data set, Table 8 shows that successive factors 1-4 explain more than 76% of the total variance and additional factors explained a marginal amount (less than 5%) of the variance. For the second data set, Table 9 shows that successive factors 1-3 explained more than 68% of the total variance. Subsequent increases explained a marginal amount of the variance (less than 5%).

The measurement model was assessed for convergent and discriminant validity and reliability using statistical formulas and SPSS. Convergent and discriminant validity was assessed by applying two

Table 6. Factor Loadings[abcde] (Data Set 1)

	BACK	CAL	KNOW	INDEN
BACK1	**0.87**			
BACK4	**0.83**			0.14
BACK5	**0.82**			
BACK3	**0.81**			
BACK2	**0.77**			0.10
CAL1		**0.90**	0.20	
CAL2		**0.89**	0.22	0.14
KNOW1		0.19	**0.87**	0.22
KNOW2		0.16	**0.86**	0.24
KNOW3		0.16	**0.89**	0.19
INDEN1	0.12		0.21	**0.82**
INDEN3		0.11	0.19	**0.84**
INDEN5			0.20	**0.86**

a. BACK = Disposition to Trust,
CAL = Calculus-based Trust,
KNOW = Knowledge-based Trust,
INDEN = Identification-based Trust
b. Extraction Method: Principal Component Analysis.
c. Rotation Method: Varimax with Kaiser Normalization.
d. Rotation converged in 5 iterations.
e. Blank cells indicate the loading was less than 0.10

Table 7. Factor Loadings[abcde] (Data Set 2)

	TA	AT	IN
TA1	**0.79**		
TA2	**0.68**		0.12
TA3	**0.67**	0.26	
AT1	0.16	**0.78**	0.21
AT3		**0.78**	0.20
AT5		**0.75**	0.10
IN2		0.17	**0.74**
IN3		0.10	**0.77**
IN4		0.14	**0.74**
IN6		0.14	**0.75**

a. TA = Taste Disclosures,
AT = Attitude Disclosures,
IN = Interpersonal Disclosures
b. Extraction Method: Principal Component Analysis.
c. Rotation Method: Varimax with Kaiser Normalization.
d. Rotation converged in 5 iterations.
e. Blank cells indicate the loading was less than 0.10

Table 8. Variance Explained (Data Set 1)

Component	Eigenvalue	% of Variance	Cumulative %	Total
1	4.26	32.77	32.77	4.26
2	3.16	24.34	57.11	3.16
3	1.43	11.04	68.15	1.43
4	1.10	8.43	76.57	1.10

Table 9. Variance Explained (Data Set 2)

Component	Eigenvalue	% of Variance	Cumulative %	Total
1	3.01	30.13	30.13	3.01
2	1.53	15.33	55.46	1.53
3	1.32	13.23	68.69	1.32

criteria: (1) the square root of the average variance extracted (AVE) by a construct from its indicators should be at least 0.707 (i.e., AVE > 0.50) and exceed correlations with other constructs (Fornell & Larcker, 1981; Barclay et al., 1995; Chin, 1998) and (2) standardized item loadings should be at least 0.707 (Compeau et al., 1999; Agarwal & Karahanna, 2000). The square root of the AVE was computed from the following formula: $AVE = \Sigma(\lambda_i)^2 / [\Sigma \lambda_i^2 + \Sigma(1 - \lambda_i^2)]$. Where λ is the standard path loading. Table 10 contains the loadings for each item. The AVE for each construct is located on the diagonal of each table and is in bold. From the table, both criteria (1) and (2) are satisfied, therefore, convergent and divergent validity is assumed.

Reliability for the seven constructs was determined using Cronbach's alpha and internal consistency reliability (ICR). ICR was computed from the formula: $ICR = \Sigma(\lambda_i)^2 / (\Sigma[\lambda_i)^2 + \Sigma(1 - \lambda_i^2)]$ where λ is the standardized component loading of a manifest indicator on a latent construct (Chin 1998). Internal consistencies (similar to Cronbach's alpha) of 0.70 or higher are considered adequate (Barclay et al., 1995; Compeau et al., 1999; Agarwal et al., 2000). ICR is considered more robust than Cronbach's alpha because it weighs items differently depending on factor loading considerations. Looking at Table 10, both ICR and Cronbach alpha were greater than 0.70, indicating high reliability.

Table 10. Cronbach's Alphas and Interconstruct Correlations

	ICR	Cronbach Alpha	1	2	3	4	5	6	7	8	9	10	11	12	13	14
1. Brand				0.01	-0.055	-0.014	0.072	0.022	-0.036	0.026	0.236****	0.363****	0.252***	0.007	0.089**	0.187****
2. Security					0.033	-0.047	-0.009	-0.009	0.004	-0.051	0.158****	0.194****	0.122****	-0.012	0.092**	0.189****
3. Personalization						0.019	-0.065	0.051	0.011	0.079**	-0.007	-0.120****	-0.093**	-0.011	0.006	0.061
4. Birth Order							0.038	0.092	-0.117	-0.252****	-0.146***	-0.164****	-0.211****	-0.071*	-0.056	-0.102**
5. Income								0.116***	-0.052	0.142****	0.037	0.055	0.071*	-0.012	0.073**	0.084**
6. Culture									-0.234****	0.037	0.009	-0.053	-0.021	0.004	0.034	0.079**
7. Religion										0.16****	0.061	-0.016	-0.024	0.035	-0.002	-0.045
8. Disposition To Trust	0.84	0.88								**0.85**	0.391****	0.255****	0.266****	0.012	0.093*	0.140*
9. Calculus-Based Trust	0.81	0.76									**0.72**	0.255**	0.211*	0.093	0.114	0.274*
10. Knowledge-Based Trust	0.76	0.77										**0.64**	0.588***	0.053	0.172**	0.374**
11. Identification-Based Trust	0.83	0.70											**0.76**	0.027	0.124*	0.365*
12. Taste Disclosures	0.75	0.73												**0.58**	0.139****	0.088**
13. Attitudinal Disclosures	0.74	0.70													**0.51**	0.3400****
14. Interpersonal Disclosures	0.71	0.77														**0.54**

* $p < 0.10$
** $p < 0.05$
*** $p < 0.01$
**** $p < 0.001$

Chapter 2
Does Self-Efficacy Matter?
Examining Online Transaction Self-Efficacy and General Self-Efficacy in B2C E-Commerce

Young Hoon Kim
Rutgers University, USA

Dan J. Kim
University of Houston Clear Lake, USA

ABSTRACT

In this study, we propose a research model examining how self-efficacy affects consumer trust in web vendors, and how self-efficacy and consumer trust influence online consumers' intentions to purchase from a certain web vendor. In particular, we separate the concept of self-efficacy into two types, general self-efficacy and domain-specific self-efficacy (i.e., online transaction self-efficacy), and we examine whether they play different roles as antecedents of trust in the realm of B2C e-commerce. The results show that online transaction self-efficacy plays an important role in consumer's trust building while general self-efficacy does not. Online transaction self-efficacy is also an important determinant of perceived risk and a consumer's intention to purchase. Although general self-efficacy does not play the same role as online self-efficacy, it is a key determinant of domain-specific self-efficacy (i.e., online transaction self-efficacy). This study provides a focused picture of trust-building and reinforcement of purchase intention in e-commerce, from the separated angle of self-efficacy. Theoretical and practical contributions are discussed.

DOI: 10.4018/978-1-60960-577-3.ch002

INTRODUCTION

Trust in online transactions (e-trust) is crucial to the success of e-commerce. Lack of trust is the main barrier to online transactions (Cole, 1998; Jarvenpaa & Tractinsky, 1999; Reichheld & Schefter, 2000; Rose, Khoo, & Straub, 1999). Since consumers tend to consider online transactions to be potentially risky and uncertainty-involving processes, e-trust has become an important issue in business-to-customer (B2C) electronic commerce. Previous studies have shown that trust is the most significant factor in the process of e-commerce (Doney & Cannon, 1997; Gefen, 2002). Trust was considered a key factor in the most effective uncertainty reduction mechanism (Gefen, 2000; Hart & Saunders, 1997). Trust had a significant effect on willingness to engage in transactions (Bhattacherjee, 2002) and purchase (Gefen). The direct effect of trust on purchase intention and behavior was proven theoretically and even empirically. The direct effect of trust on purchase intention (or behavior) can be thought of as a necessary condition of an uncertainty reduction mechanism. Jarvenpaa, Tractinsky and Vitale (2000) suggested that trust antecedes perceptions of risk, which ultimately affects willingness to buy (trust → risk perception (and attitude) → willingness to buy).

Although previous studies have taken for granted trust as an influential factor, it is becoming clearer that understanding trust itself still requires more effort. Seminal efforts have attempted to define trust in organizational and electronic commerce (Mayer, Davis, & Schoorman, 1995; 1995; McKnight & Chervany, 2002; McKnight, Choudhury, & Kacmar, 2002). Nonetheless, trust has yet to be defined adequately in the context of online transactions. The present study starts from the authors' reflection that trust requires comprehensive reconceptualizing within e-commerce settings, because an unexplored domain still remains, which we believe is associated strongly with the whole process of trust building.

The main part of our reflection on existing literature is that previous research on e-trust tends to take a trustee-centered approach, that is, it mainly focuses on the attributes of online vendors by virtue of viewing trust as "belief in an attribute of the trustee" (McKnight et al., 2002) or "willingness to believe the trustee" (Fung & Lee, 1999; McKnight et al.). Most definitions of e-trust are focused on a trustor's subjective belief of a trustee, that is, an online consumer's judgment and assessment of an online vendor with whom he or she interacts in a particular transaction (Bhattacharya, Devinney, & Pillutla, 1998; Gambetta, 1998; McKnight & Chervany, 2002). However, uncertainty reduction and trust building are an individual's perceptional process, and are influenced not only by an individual's judgment of others' attributes (i.e., ability, benevolence and integrity) but also by an individual's judgment of *his or her ability* to render matters satisfactory. Nevertheless, existing trust studies have tended to take for granted the notion that trust can be viewed from a trustee-centered perspective. Again we emphasize that a trustee-centered perspective is characterized by an individual's perception of a trustee's attributes that are fundamental to reliable and trustworthy transactions. Given that few trust studies have been done from the viewpoint of the characteristics of the trustor (i.e., online customer), this study attempts to shift focus from a trustee-centered perspective to that of a trustor attribute-centered approach, by highlighting self-efficacy in B2C e-commerce. A perspective that differentiates a trustor-centered and trustee-centered notion of trust is based on the seminal work of Mayer et al. (1995) that differentiates characteristics of trustors and trustees. In shifting the focus of trust in e-commerce, therefore, this study argues that an individual's beliefs in his or her abilities and competence should play a significant role in trust-building and uncertainty reduction. Such judgments of one's capability are conceptualized as self-efficacy, and show how a trustor judges his or her ability to deal with issues and problems in particular transactions.

This study aims to fill in the blank remaining in classical works to define e-trust: exploring other intrapersonal level factors. McKnight and Chervany (2002) provide a clear foothold for our effort to broaden e-trust horizons. They propose a conceptual framework of multiple-level trust, namely intrapersonal, institutional, and interpersonal levels. However, what is needed more is a close examination of 'intrapersonal level.' Although McKnight and Chervany referred to psychology to elicit 'dispositional trust' at intrapersonal level, their examination of intrapersonal level seems less than required. Disposition to trust, an intrapersonal factor, simply does not represent all possible conceptualizations of intrapersonal level factors which social psychology has been elaborating for decades.

The present study draws upon the concept of self-efficacy within social cognitive theory (SCT) to expand understanding of how a trustor attribute-centered approach to e-trust is possible. Social cognition research has focused on how people perceive themselves (e.g., in this study, individual online customers), and others (e.g., online businesses), in a variety of social situations. According to SCT, individuals actively think and respond to their external environment to achieve goals (McCormick & Martinko, 2004). Previous SCT-applied research (McCormick & Martinko; Stajkovic & Luthans, 1998) showed that individuals with higher self-efficacy can actively monitor their performance environment and perform well. With respect to online purchasing cases, SCT also provides a clear and powerful explanation: an individual online customer controls and directs his or her series of decisions and actions (Bandura, 1982; 1986).

Many consumers consider online transactions to be uncertain and financially risky, compared with conventional face-to-face transactions. Consumers are given little opportunity to assess the quality of goods (i.e., it is not easy to test goods through interaction with web vendors) or service (i.e., they do not know whether the service is reliable and legitimate), especially when they purchase from an unfamiliar web vendor. Ultimately, making online transactions satisfactory is a difficult task (Ba & Pavlou, 2002). Therefore, online transactions can be characterized as performance-related tasks. They are not typical work-related tasks that have been the focus of organizational studies. Social cognitive theory holds that an individual can exercise control over his or her own thoughts, emotions and actions (Bandura, 1986). For successful online transactions, individuals use their abilities to "set goals" (e.g., satisfactory purchase), "plan action" (e.g., gathering relevant information and reducing the number of online vendors), and "anticipate resultant consequences" (e.g., customer satisfaction guarantee).

Since the proposal of Bandura's socio-cognitive theory, much research has been done to explain an individual's behavioral motivations. While self-efficacy has been introduced into and utilized in a considerable amount of research in information systems (IS) and behavioral sciences (Agarwal, Sambamurthy, & Stair, 2000; Compeau & Higgins, 1995; Marakas, Yi, & Johnson, 1998; Venkatesh & Davis, 1996), little is known of the applicability of self-efficacy in the domain of e-commerce. Along with perceived usefulness and perceived ease of use, in previous IS research, self-efficacy was included as a factor in the multi-level model of technology acceptance model (Venkatesh & Davis, 1996).

The self-efficacy factor can be introduced into the domain of e-commerce in the same way as it has been in other research areas. If consumers feel too much uncertainty in e-commerce transactions, they will be reluctant to purchase from online retail websites. If, however, people are confident that they can handle potential problems that may arise during online transactions, their confidence in dealing with e-commerce will increase. Customers who see themselves as highly self efficacious are more likely to try out uncertain and possibly risky online transactions, whereas those who see themselves as having low levels of self-efficacy are less likely to engage in uncertain and risky situations.

This study addresses two research questions: (1) does self-efficacy play a role in forming and reinforcing consumers' intentions to purchase online goods? and (2) what is the structural relationship among subjective/internal factors in the formation of trust in B2C e-commerce? To this end, this study focuses on how consumers' intrapersonal level factor, self-efficacy, plays a role in trust-building and affects their intentions to purchase goods in the risky and uncertain B2C e-commerce context. In this study, self-efficacy is posited as a causal antecedent to trust in reducing uncertainty inherent in online transactions, and influences trust-building. To investigate these research questions, SEM (Structural Equation Modeling) is used to examine the proposed model of trust-building and uncertainty reduction.

TRUST

Previous research on trust in e-commerce may be categorized as follows: 1) examining the effect of trust on purchase behaviors (Jarvenpaa, Tractinsky, & Vitale, 2000; Kim, Ferrin, & Rao, 2003b; Kim, Sivasailam, & Rao, 2004); 2) exploring antecedents of trust (Bhattacherjee, 2002; Gefen, 2000; Gefen, 2002; Kim, Ferrin, & Rao, 2003a): familiarity and disposition to trust; and 3) clarifying the definition of trust in e-commerce (Mayer et al., 1995; McKnight & Chervany, 2002; McKnight et al., 2002).

Literature (Barney & Hansen, 1994; Doney & Cannon, 1997; Kim, Song, Braynov, & Rao, 2005; Zucker, 1986) has identified antecedents or determinants of e-trust: disposition to trust (Cheung & Lee, 2001; Gefen, 2000; McKnight, Cummings, & Chervany, 1998; Pavlou & Gefen, 2004), the trustor's familiarity with the trustee (Gefen, 2000; Pavlou & Chai, 2002), previous transaction experience (Pavlou & Gefen, 2004), perceived security protection (Cheung & Lee), concern for privacy (Belanger, Hiller, & Smith, 2002), perceived system reliability (Kim et al., 2003), reputation (Jarvenpaa et al., 2000; Kim et al., 2004; McKnight et al., 2002), importance of referral and word-of-mouth (Money, Gilly, & Granham, 1998; Stewart, 2003), third party seal of trust (Cheung & Lee, 2001; Kim et al., 2004), and information quality (McKnight et al., 2004).

Previous literature showed several distinct dimensions of trust: integrity, motives, consistency, openness, discreetness, functional competence, interpersonal competence, business sense, judgment (Gabarro 1978), predictability, dependability, faith (Rempel, Holmes, & Zanna, 1985), availability, competence, consistency, discreetness, fairness, integrity, loyalty, openness, promise fulfillment, receptivity (Butler, 1991), ability, benevolence, integrity (Mayer et al., 1995), keeping commitments, negotiating honesty, avoiding taking excessive advantage (Cummings & Bromiley, 1996), credibility and benevolence (Doney & Cannon, 1997), openness, congruity, shared values, autonomy (Hart, Capps, Cangemi, & Caillouet, 1986), ability, benevolence, integrity (Jarvenpaa, Knoll, & Leidner, 1998), benevolence, competence, honesty, predictability (McKnight et al., 1998). Among the above dimensions, some originally were developed to describe trust in interpersonal relationships (e.g., peer and work) so may be irrelevant to online transactions. It should be noted that some trust dimensions are applicable to e-commerce, but that some others are not.

Kim, Ferrin, and Rao (2007) have suggested a consumer decision-making model based on four antecedents to trust: cognition, affect, experience, and personality. Cognition-based trust antecedents (Chen, Chen, & Meindl, 1998; McAllister, 1995) are associated with self-observations (e.g., information quality), self-perceptions (e.g., perceived privacy protection, security protection, and system reliability) and self-interests (e.g., brand image and fancy design) of the trustee. Affect-based trust antecedents (Chen et al.; McAllister) are related to a social-emotional bond that goes beyond a regular, direct business or professional relationship with the trustee, such as inputs from others (e.g., third party seal, referral, review comments, recommendation, etc.). Experience-based and personality-oriented antecedents to trust are related to consumers' personal experiences (e.g., familiarity, e-commerce experience, etc.) and characteristics (e.g., disposition to trust and shopping style) respectively.

Trust has been conceptualized by investigating relationships among beliefs, attitudes, intentions, and behaviors (Mayer et al., 1995; McKnight et al., 1998). This direction of research is concerned with defining the trust concept in a management context, not in an interpersonal context. Schurr and Ozanne (1985) defined trust as the "belief that a party's word or promise was reliable and that a party will fulfill his/her obligation in an exchange relationship." Certainly this belief leads to behavioral intentions. Mayer et al. (1995) defined trust as "the willingness of a party to be vulnerable to the actions of another party based on the expectation that the other will perform a particular action important to the trustor, irrespective of the ability to monitor or control that other party" (p.712). McKnight et al. (2002) defined trust to mean that "one believes in, and is willing to depend on, another party" (p. 42). Gefen (2000) suggested that trust was based on previous interactions, although a supplier's previous behavior is no guarantee that he or she or it will act as expected.

Mayer et al. (1995) proposed a generic concept of trust as having three dimensions: ability, benevolence, and integrity. These three are conceptually and empirically distinct (Bhattacherjee, 2002; Gefen, 2002). Ability is defined as "that group of skills, competencies, and characteristics that enable a party to have influence within some specific domain" (Mayer et al., p.717). It reflects the trustor's perception of the trustee's competence in and knowledge of the behavior and performance that the trustor desires (Bhattacherjee). Benevolence is "the extent to which a trustee is believed to want to do good to the trustor, aside from an egocentric profit motive" (Mayer et al., p.718). It refers to the degree to which a trustee is believed to try to bring some intended results to a trustor. If a web retailer is benevolent, it is likely to exhibit empathy and receptivity toward online customers' concerns (Bhattacherjee). Integrity reflects "the trustor's perception that the trustee adheres to a set of principles that the trustor finds acceptable" (Mayer et al., p.719). Integrity can be assessed in terms of online vendors' conducts, policies that relate to customer service, and use of private information (Bhattacherjee).

McKnight and Chervany (2002) classified the definition of trust into four stages: disposition to trust, institution-based trust, trusting belief, and trusting intention. They approached the trust-building process by integrating trust-related constructs within the framework of the Theory of Reasoned Action (TRA). An issue has arisen of how the dimensionality of consumer trust should be understood. Unlike the approach that regarded consumer trust as a single-dimensional construct (Gefen & DeVine, 2001; Gefen & Straub, 2003; Jarvenpaa & Tractinsky, 1999; McKnight et al., 2000; McKnight & Chervany), Gefen (2002) proposed that e-trust should be understood as a multi-dimensional construct and showed that sub-constructs of trust were distinct from each other.

Buyers' willingness to provide their credit card numbers or other personal information will depend on their assessments of the trustworthiness of the online vendor. Trust was the result of "a set of trustworthiness beliefs" (Gefen, 2000; Mayer et al., 1995). Trust dealt with beliefs about the future behaviors and choices of others and these beliefs or trustworthiness beliefs were influenced by the individual's judgment of the other party's future actions and trading environments (Gefen).

Consumer Trust

Based on extant literature, trust can be defined as the consumer's belief that the seller, i.e., an individual or firm or Website, will fulfill its transaction as expected. Gefen (2000) showed that consumer trust influenced purchase intentions, and Reichheld and Schefter (2000) showed that consumers lacking trust in a specific online vendor were unlikely to engage in e-commerce with that vendor. Gefen adopted the idea that not only a general belief that a party can be trusted but also specific beliefs concerning its ability, integrity, and benevolence serve as antecedents of this general belief in trust. Jarvenpaa and Tractinsky (2000) suggested that trust is a critical antecedent to engaging in online transactions because it reduces the idea of risks associated with purchasing goods and services over the Internet.

In previous research, trust in others' abilities in the virtual community was positively related to willingness to give information to others and desire to obtain information from others (Ridings, Gefen, & Arinze, 2002). Trust in others' benevolence and integrity in the virtual community was positively related to willingness to give information to others and desire to obtain information from others (Ridings et al.). Trust was a significant predictor of online banking users' willingness to transact (Bhattacherjee, 2002). Attitudes and behaviors of buyers in an Internet store were shown to be affected by e-trust levels. Trust in an Internet store positively affects buyers' attitudes and negatively affects their perceptions of risks.

H1: The degree to which an individual perceives an online vendor's ability, benevolence, and integrity is positively associated with his or her willingness to purchase online.

Disposition to Trust

Deciding on whether or not to trust others depends ultimately on the individual's assessment of the other party and the situation. The consumer's individual judgment will be influenced by that consumer's intrapersonal level factor. Disposition to trust is defined as a general personality trait that exhibits a general expectation of how trusting other people should be (McKnight et al., 1998; Ridings et al., 2002). Mayer et al. (1995) viewed trust as a general personality trait as well as a domain-specific psychological state. Personality traits are subject to developmental factors irrelevant to a given context (Mayer et al.).

Ridings et al. (2002) applied disposition to trust in investigating the antecedents and effects of trust in virtual communities. They posited that, if someone is willing to trust others in general, then she or he should apply this general willingness to members of a virtual community. Mayer et al. (1995) suggested that disposition to trust can be effective when parties are unfamiliar with one another. Ridings et al. studied the role that disposition to trust plays in explaining trust in a situation where none is familiar with the another. In their study of trust in virtual communities, Ridings et al. posited that people's disposition to trust in the virtual community significantly affects their trust of other members; disposition to trust positively affects trust in other's ability, benevolence, and integrity.

McKnight et al. (2002) defined disposition to trust as the extent to which an individual showed a tendency to be willing to depend on others across various situations and persons. The more consumers are disposed to trust the other party (i.e., the vendor), the less risk they are likely to perceive, which suggests the following hypotheses:

H2-a: The degree to which an individual generally is inclined to trust others is negatively associated with the extent to which he or she perceives risk in an online transaction.

H2-b: The degree to which an individual generally is inclined to trust others is positively associated with his or her assessment of an online vendor's ability, benevolence, and integrity.

Perceived Risk

Trust plays a key role in purchases, especially when consumers look for credentials. Trust is one of the factors that influence how risk is perceived and assessed by the individual. Kathryn and Mary (2002) suggested that perceived risk associated with e-commerce was "a function of trust between a buyer and a seller" (p. 69). The level of risk inherent in a particular e-commerce situation is offset by the degree to which trust is maintained by one party. As a result, trust functions to reduce perceptions of risk. Bhattacherjee (2002) stated that trust was a significant factor of online transactions because it can be characterized by uncertainty, anonymity, lack of control, and potential opportunism. Trust is understood as a control mechanism that prevents opportunistic behaviors, encourages transactions, and supports the formation of long-term relationships (Bhattachejee, 2002).

Online consumers consider online transactions to be more uncertain and riskier than conventional transactions. Consumers are given little opportunity to verify the quality of goods on their own and it is not easy to test goods through interaction with the web vendor. When customers purchase from an unfamiliar web vendor, they are unable to assess quality, and they do not know whether or not the service is reliable and legitimate. Grabner-Kraeuter (2002) classified and characterized two types of uncertainty in e-commerce: system-dependent uncertainty, caused by functional defects or security problems in technical systems, and transaction-specific uncertainty, explained by an asymmetry in information between the transaction partners. It is meaningful to clarify that trust is essentially a means of reducing risk and uncertainty embedded in every online transaction.

Some early research suggested that perceived risk may play a small role in the adoption of online shopping (Jarvenpaa & Todd, 1996), however, consumer's risk perception has been deemed a substantial barrier to e-commerce growth. Perceived risk affects the attitude and behavior of an individual when dealing with another party. The level of risk is an important factor in forming the customer's attitude and behavior in all kinds of business transactions. Clearly a high level of risk will render it difficult for customers to utilize e-commerce. Two types of risk were categorized in the context of Internet shopping: product category risk and financial risk (Bhatnagar, Misra, & Rao, 2000). Product category risk is about the product itself. It refers to consumers' beliefs about whether products they have purchased would function according to their expectations. Financial risk is associated with an unwanted situation putting consumers at risk, like the possibility of losing money via credit card fraud.

Miyazaki and Fernandez (2001) categorized the four general categories of risk perception. The first category, privacy, contains "unauthorized sharing of personal information, unsolicited contacts from the online retailer (e.g., junk e-mail), and undisclosed tracking of shopping behavior" (p. 24). The second category, system security, includes "concerns about potentially malicious individuals who breach technological data protection devices to acquire consumers' personal, financial, or transaction-oriented information" (p. 24). The third category, online retailer fraud, refers to concerns regarding "fraudulent behavior by the online retailer, such as purposeful misrepresentation or non-delivery of goods" (p. 24). The fourth category, inconveniences of online shopping, is about other reasons for limiting online shopping behavior.

Perceived risk is thought of as the degree to which a consumer perceives a potentially negative outcome from the online transactions (Featherman & Pavlou, 2002). Kathryn and Mary (2002) suggested that perceived risk represented an individual's assessment of the relative probability of positive and negative outcomes of a given transaction or situation. Perceived risk is correlated negatively with the degree of purchasing products online (Miyazaki & Fernandez, 2001). Results showed that perceived risk toward online shopping was negatively associated with online purchase (Miyazaki & Fernandez). Perceived risk was shown to be negatively associated with willingness to buy in e-commerce (Jarvenparr et al., 2000).

H3: The degree to which an individual perceives any risk involved in an online transaction is negatively associated with his or her willingness to purchase online.

SELF-EFFICACY

There has been considerable study on self-efficacy that deals with work-related performance (Agarwal et al., 2000; Frayne & Latham, 1987; Gist, Schwoerer, & Rosen, 1989; Mitchell, Hopper, Daniels, George-Falvy, & James, 1994; Venkatesh, 2000; Wood & Bandura, 1989). These studies have sought to explore many cognitive factors having motivational effects on human action. In reality, the relationship between self-efficacy and behavior has been empirically validated in diverse domains such as education, health, and organizational tasks. In the realm of information technology, self-efficacy is regarded as a determinant of individual behavior and performance. Self-efficacy was shown to be related to the psychological aspects of the Digital Divide (Eastin & LaRose, 2000), individual behavior toward new information technology (Compeau & Higgins, 1995; Marakas et al., 1998), perceived ease of use in and on acceptance of technology (Venkatesh & Davis, 1996), and prediction of adopting a web-based information system (Yi & Hwang, 2003). Empirically demonstrated was that application-specific self-efficacy has a direct and powerful effect on ease of use and perception (Agarwal et al.).

Self-efficacy was defined as a personal judgment of "how well one can execute courses of action required to deal with prospective situations" (Bandura, 1982, p. 122). Bandura (1986) defined self-efficacy as "people's judgments of their capabilities to organize and execute courses of action required to attain designated types of performances" (p.391). And Bandura (1991) also stated that "people's beliefs in their efficacy influence the choices they make, their aspirations, how much effort they mobilize in a given endeavor, and how long they persevere in the face of difficulties and setbacks" (p.257). As Bandura (1986) pointed out, self-efficacy does not reflect skills individuals possess but rather their judgment of what they can do with the skills they have. Self-efficacy should not be understood as a measure of skill, but is concerned with the extent to which individuals believe they can perform by using their skills (Eastin & LaRose, 2000). It focuses on what people believe they can accomplish now. Self-efficacy can be understood as "beliefs in one's capabilities to mobilize the motivation" needed to manage given situational tasks (Wood & Bandura, 1989, p.408).

Gist and Mitchell (1992) pointed out that self-efficacy had three aspects. First, self-efficacy reflects individuals' comprehensive judgments of whether they are capable of completing a specific task. Second, judgment on self-efficacy changes as the individual obtains new information and experiences. Third, a self-efficacy judgment motivates the individual to act. People are neither driven solely by internal/subjective forces nor determined by external/

environmental stimuli; rather, behavior can be explained by the more comprehensive model of reciprocal relationship among subjective and external/environmental factors. Given that human behavior is explained by the interaction of internal forces and external stimuli, self-efficacy could be understood as a key mechanism that accounts for this interactive relationship between internal forces and external stimuli that affects human behavior. As Bandura (1986) pointed out, self-efficacy is a more comprehensive perception process, and it reflects the extent to which an individual adapts to accomplish under given circumstances. Thus, people who have the same skills may perform differently on the same task. Individuals who perceive themselves as highly self-efficacious tend to set out to produce, swiftly, successful outcomes, whereas those who perceive low self-efficacy are likely to cease their efforts prematurely and fail in the task.

In the context of e-commerce transactions, consumers are concerned that they might be unable to obtain relevant information about web vendors from whom they plan to purchase online. Consumers worry that if a product does not function as it should, they would be unable to return it without problems, especially in cases in which merchandise they purchased online turns out to be the wrong product or is defective. For example, if people are confident that they are usually able to purchase from web vendors the exact items they want, they are more likely to trust those web vendors. Once people are confident that defective products will be taken care of in an orderly and desirable fashion, they will be less reluctant to purchase.

This article extends the concept of self-efficacy to trust building in B2C e-commerce. While extant IS research on self-efficacy focused on self-efficacy judgment in reference to the task domain of computing (Agarwal et al., 2000), this study focuses on the impact of self-efficacy on trust in the context of online transactions. Online transactions self-efficacy is defined as the belief of a consumer in his or her ability to organize and execute certain behaviors necessary for him or her to achieve certain objectives in online purchasing (e.g., a successful and satisfactory transaction) under conditions of uncertainty. This study also suggests online transaction self-efficacy as a domain-specific self-efficacy in online transactions. Socio-cognitive theory and research to date have indicated that task-and-situation-specific self-efficacy is distinct from general self-efficacy (Bandura, 1986; Eden, 1988; Sherer, Maddux, Mercandante, Prentice-Dunn, Jacobs, & Rogers, 1982). In line with socio-cognitive research, in the realm of information technology, Marakas et al. (1998) discerned that computer self-efficacy (CSE) was a multi-level construct operating at two distinct levels: at the general computing level (general CSE) and at the specific application level (application-specific self-efficacy). Organizational behavior research (Chen, Gully, & Eden, 2001; Eden, 1988; Judge, Erez, & Bono, 1998) demonstrated that general self-efficacy predicted specific self-efficacy for a variety of tasks in various environments. Based on the interdependent relationship between general self-efficacy and domain-specific self-efficacy, self-efficacy in this research has been handled in two modes: general self-efficacy (GSE) and online transaction self-efficacy (OSE).

General Self-Efficacy

Sherer et al. (1982) provided a measure to assess self-efficacy not tied to specific situations. They approached self-efficacy as efficacy expectancies generalized from specific behavior performed by individuals to their overall behavior. Sherer et al. developed a measure for the General Self-Efficacy Scale (GSES), and obtained a factor structure with three sub-dimensions: initiation of behavior, effort in completing the behavior, and persistence in the face of difficulties. This measure is consistent with Bandura's assertion that self-efficacy expectancies determine the initial decision to set out to act, to expend effort, and to persist despite adversity (Bandura, 1986).

General self-efficacy (GSE) is not about specific situations or behaviors, but about applications across various situations (Sherer, Maddux, Mercandante, Prentice-Dunn, Jacobs, & Rogers, 1982). Individual differences in general self-efficacy exist and these are reflected in people's behaviors (Sherer et al.). GSE was defined as "a generalized trait consisting of one's overall estimate of one's ability to effect requisite performances in achievement situations" (Eden & Zuk, 1995, p.629), or as "individuals' perception of their ability to perform across a variety of different situations" (Judge et al., 1998, p. 170). GSE reveals differences among individuals in their perceptions of how well they are capable of meeting task demands in various contexts (Chen et al., 2001).

The accumulation of previous successful experiences is an important antecedent of GSE (Sherer et al., 1982). GSE is acquired and reinforced as an individual accumulates experiences, both successes and failures, across various situations (Shelton, 1990). The importance of GSE to research can be explained in terms of "1) predicting Task-and-situation specific self-efficacy (SSE) across situations and tasks, 2) predicting general and comprehensive performance criteria, and 3) buffering against the debilitating effects of adverse experiences on subsequent SSE" (Chen et al., 2001, p. 67). Reflecting the above literature, we argue thus: those with high self-efficacy are likely to choose more challenging tasks. When problems occur, they remain committed to their goals. People who believe they can produce a desired result are more likely to maintain a more active life. For example, if individuals are confident that they will be able to achieve most goals they have set for themselves, they tend not to be reluctant to try an uncertain situation. And if people are certain that they will accomplish their goals even when facing difficult tasks, they perceive less uncertainty (or risk). As a result, high self-efficacy plays a significant role in perceiving the characteristics of any tasks.

In the context of online transactions, individuals with higher general self-efficacy are expected to perceive less risk in B2C e-commerce. More specifically, if people are confident that they usually are able to purchase exactly the item they want from a Web vendor, they will be more likely to trust that web vendor and purchase in the future. If consumers are confident that, even if the vendor from whom they purchased online would not take back a defective product, they are able to solve the problem through the assistance of a third party (e.g., friends, better business bureaux, consumer advocates or relevant governmental agencies), then they are more likely to perceive a lower risk level. Therefore, it can be hypothesized that:

H4-a: The degree to which an individual believes in his or her general ability to handle any problems in everyday life is positively associated with his or her belief in capability in dealing with any problems that might arise during online transactions.

H4-b: The degree to which an individual believes in his or her general ability to handle any problems in everyday life is positively associated with his or her perception of an online vendor's ability, benevolence, and integrity for a reliable online transaction.

H4-c: The degree to which an individual believes in his or her general ability to handle any problems in everyday life is negatively associated with the extent to which he or she perceives any risk involved in an online transaction.

Online Transaction Self-Efficacy

Although Bandura (1997) stated that "an efficacy belief is not a decontextualized trait" (p.42), it should be noted that his mention does not mean that specific self-efficacy generalizes to other contexts (Stajkovic & Luthans, 1998). Previous research conceptualized and studied self-efficacy as a task-and-situation specific construct (Bandura, 1986; Gist & Mitchell, 1992; Lee & Bobko, 1994). Despite advances in theoretical and empirical research on GSE, the utility of GSE has been questioned. Stanley and Murphy (1997) questioned whether GSE was distinct from self-esteem, which is another important construct in predicting an individual's behavior. Stajkovic and Luthans

(1998) argued that the practical applicability of GSE was low. To improve the predictability of GSE, the specificity of the construct that measures self-efficacy should be matched to the specificity of the performance or task to be predicted (Chen et al., 2001).

Task-and-situation specific self-efficacy (SSE) represents "a dynamic, multifaceted belief system that operates selectively across different activity domains and under different situational demands, rather than being a decontextualized conglomerate" (Bandura, 1997, p.42). Specific self-efficacy was defined as how well one believes one could perform given the specific social context and the particular task (Stajkovic & Luthans, 1998). Specific self-efficacy has been shown to predict performance outcomes (Bandura, 1986). This is because outcomes to be measured have been highly specified. As previous research has pointed out, SSE predicts outcomes of a target situation (Bandura, 1986, 1997; Marakas et al., 1998; Yi & Hwang, 2003). What is important to SSE is to secure specificity that can be applied to specific performance situations. Based on the above argument, we argue so: if consumers are low self-efficacious, and less confident in their ability to return an item without any problem, in case the merchandise they have purchased online is defective, they are less willing to purchase online. If consumers are confident that they are able to resolve problems on their own, in case their orders do not come through satisfactorily, they are more likely to be not reluctant to purchase from a web vendor. Consumers who are highly self-efficacious are more likely to make transactions with any web vendor than are customers with low self-efficacy.

SSE is one important outcome of GSE. As pointed out by Chen et al. (2001), GSE positively influences SSE across tasks and situations. The individual's tendency to feel efficacious across situations could be applied to specific situations. General self-efficacy is defined as an individual's judgment of efficacy across various situations in everyday life, which would include online transactions, while domain specific self-efficacy is defined as an individual's perception of efficacy in completing a task in a certain situation. The more self-efficacious consumers are when dealing with an online vendor, the more likely they are to have favorable expectations of, and trust in, that vendor. This study proposes online transaction self-efficacy as a situation-specific self-efficacy influenced by the degree to which one believes in one's overall competence to effect performances across a wide variety of achievement situations. Consequently, it can be hypothesized that:

H5-a: The degree to which an individual believes in his or her capability to deal with any problems that occur during an online transaction is negatively associated with the extent to which he or she perceives any risk involved in that transaction.

H5-b: The degree to which an individual believes in his or her capability to deal with any problems that occur during an online transaction is positively associated with the extent to which he or she perceives that online vendors' ability, benevolence, and integrity.

H5-c: The degree to which an individual believes in his or her capability to deal with any problems that occur during an online transaction is positively associated with the extent to which he or she is willing to make a purchase.

Based on the above arguments on several internal/subjective factors, the research model is developed as follows (Figure 1). Testing this model is to address two research questions: whether self-efficacy plays a role in affecting trust-building and reinforcing of purchase intentions, and what kind of the structural relationship exists among relevant factors. Ovals indicate each internal factor, which is the latent variable, and arrows denote the association between two constructs.

Figure 1. Research Model

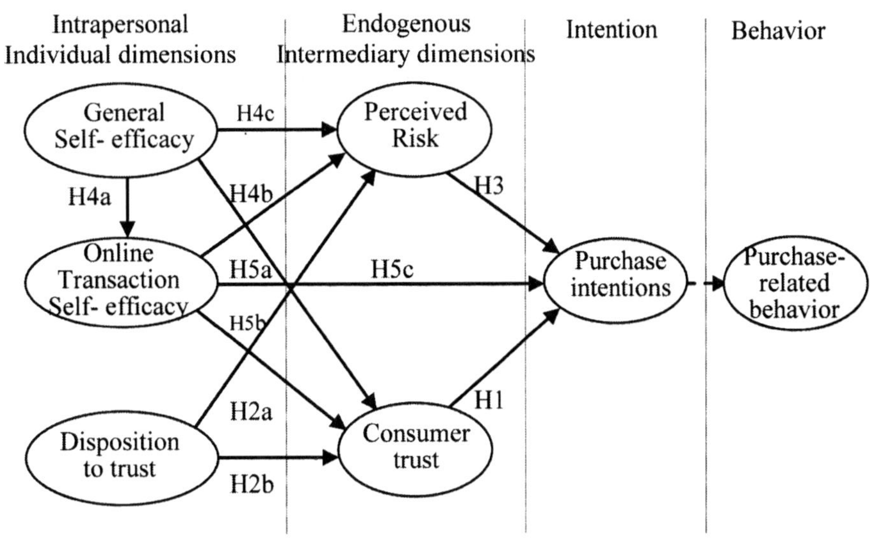

METHODS

Data collection

A cross-sectional survey was used to test the research model of the consumer experiencing a B2C retail transaction. This was because the survey is an appropriate method to test actual consumer perceptions of a B2C online transaction, and it is expected to maximize external validity. An online survey was used to collect data because of its relevant expediency and ease of data transformation to another statistical tool. The questionnaire was made on 'Angel', a Web-based class-management system accessible via Internet. Responses submitted by the end of the 15th day after the survey request, were used for this study.

The population of interest in this research is consumers involved in an actual B2C online transaction. To record respondents' experiences and perceptions, they were asked to answer each survey question based on their online purchasing experiences in the past six months. Two hundred and eighteen complete inquiries were collected from 220 students. Among those, 48 are women, 172 are men. Most respondents were in the age group 20-25 ($n = 218$).

All participants used the Internet frequently in their everyday lives and were familiar with using computers and the Internet. For questions about the extent of respondents' experience with computers and web technology (including searching, browsing, finding information, etc), the means were 5.57 and 5.86, respectively (e.g., "how would you rate your experience with computers?" (1-Novice/ 7-Expert), and "how would you rate your experience with web technology?" (1-Novice/ 7-Expert)). During a typical week, they have been shown to spend about 295 minutes on the Web and about 352 minutes using computers (including time spent on the Web).

All respondents previously had purchased online, and most were familiar with purchasing from the specific online vendor. It had been an average of 2.96 years since they began purchases on websites. The frequency with which they purchased from e-commerce Web sites was 5.82 per month.

Table 1. Degree of Internet and Computer Experience of Participants

Construct	Mean	Median	Mode
Experience with computer[a]	5.57	6.00	6
Experience with Web technology[a]	5.86	6.00	6
Average time of spending on the Web	295.52 (min.)	210.00 (min.)	180 (min.)
Average time of spending on a computer	352.39 (min.)	300.00 (min.)	300 (min.)
Duration of previous e-commerce[b]	2.96	3.00	3
Frequency of e-commerce	5.82 (times)	1.00	1

Note. a: 1 – Novice / 7 – Expert
b: 1- less than one year/ 2- two years/ 3-three years/ 4-four years/5- more than five years.

Measurement

To construct the survey instrument, existing scales from the literature were reviewed, and items were carefully adapted or developed for each construct. All items were measured with seven-point Likert-type scales ranging from *strongly disagree* to *strongly agree*. General self-efficacy can be defined as "an individual's perception of his or her ability to perform across a variety of different situations" (Judge et al., 1998, p.170). The general self-efficacy scale (Bosscher and Smit, 1998) was used to measure this variable (e.g., "When I have something unpleasant to do, I stick to it until I finish it"). For online transaction self-efficacy, no existing scale could be found to measure it in a B2C e-commerce environment. Thus, a six-item scale was developed specifically for this study (e.g., "I am confident that, in case my order does not come through in a satisfactory manner, I am able to take care of the problems on my own"). Disposition to trust can be defined as a customer's personality trait that leads to generalized expectations of trustworthiness. The scale to measure disposition to trust was assessed by using items adapted from prior studies of trust in online transaction contexts (Gefen, 2000) (e.g., "I generally trust other people"). Perceived risk can be defined as a consumer's belief about the potential uncertain negative outcomes from the online transaction. A scale measuring perceived risk of B2C retail Websites was created to utilize Jarvenpaa and Tractinsky's (1999) definition of perceived risk in the context of online transactions (e.g., "How much risk would you tolerate when deciding to make a purchase from the Web sites?"). The scale to measure consumer trust was assessed by using items adapted from previous studies on online transactions (Gefen, 2000; Jarvenpaa et al., 2000) (e.g., "I believe that the Web site vendor has my best interest in mind"). As a dependent variable, purchase intention refers to the degree to which a consumer intends to buy from a certain website. The scale to measure purchase intention was assessed by using items adapted from previous studies (Gefen, 2000) (e.g., "I am likely to purchase the product(s) from this website").

Data Analysis and Results

SEM (Structural Equation Modeling) was used to examine the proposed model of purchasing intention-behavior reinforcement. Based on data gathered, this multivariate analysis that includes relevant latent variables was conducted to test whether the proposed model showed significant structural relationships among these variables. The proposed model and hypotheses were tested using AMOS 4.0 with the maximum likelihood estimation method. This technique enables researchers to simultaneously assess measurement model parameters and structural path coefficients.

Exploratory, principal component factor analysis was conducted to determine the extent to which latent variables were discriminant. The principal component factor analysis was conducted using a Varimax rotation (see table 3). The objective of the explanatory factor analysis was to cull measurement items that did not load on the appropriate latent variable. This was accompanied by checking the internal consistency reliabilities (ICR) of the scales. Results suggested that several items should be dropped from the scales, to achieve higher levels of reliability and validity. Specifically, an item was dropped if (a) it did not meet the threshold loading of 0.40 on any factor, (b) its highest loading on an expected factor was not above 0.60, or (c) it showed a significant variance across multiple factors (Hair, Anderson, Tatham, & Black, 1998).

Confirmatory factor analysis (CFA) was conducted to examine the convergent validity of each latent variable. Convergent validity means the extent to which measures for each variable are measuring the theoretical construct (i.e., latent variable) (McKnight et al., 2002). This process was done by specifying a single factor model for each of the latent variables. Correspondence between theory and data in a CFA model was assessed using goodness-of-fit metrics such as χ^2. However, the Chi-square statistic is sensitive to the number of samples and the probability of model rejection increases as sample size increases, hence the ratio of chi-square to degree of freedom and other model fit indices should be taken into consideration (Bentler & Bonnet, 1980).

Table 4 shows overall model fit indices for each CFA model. The CFA model for three constructs (disposition to trust, perceived risk, and purchase intention) was not significant ($\chi^2 = 2.28$, $p = .68$, $\chi^2 = 2.09$, $p = 35$, and $\chi^2 = 4.35$, $p = .11$ respectively), hence it suggested that these models fit well. Unlike general hypothesis significance tests, statistically insignificant chi-square values show that the theoretical model fits actual data well. (It should be noted that the null hypothesis is that the conceptual covariance (Σ) from the theoretical relationship among constructs equals actual covariance (S) from actual data.)

Although chi-square statistics for three constructs (general self-efficacy, online transaction self-efficacy, and consumer trust) are significant, these do not well exceed the ratio of chi-square to degree of freedom (3:1). For the CFA model for general self-efficacy, χ^2/df was 2.04, suggesting acceptable model fit. Likewise, the ratio of chi-square to degree of freedom was 2.04 and 2.78 for online transaction self-efficacy and consumer trust, suggesting acceptable model fit. AMOS provides additional goodness-of-fit measures such as Comparative Fit Index (CFI), Goodness-of-Fit Index (GFI), and Root Mean Square Error of Approximation (RMSEA). CFI, based on a comparison between the model and a model that assumed independence of all variables, should exceed .90 for good model fit. GFI is a measure of the relative amount of variance and covariance in the sample, that is jointly explained by the model. If GFI equals 1, the model fits well. To fit closely, RMSEA should be .50 or less than .50. All other model fit indices satisfied the recommended level (Bhattacherjee, 2002; Byrne, 2001), indicating that the measurement items of each construct are uni-dimensional.

Table 5 shows the means, standard deviations, composite reliabilities and AVEs (average variance extracted) of each construct in this study.

Convergent validity was evaluated for the constructs using three criteria recommended by Fornell and Larcker (1981). First, all measurement factor loading should exceed .70; second, composite reliabilities are all higher than .80. Lastly, AVEs must exceed the variance due to measurement error for that construct, i.e., AVE should exceed .50. Consistent with criteria recommended by Fornell and Larcker, all measurement factor loadings exceeded .70 (see Table 2). Composite reliabilities ranged from .84 (consumer trust) to .92 (purchase intention). All composite reliabilities exceeded the recommended level of .80.

Table 2. Measurements Items for Constructs

Constructs	Measurement Items	Mean	S.D.	Loading
General Self-Efficacy	When I make plans, I am certain I can make them work.	5.42	1.24	0.73
	If I can't do a job the first time, I keep trying until I can.	5.48	1.22	0.85
	Failure just makes me try harder.	4.89	1.48	0.72
Eigenvalue				5.00
Percent of explained variance				51.11
Online Transaction Self-efficacy	I am confident that I can obtain relevant information through online sources (e.g., online discussion groups, reputation sites, etc) on the Web vendors from whom I am planning to make online purchases.	5.75	1.20	0.79
	I am confident that I am usually able to purchase exactly the item that I want from Web vendors.	5.66	1.34	0.82
	I am confident that, in case my order does not come through in a satisfactory manner, I am able to take care of the problem(s) on my own.	5.55	1.35	0.79
	I am confident that I am able to find a trustworthy Web vendor based on ratings (e.g., the numbers of stars or smiley faces) provided by other consumers.	5.35	1.38	0.75
Eigenvalue				4.99
Percent of explained variance				59.80
Disposition to Trust	I generally trust other people.	4.89	1.38	0.89
	I feel that people are generally reliable.	4.46	1.19	0.76
	I generally trust other people unless they give me reasons not to.	5.33	1.31	0.81
Eigenvalue				3.00
Percent of explained variance				67.84
Perceived Risk	Purchasing from this Web site would involve more product risk (i.e., not working, defective product) when compared with more traditional ways of shopping.	4.41	1.62	0.84
	Purchasing from this Web site would involve more financial risk (i.e., fraud, hard to return) compared with more traditional ways of shopping.	4.72	1.59	0.79
	How would you rate your overall perception of risk from this Web site?	3.42	1.52	0.81
Eigenvalue				3.00
Percent of explained variance				66.47
Consumer Trust	The Web site vendor gives the impression that it keeps promises and commitments.	5.55	1.08	0.75
	The Web site understands the market it works in.	5.62	1.09	0.75
	The Web site knows how to provide excellent service.	5.11	1.14	0.80
Eigenvalue				3.99
Percent of explained variance				57.28

continued on following page

Table 2. continued

Purchase Intention	I am likely to purchase the product(s) from this Web site again.	5.39	1.36	0.92
	I am likely to recommend this Web site to my friends.	5.40	1.34	0.86
	I am likely to make another purchase from this Web site if I need the product(s) that I am going to buy.	5.50	1.32	0.86
Eigenvalue				4.00
Percent of explained variance				75.29

Variance extracted measures ranged from .58 (online transaction self-efficacy) to .75 (purchase intention), which exceeds the recommended level of .50. Hence, all scales met the criteria for convergent validity.

Discriminant validity measures the extent to which two constructs are empirically distinct (Bagozzi, Yi, & Phillips, 1991). Discriminant validity was tested by using a chi-square difference test. To do so, the chi-square statistic of the constrained model, where correlation between the two latent variables was fixed at 1.00, was compared with that of an unconstrained model where correlation between the two constructs was freely estimated. Significant differences of the chi-square statistic between the two models indicate that the pair of constructs is distinct (Bagozzi et al.). If a chi-square difference is greater than 3.84 (6.63) at a 95% (99%) confidence interval, it suggests the two constructs are significantly distinct (Suh & Han, 2002). The discriminant validity among the all latent variables was assessed: general self-efficacy, online transaction self-efficacy, disposition to trust, perceived risk, consumer trust, and purchase intention. Results of discriminant validity testing are shown in Table 6.

Chi-square differences range from 7.58 (between disposition to trust and purchasing intention) to 90.47 (between online transaction purchasing intention). The differences are much larger than the 3.84 threshold, indicating that each pair of constructs is distinct.

Fit indices are generally within recommended guidelines, indicating that the model fits the data (χ^2 = 264.42, d.f. =159, p <.000, χ^2/df= 1.66, GFI = .89, AGFI = .86, CFI = .94, RMSEA = .055). The chi-square test of model fit is significant but the ratio of chi-square to degree of freedom is less than 2 (χ^2/df = 1.66), so it is not necessary to conclude that the proposed model does not well fit data. Other model fit indices surpassed the recommended threshold by several previous studies except GFI (Bentler & Bonnett, 1980). The RMSEA value is below the value of .06 recommended by previous research as an upper boundary (Etezadi-Amoli & Farhoomand, 1996; Hayduk, 1987), so it can be concluded that the proposed model well fits data.

The structural model and hypotheses were tested by examining the significance of the path coefficients, and the variance accounted for the antecedent constructs. Figure 3 provides the results of hypothesis testing. Inconsistent with hypothesis H4-b and H4-c, general self-efficacy had no significant effects on consumer trust (β = .08, p = .63) and perceived risk (β = -.05, p = .56). However, general self-efficacy had a significant effect on online transaction self-efficacy (β = .54, p < .001).

Despite the insignificant direct effects of general self-efficacy on perceived risk and consumer trust, it is theoretically the case that individuals with higher levels of general self-efficacy are more likely to have lower levels of risk perception and higher levels of consumer trust. This

Table 3. Factor Structure Matrix of Latent Variables (Result of Explanatory Factor Analysis)

	Components							
	1	**2**	**3**	**4**	**5**	**6**	**7**	**8**
General Self-Efficacy								
GSE1	0.002	0.003	0.139	**0.778**	0.005	-0.183	-0.000	-0.181
GSE2	-0.006	-0.001	-0.264	**0.704**	0.171	-0.005	0.004	0.007
GSE3	0.193	0.186	-0.387	**0.607**	0.005	-0.242	0.134	0.002
Online Transaction Self-Efficacy								
OSE1	0.158	**0.780**	-0.125	0.000	0.006	-0.007	0.133	-0.005
OSE2	0.002	**0.707**	-0.002	0.227	0.178	-0.003	-0.004	-0.245
OSE3	0.341	**0.675**	-0.004	-0.001	0.190	-0.009	0.122	-0.006
OSE4	0.247	**0.650**	-0.127	0.007	0.293	-0.006	0.101	0.002
Disposition to Trust								
DIS1	0.118	0.008	-0.000	0.003	0.149	-0.007	**0.838**	-0.002
DIS2	-0.003	0.009	0.001	0.006	0.002	-0.003	**0.798**	-0.004
DIS3	0.002	0.009	0.000	0.003	0.149	-0.000	**0.765**	0.003
Perceived Risk								
RIS1	-0.104	-0.003	0.138	-0.003	-0.114	-0.000	0.003	**0.824**
RIS2	-0.209	-0.148	0.002	-0.000	-0.004	-0.000	-0.001	**0.808**
RIS3	-0.336	-0.007	0.001	-0.005	-0.006	0.186	-0.007	**0.613**
Consumer Trust								
TRU1	0.114	0.008	-0.003	0.006	**0.736**	-0.183	0.122	-0.000
TRU2	0.003	0.198	-0.115	-0.001	**0.707**	-0.007	0.130	-0.009
TRU3	0.240	0.178	-0.001	0.169	**0.675**	0.001	0.006	-0.214
Purchase Intention								
INT1	**0.867**	0.215	-0.005	0.002	0.135	-0.105	0.006	-0.163
INT2	**0.819**	0.223	0.000	0.009	0.005	-0.009	0.000	-0.161
INT3	**0.806**	0.140	-0.126	0.006	0.201	-0.006	0.004	-0.148

Table 4. Overall Model Fit Indices of CFA for Convergent Validity

Construct	χ^2	**p-value**	**d.f**	χ^2**/d.f.**	**GFI**	**CFI**	**RMSEA**
General self-efficacy	103.88	.000	51	2.04	.95	.97	.05
Online transaction self-efficacy	25.02	.000	9	2.78	.99	.99	.04
Disposition to trust	2.28	.68	4	.57	.98	.98	.06
Perceived risk	2.09	.35	2	1.05	.99	.99	.02
Consumer trust	49.97	.001	24	2.08	.97	.98	.06
Purchase intention	4.35	.11	2	2.17	.99	.99	.06

Table 5. Means, Standard Deviations, and Composite Reliabilities

Construct	Number of Items	Mean	S.D.	Composite Reliability	AVE	Adapted from
General self-efficacy	3	3.39	1.44	0.86	0.61	Bosscher & Smit (1998)
Online transaction self-efficacy	4	5.48	1.35	0.88	0.58	New items
Disposition to trust	3	4.89	1.29	0.86	0.68	(Gefen, 2000)
Perceived risk	3	4.18	1.58	0.85	0.66	(Jarvenpaa & Tractinsky, 1999)
Consumer trust	3	5.45	1.12	0.84	0.57	(Gefen, 2000; Jarvenpaa et al. 2000)
Purchase intention	3	4.89	1.29	0.92	0.75	(Gefen, 2002; Jarvenpaa et al. 2000)

Table 6. Chi-Square Difference Test for Discriminant Validity

	Model with fixed correlation		Model with Correlation to be estimated			Chi-square difference
	χ^2	d.f.	Covariance	χ^2	d.f.	
GSE – OSE	63.18	20	.30	34.08	19	29.1
GSE - TRUST	33.00	14	.28	12.66	13	20.34
GSE - DISPO	17.97	14	.23	8.96	13	9.28
GSE - INTENT	50.15	14	.30	35.68	13	14.47
OSE – RISK	41.77	14	-.43	21.36	13	20.41
OSE - TRUST	101.64	14	.59	29.19	13	72.45
OSE - DISPO	50.45	14	.44	23.25	13	27.2
OSE - INTENT	115.02	14	.75	24.55	13	90.47
RISK - TRUST	32.89	9	-.48	9.10	8	23.79
RISK - INTENT	58.49	9	-.84	17.83	8	40.66
TRUST - DISPO	26.37	9	.33	10.92	8	15.45
TRUST - INTENT	87.88	9	.79	24.10	8	63.78
DISPO - INTENT	26.22	9	.34	18.64	8	7.58

conjecture prompted exploration of possible mediation effects of online transaction self-efficacy in post hoc analysis. To examine mediation effects, we followed the steps established by Baron and Kenny (1986). First, the independent variable (i.e., general self-efficacy) must be statistically significantly related to the dependent variable (i.e., perceived risk or consumer trust). Second, the independent variable (i.e., general self-efficacy) must be statistically significantly related to the mediating variable (i.e., online transaction self-efficacy). Third, the mediating variable (i.e., online transaction self-efficacy) must be statistically significantly related to the dependent variable (i.e., perceived risk or consumer trust). Last, the mediation effect of online transaction self-efficacy can be proved if, after controlling for online transaction self-efficacy,

Figure 2. Estimated Model

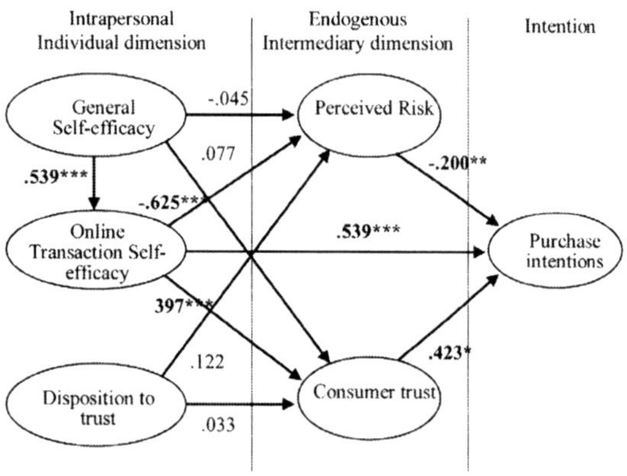

the relationship between general self-efficacy and perceived risk (or consumer trust) is no longer significant (i.e., total mediation) or the degree of the association is reduced (i.e., partial mediation).

Step 1 showed a positive relationship between general self-efficacy and consumer trust (β = .15, p = .02). But no significant relationship between general self-efficacy and perceived risk was found (β = -.03, p = .62). Regarding perceived risk, the first criterion of Baron and Kenny was not satisfied. Thus, the mediation analysis on perceived risk was dropped. Step 2 showed a positive relationship between general self-efficacy and online transaction self-efficacy (β = .15, p = .02). Step 3 showed a positive relationship between online transaction self-efficacy and consumer trust (β = .49, p < .001). For step 4, the dependent variable (i.e., consumer trust) was regressed on both the mediating variable (i.e., online transaction self-efficacy) and the dependent variable (i.e., consumer trust). The relationship between online transaction self-efficacy and consumer trust remained significant (β = .47, p <.001) while the relationship between general self-efficacy and consumer trust became insignificant (β = .08, p = .18). This result revealed that the effect of general self-efficacy on consumer trust was fully mediated by online transaction self-efficacy.

Supporting H5-a, online transaction self-efficacy had a significant effect on perceived risk (β = -.63, p < .001). Supporting H5-b, online transaction self-efficacy significantly affected consumer trust (β = .39, p < .001). Consistent with H5-c, online transaction self-efficacy significantly affected purchase intention (β = .54, p < .001). Inconsistent with H2-a and H2-b, disposition to trust had no significant effect on perceived risk (β = .12, p = .28), and this factor had no significant effect on consumer trust (β = .03, p = .31). Supporting H3, perceived risk significantly affected purchase intention (β = -.20, p < .001). The model accounted for substantial variance in online transaction self-efficacy (R^2 = .35), modest variance in perceived risk (R^2 = .29) and substantial variance in consumer trust (R^2 = .63). Consumer trust significantly affected purchase intention (β = .42, p = .04). The model accounted for substantial variance in purchase intention (R^2 = .49).

Figure 3. Mediation Effect of Online Transaction Self Efficacy

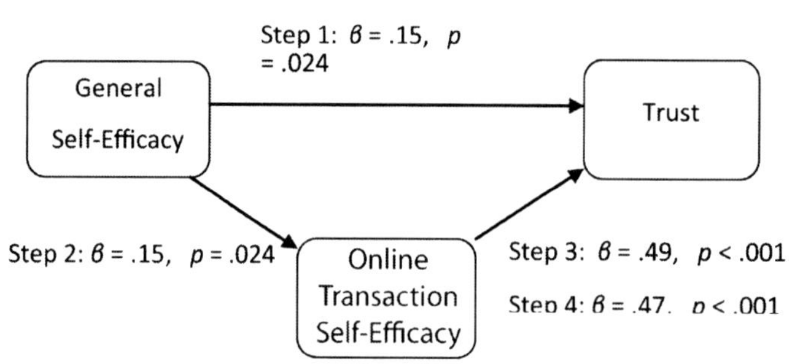

DISCUSSION

Key Findings

The effect of online transaction self-efficacy has been demonstrated in terms of its relationship with perceived risk, consumer trust, and purchase intention. Results of this study showed that online transaction self-efficacy was negatively associated with perceived risk, and positively associated with consumer trust and purchase intention.

Online transaction self-efficacy has a negative impact on perceived risk, that is, online transaction self-efficacy reduces risk perception significantly. The degree of perceived risk is negatively associated with purchase intention. The higher the degree of perceived risk, the lower the purchase intention will be. The low perception of risk in turn influences the attitude of the consumer toward the web vendor. Consistent with prior studies (Featherman & Pavlou, 2002; Gefen & Devine, 2001; Gefen & Straub, 2003), consumer trust was positively related to purchasing intention, and perceived risk was negatively related to purchase intention. It is noted that perceived risk and consumer trust account for about 49% of variance of purchase intention (R^2 = .49).

Unlike original expectations, it turned out that general self-efficacy had no direct impact on perceived risk and consumer trust. Consistent with prior literature (Chen et al., 2001), however, general self-efficacy had a positive impact on online transaction self-efficacy. It should be noted that general self-efficacy can account for about 35% of the variance of online transaction self-efficacy. Therefore, this result supports that general self-efficacy is an important antecedent of domain specific self-efficacy (i.e., online transaction self-efficacy in this study).

By differentiating domain specific self-efficacy (i.e., online transaction self-efficacy) from general self-efficacy, this study has demonstrated that these two concepts have distinct impacts. The addition of general self-efficacy has supported the argument of why a domain specific self-efficacy should be taken into account more seriously in figuring out the impact of self-efficacy. Post hoc tests showed that the effect of general self-efficacy on consumer trust was completely mediated by online transaction self-efficacy. Given that a solid theoretical linkage between general self-efficacy and domain specific self-efficacy (i.e., online transaction self-efficacy) exists, it is relevant to suspect the mediation effect of online transaction self-efficacy on the relationship between general self-efficacy and consumer trust.

It should be noted that online transaction self-efficacy is more powerful than disposition to trust in influencing consumer trust (β = .39 for online transaction self-efficacy, insignificant for disposition to trust). There are theoretical arguments (McKnight et al., 2002) and an empirical test (Gefen, 2002) showing that disposition to trust affects consumer trust. Gefen showed that disposition to trust was a significant antecedent of trust. But, in the presence of online transaction self-efficacy, disposition to trust no longer had a significant effect on perceived risk and consumer trust, indicating that online transaction self-efficacy is a stronger predictor of perceived risk and consumer trust than disposition to trust. Disposition to trust was defined as a general personality trait that encompasses a general expectation of how trusting one should be (McKnight & Chervany, 2002). This kind of general trait-related antecedent seems limited in explaining trust building. Future studies should discuss whether this construct should be included as an antecedent of trust.

These results suggested that, among other individual's perceptions, situation and task-specific self-efficacy can play a significant role as an uncertainty reduction factor when an individual would need to make a choice and behave. This study illuminated the applicability of self-efficacy in online transactions, which requires decision-making within uncertain contexts of online transactions. This model presented an insight as to how, in a context of online transactions, uncertainty reduction and purchase intention can be affected by incorporating a motivational factor such as self-efficacy into the consumer trust-building. These findings extended the scope of previous research on uncertainty reduction and purchase intention in e-commerce.

The Theory of Reasoned Action (Fishbein & Ajzen, 1975) holds that behavioral beliefs affect specific attitudes toward behavior, which affects intentions. Behavioral intentions determine behavior. Intentions, in turn, can be determined by an individual's attitude toward the behavior (Fishbein & Ajzen). Behavioral beliefs, which refer to beliefs of what will happen via particular behaviors, directly influence an individual's attitude toward his or her behavior (Fishbein & Ajzen). As McKnight and Chervany (2002) pointed out, a trusting belief is a "belief that the other party has one or more characteristics beneficial to oneself" (p. 46). Important in Mayer's three dimensions of trust is that those are the trustor's *perceptions and beliefs* of the trustees and their attributes. Those individuals' subjective perceptions of online vendors essentially represent *their expectations* of e-commerce sellers (e.g., whether the trustee is competent and knowledgeable, whether the trustee is believed to do good to the trustor, whether the trustee does what is expected). Self-efficacy directly influences such an individual's beliefs and judgment in certain situations, largely affecting outcome expectations (Stone & Henry, 2003).

In the present study, the trustor's *perceptions of and beliefs about* the trustees and their attributes are regarded as behavioral beliefs representing online customers' judgments of likely consequences of their transactions. In a continuum of The Theory of Reasoned Action, The Theory of Planned Behavior emphasizes the impact of an individual's *perceived control* over his or her behaviors (Ajzen, 2002). If online consumers form favorable beliefs about vendors through their perceived control over their actions, they are more likely to initiate the trust-building process. We argue that behavioral intentions cannot be adequately understood without considering self-efficacy, defined as individuals' perceptions of their abilities to perform particular behaviors. The greater the online customers' perceived confidence of their behaviors, and the more favorable their attitudes toward trustees (i.e., online vendors), the stronger the customers' intentions to engage in e-commerce. As discussed earlier, self-efficacy reflects people's beliefs in their abilities to influence their choices and achieve their goals. Thus, self-efficacy influences an individual's beliefs.

According to social cognitive theory (Bandura, 1997), in dealing with a given situation, an individual has two related expectations: i) outcome expectancy, belief about whether his or her behavior would result in a desirable outcome, and ii) self-efficacy, belief about whether he or she is able to perform the behavior well. Motivation for behavior(s) is the expected outcome and the expectation that a given behavior will lead to that expected outcome (Maddux & Rogers, 1982). Bandura (1986) said that "in most social, intellectual, and physical pursuits, those who judge themselves highly efficacious will expect favorable outcomes, whereas those who expect poor performance of themselves will conjure up negative outcomes" (p.25). Drawing upon the notion of Bandura's self-efficacy, we argue that the more self-efficacious consumers are with a web vendor, the more likely they will be to have favorable expectations of, and to trust, that online vendor. If an online customer lacks confidence in his or her ability to determine whether an online vendor is trustworthy, he or she might be less positive, therefore less likely to engage in an online transaction with that online seller. If an online buyer is skeptical about his or her ability to judge whether his or her online purchasing is secure and reliable, he or she might be likely to be negative about online transactions, therefore would be less likely to engage in transactions.

Figure 4 shows the effect of uncertainty reduction that trust and self-efficacy have individually and collectively. As mentioned earlier, trust is illuminated as a conventional uncertainty reduction measure, while self-efficacy will be considered as an antecedent to this uncertainty reduction mechanism. One should note that the impact of trust on uncertainty reduction is not a direct relationship; rather, any other variables can become involved in the reinforcing relationship between trust and uncertainty reduction. This study attempted to explore the factor that plays a significant role in influencing individuals' trust judgment. Thus, self-efficacy has been introduced into the argument regarding the impact of trust on uncertainty reduction.

McKnight et al. (2002) built on the integrative model by including institution-based trust, trusting intentions, trusting beliefs, and disposition to trust. They also suggested that the process of trust building could be dismantled according to each stage: dispositional, institutional, and interpersonal type trust constructs. According to McKnight et al., institution-based trust derives from a viewpoint that an individual's behavior is not determined by internal factors within the person, but by the environment surrounding him or her. Trusting intentions and trust beliefs reflect thought that social interactions among people, and an exchange of cognitive and emotional responses among them, influence an individual's behavior. Disposition to trust reflects a general propensity to trust others. Although trust building starts from an individual's intrapersonal communication level (McKnight et al.), so far little has been explored regarding intrapersonal level factors except for disposition to trust. That is, attention to an individual's intrapersonal factor has been limited to a belief in others, which is captured by disposition to trust. In this respect, this research has contributed to existing trust literature by filling in the remaining blank in McKnight and Chervany's framework (2002), intrapersonal level. By focusing on one's intrapersonal level, this study has shifted focus of trust from the perception of whether others with whom I am involved in online transactions are trustworthy to the perception of my capabilities. The belief of my capabilities refers to my perception of my own capabilities to handle uncertain and risky situations. It is argued that disposition to trust is about how one sees others whereas self-efficacy is about how one sees oneself.

This study has shown the need to explore possible antecedents and examine existing ones regarding trust building in e-commerce. Dispo-

Figure 4. The Intersection Effect of Trust and Self Efficacy

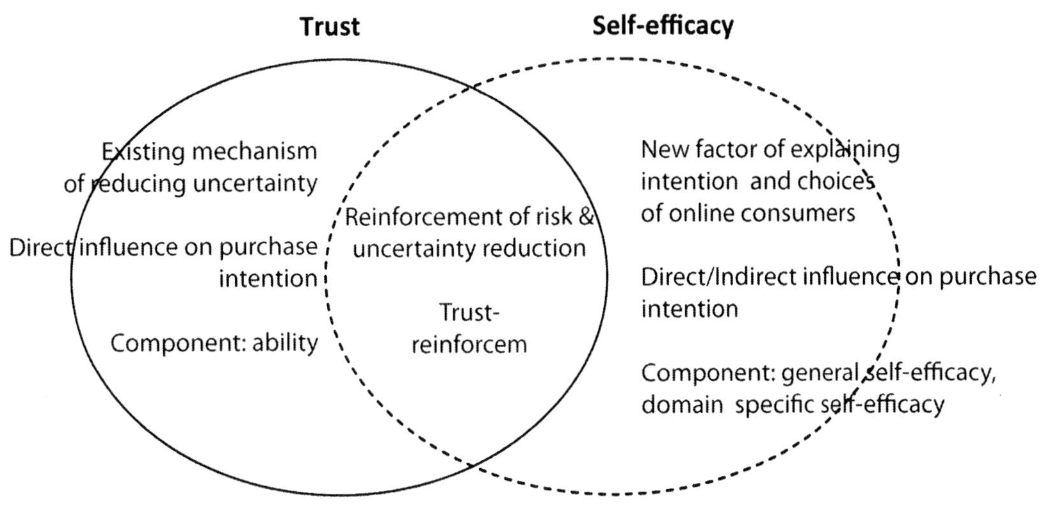

sition to trust is viewed as a general propensity to trust others, which influences an individual's beliefs and intentions about a Web vendor (McKnight et al., 2002). Contrary to perceived wisdom, at least as to perceived risk, disposition to trust which has been considered a significant variable has turned out to be an insignificant factor in the presence of self-efficacy. As mentioned earlier, disposition to trust is included as an antecedent in examining trust building in online transactions (Cheung & Lee, 2001; Gefen, 2000; Pavlou & Gefen, 2004); however, it has turned out that this factor does not play a role as an antecedent in the presence of more situation-specific factors like online transaction self-efficacy. Bhattacherjee (2002) argued that trust in e-commerce should be viewed as a domain-specific psychological state, because the general personality trait approach is more likely not to provide an adequate explanation of why an individual shows less trust toward uncertain and anonymous Web retailers. Accordingly, it should be noted that several problems exist regarding disposition to trust, an existing intrapersonal level factor. First, it is a general human trait, so lacks the domain-specificity essential to trust formation. Second, although originally it is introduced to explain trustor characteristics, it basically is oriented toward trustee attributes from the trustor viewpoint. It may reveal the extent to which a trustor is predisposed to trust *others*, but may not capture *trustor* characteristics. In more comprehensive conceptualization of trust, trustor characteristics should be taken more deeply into consideration.

Implications

These findings have several theoretical implications. First, while self-efficacy has been introduced and utilized in a considerable amount of research in IS and behavioral sciences, little is known about self-efficacy in online transactions. Understanding the nature and antecedents of trust has been a major issue for researchers and practitioners. This study also has explored possible antecedents and has examined several factors related to trust building in e-commerce. This study has demonstrated that it is important to introduce self-efficacy into research of trust in online transactions. We believe this study has illuminated a significant factor that has yet to be fully highlighted in an individual's uncertainty reduction mechanism during online transactions. Results have showed that self-efficacy is a causal antecedent to trust in reducing uncertainty inherent in online transactions and influences trust building. Whereas trust is a key of conventional uncertainty reduction mechanisms, self-efficacy is seen as a causal antecedent to this uncertainty-reduction process.

Second, this study suggests an advanced uncertainty reduction mechanism of an online consumer by investigating the inter-relationships among internal/subjective factors. A fuller understanding of the new uncertainty mechanism - beyond thc conventional wisdom that trust directly affects purchase intention - would be possible only via a systematic investigation into that relationship. To this end, this study investigated the influence of subjective/internal factors related to individual intentions to purchase goods online, and explored the interdependent relationship among these factors that are relevant to trust building in e-commerce.

Third, results have indicated that an individual's intrapersonal factors may play a role as moderators of objective trust-warranty mechanisms (e.g., reputation system, and other third-party warranty, etc.). McKnight and Chervany (2002) posited that certain situations tended to have stronger effects on interpersonal beliefs. But this does not necessarily lead to the conclusion that situations (including external safeguards or a guarantee system) influence interpersonal beliefs. Through three different measures such as information policies, guarantee policies, and reputation systems, web vendors try to make transactions more reliable (Grabner-Kraeuter, 2002). However, these instruments do not necessarily guarantee that these measures make it possible for online consumers to trust the web vendor. Kimery & McCord (2002) showed that there was no significant direct impact of a third-party seal on consumer trust in a specific e-retailer.

As McKnight et al. (2002) pointed out, trust is a complex, dynamic and multidimensional concept that could not be created by applying adequate external instruments. Consumers eventually decide on their own, despite being given any number of external measures provided by a guarantee instrument (e.g., TRUSTe) and any rating (e.g., the reputation system of eBay) offered by any other consumers. There always will be some consumers who are not confident that they can find a trustworthy web vendor, even if ratings and reputations provided by other consumers are given to them. What social cognitive theory teaches us is that external stimuli impacts do not materialize directly; rather they are realized through one's subjective mechanism that interprets and reacts to external factors (Bandura, 1982; 1986; 1991). In this vein, it is argued that externally-given, third-party, trust-warranty mechanisms do not automatically relieve online consumers from their concerns of uncertain and even risky transactions. The impact of external third party measures is moderated by the degree to which one sees oneself at the intrapersonal level. In this respect, this study has contributed to literature by examining the effect of online transaction self-efficacy.

Last, in practical respects, Web vendors and e-businesses should take into account the fact that self-efficacy of their customers can be enhanced by the extent to which they have accumulated previous purchase experiences. Although a Web vendor cannot directly engage in enhancing the degree of consumer's self-efficacy, it is evident that individual self-efficacy judgment can be positively influenced by cumulative experiences and transactions.

Limitations & Suggestions

This study has several limitations. First, it has attempted to address the applicability of self-efficacy in predicting trust building in e-commerce. As early studies may confront many problems, this research also faced obstacles common to exploratory studies: how to measure a new construct. Although this study built on measures of new task-and-situation self-efficacy in e-commerce contexts, more modifications are necessary to improve the reliability and validity of this new domain-specific self-efficacy. The composite reliability of the construct is .88. Although future studies need to refine their measures, this reliability is considered acceptable for exploratory studies.

Second, this study asked respondents to answer the measurement items based on their previous transaction experiences. It is acknowledged that, although this measuring method had the advantage of reflecting overall tendencies in the respondents' online transactions, their answers which were based on long-term (6-months) retrospection runs may discount this study's reliability. To overcome this limitation, future studies will have to focus on a shorter time frame (e.g., a week).

Third, because the web retailer was not specified to respondents, all web vendors with whom respondents have had business transactions were not unfamiliar to them. If the subjects were given an unfamiliar e-commerce vendor, the effect of online transaction self-efficacy on other constructs could be more firmly assessed. Therefore, there needs to be further research to measure the constructs with a Web site established and managed by an unfamiliar web vendor. Last, to enhance external validity of this study, research findings should be tested with samples having different demographic backgrounds. In this study, many participants were frequent users of the Internet and e-commerce, and seemed to have had somewhat positive experience with the Internet.

Suggestions for future research are as follows. First, based on findings that internal/subjective factors of trust-building play an important role, external/objective factors (e.g. the presence of a third party seal, privacy protection and security protection, etc.) should also be taken into consideration in constructing a research model. Recently, Web vendors have tried to promote trust in the Internet as well as beliefs about the specific vendor through seals from agencies such as TRUSTe. This agency assures consumers secure transactions by persuading Web vendors to adhere to its privacy policy. There is a clear effect of external/objective factors on trust building; thereby, these factors should be examined together with the internal/subjective factor. That will make for a more comprehensive approach to trust building in e-commerce.

Second, future studies should measure respondents' actual purchasing behaviors as the outcome variable. With solid theoretical basis from the Theory of Reasoned Action, this study did not measure actual purchases of the participants; rather it measured behavioral intentions (i.e., purchasing intention) and a significant antecedent of behavior. However, given that actual online purchases are the ultimate outcome in the process of trust-building, measuring actual purchases will improve the study's validity.

Third, to enhance research validity, respondents should be given two or three unfamiliar web vendors and self-retrospective questions should be avoided. This study allowed participants to recall any completed transaction with a web vendor. Resultantly, unlike other research which conducted an experiment regarding web vendors in certain retail domains such as books and travel, this study sought data across various retail domains. This procedure, however, likely biased participant responses, in a positive direction. Future studies are clearly needed to construct an experimental setting to obtain more reliable data.

ACKNOWLEDGEMENT

An earlier version of this article was presented in the HICSS 2005 and published in Journal of End User Computing 21(1), 2009.

REFERENCES

Agarwal, R., Sambamurthy, V., & Stair, R. (2000). Research report: The evolving relationship between general and special computer self-efficacy--An empirical assessment. *Information Systems Research, 11*(4), 418–430. doi:10.1287/isre.11.4.418.11876

Ajzen, I. (2002). Perceived behavioral control, self-efficacy, locus of control, and the theory of planned behavior. *Journal of Applied Social Psychology, 32*, 1–20. doi:10.1111/j.1559-1816.2002.tb00236.x

Ba, S., & Pavlou, P. (2002). Evidence of the effect of trust building technologies in electronic markets: Price premiums and buyer behavior. *Management Information Systems Quarterly, 26*(3), 243–268. doi:10.2307/4132332

Bagozzi, R. P., Yi, Y., & Phillips, L. W. (1991). Assessing construct validity in organizational research. *Administrative Science Quarterly, 36*(3), 421–458. doi:10.2307/2393203

Bandura, A. (1982). Self-Efficacy mechanism in human agency. *The American Psychologist, 37*, 122–147. doi:10.1037/0003-066X.37.2.122

Bandura, A. (1986). *Social foundations of thought and action: A social cognitive theory*. Englewood Cliffs, NJ: Prentice Hall.

Bandura, A. (1991). Social cognitive theory of self-regulation. *Organizational Behavior and Human Decision Processes, 50*, 248–287. doi:10.1016/0749-5978(91)90022-L

Bandura, A. (1997). *Self-efficacy: The exercise of control*. New York: Freeman.

Barney, J. B., & Hansen, M. H. (1994). Trustworthiness as a source of competitive advantage. *Strategic Management Journal, 15*, 175–190. doi:10.1002/smj.4250150912

Baron, R. M., & Kenny, D. A. (1986). The moderator-mediator variable distinction in social psychological research. *Journal of Personality and Social Psychology, 51*(6), 1173–1182. doi:10.1037/0022-3514.51.6.1173

Bentler, P. M., & Bonnet, D. G. (1980). Significance tests and goodness of fit in the analysis of covariance structures. *Psychological Bulletin, 88*, 588–606. doi:10.1037/0033-2909.88.3.588

Berlanger, F., Hiller, J. S., & Smith, W. J. (2002). Trustworthiness in electronic commerce: The role of privacy, security, and site attributes. *The Journal of Strategic Information Systems, 11*, 245–270. doi:10.1016/S0963-8687(02)00018-5

Bhatnagar, A., Misra, S., & Rao, H. R. (2000). On risk, convenience and Internet shopping behavior . *Communications of the ACM, 43*, 98–108. doi:10.1145/353360.353371

Bhattacharya, R., Devinney, T. M., & Pillutla, M. M. (1998). A formal model of trust based on outcomes. *Academy of Management Review, 23*, 459–472. doi:10.2307/259289

Bhattacherjee, A. (2002). Individual trust in online firms: Scale development and initial test. *Journal of Management Information Systems, 19*(1), 211–241.

Bosscher, R., & Smit, J. H. (1998). Confirmatory factor analysis of the general self-efficacy scale. *Behaviour Research and Therapy, 36*, 339–343. doi:10.1016/S0005-7967(98)00025-4

Butler, J. K. (1991). Toward understanding and measuring conditions of trust: Evolution of conditions of trust inventory. *Journal of Management, 17*(3), 643–663. doi:10.1177/014920639101700307

Byrne, B. M. (2001). *Structural equation modeling with AMOS: basic concepts, applications, and programming*. Mahwah, N.J.: Lawrence Erlbaum Associate.

Chen, C. C., Chen, X. P., & Meindl, J. R. (1998). How can cooperation be fostered? The cultural effects of individualism-collectivism. *Academy of Management Review, 23*(2), 285–304. doi:10.2307/259375

Chen, G., Gully, S. M., & Eden, D. (2001). Validation of a new general self-efficacy scale. *Organizational Research Methods, 4*(1), 62–84. doi:10.1177/109442810141004

Cheung, M. K., & Lee, M. K. O. (2001). Trust in Internet shopping: Instrument development and validation through classical and modern approaches. *Journal of Global Information Management, 9*(3), 23–35. doi:10.4018/jgim.2001070103

Cole, S. J. (1998). Testimony before the Subcommittee on Telecommunications, Trade, and Consumer Protection Committee on Commerce, U.S. House of Representatives. Retrieved on August 27, 2010, from Better Business Bureau website: www.bbb.org/alerts/cole.asp.

Compeau, D. R., & Higgins, C. A. (1995). Computer self-efficacy: Development of a measure and initial Test. *Management Information Systems Quarterly, 19*(2), 189–211. doi:10.2307/249688

Cummings, L. L., & Bromiley, P. (1996). The organizational trust inventory (OTI): Development and validation . In Kramer, R. M., & Tyler, T. R. (Eds.), *Trust in organizations* (pp. 302–330). Thousand Oaks, CA: Sage.

Doney, P. M., & Cannon, J. P. (1997). An examination of the nature of trust in buyer-supplier relationships. *Journal of Marketing, 61*(2), 35–51. doi:10.2307/1251829

Eastin, M. S., & LaRose, R. (2000). Internet self-efficacy and the psychology of the digital divide. *Journal of Computer-mediated Communication, 6*, 1. Retrieved on May 16, 2008 from http://www.ascusc.org/jcmc/vol6/issue1/eastin.html.

Eden, D. (1988). Pygmalion, goal setting, and expectancy: Compatible ways to raise productivity. *Academy of Management Review, 13*(4), 639–652. doi:10.2307/258381

Eden, D., & Zuk, Y. (1995). Seasickness as a self-fulfilling prophecy: Raising self-efficacy to boost performance at sea. *The Journal of Applied Psychology, 80*, 628–635. doi:10.1037/0021-9010.80.5.628

Etezadi-Amoli, J., & Farhoomand, A. F. (1996). A structural model of end user computing satisfaction and user performance. *Information & Management, 30*(2), 65–73. doi:10.1016/0378-7206(95)00052-6

Featherman, & Pavlou, (2002). Predicting e-service adoption: A perceived risk facets perspective 2002. *Proceedings of the Eighth America Conference on Information Systems*. Dallas, TX.

Fishbein, M., & Ajzen, I. (1975). *Belief, attitude, intention and behavior: An introduction to theory and research*. MA: Addison-Wesley Publishing Company.

Fornell, C., & Lacker, D. F. (1981). Evaluating structural equation with unobservable variables and measurement error. *JMR, Journal of Marketing Research, 18*(2), 39–50. doi:10.2307/3151312

Frayne, C. A., & Latham, G. P. (1987). Application of social learning theory to employee self-management of attendance. *The Journal of Applied Psychology, 72*, 387–392. doi:10.1037/0021-9010.72.3.387

Fung, R. K. K., & Lee, M. K. O. (1999). EC-Trust (Trust in electronic commerce): Exploring the antecedent factors. *Proceedings of the Fifth Americas Conference on Information Systems*, Miwaukee, Wisconsin, 517-519.

Gabarro, J. J. (1978). The development of trust influence and expectations . In Athos, A. G., & Gabarro, J. J. (Eds.), *Interpersonal behavior: Communication and understanding in relationships* (pp. 290–303). Upper Saddle River, NJ: Prentice Hall.

Gambetta, D. (1988). *Trust: Making and breaking cooperative relations*. Oxford, UK: Basil Blackwell.

Gefen, D. (2000). E-commerce: the role of familiarity and trust. *Omega: The International Journal of Management Science, 28*(6), 725–737. doi:10.1016/S0305-0483(00)00021-9

Gefen, D. (2002). Reflections on the dimensions of trust and trustworthiness among online consumers. *ACM SIGMIS Database, 33*(3), 38–53. doi:10.1145/569905.569910

Gefen, D., & Devine, P. (2001). Customer loyalty to an online store: The meaning of online service quality. *Proceedings of the International Conference on Information Systems*, New Orleans, Louisiana, 613-617.

Gefen, D., & Straub, D. W. (2003). Managing user trust in B2C e-services. e-Service Journal, 2, 7-24.

Gist, M. E., & Mitchell, T. R. (1992). Self-efficacy: A theoretical analysis of its determinants and malleability. *Academy of Management Review, 17*(2), 183–211. doi:10.2307/258770

Gist, M. E., Schwoerer, C., & Rosen, B. (1989). Effects of alternative training methods on self-efficacy and performance in computer software training. *The Journal of Applied Psychology, 74*, 884–891. doi:10.1037/0021-9010.74.6.884

Grabner-Kraeuter, S. (2002). The role of consumers' trust in online shopping. *Journal of Business Ethics, 39*, 43–51. doi:10.1023/A:1016323815802

Hair, J. F., Anderson, R. E., Tatham, R. L., & Black, W. C. (1998). *Multivariate data analysis*. Upper Saddle River, NJ: Prentice-Hall.

Hart, P., & Saunders, C. (1997). Power and trust: Critical factors in the adoption and use of electronic data interchange. *Organization Science, 8*(1), 23–42. doi:10.1287/orsc.8.1.23

Hayduk, L. A. (1987). *Structural equation modeling with LISREL: Essentials and advances*. Baltimore, MD: The Johns Hopkins University Press.

Jarvenpaa, S. L., Knoll, K., & Leidner, D. E. (1998). Is anybody out there? Antecedents of trust in global virtual teams. *Journal of Management Information Systems, 14*(4), 26–64.

Jarvenpaa, S. L., & Todd, P. A. (1996). Consumer reactions to electronic shopping on the World Wide Web. *International Journal of Electronic Commerce, 1*(2), 59–88.

Jarvenpaa, S. L., & Tractinsky, N. (1999). Consumer trust in an Internet store. *Information Technology Management, 5*(2), 1–35.

Jarvenpaa, S. L., Tractinsky, N., & Vitale, M. (2000). Consumer trust in an Internet store. *Information Technology Management, 1*(1-2), 45–71. doi:10.1023/A:1019104520776

Judge, T. A., Erez, A., & Bono, J. A. (1998). The power of being positive: The relation between positive self-concept and job performance. *Human Performance, 11*, 167–187. doi:10.1207/s15327043hup1102&3_4

Kathryn, M. K., & Mary, M. (2002). Third-party assurance: Mapping the road to trust in e-retailing. *Journal of Information Technology Theory and Application, 4*(2), 63–82.

Kim, D. J., Ferrin, D. L., & Rao, H. R. (2003)a. Antecedents of consumer trust in B-to-C electronic commerce. *Proceedings of the Americas Conference on Information Systems.* Tampa, FL: ACIS.

Kim, D. J., Ferrin, D. L., & Rao, H. R. (2003) b. An investigation of consumer online trust and purchase, re-purchasing intentions. *Proceedings of the International Conference on Information Systems*, Seattle, WA: ICIS.

Kim, D. J., Ferrin, D. L., & Rao, H. R. (2008). A trust-based consumer decision making model in electronic commerce: The role of trust, perceived risk, and their antecedents. *Decision Support Systems, 44*, 544–564. doi:10.1016/j.dss.2007.07.001

Kim, D. J., Sivasailam, N., & Rao, H. R. (2004). Information assurance in B2C websites for information goods/services. *Electronic Markets, 14*, 344–359. doi:10.1080/10196780412331311784

Kim, D. J., Song, Y. I., Braynov, S. B., & Rao, H. R. (2005). A multi-dimensional trust formation model in B-to-C e-commerce: A conceptual framework and content analyses of academia/practitioner perspective. *Decision Support Systems, 40*(2), 143–165. doi:10.1016/j.dss.2004.01.006

Kimery, K. M., & McCord, M. (2002). Third-party assurances: Mapping the road to trust in e-retailing. *JITTA: Journal of Information Technology Theory and Application, 4*(2), 63–83.

Lee, C., & Bobko, P. (1994). Self-efficacy beliefs: Comparison of five measures. *The Journal of Applied Psychology, 79*(3), 364–369. doi:10.1037/0021-9010.79.3.364

Marakas, G. M., Yi, M. Y., & Johnson, R. D. (1998). The multilevel and multifaceted character of computer self-efficacy: Toward clarification of the construct and an integrative framework for reason. *Information Systems Research, 9*(2), 126–163. doi:10.1287/isre.9.2.126

Mayer, R. C., Davis, J. H., & Schoorman, F. D. (1995). An integrative model of organizational trust. *Academy of Management Review*, *20*(3), 709–735. doi:10.2307/258792

McAllister, D. J. (1995). Affect- and cognition-based trust as foundations for interpersonal cooperation in organizations. *Academy of Management Journal*, *38*(1), 24–59. doi:10.2307/256727

McCormick, M., & Martinko, M. J. (2004). Social cognitive theory and leadership research: Toward a causal reasoning perspective. *Proceedings of the Southern Management Association.*

McKnight, D. H., & Chervany, N. L. (2002). What trust means in e-commerce customer relationships: An interdisciplinary conceptual typology. *International Journal of Electronic Commerce*, *6*(2), 35–59.

McKnight, D. H., Choudhury, V., & Kacmar, C. (2002). Developing and validating trust measures for e-commerce: An integrative typology. *Information Systems Research*, *13*(3), 334–359. doi:10.1287/isre.13.3.334.81

McKnight, D. H., Cummings, L. L., & Chervany, N. L. (1998). Initial trust formation in new organizational relationships. *Academy of Management Review*, *23*(3), 473–490. doi:10.2307/259290

McNight, D. H., Kacmar, C. J., & Choudhury, V. (2004). Shifting factors and the ineffectiveness of third party assurance seals: A two-stage model of initial trust in a Web business. *Electronic Markets*, *14*(3), 252–266. doi:10.1080/1019678042000245263

Mitchell, T. R., Hopper, H., Daniels, D., George-Falvy, J., & James, L. R. (1994). Predicting self-efficacy and performance during skill acquisition. *The Journal of Applied Psychology*, *79*, 506–517. doi:10.1037/0021-9010.79.4.506

Miyazaki, A. D., & Fernandez, A. (2001). Consumer perceptions of privacy and security risks for online shopping. *The Journal of Consumer Affairs*, *35*(1), 27–45. doi:10.1111/j.1745-6606.2001.tb00101.x

Money, R. B., Gilly, M. C., & Granham, J. L. (1998). Explorations of national culture and word-of-mouth referral behavior in the purchase of industrial services in the United States and Japan. *Journal of Marketing*, *62*, 76–87. doi:10.2307/1252288

Pavlou, P. A., & Chai, L. (2002). What drives electronic commerce across cultures? A cross-cultural empirical investigation of the theory of planned behavior. *Journal of Electronic Commerce Research*, *3*(4), 240–253.

Pavlou, P. A., & Gefen, D. (2004). Building effective online marketplaces with institution-based trust. *Information Systems Research*, *15*(1), 37–59. doi:10.1287/isre.1040.0015

Reichheld, F. F., & Schefter, P. (2000). E-loyalty: Your secret weapon on the Web. *Harvard Business Review*, *78*(4), 105–113.

Rempel, J. K., Holmes, J. G., & Zanna, M. P. (1985). Trust in close relationships? *Journal of Personality and Social Psychology*, *49*(1), 95–112. doi:10.1037/0022-3514.49.1.95

Ridings, C. M., Gefen, D., & Arinze, B. (2002). Some antecedents and effects of trust in virtual communities. *The Journal of Strategic Information Systems*, *11*(3), 271–295. doi:10.1016/S0963-8687(02)00021-5

Rose, G., Khoo, H., & Straub, D. W. (1999). Current technological impediments to business-to-consumer electronic commerce. *Communications of the AIS*, *1*(16), 1–74.

Schurr, P. H., & Ozanne, J. L. (1985). Influences on exchange processes: Buyer's preconceptions of a seller's trustworthiness and bargaining toughness. *The Journal of Consumer Research*, *11*(4), 939–953. doi:10.1086/209028

Shelton, S. H. (1990). Developing the construct of general self-efficacy. *Psychological Reports*, *66*, 987–994.

Sherer, M., Maddux, J. E., Mercandante, B., Prentice-Dunn, S., Jacobs, B., & Rogers, R. W. (1982). The self-efficacy scale: Construction and validation. *Psychological Reports*, *51*, 663–671.

Stajkovic, A. D., & Luthans, F. (1998). Self-efficacy and work-related performance: A meta-analysis. *Psychological Bulletin*, *124*(2), 240–261. doi:10.1037/0033-2909.124.2.240

Stanley, K. D., & Murphy, M. D. (1997). A comparison of general self-efficacy with self-esteem. *Genetic, Social, and General Psychology Monographs*, *123*, 79–100.

Stewart, K. J. (2003). Trust transfer on the World Wide Web. *Organization Science*, *14*(1), 5–17. doi:10.1287/orsc.14.1.5.12810

Stone, R. W., & Henry, J. W. (2003). The roles of computer self-efficacy and outcome expectancy in influencing the computer end-users' organizational Commitment. *Journal of End User Computing*, *15*(1), 38–53. doi:10.4018/joeuc.2003010103

Suh, B., & Han, I. (2002). Effect of trust on customer acceptance of Internet banking. *Electronic Commerce Research and Applications*, *1*, 247–263. doi:10.1016/S1567-4223(02)00017-0

Venkatesh, V. (2000). Determinants of perceived ease of use: Integrating control, intrinsic motivation, and emotion into the technology acceptance model. *Information Systems Research*, *11*(4), 342–365. doi:10.1287/isre.11.4.342.11872

Venkatesh, V., & Davis, F. D. (1996). A model of the antecedents of perceived ease of use: Development and test. *Decision Sciences*, *27*(3), 451–481. doi:10.1111/j.1540-5915.1996.tb01822.x

Venkatesh, V., & Davis, F. D. (2000). A theoretical extension of the technology acceptance model: Four longitudinal field studies. *Management Science*, *46*(2), 186–204. doi:10.1287/mnsc.46.2.186.11926

Wood, R., & Bandura, A. (1989). Impact of conceptions of ability on self-regulatory mechanisms and complex decision making. *Journal of Personality and Social Psychology*, *56*, 407–415. doi:10.1037/0022-3514.56.3.407

Yi, M. J., & Hwang, Y. (2003). Predicting the use of web-based information systems: Self-efficacy, enjoyment, learning goal orientation and the technology acceptance model. *International Journal of Human-Computer Studies*, *59*, 431–449. doi:10.1016/S1071-5819(03)00114-9

Zucker, L. (1986). Production of trust: Institutional sources of economic structure, 1840-1920. *Research in Organizational Behavior*, *8*, 53–111.

Chapter 3
Trust Restoration in Electronic Commerce

Qinyu Liao
The University of Texas at Brownsville and Texas Southmost College, USA

Xin Luo
University of Mexico, Mexico

Anil Gurung
Marshall University, USA

ABSTRACT

This paper proposes a model addressing the rebuilding of post-violation trust in B2C electronic commerce. The model uses expectation-confirmation theory and provides empirical verification for the factors affecting post-violation trust rebuilding and the association between them. The factors are perceived trustworthiness, confirmation by trust restoration, satisfaction and continuance trust intention. In accordance with exiting literature, perceived trustworthiness was found to have significant impact on continuance trust intention. The study also showed that confirmation by post-violation trust restoration activities had strong impact on satisfaction but satisfaction did not lead to post-violation continuance trust intention.

INTRODUCTION

The last decade or so has witnessed an explosive growth of electronic commerce. While the extensive use of Internet provides a new arena for marketers and retailers, the long-term profitability and survival of business to consumer (B2C) electronic commerce depend on the continued online buyers rather than the first-time users. According to Parthasarathy and Bhattacherjee (2001), it costs as much as five times more to acquire new customers than keeping the existing ones. For example, a 5% increase in customer retention in the insurance industry typically translates into 18% savings in operating costs (Crego & Schiffrin, 1995)

Trust is important for keeping continued buyers (Brynjolfsson & Smith, 2000). A customer has to trust the online business to disclose his/her private information in order to finalize a transaction. He or she has to trust the quality of the products or

DOI: 10.4018/978-1-60960-577-3.ch003

services because in most of the transactions the seller and buyer may have had never met. There are many studies that have investigated on how trust affects consumer behavior in electronic commerce (Kim & Benbasat, 2006; Morrison & Firmstone, 2000; Pennington, Wilcox, & Grover, 2003; Schoder & Haenlein, 2004). In an effort to mitigate online distrust, online companies have been using third party seals, customer feedback or comments board, reputation advertising, privacy statement and insurance to engender trust over their customers and differentiate themselves from untrustworthy competitors(Lee, Ang, & Dubelaar, 2005). Additionally, in risky online environments where information fraud and breach may exist and thereby deteriorate consumers' trust, the online merchants should also understand how trust can be rebuilt should there be a violation of trust.

While previous research has shed light on the antecedents of trust, this study focuses on the process of trust rebuilding using the expectation-confirmation theory. A theoretical model of post-violation trust rebuilding has been developed and empirically tested with data collected from a survey of online consumers. The specific research questions that we would like to address in this study are as follows: 1) what are the factors behind the online users intention to continue trusting the site even after a trust violation? 2) how do these factors influence continuance trust intention?

The paper is arranged as follows. The next section describes trust, expectation-confirmation theory and the concept of trust violation. It is followed by the development of the hypotheses and the research model. The third section outlines the research methodology that we used for this study. The fourth section presents the statistical findings, and the fifth section presents the discussions and managerial implications of the research. The last section concludes this study by mentioning the notable findings.

LITERATURE REVIEW

Trust and Trust Bebuilding

Trust has been one of the most significant research phenomena across a variety of disciplinary fields including philosophy, psychology, sociology, management, and information systems etc. Theoretical underpinning of trust has been demonstrated through a plethora of perspectives. Lumann (1979) indicates that trust refers to the belief that other people will react in predictable ways. From a social-psychological point of view, Cremer, Snyder and Dewitte (2001) argue that social interactions are pleasant and cooperative if individuals take into account others' interest because understanding trust is important in promoting cooperation across different social interactions. Trust is a bilateral relation that involves an entity manifesting trust called the trustor and an entity being trusted called the trustee. In this research, we adopt the universally acknowledged definition of trust from the work of Mayer, Davis and Schoorman (1995), who refer to trust as *the willingness of a party/trustor to be vulnerable to the actions of another party/trustee based on the expectation that the other (trustee) will perform a particular action important to the trustor, irrespective of the ability to monitor or control that other party (trustee)*.

Trust is believed to exist when one party has confidence in an exchange partner's reliability and integrity and is the perceived credibility and benevolence of a target of trust (Doney & Cannon, 1997; Morgan & Hunt, 1994). It has been considered essential for understanding interpersonal behavior because of uncertainty and information asymmetry. In conventional or off-line commerce, trust stems from the expectation of positive consequence as well as the acceptance of vulnerability, and is of crucial importance due to the difficulty of confirming another's identity and the information asymmetry between trustors and trustees. The importance of trust has been magnified in online environment, partly because of the lack of physical proximity, which, in off-line settings, can aid trust building. This viewpoint is supported by Quelch and Klein (1996) who argue that trust is a crucial factor in stimulating purchase over the Internet.

Trust enables cooperation and permits voluntary participation in mutually beneficial interactions which are otherwise costly to enforce or cannot be enforced by third parties. While previous literature has suggested that the establishment of trust is a gradual process because trust is built on the assumption that trustee can entertain estimates of trustor's trustworthiness, it does not take more than an instant to destroy trust by misfortune or a mistake and it may be costly or take a long time to rebuild trust once it is lost. We argue that trust is bound to be lessened if the trustee fails to perform the tasks to meet his/her commitments due to the lack of incentive and/or ability, or complicated circumstances beyond his/her control. The erosion of trust is believed to harm both the involved parties. The severity of trust violation depends on the magnitude of the violation, number of prior violations, and the specific dimension of trust that was violated. Notwithstanding the previous contention that trust cannot be repaired once it is violated, we argue that the broken trust can be retrieved and that rebuilding trust is a long and arduous journey even if trust violation may seriously damage or irreparably destroy trust. Our argument is based on the assumption that the trustor is willing to or has incentive to reconcile and restore trust on the trustee.

From a psychological perspective, reconciliation occurs when both trustee and trustor exert effort to rebuild a damaged relationship following an incident involving a broken promise and strive to settle the issues that led to the disruption of that relationship (Lewicki & Bunker, 1996). Defined as a deliberate decision by the trustor or victim to surrender feelings of resentment and to grant amnesty to the trustee or offender, reconciliation is viewed as a behavioral manifestation of forgiveness (Tomlinson & Lewicki, 2004). Furthermore, according to Lewicki and Bunker (1996), it is possible to forgive someone or release him/her from responsibility for damage he/she has inflicted without exhibiting a willingness to reconcile the relationship or trust him again in the future. Therefore, we believe that, following a trust violation, if the trustor or victim is willing to reconcile, rebuilding trust in the damaged relationship becomes possible.

Many factors contribute to the building of initial trust in e-commerce. Concerns for information privacy are more likely to affect the trust and willingness to transact online for a well-known merchant (Van Slyke, Shim, Johnson & Jiang, 2006). Consumer perception of certain cognitive cues (i.e., communication, opportunism, product brand equity, website attractiveness) is important predictors of initial trust in an e-retailer (Wakefield, Stocks, & Wilder, 2004). While online merchants are using trust assurance structure like third party credentialing, merchant guarantees, feedback systems, and security features to gain consumer trust (Kim & Benbasat, 2010; Lee & Lee, 2006; Utz, Matzat, & Snijders, 2009), consumer characteristics such as age, gender, culture, value, psychology and emotions as well as product characteristics (price and riskiness) can also affect trust-building in e-commerce (Kim & Benbasat, 2009, 2010; Pennanen, 2006; Riedl, Hubert, & Kenning, 2010).

While previous literature has tended to demonstrate the factors that influence trust, less attention has been paid to how trust may be rebuilt after trust is breached or violated. Trust violation occurs when the trustor's confident positive expectations of the trustee are disconfirmed. The consequence of the violation is that subsequent trust is eroded and lowered and that it may reduce the extent to which the victims of these violations will cooperate with the offender. This reflects the fundamental mechanisms of human psychology known as the asymmetry principle (Slovic, 1997). According to this principle, trust-destroying events are more noticeable, more credible, and carry much greater weight than trust-building events. For this reason, once initiated, distrust tends to reinforce itself. The asymmetry principle makes it more difficult and more costly for the learning party to obtain estimates of trustworthiness. Research within organizations has shown that trust violations stifle mutual support and information sharing, and even exert negative effects on organizational citizenship behaviors, job performance, turnover, and profits (Cremer *et al.* 2001; Jarvenpaa, Knoll & Keider, 1998; Mayers *et al.* 1995; Rousseau, Sitkin, Burt & Camerer, 1998).

Expectation-Confirmation Theory

Expectation-confirmation theory (ECT) describes the process by which consumers reach their repurchase intentions (Oliver, 1980). It has been used to study consumer satisfaction, and post-purchase behavior in consumer behavior literature (Dabolkar, Shepard & Thorpe, 2000; Oliver, 1980, 1993). The constructs in the ECT include expectation, perceived performance, confirmation, satisfaction and repurchase intention. According to the theory, consumers purchase a product or service based on initial expectation on the product or service. Satisfaction is formed if the post-purchase evaluation matches their initial expectation. Satisfied consumers finally lead to repurchase intention but dissatisfied users discontinue the subsequent use. Confirmation is inversely related to expectation and directly related to perceived performance. In a test of expectancy theory, DeSanctis (1983) found that higher levels of user expectation were related to higher levels of system use. Adopting ECT, Bhattacherjee (2001) found that continuance intention was determined by satisfaction with IS use and user satisfaction was influenced by the confirmation of consumer expectations.

Satisfaction is the summary psychological state resulting when the emotion surrounding disconfirmed expectations is coupled with the consumer's prior feelings about the consumption experience (Oliver, 1981). In the ECT, satisfaction is the key to forming and maintaining loyal consumers. The level of satisfaction depends on the baseline expectation. A high level of expectation tends to enhance one's satisfaction, while low expectation reduces consequent satisfaction. Pre-purchase expectation can change in conditions where consumers have had the first-hand experience and their post-purchase expectation will thereby provide the basis for subsequent behavior (Bhattacherjee, 2001). Others distinct satisfaction from attitude and postulate that satisfaction is a transient, experience-specific affect, while attitude is a relatively more enduring affect transcending all prior experiences (Oliver, 1980, 1981). Therefore, one may have a pleasant experience with a service, but still feel dissatisfied if it is below expectation.

Conceptual Development

Consumers' post-violation trust rebuilding in electronic commerce is similar to consumers' repurchase decision-making. Both decisions are influenced by an initial experience and followed by a confirmation experience (product/service use or trust restoring activities). Rational users most likely will go through a decision making process, similar to that in the ECT, prior to making a decisive choice. Figure 1 shows the proposed relationships among the constructs and the focus is on the post-violation trust rebuilding since this is more reflective of the trust rebuilding context. First, perceived trustworthiness is a post expectation that is important for services where expectation and perception may change with time, as is often the case with IS use. Second, perceived trustworthiness has been identified as a crucial factor in stimulating purchase over Internet (Quelch & Klein, 1996).

Following the propositions of ECT, consumers' continuance trust intention is likely to be determined by their satisfaction with prior trust restoration experience after a violation had occurred.

Figure 1. Research Model

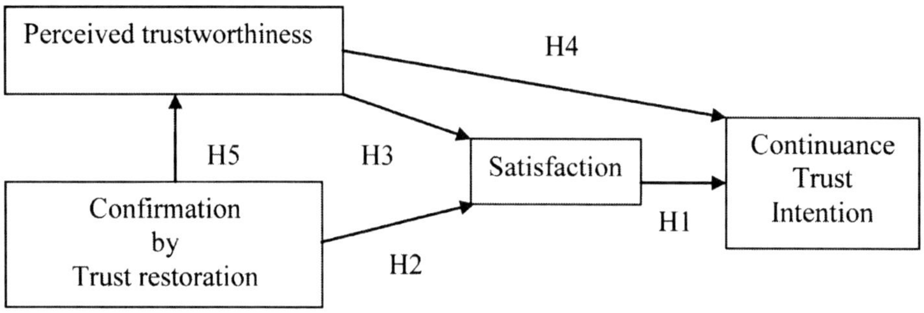

The relationship between user satisfaction and continuance intention has been confirmed by many information systems researchers (Davis, Bagozzi, & Warshaw, 1989; Karahanna, Straub, & Chervany, 1999; Taylor & Todd, 1995). The same contention can be extended to trust rebuilding in B2C electronic commerce. When the post-violation activities fulfill the assuring promises, present action consistent with their policies, or show care and concerns for damages caused by the violation, the consumers are likely to reconcile, accept the remedies, understand it as a temporary condition, and stay in the trusting relationship. Gregg and Scott (2006) found that recent negative feedback posted in an online reputation system can be used to predict future online auction activities. Therefore, the first hypothesis:

H1: Consumers' level of satisfaction with trust restoration activities is positively associated with their continuance trust intention for that online business.

The proposition of the ECT suggests that consumer satisfaction will be determined by perceived website trustworthiness and confirmation of expectation after trust violation. Since the current study focuses on the post-violation trust, the perceived trustworthiness represents the post-violation baseline expectation, against which confirmation is evaluated by consumers to determine their satisfaction. Selnes (1998) found that constructive conflict handling increases satisfaction and leads to improved trust in buyer-seller relationships. In this context, confirmation implies the realization of the expected remedies assured by the online company, while disconfirmation denotes failure to achieve expectations. This leads to the second hypothesis:

H2: Consumers' extent of confirmation is positively associated with their satisfaction with online business.

The second determinant of satisfaction, as suggested by the ECT, is perceived trustworthiness (expectation of the website's trustworthiness). In B2C e-commerce, companies use signals by trustworthy web merchants to differentiate themselves from their untrustworthy counterparts (Lee *et al.*, 2005) and add reputation advertising and structural assurance to increase the consumers' expectation of their trustworthiness, showing that their effects did not erode over time (Mcknight, Kacmar, & Chaudhury., 2004). The perceived trustworthiness can be a result of cumulated expectation through repeated transactions and probably effective trust restoration activities, which, according to Dinev and Hart (2006), can even balance out their personal information disclosure concerns. Customers with high perceived trustworthiness would be more willing to tolerate violations and open to reconciliation and, therefore, more satisfied.

H3: Consumers' perceived trustworthiness of online business is positively associated with their satisfaction with online business.

The ECT posits that expectation influence customer continuance intention. This can be explained by self-perception theory (Bem, 1972), which states that individuals continually adjust their perception (e.g., expectation) as they acquire new information about the focal behavior. The adjusted perceptions then provide the basis for subsequent behaviors. In this context, it would be the decision of whether to continue the trust on the website. If the violation was very damaging, and the consumers experienced strong negative cognitive and emotional reactions and were not willing to accept the trust restoration, the trust cannot be rebuilt.

H4: Consumers' online business continuance intention is positively associated with their perceived trustworthiness of online business.

Users may have some initial expectation (perceived trustworthiness) of a website and it will be adjusted as a result of the confirmation experience if the reality shows some discrepancies. The association between confirmation and expectation (perceived trustworthiness) postulated by the expectation-confirmation theory is based in theory of reasoned action/theory of planned behavior (TRA/TPB) (Ajzen, 1975, 1985) and can be supported by cognitive dissonance theory (Festinger, 1957). In the context of this paper, the theory holds that consumers may experience dissonance or psychological tension if their pre-violation trustworthiness perceptions are disconfirmed during actual online transaction. Rational users may try to remedy this dissonance by distorting or modifying their trustworthiness perceptions of that online vender in order to be more consistent with reality. Confirmation will tend to elevate online businesses' perceived trustworthiness and disconfirmation will reduce such perceptions. Therefore, we propose that:

H5: Consumers' extent of confirmation is positively associated with their perceived trustworthiness of online business.

METHOD

Data Collection

The empirical data for this study were collected employing a field survey of electronic commerce customers. The target respondents were drawn from students enrolled in three large universities, one in the Midwest, one in the south, and one on the eastern coast. Each customer received an email soliciting his/her participation in a survey of electronic commerce trust rebuilding. The email message outlined the purpose of the study and also provided a hyperlink to an online survey form. This method was chosen since online surveys have several advantages over traditional paper-based mail surveys, such as lower costs, faster responses, and geographically unrestricted sample (Tan & Teo, 2000). Participants were directed to the survey site by clicking on the link included in the email message. The participation in the survey was completely voluntary and the anonymity of the respondents was maintained. Any identifying information of the respondents such as IP addresses was removed before data analysis.

To ensure appropriate selection of subjects, the process of eliciting qualified subjects consisted of two steps: 1) prior to answering all other questions, subjects were first questioned whether they had shopped online or not. If not, their answers were excluded for further investigation and the survey exited. 2) Then subjects were asked whether they had encountered any trust violation problems online. Their answers were excluded for further analysis if they answered none.

Of 323 respondents to the survey, only those respondents who had bought a product from a website and have had a bad or unhappy experience were selected for data analysis. The sample size was 108 after excluding the online consumers who have not had bad experience while buying products on the web. The sample comprised of 46.3% of males and 53.7 of females. Regarding the internet experience, 14.8% reported having less than 1 year, 38.0% between 1 and 3 years, 19.4% between 3 and 5 years, and 27.8% more than 5 years.

There is no general consensus in the sample size requirements for PLS analysis. As one of the popular heuristics recommended by Chin (1998), the minimum sample size requirements is ten times the largest of these two possibilities: 1) the latent variable with the largest number of indicators or 2) the dependent variable with the largest number of independent variables. In our study, the latent variable that has the maximum number of indicators is "perceived trustworthiness" which has 10 indicators. And the dependent variable with the largest number of independent variables is either "satisfaction" or "continuance trust intention" both with two independent variables. Since the first option with the latent variable with the largest number of indicators is greater than the other option, the minimum sample requirements will be 10 multiplied by 10, resulting in a total of 100. Therefore, this research has reached the heuristics for sample size requirements. Further, it is noted to other researchers that the heuristics used in this paper should be considered with caution because smaller sample size may be subject to greater amount of estimation errors.

Instrument Development and Validation

Four constructs measured in this study are perceived trustworthiness, satisfaction, electronic commerce continuance intention, and confirmation. Constructs were measured using multi-item scales, drawn from existing trust and expectation-confirmation research, and reworded so as to relate specifically to the context of B2C electronic commerce (See Table 1). Satisfaction items were based on the seven-point semantic differential scales. All others used five-point Likert scales anchored between 1 for "strongly disagree" and 5 for "strongly agree" (Appendix).

A pre-test was first conducted to validate the instrument by administering the questionnaire to IS researchers comprising of doctoral students and the faculty. Their suggestions were accommodated in order to further refine the instrument.

RESULTS

Partial Least Squares (PLS) was employed to test the hypotheses of the proposed model. Before using PLS, data were analyzed by running

Table 1. Construct Map

Construct	Operational definition	Source of measures
Ecommerce continuance intention	Consumers' intention to continue using e-commerce	Mathieson's (1991) behavioral intention scale
Satisfaction	Consumers' feelings about e-commerce	Adapted from Spreng et al.'s (1993) overall satisfaction scale
Perceived trustworthiness	Consumer's perception of the expected trust of e-commerce	(Ba & Pavlou, 2002; Jarvenpaa, et al., 1998; Straub, Hoffman, Weber, & Steinfield, 2002)
Confirmation	Consumers' perception of the congruence between expectation of e-commerce trustworthiness and its actual trust restoring activities	Adapted from Bhattacherjee (2001)

a Principal Components Factor (PCA) analysis with varimax rotation to determine the convergent and the discriminant validity. The factor analysis resulted in four factors having eigen values above 1. The amount of variance explained was 78.92. Reliabilities of the measures were analyzed to determine that multiple measures of the constructs are measuring the respective constructs. The results of the analysis are presented followed by their discussion.

Measurement Model

The measurement model was examined by assessing the individual item reliability, internal consistency, convergent validity and discriminant validity. All measures but one had acceptable item loadings of.707, as suggested by Carmines and Zeller (1979). One item, TRU9, did not meet the requirements and was dropped. Item weights and loadings are shown in Table 2. T-Statistics for all the item loadings are significant at.001 level. Internal consistency was determined by two measures: composite reliability (CR) and average variance extracted (AVE). The composite reliabilities for all the measures exceed the 0.70 level. The AVE above the level of 0.5 indicates that the measures meet the required criteria of internal consistency (Fornell & Larcker, 1981). Table 3 shows the CR and AVE for all the measures are well above the required criteria, thus indicating that the measures are internally consistent.

The convergent validity is inferred when each measurement item correlate with its related theoretical construct. The test was performed by using the confirmatory factor analysis in PLS. Table 2 shows that the t-values of the outer model loadings are above the level of 1.96, as suggested by Gefen and Straub (2004), thus indicating that the measures meet the criteria of convergent validity.

The discriminant validity is inferred when each measurement item correlate weakly with all

Table 2. Item Weights and Loadings

Construct	Item	Weight	Loading	T-Statistic*
Perceived Trustworthiness	TRU1	.0874	.8887	33.10
	TRU2	.0849	.8736	34.64
	TRU3	.0705	.7866	17.14
	TRU4	.0851	.8656	21.10
	TRU5	.0902	.8990	39.94
	TRU6	.0926	.9204	45.03
	TRU7	.0909	.9113	44.28
	TRU8	.0811	.7253	11.92
	TRU9	.0420	.4022	2.89
	TRU10	.0894	.8969	45.82
	TRU11	.0768	.7975	15.47
	TRU12	.0986	.8816	38.65
	TRU13	.0947	.8942	38.76
	TRU14	.0904	.8985	35.26
Confirmation by Trust Restoration	CFM1	.3628	.9525	86.01
	CFM2	.3709	.9569	90.87
	CFM3	.3311	.9046	30.54
Satisfaction	SAT1	.2727	.9096	45.99
	SAT2	.2618	.9344	53.73
	SAT3	.2889	.9163	54.91
	SAT4	.2684	.9037	39.90
Continuance Trust Intention	CTI1	.5413	.9659	147.64
	CTI2	.4973	.9594	88.68

Note: T-Statistics are for loadings, not weights. *All loadings are significant at p <.001

Table 3. Correlation Matrix, Mean, Standard deviations and Average Variance Extracted for Constructs

	Mean	SD	CR	Trust	Confirmation	Satisfaction	Continuance
Trust	2.55	.99	.975	**.752**			
Confirmation	2.83	.98	.957	.786	**.883**		
Satisfaction	3.24	1.12	.954	.565	.640	**.839**	
Continuance	2.91	1.21	.962	.732	.606	.465	**.927**
Square root of AVE				.87	.94	.92	.96

Note: Average Variance Extracted (AVE) is shown on diagonals; SD = Standard Deviation; CR = Composite Reliability; Trust = Perceived Trustworthiness; Confirmation = Confirmation by Trust restoration; Continuance = Continuance Trust Intention.

the constructs except for its theoretically linked construct. Table 3 shows that the square root of AVEs of each constructs is greater than the inter-construct correlation. These tests suggest that the measures have reached the adequate level of convergent and discriminant validity.

Structural Model

Once it was determined that the measures were valid, PLS was used to generate the structural model. The PLS path coefficients of the research model are shown in Figure 2. The bootstrapping method with 200 iterations was used to determine the significance of path coefficients. The hypotheses were tested using t-tests and the results are summarized in Table 4.

The results of the PLS analysis showed that 54% of the variance in continuance trust intention was explained by perceived trustworthiness and satisfaction. Perceived trustworthiness and confirmation explained 42% of the variance in satisfaction. Further, confirmation explained 62% of the variance in perceived trustworthiness.

In hypothesis 1, we predicted that satisfaction with trust restoration activities would be positively associated with continuance trust intention. It was not supported (b=.075; p>.05). This indicates that other variables besides satisfaction were responsible for continuance trust intention of consumers to involve in doing business with the online company. The association between confirmation and satisfaction was found significant as hypothesized in the second hypothesis (b=.513; p <.01). This showed that when the consumers are confirmed by the realization of the expected remedies from the online company after their trust is violated, their satisfaction with the company will be influenced. According to hypothesis 3, perceived trustworthiness would have a positive association with satisfaction. It was not supported (b=.161; p>.05), indicating that other factors might be responsible for satisfaction. The relationship between consumers' online business continuance intention and the perceived trustworthiness of online business was found significant (b=.690; p<.01). This showed that consumers would be willing to continue the transaction with online business if they believe that the business is trustworthy. The association between confirmation and perceived trustworthiness was found significant as hypothesized in the fifth hypothesis (b=.786; p<.01). This supported

Table 4. Results of Hypothesis Tests

Hypothesis	Path Coefficient	P-value	Support
H1: SAT → CTI	.075	n.s.	x
H2: CFM → SAT	.513	<.01	y
H3: TRU → SAT	.161	n.s.	x
H4: TRU → CTI	.690	<.01	y
H5: CFM → TRU	.786	<.01	y

Legend: y = Supported; x = Not supported; n.s. = Not significant

Figure 2. PLS Analysis of Research Model

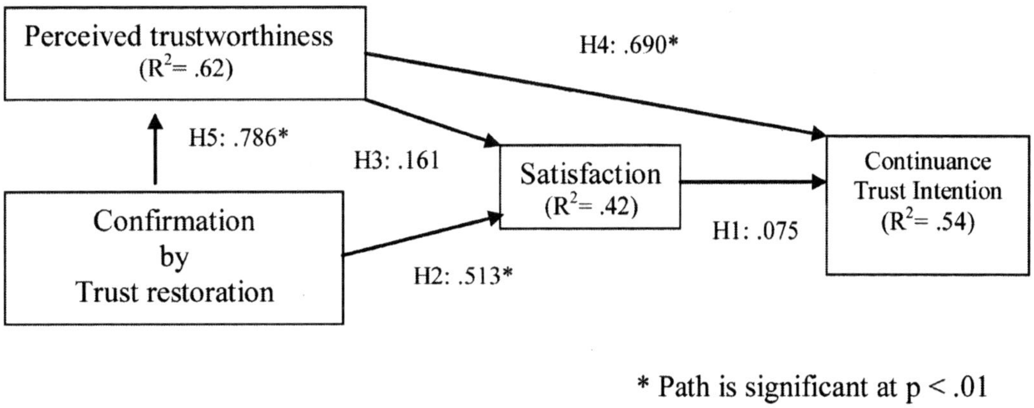

the contention that when consumers' expectation of trust restoring activities undertaken by business are confirmed then their perceived trustworthiness of business would increase. Implications of the results are discussed in the next section.

DISCUSSION

Continuance Trust Intention

Results of this study had no support for the ECT's contention that satisfaction is a significant predictor of users' continuance intention. Although prior IS studies have found satisfaction being the key to explaining the IS acceptance-discontinuance (user discontinuance of IS after its initial acceptance) and dissatisfaction is the necessary condition for IS discontinuance (Bhattacherjee, 2001), it is not confirmed by this study in the post-violation trust context. A study by Lewicki and Bunker (1996) shows that satisfaction with trust restoration activities do not always lead to the willingness to reconcile the relationship or trust the trust violator again. This agreed with the earlier discussion. Even though the customer was satisfied with online vendor's trust restoration activities, they may not immediately want to go back to the site for shopping. More measures need to be taken to regain those customers' trust. This suggests that continuance intention may have additional salient predictors than those identified in the ECT. Future studies should include satisfaction and its antecedents in order to provide a better understanding of its effect on continuance behavior in different contexts.

As proved in prior acceptance and continuance IS studies (Bhattacherjee, 2001; Davis et al., 1989; Taylor & Todd, 1995), perceived trustworthiness is a significant predictor ($R^2 = 0.51$) of continuance trust intention. While in ECT, perceived trustworthiness affects continuance intention indirectly through satisfaction, the proposed model in this study shows a direct association between the two constructs. An explanation for this is the use of post-violation expectation. Before occurrence of any violations by the online business, the user expectation of trustworthiness is based on information from referent others, popular media, or other resources, which could be biased and unrealistic. In contrast, post-violation expectation is based on users' first-hand experience, therefore, is more realistic and less susceptible to change (Fazio & Zanna, 1981). This stable and established cognitive belief about an online business acts as a strong determinant of continuance trust intention and sometimes can underplay the negative impact of the trust violation. However, studies also find that perceived trustworthiness of a vendor may not be extensible to the adoption of a new product or service offered by that vendor (Luo et al., 2010). Factors such as age, gender, culture, ethical performance of the website or the nature of a violation (morality-based or competence-based) can also influence the level of perceived trustworthiness (Pennanen, 2006; Riedl et al., 2010; Utz, et al., 2009; Yang, Chandlrees, Lin & Chao, 2009).

The findings of this research have important implications for online businesses. Because perceived trustworthiness is more important for post-violation continuance trust intention, online venders should be more careful when posting their customer claim policies and procedures. Customers prefer trust-assuring approaches that encompass market driven (reputation advertising, branding and relational marketing etc.) as well as institutional (legal binding) strategies (Pavlou & Gefen, 2004). Kim and Benbasat (2006) found that when dealing with customer complaints, claim plus data and backing can better increase consumers' trusting belief. Although the average number of trust assurances per site was as high as 5.3 (Kim & Benbasat, 2010), assurance structures were reported to be more influencial to customers when the price of product is relatively high (Kim & Benbasat, 2009). Even though customer satisfaction with post-violation handling may play a less significant role, every customer complaint should be treated as a first time violation because cumulated internet trust can be built through this process and it can balance out consumer negative concerns resulted from trust violation activities (Dinev & Hart, 2006).

Satisfaction

Satisfaction with trust rebuilding was predicted by user perceived trustworthiness ($R^2 = 0.09$) and confirmation by trust restoration activities ($R^2 = 0.33$). These two determinants jointly explain only 0.42 of the satisfaction variance, thus suggesting that there are other predictors for satisfaction other than those identified using the ECT.

Confirmation is a strong predictor of satisfaction in the ECT and has been verified by other IS studies (Bhattacherjee, 2001). According to ECT, perceived trustworthiness provides the baseline level, against which confirmation is assessed by customers to determine their satisfaction. A high level of perceived trustworthiness tends to enhance customer satisfaction. When the perceived trustworthiness level is lowered after trust violation, customers can be less satisfied. The insignificant relationship found between perceived trustworthiness and satisfaction suggests that customers can still be dissatisfied even when they are confirmed about the realization of the expected remedies for trust violations because violation involves damages at multiple dimensions as suggested by Lewicki (2003). Psychology and emotions are suggested as important dimensions in restoring trust between investors and the public (Gounaris & Prout, 2009). Trustworthiness judgments are also influenced by whether a trust violation is perceived as competence-based or morality-based. Plain apologies were more successful than denials in repairing trust (Utz et al., 2009). Violation of integrity and benevolence are likely to be experienced as more severe and damaging than violations that implicate the lack of instrumentality or ability. Examples of these natures may include intentional deception, purposefully reneging on a promise or obligation, and disrespectful treatment. If the air ticket a customer ordered online was an overbook, he/she can get cash reward or ticket for free trips as the remedy but he/she can still be dissatisfied because he/she may have to miss an important meeting or reschedule the connecting flights.

Confirmation also had a significant impact on perceived trustworthiness ($R^2 = 0.62$). Trust erodes with repetitive violations but can be restored if both trustee and trustor try to rebuild it (Lewicki & Bunker, 1996). Temporal change in perceived usefulness/expectation has been reported in IS research. This study suggests that confirmation might be one of the underlying causes for such changes.

Understanding the dynamics between confirmation by trust restoration, perceived trustworthiness and satisfaction is critical for online business. The good news from this study is that, in additional to building initial perceived trustworthiness, it is possible to improve customer perceived trustworthiness even after the trust violation. When carefully delivered, the confirmatory trust restoration activities can restore trust damages and result in better customer relationships and customers' loyalty. Trust restoration activities can also cultivate customer satisfaction. Satisfaction with post-violation restoration activities may not immediately lead to continuance trust intention but can affect perceived trustworthiness, which in turn can influence continuance trust intention.

Limitations

There are several limitations in this study. First, although the survey was designed to be administered to students in different geographical regions with equal representation of races, the online nature of the survey and the large proportion of incomplete questionnaires prevent the investigators from verifying the non-response bias.

Second, students have been used as proxy for online customer in many IS studies. The survey demographic showed 14.8% of the usable responses were from students having less than 1 year internet experience, which partially explained the low rate of violation experience. This may affect the generalizability of the outcome of the study. Future research should solicit subjects from other segments.

The third limitation is that the sample used was only confirmed of having trust violation experience but not necessarily post-violation trust rebuilding activities. This might contribute to the insignificant association between satisfaction and continuance trust intention, which is inconsistent with the literature that says "*satisfaction is a strong predictor of intention in the expectancy-confirmation theory*". When the respondents were asked about the post-violation service level, there is room for misrepresentation since the respondents may not interpret post-violation service level exactly as post-violation trust rebuilding activities. We strongly recommend that future studies include the specific trust restoration activities carried out by websites after the incidence of trust violation.

The next limitation is related to the measure of satisfaction. In this study we assessed the overall experience of the website's post-violation service. Similar to the above limitation, it will be advisable to assess the overall experience of the trust-rebuilding activities performed by the website. Just assessing the experience with the website's post-violation service may leave room for misrepresentation.

Another limitation is the need for longitudinal testing of the ECT. To capture the complex post-violation trust rebuilding process, a longitudinal comparison for trustworthiness and trust intention before and after trust violation and trust restoration would be ideal. This cross-sectional study restricted such temporal comparisons but can still be used to as a preliminary step for future research extensions.

CONCLUSION

The goal of this paper is to identify salient factors of post-violation continuance trust intention and to understand how they influence the dependent variable. ECT was adapted from the consumer behavior literature and integrated with prior IS trust research to formalize a post-violation trust rebuilding model. Data collected from online e-commerce users with violation experiences provided partial support for the proposed model. The results indicate that perceived trustworthiness is a significant factor in determining continuance trust intention with online business. Confirmation has significant impact on satisfaction and perceived trustworthiness. Contrary to prior findings, satisfaction doesn't have significant influence on continuance trust intention. As such, contribution of the study includes the empirical investigation of trust building in a post-violation context, the incorporation of perceived trustworthiness into the ECT, the validation of expectation-confirmation model, and offering an explanation for the post-violation trust rebuilding process.

As malicious intruders and online crimes are increasingly targeting electronic businesses, understanding how online businesses handle breaches or violations can be of crucial importance for safeguarding and retaining customers. In addition to initial trust-building mechanisms, strategies should also be implemented to rebuild customer trust in an effort to avail businesses with additional surviving mechanisms. In essence, the trust rebuilding approaches may differ from the ones that are used for initial trust building. Because trust is not only time-consuming to engender and cultivate, but also fragile and therefore can be destroyed. The process of continuous trust development deserves special attention (Siau & Shen, 2003) and businesses have to ensure the effect of their trust assuring and rebuilding effects don't erode over time (Mcknight et al., 2004). These mechanisms engender trust, not only in a few reputable sellers, but also in the entire community of sellers who contribute to an effective online marketplace.

REFERENCES

Ajzen, I. (1975). *Belief, attitude, intention, and behavior: An introduction to theory and research*. Reading, MA: Addison-Wesley.

Ajzen, I. (1985). From intentions to actions: A theory of planned behavior in J. K. J. Beckmann (Ed.), *Action-control: From Congnition to Behavior* (pp. 11-39). Heidelberg: Springer.

Ba, S., & Pavlou, P. A. (2002). Evidence of the effect of trust building technology in electronic markets: Price premiums and buyer behavior. *Management Information Systems Quarterly*, *26*(3), 243–268. doi:10.2307/4132332

Bem, D. J. (1972). Self-perception theory. In Berkowits, L. (Ed.), *Advances in Experimental Social Psychology* (pp. 1–62). New York: Academic Press.

Bhattacherjee, A. (2001). Understanding Information Systems Continuance: An Expectation-Confirmation Model. *Management Information Systems Quarterly*, *25*(3), 51–370. doi:10.2307/3250921

Brynjolfsson, E., & Smith, M. (2000). Frictionless commerce? A comparison of internet and conventional retailers. *Management Science*, *46*(4), 563–585. doi:10.1287/mnsc.46.4.563.12061

Carmines, E. G., & Zeller, R. A. (1979). *Reliability and validity assessment*. Beverly Hills, CA: Sage.

Chin, W. W. (1998). The partial least squares approach to structural equation modeling. In Marcoulides, G. A. (Ed.), *Modern methods for business research* (pp. 295–336). Mahway, New Jersey: Lawrence Erlbaum.

Crego, E. T. J., & Schiffrin, P. D. (1995). *Customer-centered reengineering: remapping for total customer value*. Burr Ridge, IL: Irwin.

Cremer, D. D., Snyder, M., & Dewitte, S. (2001). The less I trust, the less I contribute (or not)?: The effects of trust, accountability, and self-monitoring in social dilemmas. *European Journal of Social Psychology*, *31*, 93–107. doi:10.1002/ejsp.34

Dabolkar, P. A., Shepard, C. D., & Thorpe, D. I. (2000). A comprehensive framework for service quality: An investigation of critical conceptual and measurement issues through a longitudinal study. *Journal of Retailing*, *76*(2), 139–173. doi:10.1016/S0022-4359(00)00029-4

Davis, F. D., Bagozzi, R. P., & Warshaw, P. R. (1989). User acceptance of computer technology: A comparison of two theoretical models. *Management Science*, *35*(8), 982–1003. doi:10.1287/mnsc.35.8.982

DeSanctis, G. (1983). Expectancy theory as an explanation of voluntary use of a decision support system. *Psychological Reports*, *52*, 247–260.

Dinev, T., & Hart, P. (2006). An extended privacy calculus model for e-commerce transactions. *Information Systems Research*, *17*(1), 61–80. doi:10.1287/isre.1060.0080

Festinger, L. A. (1957). *A theory of cognitive dissonance*. Evanston, IL: Row and Peterson.

Fornell, C., & Larcker, D. F. (1981). Evaluating structural equation models with unobservable variables and measurement error. *JMR, Journal of Marketing Research*, *18*(1), 39–50. doi:10.2307/3151312

Gounaris, K. M., & Prout, M. F. (2009). Repairing relationships and restoring trust: Behavioral finance and the economic crisis. *Journal of Financial Service Professionals*, *63*(4), 75–84.

Gregg, D. G., & Scott, J. E. (2006). The role of reputation systems in reducing online auction fraud. *International Journal of Electronic Commerce*, *10*(3), 95–120. doi:10.2753/JEC1086-4415100304

Jarvenpaa, S. L., Knoll, K., & Keidner, D. E. (1998). Is anybody out there? Antecedents of trust in global virtual teams. *Journal of Management Information Systems*, *14*(4), 29–64.

Karahanna, E., Straub, D. W., & Chervany, N. L. (1999). Information technology adoption across time: A cross-sectional comparison of pre-adoption and post-adoption beliefs. *Management Information Systems Quarterly*, *23*(2), 183–213. doi:10.2307/249751

Kim, D., & Benbasat, I. (2006). The effect of trust-assuring arguments on consumer trust in internet stores: Application of Toulmin's model of argumentation. *Information Systems Research*, *17*(3), 286–300. doi:10.1287/isre.1060.0093

Kim, D., & Benbasat, I. (2009) Trust-assuring arguments in B2C e-commerce: Impact of content, source, and price on trust. *Journal of Management Information Systems, Winter*, *26*(3), 175-206.

Kim, D., & Benbasat, I. (2010). Designs for effective implementation of trust assurance in internet stores. *Communications of the ACM*, *53*(2), 121–126. doi:10.1145/1646353.1646386

Lee, B. C., Ang, L., & Dubelaar, C. (2005). Lemons on the web: A signaling approach to the problem of trust in internet commerce. *Journal of Economic Psychology*, *2*(5), 607–623. doi:10.1016/j.joep.2005.01.001

Lee, Z., & Lee, S. J. (2006). The effect of buyer feedback scores on internet auction prices. *Journal of Organizational Computing and Electronic Commerce*, *16*(1), 51–64. doi:10.1080/10919390609540290

Luo, X., Li, H., Zhang, J., & Shim, J. P. (2010). Examining multi-dimensional trust and multi-faceted risk in initial acceptance of emerging technologies: An empirical study of mobile banking services. *Decision Support Systems*, *49*, 222–234. doi:10.1016/j.dss.2010.02.008

Mathieson, K. (1991). Predicting user intentions: Comparing the technology acceptance model with the theory of planned behavior. *Information Systems Research*, *2*(3), 173–191. doi:10.1287/isre.2.3.173

Mayers, R. C., Davis, F. D., & Schoorman, J. H. (1995). An integrative model of organizational trust. *Academy of Management Review*, *30*(3), 709–734. doi:10.2307/258792

Mcknight, D. H., Kacmar, C. J., & Choudhury, V. (2004). Shifting factors and the ineffectiveness of third party assurance seals: A two-stage model of initial trust in a web business. *Electronic Markets*, *14*(1), 252–266. doi:10.1080/1019678042000245263

Morrison, D. E., & Firmstone, J. (2000). The social function of trust and implications for e-commerce. *International Journal of Advertising*, *19*(5), 599–624.

Oliver, R. L. (1980). A cognitive model for the antecedents and consequences of satisfaction. *JMR, Journal of Marketing Research*, *17*, 460–469. doi:10.2307/3150499

Oliver, R. L. (1981). Measurement and evaluation of satisfaction processes in retail settings. *Journal of Retailing*, *57*(3), 25–48.

Oliver, R. L. (1993). Cognitive, affective, and attitude bases of the satisfaction response. *The Journal of Consumer Research*, *20*, 418–430. doi:10.1086/209358

Pavlou, P. A., & Gefen, D. (2004). Building effective online marketplaces with institution-based trust. *Information Systems Research*, *15*(1), 37–59. doi:10.1287/isre.1040.0015

Pennanen, K. (2006). How consumers build trust in e-commerce: Towards a trust formation model. *Advances in Consumer Research-Latin American Conference Proceedings*, *1*, 38-43.

Pennington, R., Wilcox, H. D., & Grover, V. (2003). The role of system trust in business-to-consumer transactions. *Journal of Management Information Systems*, *20*(3), 197–226.

Riedl, R., Hubert, M., & Kenning, P. (2010). Are there neural gender differences in online trust? An fMRI Study on the Perceived Trustworthiness of eBay Offers. *Management Information Systems Quarterly*, *34*(2), 397–428.

Rousseau, D. M., Sitkin, S. B., Burt, R. S., & Camerer, C. (1998). Not so different after all: A cross-discipline view of trust. *Academy of Management Review*, *23*, 393–404.

Schoder, D., & Haenlein, M. (2004). The relative importance of different trust constructs for sellers in the online world. *Electronic Markets*, *14*(1), 48–57. doi:10.1080/1019678042000175298

Selnes, F. (1998). Antecedents and consequences of trust and satisfaction in buyer-seller relationships. *European Journal of Marketing*, *32*(3/4), 305–322. doi:10.1108/03090569810204580

Siau, K., & Shen, Z. X. (2003). Building customer trust in mobile commerce. *Communications of the ACM*, *46*(4), 91–94. doi:10.1145/641205.641211

Spreng, R. A., & Olshavsky, R. W. (1993). A desires congruency model of consumer satisfaction. *Journal of the Academy of Marketing Science*, *21*(3), 169–177. doi:10.1177/0092070393213001

Straub, D. W., Hoffman, D. L., Weber, B. W., & Steinfield, C. (2002). Measuring e-commerce in net-enabled organizations: An introduction to the special issue. *Information Systems Research*, *13*(2), 115–124. doi:10.1287/isre.13.2.115.86

Tan, M., & Teo, T. S. H. (2000). Factors influencing the adoption of internet banking. *Journal of the AIS*, *1*(5), 1–5.

Taylor, S., & Todd, P. A. (1995). Understanding information technology usage: A test of competing models. *Information Systems Research*, *6*(2), 144–176. doi:10.1287/isre.6.2.144

Tomlinson, E. C., & Lewicki, R. J. (2004). *The Effects of Reputation and Post Violation Communication on Trust and Distrust*. Social Science Electronic Publishing, Inc.

Utz, S., Matzat, U., & Snijders, C. (2009). On-line reputation systems: The effect of feedback comments and reactions on building and re-building trust in on-line auctions. *International Journal of Electronic Commerce*, *13*(3), 95–118. doi:10.2753/JEC1086-4415130304

Van Slyke, C., Shim, J. T., Johnson, R., & Jiang, J. (2006). Concern for information privacy and online consumer purchasing. *Journal of the Association for Information Systems*, *7*(6), 415–443.

Wakefield, R. J., Stocks, M. H., & Wilder, W. M. (2004). The role of website characteristics in initial trust formation. *Journal of Computer Information Systems*, *45*(1), 94–103.

Yang, M., Chandlrees, N., Lin, B., & Chao, H. (2009). The effect of perceived ethical performance of shopping websites on consumer trust. *Journal of Computer Information Systems*, *50*(1), 15–24.

APPENDIX

Intention (CTI)

1. I intend to continue trusting and using this website rather than discontinue its use.
2. My intentions are to continue trusting and using this website than use any alternative means (e.g. physical stores).
3. If I could, I would like to discontinue my trust and use of this website.

Perceived Trustworthiness (TRU)

1. This website was very concerned about the satisfaction of customers.
2. Customer satisfaction is very important to this website.
3. This website would not knowingly do anything to upset the customers.
4. This website is concerned about what is important to customers.
5. This website will do everything within its capacity to help the customers.
6. This website will do its best to be fair in dealing with customers.
7. This website has a strong sense of commitment.
8. I am never doubtful about whether this website will do what they promised.
9. I am never sure if this website is going to do what it promises or not.
10. This website displays a solid business ethics.
11. I believe this website will handle the violation according to the posted terms and conditions.
12. I feel very confident about this website's capability to settle any disputes and fulfill my needs.
13. This website seems to be successful in performing its tasks.
14. I think this website is honest.

Satisfaction (SAT)

1. How do you feel about your overall experience of this website's post-violation service:
   Very dissatisfied / very satisfied
   Very displeased/ very pleased
   Very frustrated/ very contented
   Absolutely terrible/ absolutely delighted

Confirmation (CFM)

1. My experience with this website's post-violation service was better than what I expected.
2. The post-violation service level provided by this website was better than what I expected.
3. Overall, most of my expectations of this website's post-violation service were confirmed.
   Note: Except for "satisfaction" all the items were anchored in a scale of 1 (strongly agree) to 5 (strongly disagree).

Chapter 4
Delivery and Payment Options as Antecedents to Enhanced Online Retailing

Kevin J. Shanahan
Mississippi State University, USA

Barbara Ross-Wooldridge
The University of Texas at Tyler, USA

Charles M. Hermans
Missouri State University, USA

ABSTRACT

We first measure attitudes toward a product and attitudes toward product quality when an unknown brand is associated with a well-known and trusted co-brand in the form of payment and delivery options; employing a classic co-branding strategy. Theory suggests that association with a trusted brand should lead to improved positive assessment of an unknown brand. Results suggest the popular belief that trusted brands improve respondents' assessments of unknown brands through a co-branding strategy may not be supported when there is a restriction on choice of payment and delivery options. That is, when including only a limited number of co-brands, brand associations may give the perception of restricted choice, leading to a lessened level of trust in the co-brand. We then repeat the study using a known branded product and known branded delivery and payment methods. Results show no difference in consumer perceptions between no cobrand and a full complement of cobrands. However, a restricted set of payment and delivery options leads to a more negative attitude toward the product and product quality.

INTRODUCTION

The Internet, touted as a panacea offering unbridled opportunity for lesser known small businesses, suffers from one inhibitor to their success; an inability to provide quality assurances that generates consumer trust through brand recognition. There is no doubt that Web 2.0 has been wildly successful in bringing together users from all ages, demographics and interests to the Internet, while also

DOI: 10.4018/978-1-60960-577-3.ch004

attracting both legitimate and unsavory elements profiteering from the trust exhibited by naïve users (Milam 2008). Trust, a significant factor in respect to e-commerce transactions (Stewart, 2006; Wakefield and Whitten, 2006; Alexander et al., 2006; Elliot and Speck, 2005; Shneiderman, 2000), is critical as fraud is 12 times likelier online than in brick and mortar stores (Bolton, et al., 2004).

With respect to technology mediated relationships, Fogg and Tseng (1999) define trust as a positive belief about the reliability and dependability of a person, object or process. Shneiderman (2000) further posits that branding generates trust due to familiar logos and names and therefore a Web site should attempt to create trust by obtaining certifications from third parties. Acting as a surrogate indicator for quality, positive branding is essential to an e-tailer. Jevons et al. (2001) conclude that the Internet is amplifying the effects of customer interpretation of brands and the relationship between brand image and identity. In fact, attitude toward the brand positively impacts purchase intent and site loyalty (Elliot and Speck, 2005). This poses a great challenge to small companies with unknown brands versus global companies with internationally recognized and trusted brands. As a result, business activity on the Internet has experienced a rise of brand extension, co-branding, and the increasing importance of brand association (Jevons et al., 2001). Stewart (2006) states that it is crucial to understand how different applications of technology can impact a consumer's trust online; this knowledge may help organizations develop a more effective online presence.

This chapter examines consumer attitudes towards a product and quality assessment based on the association with well-known brands. For this study the co-brand is the delivery and payment options. An experimental design utilizing a control group and an experimental group is employed to examine these differences. Specifically, we examine attitude toward an unknown product as well as quality assessment of the same product when associated with familiar and trusted brands.

DEFINITIONS OF TRUST

Trust in General

Trust has played an important role in relationships since ancient times. Many of our current traditions date back to acts of trust, such as shaking hands to illustrate that a weapon was not held to clinking of glasses for proving that wine was not poisoned (Shneiderman, 2000). Trust is important in all aspects of life and though numerous authors have defined trust (Chen and Barnes, 2007; Goodwin, 1996, Srinivasan, 2004; Harridge-March, 2006; Shneiderman, 2000) all of the definitions have several key elements; trust involves one person bestowing upon another (person, object, or process) the belief of reliability and dependability. Trust is only important in situations of uncertainty (Ha, 2004; Goodwin, 1996; Srinivasan, 2004). Uncertainty can be thought of risk and risk exists when one is less than 100% certain that something will turn out as expected (Harridge-March, 2006). The value of trust has led to the use of metaphor to illustrate its importance in our lives: it has been compared to grease that keeps the wheel turning (Goodwin, 1996) as well as to chicken soup as all sorts of positive benefits are derived when people willing to get involved (Shneiderman, 2000).

Retail Trust

The above elements of trust have been modified to suit the retail context by stating that trust is consumer confidence that the merchant will provide the product or service that the consumer has paid for in a reasonable time with an acceptable level of service (Srinivasan, 2004). Hence, trust is a key factor in respect to a company's reputation whether bricks and mortar (BAM) or e-tailer (Merrilees and Fry, 2003). Trust can be viewed as the assurance that a company will look after the interests of the consumer, it is akin to a guarantee (Merriless and Fry, 2003). Branding can be used to achieve a sustainable competitive advantage

(Ha, 2004), by creating trust via the use of familiar logos and names of companies that are perceived to have integrity (Shneiderman, 2000; Ha, 2004).

Importance of Trust in Online Transactions

Trust becomes even more of a strategic element when retailing is moved online (Chen and Barnes, 2007; Srinivasan, 2004; Merrilees and Fry, 2003, Constatntinides, 2004; Harridge-March, 2006). Trust is critical for e-tailers as it reduces the perceived level of risk associated with online transactions, increasing the likelihood of purchase (Chen and Barnes, 2007; Ha, 2004; Elliot and Speck, 2005; Kim and Benbasat 2010). Given that the initial acquisition costs of e-customers often is greater than the lifetime value of these customers, it is important to understand the role of trust in virtual environments (Ruparelia, White and Hughes 2010). Research has shown that consumers perceive risk in many purchase situations and that users of the Internet perceive purchases to be riskier there than in face-to-face encounters. This is especially true when an online retailer has neither a physical presence or is a well known brand (Harridge-March, 2006). In a sense, customers are vulnerable to the company and must believe the firm will fulfill promises and commitments and not exploit the trust customers place in the company (San Martin and Camarero 2008).

Online purchases have higher perceived risk due to time asymmetry, which is the consumer's lack of ability to verify in real-time a transaction due to physical distance, lack of personal contact, and the delinking of payment and receipt of goods (Constantinides, 2004; Chen and Barnes, 2007, Srinivasan, 2004). Thus, building trust online is key and many methods have been suggested. One way to create trust is via the use of intermediaries (Stewart, 2003; Stewart 2006; Srinivasain, 20004). Another method is interactivity which has been defined as the ability of a person to personalize a situation and can be thought of the total online shopping experience (Merriless and Fry, 2003). Both of the above methods have a common element of choice and the ability of the consumer to chose. Constantinides (2004) states that alternative payment and delivery options are needed in the development creditability of e-tailers while Merriless and Fry (2003) state that a lack of interactivity has been shown to deter the development of a positive brand attitude.

Brand Based Quality Inferences

Many e-tailers face a difficult task in transmitting trust warranting properties to consumers (Hanai and Oguchi 2009). However, companies with established brand names have strategic advantages in both electronic and traditional business environments. In either environment brand name conveys a message to the consumer about the quality of that particular brand. However, the magnitude of such effect across both shopping environments is different. For example, a recent report by Ernst and Young indicates that 69% of respondents state brand name plays a significant role in their online buying decisions (Ward and Lee, 1999). The most frequently sited reason for consumers not purchasing on line is a lack of trust (Alexander et al., 2006).

According to Ward and Lee (1999), "because of the low costs of setting up a Web site, firms that offer low quality products could potentially claim their products are of high quality, earn a profit before the ruse is uncovered, and then quickly disappear." Alexander et al. (2006) conducted in-depth interviews about consumer attitudes about shopping on line and gained the following insights from participants:

"One thing I considered [when deciding to purchase the computer] was whether [e-tailers] had the potential to rip me off and lies about the specs." (Mark);

"I worried about their honesty, like would they send me a hard drive that worked? I was a little hesitant…I had to deposit cash up front so I did wonder, 'does that site belong to a computer shop or some dodgy guy?'" (Hayden).

Because consumers cannot touch or feel products sold over the Internet, it is vital for companies selling on-line to develop a brand that is respected (McClindon, 2001).

Establishing a brand name is especially essential in electronic markets, because customers have little to rely on other than a recognized brand. Economic models based on Nelson's (1974) work show that an established brand name can signal high product quality (Klein and Leffler, 1981). Alleviating concerns over product quality by creating brand name equity is also essential in on-line transactions. Reputable brand names are linked with consumers' perceptions of product quality. The importance of brand names can be seen in the following insights:

"I trusted Amazon implicitly because they are such a big company…They have millions of customers…a really good name. I perceived the risk as really low." (Brad).

"I didn't have any worries buying from CD Now because it was well known. It wasn't 'el-cheapo'… It was up there in terms of creditability with Amazon…so I trusted them." (Helena) (Alexander et al., 2006).

Brand Associations

Companies who do not have the sufficient financial resources to establish a reputable brand name may be able to compete in the electronic marketplace by associating themselves with known brands. Smaller companies that cannot afford the capital investment necessary to establish reputable brand names may be able to take advantage of associations with other reputable brands and firms in order to lessen the consumers' product quality concerns. For example, in a study of student perceptions of brand equity Washburn et al. (2000) found that perceptions of a brand were improved when associated with other brands (co-branding). No one clear definition of co-branding has been created in the marketing literature-one over arching definition is the pairing two brands in a marketing context such as advertisements, products, product placements and distribution outlets (Leuthesser et al., 2003). Leuthesser et al. (2003) in their framework of co-branding suggest four strategies-in respect to co-branding; the applicable strategy is reaching up, it entails selecting a partner brand that contributes a positive brand image to the original product that is not essential to the functioning of the product.

Collier and Bienstock (2006) state that one aspect consumers use to judge quality in an e-tailer site is delivery of the product. In fact they state that when a consumer makes a purchase on line they enter into an implicit contract-with the assumption the e-tailer with deliver the product as promised on the webpage. This is different from brick and mortar shopping where delivery of the product is of little interest. Esper et al. (2003) in an experiment on strategic implications of delivery choices manipulated price, carrier, and website merchant. They found that willingness to buy was higher when the delivery carrier and website merchant were well known. Esper et al. (2003) found that the co-branding of a carrier with an e-tailer has a positive impact on consumer delivery-rated perceptions and expectations. Additionally, they found that FedEx, Airborne, and UPS provided a greater benefit than a non-disclosed condition, USPS or Home Direct. Though carrier results were mixed Esper et al. (2003) posit that willingness to buy is related to merchant and carrier disclosure, and they suggest further research.

Visa card has 1.6 billion cardholders worldwide and works with 24 million locations resulting in $3 trillion in purchases worldwide (Brown, 2006). Visa accounted for 50% of all sales (Brown, 2006). The use of familiar logos and names can generate trust (Shneiderman, 2000). We suggest that attitudes toward an unknown product will be improved when the unknown product is paired with a well-known brand. Additionally, quality inferences toward the unknown product are expected to be different when the unknown product is paired with a well-known brand.

In our initial study, we tested these relationships seeking to discover if positive attitudes toward an unknown product on the Internet will be greater if the product is associated with another well-known brand than when it is not associated with another brand. Additionally, we investigated consumer perceptions to see if consumers perceive an unknown product on the Internet to be of higher quality if it is associated with well-known brands than when it is not associated with another brand.

Methodology

To examine the effect of the association of an unknown brand with a well-known brand, we created two groups: an experimental group and a control group. Our methodology, mirrored that used by Stewart (2006) in her experiment to measure the influence of hyperlinks on trust. We developed a survey instrument consisting of two components 1) attitude toward the product and 2) perceived quality of the product. We then identified a cross section of Internet users in the United States and Canada, via a consumer panel, who were invited to opt in to our study. Respondents were randomly assigned to one of the two groups (experimental and control) and the survey was administered via an online survey instrument called Perseus Survey Solutions for the Web. A feature of this instrument is the identification of the Internet Protocol number, eliminating duplicate entries and faux responses (i.e., from other countries where an individual stumbled upon the survey). Additionally, there was a three day window for response to mitigate the chance that non-targeted respondents might stumble upon the survey and complete it.

Respondents were asked to examine an advertisement for a digital camera. Although product descriptions, price and a picture of the product were provided, no brand information was provided about the product. For the experimental group, logos for Visa (payment facilitation) and Federal Express (delivery facilitation) were included in the advertisement. These were omitted in the control group survey. Otherwise, the questionnaires were identical. Of the 204 surveys returned, 4 had incomplete responses for measurement scale items, however, pair-wise deletion of non-response allowed for the maximum use of the available data. Participants included 115 (56.4%) respondents in the control group (no brand association) and 89 (43.6%) in the experimental group (Visa and Fed-X brands included). Ninety-four respondents were from Canada, while 110 were from the United States. Demographic information (see Table 1) indicates a fairly good cross section of Internet users, albeit a bit heavy on male respondents.

The attitude toward the product scale employed in this study is based on Duncan and Nelson (1985) which measures positive beliefs and attitudes about a product. It was adapted to meet the needs of the current study. In a pretest, one reverse–coded item failed to load on the common factor in maximum-likelihood factor analysis. Herche and Engelland (1989) suggest reverse coded items may result in such problems for scale unidimensionality. Reliability (Chronbach, 1951) for the 3-items retained is.77 versus.61 for the original scale. This suggests the decision to drop the reverse-coded item for the main study was both appropriate and meaningful. The attitude measurement scale included three questions: 1) if I used the camera in this ad, I would probably like it, 2) I would expect that most people that use this camera are satisfied, and 3) Overall, I would describe the camera as appealing.

To identify perceptions of product quality, a new scale was created based on Zeithaml's (1988) identification of reliability and dependability as dimensions of quality measurement, along with

Table 1. Demographic information for Study One

Category	*n*		Category	*n*
Sex Male Female	134 69		Education Highschool/GED Bachelors degree Masters or PhD Technical Degree Didn't finish high school	79 69 24 21 8
Age 24 or younger 25 – 45 46 – 64 65 or older	27 135 36 4		Ehnicity American Indian/Alaskan Native Asian/ Pacific Islander Black (not of hispanic origin) Hispanic White (not of hispanic origin) Other	6 10 5 2 157 15
Income (US Dollars) $10,999 or less $11,000 - $25,999 $26,000 - $50,999 $51,000 or more	43 40 49 70		Number of Internet Purchases 0-2 3-4 5 or more	71 38 95

an overall global quality measure. These three items were 1) the camera looks like it is reliable, 2) the camera appears to be of good quality and 3) the camera appears to be dependable.

Scale reliability for these 3 items is.96. All items were measured using a 7-point Likert scale anchored with strongly disagree/strongly agree. A comparison of the 2 groups (control and treatment) across multiple dependent variables was done using Hoteling's T^2. Comparisons were made for the attitudinal measures as well as the product quality measures. The multivariate results were significant for both attitude and quality measures (Attitude: Hotelling's Trace = 15.66; F = 1043.72; df = 3, 200; p <.001; Quality: Hotelling's Trace = 9.19; F = 606.52; df = 3, 198; p <.001). Individual comparisons were also significant for all 6 items (see Table 2). However, while the difference is significant, individual means are in the opposite direction from those predicted by theory and as hypothesized in this study.

DISCUSSION

The results of this study were counter to our expectations and were contrary to the effect suggested by the extant literature on co-branding. It would appear that the positive transfer effect of using a well-known global brand to bolster unknown brands is not a truism. It appears that sometimes an association of products can result in negative consumer reactions. The literature does explain this for sullied brands (Ruth and Simonin, 2003). For example, when Ford associated the Explorer model with Firestone tires, inferiority of one product resulted in a disaster for both companies (Votolato and Unnava, 2006). Furthermore, this association yielded very negative reactions from consumers. Consumers were requesting products other than Firestone on their Ford Explorers. That is, consumers were trying to regain control over their purchases by separating the associated products. However, in this current study, we find no such past corporate malfeasance by either Fedex or Visa to suggest a negative transfer of ill will towards the brand. Thus, we looked elsewhere for possible explanations; the theory of reasoned action and the theory of psychological reactance.

The theory of reasoned action (David 1989) includes a person's subjective norms as a predictor of behavior. If those norms include a preference for Visa or UPS but only Mastercard or Fedex are offered as options, it produces friction in

Table 2. Results for Study One

Item	Group*	*n*	Mean	df	F	sig
Attitude						
If I used the camera in this ad, I would probably like it.	1 2	115 89	4.65 5.28	1, 202	7.418	.007
I would expect that most people that use this camera are satisfied.	1 2	115 88	4.63 5.28	1, 202	8.694	.004
Overall, I would describe the camera as appealing.	1 2	115 89	5.12 5.38	1, 202	1.469	.227
Product Quality						
The camera looks like it is reliable.	1 2	115 89	4.59 4.99	1,202	2.972	.086
The camera appears to be of good quality.	1 2	115 87	4.55 5.21	1,200	8.016	.005
The camera appears to be dependable.	1 2	115 89	4.41 4.87	1,202	4.107	.044

1 = co-brand; 2 = no co-brand

the transaction. One key to easing transaction friction is convenience (Ozkan, Binddusara and Hackney 2010), which can include choice of payment method.

Brehm's and Brehm's (1981) theory of psychological reactance suggests that when individuals expect to have control over a behavior and this control is threatened, psychological reactance – the motivation to regain control – is aroused. Clee and Wicklund (1980) state that consumers are accustomed to having choices; these choices are viewed as freedom, e.g. being able to choose styles of clothing that most appeal to them. Furthermore, there are two types of threats to freedom-social influence (the extent someone tries to pressure a change in behavior) and impersonal threats (barriers). Reactance causes the consumer to attempt to regain the lost freedom by being increasingly positive towards whatever freedom is threatened and becoming more negative towards that which is forced upon them (Clee and Wicklund, 1980). Clee and Wicklund (1980) found that when the consumer perceives they are being coerced-this will be met with an equal but opposite reaction. It is important to note it does not matter if the object of restricted freedom was the most preferred or not (Brehm and Cole, 1966). Edwards et al. (2002) studied reactance in respect to online pop-up ads, the authors found that reactance occurs when ads are perceived as intrusive-when the ads were perceived to ad value (either in the form of entertainment or information) they were perceived to be less of an interruption in the study and this lower reactance against the pop-up. Mazis et al. (1973) found that consumers experience reactance, when they are forced to switch brands. In fact the consumers forced to switch favored brands (detergents) demonstrated reactivity by perceiving the alternative as less attractive and the eliminated alternative as more attractive.

In the current study, the brand associations may have resulted in the perception of limited choice and unmet expectations. Specifically, there was only one form of payment (Visa only) and one form of delivery (FedEx only) for the target product, despite many alternatives such as Mastercard, Paypal, United Parcel Service etc. According to the theory of psychological reactance, three things may have happened. First, the respondents in this study may have expected to be able to make payments or take delivery by other means than those offered and were disappointed by the limited choice. Second, respondents may have felt threatened by the limited choices for payment and delivery. Finally, respondents may have responded negatively as a result of their reaction to these limited choices rather than as an evaluation of the brand association. Since the expectation of control in virtual environments is high, increase in threats to control will result in high effects of reactance. That is, consumers may form a negative attitude toward a product when payment and delivery options are restricted. This is consistent with Burke (2002) who found online consumers want to customize their own shopping experience. Thus, further study of this potential explanation was warranted, leading to our second study.

Second Study

Psychological reactance offers a plausible reason for the result of study one – a more positive result for no cobrand versus using a cobrand for an unknown product. This would suggest that unknown products employing no cobrand would be viewed more positively than those with a limited choice of known cobrands. Extending this proposition, offering a full complement of options, without restriction, should counter this psychological reactance, resulting in a more positive attitude towards the product and product quality.

Stewart (2006) suggests that reputable firms may be damaged by linking to unknown organizations and then suggests limiting and monitoring such links. Given the known effects of unknown brands on cobrands, we felt it important to ensure the results from our first study were not artifacts of the use of particular known cobrands coupled with an unknown product. As such, in our second study, we employ a known brand with known cobrands in the form of an IPOD Nano mp3 player. Thus, our treatments are a known brand coupled with 1) a control (no cobrands), 2) limited cobrand (only one delivery and payment method) and 3) a full complement of cobrands (all available choices of delivery and payment).

Methodology

Our control ad consists of a picture of a hand holding an IPOD Nano and verbage estolling the benefits of using the product with a retail price consistent with other *real* advertisements, sans any cobrand. Our limited cobrand ad consists of the control ad for the IPOD Nano with the Visa and Fedex logos appearing under the product which conveys a restricted payment and delivery system. The third ad treatment is the control ad for the IPOD Nano with logos for Visa, Mastercard, Paypal, Discover Card and American Express along with delivery options including the United States Postal Service, United Parcel Service, Fedex and DHL; offering consumers the full complement of payment and delivery systems.

We selected the IPOD Nano as our known product based upon 1) strong brand recognition and leadership in the marketplace and 2) relevance to our sample group. Recall that we used Internet enthusiasts for our initial study, drawn from the general population, to develop and test our constructs. Thus, we are confident that our constructs are valid. So, for our second study, we employed a student sample to test for differences between the three treatment groups. After all, if asked to perform a task relevant to them, students are valid respondents for exploratory studies (Calder, Phillips, and Tybout 1981; Ferber 1977). Given the exploratory nature of this study and its topical relevance (i.e., most students have purchased something online and many own an IPOD), a student sample was deemed acceptable (Churchill 1979; Yavas 1994).

Our student sample for the second study consisted of undergraduate and graduate marketing students (n = 110) enrolled at a mid-size U.S. university. Similar studies have employed student samples, particularly when the product is germane to the students (Cyr and Bonanni

2005). To encourage candid responses anonymity was assured and to encourage participation, extra credit was awarded to those who chose to participate. Participants completed the survey and a virtual receipt was provided that they could turn in for extra credit. The roughly equal male/female sample group averaged 25 years of age and was predominantly caucasian. All indicated they were fairly regular users of the Internet -- over 12 hours per week of Internet use and that they have purchased online confirming the appropriateness of this sample frame.

Data were collected using Perseus Survey Solutions for the Web, an online survey instrument that allows respondents to maintain anonymity while maximizing convenience. One feature of Perseus is the ability to identify unique IP addresses, ensuring that only one response per IP address was used in calculation. The data were ported automatically into SPSS (Statistical Package for the Social Sciences) ensuring no data entry errors. Missing data were handled by pairwise deletion to retain as much information as possible.

To test for significant differences across the three treatments, we ran a one way ANOVA and used Tukey's HSD post hoc test to identify differences for each of the variables' paired comparisons of means. This allowed us not only to test for significant differences across the three treatments, but also to identify the sources of these differences. See Table 3.

RESULTS AND DISCUSSION

The results provide strong evidence of psychological reactance. There was no significant difference between the control ad where no cobrand was used and the full complement ad. Consumers had no higher of an attitude toward the product if it was stand alone without a cobrand than if it include all delivery and payment options. However, when limited payment and delivery options were available, there was a significant difference between this treatment and the control and full complement treatments. Additionally, in every case the mean for the measures for the limited choice treatment were lower than for the control and full complement treatments.

The results for these two studies suggest important implications. The results suggest that situations exist in which brand associations can be detrimental to consumer perceptions of a target product. Brand associations or co-branding can actually result in a lower evaluation of the target product when the consumer feels restricted in their choice of payment and delivery option. The positive benefits of creditability are negated when there is a choice restriction. Additionally, negative attitudes toward the product may be transferred to the target product. Consequently, though co-branding has been found to have positive impact on perceptions of reliability and hence trust (Esper et al., 2003) an e-tailer most be careful when co-branding to not limit expected freedoms.

Limitations

As with any research study there are limitations which need to be considered when interpreting results. This one is no different. Given the Internet is placeless and available to most of the world, limiting this study to only American and Canadian Internet users -- and American students for the second study -- might seem to be a limitation; and it is to a certain extent. However, this is an exploratory study and to introduce other influences (i.e., cultural factors, poly versus monochronic time perspectives etc.) would only serve to introduce unnecessary and uncontrollable bias. To minimize these biasing intrusions, we felt it necessary to limit this initial study to only Canadian and American Internet users who share a similar cultural perspective. However, inclusion of Internet enthusiasts from Asian, Latin American and other areas would serve to establish whether or not psychological reactance is phenomenon applicable to all or if it

Table 3. Results (Tukey's HSD post hoc test)

Dependent Variable	1 = control 2 = fedexvisa 3 = full cobrand	1 = control 2 = fedexvisa 3 = full cobrand	Sig.
If I used the IPOD in this ad, I would probably like it.	1.00	2.00	.015
		3.00	.629
	2.00	1.00	.015
		3.00	.006
	3.00	1.00	.629
		2.00	.006
I would expect that most people that use this IPOD are satisfied.	1.00	2.00	.022
		3.00	.995
	2.00	1.00	.022
		3.00	.041
	3.00	1.00	.995
		2.00	.041
Overall, I would describe the IPOD as appealing.	1.00	2.00	.004
		3.00	.888
	2.00	1.00	.004
		3.00	.019
	3.00	1.00	.888
		2.00	.019
The IPOD looks like it is reliable.	1.00	2.00	.042
		3.00	.866
	2.00	1.00	.042
		3.00	.032
	3.00	1.00	.866
		2.00	.032
The IPOD appears to be of good quality	1.00	2.00	.013
		3.00	.737
	2.00	1.00	.013
		3.00	.039
	3.00	1.00	.737
		2.00	.039
The IPOD appears to be depedendable	1.00	2.00	.023
		3.00	.737
	2.00	1.00	.023
		3.00	.029
	3.00	1.00	.737
		2.00	.029

is instead limited to North Americans and others where choice is a long established expectation.

The use of a consumer panel and a student sample in the studies is both advantageous and problematic. We were able to specify the type of respondent we were seeking to employ a stratified random sample across different types of Internet users for the first study. We were also able to ensure the sample for the second study was perfectly suited to the product (i.e., the heaviest users of the Internet are college students and the most prolific purchasers of IPODs are also college students). However, those that did participate opted in and thus they could differ from those who opted out. This is not uncommon in exploratory studies, however readers need to necessarily keep this in mind when making generalizations from this study about the public at large. Future research should replicate and expand upon this study to include different groups to build on the exploratory results of this study.

CONCLUSION

We first measured attitudes toward a product and attitudes toward product quality when an unknown brand is associated with a well-known and trusted cobrand in the form of payment and delivery options; employing a classic co-branding strategy. Theory suggests that association with a trusted brand should lead to improved positive assessment of an unknown brand. Results suggest the popular belief that trusted brands improve respondents' assessments of unknown brands through a co-branding strategy may not be supported when there is a restriction on choice of payment and delivery options. That is, when including only a limited number of co-brands, brand associations may give the perception of restricted choice, leading to a lessened level of trust in the co-brand. We then repeat the study using a known branded product and known branded delivery and payment methods. Results show no difference in consumer perceptions between no cobrand and a full complement of cobrands. However, a restricted set of payment and delivery options leads to a more negative attitude toward the product and product quality.

REFERENCES

Alexander, B., Friend, L., Godwin, B., & Babis, P. (2006). Learning to trust e-tailers: Strategies used by consumers. *Journal of Research for Consumers*, *10*, 1–9.

Bolton, G., Katok, E., & Ockenfels, A. (2004). How effective are electronic reputation mechanisms? An experimental investigation. *Management Science*, *50*(11), 1587–1602. doi:10.1287/mnsc.1030.0199

Brehm, J., & Cole, A. (1966). Effect of a favor which reduces freedom. *Journal of Personality and Social Psychology*, *3*(4), 420–426. doi:10.1037/h0023034

Brehm, S., & Brehm, J. (1981). *Psychological reactance: A theory of freedom and control*. New York, NY: Academic Press.

Brown, E. (2006). Online shopping is only 3% of all retail sales. Gary Marino knows what's holding it back. *Forbes*, *178*(12).

Burke, R. (2002). Technology and the customer interface: What consumers want in the physical and virtual store. *Journal of the Academy of Marketing Science*, *30*(4), 411–432. doi:10.1177/009207002236914

Calder, B., Phillips, L., & Tybout, A. (1981). Designing research for application. *The Journal of Consumer Research*, *8*(September), 197–207. doi:10.1086/208856

Chen, Y., & Barnes, S. (2007). Initial trust and online buyer behavior. *Industrial Management & Data Systems*, *107*(1), 21–36. doi:10.1108/02635570710719034

Churchill, G. (1979). A paradigm for developing better measures of marketing constructs. *JMR, Journal of Marketing Research, 16*(February), 64–73. doi:10.2307/3150876

Clee, M., & Wicklund, R. (1980). Consumer behavior and psychological reactance. *The Journal of Consumer Research, 6*(4), 389–405. doi:10.1086/208782

Collier, J., & Bienstock, C. (2006). How do customers judge quality in an e-tailer? *MIT Sloan Management Review, 48*(1), 35–40.

Constantinides, E. (2004). Influencing the online consumer's behavior: the Web experience. *Internet Research, 4*(2), 111–126. doi:10.1108/10662240410530835

Cronbach, L. (1951). Coefficient alpha and the internal structure of tests. *Psychometrika, 16*, 297–335. doi:10.1007/BF02310555

Cyr, D., & Bonanni, C. (2005). Gender and website design in e-business. *International Journal of Electronic Business, 3*(6), 565–582. doi:10.1504/IJEB.2005.008536

David, G. (1989). Perceived usefulness, perceived ease of use and user acceptance of information technology. *Management Information Systems Quarterly, 13*(3), 319–339. doi:10.2307/249008

Duncan, C., & Nelson, J. (1985). Effects of humor in radio advertising Experiment. *Journal of Advertising, 14*(2), 33–40.

Edwards, S., Hairong, L., & Lee, J. (2002). Forced exposure and psychological reactance: Antecedents and consequences of the perceived Intrusiveness of pop-up Ads. *Journal of Advertising, 31*(3), 83–95.

Elliott, M., & Speck, P. (2005). Factors that affect attitude toward a retail website. *Journal of Marketing Theory and Practice, 13*(1), 40–51.

Esper, T., Jensen, T., Turnipseed, F., & Burton, S. (2003). The last mile: An examination of effects of online retail delivery strategies on consumers. *Journal of Business Logistics, 24*(2), 177–203.

Fogg, B., & Tseng, H. (1999). The elements of computer credibility. In proceedings of CHI'99 (Pittsburgh, May 15-20). ACM Press, New York, 80-87.

Goodwin, N. (1996). *Economic meanings of trust and responsibility*. Ann Arbor, MI: The University of Michigan Press.

Ha, H. (2004). Factors influencing consumer perceptions of brand trust online. *Journal of Product and Brand Management, 13*(5), 329–442. doi:10.1108/10610420410554412

Hanai, T., & Oguchi, T. (2009). How do consumers perceive the reliability of online shops? Cyberpsychology. *Journal of Psychosocial Research on Cyberspace, 3*(2), 1–9.

Harridge-March, S. (2006). Can the building of trust overcome consumer perceived risk online? *Marketing Intelligence & Planning, 24*(7), 746–761. doi:10.1108/02634500610711897

Herche, J., & Engelland, B. (1989). Reverse-polarity items and scale unidimensionality. *Journal of the Academy of Marketing Science, 24*, 366–374. doi:10.1177/0092070396244007

Jevons, C. Gabbott, M., & de Chernatony. L. (2001). A taxonomy of brand linkages: the brand-relationship-interaction (BRI) matrix, http://business.bham.ac.uk/business/papers/taxonomy.htm.

Kim, D., & Benbasat, I. (2010). Designs for effective implementation of trust assurances in internet stores. *Communications of the ACM, 53*(2), 121–20. doi:10.1145/1646353.1646386

Klein, B., & Leffler, K. (1981). The role of market forces in assuring contractual performance. *The Journal of Political Economy, 89*(4), 615–641. doi:10.1086/260996

Leuthesser, L. (2003). 2+2=5? A framework for using co-branding to leverage a brand. *Brand Management, 11*(1), 35–47. doi:10.1057/palgrave.bm.2540146

Mazis, M., Settle, R., & Leslie, D. (1973). Elimination of phosphate detergents and psychological reactance. *JMR, Journal of Marketing Research, X*, 390–395. doi:10.2307/3149386

McClindon, A. (2001). Strong on-line brands enhance sales, http://www.enn.ie/news.html?code=4236914.

Merrilees, B., & Fry, M. (2003). E-trust the influence of perceived interactivity on e-retailing uses. *Marketing Intelligence & Planning, 21*(2), 123–128. doi:10.1108/02634500310465461

Milam, M. (2008). The rise of brandjacking against major brands. *Computer Fraud & Security*, (October): 10–13. doi:10.1016/S1361-3723(08)70149-0

Nelson, P. (1974). Advertising as information. *The Journal of Political Economy, 82*(4), 729–754. doi:10.1086/260231

Ozkan, S., Bindusara, G., & Hackney, R. (2010). Facilitating the adoption of e-payment systems: Theoretical constructs and empirical analysis. *Journal of Enterprise Information Management, 23*(3), 305–325. doi:10.1108/17410391011036085

Ruparelia, N., White, L., & Hughes, K. (2010). Drivers of brand trust in internet retailing. *Journal of Product and Brand Management, 19*(4), 250–260. doi:10.1108/10610421011059577

Ruth, J., & Simonin, B. (2003). Brought to You by brand A and brand B. *Journal of Advertising, 32*(3), 19–30.

San Martin, S., & Camarero, C. (2008). Consumer trust to a website: Moderating effect of attitudes toward online shopping. *Cyberpsychology & Behavior, 11*(5), 549–554. doi:10.1089/cpb.2007.0097

Shneiderman, B. (2000). Designing trust into online experiences. *Communications of the ACM, 43*(1), 57–59. doi:10.1145/355112.355124

Srinivasan, S. (2004). Role of trust in e-business success. *Information Management & Computer Security, 12*(1), 66–72. doi:10.1108/09685220410518838

Stewart, K. (2003). Trust transfer on the world wide web. *Organization Science, 14*(1), 5–17. doi:10.1287/orsc.14.1.5.12810

Stewart, K. (2006). How hypertext links influence consumer perceptions to build and degrade trust online. *Journal of Management Information Systems, 23*(1), 183–210. doi:10.2753/MIS0742-1222230106

Votolato, N., & Unnava, H. (2006). Spillover of negative information on brand alliances. *Journal of Consumer Psychology, 16*(2), 192–202.

Wakefield, R., & Whitten, D. (2006). Examining user perceptions of third-party organization credibility and trust in an e-tailer. *Journal of Organizational and End User Computing, 18*(2), 1–19. doi:10.4018/joeuc.2006040101

Ward, M., & Lee, M. (1999). Internet shopping, consumer search, and product branding. *Journal of Product and Brand Management, 9*(1), 6–20. doi:10.1108/10610420010316302

Washburn, J., Till, B., & Priluck, R. (2000). Co-branding: brand equity and trial effects. *Journal of Consumer Marketing, 17*(7), 591–604. doi:10.1108/07363760010357796

Yavas, U. (1994). Research note: Students as subjects in advertising and marketing. *International Marketing Review, 11*(Winter), 35–44. doi:10.1108/02651339410069236

Zeithaml, V. (1988). Consumer perceptions of price, quality and value: A means-end model and synthesis of evidence. *Journal of Marketing, 52*(3), 2–22. doi:10.2307/1251446

Chapter 5
Swift Trust in Web Vendors:
The Role of Appearance and Functionality

Xin Li
University of North Carolina at Pembroke, USA

Guang Rong
Clemson University, USA

Michelle Carter
Clemson University, USA

Jason Thatcher
Clemson University, USA

ABSTRACT

With the growth of product search engines such as pricegrabber.com, web vendors have many more casual visitors. This research examines how web vendors may foster "swift trust" as a means to convert casual visitors to paying customers. We examine whether perceptions of website's appearance features (normality, social presence and third-party links) and functionality features (security, privacy, effort expectancy and performance expectancy) positively relate to swift trust in a web vendor. Using a quasi-experimental research design, we empirically test the proposed relationships. Based on an analysis of 224 respondents, we found appearance and functionality features explained 61% of the variance in swift trust. The paper concludes with a discussion of findings and implications.

INTRODUCTION

Trust is a key enabler of e-commerce (Kracher, Corritore, & Wiedenbeck, 2005; Lee & Turban, 2001). Extensive research has found that trust leads to online end users' reporting higher levels of purchasing intention, expressing greater loyalty to a web vendor, and engaging in actual purchasing behavior (Cyr, 2008; Gefen, 2002; Gefen, Karahanna, & Straub, 2003a; McKnight, Choudhury, & Kacmar, 2002). Given the widespread support in the literature for ties from online end users trust to their behavior, it is important to direct attention to identifying levers that foster trust and encourage online end users to complete transactions.

DOI: 10.4018/978-1-60960-577-3.ch005

Fostering trust has proven problematic among fast-moving online end users. Although search engines direct over 85% of consumers to vendor websites, 57% of consumers abandon their shopping carts prior to checkout (DoubleClick, 2004). Perhaps due to the ease of identifying alternatives through engines such as pricegrabber.com, online consumers frequently visit websites and fail to complete transactions. Thus, web vendors are under the pressure to quickly win trust, retain first time visitors and convert them to paying customers.

In this paper, we examine how web vendors may foster swift trust. Swift trust refers to trust formed quickly in a new relationship (Meyerson, Weick, & Kramer, 1996). Unlike other forms of trust, which rest on experience or familiarity with a vendor, swift trust develops quickly during a consumer's first exposure to an unfamiliar web vendor. Although first time visitors may lack experience or knowledge of a web vendor, their perceptions of the "working conditions" of e-commerce, including appearance and functionality of a website (Zhang, von Dran, Small, & Barcellos, 1999), influence their understanding of a vendor's ability to complete transactions and its trustworthiness (Corbitt, Thanasankit, & Yi, 2003; Wakefield, Stocks, & Wilder, 2004). For example, Gefen et al. (2003a) suggested that a fair and open website that clearly states due process, policies that handle the relationship, and provides clear explanations engenders consumer trust. Hence, designers emphasize a website's appearance and functionality as a means to promote swift trust.

Although substantial research has examined the implications of trust in web vendors, research has left unexplored the influence of appearance and functionality on swift trust in a web vendor. To gain deeper insight into online consumer behavior, this study examines the following research question: *How do the appearance and functionality of a website influence online consumers' swift trust in a web vendor?*

The paper unfolds as follows. First, we develop a general model tying appearance and functionality to consumer's swift trust and purchasing intention. In terms of appearance, we examine normality, social presence, and links to third-party assurance providers. In terms of functionality, we examine the roles of security, privacy, effort expectancy and performance expectancy. Next, we present the results of a quasi-experimental study that tests the proposed model. Then, we discuss our findings. The paper concludes with implications for research and practice.

LITERATURE REVIEW AND MODEL DEVELOPMENT

Trust is a complex and abstract concept. Although defined differently in many literatures, trust most commonly refers to ones willingness to depend on another based on the expectation that the other has the attributes to be trusted (Mayer, Davis, & Schoorman, 1995). Trust is driven by 1) risk and uncertainty in relationships, 2) the trusting party's vulnerability, and 3) his/her expectations of the trusted party. When these drivers are present, an individual must extend trust to another for a relationship to exist.

E-commerce researchers extended the traditional trust definition and drivers to online shopping and found that they are important in studying online end user behavior (Gefen et al., 2003a; McKnight et al., 2002) (see Table 1). For example, high uncertainty characterizes complex and anonymous online transaction processes. While traditional customers can pay at the counter and take the products home immediately, online end users do not directly observe vendors nor directly view the actual products they purchase. Given the salience of risk and uncertainty in online environments (Wang & Emurian, 2005), understanding how to foster trust becomes essential for understanding how to encourage end users to purchase goods online.

In light of risk and uncertainty, e-consumers accept some degree of vulnerability when they make online purchases. For example, when purchasing a good, a consumer accepts exposure to the chance that an unfamiliar vendor could misuse their credit card information. Consumers who accept cookies also open themselves up to having their activities tracked and information stolen. When consumers perceive higher levels of vulnerability (McKnight et al., 2002), they must extend trust to justify entering a business relationship with a web vendor.

Consumers extend trust based on their expectations of a web vendor. Expectations refer to perceptions of a vendor's trusting attributes (McKnight et al., 2002). Typically, online trust is conceived as a set of beliefs and expectations that about a vendor's a) capability to operate a business and complete transactions (i.e., competence); b) desire to positively interact with consumers (i.e., benevolence); and c) honesty and adherence to widely accepted principles (i.e., integrity) (Gefen et al., 2003a; Mayer et al., 1995; McKnight et al., 2002). When dealing with a new web vendor, consumers may not have enough direct knowledge or experience. They have to build such expectations based on other sources (Doney & Cannon, 1997; Stewart, 2003).

Swift Trust

To retain quick moving consumers, vendors must foster swift trust. Swift trust refers to trust formed quickly in new or transitory relationships

Table 1. Extending Trust Definition and Drivers to the Domain of E-Commerce

	Traditional	E-Commerce
Trust Definition	The willingness of a party to be vulnerable to the actions of another based on expectations that the other will perform a particular action important to the trustor, irrespective of the ability to monitor or control that other party (Mayer et al., 1995 p. 712).	
Prerequisite: Two parties in a social relationship.	A trusting party (trustor) and a party to be trusted (trustee) (Wang & Emurian, 2005)	The online consumer is the trustor, the web vendor is the trustee (Wang & Emurian, 2005). The relationship is predicated on the exchange of money for goods or services..
Drivers of Trust: Risk and Uncertainty	The trustor's Inability to control or monitor the trustee's behaviors, enables the trustee to act opportunistically (Kee & Knox, 1970). The greater the risks and uncertainty, the more trust is needed to enable behaviors in the context (Ruyter, Moorman, & Lemmink, 2001).	High complexity and anonymity (Wang & Emurian, 2005), as well as greater information asymmetries (Tan & Thoen, 2002), make the e-commerce environment more risky and uncertain than traditional markets.
Drivers of Trust: Vulnerability	The more a trustor will lose due to a trustee's opportunistic behavior, the more vulnerable s/he is in specific circumstances, and the higher level of trust is needed to justify the participation in such circumstances (Hosmer, 1995; Mishra, 1996).	Online customers face financial loss (e.g., credit card theft, poor quality products, etc.) and privacy loss (e.g., identity theft, spam mails, etc.) (Friedman, Kahn, & Howe, 2000; Gefen, 2002)
Drivers of Trust: Expectations	Reasonable expectation refers to a trustor's belief that the trustee can be relied on. A trustor forms a set of expectations about the trustee, including its competence, benevolence and integrity (Mayer et al., 1995). Based on these, the trustor grants trust.	Online customers form expectations of an e-vendor's competence (i.e. ability to complete transactions), benevolence (i.e. motivation to act in the customer's interests) and integrity (i.e. honesty and promise keeping) (Gefen et al., 2003a; McKnight et al., 2002).
Outcomes of Trust Trusting Behavior and Relationship	Trust leads to risk-taking behavior–the form of which is situation-dependent (Mayer et al., 1995). Trust also leads to long-term relationship and anticipated future interaction (Doney & Cannon, 1997; Mayer et al., 1995).	Trust in e-vendor leads to risk-taking behaviors, such as providing information, and making purchases (McKnight et al., 2002). It also plays an important role in fostering customer loyalty.

(Meyerson et al., 1996). It forms without the benefit of familiarity, past experience, and fulfilled promises. Swift trust is similar to initial trust in that it develops early in a relationship, reflects limited interaction between a trustor and trustee, and rests on cues derived from the environment (McKnight, Cummings, & Chervany, 1998; Meyerson et al., 1996) (see Table 2 for a comparison of forms of trust). However, unlike initial trust, swift trust is developed under time constraints due to environmental pressures or consumers' short attention span (Galleta, 2006). Jarvenpaa and Leidner (1999) argue that swift trust is characterized by short time frames, which limit trustors' ability to develop expectations of trustee. Once individuals form swift trust, they are inclined to pursue future interactions with a trustor.

Swift trust is particularly germane to understanding online consumer behavior. Product search engines usually organize results based on price. Frequently, low cost vendors use low prices to overcome a lack of name recognition. In this case, online consumers do not have past experiences or direct interactions with an unfamiliar trustee – the web vendor – suggested by a search engine. Due to their numerous shopping choices, the online consumers may expend limited time and effort exploring an unfamiliar website. To "close the deal," web vendors must foster swift trust, or lose the new customers to competitors.

Because individuals lack sufficient time to form perceptions of new trustees from scratch, swift trust is usually "imported from other settings and imposed quickly in categorical forms (Meyerson et al., 1996 p. 174)." To engender swift trust in online shopping, vendors embed cues in the website design to facilitate the importing and categorization processes. Some cues provide links for consumers to import trust from other trusted sources (i.e., trust transference, Stewart, 2003). For example, the presence of Visa and FedEx icons provides signal to consumers about safe payment and fast delivery. Other cues invoke categorization processes to speed up the trust formation. For instance, some vendors utilize page layout and menu sets similar with those known and trusted websites to encourage new consumers to categorize them as familiar. Industry certificates or awards are usually placed prominently on the homepage for consumers to label the vendors as

Table 2. Developed Trust, Initial Trust and Swift Trust

	Definition	Temporal	Studies	Trust Foundation
Developed trust	Trust built on shared experience and direct interactions between the two parties.	In an established relationship	(Ganesan, 1994; Gefen et al., 2003a)	Familiarity, Past Experiences, Direct Interactions
Initial trust	Trust in an unfamiliar trustee; a trust relationship in which the actors do not yet have credible, meaningful information about, or affective bonds with, each other.	In a new relationship	(Koufaris & Hampton-Sosa, 2004; McKnight et al., 2002)	Disposition to Trust*, Institutional-Based Trust including Situational Normality and Structural Assurances
Swift trust	Trust formed quickly in a new or temporary system, without traditional sources of trust such as familiarity, past experience, and fulfilled promises.	In a new relationship, with time constraints	(Jarvenpaa & Leidner, 1999; Meyerson et al., 1996)	Disposition to Trust*, Imported Trust and Category-Driven Trust based on quick cues
* Disposition to trust is not controllable by the web vendors and thus not examined in this study				

professional. More websites present BBB and Trust-e seals, so consumers will classify them as reliable vendors (Pennington, Wilcox, & Grover, 2003). Thus, through embedding cues in web design, new vendors can successfully foster swift trust among first time visitors.

A Model of Swift Trust in Web Vendor

Web design consists of two major dimensions – appearance and functionality (Zhang et al., 1999). Appearance features refer to the look and feel of a website. They give the first impression to the web visitors. Functionality features are more task-related. They refer to a website's ability to supply information and conclude transactions. Here, we propose a model (see Figure 1), depicting how a set of appearance and functionality features induce swift trust and purchase intention. In both appearance and functionality dimensions, we examine features that have been previously studied and are often noted as salient to fostering positive beliefs about web vendor and its website. While they are not exhaustive, the set of features will provide us some initial insight into swift trust formation. In the following sections, we discuss these appearance and functionality features and their relationships with swift trust and purchase intention.

Swift Trust and Purchase Intention

Purchase intention refers to online consumers' willingness to purchase from a web vendor (Stewart, 2003). Prior research suggests that purchase intention is influenced by consumers' trust in a web vendor (Gefen et al., 2003a; P. A. Pavlou & Fygenson, 2006; Stewart, 2003; van der Heijden, Verhagen, & Creemers, 2003; Van Slyke, Belanger, & Comunale, 2004). Although formed quickly at the early stage of a relationship, swift trust encourages further interactions and facilitates the development of purchase intention. If consumers grant swift trust towards a web vendor, they tend to believe that this vendor will protect their privacy, sell high quality products, and be capable of consummating online transactions. Thus, we hypothesize that as swift trust in a vendor grows, consumers will report higher purchase intentions.

H1: Swift trust in a web vendor positively affects purchase intention.

Appearance Features

A website is an electronic storefront of a web vendor. For a pure e-commerce company, the website is the only access point through which consumers

Figure 1. A Model of swift trust in web vendor

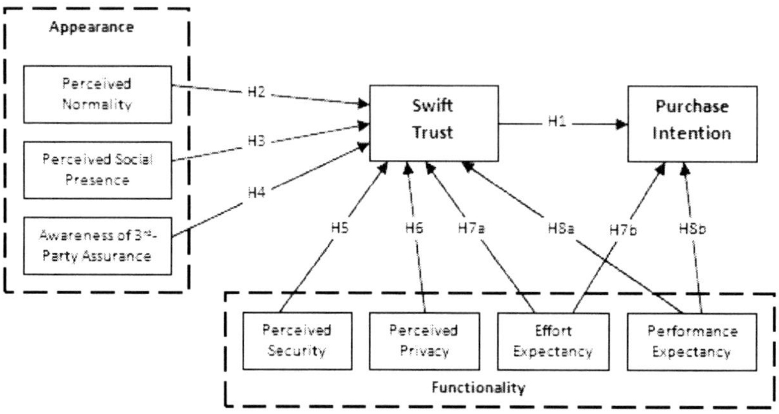

may collect information on, and interact with, the goods and services. Because of the website's centrality in the consumer/web vendor relationship, a website's appearance is an important source of signals about the vendor's trustworthiness. Prior trust literature has mentioned several appearance features that affect trust (Gefen et al., 2003a; Gefen & Straub, 2004; McKnight et al., 2002; Nadkarni & Gupta, 2007). Based on the literature, we believe online consumers will express swift trust when they perceive a website's appearance as normal and high on social presence, and they are aware of third-party assurances of trustworthiness. In the following paragraphs, we explain the logic behind these relationships.

Perceived normality. Perceived normality refers to consumers' perception that a website performs in a normal or customary manner, which is consistent with their experience with similar web vendors (Gefen et al., 2003a). Normality of a website signals to new consumers that the vendor will fulfill their expectations of a good shopping experience (i.e., product information can be easily acquired, transactions are completed smoothly and safely, and expected goods and services are received quickly) (Gefen et al., 2003a). If a website is perceived as normal, consumers will categorize it as trustworthy and extend swift trust. Alternatively, an unusual website design that is not well-known and requires learning new ways to access information may not be trusted.

When visiting a new website, consumers assess normality through their quick interaction with the website. Specifically, they evaluate their perceptions of 1) the shopping process, 2) the information required to complete a purchase, and 3) the quality of their interaction with the website (Gefen et al., 2003a; Nadkarni & Gupta, 2007). For example, most consumers are familiar with one-click shopping. If, on a new website, consumers find that they must go through a complicated process and provide unusually detailed information to complete a transaction, or they have a complicated or unpleasant communication with online representatives, they will not trust the web vendor and fail to complete a transaction. Thus, we anticipate that consumers who perceive normality of a website are more likely to form swift trust towards a web vendor.

H2: Perceived normality positively affects swift trust in web vendor.

Perceived social presence. Perceived social presence refers to consumers' perception that there is personal, sociable, and sensitive human contact and/or peer community on the website (Gefen & Straub, 2004). A website can project a social presence similar to what consumers experience in offline stores. Gefen and Straub (2004) found that when a website is perceived as having a higher level of social presence, it enables more effective interaction and communication between a consumer and web vendor, and thus, renders consumers more inclined to trust the web vendor. By projecting social presence similar to offline stores, a website may induce consumers to categorize the website as part of a trustworthy group of known, offline vendors.

In practice, although web vendors are not able to use salespersons or store assistants to physically interact with customers, they send cues or project social presence through images of high quality products, happy customers, and live-chat customer service functions (Cyr, 2008). For example, on Overstock.com, service representatives use interactive, pop-up windows to ask online consumers if they need more information, or offer to help complete a transaction. Many websites foster virtual communities, where customers can participate in peer discussions, provide product/store reviews, and receive peer assistance (e.g., newegg.com and target.com). If, during the first visit, consumers perceive a website as high on social presence, we anticipate they will extend swift trust to a web vendor.

H3: Perceived social presence positively affects swift trust in web vendor.

Awareness of third-party assurance. Awareness of third-party assurance refers to consumers' knowledge and awareness of third-party institutional mechanisms that ensure a trustworthy environment for website operations and business transactions (McKnight et al., 2002; Pennington et al., 2003). Several institutional mechanisms are widely used in e-commerce, including seal programs (e.g., Trust-e reliability and privacy seal programs, VeriSign security seal program) (Pennington et al., 2003), credit card protections (e.g., Visa card security and protection programs, Master card security and credit basics) (Miyazaki & Fernandez, 2000), and customer certified store ratings and feedback systems (e.g., BizRate.com) (P.A. Pavlou & Gefen, 2004). Prior research suggests that these mechanisms provide a safe and reliable environment for online transactions. Through prominently placing seals and icons of these mechanisms, a website encourages consumers to extend trust based on their experiences with the established institutional structures. Based on the prior studies (McKnight et al., 2002; Stewart, 2003), consumers who are quickly aware of the third-party assurance on an unfamiliar website are more likely to extend swift trust towards the web vendor.

H4: Awareness of the third-party assurance positively affects swift trust in web vendor.

Functionality Features

Online customers' impression of a website's functionality, i.e., its ability to successfully complete a transaction, influences their trust in the web vendor. Although deep understanding of functionality requires extensive interaction with a website, cues in the website design may contribute to the formation of swift trust. Based on prior research, we direct our attention to four perceptions of functionality that may influence swift trust: security, privacy, effort expectancy and performance expectancy (Gefen et al., 2003a; Miyazaki & Fernandez, 2001; Thatcher & George, 2004).

Perceived security. Perceived security refers to consumers' perception that a website can safely complete transactions (P.A. Pavlou & Chellappa, 2001). When considering a transaction with an unknown party, consumers will evaluate the vendor's ability to protect their information, successfully complete a transaction, and offer help resolving a dispute. In the online environment, consumers usually perceive additional security threats than the traditional consumers, such as credit card theft, defective products/services, and delivery failure (Featherman & Pavlou, 2003). Consumers' security concerns are the major determinant of their online perceptions and behaviors (Miyazaki & Fernandez, 2001; Salisbury, Pearson, Pearson, & Miller, 2001).

Consumers' assessment of the website's ability to safely complete transactions contributes to the formation of trust (Zhou, Dai, & Zhang, 2007). For example, Amazon.com provides notices when users sign in using the secure server. It gives customers easy access to the shipping and return policies on its homepage. By doing so, Amazon.com sends signals about its ability to facilitate safe, secure online shopping. Similarly, many web vendors send signals about security through providing order status, real-time shipping tracking, and return assistance. When first time visitors feel fewer security concerns on a website, they will be more likely to report swift trust in the vendor.

H5: Perceived security positively affects swift trust in web vendor.

Perceived privacy. Perceived privacy refers to the consumers' belief that a web vendor will protect consumers' personal and financial information (P.A. Pavlou & Chellappa, 2001). An online transaction requires consumers to provide more personal and financial information than traditional shopping channels. For example, online transactions require providing billing and shipping addresses, something that is not typically requested by brick-and-mortar stores. Also, e-commerce companies often use cookies to collect information and provide customized recommendations to consumers. Due to demands for consumer information, as well as a web vendor's ability to collect information without consumers' notice, privacy concerns have become a defining issue for many web consumers (Malhotra, Kim, & Agarwal, 2004; Miyazaki & Fernandez, 2001).

When considering a transaction with an unfamiliar store, privacy may be a salient issue for a consumer (Liu, Marchewka, Lu, & Yu, 2005). A website may address privacy concerns through prominently featuring links to the privacy notice or policies, by briefly stating how they collect data on consumers, and by illustrating how such data may be used by the firm (Gefen et al., 2003a; Gefen, Rao, & Tractinsky, 2003b). When consumers quickly recognize that a web vendor complies with fair information practices and commits to protect its customers' privacy, they are more likely to express swift trust. Hence:

H6: Perceived privacy positively affects swift trust in web vendor.

Effort expectancy and performance expectancy. Within the domain of e-commerce, effort expectancy and performance expectancy have been tied to trust and purchase intentions (Gefen et al., 2003a; P.A. Pavlou, 2003). Effort expectancy (also referred to as ease of use (Venkatesh, Morris, Davis, & Davis, 2003)) refers to the degree to which the consumers believe that using a new website would be free of effort (Gefen et al., 2003a). Performance expectancy (also referred to as perceived usefulness (Venkatesh et al., 2003)) refers to the degree to which the consumers believe that using a new website would enhance their ability to safely, effectively purchase goods (Gefen et al., 2003a). Gefen et al. (2003a) found that customers' effort expectancy in using a website influence their trust. Their findings also indicate that trust, effort expectancy, and performance expectancy influence customers' usage intentions towards the website. Consistent with prior research, we hypothesize that when a new website is perceived as low on effort expectancy, consumers will be more likely to report swift trust as well as intentions to use a website. Hence:

H7a: Effort expectancy negatively affects swift trust in web vendor.

H7b: Effort expectancy negatively affects purchase intentions.

In a departure from Gefen et al. (2003a), we argue that performance expectancy will positively influence swift trust. Because first time visitors lack extensive experience with the tools provided by a web vendor, expectations about performance reflect how they interpret cues embedded in a website. For example, a standard "useful" feature of a shopping site is the ability to search for products. Similarly, a comparison tool can help consumers compare similar products in terms of price, specifications and features in a more effective way. When consumers perceive that a website possesses tools that enable searching for and acquiring products, they will be more likely to express positive expectations of performance (Ranganathan & Ganapathy, 2002). Given that swift trust reflects limited interaction with a website, we anticipate that the presence of these "useful" tools positively influences swift trust and purchase intention. Hence:

H8a: Performance expectancy positively affects swift trust in web vendor.

H8b: Performance expectancy positively affects purchase intention.

METHOD

A quasi-experimental survey design was used to test the research model. We used Overstock.com as our target website as it is a pure e-commerce company. Subjects would not confound trust in Overstock.com with their experiences at a real-world brick-and-mortar or click-and-mortar business.

We collected data at three public universities in the United States. Junior and senior levels college students participated in the study. Although student samples have been criticized in many IS research contexts, evidence suggests that college students are active online shoppers, who do not differ from their working peers (Sen, King, & Shaw, 2006), and thus, represent a useful sample for testing our research model (Suh & Lee, 2005).

Study Procedure

The study consisted of a task and a survey. Participants were assigned a shopping task on Overstock.com. Specifically, subjects were asked to shop for a birthday gift for their significant others. They were given 10 minutes to view the web pages and research a purchase. No actual purchase was required in the shopping task. Following completion of the task, subjects were asked to complete a survey about their experiences on Overstock.com. The survey collected data on all constructs in the research model and demographic information. Respondents were required to complete the task and survey in 25 minutes, thus engendering time pressure characteristic of situations involving swift trust.

Measurement Development

Where possible, we adapted measures from prior online trust research. Each item was measured using a 7-point Likert-type scale (anchored with 1 = strongly disagree, 7 = strongly agree). Purchase intention was measured using 4 items adapted from Pavlou's work (P.A. Pavlou, 2003; P.A. Pavlou & Gefen, 2004) (see Appendix I for the items).

Swift trust was operationalized as a second-order construct. It is comprised of three dimensions – competence, benevolence, and integrity. Each dimension was measured using 3-4 items adapted from McKnight et al. (2002).

Measures of most appearance features were adapted from prior studies. Perceived normality was measured by items adapted from Gefen et al. (2003a). Perceived social presence was measured by items adapted from Gefen and Straub (2004). To measure awareness of third-party assurance, we developed four-items that directed attention to the presence of icons and links to trusted third parties such as VeriSign security seal program or credit card partners that appear on Overstock.com.

Functionality features measures were adapted from prior research. Effort expectancy and performance expectancy were adapted from Gefen et al. (2003a). Perceived security and perceived privacy were adapted from Salisbury et al. (2001), Yang and Jun (2002), and Smith et al. (1996).

Pilot Study and Data Collection

We conducted a pilot study to validate the measurement instruments and our quasi-experiment design. The instrument and task were well received by the pilot study participants. Minor changes were made in wording and the order of items. Also, we received feedback that our task was meaningful and induced a feeling of time pressure among our respondents.

281 students participated in this study. We dropped fourteen responses due to missing values. Also, we dropped forty-three subjects because they reported prior experience with Overstock.com. This yielded a usable sample of 224 respondents that included 118 females and 106 males, with substantial Internet and online shopping experience. T-tests revealed that sample characteristics and responses across research sites were not

significantly different. Table 3 presents sample characteristics.

RESULTS

We used Partial Least Square (PLS), a structural equation modeling technique, to evaluate the hypotheses. Although a debate is emerging in the MIS literature on the merits of PLS, in the broader methods literature, PLS is considered a useful tool for theory building, specifically when one seeks to establish predictive validity in a structural model (Chwelos, Benbasat, & Dexter, 2001). As a result, we believe PLS is an appropriate tool for estimating our measurement and structural models. In the following sections, we present the results in two steps - measurement model and structural model.

Measurement Model

Following Agarwal and Karahanna's (2000) approach, two measurement models were evaluated. First, we evaluated the measurement model for swift trust – a second order construct. Swift trust is formed by three reflective sub-dimensions - competence, benevolence and integrity. All items yielded high loadings (ranging from 0.855 to 0.948, $p < 0.000$) on the appropriate sub-dimension. Also, each sub-dimensions' internal consistency score (ranging from 0.908 to 0.941) and composite reliability score (ranging from 0.943 to 0.958) were high. The detailed item loadings and reliability scores are reported in Appendix II (a) and Table 4, respectively. a confirmatory factor analysis was performed to assess the convergent and discriminant validity of the measures (see Appendix II (a) and Table 4). Briefly, all items load higher on the corresponding sub-dimensions than on other sub-dimensions, and each sub-dimension has a square root of the AVE (ranging from 0.832 to 0.852) greater than its correlations with other sub-dimensions. Hence, our analysis indicates adequate reliability, convergent, and discriminant validity of the swift trust measurement model.

Next, we used the factor scores of the above three sub-dimensions as direct measures of swift trust to assess the full measurement model. Results are presented in Table 5 and Appendix II (b). All indicators load on the construct of interest, with loadings ranging from 0.829 to 0.965 ($p < 0.000$). Internal consistency scores range from 0.892 to 0.953. The composite reliability scores range from 0.927 to 0.964. All indicators loaded higher on the construct of interest than other constructs. Every construct has square root of AVE (ranging

Table 3. Sample characteristics

Char.	Number	Percentage	Char.	Number	Percentage
Gender			**Internet Experience – Years of Use**		
Female	118	52.7%	0-3 years	5	2.2%
Male	106	47.3%	4-7 years	103	46.0%
Age			8 years or above	116	51.8%
Under 21	85	37.9%	**Internet Experience - Often**		
21 - 45	133	59.4%	Once a day or less	16	7.1%
Above 45	6	2.7%	Many times a day	208	92.9%
Internet Level			**Online Shopping Experience – in past 2 years**		
Beginner	2	0.9%	0-2 times	31	13.8%
Intermediate	34	15.2%	3-10 times	67	29.9%
Proficient	188	83.9%	11 time or above	126	56.3%

from 0.864 – 0.942) greater than its correlations with any other constructs. Hence, our analysis indicates adequate convergent and discriminant validity for the overall measurement model.

Structural Model

Figure 2 presents the structural model results. Appearance and functionality features explain 61% of the variance in swift trust. Also, swift trust, effort expectancy, and performance expectancy explained 40% of the variance in purchase intention.

Swift Trust. In terms of appearance features, we found perceived normality (H2:.19, p<.01), perceived social presence (H3:.13, p<.01), and awareness of 3rd party assurance (H4:.28, p<.01) positively relating to swift trust. In terms of functionality features, perceived security (H5:.26, p<.01) positively related to swift trust while effort expectancy (H7a: -.13 p<.05) negatively related to swift trust. Perceived privacy (H6: n.s.) and performance expectancy (H8a: n.s.) were not significantly related to swift trust. Collectively, our results provide evidence that a website's appearance and functionality attributes influence swift trust.

Purchase Intention. The overall model explains 40% of the variance in purchase intention. Swift trust (H1:.36, p < 0.01) and performance expectancy (H8b:.44, p < 0.01) positively relates to purchase intention. Effort expectancy (H7b: -.12, p < 0.05) negatively relates to purchase intention.

Table 4. Swift Trust: Means, Reliability and Average Variance Extracted

Dimension	Mean	SD	CR	Alpha	1	2	3
1. Competency	5.516	0.949	.952	.931	**.832**		
2. Benevolence	5.022	1.095	.943	.908	.707	**.848**	
3. Integrity	5.142	1.010	.958	.941	.698	.797	**.852**

Diagonal elements in the 'correlation of constructs' matrix are the square root of the average variance extracted. For adequate discriminant validity, diagonal elements should be greater than corresponding off-diagonal elements.

Table 5. Overall Measurement Model: Means, Reliability and Average Variance Extracted[1]

	Mean	SD	CR	Alpha	1	2	3	4	5	6	7	8	9
1. Transaction Intention	5.008	1.348	.961	.944	**.928**								
2. Trust in Online Store	5.227	0.924	.933	.892	.533	**.907**							
3. Perceived Normality	5.961	1.028	.959	.935	.340	.538	**.942**						
4. Perceived Social Presence	4.231	1.351	.964	.953	.364	.396	.070	**.918**					
5. Awareness of 3rd-party	5.056	1.057	.927	.894	.414	.635	.400	.360	**.872**				
6. Effort Expectancy	6.221	0.921	.964	.949	.341	.520	.717	.119	.375	**.933**			
7. Performance Expectancy	5.498	1.144	.957	.940	.566	.530	.501	.338	.392	.583	**.921**		
8. Perceived Security	4.479	1.324	.960	.944	.413	.596	.316	.361	.545	.274	.349	**.926**	
9. Perceived Privacy	2.908	1.311	.947	.932	.064	.211	.185	.042	.184	.145	.087	.313	**.864**

Diagonal elements in the 'correlation of constructs' matrix are the square root of the average variance extracted. For adequate discriminant validity, diagonal elements should be greater than corresponding off-diagonal elements

Figure 2. Research model with PLS results

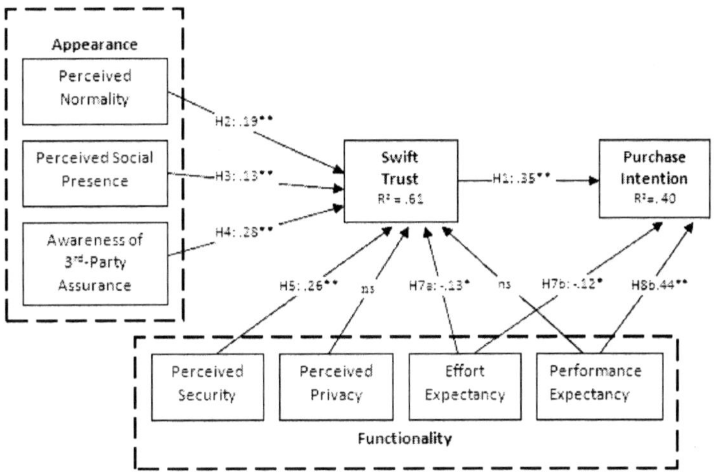

DISCUSSION

This study examined sources and consequences of swift trust in web vendors. In the following paragraphs, we discuss our findings and the implications.

Appearance Features and Swift Trust

All three appearance features that we examined positively relate to swift trust. The study findings show that perceived normality has a significant positive relationship with swift trust (H2: Supported). Similar to other groups of online consumers, our respondents had significant Internet and e-commerce experience. Among our study participants, similarity with familiar websites engendered their swift trust in an unfamiliar website. This finding suggests that web designers should carefully consider how they visually and structurally differentiate their website from competitors. If a website employs an unusual or novel design, first time visitors may not extend trust to a web vendor. For new web vendors, in addition to relying on low price or novelty of product lines/business models, our findings suggest patterning websites after successful e-commerce businesses in their market as a means to engender swift trust for first time visitors.

The study also shows that social presence positively related to swift trust in a web vendor (H3: Supported). An unfamiliar website that projects social presence similar to real-world salespersons and customer service representatives engenders feelings of competence, benevolence, and integrity in online consumers (Gefen & Straub, 2004). Overstock.com uses images of satisfied customers and content employees to convey social presence. In addition, when customers check a product, a live assistance chat window frequently pops up and offers to provide more information or help completing a transaction. Further, below the item description, customers can read the product reviews posted by other customers or post their own reviews. All these features give consumers the feeling like they were shopping at a physical store with helpful service representatives, and they were part of a community of shoppers (Thatcher & George, 2004). Thus, we suggest prominently projecting social presence as a useful means to foster consumers' swift trust.

First time visitors reported higher levels of swift trust when they were aware of the third-party assurance (H4: Supported). Overstock.com places icons of third party assurance providers on every webpage – including icons from credit card companies, payment options, VeriSign BBB Online, and BizRate.com. Our findings confirm that third party icons signal that Overstock.com is operated in a safe and reliable environment, and the transactions in the environment are well protected (McKnight, Kacmar, & Choudhury, 2004). For practice, this finding directs web designers to carefully consider the placement of third-party assurance icons and seals. If properly sized, placed at directly visible positions, repeated on different pages or different sections, the third party assurance icons engender consumers' swift trust (McKnight et al., 2004).

Overall, appearance features are salient to understanding swift trust. This is probably because the appearance features are mostly visible to the first time website visitors under time pressure. Our findings suggest that consumer perceptions of normality, social presence, and third-party assurances lead to swift trust in a web vendor. For web designers, these findings suggest that the look and feel of a website can be used to foster swift trust and convert first time visitors to paying customers.

Functionality Features and Swift Trust

We found mixed results for functionality features' relationship with swift trust. Perceived security positively related to swift trust (H5: supported). Consumer perceptions of a website's capability to perform secure transactions influence their perceptions of the web vendors' competence, benevolence, and integrity. Fully understanding the security features on a website may require time and extensive interaction. However, web vendors can quickly signal their intention and ability to provide a safe shopping experience to the first time visitors through security cues. For example, Overstock.com provides prominent links to order tracking, shipping and return policies on its homepage. The transparent transaction processes may create a sense of security for online consumers. In addition, the "golden lock" signs on the login and check-out pages, as well as the time-outs and re-login requests, also provide quick signals of a website's security. If these security cues are prominently placed, first time visitors can quickly perceive good protection and make quick inferences about the trustworthiness of a web vendor. While most web vendors expend significant efforts in developing security features that consumers may not directly see or understand, we suggest, to foster swift trust, web vendors should give special attentions to how to signal the presence of the security features to online consumers.

Contrary to our expectations, perceived privacy was not significantly related to swift trust (H6: not supported). This finding may be a function of the task we used in our study. Participants searched for information and assessed features of a website; but they did not provide personal information required to complete a transaction. Perhaps due to the short and anonymous visit, our participants were not concerned with privacy issues associated with completing a purchase on Overstock.com. Because swift trust develops prior to making a purchase, we are comfortable with the strength of our research design. However, future research should examine ties between swift trust and an antecedent to privacy concerns. Hence, even though we did not find a relationship between privacy and swift trust, there remains room for future research on privacy and swift trust.

Effort expectancy negatively related to swift trust (H7a: Supported) and purchase intention (H7b: Supported). When using a website was perceived as relatively free of effort, consumers were more likely to perceive the web vendor as competent, benevolent and high on integrity. While consistent with prior online consumer behavior research (Gefen et al., 2003a), our findings confirm the nomological net of relationships between effort expectancy, trust, and purchase intention. For practice, our findings underscore the importance of designing websites to be easy to navigate, easy to find product information, and easy to conclude transactions.

Performance expectancy was not related to swift trust (H8a: Not Supported) and it was related to purchase intention (H8b: Supported). Performance expectancy's influence on swift trust may have been washed out by perceived normality, perceived social presence, perceived security, and effort expectancy. While other perceptions refer to specific aspects of a website, performance expectancy requires consumers to make global assessments of a website. In light of this, it makes sense that perceptions of specific website attributes would exert greater influences on swift trust than a global assessment of a website. An alternative explanation for this finding may be that it requires consumers' substantial experience to form perceptions of performance expectancy. Because swift trust reflects only limited interaction with a website, online consumers may lack the experience to form beliefs about performance expectancy. Thus, it is not surprising that performance expectancy is not an antecedent to swift trust in a website. However, purchasing a product rests on general, well-developed perceptions of a website's functionality. Hence, performance expectancy, as expected, directly influences purchase intention (Gefen et al., 2003a).

Overall, online consumers report higher levels of swift trust when they report positive perceptions of a website's security and low levels of effort to use. The other functionality features may require more interactions to be realized and contribute to trust formation. Although perceptions of the features may evolve over time, web vendors who embed noticeable signals that they are capable to complete secure, easy transactions are likely to engender consumers' swift trust and purchasing intention in their websites.

Swift Trust and Purchase Intention

Swift trust positively relates to purchase intention (H1: Supported). When online consumers quickly form trust, they are more likely to participate in further interaction with the website and eventually make actual purchases from the vendor. This finding is consistent with prior trust research (Gefen, 2002b; see Gefen et al., 2003a; Gefen et al., 2003b; P.A. Pavlou & Gefen, 2004). Our finding also supports the idea that trust is relevant to purchasing intention even when consumers have limited time to familiarize themselves with a web vendor. Hence, this finding underscores the importance of the previous findings on how appearance and functionality features influence the formation of swift trust in a web vendor. For practice, although the casual visitors led by search engines may have many alternatives and move fast, web vendors still can successfully foster swift trust and convert them to paying customers through the proper use of the appearance and functionality features.

CONCLUSION

This study examined swift trust in web vendors. To induce conditions necessary for the formation of swift trust, we constrained study participants' time to visit a website. Further, we dropped responses from study participants with experience with our target website – Overstock.com. This study found substantial support for appearance and functionality features positively relating to swift trust. We also found support for our hypotheses that swift trust, effort expectancy, and performance expectancy influence purchase intention.

For research, this study provides initial evidence that swift trust has different antecedents than other forms of experience based trust identified in the e-commerce literature – it was not affected by perceived privacy or performance expectancy. This suggests that future research examine additional factors that shape the development of swift trust. For practice, our research underscores the importance of fostering swift trust as a means to increase purchase intention. Our findings direct attention to approaches under managerial control such as normality (i.e., using website designs similar to known vendors) and social presence (i.e., engendering a sense of community or having interactive help features) that positively influence the formation of swift trust.

In light of our findings, it is important to note limitations and opportunities for extending this research. An important limitation of this study is the use of a single website – Overstock.com. We used this approach to control for variance in how website's features and respondents' experience influence swift trust. Overstock.com possesses many favorable features such as recommendation agents, icons, and product descriptions that may foster swift trust. In future research, it would be useful for researchers to examine how manipulating these features would influence consumers' swift trust in other unfamiliar web vendors.

Also, future research should examine how to foster swift trust in diverse populations of online consumers. In this research, we drew on students who are active online consumers to examine swift trust. Although students are a valid sample for the current study, a pure student sample may include less variance in age, occupation, and Internet experience. For example, research suggests that age influences perceptions of technology among members of the workforce (Morris & Venkatesh, 2000). Hence, future research should examine differences in demographic factors such as age, income or occupation, which may relate to the formation of swift trust in e-commerce.

REFERENCES

Agarwal, R., & Karahanna, E. (2000). Time flies when you're having fun: Cognitive absorption and beliefs about information technology usage. *Management Information Systems Quarterly*, *24*(4), 665–694. doi:10.2307/3250951

Chwelos, P., Benbasat, I., & Dexter, A. S. (2001). Research report: Empirical test of an EDI adoption model. *Information Systems Research*, *12*(3), 304–321. doi:10.1287/isre.12.3.304.9708

Corbitt, B. J., Thanasankit, T., & Yi, H. (2003). Trust and e-commerce: A study of consumer perceptions. *Electronic Commerce Research and Applications*, *2*, 203–215. doi:10.1016/S1567-4223(03)00024-3

Cyr, D. (2008). Modeling Web site design across cultures: Relationships to trust, satisfaction, and e-loyalty. *Journal of Management Information Systems*, *24*(4), 47–72. doi:10.2753/MIS0742-1222240402

Doney, P. M., & Cannon, J. P. (1997). An examination of the nature of trust in buyer-seller relationships. *Journal of Marketing*, *61*, 35–51. doi:10.2307/1251829

DoubleClick. (2004). [*Ad Serving Trend Report*: Doubleclick.com.]. *DoubleClick*, *Q3*, 2004.

Featherman, M. S., & Pavlou, P. A. (2003). Predicting e-services adoption: A perceived risk facets perspective. *International Journal of Human-Computer Studies*, *59*(4), 451–474. doi:10.1016/S1071-5819(03)00111-3

Friedman, B., Kahn, P. K., & Howe, D. C. (2000). Trust online. *Communications of the ACM*, *43*(12), 34–40. doi:10.1145/355112.355120

Galleta, D., Henry, R., McCoy, S., & Polak, P. (2006). When the Wait Isn't So Bad: The Interacting Effects of Web Site Speed, Familiarity, and Breadth. *Information Systems Research*, *17*(1), 20–37. doi:10.1287/isre.1050.0073

Ganesan, S. (1994). Determinants of long-term orientation in buyer-seller relationships. *Journal of Marketing, 58*(2), 1–19. doi:10.2307/1252265

Gefen, D. (2002). Customer loyalty in e-commerce. *Journal of the Association for Information Systems, 3*, 27–51.

Gefen, D. (2002b). Customer loyalty in e-commerce. *Journal of the Association for Information Systems, 3*, 27–51.

Gefen, D., Karahanna, E., & Straub, D. W. (2003a). Trust and TAM in online shopping: An integrated model. *Management Information Systems Quarterly, 27*(1), 51–90.

Gefen, D., Rao, V. S., & Tractinsky, N. (2003b). *The conceptualization of trust, risk and their relationship in electronic commerce: The need for clarifications.* Paper presented at the 36th Hawaii International Conference on System Sciences, Big island, Hawaii.

Gefen, D., & Straub, D. W. (2004). Consumer trust in B2C e-commerce and the importance of social presence: experiments in e-products and e-services. *Omega, 32*, 407–424. doi:10.1016/j.omega.2004.01.006

Hosmer, L. T. (1995). Trust: The connecting link between organizational theory and philosophical ethics. *Academy of Management Review, 20*(2), 379–403. doi:10.2307/258851

Jarvenpaa, S. L., & Leidner, D. E. (1999). Communication and Trust in Global Virtual Teams. *Organization Science, 10*(6), 791–815. doi:10.1287/orsc.10.6.791

Kee, H. W., & Knox, R. E. (1970). Conceptual and methodological considerations in the study of trust and suspicion. *The Journal of Conflict Resolution, 14*(3), 357–366. doi:10.1177/002200277001400307

Koufaris, M., & Hampton-Sosa, W. (2004). The development of initial trust in an online company by new customers. *Information & Management, 41*, 377–397. doi:10.1016/j.im.2003.08.004

Kracher, B., Corritore, C. L., & Wiedenbeck, S. (2005). A foundation for understanding online trust in electronic commerce. *Information. Communications and Ethics in Society, 3*(3), 131–141. doi:10.1108/14779960580000267

Lee, M. K. O., & Turban, E. (2001). A trust model for consumer internet shopping. *International Journal of Electronic Commerce, 6*(1), 75–91.

Liu, C., Marchewka, J. T., Lu, J., & Yu, C. S. (2005). Beyond concern - A privacy-trust-behavioral intention model of electronic commerce. *Information & Management, 42*, 289–304. doi:10.1016/j.im.2004.01.003

Malhotra, N. K., Kim, S. S., & Agarwal, J. (2004). Internet Users' Information Privacy Concerns (IUIPC): The Construct, the Scale, and a Causal Model. *Information Systems Research, 15*(4), 336–355. doi:10.1287/isre.1040.0032

Mayer, R. C., Davis, J. H., & Schoorman, F. D. (1995). An integrative model of organizational trust. *Academy of Management Review, 20*(3), 709–734. doi:10.2307/258792

McKnight, D. H., Choudhury, V., & Kacmar, C. (2002). Developing and validating trust measures for e-commerce: An integrative typology. *Information Systems Research, 13*(3), 334–359. doi:10.1287/isre.13.3.334.81

McKnight, D. H., Cummings, L. L., & Chervany, N. L. (1998). Initial trust formation in new organizational relationships. *Academy of Management Review, 23*(3), 473–490. doi:10.2307/259290

McKnight, D. H., Kacmar, C., & Choudhury, V. (2004). Shifting factors and the Ineffectiveness of third party assurance seals: A two-stage model of initial trust in a web business. *Electronic Markets, 14*(3), 252–266. doi:10.1080/10196780420000245263

Meyerson, D., Weick, K. E., & Kramer, R. M. (1996). Swift trust and temporary groups. In Kramer, R. M., & Tyler, T. R. (Eds.), *Trust in Organizations: Frontiers of Theory and Research* (pp. 166–195). Thousand Oaks, CA: Sage Publications.

Mishra, A. K. (1996). Organizational responses to crisis: The centrality of trust. In Kramer, R. M., & Tyler, T. (Eds.), *Trust in Organizations* (pp. 261–287). Newbury Park, CA: Sage Publications.

Miyazaki, A. D., & Fernandez, A. (2000). Internet privacy and security: An examination of online retailer disclosures. *Journal of Public Policy & Marketing*, *19*(1), 54–61. doi:10.1509/jppm.19.1.54.16942

Miyazaki, A. D., & Fernandez, A. (2001). Consumer perceptions of privacy and security risks for online shopping. *The Journal of Consumer Affairs*, *35*(1), 27–44. doi:10.1111/j.1745-6606.2001.tb00101.x

Morris, M. G., & Venkatesh, V. (2000). Age differences in technology adoption decisions: Implications for a changing workforce. *Personnel Psychology*, *53*(2), 375–403. doi:10.1111/j.1744-6570.2000.tb00206.x

Nadkarni, S., & Gupta, R. (2007). A Task-Based Model of Perceived Website Complexity. *Management Information Systems Quarterly*, *31*(3), 501–524.

Pavlou, P. A. (2003). Consumer acceptance of electronic commerce: Integrating trust and risk with the technology acceptance model. *International Journal of Electronic Commerce*, *7*(3), 101–134.

Pavlou, P. A., & Chellappa, R. K. (2001). The role of perceived privacy and perceived security in the development of trust in electronic commerce transaction. Unpublished Working paper.

Pavlou, P. A., & Fygenson, M. (2006). Understanding and predicting electronic commerce adoption: An extension of the theory of planned behavior. *Management Information Systems Quarterly*, *30*(1), 115–143.

Pavlou, P. A., & Gefen, D. (2004). Building effective online marketplaces with institution-based trust. *Information Systems Research*, *15*(1), 37–59. doi:10.1287/isre.1040.0015

Pennington, R., Wilcox, H. D., & Grover, V. (2003). The role of system trust in business-to-consumer transactions. *Journal of Management Information Systems*, *20*(3), 197–226.

Ranganathan, C., & Ganapathy, S. (2002). Key dimensions of business-to-consumer web sites. *Information & Management*, *39*(6), 457–465. doi:10.1016/S0378-7206(01)00112-4

Ruyter, K. D., Moorman, L., & Lemmink, J. (2001). Antecedents of commitment and trust in customer–supplier relationships in high technology markets. *Industrial Marketing Management*, *30*, 271–286. doi:10.1016/S0019-8501(99)00091-7

Salisbury, D. W., Pearson, R. A., Pearson, A. W., & Miller, D. W. (2001). Perceived security and World Wide Web purchase. *Industrial Management & Data Systems*, *101*(3/4), 165–176. doi:10.1108/02635570110390071

Sen, R., King, R. C., & Shaw, M. J. (2006). Buyers' choice of online search strategy and its managerial implications. *Journal of Management Information Systems*, *23*(1), 211–238. doi:10.2753/MIS0742-1222230107

Smith, H. J., Milberg, S. J., & Burke, S. J. (1996). Information privacy: Measuring individuals' concerns about organizational practices. *Management Information Systems Quarterly*, *20*(2), 167–196. doi:10.2307/249477

Stewart, K. J. (2003). Trust transfer on the World Wide Web. *Organization Science*, *14*(1), 5–17. doi:10.1287/orsc.14.1.5.12810

Suh, K. S., & Lee, Y. E. (2005). The effects of virtual reality on consumer learning: An empirical investigation. *Management Information Systems Quarterly*, *29*(4), 673–697.

Tan, T. H., & Thoen, W. (2002). Formal aspects of a generic model of trust for electronic commerce. *Decision Support Systems*, *33*, 233–246. doi:10.1016/S0167-9236(02)00014-3

Thatcher, J. B., & George, J. F. (2004). Commitment, trust, and social involvement: An exploratory study of antecedents to web shopper loyalty. *Journal of Organizational Computing and Electronic Commerce*, *14*(4), 243–268. doi:10.1207/s15327744joce1404_2

van der Heijden, H., Verhagen, T., & Creemers, M. (2003). Understanding online purchase intentions: Contributions from technology and trust perspectives. *European Journal of Information Systems*, *12*, 41–48. doi:10.1057/palgrave.ejis.3000445

Van Slyke, C., Belanger, F., & Comunale, C. L. (2004). Factors influencing the adoption of web-based shopping: the impact of trust. *ACM SIGMIS Database*, *35*(2), 32–49. doi:10.1145/1007965.1007969

Venkatesh, V., Morris, M., Davis, G., & Davis, F. D. (2003). User acceptance of information technology: toward a unified view. *Management Information Systems Quarterly*, *27*(3), 425–478.

Wakefield, R. L., Stocks, M. H., & Wilder, W. M. (2004). The role of web site characteristics in initial trust formation. *Journal of Computer Information Systems*, *45*(1), 94–103.

Wang, T. D., & Emurian, H. H. (2005). An overview of online trust: Concepts, elements, and implications. *Computers in Human Behavior*, *21*, 105–125. doi:10.1016/j.chb.2003.11.008

Yang, Z. L., & Jun, M. J. (2002). Consumer perception of e-service quality: From Internet purchaser and non-purchaser perspectives. *The Journal of Business Strategy*, *19*(1), 19–41.

Zhang, P., von Dran, G. M., Small, R. V., & Barcellos, S. (1999). *Websites that satisfy users: A theoretical framework for Web user interface design and evaluation.* Paper presented at the the 32nd Hawaii International Conference on System Sciences, Maui, HI.

Zhou, L., Dai, L., & Zhang, D. (2007). Online Shopping Acceptance Model - A Critical Survey of Consumer Factors in Online Shopping. *Journal of Electronic Commerce Research*, *8*(1), 41–62.

APPENDIX A: SURVEYS AND MEASURES

Table 6.

Construct	Items
Appearance Features	
Perceived Normality	The steps required at this website to search for products and make orders are typical of other similar type websites.
	The information requested of me at this website is the type of information most similar type websites request.
	The nature of the interaction with this website is typical of other similar type websites.
Perceived Social Presence	There is a sense of human contact in this website.
	There is a sense of personalness in this website.
	There is a sense of sociability in this website.
	There is a sense of human warmth in this website.
	There is a sense of human sensitivity in this website.
Awareness of Third-Party Assurance	The display of the VeriSign icon on Overstock.com makes me feel that this website is trustworthy.
	The display of the BBBOnline icon on Overstock.com makes me feel that this website is trustworthy.
	The display of the Visa, MasterCard, American Express, and DiscoverCard icons on Overstock.com makes me feel that this website is trustworthy.
	The display of the BizRate.com icon on Overstock.com makes me feel that this website is trustworthy.
Functionality Features	
Effort Expectancy ***(Reverse Coded)***	I find this website easy to use.
	It would be easy for me to become skillful at using this website.
	Learning to use this website would be easy to me.
	My interaction with this website is clear and understandable.
Performance Expectancy	I find this website useful.
	Using this website can improve my shopping performance.
	Using this website can enhance my shopping effectiveness.
	Using this website can increase my shopping productivity.
Perceived Security	I feel secure in providing sensitive information (e.g., credit card number) when transacting with Overstock.com.
	I would feel totally safe providing sensitive information about myself to Overstock.com.
	I would feel secure sending sensitive information to Overstock.com.
	Overall, Overstock.com is a safe place to send sensitive information.
Perceived Privacy ***(Reverse Coded)***	I am concerned that Overstock.com is collecting too much information about me.
	It bothers me when Overstock.com asks me for personal information.
	I am concerned about my privacy when browsing Overstock.com.
	I have doubts as to how well my privacy is protected on Overstock.com.
	My personal information could be misused when transacting with Overstock.com.
	My personal information could be accessed by unknown parties when transacting with Overstock.com.
Swift Trust in Online Store	

continued on following page

Table 6. continued

Construct	Items
Appearance Features	
Competence	I believe this online store is effective in assisting and fulfilling my purchases.
	This online store performs its role of e-vendor very well.
	Overall, this online store is a capable and proficient e-vendor.
	In general, this online store is very knowledgeable about the business it operates.
Benevolence	I believe that this online store would act in my best interest.
	If I required help, this online store would do its best to help me.
	This online store is interested in my well-being, not just its own.
Integrity	This online store is truthful in its dealings with me.
	I would characterize this online store as honest.
	This online store would keep its commitments.
	This online store is sincere and genuine.
Purchase Intention	
	Given the need, I intend to transact with Overstock.com.
	Given the chance, I think that I would consider making purchases from Overstock.com.
	I would probably purchase from Overstock.com when I have a need.
	It is likely that I will actually buy products from Overstock.com in the near future.

APPENDIX B: CONFIRMATORY FACTOR ANALYSES: FACTOR LOADINGS & CONVERGENT VALIDITY

Table 7. (a) First-Order Constructs

	Com	Ben	Int
Com1	**0.855**	0.568	0.581
Com2	**0.948**	0.664	0.650
Com3	**0.929**	0.679	0.678
Com4	**0.915**	0.666	0.636
Ben1	0.693	**0.935**	0.755
Ben2	0.664	**0.914**	0.706
Ben3	0.597	**0.914**	0.741
Int1	0.639	0.743	**0.917**
Int2	0.689	0.746	**0.947**
Int3	0.633	0.706	**0.895**
Int4	0.616	0.748	**0.933**

Table 8. (b) Second-Order Constructs

	Intent	Trust	Normality	Social Presence	Aware-ness	Effort Expect.	Perf. Expect.	Security	Privacy
Intent1	**0.936**	0.489	0.336	0.309	0.370	0.298	0.475	0.382	0.080
Intent2	**0.947**	0.565	0.401	0.330	0.439	0.397	0.553	0.397	0.054
Intent3	**0.958**	0.498	0.344	0.353	0.395	0.350	0.556	0.395	0.084
Intent4	**0.885**	0.430	0.175	0.365	0.332	0.214	0.522	0.366	0.020
Com	0.479	**0.886**	0.561	0.267	0.567	0.532	0.480	0.494	0.206
Ben	0.499	**0.925**	0.449	0.405	0.562	0.445	0.505	0.566	0.214
Int	0.480	**0.922**	0.463	0.408	0.607	0.445	0.463	0.568	0.158
WN1	0.307	0.507	**0.946**	0.055	0.356	0.698	0.486	0.281	0.180
WN2	0.347	0.527	**0.938**	0.115	0.440	0.641	0.462	0.343	0.204
WN3	0.308	0.493	**0.955**	0.026	0.335	0.697	0.474	0.271	0.138
SP1	0.368	0.382	0.048	**0.916**	0.344	0.101	0.331	0.332	0.083
SP2	0.334	0.360	0.097	**0.888**	0.368	0.135	0.333	0.321	0.070
SP3	0.319	0.376	0.070	**0.940**	0.330	0.093	0.289	0.350	0.036
SP4	0.331	0.338	0.045	**0.931**	0.306	0.106	0.281	0.305	-0.044
SP5	0.326	0.368	0.064	**0.937**	0.311	0.115	0.324	0.354	0.041
AW1	0.348	0.612	0.410	0.289	**0.893**	0.397	0.354	0.500	0.214
AW2	0.307	0.544	0.289	0.274	**0.886**	0.317	0.364	0.444	0.164
AW3	0.374	0.537	0.393	0.322	**0.848**	0.328	0.311	0.445	0.119
AW4	0.426	0.524	0.301	0.384	**0.875**	0.261	0.342	0.519	0.138
PEOU1	0.334	0.520	0.688	0.128	0.368	**0.950**	0.583	0.273	0.186
PEOU2	0.302	0.474	0.706	0.080	0.361	**0.921**	0.531	0.233	0.123
PEOU3	0.306	0.444	0.619	0.103	0.280	**0.923**	0.512	0.217	0.136
PEOU4	0.333	0.505	0.672	0.133	0.391	**0.953**	0.554	0.300	0.098
PU1	0.482	0.480	0.478	0.271	0.340	0.589	**0.836**	0.330	0.159
PU2	0.548	0.496	0.463	0.299	0.386	0.512	**0.965**	0.315	0.041
PU3	0.538	0.500	0.450	0.337	0.373	0.541	**0.958**	0.317	0.026
PU4	0.526	0.485	0.466	0.343	0.350	0.519	**0.936**	0.332	0.102
Secu1	0.410	0.542	0.315	0.278	0.451	0.235	0.273	**0.897**	0.296
Secu2	0.364	0.511	0.251	0.378	0.493	0.217	0.338	**0.939**	0.300
Secu3	0.389	0.531	0.266	0.341	0.507	0.245	0.314	**0.961**	0.310
Secu4	0.375	0.620	0.335	0.347	0.567	0.312	0.367	**0.924**	0.263
Priv1	0.085	0.153	0.237	-0.057	0.174	0.230	0.098	0.218	**0.829**
Priv2	0.054	0.178	0.190	-0.001	0.179	0.174	0.095	0.273	**0.839**
Priv3	0.051	0.174	0.160	0.041	0.170	0.132	0.058	0.265	**0.878**
Priv4	0.061	0.219	0.174	0.019	0.167	0.133	0.095	0.321	**0.929**
Priv5	0.025	0.187	0.112	0.096	0.154	0.051	0.040	0.280	**0.877**
Priv6	0.062	0.182	0.104	0.107	0.117	0.057	0.068	0.259	**0.855**

Section 2

Chapter 6
An End–User's Journey of System Use:
A Change in Attitudes and Behavior Over a Period

Zahid Hussain
University of Bradford, UK

Khalid Hafeez
The University of York, UK

ABSTRACT

Using a new information system is a journey that end-users follow, sometimes by choice and at other times by obligation. This journey changes their attitudes and behavior as they explore the system and discover its workings. In this chapter we map such a journey using Morgan's (1986, 1997) metaphors by tracking a change in end–user attitudes and behavior. We use a longitudinal case study approach to follow this journey, report the direction and any shifts in end-users' conceptual position. Our results show that within a space of eighteen months the organization's overall metaphorical stance shifted from the organism to the machine metaphor. This reflects the end-user's initial optimism for the change to enable ease of working to that of efficiency dictated by the senior management towards the end. This shift was due to organizational conditional factors, such as the ISD methodology.

1. INTRODUCTION

This chapter describes our use of Morgan's (1986, 1997) metaphors in describing the end-user's journey of system use by tracking a change in their *attitudes* and *behavior* over a period at a UK National Health Service (NHS) hospital. We use a case study approach, within which we elicit the *attitudes* using a questionnaire and infer the *behavior* using observations and interviews. We

DOI: 10.4018/978-1-60960-577-3.ch006

created a research instrument based on the eight metaphors of Morgan and four organizational paradigms of Burrell and Morgan (1979), and draw upon the work of Hirschheim et al. (1995).

We present the results in the form of a journey for the end user, tracking the metaphorical shift for each end-user, over the project duration. We show how individual journeys can be combined to capture organizations' shift in metaphorical position. Our results show that within a space of eighteen months the organization's overall metaphorical stance shifted from the *organism* to the *machine* metaphor. This reflects the end-user's initial optimism for the change to enable ease of working to that of efficiency dictated by the senior management towards the end. We also found that this shift was due to organizational conditional factors, such as the ISD methodology. We believe that such use of metaphors, for making sense of end-user *attitudes* and *behavior,* is rare but very valuable to researchers and practitioners.

Metaphors are useful communication devices in our daily conversations. They are conceptual tools that we use to make sense of the world and interpret meaning (Pepper, 1942; Ortony, 1975; Smith & Simmons, 1983; Oswick & Grant, 1996). Using analogies, metaphors create mental pictures that help to interpret the world, such as viewing the working of an organization as a *machine*. Lakoff & Johnson (1980) and Morgan (1986) believe that by creating certain types of realities within our minds metaphors assist us to contextualize the world in ways that we may not have envisaged before. Morgan (1986) provides eight metaphors for organizations: *machine, organism, brain, culture, political system, psychic prison, flux and transformation*, and *instruments of domination*. A detailed description of these is given in Appendix 1. These metaphors help to make sense of organizational structure, management control, management style and behavior by associating certain meanings to them. On the other hand, these metaphors encapsulate perceptions of individuals by expressing their motives, desires, attitudes, needs and dedication towards the organization.

Orlikowski & Gash (1994) suggest that attitudes, mental frames or cognitive structures have a key effect in shaping the information system development (ISD) related *behavior* of individuals. End-user involvement and satisfaction is crucial for system success (Harris, 2000; Butler & Fitzgerald, 2001; McGill, 2004; Adams, 2004) especially in public sector organizations (Lau & Herbert, 2001; Aladwani, 2002). However, understanding of end-user *attitudes* and *behavior* during their involvement in ISD is a difficult and complex task, as end-users' views can be deep-rooted or hidden (Shaw et al., 2003) while they are still learning about the system and its proposed use (Stein & Vandenbosch, 1996; Wagner, 2000; Tiwana & McLean, 2005). We believe that metaphors can be very useful in dealing with such complexities (Xia & Lee 2005). In the past, metaphors have been used by IS researchers in *making sense* of organizational context. However, most researchers only used one or two metaphors in their study (see for example, Boland & Greenberg, 1992; Heiskanen, 1993; Kling & Iacono, 1984; Mumford & Weir, 1979; Wilson, 1994). However, we concur with Walsham (1991, 1993) and Oates & Fitzgerald (2007) that applying several metaphors would help in making a better sense of the research situation.

Therefore, in this research we use all eight of Morgan's (1986, 1997) metaphors in making sense of the *attitudes* and *behaviors* of end-users, during their involvement in an ISD project, in a UK National Health Service (NHS) hospital. Using our research instrument (Appendix 1) we mapped Morgan's (1986, 1997) eight metaphors onto Burrell & Morgan's (1979) paradigms. This enabled us to link each of these eight metaphors to their philosophical underpinning. We conducted a *gap analysis* between the underlying *attitudes* and *behavior* of several key end-users at the beginning and towards the end of the project. This allowed us to identify a *metaphorical journey,* for each end-user, during the ISD. For the purpose of this research we define *attitudes* as the mental concepts (constructs) or assumptions of end-users. Whereas *behavior* relates to any demonstrable physical actions as well as decision-making observed by us or narrated by the end-users (as a reflective or experiential account of the situation). We explain the choice of particular metaphors for each end-user and track their journey by using graphical representation. We use Walsham's (1993) organizational conditional factors (namely, context, process and content or nature of the system) in explaining the metaphorical choices of end-users, hence their metaphorical journey.

The structure of this paper is as follows: section 2 provides a literature review on the use of metaphors in the IS field. Section 3 provides a brief overview of the case organization. Section 4 describes the research methodology, data collection and analyses. The subsequent sections comprise: research results, discussion, implications for research and practice, and, conclusions.

2. METAPHORS AND INFORMATION SYSTEMS: A LITERATURE REVIEW

Many researchers have used metaphors to understand and explore beliefs and perceptions of organizational stakeholders. For example, Gibson & Zeller-Bruhen (2001) use metaphors to explain organizational teamwork in different contexts. Polley (1997) uses the metaphors of *bifurcation* and *mathematical chaos* to explain organizational dynamics. Sushil (2001) uses ten metaphors to describe managerial flexibility. Morgan (1980) and Bryant (1993) employ metaphors as problem solving devices and for making general sense of organizations. Morgan (1986, 1997), of course, uses eight metaphors as to capture human presuppositions and assumptive structure regarding the nature of organizations.

The popularity of the metaphor is reasoned as a way of conveying meaning in a powerful, imagery-rich manner (Ricoeur, 1978; Sacks, 1978). Within metaphors, thought, emotion, social action space and time are interwoven, making the metaphor a powerful means to capture some or many aspects of multidimensional meaning, and importantly, *meaning making.* Morgan (1986, 1997) stresses the significance of the metaphor, not just as a device for embellishing discourse, but the use of metaphor implies *a way of thinking* and *a way of seeing* that pervades how we understand the world generally (1997:4).

2.1 Metaphors and IS

Metaphors are recognized in the (IS) literature (Walsham, 1991; Kendall & Kendall, 1993; Oates & Fitzgerald, 2007) as mental constructs that express the *minds* and the *behavior* of end-users. Metaphors may relate to the organization's social reality, such as IS goals and the role of stakeholders, or choice and performing of IS activities, etc. Metaphors also come into play when there is a possible conflict of fit between the developers' underlying *attitudes*, against which the system is developed, and the perceptions and *behavior* of end users (see for example, Shaw, et al., 2003; Adams, et al., 2004). Some other examples of metaphor use in IS research are provided in Table 1.

2.2 Organizational Conditional Factors

Walsham (1993) advocates the importance of *interpretivism* and *social behavior* approaches (like metaphors) for evaluating the role of IS and its development in organizations. He emphasizes three conditional factors that could affect *attitudes* and *behavior* of end-users, namely, *content, context* and *process. Content* concerns the problem being addressed, such as the nature of the system in question. *Context* concerns the environment within which something would take place. This may include hindering and enabling factors in the organization (Constantinides & Barrett, 2006)

Table 1. Use of metaphors by information systems researchers

Researchers	Applications
Kling (1978)	Looks at how a *mechanistic* metaphor may be used for understanding computer-based technologies and systems.
Kling & Iacono (1984)	Look at the use of power and social relationships in implementing manufacturing requirements purchasing system. They use a *political system* metaphor to explain key *behavioral* aspects, such as campaigns for building support and quieting opposition to maintain their control over system development.
Madsen (1989)	Uses metaphors in assisting system design by enabling organizational participants to reflect upon and "break down" their work into simpler tasks.
Baskerville (1991)	Uses a model of knowledge acquisition attitudes, based on a continuum consisting of instinctive (non-positivist) to mechanistic (positivist) dimensions, to classify the philosophical assumptions of IS designers from their comments and behavior.
Hirschheim & Newman (1991)	Describe ways of developing systems that may be understood by means of metaphors.
Keys (1991)	Uses metaphors to look at Operational Research and its role in organizations.
Boland & Greenberg (1992)	Employ *machine* and *organism* metaphors to show how they can influence an IS design.
Couger *et al.* (1993)	Illustrates how metaphors may assist IS designers to be more creative in problem-solving.
Kendall & Kendall (1993)	Use metaphors to analyze several well-known ISD methodologies using six metaphors, namely: *journey, war, game, organism, society* and *machine*. They concluded that the IS developers should choose appropriate ISD methodology to suit the metaphors of eventual system users.
Wilson (1994)	Uses the *brain* metaphor to design IS in their research organization.
Kaarst-Brown & Robey (1999)	Use metaphors to reveal assumptions (i.e. how the use of IT may unearth any cultural differences across the organization).
Porra et al. (2005)	Use *mechanistic, organic* and *colonial* metaphors within a General Systems Theory framework to investigate inconsistencies between the deployment of IT resources and the mismatch with organizational operations at Texaco.

like organizational culture (Heracleous, 2001). Whereas, *process* concerns the logic in which something would happen, such as developing IS. According to Walsham, these conditional factors interact with one another and a combination of these then determine the outcome, for example development and use of IS.

Doherty and King (1998), on the other hand, emphasize the need to understand the influence of technology on the organization and its contextual factors. For instance, the generation of a new power structure in an organization, as a result of the acquired IS, could reveal the impact of IS on organizational factors (Bloomfield and Coombs, 1992; Nadan, 1997; Hussain and Taylor, 2007). In this research we also focus on the role of conditional factors in influencing the *mindsets* and *behavior* of end-users as developers.

2.3 Burrell and Morgan's Paradigms

Burrell and Morgan's (1979) work on organizational paradigms has had an important impact on Morgan's (1980, 1986, 1997) work on metaphors. In this paper, we use both Burrell and Morgan's organizational paradigms and Morgan's metaphorical images, in order to make a better sense of end-user *attitudes* and *behaviors*. We aim to use Burrell and Morgan's organizational paradigms for classifying Morgan's metaphors based on their orientation.

Burrell and Morgan (1979) put forward four organizational paradigms using five sets of assumptions that are prevalent in organization studies. The first of the five assumptions is *ontological*, and concerns the nature of the social world. On one hand the social world is considered external to the individual: 'reality' is objective (realism). On the other hand, the social world is considered to be the product of individual consciousness: 'reality' is subjective (nominalism). The second assumption is *epistemological*, which concerns the grounds of knowledge. At one end, knowledge is real and tangible: it can be communicated explicitly (positivism). At the other end, knowledge is soft, subjective, and spiritual: it can only be experienced (anti-positivism). The third is *human nature* and associated human relationships within the social environment. At one extreme, human beings are viewed as being conditioned by their environment (determinism). At the other extreme, human beings are viewed as the creators of their environment as they possess free will (voluntarism). The fourth assumption concerns the *method* used to investigate and obtain knowledge of the social world. At one extreme, method views the social world as external consisting of objective reality (nomothetic). At the other extreme, method views the social world as created by the subjective experience of individuals (ideographic). The fifth assumption concerns the nature of society and the degree of *regulation*: whether or not the social world is stable, cohesive and integrated with underlying unity.

These assumptions underpin four organizational paradigms*: interpretivism, functionalism, radical humanism* and *radical structuralism*, which provide the foundation for sixteen original metaphors by Morgan (1980), and now the ubiquitous 'images of organization' (Morgan, 1986, 1997) containing eight metaphorical images that provide an important springboard for the use of metaphors in organizational research, looking at IS.

3. CASE ORGANIZATION

Our research organization, referred to as Newtown hospital, is a UK National Health Service (NHS) hospital. The NHS is one of the largest employers in Europe, with over 1.3 million staff. Over the last ten years, the NHS has undergone rapid changes to meet the requirements of a variety of stakeholders (e.g. government, legal, professional, and consumer). IS has been identified as a key agent for achieving radical change. Newtown hospital is located in a major northern city in the UK comprising around 5,000 staff, including full time professionals and part-time contract staff. The hospital experienced a series of organizational changes over the years, dictated by NHS reforms. As with other NHS trust hospitals IS is considered either a key driver or a key agent for these changes. For example, within the pharmacy department the system would change its processes. The pharmacy department investigated comprised 36 full time staff. The project was to replace an outdated system with a new system. We recruited nine end-users for our case study, seven of whom were the primary end-users and two were secondary or technical end-users (the IT Manager and the Project Manager).

3.1 Project Context

The project concerned the development of a new information system for the pharmacy department (the pharmacy) of the organization. This was to replace an old outdated system, which was incapable of dealing with the current service standard and the volume of work. The old system was bought in 1985 from another hospital and was already out-of-date at the time of purchase. Furthermore, due to the growth in the number of patients, the pharmacy had recruited more staff over the years. The transaction traffic on this non-upgradeable system had increased dramatically, resulting in regular system shutdowns or at best a very slow system response. The Pharmacy Management, under stress due to lack of workspace, storage space, a high amount of wastage and the slow response of IS, expressed their concern to the Strategic Management. The Pharmacy Management were asked to present a business case highlighting general improvements to be met by the new IS. Eventually, the Strategic Management approved the business case, and the pharmacy was granted permission to raise a tender document for the new information system.

The project began as a replacement for an old pharmacy system, however, it resulted in the initiation of wider changes to the pharmacy. The project involved (1) implementation of new pharmacy system, (2) a general change in the pharmacy set-up/layout and (3) a change in its current work procedures and routines. Firstly, the new system had to perform all the tasks performed by the old system, such as printing labels, stock keeping and producing basic financial statements. However, all new systems available in the market offered much more advanced functions, hence the Pharmacy Management decided to rethink the processes and reconsider their initial requirements. Embracing the extra functionality offered by the new system would involve a change in the current methods of dispensing, stock control, ordering, generating reports and financial statements and other tasks. It would, therefore, affect how staff (especially the administration staff) performed their daily duties. The Pharmacy Management therefore concluded that the new IS would form the backbone of a new administration system by supporting the daily tasks of all subsections of the pharmacy.

Secondly, acquiring the new IS would result in changing the pharmacy layout. For example, the new system would cut down the stock levels by automating and ordering nearer the time. It required placing computer terminals at different locations of the pharmacy to accommodate the speedier processing of customer prescriptions. The way a prescription was received and the way the related hospital ward was to be notified had to be changed. This required placing terminals in each of the ward. Such change affected staff working practices, whereby some staff members were affected more than others.

Thirdly, due to added functionality of the new system, this led to different kinds of resource and other management controls. The management could now access to up-to-the-minute information on staffing, stock levels, consultants, patients and even orders placed with particular supplier. The new system also affected the pharmacist role in checking the prescription, selecting different ingredients in drug preparation, and checking the prescription against the patient's profile for accurate dispensing. In all, the entire project had much wider implications than originally planned. In many respects, the new IS system led to re-engineering working practices.

As part of our research, we gained access to a number of policy and administrative documentation associated with this project, such as, IS procurement policy, IS strategy, IT architecture, health and safety, etc. We found that all stakeholders (including end-users) had to conform to appropriate NHS and Newtown standards and procedures. A list of the key stakeholders (including end-users) involved with the project together with a summary of their underlying aims in relation to the new system are provided in Table 2.

The decision to purchase a new system was largely the responsibility of the Chief Pharmacist and the Pharmacy Manager. They were the authors of IS requirements for the new system. The final IS requirements were gathered from three main sources: (1) looking at the old system and its use in the pharmacy, (2) visits to local hospitals, and (3) vendor suggestions. Initially, they only sought a simple system that would allow them to print labels, manage stock, allow order production and print certain types of financial and management reports. After tendering the functional need, they found that the systems in the market offered much more than they expected. Therefore they were encouraged to reconsider the functional requirements. They then followed the prescription handling process from start to end. The IS was to be used for prescription handling, stock control, order management, financial control, drug manufacturing, prescription checking, referring to the drugs dictionary and referencing, etc. As far as the usability is concerned the old IS had no

Table 2. Aims of the key stakeholders at Newtown

Key Stakeholders (end-users)	Aims/assumptions
Strategic Management *(Managing Director, Medical Director, Executive Director of Nursing, Executive Director Finance and Business Planning, Executive Director Personnel, Director of Estates, Director of Management Contracts, Director of Contracts and Information)*	Initially, to expedite this project over other pending projects. Get the most cost effective solution to replace the existing system. Help the pharmacy department to save costs in the long run. Monitor the quality of prescriptions and costs incurred through carelessness of medical staff.
Pharmacy Management *(primary end-users)* *(Chief Pharmacist and Pharmacy Manager)*	Replace the existing pharmacy system to minimize system downtimes and resulting disruptions. Save costs in the long run through IS. Monitor the workforce more closely. Monitor the quality of prescriptions. 'Prepare' special drugs more quickly with the help of IS.
Pharmacy Workers *(primary end-users)* *(Pharmacists, Pharmacy Technicians, Pharmacy Assistants, Administration Staff, Ward Workers involved in ordering drugs)*	Avoid system downtime problems and switching back to the manual system. Use the system if it is easy to use, and if sufficient training is provided. Not to appear as hindering the objectives of the Pharmacy Management.
IT Management *(secondary end-users)* *(IT Manager, Contracts Manager)*	Acquire a system that links well with the main organizational systems. Provide a minimum input into the project. Dedicate minimum resources to the pharmacy processes. Provide basic help in maintaining the new system.
External Stakeholders *(Project Manager (secondary end-user), Vendors, Local Organizations, Researchers, NHS Executive (Headquarters))*	Project manage to ensure success by setting milestones. Document requirements systematically using POISE methodology. Draw up a purchase contract between the organization and the vendor.
Customers *(Internal and external)*	Quicker service and processing of prescriptions. Better quality service and more accurate dispensing. Better checks on those involved in prescribing and processing a prescription.

graphical outputs. It was therefore acknowledged that most of the end-users would like the new graphical features. However, they were cautious about having a technically advanced system with an abundance of new functionalities – as most of these end-users were IT illiterate.

The Chief Pharmacist and the Pharmacy Manager initially specified the IS requirements in a narrative form, which were then re-written by the Project Manager, with their assistance, using the POISE (Procurement of Information Systems Effectively) format. POISE is a structured systems development methodology in which requirements are rationally constructed and formally written so that the customers and their vendor can check through this specification and tick off the elements that they could fulfill. POISE is sequential in nature and requires a step by step completion of tasks. It requires high volumes of documentation to be kept with justification for future clarity, thus it takes longer to develop IS and also costs more. With this project, POISE was divided into two parts – schedules A and B. Schedule A was used as an initial discussion document between the hospital and the vendor supplying the system. Once the requirements were finalized, schedule B was produced detailing other refined requirements.

4. RESEARCH METHODOLOGY

We employ a *longitudinal case study* approach that is interpretivist in nature in order to obtain knowledge of the participants' social constructs (Constantinides & Barrett, 2006). According to Walsham (1993): *"An interpretive perspective seeks to understand social contexts and how this relates to the reasons why an actor takes a particular course of action"*. Orlikowski & Baroudi (1991:15) also suggest: *"The* [interpretive] *empirical work is based on the assumptions that people create and associate their own subjective and inter-subjective meanings as they interact with the world around them"*. Therefore, an interpretivist case study approach is commonly used by IS researchers in obtaining deeper insights. For example, Wagner & Newell (2006:44) used the longitudinal case study approach along with conceptual ideas of Fuller (1978) to look at controversial episodes during the implementation of IT (Enterprise Resource Planning system (ERP)) in an organization. Wagner & Newell's (2006) experience of using this research approach suggests that: *"... narrative data are helpful when exploring controversies because individual stories of negotiation speak on behalf of a network of interests and highlight conflicting agendas at work. So when analyzing the visionary narratives of a powerful stakeholder, one would interpret his or her words as representing a particular ontological network"*. Harley et al. (2006) employed case study approach to look at *attitudes* and reactions of management during technology (ERP) led organizational change in two research organizations.

So we chose the case study approach to focus on organizational conditional factors and evaluate the impact of these on the *attitudes* and *behavior* of end-users, as project stakeholders over longitudinal period. We use Morgan's (1997) metaphors as sensitizing devices and theory generation tools (Eisenhardt, 1989).

4.1. Research Framework

In this case study we employ two key data collection approaches, the first involving *operationalisation* of Morgan's metaphors to investigate end-users' *attitudes*. The second involving *application of* Morgan's metaphorical definitions to the research situation in order to make sense of end-users' *behavior*. Subsequently, the results of both applications are compared to determine whether or not the metaphorical *assumptions* held by end-users influence their *behavior*. We recognize that given the highly subjective nature of metaphors, they can be misinterpreted. In our view this is why Morgan (1980) himself related his metaphors to the organizational paradigms of Burrell & Morgan (1979). So for this research we mapped Morgan's (1986, 1997) metaphors to paradigms to help us devise an effective tool for data generation and analyses. We map Morgan's (1986, 1997) metaphors against Burrell & Morgan's (1979) paradigms by matching the individual characteristics of each metaphor with paradigms (see Appendix 1). Figure 1 shows an account of this mapping based on our understanding. This allows us to illustrate and map particular ontological and epistemological positions of Morgan's metaphors. For example, we place the - *machine* (M), *psychic prison* (Ps) and *brain* (B) metaphors in the *Functionalism* quadrant of Burrell & Morgan. We also take into account the relative strength of *Objective-Subjective* and *Order-Conflict* aspects in positioning them in their respective quadrant. Similarly, the *culture* (C) metaphor is placed in the *Interpretivism* quadrant, the *instrument of domination* (IofD) in the *Radical Structuralism* quadrant, and the - *flux and transformation* (F+T), *organism* (O) and *political system* (Po) metaphors are placed in the *Radical Humanism* quadrant. We aim to generate data concerning end-users' *attitudes* and *behavior* and represent it on this metaphor map, as explained in the subsequent subsections.

4.1.1. Elicitation of Metaphorical Attitudes of End-Users

A questionnaire was developed to ascertain metaphorical *attitudes* held by end-users (Boland & Greenberg, 1992). It contained five questions based on ontological, epistemological, human nature (subjective-objective dimension), change and conflict (order-conflict dimension) assumptions (see Appendix 2) of Burrell & Morgan (1979).

Figure 1. Mapping Morgan's (1997) metaphors onto Burrell & Morgan's (1979) paradigms

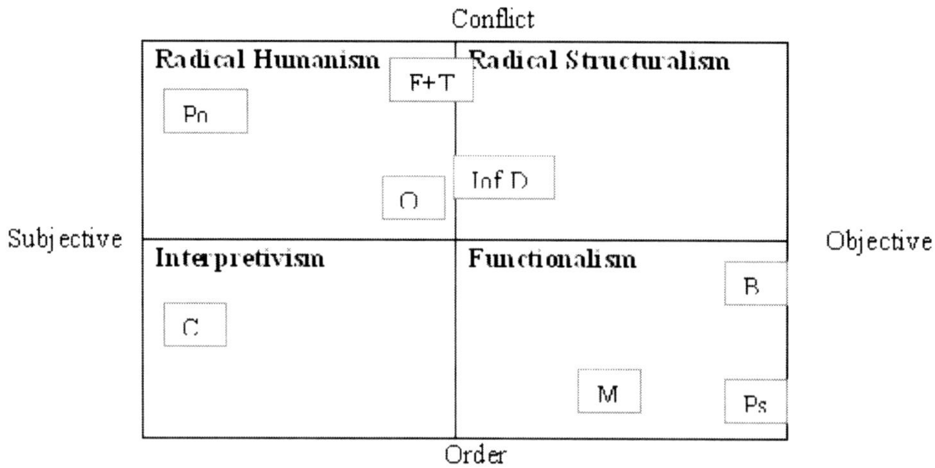

Key: M - *Machine*, O - *Organism*, B - *Brain*, C - *Culture*, Po - *Political system*, Ps - *Psychic prison*, F+T - *Flux and transformation*, IofD - *Instrument of domination*

We prepared a *reference answer* as a response for each metaphor in each of the five questions. Each response was to represent an end-user's viewpoint and experience of their involvement in the project, encapsulating the "real" world situation. Each end-user was interviewed individually by, first explaining the purpose of our research, followed by a discussion about their association and experiences with the organization, and challenges in their present job role. Subsequently, the specific role of the IS in their work was discussed. Each respondent filled-in the research questionnaire, and where required, sought clarifications. This *operationalisation* exercise was conducted twice, first at the *requirement construction stage* and subsequently the *system implementation stage*. This time duration helped us to investigate the change in end-user *attitude*. In order to get an unbiased response (and cooperation), each end-user was informed about the confidentiality, anonymity, academic value, and non-management involvement in this piece of research.

4.1.2. Elicitation of Metaphorical Behavior of End-Users

We employed a range of methods in looking at end-user *behavior*. As Table 3 shows observations of end-users' *behavior* and inferences of actions were made throughout the research period by attending project-related in/formal meetings, discussions, seminars and other events. We also used interviews and previous minutes of project meetings and other related documents. This use of multiple methods allowed for *triangulation*, where we could compare, for example, documented evidence against observed actions. Although, we gave higher importance to data generated through interviews and meetings; as these contained the explicit use of metaphorical discourse by individual end-users.

We conducted 55 interviews over a period of eighteen months. In these interviews we posed different scenarios to illustrate various aspects of ISD-related activities (Hirschheim et al., 1995) with end-users. We followed the thread of conversations by asking further explanations to unfold relevant actions, issues and viewpoints. This use

Table 3. Data collection for measuring metaphorical behavior

Data Source	Method	Description
Formal project meetings	Observation	Project related meetings attended by developers and one researcher attending as an observer.
Pre-arranged interviews	Unstructured questioning	Attended by individual developers and the researcher.
Informal meetings, events and scenarios	Observation, unstructured questioning	Spontaneous meetings attended by one or more developers and the researcher.
Documents	Content analysis	Project documents, minutes and meetings.

of a range of *behavior* elicitation methods enabled us to develop rich insights. Subsequently, we analyzed *words* and *phrases* to elicit the *metaphors* according to a data codification scheme, as explained in the subsequent section.

To assist us in matching appropriate metaphors to end-user *behavior*, we used metaphorical definitions created from Morgan (1986, 1997) and took into account Burrell and Morgan's (1979) paradigms. Because the latter have influenced Morgan's (1980, 1986, 1997) work. For example, Morgan (1980) locates his *machine* metaphor within Burrell and Morgan's (1979) *functionalist* paradigm, which also fits into the functionalist paradigm of Hirschheim, et al. (1995). We illustrate the metaphorical *behavior* using four ISD-related activities of Hirschheim, et al. (1995), namely, the role of IS designer, objectives for design and use of IS, control of users, and organizational implementation.

4.2 Data Codification

Data codification in interpretive research usually serves to classify the acquired responses under different categories (Harley et al., 2006). In this research, a comprehensive data classification regime was followed. The data, collected using observations (of meetings, seminars, events and discussion) and questionnaires (end-user profiles, records and project evaluation documents), were codified and mapped against Morgan's description of metaphors. A key criterion for this classification was to make sense of the ISD-related activities using metaphors. Where the data collection was carried out by a single researcher, the data was checked and classified with help of another researcher. Here the researchers ascribed theoretical meanings to *attitudes* and *behavior*. Sometimes an end-user response conformed to more than one metaphor. In such a scenario we rechecked the meaning against the text of Morgan (1986, 1997) and even Burrell & Morgan (1979) while using Morgan's (1980) previous work as a guide. At times we also arranged further meetings to clarify and confirm any aspect of *behavior* that we found ambiguous in order to provide a 'best approximation to truth'.

For example, Golden-Biddle & Locke (1993) suggest that research validity is the 'best approximation to truth' and helps to make sure that data is reliable and the findings are valid (Bryman, 2001). Klein & Myers (1999) propose a number of principles for evaluating interpretive field research, especially case studies. These include contextualization, interaction between the researchers and the subjects, abstraction and generalization, dialogical reasoning, multiple interpretations and suspicion. These were applied for validating our case study research. Furthermore, we carried out research validity checks on 33% of the research subjects to ensure data quality.

5. RESEARCH RESULTS

5.1. Metaphorical *Attitudes* of End-Users

The metaphorical *attitudes* of end-users, elicited at the *requirement construction stage* and at the project *implementation stage* of ISD are provided,

Table 4. Metaphorical attitudes in the case organization: the requirements stage

End-users	Q 1 Ontology	Q 2 Epistemology	Q 3 Order	Q 4 Conflict	Q 5 Determinism	Predominant Metaphor
A: Pharmacy Manager (MD)	O/F	Po	O	Po	O	O
B: Ordering Clerk (AM)	B	M	O	O	B	O/B
C: Clerical Officer (JH)	B	IofD	O	O	O	O
D: IT Manager (KT)	O	IofD	B	B	B	B
E: Project Manager (PM)	M	B	O	C	O	O
F: Chief Pharmacist (DM)	O/Po	C	F	O	O	O
G: Pharmacy Technician (DJ)	M	M	F	IofD	B	M
H: Pharmacist (SM)	B	M	F	Po	B	B
I: Assistant Administration Officer (CR)	O	B	C	O	B	O
					Overall	**O**

Key: M - *Machine*, O - *Organism*, B - *Brain*, C - *Culture*, Po - *Political system*, Ps - *Psychic prison*, F+T - *Flux and transformation*, IofD - *Instrument of domination*

respectively, in Tables 4 and 5. Table 4 shows predominance of the *organism* metaphor followed by the *brain* metaphor at the *requirement construction stage*. Table 5 shows the predominance of the *machine* metaphor followed by the *brain* metaphor at the *implementation stage*. The 'predominant metaphor' for each respondent (see Tables 4 & 5) was determined after looking at the metaphorical choices made by each respondent for Q1 to Q5 (see Appendix 1) and counting across horizontally. The predominance of the 'overall' organizational metaphor was determined by counting the predominant metaphors of end-users (see Tables 4 & 5).

The pharmacy had a long history of over three decades, in the hospital environment. During this period the number of staff increased dramatically. The choice of the *organism* metaphor by end-users represents a genuine belief that the need for a new system had evolved naturally, since the old system had become outdated and inefficient. So a point was reached where a change was deemed essential to sustain the pharmacy. The *brain* metaphor was the second most dominant choice at the requirements stage, where a high degree of control and co-ordination was seen as important, for example, the Pharmacy Management observed the pharmacy operations, visited other hospital pharmacies, and took advice from the software vendors.

During the second operationalisation (at the IS implementation stage) the predominant metaphor changed. The initial 'optimism' of the *organism* metaphor that the required changes would evolve naturally without any specific interventions had to give way to the *machine* and the *brain* metaphors. This can be linked to the added functionality aimed at yielding greater value. The new system would serve as a technical backbone to support the pharmacy processes and raise efficiency. The system was also intended to provide information to help management plan and co-ordinate their activities and automate management tasks, such as reporting and checking the accuracy of prescriptions. For example, with the new system the intervention of a pharmacist is required only if a mistake is identified in the prescription.

Finally, the concept of a 'predominant' metaphor is useful in understanding the ways in which end-users perceive organizational situations, the social context within which IS is developed (Couger et al., 1993). The predominant metaphors

Table 5. Metaphorical attitudes in the case organization: the implementation stage

End-users	Q 1 Ontology	Q 2 Epistemology	Q 3 Order	Q 4 Conflict	Q 5 Determinism	Predominant metaphor
A: Pharmacy Manager (MD)	Ps	M	F	M	M	M
B: Ordering Clerk (AM)	M	M	B	B	M	M
C: Clerical Officer (JH)	M	M	B	O	O	M/O
D: IT Manager (KT)	M	M	F	B	O	M
E: Project Manager (PM)	B	B	M	M	F	B/M
F: Chief Pharmacist (DM)	M	C	F	F	F	F
G: Pharmacy Technician (DJ)	M	B	B	O	B	B
H: Pharmacist (SM)	M	Po	F	Po	Po	Po
I: Assistant Administration Officer (CR)	X	X	X	X	X	X
					Overall	M

Key: M - *Machine*, O - *Organism*, B - *Brain*, C - *Culture*, Po - *Political system*, Ps - *Psychic prison*, F+T - *Flux and transformation*, IofD - *Instrument of domination; X - Not involved or absent*

may bear close relationships to value systems as advocated by Jayaratna (1996), and may explain why end-users view a particular situation problematic.

5.1.1. Metaphorical Change Overtime

As mentioned earlier, we used Burrell and Morgan's paradigms for mapping out metaphorical journeys of different end-users. Figure 2 (A-H) illustrates the metaphorical journeys of the eight end-users involved in the IS project over eighteen months (starting at the *requirement construction stage* and finishing at the *project implementation stage*). One exception is the Assistant Administration Officer (CR) who left the organization before the project *implementation stage*. Relevant data for each end-user is also provided in Figure 2. The *tail* (or the start point) of the arrow indicates the *predominant metaphorical* position of an end-user at the start (*the requirement construction stage*) of the project. The *head* of the arrow indicates the *predominant metaphorical* position of the end-user at the end (*project implementation* stage). The shape of the arrow line indicates the strength (or influence) of other metaphors during this start-to-end metaphorical journey. The overall direction of the journey is determined after taking into account the metaphorical choices made during both operationalisations.

Due to space limitations, we only describe the journey of a few end-users in more detail. For example, Figure 2(A) provides the metaphorical journey undertaken by the Pharmacy Manager (MD). As indicated in Table 4, at the start of the project, the Pharmacy Manager had a bias towards the *organism* metaphor as he believed that (at least) the functioning of the pharmacy was made up of social beliefs (see Q1) and the change was necessary to meet the changing needs of the pharmacy and its aging technology (see Q3). He was under the impression that he had maneuverability with regards to decision-making for ensuring smooth operations. However, he was conscious of the political needs (the *Political systems* metaphor (Po)) for the pharmacy to collaborate and communicate with other parts of the hospital to operate effectively (see Q2). For him 'conflict' with other parts of the organization was positive and healthy for improving the working of the system as shown in the top left hand quadrant of the Burrell and Morgan paradigm (Figure 2-A).

Figure 2. Individual journey maps

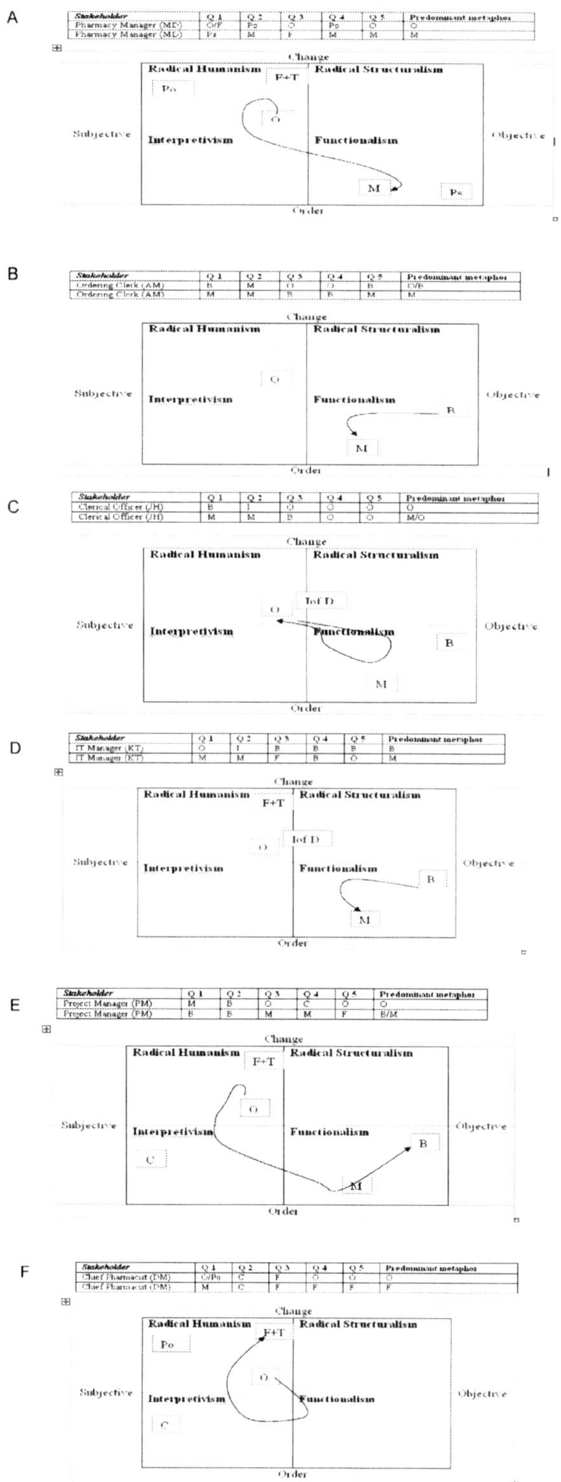

As an illustration, the relative shape and direction of the arrow from different metaphors in the quadrants gives a rough measure of the respective metaphorical influences on his metaphorical journey.

As shown, at the *implementation stage*, the Pharmacy Manager's *behavior* conforms to the *machine* metaphor (Figure 2-A, bottom-right quadrant). This was due to him having to follow the set rules, procedures and processes aimed at yielding maximum efficiency and cost savings (see Q2 in Table 5). However, this experience reinforced his beliefs further that change is highly desirable (especially at the top level) to achieve greater organizational effectiveness (see Q3 in Table 5). He soon realized that the top management do not encourage conflict, for example, considering an alternative plan for a situation (see Q4) by the junior staff. Also it became evident that with regards to IT implementation he and other pharmacy staff had to sacrifice the freedom they had enjoyed for many years and in future they would have little choice to determine their own ways of working (Q5). Thus he felt that Newtown at times was like a *psychic prison* (Ps) with little room to maneuver in the lower right hand quadrant in Figure 2-A).

Similarly the metaphorical journey for the other end-users can be explained. For example, Figure 2(C) shows that the Clerical Officer's (JH) predominant starting metaphor was *organism.* Her final destination was also the *organism* (O) metaphor. Although, her metaphorical journey draws upon the influences of other metaphors during the different phases of the project. For example, JH's second most influencing metaphor was *machine* (M); however, the *brain* metaphor had some influence on her choice. Whereas, Figure 2-G indicates the *attitudes* of the Pharmacy Technician (DJ) selecting the *machine* metaphor as predominant at the *requirements stage*, and ultimately choosing the *brain* (B) metaphor at the *implementation stage*. Also during this transition he was somewhat exposed to the - *instrument of domination* (IofD), *organism* (O), and *flux and transformation* (F+T) metaphors. Therefore, the journey loop (arrow skewed upward towards IofD) illustrates these influences.

The metaphorical journey for the Chief Pharmacist (DM), shifted from the *organism* (O) to the *flux and transformation* metaphor, while there was also an influence of the *machine* (M) metaphor. However, the metaphorical journey of the Pharmacist (Figure 2-H) shows more dramatic shift, from the *brain* (b) metaphor inspired by logic and order, to that of the *political system* (Po) metaphor. One explanation for this may be that the Pharmacist felt the biggest impact from this system being a regular user. Before the automation, she was the most active member of the pharmacy in decision-making for prescriptions, and related affairs. A loss of control over the situation, and perhaps more importantly, profound change to her work practices where she was no longer needed to make routine decisions, made her role less important in the organization, or at least to her. In this context, she felt that political maneuvering was necessary to remind others of her worthiness.

5.1.2. Overall Metaphorical Journey

The individual journeys (provided in Figure 2A-H) were subsequently combined to determine the overall change in metaphorical position (Figure 3). Figure 3, shows that the journey started at the *organism* (O) metaphor and ended at the *machine* (M) metaphor, while being influenced by other metaphors, for example, the *flux and transformation* (F+T) and the *instrument of domination* (IofD), with relatively marginal sensitivity to the *culture* (C) and the *political system* (Ps) metaphors. In fact the predominant metaphor column of Tables 4 and 5 explains how the individual metaphors shaped the metaphoric stance for the whole organization. This shift occurred over a period of 18 months and was influenced by various organizational conditional factors (to be explained shortly).

5.2. Metaphorical *Behavior* of End-Users

5.2.1. Role of IS Designer

There were three senior end-users involved in the pharmacy project: the Chief Pharmacist (DM), the Pharmacy Manager (MD) and the Project

Figure 3. Overall metaphorical journey for the Newtown case organization

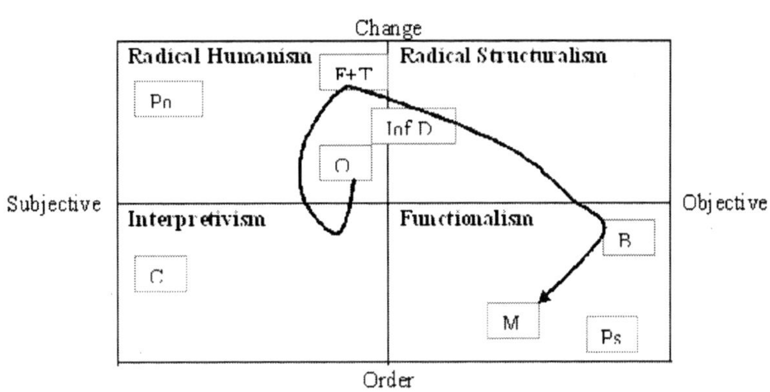

Key: M - *Machine*, O - *Organism*, B - *Brain*, C - *Culture*, Po - *Political system*, Ps - *Psychic prison*, F+T - *Flux and transformation*, IofD - *Instrument of domination*

Manager (PM) as an external consultant. At the beginning of the project, the *behavior* of these end-users conformed to the *organism* metaphor, as the development of this system required a lot of mental and practical changes and planning involving vertical and horizontal communications. The need for communication and meticulous planning became essential when it was realized that the purpose of the project had changed a little, as it was now not only going to replace the old information system, but to substitute it with a much more sophisticated system that would automate a large part of the pharmacy. As the Pharmacy Manager (MD) indicated: *"Although the process of acquiring the system seems simple and straightforward, it was complex and difficult; for example, it involved selling the idea to workers and management* [the Strategic Management], *and then planning the pharmacy change while taking into account a large number of internal and external factors"*. In fact the adoption of the new system resulted in a number of changes to the pharmacy processes and workings of its staff.

At the end of the project, the *behavior* of most end-users conformed to the *machine* metaphor. As a considerable amount of attention was paid to streamling the work processes in order to facilitate integration between the pharmacy processes to yield efficiency. Also, the end-users were concerned with the system functionality to be able to run the pharmacy once the old system ceased working. This involved following the prescription handling process from start to finish, in order to analyze, simplify and automate these. This could relate to efficiency driven success measures of the project, as all efforts were made to transfer old data, as quickly and efficiently as possible. As the Chief Pharmacist (DM) said: *"We had little room to discuss anything other than the processes that needed to be computerized; on the other hand, workers lacked the knowledge required to undertake such change"*.

5.2.2. Objectives for the Design and Use of IS

Initially, the *organism* metaphor was applicable at the *requirement construction stage*, as the need to replace the existing pharmacy system had evolved naturally. This was the main justification put forward by the Pharmacy Management for replacing the old system which was inefficient and slow. Most of the end-users that we interviewed, understood the then need for a new system, and agreed with the Pharmacy Management's concerns. Although, as per Newtown's norms, senior management asked the Pharmacy Management to present and justify the business case, which was approved without much deliberation. At the *implementation stage* the objectives for adopting the new system became very much *mechanistic*, as the Pharmacy Management had to quantify the benefits in business terms, by making the main objectives precise and measurable. The final (post implementation) use of the system was mechanistic as well, with emphases placed on quicker processing of prescriptions through computerized routines and mechanistic decision-making. As the Clerical Officer (JH) told us: *"The system has replaced what little thinking we used to do, even the pharmacists seem to do less than they used to"*. The system replaced the most routine decision-making for workers, and streamlined the pharmacy operations to process prescriptions much more quickly.

5.2.3. Control of Users

The *machine* metaphor described the degree of control over lower-level end-users throughout the project. They had little choice but to use this system to keep the pharmacy running. The system gave them very little allowance for decision-making. It reinforced the established organizational hierarchy by acting as a monitoring and control tool for pharmacy operations. One repercussion of this regime was that the senior pharmacy staff became more distanced and had considerably reduced interaction with the junior staff, as the former could make the changes such as resource allocation on-line, without needing any face to face interaction. As the Chief Pharmacist suggested: *"The system is comprehensive and if used more fully it can help us to manage more effectively as well as enabling the pharmacy tasks".*

5.2.4. Organizational Implementation

A systematic implementation was undertaken to verify the output of the new systems with the old system. Once the new system was implemented, a lot of effort was put into conducting data integrity checks. In our view, therefore, the prevalence of the *machine* metaphor is justified as the bulk of the end-users' efforts were focused on checking and aligning the system outputs, while paying little attention to social factors and user training needs. As the Pharmacy Manager remarked at the *post implementation stage*: *"We had to carry out a tremendous amount of checking with help from staff to make sure that the same output was produced by the old and the new systems. We did find lots of problems that were corrected".*

5.3. Comparison of *Attitudes* and *Behavior*

The predominance of the *organism* metaphor at the *requirement construction stage* confirms the end-users' initial *attitudes* and *behavior* representing their views that the change had evolved naturally to overcome IS related problems, as well as other departmental inefficiencies. But as the project progressed, most end-users became skeptical about the way the project was managed, as much attention was focused towards the physical set-up and running of the pharmacy with a particular focus on costs. Hence we found that the *machine* metaphor influenced the *attitudes* and *behavior* of the end-users at the implementation stage because little attention was paid to social aspects. However, at both stages of the project, the second most dominant metaphor was the *brain* metaphor, reflecting the fact that the project was planned while adhering to and communicating appropriate organizational 'norms' and practices.

6. DISCUSSION

In general there was a transition in the *attitude* from the predominant *organism* and *brain* metaphors at the *requirements stage* to the *machine* metaphor at the *implementation stage.* This was matched by a similar transition for *behavior*, as shown in Table 6.

The selection of the *machine* metaphor was due to overwhelming emphasis being placed on making sure that new system worked correctly, while, neglecting the social issues such as the impact of work practice changes on individuals. Consequently, it expressed the fact that the end-users were dissatisfied with the new system, as they were:

- compelled by the Pharmacy Management to use the new system. The end-users were told that the system was needed for the essential operations of the Department and also to make much needed improvements to meet Newtown's overall efficiency drive.

Table 6. Summary of predominant metaphorical attitudes and behavior

	Project Stage	Predominant Metaphor
Attitude	Requirements Stage	1. *Organism*, 2. *Brain*
	Implementation Stage	1. *Machine*, 2. *Brain*
Behavior	Requirements Stage	1. *Organism*, 2..*Brain*, 3. *Machine*
	Implementation Stage	1. *Machine*

- the Pharmacy Management were to use the system as a control device (although this was not an explicit). The Pharmacy Management asked the vendor to provide the 'prescription monitoring functionality' to allow them to monitor their subordinates. Therefore exercise greater management and control.

End-users had to learn new IT skills at their own initiative and deal with usability problems. Furthermore, as the efficiency goals of the new system became evident, it was realized that they needed to recruit a new system manager to exploit the system more fully and to identify how to automate additional pharmacy processes. Subsequently, the Chief Pharmacist advertised the new post. Overall the end-users viewed it as a senior management tool to further their monitoring and control regimes.

One metaphor, albeit apparent to the researchers from *behavior* and observation, but rarely selected by end-users, was the *political system*. The majority of the end-users participated did not select this metaphor as perhaps politics were taken for granted; or they thought that this (despite constant reassurance) might be conveyed to the management or outside world (Walsham, 1993). Another plausible explanation for this could be that there seems to be a negative connotation attached with this word, and being aware of this the individuals' made a cautious effort not to relate to this. This could possibly raise a question concerning the selection (or the lack) of other, similarly 'radical' metaphors, such as the *instrument of domination* metaphor. It would be a challenge to devise appropriate questions to capture the existence of such metaphors, if present.

However, we believe that the key factors affecting end-users' *attitudes* and *behavior* were organizational conditional factors, such as the organizational context, the process and the system or its content. In our view, there were a number of contextual factors affecting the IS project in Newtown, such as its long history (more than five decades), the rigid structure, strong top-down leadership, its narrowly defined IS strategy and a strong culture with many sub-cultures. The key process factors affecting the development of the system were: the standard ISD methodology and procedures, minimum user involvement and drive for efficiency. In addition, the IS nature or content related aspects were: the fluid scope of the system, automation of tasks, and much enhanced monitoring and control. Therefore, we suggest that the course of the end-users' metaphorical journey was influenced by the organization conditional factors. The conditional factors are detailed in

Table 7. Conditional factors and paradigmatic categorization (Source: Walsham 1993)

Conditions	Factors that impact metaphor change
Context (Cx)	Cx1: Organizational history, rituals and stories, culture. (**Interpretivist**) Cx2: Organizational structure. (**Functionalist**) Cx3: Organizational leadership. (**Functionalist**) Cx4: Organizational and IS strategy and organizational policies. (**Functionalist**) Cx5: End-user norms and values. (**Radical structuralist**)
Process (P)	P1: IS methodology followed. (**Functionalist**) P2: IS related policies and procedures. (**Functionalist**) P3: Publicity and user involvement in IS project. (**Functionalist**) P4: Legitimation of IS project for end-user. (**Radical structuralist**)
Content (Co)	Co1: Automation of particular work processes. (**Functionalist**) Co2: Type of systems and its different uses at different levels. (**Functionalist**) Co3: Personal domination or the IT expertise resulting from system use and adoption. (**Radical structuralist**) Co4: Impact of IS on jobs. (**Functionalist**)

Table 7, where each factor is classified using paradigmatic labels used in Figures 1, 2 and 3 for classifying metaphors.

So Table 7 shows that most of the organizational context, process and content factors for our case organization had the *functionalist* orientation. This is where the *machine* and *brain* metaphors are located (as shown in Figure 1). Thus, the predominance of the *machine* and the *brain* metaphors, illustrated in Figure 4.

We believe that the presence of these factors in a particular paradigm could help us to extrapolate the impact of conditional factors on metaphorical journey. As we see, most of the conditional factors for Newtown map onto the *functionalist* paradigm. This could explain why the main organizational emphases were on achieving efficiency and effectiveness, rather than pursuing end-user satisfaction. For example, being a typical NHS hospital this organization was based on clearly defined rules, well regulated policies, procedures and strategies. It was very tightly controlled like a machine. The lines of hierarchy were clearly followed and functional operations were given a priority. The system was developed using a structured methodology that involved creating a business plan, followed by analysis, technical design and implementation. There was limited worker involvement at the initial stages, where the Chief Pharmacist promised them better pharmacy and work related improvements. However, subsequently the system objectives moved towards efficiency orientation aimed at saving time while automating the work processes. Furthermore the system would monitor and even control the work and check worker efficiency. It was used as a device to automate and streamline the processes.

7 IMPLICATIONS FOR RESEARCH AND PRACTICE

7.1 Implications for Research

We noted that one of the key reasons why the end-users changed their metaphorical position over time is due to the organizational conditional factors. Under the circumstances, perhaps, a metaphor in itself does not express a fixed, normative stance, but merely reflects upon end-users' current perceptions of the social situation (Davidson, 2006). So, subsequently, in this context, it would be interesting to track end-users' changing metaphors in a longitudinal study (and perhaps over several projects), asking at different stages, what was their perceived reason for the change in their *attitude* and *behavior*. This may further reveal the underlying dynamics and change associated with metaphor selection over a time period, which we noted in our research.

Figure 4. Mapping context, process and content to paradigms

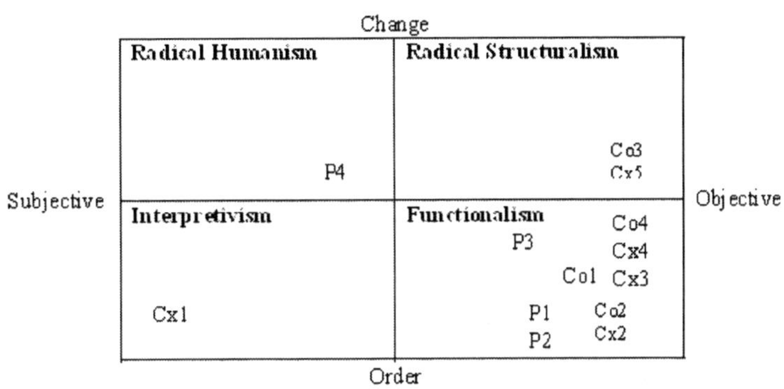

Further research is also required in other voluntary as well as commercial organizations. An investigation as to which metaphors end-users perceive as contradictory, and which they perceive as (partially) overlapping, may lead to refinement of the original set of eight metaphors (McCourt, 1997). This would help to understand how different, and sometimes contradictory, metaphors co-exist within an end-user's mind; and would investigate whether an end-user prioritizes between different metaphors, or whether s/he only prioritizes when s/he perceives contradictions between metaphors.

7.2 Implications for Practice

Our findings have a number of implications for practice. Firstly, those undertaking change would gain a better understanding of organizational context and underlying metaphorical *attitudes* and *behavior* of end-users. They can then plan and strategize how to move from the current situation to a desired position. This would require formulating appropriate interventions and actions; while weighing up the needed measures and resources. Secondly, those in-charge of managing IS led change could use appropriate metaphors in their discourse to explain the need for change; and thereby motivate the end-users by affecting their interpretive schemes (Bartunek, 1984; Scroggins, 2006). Furthermore, the metaphors can serve as devices for communicating the need for change. Therefore metaphors can help to legitimate the need for the change and help to increase end-user's ownership of change, thereby enhancing the chances of success.

8. CONCLUSION

We found that metaphors are powerful tools for making sense of organizations and in revealing complexities. In this research we revealed the *attitudes* and *behavior* of end-users involved in the development of a new pharmacy system. We also reveal the metaphorical journey of end-users where their overall metaphor shifted from the *organism* to the *machine*; while having an influence of the - *flux and transformation, culture, political system* and *brain* metaphors. We believe that this journey was largely affected by organizational conditional factors, which had a strong *functionalist* orientation.

Our use of metaphors, to unearth end-users' *attitudes* and *behavior,* in an explicit manner, is rare but useful. We believe that our systemic approach can serve as a *method* for other researchers and practitioners in making sense of the end-user biases during ISD. It would also better equip them in dealing with organizational conditional factors.

REFERENCES

Adams, B., Berner, E. S., & Rousse, J. (2004). Applying strategies to overcome user resistance in a group of clinical managers to a business software applications: A case study. *Journal of Organizational and End User Computing, 16*(4), 55–64. doi:10.4018/joeuc.2004100104

Aladwani, A. M. (2002). Organizational actions, computer attitudes, and end-user satisfaction in public organizations: An empirical study. *Journal of End User Computing, 14*(1), 42–49. doi:10.4018/joeuc.2002010104

Bartunek, J. M. (1984). Changing interpretive schemes and organizational restructuring: The example of a religious order. *Administrative Science Quarterly, 29*, 355–372. doi:10.2307/2393029

Baskerville, R. (1991). Practitioner autonomy and the bias of methods and tools. In H.E. Nissen., H. K. Klein., & R. Hirschheim (Eds.), *Information systems research: Contemporary approaches and emergent traditions,* Amsterdam: North-Holland, 673-697.

Bloomfield, B. P., & Coombs, R. (1992). Information technology, control and power: The centralization and decentralization debate revisited. *Journal of Management Studies*, *29*(4), 459–484. doi:10.1111/j.1467-6486.1992.tb00674.x

Boland, R. J., & Greenberg, R. H. (1992). Method and metaphor in organizational analysis. *Accounting. Management and Information Technology*, *2*(2), 117–141. doi:10.1016/0959-8022(92)90004-C

Bryant, J. (1993). OR Enactment: The theatrical metaphor as an analytical framework. *The Journal of the Operational Research Society*, *44*(6), 551–561.

Bryman, A. (2001). *Social research methods*. Oxford: Oxford University Press.

Burrell, G., & Morgan, G. (1979). *Sociological paradigms and organizational analysis*. London: Heinemann.

Butler, T., & Fitzgerald, B. (2001). The relationship between user participation and the management of change surrounding the development of information systems: A European perspective. *Journal of End User Computing*, *13*(1), 12–25. doi:10.4018/joeuc.2001010102

Constantinides, P., & Barrett, M. (2006). Large-Scale ICT innovation, power, and organizational change: The case of a regional health information network. *The Journal of Applied Behavioral Science*, *42*(1), 76–90. doi:10.1177/0021886305284291

Couger, J. D., Higgins, L. F., & McIntyre, S. C. (1993). (Un)Structured creativity in information systems organizations. *Management Information Systems Quarterly*, *17*(4), 375–397. doi:10.2307/249584

Davidson, E. (2006). A technological frames perspective on information technology and organizational change. *The Journal of Applied Behavioral Science*, *42*(1), 23–39. doi:10.1177/0021886305285126

Doherty, N. F., & King, M. (1998). The importance of organizational issues in systems development. *Information Technology & People*, *11*(2), 104–123. doi:10.1108/09593849810218300

Eisenhardt, K. M. (1989). Building theories from case study research. *Academy of Management Review*, *14*(4), 532–550. doi:10.2307/258557

Gibson, C. B., & Zellmer-Bruhn, M. E. (2001). Metaphors and meaning: An intercultural analysis of the concept of teamwork. *Administrative Science Quarterly*, *46*(2), 274–303. doi:10.2307/2667088

Golden-Biddle, K., & Locke, K. (1993). Appealing work: An investigation of how ethnographic texts convince. *Organization Science*, *4*, 595–616. doi:10.1287/orsc.4.4.595

Harley, B., Wright, C., Hall, R., & Dery, K. (2006). Management reactions to technological change: The example of enterprise resource planning. *The Journal of Applied Behavioral Science*, *42*(1), 58–75. doi:10.1177/0021886305284857

Harris, R. W. (2000). Schools of thought in research into end-user computing success. *Journal of End User Computing*, *12*(1), 24–34. doi:10.4018/joeuc.2000010103

Heiskanen, A. (1993). Organizational metaphors and information systems practice: a case example of implementation strategy formulation. In Avison, D., Kendall, J. E., & DeGross, J. I. (Eds.), *Human, organizational, and social dimensions of information systems development* (pp. 399–417). Amsterdam: North-Holland.

Heracleous, L. (2001). An ethnographic study of culture in the context of organizational change. *The Journal of Applied Behavioral Science*, *37*(4), 426–446. doi:10.1177/0021886301374003

Hirschheim, R., Klein, H. K., & Lyytinen, K. (1995). *Information systems development and data modeling*. Chichester: Cambridge University Press.

Hirschheim, R., & Newman, M. (1991). Symbolism and information systems development: myth, metaphor and magic. *Information Systems Research*, *2*(1), 29–62. doi:10.1287/isre.2.1.29

Hussain, Z., & Taylor, A. (2007). Evaluating the Behaviour of Information Systems Developers: The relevance and utility of paradigms. *Behaviour & Information Technology*, *26*(3), 221–236. doi:10.1080/01449290600877413

Jayaratna, N. (1996). Choice of a methodology for information systems development! P*roceedings of the Fourth Conference of the British Computer Society Information Systems Methodologies Specialist Group*, 12-14 September. Cork, Ireland, 23-28.

Kaarst-Brown, M. L., & Robey, D. (1999). More on myth, magic and metaphor: Cultural insights into the management of information technology in organizations. *Information Technology & People*, *12*(2), 192–217. doi:10.1108/09593849910267251

Kendall, J. E., & Kendall, K. E. (1993). Metaphors and methodologies: Living beyond the systems machine. *Management Information Systems Quarterly*, *17*(2), 149–168. doi:10.2307/249799

Keys, P. (1991). Operational research in organizations: A metaphorical analysis. *Journal of Res. Soc*, *42*(6), 435–446.

Klein, H. K., & Myers, M. D. (1999). A set of principles for conducting and evaluating interpretive field studies in information systems. *Management Information Systems Quarterly*, *23*(1), 67–93. doi:10.2307/249410

Kling, R. (1978). Automated welfare client-tracking and service integration: the political economy of computing. *Communications of the ACM*, *21*(6), 484–493. doi:10.1145/359511.359528

Kling, R. (1980). Social analyses of computing: Theoretical perspectives in recent empirical research. *ACM Computing Surveys*, *12*(1), 61–110. doi:10.1145/356802.356806

Kling, R., & Iacono, S. (1984). The control of information systems developments after implementation. *Communications of the ACM*, *24*(12), 1218–1226. doi:10.1145/2135.358307

Lakoff, G., & Johnson, M. (1980). *Metaphors we live by*. Chicago: University of Chicago Press.

Lau, F., & Herbert, M. (2001). Experiences from health information system implementation projects reported in Canada between 1991 and 1997. *Journal of End User Computing*, *13*(4), 17–25. doi:10.4018/joeuc.2001100102

Madsen, K. H. (1989). Breakthrough by breakdown: metaphors and structured domains. In H.K. Klein., & K. Kumar (Eds.), *Systems development for human progress*. Amsterdam: North-Holland, 41-53.

McCourt, W. (1997). Discussion note: using metaphors to understand and to change organizations: A critique of Gareth Morgan's approach. *Organization Studies*, *18*(3), 511–522. doi:10.1177/017084069701800307

McGill, T. (2004). The effect of end user development on end user success. *Journal of Organizational and End User Computing*, *16*(1), 41–58. doi:10.4018/joeuc.2004010103

Morgan, G. (1980). Paradigms, metaphors and puzzle solving in organization theory. *Administrative Science Quarterly*, *25*(4), 605–622. doi:10.2307/2392283

Morgan, G. (1986). *Images of organization*. USA: Sage Publications.

Morgan, G. (1997). *Images of organization. New edition*. USA: Sage Publications.

Mumford, E., & Weir, M. (1979). *Computer systems in work design:The ETHICS method*. New York: Wiley.

Nadan, R. K. (1997). *The dialectic of management control: The Case of the Fiji Development Bank*, PhD Thesis. UK: Bristol University, 1997.

Oates, B. J., & Fitzgerald, B. (2007). Multi-metaphor method: organizational metaphors in information systems development. *Information Systems Journal*, *17*(4), 421–449. doi:10.1111/j.1365-2575.2007.00266.x

Orlikowski, W. J., & Baroudi, J. J. (1991). Studying information technology in organizations: research approaches and assumptions. *Information Systems Research*, (2): 1–28. doi:10.1287/isre.2.1.1

Orlikowski, W. J., & Gash, D. C. (1994). Technological frames: Making sense of information technology in organizations. *ACM Transactions on Information Systems*, *12*(2), 174–207. doi:10.1145/196734.196745

Ortony, A. (1975). Why metaphors are necessary and not just nice. *Educational Theory*, *25*, 45–53. doi:10.1111/j.1741-5446.1975.tb00666.x

Oswick, C., & Grant, D. (1996). *Organisation development - metaphorical exploration*. London: Pitman.

Pepper, S. (1942). *World Hypotheses: a study in evidence*. California: University of California Press.

Polley, D. (1997). Turbulence in organizations: New metaphors for organizational research. *Organization Science*, *8*(5), 445–457. doi:10.1287/orsc.8.5.445

Porra, J., Hirschheim, R., & Parks, M. S. (2005). The history of Texaco's corporate information technology function: A general systems theoretical interpretation. *Management Information Systems Quarterly*, *29*, 721–746.

Ricoeur, P. (1978). The metaphorical process as cognition, imagination and feeling. In Sacks, S. (Ed.), *On metaphors*. Chicago: University of Chicago Press.

Sacks, S. (Ed.). (1978). *On metaphors*. Chicago: University of Chicago Press.

Scroggins, W. A. (2006). Managing meaning for strategic change: The role of perception and meaning congruence. *Journal of Health and Human Services Administration*, *29*(1), 83–103.

Shaw, N., & Lee-Partidge, J.-E. (2003). Understanding the hidden dissatisfaction of users towards end-user computing. *Journal of End User Computing*, *15*(2), 1–22. doi:10.4018/joeuc.2003040101

Smith, K. K., & Simmons, V. M. (1983). A rumpelstiltskin organization: Metaphors or metaphors in field research. *Administrative Science Quarterly*, *28*(3), 377–392. doi:10.2307/2392248

Stein, E. W., & Vandenbosch, B. (1996). Organizational learning during advanced systems development: Opportunities. *Journal of Management Information Systems*, *13*(2), 115–136.

Sushil. (2001). Flexibility metaphors. Systems Research and Behavioural Science, 18, 569-575.

Tiwana, A., & McLean, E. R. (2005). Expertise integration and creativity in information systems development. *Journal of Management Information Systems*, *22*(1), 13–44.

Wagner, C. (2000). End user as expert developer? *Journal of End User Computing*, *12*(3), 3–13. doi:10.4018/joeuc.2000070101

Wagner, E. L., & Newell, S. (2006). Repairing ERP: Producing social order to create a working information system. *The Journal of Applied Behavioral Science*, *42*(1), 40–57. doi:10.1177/0021886305284290

Walsham, G. (1991). Organizational metaphors and information systems research. *European Journal of Information Systems*, *1*(2), 83–94. doi:10.1057/ejis.1991.16

Walsham, G. (1993). *Interpreting information systems in organizations*. Chichester: John Wiley & Sons.

Wilson, F. A. (1994). Computer-based systems and organizational structures: designing the ghost in the machine. In R. Baskerville., O. Ngwenyama., S. Smithson., & J.I. DeGross, (Eds.), *Transforming organizations with information technology*. Amsterdam: North-Holland, 343-355.

Xia, W., & Lee, G. (2005). Complexity of information systems development projects: conceptualization and measurement development. *Journal of Management Information Systems*, *22*(1), 45–83.

APPENDIX A

QUESTIONS USED FOR OPERATIONALISATION OF MORGAN'S METAPHORS

Table 8.

Questions	Machine (M)	Organism (O)	Brain (B)	Culture (C)	Political System (Po)	Psychic Prison (Ps)	Flux and Transformation (F+T)	Instrument of Domination (IofD)
Ontology **Q1**: Do you see your organization as having a relatively objective existence or as a collection of beliefs and values of the individuals who control the organization?	Organization is a concrete entity that is organized to yield most value.	Organisation is made up of social beliefs and values.	Organisation is a concrete entity that is systematically organized.	Organization is made up of group beliefs.	Organisation is made up of political beliefs.	Organisation is a concrete entity that traps people within it.	Organisation is seen as changing patterns of belief.	Organisation is a concrete entity that exploits the workers and environment.
Epistemology **Q2:** Do you view the nature of knowledge in your organization as tangible or intangible?	Knowledge is tangible and should only be accessed by those higher up the hierarchy.	Knowledge is intangible and is created and learnt through communication.	Knowledge is tangible and has to be obtained in a systematic way.	Knowledge is intangible and has to be learnt within cultural framework.	Knowledge is intangible and the more knowledge one has the more power will one have.	Knowledge is tangible with limited access.	Knowledge is intangible and is updated regularly to match the environment and increase choice of survival.	Knowledge is tangible and can only be obtained by those higher up the organizational hierarchy.
Order **Q3:** Do you see your organization as one where fundamental changes occur frequently or only rarely?	Change is seen as negative and stability is a basic necessity.	Change is natural and is necessary for stability.	Change is planned by strategic management.	It may be difficult to change organizational culture.	Change is likely due to power shifts.	Change is highly discouraged.	Change is highly valued as it results in greater efficiencies.	Change is allowed for that preserves organizational goals.
Conflict **Q4:** What role does conflict play within your organization?	Conflict is highly undesirable and should be eliminated at every stage.	Conflict is positive because it can encourage groups to improve situations.	Conflict is seen as negative and should be resolved strategically.	Conflict is undesirable but should be managed.	Conflict seen as aspiration for change.	Conflict is highly discouraged.	Conflict is highly desirable as it generates necessary change.	Conflict repressed but there is likely to be high level of implicit conflict.
Determinism **Q5:** How important is it for workers to determine some or all aspects of their work at your organization?	Workers should not have a right to determine their own work.	Allow a great degree of flexibility (often in decentralized organizations)	Workers can not determine their own actions successfully but learning is encouraged.	Some cultures give greater responsibility to workers than others do.	Most political situations do not allow workers to determine their own work.	Workers should not determine their own work.	Usually workers are given a degree of initiative.	The worker should not be allowed to control any aspect of their work.

APPENDIX B

FOUR PARADIGMS OF BURRELL AND MORGAN (1979)

A summary of the paradigms characteristics used to interpret the conditional factors..

Figure 5.

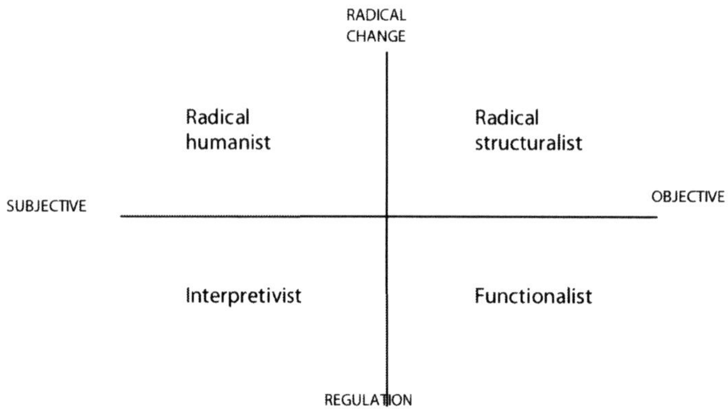

Table 9.

Functionalist	Interpretivist	Radical Structuralist	Radical Humanist
Realist, positivist, determinist, nomothetic. Status quo. Social order. Consensus. Social integration. Solidarity. Need satisfaction e.g. functional needs. Actuality. Structural set-up of society and organizations. Value of scientific enquiry.	Nominalist, anti-positivist, voluntarist, ideographic. Implicit links with sociology of regulation. Status quo. Social order. Social Integration, cohesion and consensus. Solidarity. Actuality. Understand social desires causes and effects. Reality is made up of collective human beliefs and values. Consciousness. Language and communication.	Realist, positivist, determinist, nomothetic. Radical change built into the structure of society and it happens through political and economic crises. Emancipation. Potentiality. Structural relationships. Structural conflict. Mode(s) of domination. Contradiction. Deprivation through objectively determined tools and mechanisms, e.g. machinery.	Nominalist, anti-positivist, voluntarist, ideographic. Continuous change. Mode(s) of domination. Emancipation. Deprivation. Potentiality. Human consciousness (self-consciousness). Need for self-representation. Language and communication.

Chapter 7
End User Authentication (EUA) Model and Password for Security

George S. Oreku
Harbin Institute of Technology, China

Jianzhong Li
Harbin Institute of Technology & Heilongjiang University, China

ABSTRACT

Authentication is one among a set of services that constitute a security subsystem in a modern computing or communications infrastructure. End User Authentication flexibility model proposed in this article will allow the user to have multiple authentications with varying levels of guarantee, and for suppliers to request and rely on mechanisms appropriate to the service requested. We describe the ticket used by clients, servers, model and algorithm to achieve authentication toward prevention of unauthorized access to in sourced data on applications level. An authentication to end-user proposed in this article is a simple three level ticket request model solution in an open distributed environment. We also develop an analytical password for the proposed mechanism and validate this approach through experiment. Furthermore, we explore this approach to end user authentication and demonstrate the conception of a textual password which in many cases improves the security. We analyze Deffie-Hellman exchange weakness and present how it can be made robust against attacks. Our approach is based on the use of the Kerberos authentication technique and the Diffie-Hellman Key exchange.

MOTIVATIONS

The frontline of defense against intruders is the password system. Virtually all multiuser systems require that a user provide not only a name or identifier (ID), but also a password. The password serves to authenticate the ID of the individual logging on to the system. To understand the nature of the threat to password-based systems one should consider a scheme that is widely used on UNIX, in which passwords are never stored in clear text. The problem is that many users choose a password that is too short or too easy to guess. At the other extreme, if users are assigned passwords consisting of eight randomly selected printable characters, password cracking is effectively impossible. Our goal, then, is to eliminate guessable passwords while allowing the user to select a password that is memorable.

If a set of users is provided with dedicated personal computers that have no network connections, then a user's resources and files can be protected by physically securing each personal computer. When these users instead are served by a centralized time-sharing system, the time-sharing operating system must provide the security. Currently these requirements are being overridden in the interests of efficient, standardized commercial arrangements. Thus, a corporate IT infrastructure would want to authenticate that the user of a certain requested online service is authorized for certain services prior to granting privileged sensitive access (perhaps by means of a user password and a smartcard). However the operating system can enforce access control policies based on user identity and use the logon procedure to identify users.

Today neither of these scenarios is typical. More common is a distributed architecture consisting of dedicated user workstations (clients) and distributed or centralized servers. In an unprotected network environment any client can apply to any server for service. The obvious security risk is that of impersonation. An opponent can pretend to be another client and obtain unauthorized privileges on server machines. To counter this threat we would like to minimize the number of times that a user has to enter a password by a sign on password. The second problem is that the earlier scenario involved a plain text transmission of the passwords which may cause an eavesdropper to capture the password and use any service accessible to the victim. To solve this problem we introduce a scheme for avoiding plain text passwords and a new server model.

In our DBMS model key exchange tickets storage for communication authentications, we would only want to grant access to those users whose accounts are (current). For example we would not permit users to access the system using a stolen credit card.

Many systems currently lack the expertise in an increasingly distributed environment (i.e., Internet services) in which it is likely to become harder to provide users with understandable and effective controls over their data use. With that idea in mind, three approaches to security can be envisioned:

1. Rely on each individual client workstation to assure the identity of its user or users and rely on each server to enforce a security policy based on user-based identifications (ID).
2. Require that client systems authenticate themselves to servers, but trust the client systems concerning the identity of their users.
3. Require the user to prove identity for each service invoked. Also require that servers prove their identity to clients.

Raising questions to ecommerce security, this article presents authentication and authorization service model algorithms to an end user by the use of textual passwords and authentication. We extend the use of the last models by Diffie-Hellman, "Key Exchange A Non-Mathematician's Explanation" (Palmgren, 2005) and *Kerberos* authentication model (Steiner, Neuman, & Schiller, 1988) quoting at length to place authentication in proper systems context use.

LITERATURE REVIEWS

Since the introduction of public key cryptography in the 1970's (Deffie & Hellman, 1976), many cryptosystems have been proposed and many cryptographic schemes have been broken. The most used cryptosystems rely on a number of theoretical problems like the factorization problem (Rivest et al, 1978) and the discrete logarithm over suitable group (ElGamal, 1985). For the vast majority of computer systems, authentication for users and passwords are the method of choice for access control security mechanisms. In consumer applications as diverse as financial transactions, remote computer login, building access control, and keyless entry, it is extremely important to prove that a person is who that person claims to be.

Kerberos provides a centralized authentication server whose function is to authenticate users to servers and servers to users (Stallings, 2003). Although this method is used by many systems, it is not very desirable. Each server needs to store the passwords of every potential client. An intruder could then get the list of passwords and break the security of the system. Moreover, every time a new user joins the network, that user's password must be added to all the servers. In addition, after a security breach, all the passwords and password files need to be changed. These shortcomings are remedied by using a third party to store the passwords. Kerberos is such a third-party authentication system.

Using Kerberos, when Alice wants to communicate with Bob, she gets a "ticket" valid for the session with Bob. Before getting tickets Alice registers with Kerberos by providing her password. This registration is valid for as long as Alice remains logged on.

Passwords continue to be the most prevalent form of user authentication (Steiner et al., 1988; Yl¨onen, 1996), but recent years have seen an increasing number of phishing attempts (see the RSA Buys Consumer Authentication Specialist Website EWeek.com; Computer World Website www.computerworld.com; McMillan, 2005). Conventional wisdom suggests that server-side authentication will solve the problem, for example by using the single sign on password. One issue with this solution is the fact that users rarely check certificates or heed warnings, so a phisher may easily capture passwords with a false SSL-based Website. RSA Laboratories has suggested a technique to mitigate this risk with a strategy of altering the password before sending it to the Website. For example, the password may be hashed with an SSL public key or with the destination URL (Kocher, 1996; Yee & Sitaker 2006) Digital Rights Management (DRM) privacy requirements also imply the need for additional controls that enable elective access to data to perform designated operations without making data available for other purposes (Linn, 2005). Generally these needs are in a distributed architecture consisting of dedicated user workstations (client) and distributed servers.

Many model algorithms and password solutions for security have been proposed (Dhamija & Tygar, 2005; Halderman, Waters, & Felten., 2005; Ross, Jackson, Miyake, Boneh, & Mitchell, 2005) but this presentation utilizes Diffie-Hellman, "Key Exchange A Non-Mathematician's Explanation" (Palmgren, 2005) and PKI *Kerberos* (Della-Libera et al., 2003) which covers a wide range of applications for the design of end user authentication security model algorithms.

Methodology

On the basis of the nature of our investigations, this study can be classified as experimental and nonexperimental. Nonexperimental parts absorb the literature reviewed and sources cited related to this finding. In experimental we tested particular password design requirements based on the level of the key length. With regards to literature evaluation in this study a Kerberos-like user authentication scheme is proposed. This model consists of three-leveled identity verification, ticket request exchange, and a one-time password designed to reach a security authentication system.

We introduce the cause of password failures in order to realistically assess the EUA, Kerberos and Diffie-Hellman exchange section.

We presented an alternative approach to solve the Deffie-Hellman exchange and Kerberos problems mathematically on security consideration section. The algorithm presented explains the ticket message exchange for access to an end user in distributed systems and password design.

However we observed the phenomenon and attempted to establish what caused it. We started to analyze the effects and outcomes and attempted to determine causations. Our experiment was carried out in a controlled environment where the independent variables were introduced by our findings. We placed our findings in the context of what others have discovered.

END USER AUTHENTICATION (EUA) ACCESS CONTROL MODEL ARCHITECTURE

End User Authentication model and algorithms are creating more automated and fluid security infrastructure identity management, which is also referred to as user provisioning indicated to three levels/ units in our model. Our model is built on the premise that defensive, or exclusionary, security must be aligned with inclusionary tools and practices that allow users to access systems and information anytime, anywhere (flexibility). With this, users and administrators will not need to deal with maintaining numerous authorization and authentication schemes to access applications or DNS locations as all are being stored in the DBMS.

Ubiquitous computing in which users can move seamlessly within and between networks is the revolutionary driver for eCommerce. With increasing number of mobile and wireless networks, mechanisms that prompt fast handover between different wireless and network technologies are needed in order to ensure end users move with minimum service interruptions. One of the obstacles for fast handover is end user authentication. Basically a user needs to be clearly identified within the network and billed according to the requested network service provider whether it is from WLAN or LAN. Currently different eCommerce technologies require different forms of identification. Consequently, it is not possible to comply with the requirement of fast handoff for future multinetwork environments. For example, in WLAN the authentication mechanism is based on an allowed Medium Access Control (MAC) list together with a static Wired Equivalent Privacy (WEP) key and/or network key.

In our model, end user authentications at system and network level are investigated. The methodology is unique because unlike other available methodologies, it is both user-centric and performance based. The immediate use of it is to assist end user designers in the commercial field to locate and use established UI patterns more efficiently and effectively. Our end user introduces a new form of identification which can be recognized by any network. Furthermore, it can enhance network capabilities in term of mobility, uniformity and scalability. Automation of this process enables a wider adoption of performance evaluation techniques contrary to eCommerce generation authentications mechanism on place for enterprise systems which are costly and time consuming processes because of complicated infrastructure code. While the EUA user is presented with a rather simple solution to the problem, the difficulty in this model has been in dealing with the backend complexity you have already stated "in this model."

We illustrate the architecture of the access for an end user authentication, detailed use of ID and Certificate Authority (CA) as well as authentication procedure at the network level as follows:

1. The early request ticket for the key exchange authentication from the DBMS unit that provides early access to the first level,

Figure 1. Architecture of an End user Authentication access model

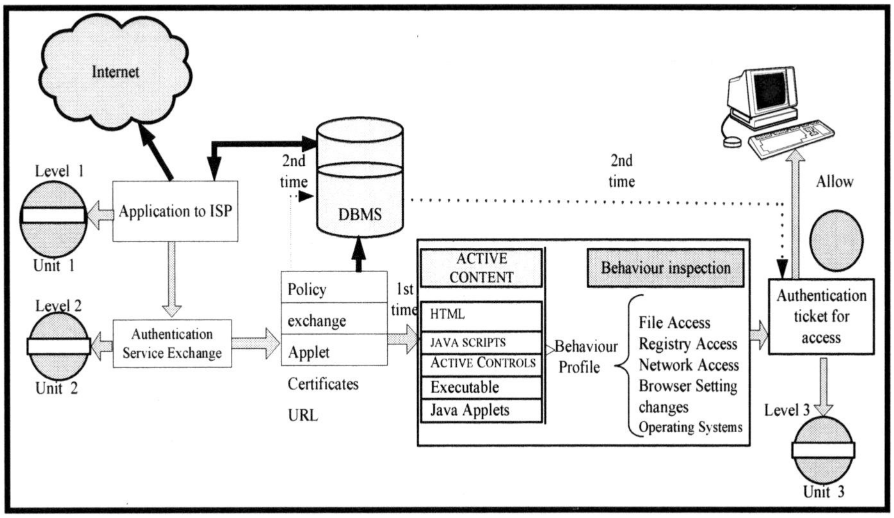

information about next level, and receives tickets for key in order to exchange enter the active contents. This provides identification that lives beyond the span of single first level authorizations or interactions.

2. Level two makes it possible to associate successful messages or requests to the third level. This section manages the early interaction between the user and the server allowing the user to view some of the site details such as policies and active contents. Individual identities are recognized as part of the ordinary ticket exchange with the responsible authority (DBMS). For example when a user initially enters their ID it is immediately recognized as valid on the network. This information might be accessible by administrator or in response to legal process.
3. The single use authorization, which conceals user's identities and also limits linkage among given users successive actions, is in the third part. The third level service unit provides secure access service to enterprise commercial service's sites or requested link.

The authentication End User Model consists of the following components:-

1. Incoming Interment applications from server providers (ISP).
2. Database Management Systems (DBMS).
3. Active content and behaviors inspections.
4. Level one, two and three.

The "incoming internet applications from server" in Figure 1 is a request for access to a service from servers that end-user applies to enterprise sites or Web source. We do not need to secure the servers since that is beyond the scope of this work.

Database Management systems (DBMS) in this model a universal Web-based database intended to work in Internet/Intranet networks. It allows quick access and manipulation of any database via the Internet.

Active content and behavior inspections based on our model protects commercial Websites and companies from new, unknown attacks and to analyze content, deduce the type of behavior and thus proactively block malicious or inappropriate content while allowing appropriate content to flow in a transparent manner.

Behavior analysis is in the application level, which means it determines the full set of behaviors that a given element of content will exhibit when

Figure 2. Basic authentication (left): Alice confirms her identity to Bob by providing password. Third party system (right): Kerberos verifies the password and provide the ticket for the session

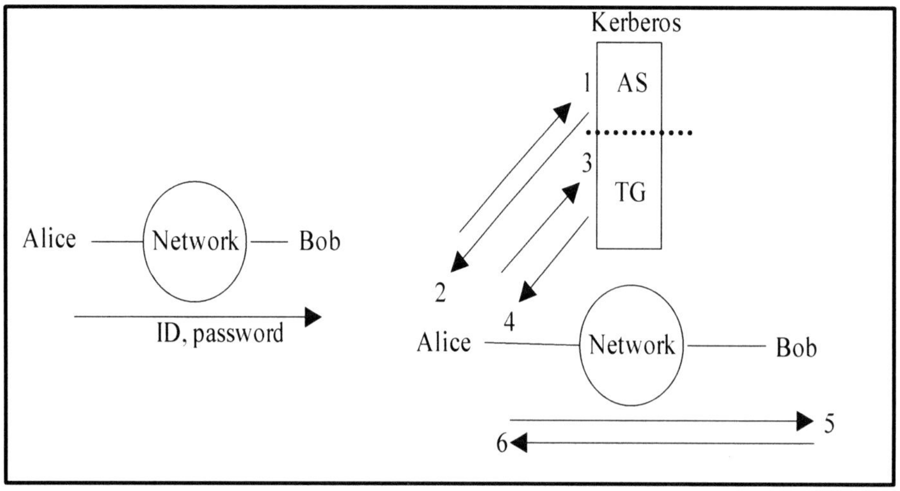

loaded into the target application, (e.g., a Web browser or e-mail program). Then, in accordance with each organization's specific security policy the system decides whether or not to allow the access.

The three different units (Unit 1, Unit 2 and Unit 3) verify the user in the application-level by sending different requests in each unit. In level one, the user will log into Website for service access and the request module will send these applications to the Database requesting the user's ID and password which are stored in the database.

The following takes place in the whole process:

1. The Client/user makes a request; DBMS sends the ticket that includes the user's ID and username. Ticket is encrypted and shared with the DBMS and user.
2. Encrypted *ticket* is sent back to Client (C).
3. With the newly generated ticket C can now apply to WS for service by sending a message to WS containing C's ID and the ticket.
4. With the ticket C can now apply to WS for service by sending a message to WS containing the C's ID and the ticket.
5. WS decrypts the ticket and verifies that the user ID in the ticket is the same as the unencrypted user ID in the message.
6. If the two match, (the user is considered valid and access is granted to the requested service).

ALGORITHMS FOR MESSAGE EXCHANGES

In this section, we describe the algorithms module that is used in encrypted ticket key exchange. (The main idea of ticket exchange is to enforce the login certificates and make sure that security level is provided by strong end user authentication). We analyze the semantics basing on *Kerberos* authentication technique key exchange (Schechter, 2005) and (Della-Libera et al., 2003) and Diffie-Hellman Key exchange of each security transcoding by using an online contracting scenario. For clearly clarifying the notes for ticket exchange, we will recall the security notion of Kerberos message exchange (Stallings, 2003). Full service Kerberos environments consist of a Kerberos server, a number of clients, and a number of application servers. The procedure, shown in the right part of figure 2, is based on a secret key. Here are the steps of the procedure:

1-2: When Alice logs on; she requests a "session key" from the authentication server (AS). This session key remains valid while Alice is logged on.
3-4: Before requesting a service from Bob, Alice asks the ticket-granting server (TG) for a "service ticket."
5-6: Alice can then ask Bob for the service by showing him the ticket.

We examine these steps in more detail.

The AS shares a secret key with each user of Kerberos. For instance, say that *K*(*Alice*) is the secret key of Alice. When Alice logs on, her workstation asks (step 1) AS for the session key *S*(*Alice*), which AS provides in an encrypted message *E*(*M, K*(*Alice*)) (step 2) where

M = [*S*(*Alice*), *T* = *E*(*Alice, S*(*Alice*), *Expiration time; K*(*AS*))].

Alice's workstation decrypts the message using K(Alice) and remembers S(Alice) and T.

Next, Alice wants to talk to Bob. She sends the following message to *TG* (step 3):

"I want to talk to Bob": (*T, Bob*).

TG decrypts *T* using the key *K*(*AS*) and uses (*Alice, S*(*Alice*), *Expiration time*) to verify that Alice is a legitimate user and to obtain the session key *S*(*Alice*) of Alice.

TG then provides the service key *S* (*AB*) to Alice for the A-B session between Alice and Bob by sending the following message (step 4):

E(*S*(*AB*)*; S*(*Alice*)), *E*(*Alice*, *S*(*AB*)*;K*(*Bob*)).

Alice decrypts the first part of the message to get *S* (*AB*) and then sends Bob the second part of the message (step 5):

Hi Bob, *E* (*Alice, S* (*AB*)*; K*(*Bob*)).

When it gets that message, Bob can decrypt it and find (*Alice, S* (*AB*)) to learn that the session *S*(*A B*) will be used for this session between Alice and Bob. Alice and Bob can then talk using the key *S* (*AB*).

Note that the keys *S* (*Alice*) and *S*(*A B*) are time-limited, which reduces the chance that these keys will be discovered. The steps presented are mapped to our model and consider an example that there is an end user requesting for a service and:

1. The Kerberos server must have the user ID (UID) and hashed password of all participating users in its database while users are registered with the Kerberos server.
2. The Kerberos server must share a secret key with each server and all servers are registered with the Kerberos server.

As providing an end user authentication service (EUA) to authenticate users to Web source and users to database relies on conventional encryption, making no use of public-key encryption, we analyze the steps as follow:

Notation

For clarity, we list the symbols used in this section.

C = Client, **ADBMS** = Authentication database management system, **WS** = Web source, **IDc** = Identifier of user on **C**, **Idws**= Identifier of Web source, $\mathbf{P_C}$ = Password of user on **C**, **Kws** = Secret encryption key shared by **ADBMS** and **WS**, **TS** = Timestamp, || = Concatenation

Steps (1):

1. User logs into a commercial Website and requests access to Service Web source.
2. Client module **(C)** in the workstation (Database) requests the user's password and then sends a message to the Authentication

Database Management System **(ADBMS)** that includes the user's **ID**, the database **ID**, and the user's password.

3. **(ADBMS)** checks its database for proper authentication, and whether user has authorization to access **(WS)**.
4. If both tests are passed, the **(WS)** accepts the user as authentic and must now convince the host system **(WS)** that the user is authentic.
   (4.1) **(ADBMS)** creates a ticket that includes user's **ID** and network address and the server's **ID**. Ticket is encrypted and shared and the key is shared by **(ADBMS)** and **(WS)**
   (4.2) Encrypted *ticket* is sent back to Client **(C)**
5. With the newly generated ticket, **C** can now apply to **(WS)** for service by sending a message to **(WS)** containing the **C's ID** and the ticket.

Steps (2):

6. With the ticket, **C** can now apply to **(WS)** for service by sending a message to **(WS)** containing **C's** ID and the ticket.
   (6.1) **(Ws)** decrypts the ticket and verifies that the user **ID** in the ticket is the same as the unencrypted user **ID** in the message.
   (6.2) If the two match, the server considers the user authenticated and grants the requested service.
7. Simply stated:
   (6.1) C Ú ADB: IDc || P_c || IDws
   (6.2) ADBMS Ú C: Ticket
   (6.3) C Ú WS: IDc || Ticket

- *Authentication Service Exhange: To obtain Ticket-Granting Ticket.*

1. C Ú ADBMS: IDc || IDtgs ||TS1
2. ADBMS Ú C: E_{Kc} [$K_{c,tgs}$|| IDtgs || TS_2 || $Lifetime_2$ || Tickettgs]

- *Ticket-Granting Service Exchange: To obtain Service-Granting Ticket.*

3. C Ú TGS: IDv ||$Ticket_{tgs}$ ||Authenticatorc
4. TGS Ú C: E_{Kc} [$K_{c,¨ws}$|| IDws || TS_4 || Ticketv]

- *Client/WebService Authentication Exhange: To Obtain Service*

5. C Ú WS: $Ticket_V$ || Authenticatorc
6. WS Ú C: EKc,v[TS5 +1]

TOWARDS A REALISTIC ASSESSMENT OF THE EUA, KERBEROS AND DIFFIE-HELLMAN EXCHANGE

Considering today's pervasiveness of malicious software (viruses, trojan horses) and phishing attacks, any authentication solution must be resistant against offline credential stealing attacks. For this a challenge/response-based one-time password authentication is proposed. Ideally the user should not be aware that authentication is taking place beyond the requirement to enter a password. EUA model leverages the power of your existing access infrastructure and increases login security with a strong three level authentication solution. Three level verification provides a pathway to legislative compliance by ensuring the protection of sensitive data from unauthorized access through textual password.

There are a number of challenges and open problems associated with the *Kerberos* authentication mechanism. Among the issues are that both Kerberos versions are vulnerable to password and key session attacks. An opponent can capture the exchange message and attempt to decrypt it by trying various passwords. If the results of a test decryption is of the proper form, then the opponent has discovered the client password and may subsequently use it to gain authentication credentials. Secondly, each ticket includes a session key that is used by the client to encrypt the authenticator sent to the service associated with that ticket. The session key subsequently may be used by client and the server to protect messages passed during the session. Since the same ticket may be used repeatedly to gain service from a particular server, there is the risk that an opponent or another user with root access could replay a message from an old session to the client or the server. Being inspired with the aforemetioned issues, we have proposed one time passwords, based on key length which can be applied within a specific time period.

Diffie-Hellman exchange strategy was named after its inventors. Alice and Bob first agree on a pair of numbers (z, p).These numbers can be made public. Alice then chooses a number α and Bob chooses a number b. Alice computes $\alpha = z^{\alpha} \bmod p$ and sends it to Bob who computes $\alpha^{b} \bmod p$. Similarly, Bob computes $\beta = z^{\alpha} \bmod p$ and sends it to Alice who computes $\beta^{a} \bmod p$.

However there are some draw backs in this approach and to combat the weaknesses in Deffie-Hellman exchange we claim that:

$$\alpha^{b} \bmod p = \beta^{a} \bmod p = z^{ab} \bmod p :k. \qquad (1)$$

Moreover, it is difficult to calculate a from α and b from β, so that an eavesdropper who knows (Z, P) and observes (α,β) cannot compute K.

To show (1), we first note that $\alpha = z^{\alpha} \bmod p$ so that $\alpha = z^{\alpha} + mp$ for some integer m. Consequently,

$$\alpha^{b} = (z^{a} + mp)^{b} =$$

$$z^{ab} + bz^{a(b-1)}mp + \frac{b(b-1)}{2} =$$

$$z^{a(b-2)}(mp)^{2} + \cdots + bz^{a}(mp)^{b-1} + (mp)^{b}.$$

This equality proves formula (1). It turns out that the Diffie-Hellman exchange is not robust to a "person-in-the-middle" attack as we explain next. Imagine that an eavesdropper Eve intercepts the Diffie-Hellman exchange between Alice and Bob. Eve can communicate with Alice as if she were Bob and agree with Alice on a common secret key. In the same way, Eve can agree on a secret key with Bob as if she were Alice. At that point, Eve can intercept the messages from Alice to Bob, read them or change them and re-encrypt them for Bob. Alice and Bob are unaware of the existence of Eve.

Another weakness of the Diffie-Hellman exchange is that Eve can intercept the message α from Alice to Bob and replace it by 0. Similarly, when the message β comes from Bob to Alice, Eve can replace it with 0. As a result, Alice and Bob end up agreeing on the common key 0 that Eve knows. (Eve could have used 1 or - 1 instead of 0.) To prevent this simple attack, the system should verify that the numbers exchanged are not 0, 1, or -1.

A more subtle attack by Eve is as follows. Eve chooses some prime number q that divides $p-1$. She intercepts α from Alice to Bob and replaces it with α^{q}. She also intercepts β from Bob to Alice and replaces it with β^{q}. As a result, Alice and Bob end up agreeing on the key k^{q} instead of the key K. Although Eve does not know k^{q}, she knows that the key belongs to a smaller subgroup of keys (the exact qth powers) on which the search is considerably easier.

The Diffie-Hellman exchange can be made robust against this attack. When signing the exchange, Alice sends α to Bob and Bob sendsβ to Alice. Alice then signs (α, β) and sends it to Bob. Bob also signs (α, β) and sends it to Alice. Eve cannot fake the signatures.

By definition, a prime number p is a safe prime if $p' := (p - 1) / 2$ is also prime. In that case, one can show that the only multiplicative subgroups of $\{1, 2,..., p - 1\}$ are $\{ 1 \}$, $\{- 1, 1 \}$, and $\{ 1, 2...., p - 1 \}$. It is sufficient in the Diffie-Hellman exchange to check that the numbers exchanged are not 0, 1, or - 1.

Also the simplest mechanism for identification is to use a password. To certify her identity, Alice has a secret password K and she sends *(Alice, K)* to Bob. Bob maintains a list of names with hashed passwords. This list contains *(Alice, H(K))* and Bob can thus verify that Alice is who she claims to be. Bob does not keep the list of pairs *(Alice. K)* for obvious reasons. The weakness of the password mechanism in this situation is that Bob and the communication line both see the secret password *K* of Alice.

We propose *Single sign-on Passwords* to meet the mentioned challenge in the previous paragraph. The authentication process password needs to obtain the authentication information from an entity, analyze the data and determine if it is associated with that entity. This means that the computer must store some information about the entity and required mechanisms for managing the data. We represent these requirements in our single sign on password design which consist of five components:

1. The set A of **authentication Information** is the set of specific information with which entities prove their identities.
2. The set C of **complementary Information** is the set of information that the system stores and uses to validate the authentication information.
3. The set F of **complementation functions** that generate the complementary from the authentication information that is:
   For $f \in F$, $F: A \rightarrow C$
4. The set L of authentication functions that verify identity. That is for
   $| \in L$, $|$: $\mathbf{A \times C \rightarrow \{true, false\}}$
5. The set S of **selection functions** that enable an entity to create or alter the authentication and complementary information.

The goal of an authentication system is to ensure that entities are correctly identified. If one entity can guess another's password, then the guesser can impersonate the other (Bishop, 1991; Jermyn, et al., 1999). The *Single sign on Passwords* presented provides a systematic way to analyze this problem (passwords). The goal is to find $\in A$ such that, for $f \in F$, $f(a) = c \in c$ and c is associated with a particular entity (or any entity). Because one can determine whether a is associated with an entity only by computing f (a) or by authenticating via | (a) we have two approaches for protecting the password used simultaneously:

1. Hide enough information so that one of *a, c*, or *f* cannot be found.
2. Prevent access to the authentication functions **L**.

SECURITY CONSIDERATIONS TO PROPOSED APPROACH

Only the ticket exchange request would have to be extended to allow the server to ask for an appropriately derived part of the login certificate challenge to be displayed on the user screen, and an appropriate response or short-time password to be gathered from the user keyboard. The challenge and response length and format hereby are independent parameters (e.g., equal to or greater than a six-digit numeric character challenge). Each of these approaches leads to different types of attack and defenses (i.e., countering password guess, rewires either set of complementation functions and complementary information or access to the authentication functions). In both approaches, the goal of the defenders is to maximize the time needed to guess the password. A generalization of Anderson's Formula (Anderson, 1972) provides the fundamental basis:

- Let P be the probability that an attacker guesses a password in a specified period of time
- Let G be the number of guesses that can be tested in one time unit
- Let T be the number of time units during which guessing occurs
- Let N be the number of possible passwords

Then $P \geq \frac{TG}{N}$

Example 1: *Lets password be composed of characters drawn from an alphabet of 96 characters.*

Assume that 10^4 guesses can be tested each second. We wish to estimate the probability of a successful guess to be 0.5 once per 365-day period. What is the minimum password length that will give us this probability?

From this formula, we want

$$N \geq \frac{\text{TG}}{\text{P}} = \frac{(365 \times 24 \times 60 \times 60)10^4}{0.5}$$

$= 6.31 \times 10^{11}$.

Thus we must choose an integer s such that

$$\sum_{i=0}^{s} 96^i \geq N$$

This holds when $s \geq 6$ so, in order to meet the minimum required password conditions of at least **6** characters is required.

Assumptions underlie example:-

1. The time required to test a password is constant
2. All passwords are equally likely to be selected

Proof:

a. The first is reasonable, because the algorithms used to validate password are fixed and either the algorithm is independent of the password's length or the variation is negligible.
b. The second assumption is a function of the password selection mechanism (Morris & Thomson, 1979).

ONE-TIME PASSWORDS

We based our approach on a one-time password. One time password is a password that is invalidated as soon as it is used. A security system that requires a new password every time users authenticate themselves, thus protecting against an intruder replaying an intercepted password. S/Key (Haller, 1994) implements a one-time password scheme. It uses techniques first suggested to generate the password (Lamport, 1981).

With this technology our approach takes the "seed" the user enters and generates a list of *n* passwords. The implementations present each password as a sequence of six or more shorts words (but, the internal presentation is an integer). The user can generate a numbered list of these sequences. The system initializes a database, called a "ticket" file, with the number of the next passwords correctly supplied.

The exchange proceeds as follows:

1. User supplies his name to the server
2. The server replies with the number ***i*** stored in the "*ticket*" file
3. User supplies the corresponding password *pi*
4. The server computes $h(p_i) = h(k_{ni+1}) = k_{ni+2} = P_{i1}$ and compares the results with the stored password.

If they match, the ticket file to *i*1 and stores *Pi* in the file. If the authentication fails the ticket file is left unchanged.

Note: h – one-way hash function and K – Seed

PERFORMANCE ANALYSIS

We analyze the robustness of our passwords capabilities against forgery and time session. We will derive the probability that an unauthorized end-user will be able to forge (by guessing) the appropriate capability to allow its login typed keys to be authorized within a particular time.

Parameters: X: password length and Z: time.

The probability that randomly guessed capability will pass a particular authorization is given by

Table 1. Evaluation of P(x, z) (the probability to pass one login with a forged authorization) for a common values of X and Z

	X=2	X=3	X=4	X=5	X=6
Z=1	0.7500	0.8750	0.9375	0.9688	0.9844
Z=2	0.4375	0.5781	0.6836	0.7627	0.8220
Z=3	0.2344	0.3301	0.4138	0.4871	0.5512
Z=4	0.1211	0.1760	0.2275	0.2758	0.3210

Figure 3. Inputs per time

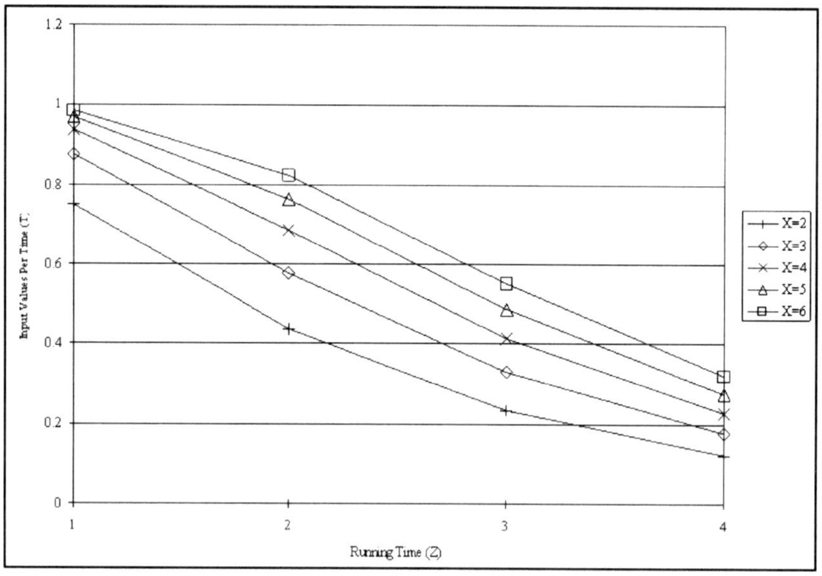

$$P(X, Z) = 1 - \left(1 - \frac{1}{2^Z}\right)^X$$

and the probability that a randomly guessed capability will pass all *d* authorization in a system is simply $p(x, z)^d$. Recall that the capability password authorization *must* be equal to or > than 6 symbols (characters). Table 1 shows *P*(*x*, *z*), the probability of successfully forging, capable passwords, for reasonable values of *(X) key length* and *(Z) time taken.*

(Figures 3 and 4 depict password log in performance over time in conjunction with the length of the password. To analyze the performance of our one-time passwords we select attackers at random and have them try to login with randomly forged key capabilities. We leave the exact timing decisions to 1 ≥ 6 symbols, and simply assume in our experiments that x is likely to be from two to six. With the ideal log in the DBMS automatically drops all attack passwords < 6 characters. From the graph we see a correlation between the length of the password and the amount of time required to correctly guess the password. The performance is excellent, 97.14% of the attacks using short key length per log in from (z = 1), and increasing probability to 100% of login match to key length ≥ six with running time of (z ≥ 4). We show the results of our experiment only from a mathematical aspect since it involves human interactions. Furthermore, although not shown in

Figure 4. Passwords length per input values

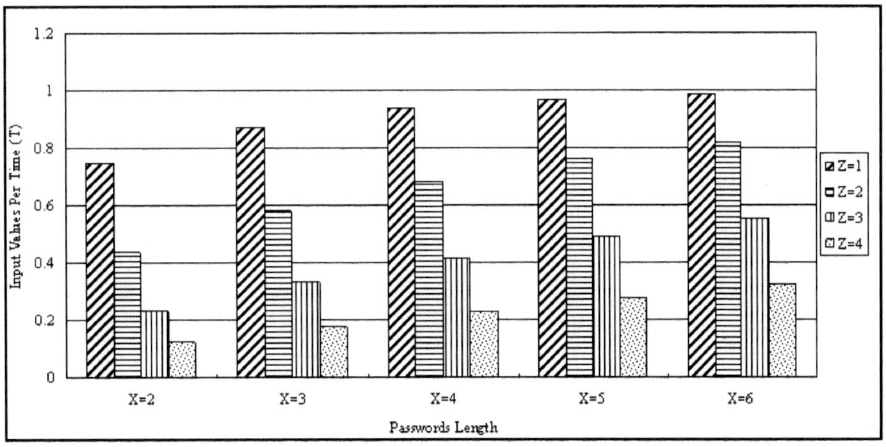

the figures, it is intuitive that the effect of validity x decreases as z increases which means that with the increase of time the probability of successfully logging is realized.

Choosing a value for *X* (the maximum number of keys that are valid at any one time login) presents a tradeoff. As we show in the table, *X* must be at least *2*, because a valid capability is 100 % that matches any of the *X* capabilities in the DBMS, small value of *X* provides the smallest probability that a random hacker with adequate capability will compromise the password (Table one shows this effect).

The value of *X* also affects the time needed to compromise the password. The minimum valid time (min_m) *is* (min_m) = $(x-1).\ T_k$, where T_k denotes the time during which a key is typed. The maximum valid time (max_m)= $X.T_k$. Ideally, we would like to get small intervals for the valid time so that we can tightly control the validity period. Thus we would like large X values to minimize the difference between (min_m) *and* (max_m). So we can determine X from Minm and Maxm

$$X = \frac{\max_m}{\max_m - \min_m}$$

The max_m metric defines the longest amount of time that password matches can remain idle and still have a valid capability. Put in another way, max_m defines the maximum amount of time that an attacker can login with particular capability before the capability is rejected by authentications.

Because the (login denial) rejection probabilities are independent *Bernoulli trials,* the probability that the end user/client and server will be able to establish correct passwords after one try (by exchanging password is):-

P (connect after 1 try) $= (1- \in_i)^i$

The probability that client will connect after K tries is:-

P (connection after K tries)

$= 1 - (1 - P\ (connect\ after\ 1\ try))\ k$

$= 1 - (1 - \in_i)^i)k$

For a given desired connection probability, *P (connect)* the required number of connection attempts are:-

$$K = \frac{\log\left(1 - P\ (connect)\right)}{\log\left(1 - (1 - \in_i)^i\right)}$$

A nice feature of this formula is that the expected number of connection attempts depends logarithmically on the matches' probability, which indicates that, even for large $\in_i$, a determined client can get connected after a moderate waiting time.

FUTURE WORK

Future work on Web service authentications includes an XML- based logic for Web service authentications (Bhargavan, Fournet, & Gordon, 2004; Gordon, Bhargavan, Fournet, & Pucella, 2003) that is embedded within the applied Pi-calculus (Fournet & Abadi, 2003) allowing verification of Web service security protocols via both human and machine proof techniques. It is likely that their approach will be relevant to future considerations of Web service request authentication for our model.

The most obvious direction is the development of end user authentications through long key length passwords including an extension of message exchange algorithms comprised of access control architecture implementations. In addition to stand alone Web services, authorizations for composite Web services (Christophides, Hull, Karvounarakis, Kumar, Tong, & Xiong, 2001; Hull & Su, 2004) also promises to be an interesting topic for future work; access control in that setting presents a number of unique issues for investigation. With regard to changing legislation and the spreading of e-ID's among customers, the solution nonetheless remains a highly attractive and valuable alternative for the future (Hiltgen et al., 2004).

CONCLUSION

In this article, a Kerberos-like user authentication scheme is proposed. In this scheme, a model combining three leveled identity verification, ticket request exchange, and one time password is designed to fulfill security authentication system. However, the alternative and better approach to solve the Deffie-Hellman exchange and Kerberos problems has been presented.

Generally, authorization services focus on representing and enforcing decision rules, with the characteristics of requestors used to protect objects comprising inputs to those rules. While a variety of powerful and relevant methods are available to protect identity, significant challenges remain for technology and standards developers. The primary need is for technical measures to strengthen security polices of EUA that might reduce the trust level to a user.

We have presented an algorithm that explains the ticket message exchange for access to an end user in distributed systems. We classify the access control entries of active content and behavior monitoring in our modeling as not a final access authority but pre access to a third unit for full authentication to the service requested. Moreover, it should be noted that while only a user is actively using her/his access (i.e., while logged in) are valid mappings in place and therefore any form of attack is limited to when the user in question is logged in. When a user is not logged in, no amount of IP address forgery will permit unauthorized access to her/his access.

Challenge-passwords matching within a specific time (login sessions) allow the system to vary the password and less vulnerable to compromise because the password is never transmitted in the clear. One-time passwords are particularly effective against guessing attacks because even if a password is guessed, it may not be reused due to the time limitations. This can combat the problems in case of time out with no matches on passwords, back off techniques, disconnection, disabling passwords, aging and jailing.

The conventional textual password schemes presented achieve better security. Our approaches exploit the input capabilities of logging that allows us to determine the input time needed from the password and the length in which it occurs. Presented security mathematically arguments analyzes the information content of the resulting password used. More sophisticated client-platform attacks conceivable in the future for instance; activating the ready-to-use transaction signing option can simply thwart content manipulation attacks.

REFERENCES

Abadi, M. et al. (2004). Private authentication. *Theoretical Computer Science, 322*(3), 427-476)

Anderson, J. (1972). Information security in a multi-user computer environment. M. Rubinoff (Ed.), *Advances in computer 12.* New York: Academic Press.

Bhargavan K., Fournet, C., & Gordon, A. D. (2004). A semantics for web service authentications. In *Proceedings of the 31st ACM SIGPLAN-SIGACT Symposium on Principals of Programming Languages* (pp. 198-209). ACM Press.

Bishop, M. (1991). Password management. In *Proceedings of COMPCON '91* (pp.167-169).

Christophides, V., Hull, R., Karvounarakis, G., Kumar, A., Tong, G., & Xiong, M. (2001). Beyond discrete e-services: Composing session-oriented service in telecommunications. In *Proceedings of the Workshop on Technologies for E-Services (TES)*, Rome, Italy.

Deffie, W. & Hellman, M. E. (1976). New directions in cryptography. *IEEE Transactions on Information Theory, 22*(6), 644-654,.

Della-Libera, G. et al. (2003). Web services security Kerberos binding. IBM Corporation Microsoft Corporation. Retrieved November 4, 2008, from *http://msdn.microsoft.com/library/default*

Dhamija, R. & Tygar, J. D. (2005). The battle against phishing: Dynamic security skins. In Proceedings of the Symposium on Usable Privacy and Security

ElGamal, T. (1985). A public-key cryptosystem and a signature scheme based on discrete logarithms. Advances in Cryptography, Crypto'84, pp.10-18.

EWeek.com (2006, Aril). RSA buys consumer authentication specialist.

Fournet, C. & Abadi, M. (2003). Hiding names: Private authentication in the pi calculus. In *Proceedings of the International Symposium on Software Security* (pp. 317-338). Springer-Verlag.

Gordon, A., Bhargavan, K., Fournet, C., & Pucella, R. (2003). Tulufale: A security tool for web service. In Springer (Ed.), *Formal methods for Components and Objects.*

Halderman, J. A., Waters, B., & Felten, E. (2005). A convenient method for securely managing passwords. In *Proceedings of the 14th International World Wide Web Conference (WWW)*

Haller, N. (1994). The s/key one-time password system. In *Proceedings of the 1994 symposium on Network and Distributed System Security* (pp.151-157).

Hull, R.& Su, J. (2004). Tools for design of composite web service. In *ACM SIDMOD* (pp. 958-961).

Hiltgen, A. et al. (submitted). Secure internet banking authentication. Retrieved November 4, 2008, from www.zurich.ibm.com/pdf/csc/SecureInternetBankingAuthentication.pdf

Jermyn, I. et al. (1999). The design and analysis of graphical passwords. In *Proceeding of the 8th USENIX Security Symposium.*

Kocher, P. (1996). Personal communication

Linn, J. (2005). Technology and web user data privacy: A survey of risks and countermeasures. *Security & Privacy, 3*(1), 52-58.

Lamport, L. (1981). Password authentication with insecure communication. *Communication of the ACM, 24*(11), 770-771.

McMillan, R. (2005). Ebay tricked by phony e-mail, by, InfoWorld

Morris, R. & Thomson, K. (1979). Password security, A case history. *Communications of the ACM, 22*(11), 594-597.

Palmgren, K. (2005). Diffie-Hellman key exchange – *A Non-Mathematician's Explanation*

Rivest, R. L. et al. (1978). A method for obtaining digital signatures and public key cryptosystems. *Communications of the ACM, 21*(2), 120- 126.

Ross, B., Jackson, C., Miyake, N., Boneh, D., & Mitchell, J. C. (2005). Stronger password authentication using browser extensions. In *Proceedings of the 14th Usenix Security Symposium.*

Schechter, S. E. (2005). Toward econometric models of the security risk from remote attack. *Security & Privacy, 3*(1), 40-55.

Steiner, J. G. et al. (1988). *Kerberos: An authentication service for open network systems,*

Steiner, J. G., Neuman, B. C., & Schiller, J. I. (1988). Kerberos: An authentication service for open network systems. In *Proceedings of the Winter 1988 USENIX* (pp. 191–202). Dallas, TX: USENIX.

Stallings, W. (2003). *Network security essentials: Applications and standard* (2nd ed). Upper Saddle River, New Jersey: Prentice Hall.

www.computerworld.com (2005). Bank of America's move to stronger authentication delayed. Computer World. Retrieved November 4, 2008, from *http://www.computerworld.com/securitytopics/security/story/0,10801,105620,00.html*

Yl¨onen, T. (1996). SSH – Secure login connections over the Internet. In *Proceedings of the 6th USENIX Security Symposium* (pp. 37–42). San Jose, CA.

Yee, K. P. & Sitaker, K. (2006). Passpet: Convenient password management and phishing protection. In *Proceedings of the 2nd Symposium on Usable Privacy and Security* (pp. 12-14). Pittsburgh, PA: ACM Press. Retrieved November 4, 2008, from http://cups.cs.cmu.edu/soups/2006/proceedings/p32_yee.pdf

This work was previously published in Journal of Organizational and End User Computing (JOEUC) 21(2), edited by Mo Adam Mahmood, pp. 28-43, copyright 2009 by IGI Publishing (an imprint of IGI Global).

Chapter 8
A Model of the Relationship among Consumer Trust, Web Design and User Attributes

Xiaoni Zhang
Northern Kentucky University, USA

Victor R. Prybutok
University of North Texas, USA

Sherry Ryan
University of North Texas, USA

Robert Pavur
University of North Texas, USA

ABSTRACT

One important aspect of consumer relationships is trust. Conducting business on the Web is relatively new compared to traditional business and many of the factors related to consumer trust related to the Web remained unexplored. To increase our understanding about trust building on the Internet, this article studies trust with a focus on its relationship to Web design characteristics, specifically perceived quality of presentation, perceived ease of navigation, and several user attributes: prior internet experience, Web users' self efficacy, and gender differences. A research model is proposed that builds upon prior research on trust. A survey is developed based on the constructs and relationships in the model. The data analysis and results confirm five out of eight of the hypotheses associated with the model. Theoretical and practical implications are provided.

INTRODUCTION

Numerous researchers suggest that trust is the foundation upon which people base their purchase decisions. When a customer trusts a company, they anticipate that company will fulfill their needs and expectations (Bauer, 2002; Bhattacherjee, 2002). A consumer's purchase decision to buy on the Internet is complex and sophisticated, but trust is a relevant factor (McKnight & Chervany,

DOI: 10.4018/978-1-60960-577-3.ch008

2001-2002; McKnight, Choudhury & Kacmar, 2002). Because online consumers rely on Website information, the information presented has to be conducive for making decisions and selecting products that match customers' tastes and needs. While there are differences between traditional and Internet sales, in both, the presentation and shopping experience provide cues that affect the development of trust (Giddens, 1990). Professional looking design and the way in which the site interacts with the customer are sources for building online trust. Such interface cues can induce and inspire a customer to trust a Website and its products or services.

From the corporate perspective, managers are faced with decisions that impact the effectiveness of their firm's Web strategy, one of which is how to design Web interactions so customer relationships will be enhanced. The lack of trust has been identified as a key inhibitor in the Business-to-Consumer (B2C) environment (Debreceny, Putterill, Tung, & Gilbert, 2003). Because trust results from an extended set of encounters between a company and its customers, trust is hard to build but easy to lose. Continuously building and maintaining trust is essential to institutional reputation (Lewicki & Bunker, 1996). In fact, a single violation of trust can destroy years of slowly accumulated credibility. In the virtual environment, trust is the user's willingness to risk time, money, and personal data on a Website.

Understanding trust-related Web design and content can help managers make better decisions in electronic commerce investments. Recently, research has found that an overall perception of a Website's ease-of-use was significantly related to trust (Gefen, Karahanna, & Straub, 2003). However, the need remains for additional assessment of effective Web designs and the relationship between various design elements and trust (Katerattanakul & Siau, 1999; Rosen & Purintin, 2004). Thus, the roles that Web content and other design factors play in affecting trust in an e-commerce environment needs to be investigated.

Gender research is also of particular interest to companies as they use such information to design target marketing. Numerous studies have examined gender issues in learning, cognitive style, information processing and decision making (Jackson, Ervin, Gardner & Schmitt, 1992; Maccoby & Jacklin, 1974; Meyers-Levy & Sternthal, 1991; Meyers-Levy & Maheswaran, 1991). In technology adoption areas, significant gender differences were found in social norms, attitude toward technology, technology usage, and perceived behavioral control (Gefen & Straub, 1997; Venkatesh & Morris, 2000; Venkatesh, Morris & Ackerman, 2000). In Internet usage, men were found to spend more time downloading and browsing than women (Teo & Lim, 2000). However, gender issues related to trust and Web design are an under-researched area. To enrich our understanding on the effect of interface design and its interaction with gender, this article studies trust from the customer's perceptive of two key Web design elements: perceived quality of presentation and the perceived ease of navigation. In doing so, we significantly contribute to the literature in several ways.

First, we propose and test a theoretical model that shows the relationships among trust, the quality of presentation, perceived ease of navigation, and two antecedents of perceived ease of navigation: prior experience, and Web self-efficacy. Second, we investigate how gender affects the perception of Website design and content elements. And third, we discuss the implications of our findings for both theory and practice.

THEORETICAL BACKGROUND AND HYPOTHESES

Trust

A substantial amount of research has investigated IT-related trust, some of which has addressed trust issues on the Internet (Gefen, Karahanna, &

Straub 2003; McKnight & Chervany, 2001-2002). Much of the published work on trust has focused on general trust. However, this work examines trust from a cognitive perspective because, from a design standpoint, a cognitive state of trust is important in ensuring that human-computer interactions proceed smoothly (Bevin, 2000).

No single, universally accepted definition of trust exits, yet there is general agreement that to engender trust one must act in a dependable, ethical, and desirable manner (Hosmer, 1995; Rotter, 1971). Trust implies that the other party can be believed (Gefen, 2000; Gefen, 2002b; Gefen, Karahanna, & Straub, 2003; Hoffman, Novak, & Peralta, 1999). When we apply this definition to a Web context, trust means what is on a Website is trustworthy and believable. Rousseau et al. (1998) defines trust as a state "comprising the intention to accept vulnerability based on positive expectations of the intentions and behaviors of the others." Building upon Rousseau et al.'s (1998) work we define trust as positive expectations of the substance and behaviors of a Website. Support for this definition in the literature traces back to Lewicki and Bunker (1996) who propose that trust is situational and context-specific. Positive impressions can be developed under certain situations and within a given context. Pavlou's (2003) recent work supports the importance of trust in an e-commerce environment and shows that trust creates positive attitudes.

Prior studies in e-commerce-related trust and consumer decision-making are diverse. One stream of trust-related research has been technical in nature, focusing on security issues such as the role public key encryption and digital signatures play in ensuring trust in electronic commerce (Fernandes, 2001). In the virtual environment, transaction trust is a combination of an agent's trust in the other party and the agent's trust in the control mechanism (Tan & Thoen, 2002). Trust can be fostered by the usage of digital certificates (Ba, 2001; Kimery & McCord, 2002). The trusted third party performs the roles of issuing digital certificates and punishing cheating behavior.

Other, more general, research has also found that trust affects the willingness of consumers to make online purchases (McKnight, Choudhury, & Kacmar 2002; McKnight & Chervany, 2001-2002). While a large percentage of users believe that trust of a site's information is important, only 29% of users say they trust Websites that sell products and services (http://www.consumerWebwatch.org/news/1_credibility.htm). Consumers who are suspicious about the vendor obeying the rules of commerce or keeping its word are unlikely to conduct business with that vendor (Gefen, Karahanna, & Straub, 2003). Some even suggest that consumers who have doubts about an online vendor will not rely on the information that vendor provides (window-shopping) and will not conduct transactions (Reichheld & Schefter, 2000). While these issues apply to any vendor, they are more pronounced with online vendors because consumers cannot rely on physical cues when assessing the integrity, benevolence or ability of the vendor. Further complicating the trust relationship is that customers must pay vendors before the service or merchandise is rendered.

Whether Web savvy or relatively inexperienced, Internet surfers want the sites they visit to provide easy-to-find and clearly stated information that helps them judge a site's credibility. These Website design and quality characteristics are critical to increasing the likelihood that customers will shop at that site. A few studies have investigated the relationship between trust and the quality of Website design. Important characteristics of the World Wide Web, such as its interactive structure and information quality, have a significant effect on relationship marketing, commitment, satisfaction and trust (Bauer, 2002). Customers would withdraw their trust if their expectations with regard to these characteristics were not met. Others found that site quality, trust, and positive affect toward the site are critical in explaining both the purchase intentions and loyalty of visitors to the site (McKnight & Chervany, 2001-2002; McKnight, Choudhury, & Kacmar 2002a; McKnight, Choudhury, & Kacmar, 2002b). Wang and Strong (1997) suggest that evaluation criteria for the quality of Website design include structure and layout (presentation) and navigation. We follow this suggestion and propose and test a model that hypothesizes relationships between these two key design factors and trust (see Figure 1).

Perceived Presentation Quality and Trust

Bevin (2000) emphasized high quality content as an important Website design goal. Previous research contains different definitions of content quality. Huizingh (2000) claims that content quality refers to the usefulness of the information provided by the Website and shows that information, transaction and entertainment are important in Web content whereas Chau et al. (1995) use relevancy and the amount of information to measure content quality. Content was defined as relevance, media use, depth and breadth and current and timely information (Agarwal & Venkatesh, 2002). Agarwal and Venkatesh (2002) found a positive relationship between content quality and consumers' satisfaction.

Presentation of information on a Website must take into consideration graphics, colors, the amount of information displayed and the way that the information is organized. Presentation issues consist of (1) where information is located, (2) how graphics are used, and (3) what elements on the site are distracting (McClure, Wyman, Beachboard, & Eschenfelder, 1997). The importance of how information is displayed to attract customers is of fundamental importance in e-commerce. A common look and feel to the information display and navigation are important properties of Websites (Rather & Grose, 1996). Websites must be aesthetically appealing and Web designers must take care in the presentation of the information on the home page to entice the user to continue further into the Website, and to feel comfortable sharing personal information, making purchases,

Figure 1. Research model

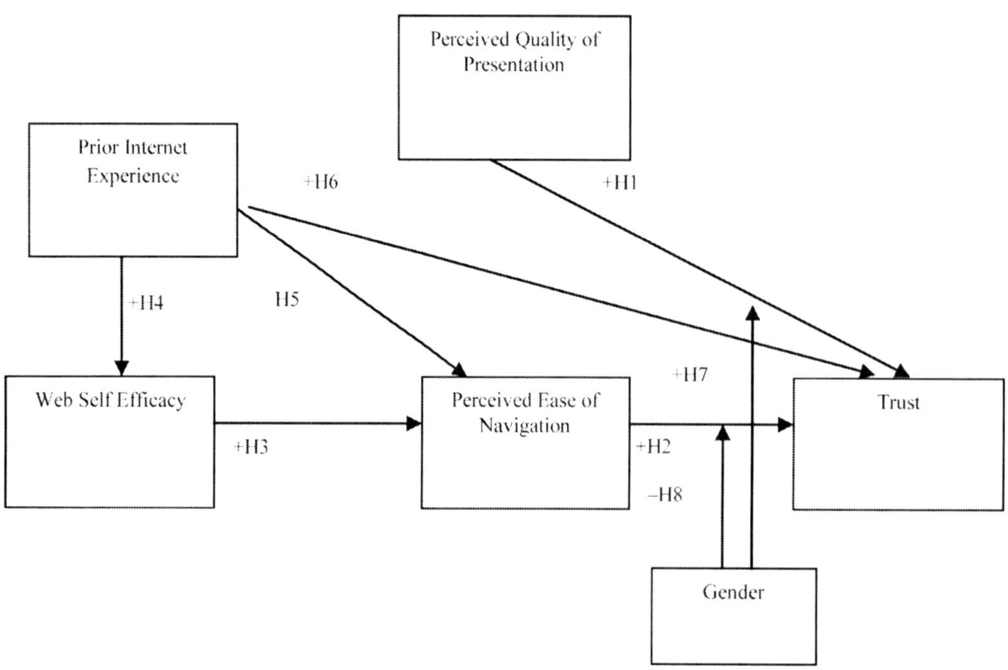

and acting on Web vendor advice. These trusting behaviors are essential to widespread adoption of e-commerce sites.

During interpersonal interactions, people subconsciously look for cues as to whether they can trust the other party (Benassi, 1999). We can extend this idea to human-computer interactions. People use information cues available on the Web to build their trust. Content, information amount, and graphics are information cues. The presence of these cues on a Web page increases consumer trust (Baron & Kenny, 1986). Yoon (2002) found that site content, the equivalent of presentation in our study, is the antecedent of trust. Conversely, customers withdraw their trust if their expectations with regard to these characteristics are not met (Bauer, 2002).

Prior studies have used different terms such as the Web content, Web characteristics, site quality and presentation, but these terms are used in a context that convey the meaning of capturing the quality of content, information, and graphics on the Website. Thus, Websites can improve user trust by content control (Heijden, Tibert, & Creemers, 2003). We therefore propose:

H1: *Perceived presentation quality is positively related to trust.*

Perceived Ease of Navigation and Trust

Navigation is defined as the sequencing of Web pages but require that this be done in a manner that is consistent and well organized (Pavlou, 2003). In essence, navigation measures the effort one spends on performing tasks. According to consumer WebWatch, 80% of the respondents to their survey state that it is important that a site is easy to navigate (http://www.consumerwebwatch.org/news/1_credibility.htm). Navigation issues include understanding what the navigation icons mean, the ease in which graphics helped the navigation process, and the ability to find pertinent information without relying on chance (McClure, Wyman, Beachboard & Eschenfelder, 1997). Navigation and presentation are important Web design elements (Huizingh, 2000). Making navigation easier eliminates user frustration. Chau, Au and Tam (1995) use the dimensions of navigation, structure, and presentation to define the construct interaction quality in their study. They found that interaction quality is positively related to consumer satisfaction, an attitudinal attribute of consumers.

Web usability experts suggest that organization and navigation is important to outcomes (Nielsen, 2000). Websites can also improve user trust by streamlined navigation (McKnight, Choudhury, & Kacmar, 2002). Yoon (2002) proposed that navigation, in the form of ease of use, affects online trust. In Yoon's study, ease of use is defined by the items: I find the system to be easy to use, I find it easy to get the system to do what I want it to do; interacting with the system does not requires a lot of my mental effort.

Other e-commerce researchers have also borrowed from the Technology Acceptance Model's (TAM) terminology "ease of use". Agarwal and Venkatesh (2002) included ease of use in their Web usability instrument. However, they operationalized ease of use as goals, structure and feedback rather than focusing exclusively on the navigation aspects.

Several studies using TAM established the relationship between perceived ease of use and trust (Gefen, Karahanna, & Straub, 2003; Jarvenpaa & Todd, 1997). Gefen et al.'s (2003) study links TAM to trust. They concluded that perceived ease of use positively impacts trust. Perceived ease of use is an antecedent of trust (Pavlou, 2003). In a study of consumer acceptance of e-commerce, Pavlou (2003) confirmed that perceived ease of use is positively correlated with trust and supports the relationship between trust and ease of use. However, Pavlou uses trust as an antecedent to ease of use while in the context of our model we use ease of use as an antecedent to trust. Such discrepancies are potentially due to the complexity of the interrelationships among the other variables that are different within the models. We use the construct perceived ease of navigation to customize "ease of use" explicitly for the Web environment and to focus on the design element of navigation. Thus we propose:

H2: *Perceived ease of navigation is positively related to trust.*

Web Self-Efficacy

In this study, we evaluate self-efficacy pertaining to the Internet experience and use the term Web self-efficacy. Web self-efficacy is defined as an individual's beliefs in their ability to use the Web to perform a task. The construct of self-efficacy was developed by Bandura (1977, 1982, 1997). Bandura's Social Cognitive Learning Theory defined self-efficacy as people's beliefs in their ability to organize and execute the courses of action required to attain designated levels of a particular task performance. Bandura argued that beliefs of personal efficacy constitute the key factor of human agency. This reflects an individual's subjective confidence in his/her capabilities to exercise control over events rather than an objective evaluation of skills or performance. Efficacy beliefs also influence an individual's thought patterns and emotional reactions. Efficacy beliefs also help determine how much effort people will expend on an activity, how long they will persevere when facing obstacles. It is also known that self-efficacy is positively correlated with effort, persistence, and resilience. Self-efficacy has received support from diverse fields (Bandura, 1997; Madduxtanley, 1986; Multon, Brown & Lent, 1991). For example, self-efficacy was the focus of studies on clinical problems such as phobias (Bandura, 1982) and social skills (Multon, Brown & Lent, 1991).

Furthermore, self-efficacy was extended to the computer usage area, in which, a number of studies have been performed (e.g., Marakas et al., 1998; Marakas et al., 2007). It was repeatedly reported to constitute a major factor in understanding the frequency and success with which individuals use computers. Individuals with high self-efficacy used computers more often and with pleasure; consequently, they experienced less computer related anxiety (Compeau & Higgins, 1995). Level of enjoyment and anxiety levels were also significant predictors of computer use. Similar research by Hill, Smith and Mann on self-efficacy on computer use shows that self-efficacy explains computer use because self-efficacy affects an individual's intention to use computers (Hill & Hannafin, 1997; Hill, Smith, & Mann, 1987). Hasan (2007) concludes that computer self-efficacy and system complexity have significant direct effects on perceived usefulness and perceived ease of use as well as indirect effects on attitude and behavioral intention.

Self-efficacy beliefs are recognized as a factor that contributes to the success of completing a task. People with low self-efficacy potentially believe that things are harder than they are capable of accomplishing. High self-efficacy, on the other hand, increases people's confidence in doing a task and completing it successfully. Because self-efficacy is based on self-perceptions regarding particular behaviors, the construct is considered situation specific or domain sensitive. Because of the increasing reliance on the Internet technologies in all aspects of life, it is relevant to include the study of self-efficacy in relationship to Website issues.

Web Self-Efficacy and Navigation

People are generally more interested in performing activities in which they have high self-efficacy (Ren, 2000). As a result it is inferred that people with high Web self-efficacy are more likely to take advantage of what the Web has offered and used them more frequently. Higher self-efficacy translated in higher search efficiency, success and satisfaction (Nahl & Tenopir, 1996). High search efficiency is inferred to be the same as high navigation skills. In a study of library instruction and self-efficacy, Ren (2000) provides evidence of a positive correlation between a student's self-efficacy and the frequency of use of the library electronic resources. Using electronic resources involves the activities of navigation. The implication from Ren's study is that self-efficacy is related to navigation. In Ren's work prior Internet experience was the strong predictor of Internet self-efficacy. In several other research works using the TAM, self-efficacy and perceived ease of use was tested (Chau, Au, & Tam, 1995; Venkatesh & Davis, 1996). Because the perceived ease of use measure is similar to our perceived ease of navigation measure, we infer a relationship between self-efficacy and perceived ease of navigation as stated in the following hypothesis:

***H3:** Web self-efficacy has a positive effect on perceived ease of navigation.*

Prior Internet Experience

Prior experience is an antecedent of self-efficacy (Lewis, 1985). Through experiences people learn and gain skills (Bandura, 1982; Oliver & Shapiro, 1993). Therefore, prior experience with the Internet and related skills should be positively related to Internet self-efficacy. A positive relationship between prior experience and Internet self-efficacy were confirmed (Eastin & Robert, 1997). Self-efficacy is an essential part of the human functioning reciprocally motivating and perpetuating the individual's behavior (Bandura, 1982). The concept of self-efficacy is considered a theoretical foundation in determining the individual differences. According to Bandura (1982), self-efficacy is the concept by which each person's experiences, abilities, and thoughts merge. Still others have found that prior Internet experience is a strong predictor of Internet self-efficacy (Ren, 2000). This suggests our fourth hypothesis as follows:

***H4:** Prior Internet experience is positively related to Web self-efficacy.*

In Venkatesh and Davis's study (1996), experience is one of the antecedents of perceived ease of use. Hackbarth, Grover and Yi (2003) also confirmed the positive relationship between experience and ease of use. Given that perceived ease of navigation is a special case of ease of use, we therefore posit:

***H5:** Prior Internet experience is positively related to perceived ease of navigation.*

In the literature, there is recognition that familiarity is a predictor for trust (Gefen, Karahanna, & Straub, 2003; Luhmann, 1988). Bhattacherjee (2002) defines familiarity as "one's understanding of another's behavior based on prior interactions or experiences." Several other researchers (Rempel, Holmes, & Zanna, 1985; Schonberg, Hoch, Podlaseck, & Spraragen, 2000) state past experience may foster or detract trust. Positive experience strengthens the trust relationship and negative experience weakens it. Furthermore, McKnight, Choudhury and Kacmar (2002) confirmed the positive relationship between Web experience with trust beliefs and site quality with trust beliefs and intention. According to Consumer Web Watch (http://www.consumerwebwatch.org/news/1_credibility.htm), the most experienced Internet users generally trust e-commerce sites more than novice users. Both academic and practitioner support suggests that Web experience relates to trust on the Internet (Gefen, Karahanna, & Straub, 2003; McKnight, Choudhury, & Kacmar 2002). Therefore, our sixth hypothesis is as follows:

***H6:** Prior internet experience is positively related to trust.*

Gender

Gender differences have been examined from various dimensions, for example, investigating differences in *emotional* intelligence abilities between age and *gender* groups (Kafetsios, 2004), discrimination and salary differences between men and women (Auster, 1989; Larwood, Gutek, & Gattiker, 1984), and differences in learning strategies (Carr & Jessup, 1997). The numerous gender-related studies provide mixed results. However, much of this literature supports the contention that different genders exhibit different behaviors. For example, Bailey (2005) found significant differences between genders for online product review Websites. Males are more aware of the product review Websites, are more likely to visit a product review Website before and visit a product review Website prior to purchase.

Imhoff, Vollmeyer and Beierlein (2007) conclude that the gender gap is closing for computer access and self-efficacy. When comparing computer usage, female and male students are comparable. Yet, male students outperform female students at a computer task (remastering of Power-Point slides) and males spend more time at the computer for personal purposes.

Specifically related to Internet purchases, a shopping behavior study found that categories of products purchased and other shopping attributes varied significantly by gender (Kim & Kim, 2004). Their study identified predictors of the intention to purchase clothes, jewelry, or accessories based on online shopping attributes and demographic variables. Women enjoy shopping more than men and women are more thoughtful than men (Cleveland, Babin, Laroche, Ward & Bergeron, 2003). Men like to shop for functional products and women like to shop for aesthetics products. Generally speaking, women hold more positive attitudes toward shopping and hold more positive images of store shopping and catalog shopping than do men (Compeau & Higgins, 1995). Prior studies provide empirical evidence that important differences exist in information processing styles between men and women (Fischer & Arnold, 1994; Zeithaml, 1985). When shopping online, consumers use information display on the Website to judge product quality and make shopping decisions. A significant interactive effect between format and gender has been identified (Togo & Hood, 1992). Prior studies indicate women pay more attention to the physical appearance than men. For example, when evaluating service quality, women rate the physical environment more highly than men (Hofstede, 1980). The same attention to the physical layout can be extended to the online environment. Online stores are pictured with colors, graphics, animations, texts or videos. These physical elements perform the same cues regarding quality in an online environment that physical layout or product arrangement does in a "brick and mortar" store. In addition, women have been found to be more "emotionally intelligent" than men (Kafetsios, 2004; Petrides, Furnham, & Martin, 2004). The stimuli on the Website such as colors, graphics and overall layout may create a stronger emotional effect for women than for men resulting in stronger perceptions regarding quality, and in turn, whether the Website can be trusted. We therefore propose:

H7: *Perceived presentation quality will influence trust more strongly for women than men.*

Research has found differences in the level of spatial ability among males and females resulting from differences in the development of the brain hemispheres (McGee, 1979; Peter, 1995). Therefore, due to neuropsychological differences, the results of several studies have indicated that males outperform females on spatial tasks (Cochran & Wheatley, 1989). When implementing spatial tasks, men and women use different cognitive strategies (Bosco, Longoni, & Vecchi, 2004). Successful task performance is also more consistent with the male stereotype than with the female stereotype. Task-oriented factors are more important for men than for women (Multon, Brown, & Lent, 1991). Men are more achievement oriented and would like to engage in activities that weigh more heavily on factors affecting task completion (Venkatesh & Morris, 2000). Navigation is a task-oriented activity. One study showed that females take more linear steps than males in navigation (Reed & Oughton, 1997). Men show different Web use patterns than women (Jackson, Ervin, Gardner, & Schmitt, 1992). Men like to search and women like to communicate. These different usage patterns suggest that men weigh the importance of navigation more heavily than women. It is reasonable to extend prior studies on gender difference to a Website context. We expect gender differences still exist on Web information search and judgment formation. These different gender-related Web habits moderate the relationships between trust and navigation. We therefore propose:

H8: *Perceived ease of navigation will influence trust more strongly for men than for women.*

METHODOLOGY

Website Selection

Ten industries selected were: (1) general merchandiser, (2) computer software, (3) electronics and electrical equipment, (4) telecommunications, (5) commercial banks, (6) food and drug, (7) wholesalers, (8) motor vehicles and parts, (9) specialist retailers and (10) forest products. These industries were selected for two reasons: (1) they are a very diverse group of industries and (2) at least 20 Fortune 500 companies were found in each industry. Two hundred Fortune 500 companies, 20 from each category, were randomly selected for Website evaluation. Fortune 500 were chosen because business students are probably familiar with these companies. Also, because Fortune 500 are considered in the same high revenue bracket it was deemed likely that their technology capability and available resources did not restrict their ability to deliver a desired Website. Because of the randomization process in assigning Websites to respondents, there should be little effect due to subjects themselves in determining differences among clusters of companies.

Research Participants

About 800 junior and senior level business students were notified of the opportunity to participate in the Web evaluation project. Participation in this project was voluntary although a few extra credit points were given to those who participated. Subjects were notified of this opportunity in class by their instructors. Basic computing skills including Internet competencies are incorporated into mandatory lower-level courses in the Business College. Based on the subjects' ages and demographics, the participants from this group constitute subjects with high likelihood of being frequent Web uses and purchasers. In partial support of this group's capability of evaluating Websites our data show that most of them have made or considered making Web purchases in the recent past. In addition, a reasonable body of work exists that suggests that the college student population resembles real Web users and that college students are appropriate subjects for Web evaluation (Gefen, Karahanna, & Straub, 2003; Hackbarth, Grover & Yi, 2003; McKnight & Chervany, 2001-2002; McKnight, Choudhury, & Kacmar 2002).

Pilot Study

A pilot study of 10 junior and senior level students was used to test a preliminary version of the questionnaire. Each respondent completed the questionnaire and provided feedback to the researchers. Items 13 and 14 were reworded after reviewing the pilot study so that they would be more relevant to determination of the perceived ease of navigation. Researchers in this study felt that respondents were not showing bias towards specific types of firms because feedback from the students indicated that they were judging each Website on its own merit.

Protocol

Twenty Fortune 500 companies were randomly selected for each participant using a visual basic program. A cover letter describing the purpose of Web evaluation was distributed to the interested respondents in class. The cover letter and the Excel Web evaluation file containing links to 20 Fortune Company Web addresses were emailed separately to about 800 subjects. The Excel file contained 19 columns with the first column holding the links to 20 Fortune companies and the remaining 18 columns containing the survey items for each company. They were given 3 weeks to finish the evaluation. The cover letter told the respondent to use the 1-7 Likert scale to evaluate each of the 20 Websites. Respondents were asked to input their answer into the Excel file that was provided. Upon completing the evaluation of the 20 Websites, the respondents then sent an email with their Excel file to the researchers.

At the end of the 3-week period, the researchers received 216 e-mails with Excel file attachments from the respondents. In addition to the instrument, demographic questions were asked. With this restriction, there were 3535 usable Website evaluations. Therefore the Websites were evaluated by respondents who self-reported that they had reasonably good skills in evaluating Websites. During the data collection procedure, it was discovered that some Websites were down or took an unusually long time to be displayed. Occasionally, the browser would even "crash" as a Website was starting to be displayed. Hence, participants did not respond to the evaluation of Websites in which difficulty was encountered in opening the site.

The demographics of the respondents include 48.3% males and 51.7% females. In this sample 51.4% of the respondents made prior purchases online. The subjects in this study were students that can access the Internet at school and all have experience with the Internet. The basic issues of user interface, layout, and navigation structure are not new to these respondents. With respect to the age distribution, 75.8% of the respondents are under 25, 18.3% of the respondents are between 26-35, and 5.9% of the respondents are over 36.

Measures

The items used in our instrument are shown in Table 1 (Zhang et al., 2000). We used three items to assess trust based on Rousseau et al.'s (1998) definition: "A psychological state comprising the intention to accept vulnerability based on positive expectations of the intentions and behaviors of the others." This is supported by prior literature (e.g., Meyerson et al., 1996; Wrightsman, 1991). To measure the quality of the presentation, we included items on colors, graphics, and the amount of information displayed and the appeal of the layout. These dimensions were researched in prior studies (Huizingh, 2000; McClure et al., 1997). To measure perceived ease of navigation, we included items that captured the ease of locating information, the meaningfulness of graphics, user' expectation of links, and the ease of identifying links (McClure et al., 1997). To measure Web self-efficacy, we used three items about confidence level in navigating the Internet, confidence level in evaluating Web design and confidence level in evaluating Web content. A seven-point Likert was used for all the items with 1 representing strongly disagree and 7 corresponding to strongly agree.

We performed t-tests on the key constructs: Web self-efficacy, navigation and trust. The results show no significant differences between the groups who purchased online with those who did not purchase online for navigation and trust but there was a significant difference for Web self-efficacy. In purchasing items on a Website, buyers are usually required to enter additional information and navigate through extra screens that the non-pur-

Table 1. Description of survey items

Item Description
Information appears to be believable.
I would recommend this site to a colleague
Viewing this site gives me a good image of the company
Please rate your skills in navigating Websites
Please rate your skills in evaluating Website design.
Please rate your skills in evaluating web content
The use of graphics is very appropriate for this site
This site is appealing.
The amount of information displayed is just right
The colors in this Website are pleasant
Information links are located where I would expect them to be.
This site organized its information in a way that is easy for me to understand.
The graphical presentation appears to be helpful in navigating
Someone without knowledge about this company could easily find information

chasers do not. According to Social Cognitive Theory, experiences such as this which provide feedback and allow the individual to successfully complete a task (i.e., transacting an online purchase) can build self-efficacy through the process of enactive mastery.

As with any survey, nonresponse bias and common method variance are the limitations of this study. To assess nonresponse bias, we followed the method suggested by Armstrong and Overton (1977) and compared the last 20% of the respondents with early respondents on trust, perceived quality of presentation and perceived ease of navigation constructs. The t values are 1.22, 1.45, and 1.56 respectively. These values were not significant and support the contention that nonresponse bias is not a concern to this study.

The widely used Harman's single-factor test was conducted to check the issue of common method variance (Anderson & Bateman, 1997; Greene & Organ, 1973). Exploratory factor analysis was used to analyze all latent constructs. Results show that four eigenvalues exceed 1 (ranging from 1.02 to 10.9) and account for 66.6% of variance in the items. Eigenvalue value results appear to be supportive for four factors.

Care was taken to ensure the validity and reliability of the measures. First, we interviewed experts to ensure the clarity and appropriateness of these items. Next, we conducted a pilot study to further refine the items and establish content validity. In addition, we assessed construct validity and reliability (Cook & Campbell, 1979). Partial least squares (PLS) was used to analyze data. PLS is regularly employed for confirmatory testing in IS research It is viewed as an alternate approach to SEM and will converge to parameter estimates when maximum likelihood estimators cannot be found. According to Barclay et al. (1995), a generally accepted rule of thumb for acceptable loadings is 0.70 or above. Table 2 shows the factor loadings, composite reliability and average variance extracted. All the PLS loadings are greater than 0.7 and are statistically significant. The average variances extracted are greater than 0.5 for all the constructs and these results along with statistically significant and high loadings provide evidence of convergent validity and discriminant validity.

In addition, we also checked the most widely used internal consistency reliability coefficient, Cronbach's alpha. Some suggest that the acceptance level for coefficient alpha is at least 0.7 (Robinson, Shaver, & Wrightman, 1991). Table 3 shows the reliability scores and descriptive statistics for the constructs in this work. All the constructs show reliability scores that range from 0.81 to 0.94, thus demonstrating adequate reliability. Table 4 shows correlations between constructs.

Results

Our purpose is to confirm the relationships proposed in our research model within the context of this study and this simultaneously tests the transference of these concepts to trust on the Internet.

Table 2. Survey items and factor loadings

	Items	Loadings	t-value	AVE	Reliability
Presentation	p1	0.82	106.59	0.68	0.90
	p2	0.82	128.77		
	p3	0.79	79.85		
	p4	0.88	171.15		
Navigation	n1	0.86	146.74	0.74	0.90
	n2	0.86	34.24		
	n3	0.87	110.38		
Trust	t1	0.83	104.17	0.77	0.91
	t2	0.89	194.10		
	t3	0.90	234.73		

Table 3. Descriptive statistics and reliability of constructs

Constructs	Number of Items	Alpha	Means	S.D.
Perceived Quality of Presentation	4	0.93	5.05	1.19
Perceived Ease of Navigation	4	0.94	5.06	1.23
Trust	3	0.92	5.07	1.29
Web Self Efficacy	3	0.81	2.05	0.92
Prior Internet Experience	1		2.91	1.72

We analyze our path model and our analysis shows the R^2 is 71.7% when experience, perceived quality of presentation and perceived ease of navigation are used to predict trust; R^2 is 15% when prior Internet experience is used to predict Web self-efficacy; R^2 is 5% when Web self-efficacy and prior Internet experience is used to predict perceived ease of navigation. Figure 2 shows the significant paths as solid lines and the nonsignificant paths as dashed lines. Table 5 shows the relationships among the constructs, coefficients and *t* values. Table 5 also shows that only the relationships between trust and perceived ease of navigation, trust and perceived quality of presentation, experience and perceived ease of navigation, experience and Web self-efficacy are significant. The coefficient of 0.48 with a 0.001% significance level from perceived ease of navigation to trust suggests the importance of navigation on the Web. This implies that deadlinks or links of a different context or beyond the consumers' expectation are detrimental to virtual companies. The coefficient of 0.43 between trust and perceived quality of presentation with a 0.001% significance level demonstrates the importance of presentation in determining the consumers' perception of trust. On the Web, how information is organized, the amount of information displayed, and how graphics are created and displayed are different dimensions of trust of virtual companies. If a Website makes consumers uncomfortable, it is hard for them to think the Website is reliable and trustworthy. Figure 2 and the results show confirmation of H1 and H2, H4, H5 but that H3 and H6 were not confirmed.

Table 4. Correlations between constructs

	Web Self-Efficacy	Perceived Quality of Presentation	Perceived Ease of Navigation	Trust	Prior Internet Experience
Web Self-Efficacy	1				
Perceived Quality of Presentation	0.06 (p=0.05)	1			
Perceived Ease of Navigation	0.07 (p=0.04)	0.74 (p<.001)	1		
Trust	0.07 (p=0.04)	0.79 (p<.001)	0.82 (p<.001)	1	
Prior Internet Experience	0.80 (p<.001)	0.07 (p=0.04)	0.07 (p=0.04)	0.05 (p=0.06)	1

Table 5. PLS path coefficients and t-values

	Coefficient	t-value	R^2
Trust = Experience + Perceived quality of presentation+ Perceived ease of navigation	-0.01 0.43 0.48	0.82 27.16*** 37.66***	71.7%
Perceived ease of navigation = Web Self Efficacy + Prior Internet Experience	0.02 0.08	0.88 3.52***	5%
Web self efficacy = Prior Internet Experience	0.39	29.12***	15%

* p < 0.05; **p < 0.01; ***p < 0.001

Figure 2. Basic model paths

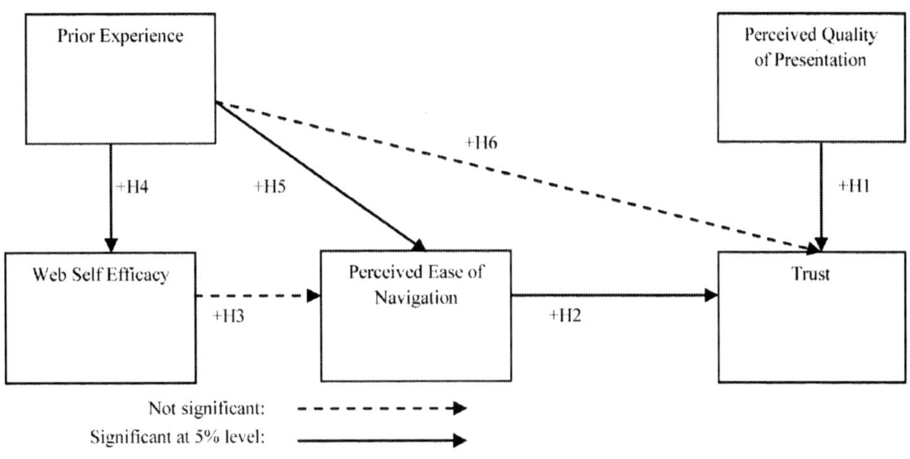

Examining the Moderating Effect of Gender

To examine the moderating effect of gender in our model on the relationship between perceived quality of presentation and trust and perceived ease of navigation and trust, the data set was split into two with one set containing only male responses and the other set containing only female responses. The model was then run separately using both data sets (Baron & Kenny, 1986). Table 6 shows the results for the two split data sets. A regression

Table 6. Regression coefficients for gender moderating the relationship with trust

	Female		Male	
Independent Variable	**Coefficient**	**t-value**	**Coefficient**	**t-value**
Perceived quality of presentation	0.57	8.9**	0.29	24.04**
Perceived ease of navigation	0.16	2.6*	0.39	17.9**

* $p < 0.05$; ** $p < 0.01$; *** $p < 0.001$

analysis on the split data sets was performed. By comparing the results between the two data sets, the coefficient of perceived quality of presentation is 0.57 for female whereas 0.29 for male; the coefficient of perceived ease of navigation is 0.16 for female whereas the coefficient of that is 0.39 for male. Although both perceived quality of presentation and perceived ease of navigation are significant predictors of trust, the magnitude of the difference in the coefficients indicates that females and males have different preferences or weights assigned to these variables. The magnitude of the coefficients shows that females weight perceived quality of presentation more heavily than males, while males consider perceived ease of navigation more important than perceived quality of presentation.

Joreskog and Wold (1981, p.270) suggest that "PLS is primarily intended for causal-predictive analysis in situations of high complexity but low theoretical information." In addition, Chin et al. (2003) state that PLS is appropriate for predictive analysis. We used PLS to perform a structural model analysis that examined the hypothesized relationships among presentation, navigation, trust, prior experience, as well as the interaction effects between gender and presentation and gender and navigation. The overall model is significant: trust = 0.35 presentation + 0.43 navigation - 0.12 gender + 0.07 prior experience + 0.13 gender*presentation + 0.07 gender*navigation. The R^2 is 72.1%, which indicates good model fit. The interaction is significant between gender and presentation but not significant between gender and navigation. The results confirmed H7 but not H8.

DISCUSSION AND IMPLICATIONS

This study proposed and tested a model of trust in an e-commerce environment. Our hypotheses confirm the positive relationships between perceived quality of presentation and trust and perceived ease of navigation and trust. We also identified interactive effects showing that perceived presentation quality influences trust more strongly for women than men and perceived ease of navigation influences trust more strongly for men than women. In addition, we found that experience and Web self-efficacy are antecedents to perceived ease of navigation. All hypothesized relationships except the relationship between prior experience and trust were significant. These results provide a number of theoretical and practical implications.

Our study extends previous research that found Website ease-of-use was significantly related to trust by investigating specific Web interface design factors. We provide evidence that both the users' perceptions of Website presentation quality as well as ease of navigation are key elements in building customer trust. Web users come to a Website with a purpose but want to be sure that they can trust the Website. The layout of the information and graphics gives users impressions about the care and convenience and provides information cues of the overall quality of presentation, designed into the site. Because Web stores cannot be physically contacted, their perceived quality of presentation

Table 7. PLS results of model showing the interactive effects of gender

	Coefficient	t-value
Perceived Quality of Presentation	.0.29	16.02***
Perceived Quality of Navigation	.43	13.31***
Gender	-.12	3.32**
Prior experience	0.07	0.59
Gender* Perceived Quality of Presentation	.13	5.04***
Gender* Perceived Ease of Navigation	0.07	1.34

* $p < 0.05$; ** $p < 0.01$; *** $p < 0.001$

is akin to certain features of brick-and-mortar stores. Users may come to a Website with some preconceived expectations for that site. Upon judging the Web pages appearance and elements such as how product information is presented or business policies displayed, Web users are further formulating their evaluation of the trustworthiness of the Website. It is easier for users to visit a different site via a click than visit another brick and mortar store. Shim, Shin, and Nottingham (2002) show that disconfirmation of expectations about a site's perceived quality of presentation causes the customer to discontinue shopping at that site.

Perceived ease of navigation is also important in building trust. In general, navigation facilitates the locating of the desired information with ease. Users lose patience if they are unable to find the information they are looking for quickly and, as a result, they may leave the site. Such experiences also result in negative recommendations to friends about the site or future visits to the site. Navigation is represented on the Website via textual links or graphical links. The metaphor of the texts and graphics should match the users' mental model. Navigation was recognized as a factor influencing users' attitude toward online shopping (Yoon, 2002). Simply viewing the links, users can guess what kind of information may be found on the following page. Navigation is efficient and effective if the user is able to quickly access what he or she wants. Having navigational indicators readily apparent and well laid out provides the user with a sense that the Website's organization was planned with care and that the company is cognizant of the users' need to access information without difficulty. Our results imply that Websites designed in such a way engender trust.

Our data also showed that gender variations were significant. The difference in magnitude of the coefficients of presentation and perceived ease of navigation between males and females suggests that Websites should put more efforts into their presentation if the sites are tailored toward women. Therefore, sites that sell items that are generally of more interest to female shoppers than males such as cosmetic, clothes, and health products are appropriate for greater investment in the presentation area. On the other hand, sites that sell auto parts, automobiles, computers and electronics have a majority of male customers. To better address consumers' perceptions of Websites and produce trust in Websites, these male dominated sites would be better served by shifting limited resources toward a greater focus on the metaphor used for navigation and its structure.

Our study provides additional evidence that gender differences exist and should be taken into consideration when designing Websites. However, more research should be done in this area because past research results have been mixed. For example, Simon and Peppas' (2005) findings that males possess more positive attitudes than females toward media rich Websites may appear to contradict our findings that females are more attuned to Website presentation issues. However, two important differences exist between our study and this prior one. First, in our study, one aspect of presentation quality was that, "The amount of information displayed is just right." It is possible that intensively media rich Websites may overwhelm at least some females and cause them to distrust the site. Future study is needed to confirm this supposition. Second, our study specifically investigates the relationship between design variables and trust, not just general attitudes. Most of the prior studies regarding gender differences and Web design have examined attitudes or affect rather than trust. Thus, our empirical investigation of the moderating effect of gender and Website design on trust represents an important contribution to the literature.

Self-efficacy was shown to be a direct antecedent of perceived ease of navigation and prior experience a direct antecedent of self-efficacy. This highlights the notion that Websites for novice or new computer users must be extremely easy to navigate. While our sample was composed of U.S. participants, companies whose target market includes less computer- experienced populations would do well to focus on the navigational aspects of their Websites.

Our hypothesis stating that prior internet usage was related to trust was not supported. Our finding is contrary to Jarvenpaa and Todd's (1997) suggestion that greater experience with the Web is associated with lower trust and higher risk in evaluating a particular merchant. However, our finding is consistent with the work of Schoenbachler and Gordon (2002). In addition, several researchers (Reichheld & Schefter, 2000; Schoenbachler & Gordon, 2002) state that past experience fosters or detracts from the perception of trust. Therefore, two possible explanations are provided for the failure to support H6. First, the nonsignifcant relationship between prior experience and trust could be because of the relative nature of the respondents' past experiences. Positive experience strengthens the trust relationship and negative experience weakens trust relationship. Given such a situation the experiences within a group of individuals can be either biased or mixed. Another possible reason for the disconfirmation of H6 is that experienced Internet users rely on visual cues to develop trust with a particular Website instead of using past experience. Experienced users visit many different Websites and have different evaluations of those Websites. A respondent's general trust impression on the Internet may be mixed and they may deal with site evaluation on case-by-case basis.

Overall, this work has implications for commercial applications because if a Website gains the users' trust, there are considerable benefits because trust can transform to loyalty and loyalty translates into revenue (Gefen, 2002a). Loyalty translates into revenue because it results in a stable and increasing customer base. Companies can focus on designing Websites in a manner that evokes trust in an effort to obtain the associated loyalty and potential revenue.

Limitations

This study examines trust from the consumers' perspective by investigating the relevance of perceived quality of presentation and perceived ease of navigation features of a Website. There are several limitations associated with this study. First, the respondents in this study are students in a business college. In terms of their demographics, student samples are usually more homogeneous than the general population. However, as noted earlier, previous research has found that college students are appropriate subjects for Web evaluation (Gefen, Karahanna, & Straub, 2003; McKnight, Choudhury, & Kacmar 2002). Second, we notified the respondents that the Websites they were to evaluate are Fortune 500 companies (200 of Fortune 500 companies were evaluated). This knowledge potentially created positive expectations before the actual evaluation started because the respondents' knowledge of the size and reputation of the company potentially transferred to its Website. Despite this potential positive affect, the data showed differences between the Websites based upon the constructs defined in our model. Third, we suffer mono-method bias because our operationalization of prior Internet experience relied on one item. Fourth, our measure for perceived ease of navigation assessed the opinions or perceptions subjects gathered from the Websites' homepage. Respondents evaluated whether the information links were in the expected location, the organization and graphical presentation appeared helpful in navigating, and navigational aides, in general, were in place to easily find information. To examine *actual* navigation, autonomous software tools such as used by Scharl and Bauer (1999) may be useful. However, consistent with the substantial body of literature on perceived ease of use, we also investigated perceived rather than actual navigation.

Future Research Directions

With advancements in Web development and technology, the Web increasingly plays a role in business operations and trust of the Website is becoming more critical. In customer relationship management, Websites can build connections and provide interactions with Web users or potential customers. The customer experience is improved through providing information in a form that is easy to navigate and that lets customers make buying decisions at their own pace and schedule (McKnight, Choudhury & Kacmar 2002; McKnight & Chervany, 2001-2002). Customer relationship management tools are designed to help companies track, report and automate customer interaction. Recent progress includes using the Web to address the collaborative requirements of cross-functional customer-support teams. An area for further investigation is the exploration of the role of trust in these cross-functional customer-support teams and how the Web design of the systems they use impacts trust.

Another potential research area is trust in Web services. As this study confirms the positive relationship between presentation and trust, a professional looking Website does create impressions of credibility. Web services rely on the Web to deliver software applications. Trust is of utmost importance in the success of Web services. The design of such interface affects users' acceptance of Web services. Users tend to trust sites that are well-designed and well-organized. Providing the third party trust symbol on the Website enhances the users' trust building process. As companies depend on Web interfaces to reach their business potential, more effort needs to be devoted to creating interface designs that foster trust. Web services are currently a popular trend; trust and security are issues that hinder wide adoption of Web services. Ensuring security and inspiring trust between Web services providers and users could help the development of this trend.

An additional avenue of future research would be to conduct a study similar to the present one but in a lab environment where more objective measures could be gathered. For example, capturing time related information such as how long participants spend on each site, how long the site evaluations take, and how it takes for a visitor to determine trustworthiness might add valuable insights.

CONCLUSION

This work contributes to the Web usability literature and trust literature by exploring how Web interface design factors and their interaction with gender effects trust in an e-commerce environment. Additional relationships of interest were Web self-efficacy and the effect of prior experience. We proposed a research model that posits the relationships among the constructs and tested these hypothesized relationships. This study confirmed five of the eight proposed hypotheses. The confirmation of perceived quality of presentation and ease of navigation significantly influencing trust suggests to practitioners the importance of the interface in trust building. Although practitioners well recognize the importance of a Website's look and feel, interface design is usually approached from an aesthetics perspective rather than focusing on trust building mechanisms. Our study provides an alternative perspective, stressing the importance of Website design in creating trust. Companies need to leverage the findings provided by this study because trust leads to cooperative behaviors that are conducive to marketing success.

Gender differences also significantly interact with Website design elements. Presentation quality is more influential in fostering trust in women whereas ease of navigation is more important for men. Given these findings, companies can allocate limited Website design resources most effectively by understanding the demographics of their customer base.

REFERENCES

Agarwal, R., & Venkatesh, V. (2002). Assessing a firm's web presence: A heuristic evaluation procedure for the measurement of usability. *Information Systems Research, 13*(2), 168–186. doi:10.1287/isre.13.2.168.84

Anderson, L. M., & Bateman, T. S. (1997). Cynicism in the workplace: Some causes and effects. *Journal of Organizational Behavior, 18*, 449–469. doi:10.1002/(SICI)1099-1379(199709)18:5<449::AID-JOB808>3.0.CO;2-O

Armstrong J. S. & Overton, T. S. (1977). Estimating nonresponse bias in mail surveys. *ournal of Marketing Research, 14*(3), 396-402.

Auster, E. (1989). Task characteristics as a bridge between macro and micro research on salary inequality between men and women. *Academy of Management Review, 14*(2), 173–193. doi:10.2307/258415

Ba, S. (2001). Establishing online trust through a community responsibility system. *Decision Support Systems, 31*(3), 323–336. doi:10.1016/S0167-9236(00)00144-5

Bailey, A. A. (2005). Consumer awareness and use of product review websites. *Journal of Interactive Advertising, 6*(1), 90–108.

Bandura, A. (1977). *Social learning theory.* Englewood Cliffs, NJ: Prentice-Hall.

Bandura, A. (1982). Self-efficacy mechanism in human agency. *The American Psychologist, 37*, 122–147. doi:10.1037/0003-066X.37.2.122

Bandura, A. (1997). *Self-Efficacy: The exercise of control.* New York: Freeman.

Barclay, D., Thompson, R., & Higgins, C. (1995). The partial least squares approach to causal modeling: Personal computer adoption and use as an illustration. *Technology Studies: Special Issue on Research Methodology, 2*(2), 285–324.

Baron, R. M., & Kenny, D. A. (1986). The moderator-mediator variable distinction in social psychological research: Conceptual, strategic, and statistical considerations. *Journal of Personality and Social Psychology, 51*, 1173–1182. doi:10.1037/0022-3514.51.6.1173

Bauer, H. H. (2002). Customer relations through the internet. *Journal of Relationship Marketing, 1*(2), 39. doi:10.1300/J366v01n02_03

Benassi, P. (1999). TRUSTe: An online privacy seal program; Association for computing machinery. *Communications of the ACM, 42*(2), 56–58. doi:10.1145/293411.293461

Bevin, N. (2000). Usability issues in web site design. In *Proceedings of 6m Interactive Publishing*, Serco Usability Services (pp. 1-7).

Bhattacherjee, A. (2002). Individual trust in online firms: Scale development and initial test. *Journal of Management Information Systems, 19*(1), 211–241.

Blau, P. M. (1964). *Exchange and power in social life.* New York: John Wiley & Sons.

Bosco, A., Longoni, A. M., & Vecchi, T. (2004). Gender effects in spatial orientation: Cognitive profiles and mental strategies. *Applied Cognitive Psychology, 18*(5), 519–532. doi:10.1002/acp.1000

Carr, M., & Jessup, D. L. (1997). Gender differences in first-grade mathematics strategies: Social and metacognitive influences. *Journal of Educational Psychology, 89*(2), 318–328. doi:10.1037/0022-0663.89.2.318

Chau, P. Y. K. (2001). Influence of computer attitude and self-efficacy on it usage behavior. *Journal of End User Computing, 13*(1), 26–33. doi:10.4018/joeuc.2001010103

Chau, P. Y. K., Au, G., & Tam, K. Y. (1995). Impact of information presentation models on online shopping: An empirical evaluation of a broadband interactive shopping service. *Journal of Organizational Computing and Electronic Commerce, 10*(1), 1–22.

Chin, W. W., Marcolin, B. L., & Newsted, P. R. (2003). A partial least squares latent variable modeling approach for measuring interaction effects: Results from a Monte Carlo simulation study and an electronic-mail emotion/adoption study. *Information Systems Research, 14*(2), 189–217. doi:10.1287/isre.14.2.189.16018

Cleveland, M., Babin, B. J., Laroche, M., Ward, P., & Bergeron, J. (2003). Information search patterns for gift purchases: A cross-national examination of gender differences. *Journal of Consumer Behaviour, 3*(1), 20–47. doi:10.1002/cb.120

Cochran, K. F., & Wheatley, G. H. (1989). Ability and sex-related differences in cognitive strategies on spatial tasks. *The Journal of General Psychology, 116*(1), 43–55. doi:10.1080/00221309.1989.9711109

Cohen, J., Cohen, P., West, S. G., & Aiken, L. S. (2003). *Applied multiple regression/correlation analysis for the behavioral sciences* (3rd ed.). Mahwah, NJ: Lawrence Erlbaum.

Compeau, D. R., & Higgins, C. A. (1995). Computer self efficacy: Development of a measure and initial test. *Management Information Systems Quarterly, 19*(2), 189–211. doi:10.2307/249688

Cook, T. D., & Campbell, D. T. (1979). *Quasi-experimentation: Design & analysis issues for field settings*. Boston, MA: Houghton Mifflin Co.

David, P., Song, M., Hayes, A., & Fredin, E. S. (2007). A cyclic model of information seeking in hyperlinked environments: The role of goals, self-efficacy, and intrinsic motivation. *International Journal of Human-Computer Studies, 65*(2), 170–182. doi:10.1016/j.ijhcs.2006.09.004

Debreceny, R., Putterill, M., Tung, L., & Gilbert, A. L. (2003). New tools for the determination of e-commerce inhibitors. *Decision Support Systems, 34*(2), 177–195. doi:10.1016/S0167-9236(02)00080-5

Eastin, M. S., & Robert, L. L. (2000). Internet self efficacy and the psychology of the digital divide. *Journal of Computer Mediated Communication, 6*(1). Retrieved November 4, 2008, from http://www.ascusc.org/jcmc/vol6/issue1/eastin.html

Fernandes, A. D. (2001). Risking "trust" in a public key infrastructure: Old techniques of managing risk applied to new technology. *Decision Support Systems, 31*(3), 303–322. doi:10.1016/S0167-9236(00)00139-1

Fischer, E., & Arnold, S. J. (1994). Sex, gender identity, gender role attitudes, and consumer behavior. *Psychology &. Marketing, 11*(2), 163–182.

Gefen, D. (2002a). Customer loyalty in ecommerce. *Journal of the Association for Information Systems, 3*, 27–51.

Gefen, D. (2002b). Reflections on the dimensions of trust and trustworthiness among online consumers. *The Data Base for Advances in Information Systems*, *33*(3), 38–54.

Gefen, D., Karahanna, E., & Straub, D. W. (2003). Trust and TAM in online shopping: An integrated model. *Management Information Systems Quarterly*, *27*(1), 51–90.

Gefen, D., & Straub, D. W. (1997). Gender differences in the perception and use of e-mail: An extension of the technology acceptance model. *Management Information Systems Quarterly*, *21*, 389–400. doi:10.2307/249720

Giddens, A. (1990). *The consequences of modernity*. Oxford: Polity Press.

Greene, C. N., & Organ, D. W. (1973). An evaluation of causal models linking the received role with job satisfaction. *Administrative Science Quarterly*, *18*, 95–103. doi:10.2307/2391931

Hackbarth, G., Grover, V., & Yi, M. Y. (2003). Computer playfulness and anxiety: positive and negative mediators of the system experience effect on perceived ease of use. *Information & Management*, *40*, 221–232. doi:10.1016/S0378-7206(02)00006-X

Hasan, B. (2007). Examining the effects of Computer self-efficacy and system complexity on technology acceptance. *Information Resources Management Journal*, *20*(3), 76–88. doi:10.4018/irmj.2007070106

Heijden, H., Tibert, V., & Creemers, M. (2003). Understanding online purchase intentions: contributions from technology and trust perspectives. *European Journal of Information Systems*, *12*(1), 41–48. doi:10.1057/palgrave.ejis.3000445

Hill, J. R., & Hannafin, M. J. (1997). Cognitive strategies and learning from the world wide web. *Educational Technology Research and Development*, *45*(4), 37–64. doi:10.1007/BF02299682

Hill, T., Smith, N. D., & Mann, M. F. (1997). Role of efficacy expectations in predicting the decision to use advanced technologies: The case of computers. *The Journal of Applied Psychology*, *72*(2), 307–313. doi:10.1037/0021-9010.72.2.307

Hoffman, D. L., Novak, T. P., & Peralta, M. (1999). Building consumer trust online; Association for computing machinery. *Communications of the ACM*, *42*, 480–486.

Hofstede, G. (1980). *Culture's consequences: International Differences in Work Related Values*. London: Sage.

Hosmer, L. T. (1995). Trust: The connecting link between organizational theory and philosophical ethics. *Academy of Management Review*, *20*(2), 379–403. doi:10.2307/258851

Hsu, Yu-chang. (2006). Better educational website interface design: The implications from gender-specific preferences in graduate students. *British Journal of Educational Technology, 37*(2), 233-242.

Huizingh, E. (2000). The content and design of Websites: An empirical study. *Information & Management*, *37*, 123–134. doi:10.1016/S0378-7206(99)00044-0

Imhof, M., Vollmeyer, R., & Beierlein, C. (2007). Computer use and the gender gap: The issue of access, use, motivation, and performance. *Computers in Human Behavior*, *23*(6), 2823–2837. doi:10.1016/j.chb.2006.05.007

Jackson, L. A., Ervin, K. S., Gardner, P. D., & Schmitt, N. (2001). Gender and the Internet: Women communicating and men searching. *Sex Roles*, *44*(5/6), 363–379. doi:10.1023/A:1010937901821

Jarvenpaa, S., & Todd, P. (2004). Consumer reactions to electronic shopping on the World Wide Web. *International Journal of Electronic Commerce*, *1*(2), 59–88.

Joreskog, K. G., & Wold, H. (1981). The ML and PLS techniques for modeling with latent variables: Historical and comparative aspects. In Joreskog, H. W. A. K. (Ed.), *System under indirect observation: Causality, structure and prediction* (pp. 263–270). Amsterdam: North-Holland.

Kafetsios, K. (2004). Attachment and emotional intelligence abilities across the life course. *Personality and Individual Differences*, *37*(1), 129–146. doi:10.1016/j.paid.2003.08.006

Karacapilidis, N., & Moraïtis, P. (2001). Building an agent-mediated electronic commerce system with decision analysis features. *Decision Support Systems*, *32*(1), 53–69. doi:10.1016/S0167-9236(01)00100-2

Katerattanakul, P., & Siau, K. (1999). Measuring information quality of web sites: Development of an instrument. In *Proceedings of the Twentieth International Conference on Information Systems* (pp. 279-285), Charlotte, North Carolina.

Kim, E. Y., & Kim, Y. (2004). Predicting online purchase intentions for clothing products. *European Journal of Marketing*, *38*(7), 883–907. doi:10.1108/03090560410539302

Kimery, K. M., & McCord, D. M. (2002). Third-party assurances: The road to trust in online retailing. *In Proceedings of the 35th Hawaii Conference on System Sciences*, Hawaii.

Larwood, L., Gutek, B. A., & Gattiker, U. E. (1984). Perspective on institutional discrimination and resistance to change. *Group and Organizational Studies*, *9*, 333–352. doi:10.1177/105960118400900303

Lewicki, R. J., & Bunker, B. B. (1996). Developing and maintaining trust in work relationships. In Kramer, R. M., & Tyler, T. (Eds.), *Trust in organizations: Frontiers of theory and research* (pp. 114–139). Thousand Oaks, CA: Sage.

Lewis, C. (1985). An exploratory study of the influences of self efficacy on the personal computer learner. *Dissertation Abstracts International*.

Luhmann, N. (1988). Familiarity, confidence, trust: Problems and alternatives. In Gambetta, D. G. (Ed.), *Trust* (pp. 94–107). New York: Basil Blackwell.

Maccoby, E., & Jacklin, C. (1994). *The psychology of sex differences*. New York: University Press.

Maddux, J. E., & Stanley, M. A. (1986). Self efficacy theory in contemporary psychology. *Journal of Social and Clinical Psychology*, *4*(3), 347–382. doi:10.1521/jscp.1986.4.3.249

Marakas, G., Yi, M. Y., & Johnson, R. D. (1998). The multilevel and multifaceted character of computer self-efficacy: Toward clarification of the construct and an integrative framework for research. *Information Systems Research*, *9*(2), 126–163. doi:10.1287/isre.9.2.126

Marakas, G. M., Johnson, R. D., & Clay, P. F. (2007). The evolving nature of the computer self-efficacy construct: An empirical investigation of measurement construction, validity, reliability and stability over time. *Journal of the Association for Information Systems*, *8*(1), 15–46.

McClure, C. R., Wyman, S. K., Beachboard, J. B., & Eschenfelder, K. R. (1997). Developing system-based and user-based criteria for assessing federal websites. *Journal of the American Society for Information Science American Society for Information Science*, *34*, 78–88.

McGee, M. (1979). Human spatial abilities, psychometric studies and environmental, genetic, hormonal, and neurological influences. *Psychological Bulletin*, *86*, 889–918. doi:10.1037/0033-2909.86.5.889

McKnight, D. H., & Chervany, N. L. (2001-2002). What trust means in e-commerce customer relationships: an interdisciplinary conceptual typology. *International Journal of Electronic Commerce*, *6*, 235–260.

McKnight, D. H., Choudhury, V., & Kacmar, C. (2002a). Developing and validating trust measures for e-commerce: An integrative typology. *Information Systems Research*, *13*(3), 334–362. doi:10.1287/isre.13.3.334.81

McKnight, D. H., Choudhury, V., & Kacmar, C. (2002b). The impact of initial consumer trust on intentions to transact with a web site: A trust building model. *The Journal of Strategic Information Systems*, *11*(3/4), 297–323. doi:10.1016/S0963-8687(02)00020-3

Meyers-Levy, J., & Maheswaran, D. (1991). Exploring differences in males' and females' processing strategies. *The Journal of Consumer Research*, *18*(1), 63–70. doi:10.1086/209241

Meyers-Levy, J., & Sternthal, B. (1991). Gender differences in the use of message cues and judgments. *JMR, Journal of Marketing Research*, *28*(1), 84–96. doi:10.2307/3172728

Multon, K. D., Brown, S. D., & Lent, R. W. (1991). Relation of self efficacy beliefs to academic outcomes: A meta-analytic investigation. *Journal of Counseling Psychology*, *38*, 30–38. doi:10.1037/0022-0167.38.1.30

Nahl, D., & Tenopir, C. (1996). Affective and cognitive searching behavior of novice end-users of a full-text database. *Journal of the American Society for Information Science American Society for Information Science*, *47*(4), 276–286. doi:10.1002/(SICI)1097-4571(199604)47:4<276::AID-ASI3>3.0.CO;2-U

Nielsen, J. (2000). *Design web usability*. Indianapolis, IN: New Riders Publishing.

Oliver, T. A., & Shapiro, F. (1993). Self efficacy and computers. *Journal of Computer-Based Interactions*, *20*, 81–85.

Pavlou, P. A. (2003). Consumer acceptance of electronic commerce: Integrating trust and risk with the technology acceptance model. *International Journal of Electronic Commerce*, *7*(3), 101–134.

Peter, M. (1995). Spatial ability, student gender, and academic performance. *Journal of Engineering Education*, *84*(1), 69–73.

Petrides, K. V., Furnham, A., & Martin, G. N. (2004). Estimates of emotional and psychometric intelligence. *The Journal of Social Psychology*, *144*(2), 149–162. doi:10.3200/SOCP.144.2.149-162

Rather, J., & Grose, E. M. (1996). Characterization and assessment of HTML style guides. *CHI*, *96*, 115–116.

Reed, W. M., & Oughton, J. M. (1997). Computer experience and interval-based hypermedia navigation. *Journal of Research on Computing in Education*, *30*(1), 38–42.

Reichheld, F., & Schefter, P. (2000). E-loyalty: Your secret weapon on the web. *Harvard Business Review*, 105–113.

Rempel, J. K., Holmes, J. G., & Zanna, M. P. (1985). Trust in close relationships. *Journal of Personality and Social Psychology*, *49*, 95–112. doi:10.1037/0022-3514.49.1.95

Ren, (2000). Library instruction and college student self-sufficiency in electronic information searching. *Journal of Academic Librarianship*, *26*(5), 323-328.

Rosen, D. E., & Purinton, E. (2004). Website design: Viewing the web as a cognitive landscape. *Journal of Business Research*, *57*(7), 787–794. doi:10.1016/S0148-2963(02)00353-3

Rotter, J. B. (1971). Generalized expectancies for interpersonal trust. *The American Psychologist*, *26*, 443–452. doi:10.1037/h0031464

Rousseau, D., Sitkin, S. B., Burt, R. S., & Camerer, C. (1998). Not so different after all: A cross-discipline view of trust. *Academy of Management Review*, *23*(3), 393–404.

Scharl, A., & Bauer, C. (1999). Explorative analysis and evaluation of commercial web information systems. In *Proceedings of the Twentieth International Conference on Information Systems* (pp. 534-539), Charlotte, North Carolina.

Schoenbachler, D. D., & Gordon, G. L. (2002). Trust and customer willingness to provide information in database-driven relationship marketing. *Journal of Interactive Marketing*, *16*(3), 2–16. doi:10.1002/dir.10033

Schonberg, T. R., Hoch, M., Podlaseck, M., & Spraragen, S. (2000). Measuring success. *Communications of the ACM*, *43*(8), 53–57. doi:10.1145/345124.345142

Sharma, S., Durand, R. M., & Gurarie, O. (1981). Identification and analysis of moderator variables. *JMR, Journal of Marketing Research*, *18*(3), 291–300. doi:10.2307/3150970

Sheikh, K. (2004). Predicting risk among non-respondents in prospective studies. *European Journal of Epidemiology*, *2*(1), 39–43. doi:10.1007/BF00152716

Shim, S. B., Shin, Y. B., & Nottingham, L. (2002). Retailer web site influence on customer shopping: An exploratory study on key factors of customer satisfaction. *Journal of the Association for Information Systems*, *3*, 53–76.

Simon, S. J., & Peppas, S. (2005). Attitudes towards product website design: A study of the effects of gender. *Journal of Marketing Communications*, *11*(2), 129–144. doi:10.1080/1352726042000286507

Tan, Y., & Thoen, W. (2002). Formal aspects of a generic model of trust for electronic commerce. *Decision Support Systems*, *33*(3), 233–246. doi:10.1016/S0167-9236(02)00014-3

Teo, T. S. H., & Lim, V. K. G. (2000). Gender differences in Internet usage and task preferences. *Behaviour & Information Technology*, *19*(4), 283–295. doi:10.1080/01449290050086390

Thong, J. Y. L., Hong, W., & Tam, W. Y. (2004). What leads to user acceptance Of digital libraries? *Communications of the ACM*, *47*(11), 78–83. doi:10.1145/1029496.1029498

Togo, D. F., & Hood, J. N. (1992). Quantitative information presentation and gender: An interaction effect. *The Journal of General Psychology*, *119*(2), 161–167. doi:10.1080/00221309.1992.9921169

Venkatesh, V., & Davis, F. D. (1996). A model of the antecedents of perceived ease of use: Development and test. *Decision Sciences*, *27*(3), 451–481. doi:10.1111/j.1540-5915.1996.tb01822.x

Venkatesh, V., Morris, M., & Ackerman, P. (2000). A longitudinal field investigation of gender differences in individual technology adoption decision-making processes. *Organizational Behavior and Human Decision Processes*, *83*, 33–60. doi:10.1006/obhd.2000.2896

Venkatesh, V., & Morris, M. G. (2000). Why don't men ever stop to ask for directions? Gender, social influence, and their role in technology acceptance and usage behavior. *Management Information Systems Quarterly*, *24*(1), 115–139. doi:10.2307/3250981

Wang, R. Y., & Strong, D. M. (1997). Beyond accuracy: What data quality means to data consumers. *Journal of Management Information Systems*, *12*(4), 5–34.

Wang, W., & Benbasat, I. (2005). Trust in and adoption of online recommendation agents. *Journal of the Association for Information Systems*, *6*(3), 72–101.

www.consumerwebwatch.org/news/1_credibility.htm (2000). A matter of trust: What users want from web sites credibility and trust online.

Yoon, S. (2002). The antecedents and consequences of trust in online-purchase decisions. *Journal of Interactive Marketing*, *16*(2), 47. doi:10.1002/dir.10008

Zeithaml, V. A. (1985). The new demographics and market fragmentation. *Journal of Marketing*, *49*(3), 64–75. doi:10.2307/1251616

Zhang, X., Keeling, K., & Pavur, R. (2000). Information quality of commercial web site: An explorative analysis. In *Proceedings of the International Conference on Information Systems (ICIS)*, Brisbane, Australia.

This work was previously published in Journal of Organizational and End User Computing (JOEUC) 21(2), edited by Mo Adam Mahmood, pp. 44-66, copyright 2009 by IGI Publishing (an imprint of IGI Global).

Chapter 9
Capturing and Comprehending the Behavioral/Dynamical Interactions within an ERP Implementation

James R. Burns
Texas Tech University, USA

Don G. Jung
MyongJi University, Korea

James J. Hoffman
Texas Tech University, USA

ABSTRACT

The behavioral and dynamic implications of an ERP deployment are, to say the least, not well understood. Getting the switches set to enable the ERP software to go live is tedious. But the difficult part is understanding all of the dynamic interactions that accrue as a consequence. Connectionist and causal models are proposed in this article to facilitate an understanding of the dynamics and to enable control of the information-enhanced processes to take place. The connectionist model facilitates the understanding of the dynamic behavioral implications of the larger ERP implementation installation per se. The underlying connectionist model will observe and detect information transfers and workflow. Once maps of the total infrastructure are determined by the models, an analyst can suggest improvements. The models become decision support aids for process analysts in situations where ideal process flows/information transfers are sought.

INTRODUCTION

A class of packaged application software called Enterprise Resource Planning systems (ERP) seeks to integrate the complete range of a business's processes and functions in order to present a holistic view of the business from a single information and IT architecture. ERP systems are integrated, enterprise-wide systems that automate

DOI: 10.4018/978-1-60960-577-3.ch009

core corporate activities such as manufacturing, human resources, finance/accounting and supply chain management (Klaus, Roseman, & Gable, 2000). A brief history of ERP is provided by Jacobs and Weston (2007). Additionally, a discussion of a recent ERP implementation with focus on end-user training can be found at www.diplomica.com (2007).

From a research perspective, several longitudinal studies have been conducted of ERP systems to ascertain how well they achieved their objectives (Holsapple & Sena, 2003a; Holsapple & Sena, 2003b; Lonzinsky, 1998). Other more recent studies have examined research questions such as: (1) how change management issues relate to federated ERP systems (Abels, Brehm, Hahn, & Gomez, 2006); (2) what determinants of ERP implementation success are (Cegielski, Hall, & Rebman, 2006); (3) what factors bring about a successful implementation of a collaborative technology that results in productivity improvements in small businesses (Jones & Kochtanek, 2004); and (4) how organizational knowledge is shared during ERP implementation (Jones & Price, 2004). Hendricks, Singhal and Stratman (2007) provide an excellent discussion of how enterprise systems (ERP) affect corporate performance.

ERP is an important area of study since large organizations world-wide have already adopted ERP and increasingly, small- and medium-sized enterprises (SMEs) too are finding it cost effective and a competitive necessity to follow suit. Current ERP solutions are based on a three-tier client-server architecture, in which the data, the applications and the presentation layers form three logically independent levels, each distributed from the other. Typically, the data management layer contains the database and the applications layer contains the business logic, with each allocated to separate distributed servers. The applications server often contains a portion of the presentation layer in that it serves out Web pages. The final physical component is simply the Web browser which is also a part of the presentation layer, but resides on a different processor—the client.

The comprehensive functionality of any ERP system requires a corresponding reference model for the whole enterprise. In addition to the usual software documentation, the supported processes and organizational structures as well as the structure of the data and objects are usually depicted in a reference model called the Enterprise Model. This model enables rapid access to the functionality and allows navigation through different abstraction levels and between different views in the Enterprise Model.

Enterprise Modeling is the construction of an enterprise model as a limited system that represents the larger system in question. The purpose of Enterprise Modeling is to understand and improve the enterprise, that is, to improve the symbiosis of the individual business processes and objects. In this sense, improvement means any change in coordination among the business processes and between objects that increases the benefits of symbiosis. The methodology of Enterprise Modeling is the construction of a set of views of the enterprise considered as a system. The resulting enterprise model contains business processes and objects and their relationships. Enterprise Modeling is the tool of business engineering and reengineering.

Enterprise Modeling has been one of the main themes of research in ERP, BPR, Software Engineering and IT Project Management areas, and as a consequence there are many different reference models and methodologies for enterprise modeling. Although there are numerous models and methodologies for enterprise modeling, their general structures are all similar and one of the most important components that they usually include is the business process model.

In this article, our purpose is (1) to present an efficient and robust mechanism that can capture the patterns of information transfer between business processing entities and (2) to extract behavioral implications from them within an ERP framework.

For the purpose of this research, we integrated existing practice results from ERP enterprise and business process modeling with research we did on CIROS (Connectionist Inexact ReasOning System) for inexact reasoning (Jung, 1990; Jung & Burns, 1993).

This article consists of the following contents: in the next section (section two), we examine business process models for BPR within an ERP framework. In doing so, we focus on the problems and misuses and the possible causes for those problems and misuses in existing ERP systems. Also, we briefly review existing and industry-wide-adopted business process models.

In the third section, we present an information architecture for the prototype system to be proposed and suggest how this system would exist as a software layer juxtapositioned between other software layers so it can capture transaction traffic. We suggest that this layer will serve as a silent observer/recorder of all that goes on in terms of information transfer and workflow within the larger ERP system.

In the fourth section, we present a simplified business process model for our research purpose by modifying existing ones. The result is a Simplified Business Process Model (SBPM). Although it has a simple network structure, consisting of only two components—process nodes and links between nodes—we believe it serves well our research purpose and has enough scale-ability for practical applications.

In the fifth section, we briefly review the CIROS model and its underlying theoretical elements, and then modify the CIROS model to fit our current research concern. We combine the SBPM and CIROS models, and the result is a new connectionist model, called CLEAROS (Connectionist LEArning and ReasOning System), that has the capability of inferencing and learning for BPR[1] within an ERP framework.

In the sixth section, we suggest some further possible analyses that can be done based on the outputs of CLEAROS. In the seventh section, we provide an illustrative scenario of how the methodology could be used. In the final section, we summarize the research concepts and present some further issues extending the research result here.

BUSINESS PROCESS

Models for BPR Within an ERP Framework

The languages and methodologies for describing/modeling business processes are very diverse.[2] The types of models required to design, analyze and operate business enterprises have been discussed by numerous researchers (Jonkers & Franken, 1996; Kettinger & Grover, 1995). The general conclusion is simply that different models are required for different purposes. Thus, a critical research issue is to identify which type of model should be used for what purpose.

As stated previously, business processes can be described or modeled in various different ways for various purposes. However, our primary concern is the patterns of information flow between/among business processes and the behavioral ramifications that are consequences of these patterns, within an ERP framework. For that purpose, we are going to review a real business process model from an ERP software company and then, we build and present a business process model for our research purpose by simplifying it, which is the task described in Section 3. In the following, we briefly review and describe the business process model from SAP R/3 known as Business Blueprint (Curran & Keller, 1998).

SAP R/3 Business Process Model

A tool for business process engineering (and re-engineering) in the SAP R/3 system is Business Blueprint. It includes various components for BPR. The language and methodology of Business Blueprint is based on a concept called EPC (Event-driven Process Chaining).

EPC is based on four key elements: events (when should something be done?); tasks or functions (what should be done?); organization (who should do what?); and communication (what information is required to do the right task?). Events are the driving force behind a business process, prompting one or more activities to take place. The EPC provides the interconnections between tasks, data, and organizational units and the logical time sequence involved to define a business process.

An event always triggers a task. It is important for each task to begin with at least one event (the start event) and to end with at least one final event (the finish event). The organizational units (departments, people, etc.) responsible for doing the task are added to the model of the business process to show a complete picture of how the business process is structured and performed.

When companies are faced with the complexities of creating a business information construct, however, different issues require different analyses of aspects of the business. To fill this need, the Business Blueprint of the SAP R/3 system provides the users with the capability of modeling from various viewpoints the business functions and application components, business organizations, data, business processes, and interactions of the various components. Each view answers a distinct question about the interaction of business processes. Accordingly, the users of the Business Blueprint can produce different models from each view, (i.e., application component model, organization model, data model, process model and interaction model). Among these the process view is the central view, and hence the process model incorporates the other models to give the users an integrated view of the whole enterprise under consideration.

Problems with Existing ERP Systems for BPR

ERP software projects often deliver disappointing organizational results, even if the information systems work well technically. One explanation is that companies use technology to automate old, ineffective processes. Moreover, BPR has had a high failure rate with consultants estimating that as many as 70% of BPR projects fail (Hammer & Champy, 1993).

It is well known that the implementation of any ERP software system will drive changes to existing processes. Necessarily, those business processes must morph to accommodate the new software system. The real question is, did the changes required result in any improvement in overall performance? A study described in Gattiker and Goodhue (2002) suggests that the process changes necessitated by the implementation did NOT result in any improvement in overall performance, in spite of the fact that the ERP-imposed processes were supposed best practices. The study rejected the hypothesis that ERP-driven changes in business practices resulted in positive performance impacts from using the software. These results illustrate just how much more work needs to be done to truly discover how to maximize the potential benefits of ERP systems.

Research in artificial intelligence and expert systems (Holsapple & Whinston, 1996, pp. 462-490) suggests that if one were to ask managers how they react to a given scenario or situation, they could tell you, albeit incorrectly. It becomes necessary, therefore, to observe the managers at work and to record their responses from what is observed rather than from what they might say. This becomes even truer when more than one human decision maker or manager is involved in making a complex, chain-of-organizational decisions. Such "distributed human organizational knowledge" can only be captured through repeated observation. The concept of using artificial intelligence to comprehend the collective decision-making paradigms of an entire organization has yet to fully emerge as a discipline. In this work, we propose a mechanism for doing just that—undoing the reductionist approach to distributed decision-making by capturing the actions of every decision-making node in the entire process and performing analysis upon those actions. By examining the actions of the whole process, the collective behavior and dynamics of the whole process can be understood. In the next section, we present an architecture for capture and comprehension of the individual actions/decisions leading to an understanding of the organizational performance as a whole.

An Information Architecture for this Research

We are proposing that a connectionist model and its data-capture/storage module exist as a "layer" of software that interoperates between the business logic and the data management components of any ERP application. The layered information architecture for the system is exhibited in Figure 1. The dark layer, labeled the "Capture and Comprehension Layer" in Figure 1, is placed between the data management and business logic management layers of the traditional ERP architecture so that it is in a position to observe all the transaction traffic. Transaction traffic would include all client-initiated queries, all e-mails and their attachments, all purchase orders/invoices as well as other business documents, all "pushed" as well as "pulled" content.

The Capture and Comprehension Layer exhibited in Figure 1 observes all of the transaction activity and records the origin and destination of every such transaction, the time and date of the transaction, while classifying the transaction as to type and content. Each transaction is seen as an output from an origin node and as an input to a destination node. From these output/input records involving a pair of nodes, the proposed "system" will infer input/output records for any given process node. Moreover, input/output records are constructed for an entire network of nodes (to be defined subsequently). It is these collections of input/output ((or stimulus/response) records that

Figure 1. Location of the capture and comprehension layer (black) within the ERP architecture (grey)

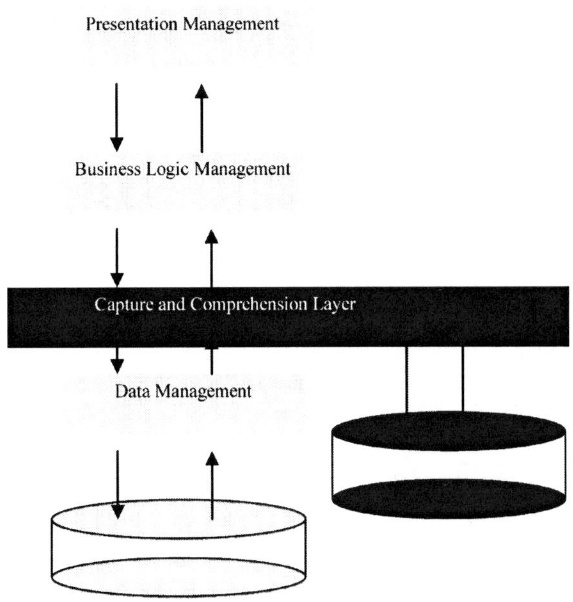

the "system" uses to create a picture of what is related to what and who is making what decisions in terms of stimulus/response. How the collective decision-making is affecting the overall dynamical behavior of the organization in question is discussed next.

A Business Process Model for this Research

In this section, we define a generic business process, identify some important components of a business process, and then present a Simplified Business Process Model (SBPM) for our research purpose. The SBPM is based on SAP's Business Process Reference Model and the definition/characteristics of the prototypical business process as specified in the next section.

Definition: Business Process. A business process is a specified activity in an enterprise that is executed repeatedly. Business processes have the following characteristics (Martin, 1993; Taylor, 1996; Scheer, 1992, 1994).

- Business processes have definable beginning and end points, called nodes.
- Nodes exist wherever processing takes place; the nodes pass information to each other vis-à-vis a network.
- Business process nodes have inputs consisting of information, material, energy, and so forth, which they transform into outputs that also consist of information, material, energy, and so forth The transformation adds value to the outputs.
- Business processes are created by higher level business processes that monitor and control their operation (i.e., business processes are structured in hierarchical organizations).
- Business processes consume resources that are allocated to them by their higher level controlling business processes.
- Business processes report their status to their higher level controlling business processes.
- Business processes consist of sequences of events—instants in time at which the process undergoes state change

Accordingly, a business process model should incorporate a network structure and include process nodes and the relationships between the process nodes as a minimum. In addition, events, resources such as information, actor or owner, and information storages can be included as the modeler requires.

Process structure. A given business process can be thought of as a network of processing nodes. The process dependency model shows how business processes relate to each other and how they are dependent on each other. A given process is dependent on another process in the sense that the process in question cannot take place until the other process has completed for whatever reason. Basically, process dependency is determined by the business rules of the enterprise. Because business rules are very important in building the business process model, a thorough explanation will be given next. For the description of the process dependency, we use an example of a business process diagram shown in Figure 2.

There can be several forms of process dependency. In Figure 3, the single arc proceeding from process node 2 to process node 3 exhibits one-to-one process dependency. Node 5, with its many inputs from Nodes 1, 2 and 4, exhibits many-into-one dependency. Node 2 initiates nodes 3 and 5 and thus exhibits one-into-many dependency. We will visit Figure 2 again when we discuss a possible scenario involving our system in the last section.

What we wish to propose in this article is mechanisms to capture and comprehend the transaction traffic between the nodes.

The business rules. The enterprise has a set of business rules representing the conditions, con-

Figure 2. A business process diagram

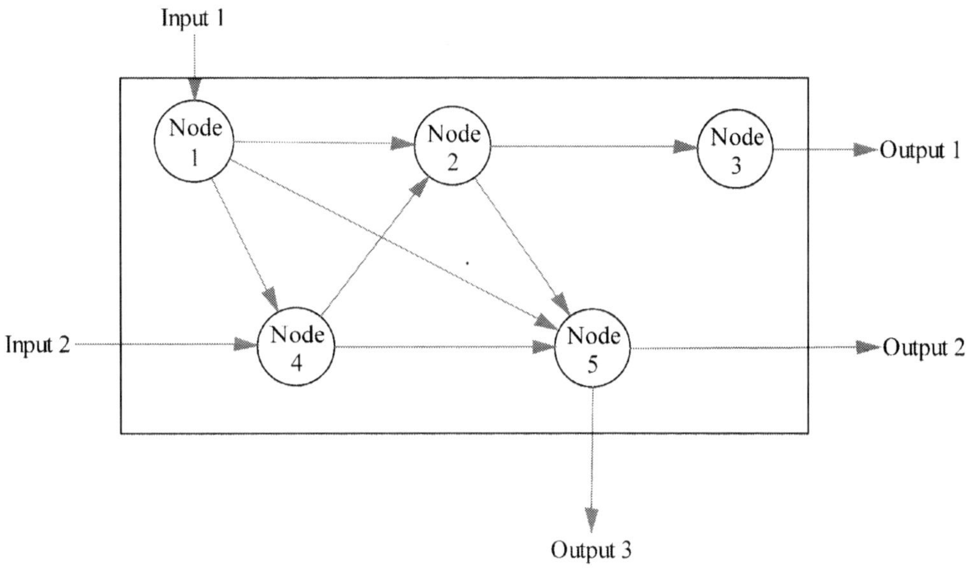

straints, and policies that control its organization, direction, and operation. Business rules are, in a sense, a shorthand language for expressing the business knowledge. One place business rules can be found is in the policy and procedure manuals of the organization. Such manuals contain the written operating policies of the firm. Carried to its logical extreme, the set of business rules of an enterprise can act as the declarative script of the enterprise. No matter what happens, one or more business rules would control what happens after that (Gale & Eldred, 1996). A contemporary discussion of business rules can be found in Von Halle, et al. (2006). Debevoise (2005) provides an excellent discussion of business process management utilizing a business rules approach.

Figure 3. Process node architecture

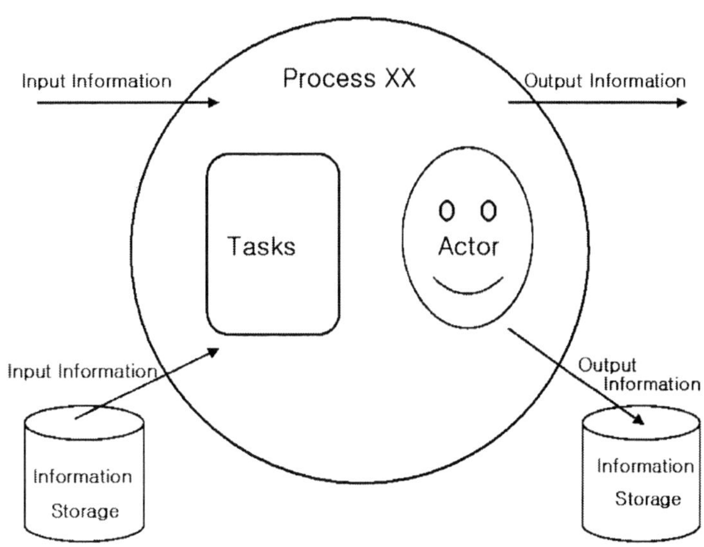

The enterprise is an example of a general system. Any general system can be analyzed in terms of three perspectives: a structural perspective, a functional perspective, and a behavioral (or dynamical) perspective. Business rules apply to any or all of the enterprise perspectives. Thus, a given business rule may roughly be classified in one of the three perspectives.

Structural business rules are related to the structure of the enterprise. The structure of the enterprise is its set of entities and their relationships at a specific point of time. Structural business rules maintain the integrity of enterprise entities. Examples of structural business rules are as follows:

- The enterprise should consist of: marketing department, personnel department, finance department, accounting department, and customer service department. (Organization rule)
- Annual Total Profit = Annual Total Revenue – Annual Total Expense (Entity definition)

Functional business rules are the business rules that specify the goals and objectives of the enterprise. Basically, they collectively define the "what should be done (by whom)". Examples of these rules are:

- The marketing department should maintain at least 35% of the domestic market of product A.
- The management of human resources is the responsibility of the managers throughout the company (as opposed to being established as a separate organizational unit).

Behavioral business rules are used to control the preconditions and post-conditions of the state changes of the enterprise. A typical behavioral business rule has the following form: when certain events occur and certain conditions hold true, then the system states change. Behavioral business rules are closely related to the business process chains. In fact, the relationships between different business processes and chaining of the business processes are solely determined by the behavioral business rules of the enterprise in our Simplified Business Process Model (see the following subsection).

A Simplified Business Process Model (SBPM)

A simplified business process model that is sufficient for our purpose can be constructed as follows. The whole business process under consideration consists of smaller (sub) process nodes and relationships between them. The relationship type between two process nodes that is captured in this model is the triggering control sequence. That is, there should be an event or a set of events between the two process nodes that satisfy some predefined (according to some business rules) pre- and post-conditions for the relationship between the two nodes.

Moreover, because the relationship type is a kind of triggering control sequence, it should have some temporal sequence (i.e., the process node before the occurrence of the event (or transaction) originates the event and then the other process node after the occurrence is the destination) and therefore can be represented as a directed link. If we represent the process node as a circle and the relationship between two nodes as a directed link, a typical business process can be diagrammed as in Figure 2. We shall refer to this as a "knowledge network" and it is logically structured to cohere with our knowledge of the physical system that it represents. Thus, every transaction will have an origination node and a destination node.

Each process node must have as its components a task function that is basically a set of services that are expected to be done at this node: an actor who is in charge of or responsible for the task of this process node (an actor may be a person, an organizational unit, or an artificial software agent), and information storage(s) to read input information from or to store output information in. Here, the output information simply means the information resulting from the execution of the node's task (or function). The information storage(s) and the information stored in the storage(s) may be owned (or used) by the process node only, but is usually shared by other process nodes.

The input information may be an input from another node (or from outside of the whole business process in consideration) or read-in records or documents from the permanent storage(s) used by the node. The output information may be some temporary results to be delivered to the nodes that are linked to this node, or some permanent results that should be recorded and kept in a database as a record of a table or a document. Therefore, output information of a process node can be either temporary or permanent and, if permanent, must be deposited in the information storage. The structure of our Business Process Model is shown in Figure 2. Additionally, each business process node will have a very simplified internal architecture as shown in Figure 3. This figure shows us where we can insert a monitoring mechanism that will capture the transaction traffic; clearly, this will occur at the points where we see an input or output arrow. Software that can capture this traffic works as follows; the transaction is sent, not only to its destination but also to a system that records the origin and the destination of the transaction. The software is also capable of detecting the type of transaction as well as important content within the transaction. Additionally, each transaction is date-stamped and time-stamped so that durations can be determined. Of interest would be the length of time an information packet spends in some non-value adding activity such as in storage. All of this data would be placed in database tables, as suggested in Figure 1, utilizing standardized records. This concludes our discussion of the detection and capture mechanism; we describe next several possible comprehension mechanisms.

A Connectionist Approach to Business Problem-Solving and BPR

In this section of the article, we consider the network structure (topology) of the whole business process. Usually, this network of process nodes will have a mesh topology and might contain loops or cycles. We use the term "loop" to mean the link starts from a node and comes back directly to the same node. On the other hand, a cycle is a path (a sequence of links) on the network that starts from a node and ends with the same node but with at least one visit to another node. These definitions are used in the material to follow.

The fundamental structure of CLEAROS is exhibited in Figure 4. It is basically a layered, acyclic knowledge network. At the bottom is the input layer that represents the collection of source or input process nodes. The top layer is the output layer that represents the collection of target or output process nodes. Between the two layers are one or more intermediate layers that represent various classes of intervening process nodes. ERP process analysts will decide upon the initial structure of CLEAROS, in which each node represents a process of interest, possibly through use of SAP Business Blueprint and commercial tools like it. The structure must be acyclic because the learning (training) and inferencing algorithms require acyclic networks.

To capture and represent knowledge about the behavior of the ERP system, CLEAROS uses a connectionist model (Waltz & Feldman, 1988—see Appendix A for further discussion of connectionist models and of how CLEAROS works operationally) that makes the following assumptions:

1. The domain knowledge (K) consists of two components, the set (V) of business process nodes and the set (E) of relationships (links) among the business process nodes. Mathematically, K is a diad of V and E (K = <V, E>). The links of the digraph may

Figure 4. Connectionist structure of CLEAROS

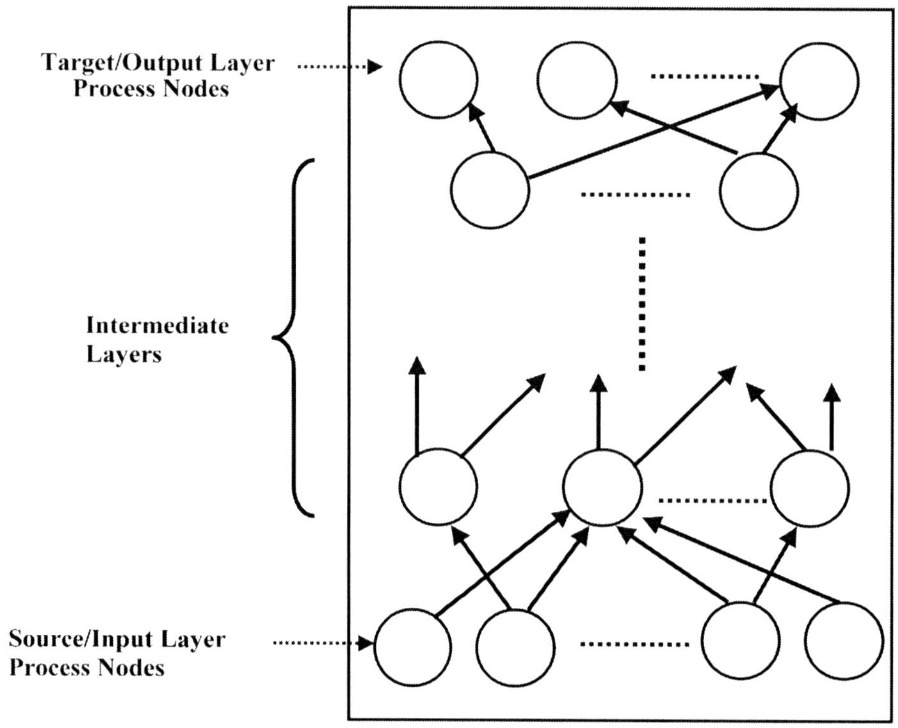

represent any natural cognitive ordering that is consistent, meaning each link must represent the same relation.

2. The whole node set consists of three mutually exclusive subsets: input (or source) process node set, output (or target) process node set, and intermediate process node set. A process node in CLEAROS should belong to exactly one of these subsets at a time (or in a session of running). See Figures 4 and 7 for depictions of how these nodes interact. An input (or source) process node represents a business process that captures or generates ultimate source information in the ERP system. Ultimate source inputs are generated and captured inside of the whole business process under consideration. One possible source input would be POS (Point-Of-Sale) data; another is EDI (Electronic-Data-Interchange) data that is transported across organizational boundaries.
   An output (or target) node represents a point at which transactions leave the system of interest. It is a point where measurements are taken because managers or analysts have concerns. It may also be a "natural" output of the collection of processes networked together—the end product of a supply chain, for example.
   An intermediate process node represents one of the middle steps to reach the target process node from the input nodes. Since there are usually many intermediate nodes by which to reach the target, they collectively determine the behavior of the target.
3. The relationships taken into account in CLEAROS may represent information transfers or actual flows or money, material or product. The relationship between two process nodes in CLEAROS represents a triggering (or "invoking" in programming terminology) sequence (i.e., if the preceding

process is finished and a certain condition holds true then the (directly) succeeding process should follow):

As we have seen in the BPM section of this article, the relationship between two process nodes is determined by the business rules of the enterprise. In fact, the whole business process dependency structure of an enterprise is determined by the whole set of business rules of the enterprise and represented as a network topology (See the item (1) in the following description).

Based on the fundamental assumptions about the knowledge of enterprise business processes, CLEAROS represents its knowledge as follows (design constructs of CLEAROS).

1. **Network representation of knowledge:** Knowledge about the enterprise's business processes may be represented in a network of process nodes and directed links (some other authors use the term "arc" or "connection" or "edge" instead of "link," but in this article, the term link is used consistently). The process nodes and their links constitute the network topology. The knowledge network initially constructed within CLEAROS is patterned after the enterprise's actual business process network as discerned by use of SAP's Business Blueprint.
2. **Representing the influence of a link by weight values (learning):** Associated with each link is its value from the continuous range of [0, +1], called the "weight value" or WV. The weight of a link in CLEAROS measures and reflects the relative degree of influence by the preceding process node on the succeeding process node. The weight value +1 of the link from the preceding process node to the succeeding process means that the preceding process node has the maximum degree of influence on the performance of the succeeding process node. Zero weight means that the preceding process node has no influence on the succeeding process node.
3. **Representing the relative importance of each process node (inferencing):** Associated with each node is its value taken from the continuous range of [0, +1], that represents the degree of the importance of the process node in terms of its relative criticalness over the whole business process (under consideration), where the value +1 means that it is a process with the highest degree of importance over the whole business process under consideration, and where the value 0 means that the process has no contribution (no value addition) to the whole business process under consideration. This number will be called the "PF" (Performance Factor) of the process node and will represent the degree of the contribution (value addition) to the whole business process under consideration.
4. **Acyclic layered network:** As discussed in the BPM section of this article, the original business process diagram under consideration, if represented in a network, might involve loops or cycles, and thus violates the assumptions made in CLEAROS. So it will be assumed, initially, that our business process model does not involve any loop or cycle. If a business process appears to involve loops or cycles, this concern can be addressed by consideration of the abstraction level of the process nodes. A method that can resolve the problem of loops is suggested in (Jung & Burns, 1993) and in the Appendix to this article. By picking a high-enough abstraction-level, the loops and cycles disappear as they are contained within the process nodes. In any case, the knowledge network in CLEAROS will be assumed to be an acyclic network. Causal models of the enterprise will, however, contain the cycles and loops, thereby enabling analysis both with and without loops. This approach offers

the best potential for fully understanding the interactions between nodes.

5. **Knowledge update by inferencing (update of fact-type knowledge):** CLEAROS changes (or updates) its knowledge in two ways: (1) by learning, and (2) by inferencing. Knowledge updates by inferencing in CLEAROS mean changing (or updating) the PF values of its nodes.
6. **Knowledge update by learning (update of rule-type knowledge):** CLEAROS can modify its pattern of connectivity as a part of its learning process. Modifying the pattern of connectivity (thus learning) means changing (or updating) all or part of the weight WV values associated with the links in CLEAROS.

Initialization of the CLEAROS Knowledge Network

For CLEAROS to do its main job, inferencing, its knowledge network (knowledge base) should first be structured and then initialized. The starting rule used for structuring the knowledge network is to use a separate node for each process and/or processor in the real network. Once the node structure is determined, the initialization of the CLEAROS knowledge base is just the initialization of all its weight values. The weight values initialization in CLEAROS can be done basically in three ways.

One way is assigning a weight value for each link. The initial weight value of each link may be supplied by human experts who are in charge of the process. Another way is that we calculate the data traffic rate for each link between two process nodes and normalize it, and then assign the normalized value to the weight. The last method is by using the CLEAROS learning mechanism. To use the CLEAROS learning system, we should have enough learning records. The specific learning method of CLEAROS is explained next.

Learning

Learning requires building and updating the knowledge structure. Because CLEAROS represents its knowledge structure as a network of process nodes and relationships between these nodes, its structural change assumes adjustment and update of relationships between the process nodes. In CLEAROS, this is done by adjustment of weight values between the nodes in different layers. Therefore, learning in CLEAROS requires updates of its weight values. These adjustments permit CLEAROS to perform correct inferencing.

Learning in CLEAROS takes place as follows. Once the structure of the knowledge network has been determined and initialized, learning is required to establish the weight values of the links. Learning requires a table of input/output records. CLEAROS is exercised by exposing it to each set of inputs in a single record, one record at a time. The outputs produced by CLEAROS are then compared with the actual outputs contained in each record. Learning takes place through adjustment of the weight values so as to minimize the error between the predicted outputs of CLEAROS and the actual outputs.

There are many theories, methods and algorithms for learning in the connectionist paradigm. The learning method adopted in CLEAROS is the Generalized Delta Rule or back-propagation algorithm as suggested in Rumelhart, Widrow and Lehr (1994). Back-propagation is currently the most important and most widely used algorithm for connectionist learning. It is an algorithm for learning in feed-forward networks (like CLEAROS) using MSE (Mean Squared Error) and gradient descent. For a detailed introduction to the back-propagation method, readers may consult chapters 11 and 12 of Gallant (1993). For a detailed explanation about the application of the back-propagation method to reasoning system designs, readers are referred to Jung (1990). A thorough illustration of initialization, learning and usage of connectionist models like CLEAROS is found in Jung and Burns (1993).

Inferencing

This step can be applied after initialization and learning have been undertaken. One of the main purposes of CLEAROS is to find the relative degree of performance (i.e., the PF) of a business process node and the relationships among different process nodes in terms of contribution or value addition (again, the PF). In other words, managers or analysts who are concerned about the overall performance of the whole business process (under consideration) may want more detailed information about the relative performance or contribution of each component process and once they get this information, they can do whatever they think appropriate based on the information.

The inferencing mechanism of CLEAROS can provide that kind of information that managers or analysts need. There are basically two types of inferencing tasks that are possible in CLEAROS. These inferencing tasks in CLEAROS can be grouped into two groups. The first group involves forward-chaining computation and the second group involves backward-chaining computation. For fundamental computational mechanisms of connectionist models like forward- and backward chaining and for various learning models, readers may consult Gallant (1993). For hyper-fast inference engine architectures see Burns, Winstead and Hayworth (1989).

1. Forward-chaining computation:
    - Find the effect of input/source process nodes;
    - Calculate the Performance Factor of the target process nodes;
2. Backward-chaining computation
    - Find the causes or paths for a target process node; and
    - Produce justifications/explanations for the conclusion.

Finding the effect of input/source process nodes means finding the paths from a given source process (or set of source nodes) to the target process nodes. This task is needed when managers or analysts want to understand the exact (partial) process chain and the effect of change in some processes. Calculating the effect of input/source process nodes is needed when a manager or analyst wants to get information on the effect of the source process' PF (or the change of their values) on the target process.

Finding the causes or paths for a target process node is similar to the task of finding the effect of input/source process nodes but, in this case, search direction is the opposite one (from target/top to source/bottom). This task is needed when managers or analysts want to find an answer to the question such that "Given a process with a problem, what process chain do I need to address to resolve the problem?" Producing justification/explanation is similar to the task of finding the causes or paths but during learning, CLEAROS calculates the weight values WV of all the links and the performance factor PF values of all the nodes along the chain and shows them to the users. For a more detailed explanation about each of the inferencing tasks presented in this article, readers should consult Jung and Burns (1993).

Analysis of the Discovered Knowledge Network

Three-pronged analyses of the knowledge network created by CLEAROS are possible. First, through the use of simulation and system dynamics (see Sterman (2000), Senge (1990)), the performance and behavior of the associated processes will be assessed. The assessment begins with a determination of the criteria by which performance is assessed (what is the bottom line)? Once the criteria are known, a performance criterion can be constructed. The basic causal structure of the system dynamics model can be discerned from the density/character of the transaction traffic between the identified nodes. A stock-and-flow diagram and subsequent simulation model could then be constructed, tested and utilized to comprehend the underlying dynamics. Are there other networks/rules that might achieve better performance? What is the bottleneck or impediment that prevents performance from being better? Are there networks that might perform equally well at considerably less cost? This analysis type would address such questions.

A second possibility is to perform value analysis[3] on the implied value chain embedded within the knowledge network. Nodes with low PF's and/or links directed toward or away from them with low WV's would be good candidates for elimination. Such an analysis might reveal that a particular node adds no customer-perceived value and thence can be removed. Another possibility might reveal that a simplified knowledge network will achieve the same result, reducing process cost, cycle time while improving quality. Value analysis can contribute significantly to the simplification of the knowledge network. The problem of complexity in large ERP systems is a huge one and this analysis type alone can have a significant impact on the bottom line. It is complexity that adds so much cost and time to the testing and debugging effort. As the ERP software system increases in complexity, the expected time to find a bug increases from days to months.

Still, a third possibility is to perform carbon/silicon replacement analysis on the network. Such analyses might reveal where an expensive carbon-based processor (i.e., a human) or node could be replaced with an inexpensive silicon-based one (i.e., a computer). This might be possible when the business rules of a carbon-based processor are observed to be deterministic and programmable.

THE METHODOLOGY IN PRACTICE: A STEP-BY-STEP EXAMPLE

In what follows, we shall use the word "training" to connote learning as discussed earlier. The basic steps of the methodology would be the following:

1. Determine the structure of the knowledge network and initialize all of its WV's and PF's
2. Monitor the transaction traffic for at least a month
3. Study the transaction traffic and create input/output records for training
4. Layer the knowledge network based on the transaction traffic
5. Train the connectionist network to the transaction traffic using CLEAROS so that values are established for all WV's
6. Perform inferencing on the trained network so as to find all of the PF's
7. Analyze the fitted network using the analyses suggested (system dynamics, value analysis, carbon/silicon replacement)
8. Propose a simplified/restructured knowledge network
9. Test the simplified/restructured knowledge network in off-line simulative fashion
10. Implement the simplified knowledge network
11. Monitor and measure the simplified/restructured knowledge network to ascertain if it achieves goals

We will begin with the process diagram shown in Figure 2. Assume that the knowledge network exhibited in Figure 2 produces the following record of transaction traffic shown in Table 1 next. The nodes correspond to the following functions. Node 1 receives returned items. Node 2 does all manufacturing and rework. Node 3 ships returned items back to customer. Node 4 receives incoming purchase orders. Node 5 does all outgoing new order shipping.

In analyzing the transaction traffic, we learn that a rework item was inputted to Node 1. Node 1 logs in the item, examines the item and decides whether the item can be reworked or not. If the item can be reworked, it is transferred to node 2, where manufacturing reworks the item. If the item cannot be reworked, it is discarded and a notice is sent to Node 4 resulting in the manufacture of a new item as a replacement. Once reworked at Node 2, the item is transferred to Node 3. At Node 3, the reworked item is then packaged and shipped back to the customer.

In Table 1, we also see that a purchase order was entered at Input 2. This resulted in orders being transmitted to Nodes 2 and 5. As can be seen, the knowledge network processes returns and purchase orders coming in from customers. However, it does not do it efficiently. For example in Table 1, we see that more than a month was required to process order #21345 (from 8/15/2007 until 9/26/2007) and roughly three weeks were required to process the returned item (from 8/13/2007 until 8/29/2007). Most of that time is consumed at Node 2. Thus, there is clearly a bottleneck at Node 2.

Next, we examine the transaction counts for a period of a month, as shown in Table 2 (step 2).

We learn that there were 395 product returns during the month and 1945 purchase orders. We also observe that of the 395 returns, 295 were reworkable and 100 had to be discarded, resulting in new products being built for the customer. We can discern this by observing that Node 1 transferred 295 transactions to Node 2, and 100 transactions to Node 4. We also notice that during this month, only 90 reworked items were returned to their owners, while 1788 new items were shipped out. Clearly, there is a significant number of orders-in-process as well as rework-in-process, but we cannot tell how much. It is impossible to tell from the transaction counts how much product is currently "in the system" because we don"t know how many transactions were in the system to begin with.

Training the connectionist model CLEAROS with an identical network topology to that of Figure 2 yields the result shown in Figure 5 in which the thick, bold arcs/nodes show us what arcs/nodes received the most weight as a result of the training and inferencing. The training (step 5) utilized the data in Tables 1 and 2 after that data had been reorganized into input/output pairs (step 3). This picture, again suggests that Node 2 is a bottleneck as it is given the highest weight among all of the

Table 1. Transaction traffic for simple knowledge network exhibited in Figure 2

Input Node	Output Node	date	time	Urgency	Content	Order #
Input 1	1	8/13/2007	8 a.m.	Expedite	Rework	225
Input 2	4	8/15/2007	9 a.m.	Normal	Purchase Order	21345
1	2	8/16/2007	8:10 a.m.	Immediate	notice	225
1	4	8/17/2007	2:00 p.m.	Normal	notice	None
1	5	8/16/2007	8:15 a.m.	Normal	notice	None
2	3	8/29/2007	4:30 p.m.	Normal	notice	225
2	5	9/5/2007	4 p.m.	Normal	notice	21345
3	Output 1	8/29/2007	5 p.m.	Normal	Rework Returned	225
4	2	8/19/2007	1:30 p.m.	Normal	order	21345
4	5	8/19/2007	1 p.m.	Normal	order	21345
5	Output 2	9/26/2007	4:30 p.m.	Normal	order filled/shipped	21345
5	Output 3	9/16/2007	5 p.m.	Normal	adj AP & Cash	21345

Table 2. Transaction counts for all arcs in Figure 2 over the period of a month

ARC	Input Node	Output Node	Traffic/mo
Input 1 to 1	Input 1	1	395
input 2 to 4	Input 2	4	1945
1 to 2	1	2	295
1 to 4	1	4	100
1 to 5	1	5	10
2 to 5	2	5	1895
2 to 3	2	3	92
3 to Output 1	3	Output 1	90
4 to 2	4	2	1822
4 to 5	4	5	25
5 to Output 2	5	Output 2	1788
5 to Output 3	5	Output 3	1788

nodes. Evidently, CLEAROS ignores transaction counts of 25 or less as being too insignificant to be considered here, eliminating arcs 1 to 5 and 4 to 5. CLEAROS would tell us (step 6) that purchase order transactions starting at Input 2 result in shipped orders coming out at Output 2 about a month later. CLEAROS also tells us that rework transactions result in reworked product being shipped back to the customer 75% of the time (at Output 1) and in new product replacements 25% of the time, coming out at Output 2. Further, observations at Node 2 revealed that rework jobs essentially brought the line to a halt while technicians diagnosed and then repaired each reworked unit. The rework jobs were curtailing throughput of the new orders.

Based on the information highlighted in this example, process analysts would decide (step 7) to separate the Rework from the Purchase Order Fulfillment and simplify the total process, as shown in Figure 6. In Figure 6, Nodes 1, 2 and 3 do all of the Rework processing while Nodes 4, 5 and 6 do all of the purchase order processing. Obviously, Nodes 1 and 3 would do the receiving, Nodes 2 and 4 the rework or manufacturing, while Nodes 3 and 6 would do the shipping. This improved knowledge network (step 8) would then be tested in an off-line, simulative fashion (step 9).

By comparison with Figure 5, Figure 6 is referred to as "layered". Layering often helps process analysts to gain additional insight, to see their processes in a whole new way. Algorithms for layering are discussed in Jung (1990) and Jung and Burns (1993) as well as the Appendix.

Figure 5. Result of applying the connectionist model to the data in Tables 1 & 2

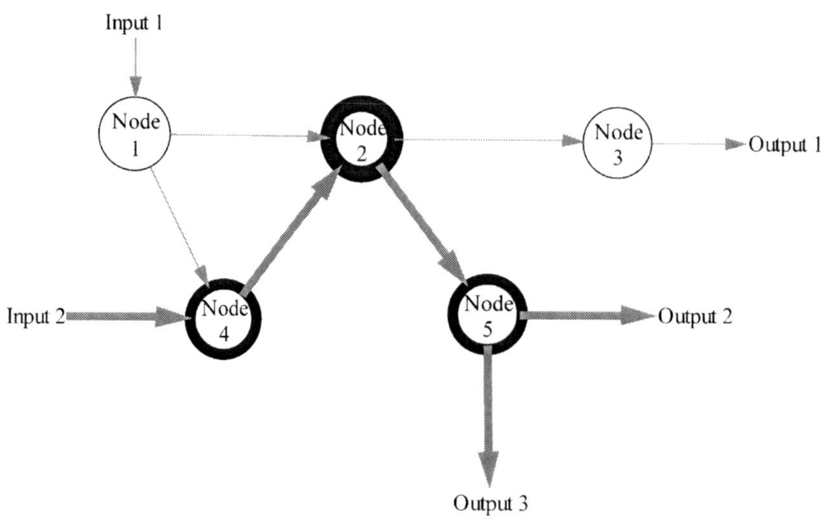

Simulation studies of the reengineered processes shown in Figure 6 might suggest that purchase order cycle time could be reduced from one month to three days, mostly as a result of eliminating the bottleneck at Node 2. Substantial improvements in throughput would then be realized as well. The simulation studies also might suggest that increases in the capacity at Node 2 would further reduce purchase order cycle time without creating too much resource idleness. In addition, improvements in outgoing quality would be significant now that manufacturing has segregated its rework from its primary responsibility of filling orders. Finally, by placing the Receiving (Nodes 1 and 4), Manufacturing (Nodes 2 and 5) and Shipping (Nodes 3 and 6) nodes in close proximity, it is possible to utilize sharing of resources. The revised, simplified knowledge network would be implemented (step 10) and monitored to ascertain that it achieves its objectives (step 11).

SUMMARY

In this article, an enterprise architecture that automates the process of capturing what information/data professional people and managers are using, and comprehending how they are reacting/responding to that information, is described. The basic idea is to (1) capture all of the transaction traffic between and among the nodes of an ERP system and then (2) to use various models including a connectionist model as discussed in Jung (1990) and Jung and Burns (1993) to "comprehend" the structure of the interactions that exist within the process. The Capture and Comprehension Layer exhibited in Figure 1 observes all of the transaction activity and records the origin and destination of every such transaction. The transaction is seen as an output from an origin node and as an input to a destination node. It is thus able to construct input/output records for any given node. Moreover, input/output records are constructed for an entire network of nodes as defined by CLEAROS. It is these collections of input/output ((or stimulus/response) records that CLEAROS uses to create a picture of what is related to what and how the collective decision-making is affecting the dynamical behavior of the organization in question.

With regard to process structure, the unknowns are the human information processors in terms of

Figure 6. Re-engineered processes to accommodate shortened cycle times, increased throughput and improved product quality

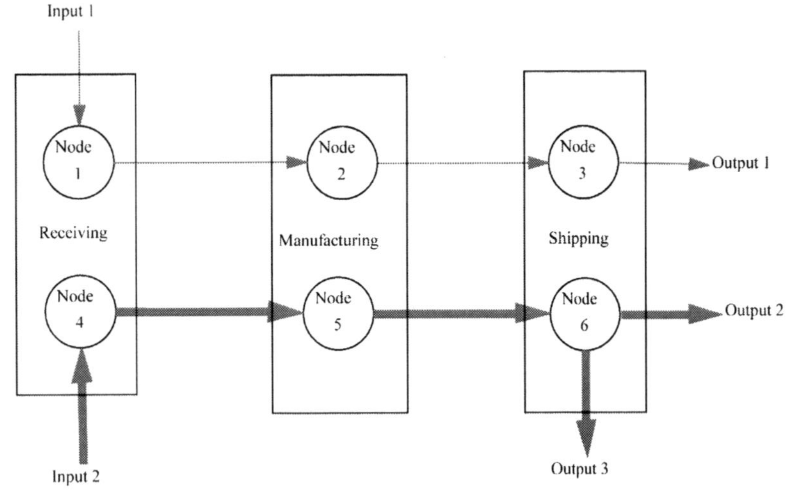

what information they take in as inputs and the information they put out as outputs. The rest is reasonably well known; specifically, the business rules are known. Once the process structure is known, there is opportunity to understand why the total process behaves as it does and why performance is less than desirable, as well as how performance can be improved.

Analysis of the process begins once the total process is known. Three-pronged analyses are possible in which overall process performance is assessed first. First, process dynamics can be understood using system dynamics. Alternate process structures can be modeled and tested for possible improvements in performance. Then, value analysis of the implied value chain is possible, revealing where processing at certain nodes adds no customer-perceived value. Finally, carbon/silicon replacement analyses can be performed, resulting in substantial reductions in cost as carbon-based units are replaced with silicon ones.

Overall, it is hoped that this article has highlighted the challenges associated with ERP implementation. Additionally, it is hoped that the ideas developed in this article aid researchers and managers in better understanding how to successfully implement ERP in organizations.

Finally, this article launches an entirely new discipline, which we refer to as distributed natural/artificial intelligence. By our definition, distributed natural/artificial intelligence studies the collective performance implications coming forth from a network of intelligent nodes, each making decisions that affect the overall performance of the larger network as a whole. In this way, we hope to comprehend why certain behaviors, dynamics are being observed in the system.

REFERENCES

Abels, S., Brehm, N., Hahn, A., & Gomez, J. (2006). Change management issues in federated ERP systems: An approach for identifying requirements and possible solutions. *International Journal of Information Systems and Change Management*, *1*(3), 318–335. doi:10.1504/IJISCM.2006.011202

Agerfalk, P., & Goldkuhl, G. (2001). Business action and information modeling – The task of the new millenium. In Rossi, M., & Siau, K. (Eds.), *Information Modeling in the New Millenium* (pp. 110–137). Hershey, PA: Idea Group Publishing. doi:10.4018/9781878289773.ch007

Beaty, R., & Williams, C. (2006). ERP II: Best practices for successfully implementing an ERP upgrade. *Communications of the ACM*, *49*(3), 105–109.

Burns, J., Winstead, W., & Hayworth, B. (1989). Semantic nets as paradigms for both causal and judgmental knowledge representation. *IEEE Transactions on Systems, Man, and Cybernetics*, *SMC-19*(1), 58–68. doi:10.1109/21.24531

Cegielski, C., Hall, D., & Rebman, C. (2006). Enterprise resource planning systems implementation success. *International Journal of Information Systems and Change Management*, *1*(3), 301–317. doi:10.1504/IJISCM.2006.011201

Cost, K., & Slaughter, K. (1997). *Best Business: Spanning the boundaries of business and IT. Vanenburg*. Putten, The Netherlands: Baan Institute Press.

Curran, T., & Keller, G. (1998). *SAP R/3 business blueprint*. Upper Saddle River, NJ: Prentice Hall.

Debevoise, T. (2005). *Business process management with a business rules approach: Implementing the service oriented architecture*. Canada: Business Knowledge Architects, Arbor Books.

Gale, T., & Eldred, J. (1996). *Getting results with the object-oriented models*. New York: SIG Books.

Gallant, S. I. (1993). *Neural network learning and expert systems*. Cambridge: MIT Press.

Gattiker, T., & Goodhue, D. (2002). Software-driven changes to business processes: An empirical study of impacts of enterprise resource planning (ERP) systems at the local level. *International Journal of Production Research, 37*(9), 2093–2108.

Hammer, M., & Champy, J. (1993). *Reengineering the corporation: A manifesto for business revolution*. New York: Harper.

Harary, H., Norman, Z., & Cartwright, D. (1965). *Structural models: An introduction to the theory of directed graphs*. New York: Wiley.

Hendricks, K., Singhal, V., & Stratman, J. (2007). The impact of enterprise systems on corporate performance: A study of ERP, SCM, and CRM system implementations. *Journal of Operations Management, 25*(1), 65–82. doi:10.1016/j.jom.2006.02.002

Holsapple, C., & Sena, M. (2003a). The decision support characteristics of ERP systems. *International Journal of Human-Computer Interaction, 16*(1), 101–123. doi:10.1207/S15327590IJHC1601_7

Holsapple, C., & Sena, M. (2003b). ERP plan and decision-support benefits. *Decision Support Systems, 38*(3), 575–590.

Holsapple, C. & Whinston, M. (1996). Decision support systems: A knowledge-based approach. St. Paul, MN: West Publishing company. *Implementation of an Enterprise Resource Planning system with Focus on end-User Training*, (2007) [http://www.diplomica.com/db/diplomarbeiten1906.html], April.

Jacobs, F., & Weston, F. (2007). Enterprise resource planning (ERP)—A brief history. *Journal of Operations Management, 25*, 357–363. doi:10.1016/j.jom.2006.11.005

Jones, M., & Price, R. (2004). Organizational knowledge sharing in ERP implementation: Lessons from industry. *Journal of Organizational and End User Computing, 16*(1), 21–41. doi:10.4018/joeuc.2004010102

Jones, N., & Kochtanek, T. (2004). Success factors in the implementation of a collaborative technology and resulting productivity improvements in a small business: An exploratory study. *Journal of Organizational and End User Computing, 16*(1), 1–20. doi:10.4018/joeuc.2004010101

Jonkers, H., & Franken, H. (1996). Quantitative modeling and analysis of business processes. In *Proceedings of 8th European Simulation Systems: Simulation in Industry*, Vol. 1, 175-179.

Jung, D. (1990). *Design of inexact reasoning systems for managerial problem diagnosis*. Unpublished doctoral dissertation, Texas Tech University, Lubbock, TX.

Jung, D., & Burns, J. (1993). Connectionist approaches to inexact reasoning and learning systems for executive and decision support. *Decision Support Systems, 10*, 37–66. doi:10.1016/0167-9236(93)90004-M

Kettinger, W., & Grover, V. (1995). Toward a theory of business process change management. *Journal of Management Information Systems, 12*(18), 9–12.

Klaus, H., Roseman, M., & Gable, G. (2000). What is ERP. *Information Systems Frontiers, 2*(2), 141–162. doi:10.1023/A:1026543906354

Koulopoulos, T. (1995). *The workflow imperative*. New York: Van Nostrand Reinhold.

Lonzinsky, S. (1998). *Enterprise-wide software solutions: Integration strategies and practices*. Reading, MA: Addison Wesley.

Martin, J. (1993). *Principles of object-oriented analysis and design*. Upper Saddle River, NJ: Prentice-Hall.

Rohloff, M. (1996). Reference model and object oriented approach for business process design and workflow management. In *Proceedings of IEEE*.

Rumelhart, D. & McClelland, J. & PDP Research Group (1986). *Parallel distributed processing: Explorations in the microstructure of cognition* (Vol. 1)*: Foundations*. Cambridge: MIT Press.

Rumelhart, D., Widrow, B., & Lehr, M. A. (1994). The basic ideas in neural networks. *Communications of the ACM*, *37*(3), 87–92. doi:10.1145/175247.175256

Scheer, A. (1989). *Enterprise-wide data modeling: Information systems in industry*. Berlin, Germany: Springer-Verlag.

Scheer, A. (1992). *Architecture of integrated information systems: Foundations of enterprise-modeling*. Berlin, Germany: Springer-Verlag.

Scheer, A. (1994). *Business process engineering: Reference models for industrial enterprises* (2nd ed.). Berlin, Germany: Springer-Verlag.

Senge, P. (1990). *The fifth discipline: The art & practice of the learning organization*. New York: Doubleday Currency.

Sterman, J. (2000). *Business dynamics: Systems thinking and modeling for a complex world*. Boston: Irwin McGraw-Hill.

Taylor, D. (1996). *Business engineering with object technology*. New York: Wiley.

van Es, R., & Post, R. (1996). *Dynamic enterprise modeling: A paradigm shift in software implementation*. Baan Business Innovation.

Von Halle, B., Goldberg, L., & Zachman, J. (2006). *Business rule revolution: Running business the right way*. Silicon Valley, CA: Happy About.

Waltz, D., & Feldman, J. (1988). *Connectionist models and their implications: Readings from cognitive science*. Norwood, New Jersey: Ablex Publishing Corp.

Wikipedia (2006). *Business process management*. Retrieved November 5, 2008, from wikipedia.org/wiki/Business_Process_Management

Wikipedia (2006). *Product life cycle management*. Retrieved November 5, 2008, from en.wikipeida.org/wiki/Product_Lifecycle_Management

ENDNOTES

1. Business Process Re-engineering—a topic about which much has been said and studied during the last two decades.
2. See Koulopoulos (1995); Linzinsky (1998); Martin (1993); Rohloff (1996); Scheer (1989); Taylor (1996); and van Es, R. & Post, R. (1996)
3. Industrial engineers call this "value stream mapping."

APPENDIX A

The generic structure of CLEAROS follows that of a connectionist model. CLEAROS uses a connectionist model rather than a neural model because synapse firings do not contribute to our understanding of the process being modeled.

As mentioned in the main body of this article, two steps are required to formulate the CLEAROS connectionist model. A third step is the one that actually uses CLEAROS to model/simulate the distributed infrastructure. The steps are: (1) initial structure and weight values WV; (2) learning; (3) inferencing. We discuss each of these in turn.

Initial Network Structure and Weights

The initial structure of the acyclic knowledge network is determined by process analysts who may use commercial products like SAP's Business Blueprint. Additional input to this process is the expert knowledge of the process analysts. The output of this process is a knowledge network that is free of loops/cycles and is a layered network. The network structuring and initial weight determination process consists of three tasks: structuring the initial network, removing all loops/cycles in the initial network, layering the network and establishing the initial weights.

Next, the structure must be examined. The original knowledge structure, if represented in a network, might involve loops of cycles. In CLEAROS, it is restructured to resolve the abstraction level imbalances of the variables that are represented by cycles or other contradictions to the assumptions before it performs any inference or learning process. Thus, cycles/loops must be removed by "condensing" them down to a single node. Layering the network means (1) that all layers have the same number of nodes and (2) no link extends for a distance longer than the next succeeding layer. Thus, links cannot extend to nodes that are not in the next immediate layer, if the structure is to be "layered." This is the way we have drawn the structure in Figure 7.

Figure 6 would be considered "layered" but Figure 5 would not be. Actually, layering is optional, but for large networks becomes necessary in order to keep the computational time for learning and inferencing within reasonable bounds. Assume a structure with L layers and N nodes. Without layering, the computational complexity is of the order of O[N(L-1)], whereas the computational complexity of a layered network is of order O[N]. Layering frequently results in additional nodes being added. As was observed in the main body of the article, layering actually helps analysts to gain additional insight into their processes as each layer is given meaning in the context of the entire knowledge network. Thus, new perspectives and perceptions can be gained from this step. In summary, what the initial structuring step does is to take unstructured, messy managerial knowledge and arrange that into a logical, sound, layered hierarchical structure that facilitates computerized learning and inferencing.

Learning

Learning involves finding the weight values WV through fitting to input/output records of data. Based on these values, a new structure may emerge. Structural change involves adjustment and update of the relationships between variables. In CLEAROS, this is done by adjustment of weight values between cells in different layers (recall that weight values are associated with the links in the knowledge network). The learning method adopted for CLEAROS is the generalized delta rule or back-propagation algorithm as suggested in Rumelhart et al. (1986). This algorithm finds weight values WV that enable the outputs of the knowledge network to match the outputs in the input/output records when the knowledge network is stimulated with the corresponding inputs. Associated with each link is a weight value from the continuous range of [-1, 1]. The value 1 means a perfect (positive) correlation between the two variables that are connected by a link and -1 means a perfect (negative) correlation between the two variables. Zero weight means no correlation (or independence) between the two variables. By weight, we mean that strength of connection of the degree of belief in the (causal) relationship between two variables that is represented as a link in network representation of knowledge.

Inferencing

The main purpose of CLEAROS is to find causes within the frame of discernment for the observed symptoms. In pursuit of this purpose, CLEAROS infers the performance factors (PF) associated with the nodes, especially those nodes representing causes. Each node or cell in CLEAROS represents a single process or processor (silicon or carbon). It does not incorporate distributed representations of a process or processor. The inferencing is actually a computational algorithm for finding the ultimate causes. The task is the following. In the Cartesian space S x C, where S is the space of all possible symptom elements and C is the space of all possible cause elements, find a subset of S x C that correctly captures the symptom/cause pairs. This task is a problem of graph search, involving either breadth-first or depth-first search. Both algorithms have the same computational complexity: O(max[n,e]), where n is the total number of nodes and e is the number of links in the digraph. Both lines of reasoning can be pursued in parallel because of the natural parallel computational structure employed by CLEAROS. For the calculation of performance factors, it is computationally more convenient and efficient to use a completely layered knowledge network like that shown in Figures 4, 6 and 7. In what follows, a mathematical formulation of the computation process is presented, followed by an example.

The inference computation process can be mathematically expressed as a system of equations that involve a weight matrix $\mathbf{W}_k$ for each layer k. In addition, the inference algorithm also needs as input, an activation level for each cell, represented by y_{ki} of the ith cell in the kth layer. The standard graph-theoretic formula (Harary, Norman, & Cartwright, 1965) is known to be

$$y_{ki} = \sum_{j=1}^{N_{(k-1)}} w_{kij} y_{(k-1)j} \quad k = 1, \ldots, L, \; i = 1, \ldots, N_k, \tag{1}$$

where w_{kij} is the weight of link ij directed from the jth cell in the (k – 1)th layer to the ith cell in the kth layer, and $y_{(k-1)j}$ is the output level of the jth cell in the (k – 1)th layer. If vector/matrix notation is used, Eq. (1) becomes

$$\mathbf{y}_k = \mathbf{W}_k \mathbf{y}_{k-1}, \; k = 1, \ldots, L, \tag{2}$$

where y_{k-1} is the activation vector of the k-1th layer, $\mathbf{W}_k$ is the weight matrix, and $\mathbf{y}_k$ is output vector, both for the kth layer

Figure 7. This is Figure 6 with all nodes labeled using the appropriate mathematical notation. A link from Node 1 to Node 5 is shown because the learning step found a relationship (a relatively strong WV) there

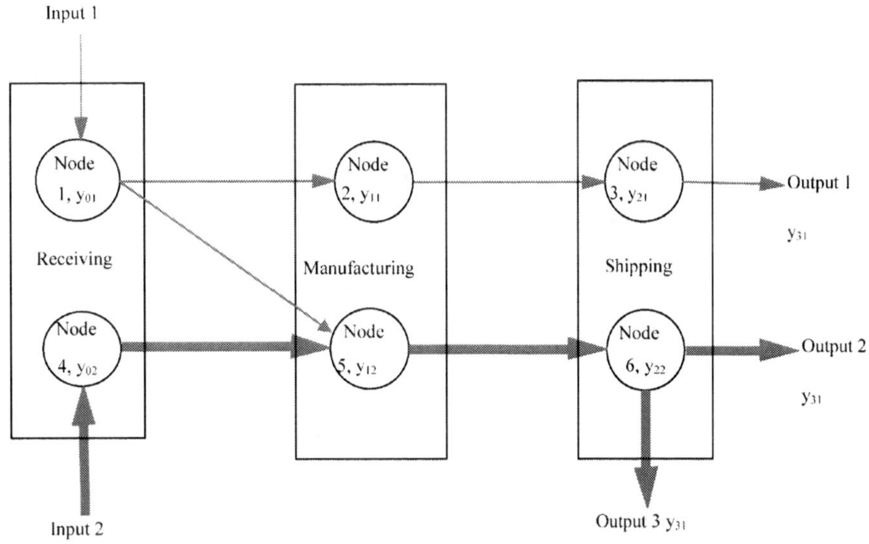

For a computational example, we shall consider the knowledge network depicted in Figure 6. In this case, the input set Y = {returns, purchase orders}. Assume that the input vector is $\mathbf{y}_o = [\ 100, 500]^T$.

These values connote weekly returns and weekly purchase orders. Then, iteratively and successively, the activation level of layer 1 is $[100, 500]^T$. This can be interpreted as the net influences of the input set on the two receiving nodes (see Figure 7), nodes 1 and 4. For simplicity, the output values coming out of Nodes 1 and 4 are simply the input values going into nodes 2 and 5; thus, $\mathbf{y}_1$ is a function of $\mathbf{y}_o$, $\mathbf{y}_1 = \mathbf{f}(\mathbf{y}_o)$, and we will assume that function to be simply a linear function. Thus,

$$\mathbf{y}_1 = \mathbf{W}_1\mathbf{y}_0 = \begin{bmatrix} .99999 & 0.00001 \\ 0.00001 & .99999 \end{bmatrix} * \begin{bmatrix} 100 \\ 500 \end{bmatrix} = \begin{bmatrix} 100.004 \\ 499.996 \end{bmatrix}$$

Assume that learning (back propagation) has found weight values for $\mathbf{W}_1$ to be $\begin{bmatrix} .99999 & 0.00001 \\ 0.00001 & .99999 \end{bmatrix}$

Next,

$$\mathbf{y}_2 = \mathbf{W}_2\mathbf{y}_1 = \begin{bmatrix} .75 & 0.00001 \\ .25 & .99999 \end{bmatrix} * \begin{bmatrix} 100.004 \\ 499.996 \end{bmatrix} = \begin{bmatrix} 75.008 \\ 524.992 \end{bmatrix}.$$

Assume that learning has found weight values for $\mathbf{W}_2$ to be $\begin{bmatrix} .75 & 0.00001 \\ .25 & .99999 \end{bmatrix}$.

Notice, in Figure 7, that learning has found a relationship between node 1 and node 5 of weight.25. Next,

$$\mathbf{y}_3 = \mathbf{W}_3\mathbf{y}_2 = \begin{bmatrix} .99999 & 0.00001 \\ 0.00001 & .99999 \end{bmatrix} * \begin{bmatrix} 75.008 \\ 524.992 \end{bmatrix} = \begin{bmatrix} 75.0125 \\ 524.9875 \end{bmatrix}$$

Assume that learning has found weight values for $\mathbf{W}_3$ to be $\begin{bmatrix} .99999 & 0.00001 \\ 0.00001 & .99999 \end{bmatrix}$

It should be apparent from the earlier that, in the manufacturing stage, it is discovered that roughly 1 out of 4 returned items cannot be repaired, so that customer gets a new one. The result is, an initial order vector of 100 returned items and 500 new orders actually results in 75 returned items being repaired and returned to customers and 525 new items being sent out. Clearly,

$$\mathbf{y}_3 = \mathbf{W}_3\mathbf{y}_2 = \mathbf{W}_3\mathbf{W}_2\mathbf{y}_1 = \mathbf{W}_3\mathbf{W}_2\mathbf{W}_1\mathbf{y}_0 = \mathbf{W}\,\mathbf{y}_0.$$

When we carry out the indicated multiplications in $\mathbf{W}_3\mathbf{W}_2\mathbf{W}_1$, we get the following result:

$$\mathbf{y}_3 = \mathbf{W}\,\mathbf{y}_0 = \begin{bmatrix} .7499875 & 0.000029999 \\ 0.250012 & .99997 \end{bmatrix} * \begin{bmatrix} 100 \\ 500 \end{bmatrix} = \begin{bmatrix} 75.01375 \\ 524.9863 \end{bmatrix}.$$

The same result is obtained for the output vector $\mathbf{y}_3$.

What we conclude from this series of vector/matrix multiplications is that reworked returns are strongly influenced by the number of incoming returns and the number of manufactured products is strongly determined by the number of incoming purchase orders. Further about 25% of returned items cannot be reworked, so they are replaced with a new one. Notice, though that the relationships are not perfect in the sense that very weak connections of the order.000001 were found. These are just computational errors.

Functional Comparison of CLEAROS with Other Analysis Tools

The overall architecture of CLEAROS resembles causal diagrams used in system dynamics or other causal modeling methodologies. However, there are a number of important differences between CLEAROS and these causal models: (1) the main purpose of building CLEAROS is to capture unknown organizational knowledge (that is heuristic and experiential) and then do subsequent inferential computation on it. On the other hand, the principal purpose of casual models is to capture the causality inherent in systems; (2) CLEAROS is designed to handle a large number of relevant variables, and more importantly the relationships between these variables need not be limited to causal relationships, while those in causal models are; (3) CLEAROS assumes hierarchical, layered and acyclic network structures with synchronous timing in updating their status. On the other hand, causal models assume general network structures with asynchronous timing in updating their status; (4) CLEAROS supports weighted relationships (representing degree of influence) whereas the signed digraphs utilized in causal models do not.

This work was previously published in Journal of Organizational and End User Computing (JOEUC) 21(2), edited by Mo Adam Mahmood, pp. 67-89, copyright 2009 by IGI Publishing (an imprint of IGI Global).

Section 3

Chapter 10
An Empirical Study of Computer Self-Efficacy and the Technology Acceptance Model in the Military:
A Case of a U.S. Navy Combat Information System

Yair Levy
Nova Southeastern University, USA

Bruce D. Green
The GBS Group, USA

ABSTRACT

The U.S. Navy continues to be a major developer and procurer of information systems (ISs), yet very limited research has been done to determine the factors that influence technology acceptance by naval personnel. Literature suggests that efforts to embrace information technology in improving decision making and reducing workload depend heavily on the use of such systems. Moreover, previous research has shown the validity of the technology acceptance model (TAM) and computer self-efficacy (CSE) to model technology acceptance in numerous environments. However, very little research was done specifically addressing such technology acceptance with military combat ISs. Thus, this study examines the applicability of the extended TAM with a CSE construct model to the U.S. Navy's combat ISs. A survey sample of 237 sailors from five different U.S. Navy aircraft carriers was used to assess such an extended model on a U.S. Navy's combat IS. Results indicate that perceived ease of use, perceived usefulness, and CSE were valid antecedents of technology acceptance (as indicated by intention to use). Moreover, high Cronbach's alpha was observed on all measures, indicating reliability of the measures in the context of military organizations.

DOI: 10.4018/978-1-60960-577-3.ch010

INTRODUCTION

Understanding the factors that influence individual adoption and usage of information systems (ISs) continues to be a central interest for IS researchers (Thompson, Compeau, & Higgins, 2006, p. 25). Over the past two decades, a large body of research regarding technology acceptance of IS has been conducted (Chau, 1996; Chau & Hu, 2001; Davis, 1989; Hu, Chau, Sheng, & Tam, 1999; Legris, Ingham, & Collerette, 2003; Ma & Liu, 2004; Venkatesh, Morris, Davis, & Davis, 2003; King & He, 2006). One of the highly cited models is the technology acceptance model (TAM) introduced by Davis (1986). According to Compeau et al. (2006), it is the simplicity of TAM and its measures that made it fertile ground for the flourishing research stream that resulted.

Since the late 1980s, technology acceptance studies have been successfully replicated in many environments (Venkatesh et al., 2003). Such environments include a public hospital system (Chau & Hu, 2001), a construction-engineering environment (Lowry, 2002), technology adoption in Arab nations (Rose & Straub, 1998; Elbeltagi, McBride, & Hardaker, 2005), online gaming (Hsu & Lu, 2004), and a large corporation undergoing ERP implementation (Amoako-Gyampah & Salam, 2004). Moreover, many technology acceptance models and studies have been conducted in academic settings (Davis, 1989; McFarland & Hamilton, 2006; Taylor & Todd, 1995). Furthermore, others criticized most of the key TAM studies for the use of students as study participants and recommended that further validations are needed using other types of participants (Legris et al., 2003). However, researchers noted that it is important to study existing technology acceptance models in those IS contexts that "target highly specialized individual professionals" (Chau & Hu, 2001, p. 700).

Additionally, researchers have recommended replication of instruments and revalidation of technology acceptance models for unique environments (Amoako-Gyampah & Salam, 2004). Furthermore, others criticized previous TAM studies for the use of office-related applications as the IS and noted that research would benefit from the investigation of managerial or process-level applications, as well as other professional systems (Legris et al., 2003). Yet, despite the fertile work on technology acceptance in IS research, very little attention has been given to the investigation of technology acceptance in military environments (Briggs et al., 1999; Simon & Paper, 2007).

Hutchins (1996) details the dangers associated with tactical decision making in the military. Such unique context, especially during combat situations or when dealing with combat-related decisions where outcomes can have life-and-death as well as international relations consequences, may warrant the examination of existing technology acceptance models. In the past decade, the U.S. Navy has been spending a substantial amount of resources on the development of customized and unique Naval IS. In 2005, the U.S. Navy awarded more information technology contracts than any other federal agency, including all other branches of the military. The U.S. Navy awarded approximately $54 billion worth of prime technology contracts in 2005 through the Seaport program, which includes 500 vendor corporations ("Navy and Marines Lead Federal IT Spending," 2005). One of the key goals of such spending is to reduce shipboard manning by the use of IS. Achievement of this goal requires the development and integration of improved systems (Bisantz et al., 2003). Thus, considering the substantial funds being applied to IS projects by the U.S. Navy and the observed limitations of prior key TAM studies noted above, a model for technology acceptance and the factors that influence IS usage are warranted for the military.

This study explored the factors that influence sailors' intention to use the combat IS aboard U.S. Naval aircraft carriers. Specifically the model examined by this study is the revised TAM with computer self-efficacy (CSE) (Chau, 2001; Chau

& Hu, 2001). The next section provides a review of the theoretical foundation used for the study including literature related to TAM and CSE. Then, the research model, study's hypotheses, and the instrument are reviewed. Next, the methodology used for this study is discussed including a review of the specific system investigated; this is followed by data analysis of the results. Then, discussions about the implications of the results for the practice and research as well as the limitations of the study are presented. The article concludes with suggestions for future research given the findings from this study.

THEORETICAL BACKGROUND

Technology Acceptance in the U.S. Navy

Researchers have found that there are unique aspects to decisions made by personnel in a combat department on a U.S. Navy ship due to the potential for political or lethal impacts from those decisions (Hutchins, 1996). Acceptance of naval combat IS has not been explored previously, but studies about the acceptance of general technology aboard U.S. Navy ships have found the TAM to be a good basis for research (Briggs et al., 1999; Simon & Paper, 2007). Simon and Paper (2007) studied technology acceptance of a voice recognition system by engineering and medical personnel aboard a U.S. Navy aircraft carrier. They extended TAM with subjective norms based on findings from a focus group which suggested that social pressures would be a large influence on system usage. Simon and Paper (2007) recount that the body of literature on subjective norms as a significant external variable to the TAM is mixed with a few studies showing significance, while most other studies drop the variable altogether. They concluded that the TAM extended with subjective norms is "a robust model with excellent ability to predict system use" (p. 39). One key fundamental difference exists between Simon and Paper's (2007) study and our study which is the type of system under investigation. In our study, the IS under investigation deals with situational awareness used in combat, while the Simon and Paper (2007) study addressed a voice recognition system used by engineering and medical personnel aboard an U.S. Navy aircraft carrier. Thus, although the users investigated by Simon and Paper (2007) are specialized professionals aboard an U.S. Navy aircraft carrier, the specific type of system investigated by them appears to be less strategic in nature than the one investigated in this study. Thus, subjective norms appear to be less important for the acceptance of combat IS.

Briggs et al. (1999) studied the acceptance of a group support system (GSS) using a modified version of the TAM called the technology transition model (TTM). Based on a qualitative study, they found that occasional users of the GSS saw less benefit than did regular GSS users. They recommended that system specialists be made available to aid the occasional user. Though Briggs et al. (1999) do not make the explicit connection, the different perceptions of regular users and occasional users toward the system could be attributed to difference in computer self-efficacy. Thus, this study investigated U.S. Navy sailors' computer self-efficacy and its impact on their TAM-related perceptions in the context of combat IS aboard aircraft carriers.

Technology Acceptance Model

The TAM has been studied extensively with many variations and in many different environments (Al-Gahtani, 2001; King & He, 2006; Legris et al., 2003; Venkatesh et al., 2003). King and He (2006) performed a meta-analysis of 88 TAM studies and found the model to be a strong predictor of user acceptance. Likewise, Legris et al. (2003) performed a meta-analysis of 28 TAM studies and found strong support for the model. Venkatesh et al. (2003) provided an extensive literature review of different variations and revised models of technology acceptance including the original TAM. They found the original TAM to be a good predictor of system acceptance.

Davis, Bagozzi, and Warshaw's (1989) original TAM is grounded on the theory of reasoned action (TRA) proposed and validated by Ajzen and Fishbein (1975). The essence of the TAM is in using users' perceptions about usefulness, ease of use, and attitude toward a specific technology in order to predict users' intention to use, as well as actual usage of the technology. The overall approach of the TAM is predictive in nature, attempting to uncover the constructs that impact users' intentions to use technology. Figure 1 provides an overview of the original conceptual map proposed by Davis et al. (1989).

The factors in TAM that predict usage are perceived usefulness (PU), perceived ease of use (PEOU), and attitude. *Perceived usefulness* is defined as "the degree to which a person believes that using a particular system would enhance his or her job performance" (Davis, 1989, p. 320). *Perceived ease of use* is defined as "the degree to which a person believes that using a particular system would be free of effort" (Davis, 1989, p. 320). *Attitude* has been defined by Yang and Yoo (2004) as a combination of "how much the person likes the object of thought" and "specific beliefs related to the object" (p. 20).

Behavioral intention (BI) or *intention to use* refers to whether one intends to use a technology (Chau & Hu, 2001). BI has been used as the dependent variable in technology acceptance studies and found to be a valid predictor of actual system use (Simon & Paper, 2007; Venkatesh et al., 2003). Simon and Paper (2007) found a significant path coefficient from BI to actual system use (0.90, $p<0.001$) in their longitudinal study of technology acceptance on a U.S. Navy aircraft carrier. The advantage of using BI instead of actual use as the dependent variable is that BI can be collected in a cross-sectional study (Chau & Hu, 2001), whereas actual use requires a longitudinal data collection (Agarwal & Prasad, 1999; Taylor & Todd, 1995; Venkatesh et al., 2003). Moreover, in the event of a sensitive type of IS, such as combat IS in this study, BI appears to be a more appropriate dependent variable to measure than actual system use, as system use measure for such a system is challenging due to context of the system.

Previous studies of TAM have investigated the external variables, or antecedents of PU and PEOU (see Figure 1), in an effort to gain a better understanding of the actions that can be taken to improve predictability of technology acceptance (Amoako-Gyampah & Salam, 2004; Venkatesh & Davis, 2000). To that end, researchers have extended TAM with external variables such as cognitive absorption (Agarwal & Karahanna, 2000), task technology fit (Dishaw & Strong, 1999), technical support (Elbeltagi et al., 2005), compatibility (Chen & Tan, 2004), and trust (Gefen, Karahanna, & Straub, 2003). An extension to the TAM that has been studied repeatedly

Figure 1. Davis et al.'s (1989) conceptual map of the TAM

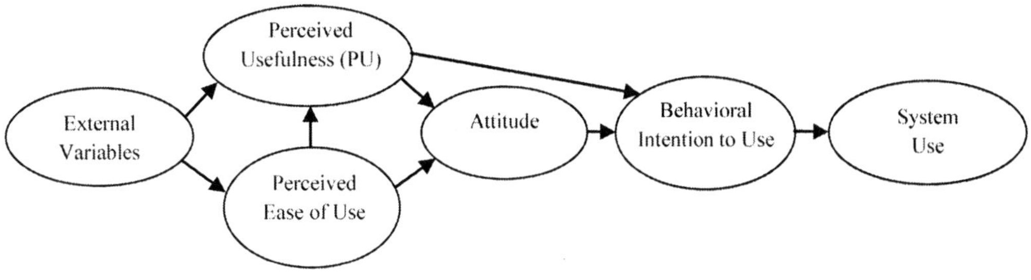

is CSE (Chau, 2001; Wang, 2002; Venkatesh & Davis, 1996).

The construct of CSE proposed by Compeau and Higgins (1995) emerged from the general concept of self-efficacy that was founded on social cognitive theory (Bandura, 1977, 1982, 1984). CSE is defined as "an individual's perception of his or her ability to use a computer in the accomplishment of a job task" (Compeau & Higgins, 1995, p. 193). Literature suggests that CSE has a very high reliability and strong validity across different contexts (Agarwal, Sambamurthy, & Stair, 2000; Chung, Schwager, & Turner, 2002; Marakas, Yi, & Johnson, 1998; Sheng, Pearson, & Crosby, 2003; Stone, Arunachalam, & Chandler, 1996; Stone & Henry, 2003; Thatcher & Perrewe, 2002; Yi & Im, 2004). Moreover, CSE has been validated in numerous studies as an external variable for the TAM, though these studies were done in the context of non-military IS (Hasan, 2006b; Igbaria & Iivari, 1995; Venkatesh, 2000; Venkatesh & Davis, 1996).

Igbaria and Iivari (1995) studied the TAM extended with CSE using a sample of 450 personal computer users. They found that CSE influences PEOU. Similarly, Venkatesh and Davis (1996) studied the acceptance of IS by measuring CSE, usability, experience, and their impact on TAM constructs using a sample of 108 students. They found that CSE strongly influences PEOU. Agarwal and Karahanna (2000) conducted a study of the influence of cognitive absorption on technology acceptance of the Internet using a sample of 288 students. They incorporated CSE in their research model, while their results provide support that CSE influences PU and PEOU, which in turn influence BI.

Other studies also demonstrated the significant influence of CSE on PEOU (Hasan, 2006a, 2006b). In one study, Hasan (2006a) investigated how well 78 students learned Unix commands and the influences of CSE and anxiety on PEOU. He found that CSE had a significant influence on PEOU. In a separate study, Hasan (2006b) studied TAM extended with CSE of a Unix-based computer text editor using a sample of university students. In this study as well, he found that CSE demonstrated a significant influence on PEOU for the students. Chau (2001) conducted a study of extending the TAM model with CSE on 360 business students. Although providing validation for Davis et al.'s (1989) original TAM model, his study suggests that CSE is a key external construct that influences PEOU and PU. Celuch, Taylor, and Goodwin (2004) investigated insurance professionals and an online insurance quote system using the external construct of CSE. Celuch et al.'s (2004) study included CSE and its influence on BI. They also confirmed CSE to be a significant construct to influence BI.

While there is evidence from literature to support the belief that CSE may serve as a strong external variable and a contributor to PEOU and PU as noted above, there is very little attention in literature for validating the original TAM model with CSE in the context of military IS. As noted previously, Briggs et al. (1999) found that occasional U.S. Navy users of a group support system needed help from regular users to utilize the system. This warrants future investigation of U.S. Navy technology users, specifically with an investigation of their PEOU and CSE.

Legris et al. (2003) concluded in their meta-analysis of TAM studies that "research would benefit from examining the introduction of business process applications" (p. 202). Table 1 indicates that although there have been many technology acceptance studies published, the majority of studies have concentrated on generic or commercially available systems, while very few studies investigated highly specialized systems combined with specialized professional users. Table 1 provides a list of 73 technology acceptance studies that were reported in 66 published articles. The study applications included 23 related to the acceptance of the Internet or specific Internet application; 15 studies are related to the acceptance of generic office applications (word processors, spreadsheets, graphics, etc.); 20 studies are related to the acceptance of applications that are specific to a particular business or profession and a specific process; and 15 studies are related to the acceptance of miscellaneous technologies such as general computer use.

Table 1 also includes an indication for the environments in which these given technology acceptance studies were conducted. Thirty-seven (37) out of the 73 were conducted in corporate environments; 22 were conducted in university settings (i.e., using students as participants); seven were conducted in other miscellaneous environments; and seven were conducted in specialized environments such as government, hospital, or military, of which only two (Briggs et al., 1999; Simon & Paper, 2007) were conducted in the context of the U.S. Navy. It is evident that very few technology acceptance-related studies were conducted in specialized contexts. These include the Colvin and Goh (2005) study of the acceptance of patrol car laptops by 430 police officers, the Lowry (2002) study of building management system acceptance by 58 engineers, the Celuch et al. (2004) study of acceptance of an online insurance quote system by 734 insurance professionals, and the Lucas and Spitler (1999) study of broker workstation acceptance by 107 stockbrokers. These examples further support the notion that although technology acceptance studies with specialized contexts were conducted, the majority of technology behind such studies appears to be generic in nature.

The two studies by Hu et al. (1999) and Chau and Hu (2001) are among the few that investigated specialized contexts with specialized professional users. In their study, Hu et al. (1999) investigated the acceptance of a telemedicine system by 408 physicians in Hong Kong by measuring PU, PEOU, attitude, and BI. They found that the TAM was applicable to this group of specialized professional physicians in a hospital environment, and that physicians' attitudes towards the telemedicine system had a significant influence on intention to use the system. In contrast, they found that PEOU did not have a significant influence on PU and attitude in this specialized context. Hu et al. (1999) concluded that "the explanatory power of TAM, particularly the PEOU factor, may weaken as the competency of the users increases" (p. 106). This finding suggests that "competency" or CSE should be further investigated as an external variable to the TAM, particularly when exploring specialized systems.

Thus, our study attempted to add to the body of knowledge by providing additional empirical results about an investigation of a specialized system (i.e., combat IS) in the context of professional users (i.e., U.S. Navy sailors). Moreover, the study attempted to add to the body of knowledge by investigating the influence of CSE as an external variable on the original TAM constructs in such specialized context.

RESEARCH MODEL, HYPOTHESES AND INSTRUMENT

The proposed research model examined in this study is based on the original TAM proposed by Davis (1986), augmented by CSE as suggested by Chau (2001), Chau and Hu (2001), McFarland and Hamilton (2006), as well as Venkatesh and Davis (1996). Figure 2 provides a conceptual map of the research model examined in this study. This modified model is based on the relationships proposed in the extension of the TAM with CSE.

A substantial number of TAM-related studies have documented the significant influence of BI on actual system use. According to Legris et al. (2003), out of 27 TAM-related studies reviewed, 10 studies indicated a significant positive relation between BI and actual system use. One study showed non-significant positive relation, and none of the studies reviewed by Legris et al. (2003) showed negative relation between BI and actual system use, while 17 out of the 28 TAM-related studies reviewed by Legris et al. (2003) were done

Table 1. Literature summary table for technology acceptance studies

Author(s)	Target System(s)	Sample	Model	Environment
Adams, Nelson, & Todd, 1992	Voicemail, E-Mail, WordPerfect, Lotus 1-2-3, Harvard Graphics	118 Professionals	TAM	Corporate Environment
Agarwal & Karahanna, 2000	Internet	288 Students	TAM + Cognitive Absorption, CSE, Innovativeness, Playfulness	University Environment
Agarwal & Prasad, 1999	Command-Line I/F & GUI	230 Employees	TAM + Individual Differences	Corporate Environment
Al-Gahtani & King, 1999	Spreadsheet	329 Students	TAM + End-User Computer, Satisfaction + Compatible, Image, Support	University Environment
Al-Gahtani, 2001	Spreadsheet	324 Students	TAM	University Environment
Amoako-Gyampah & Salam, 2004	ERP System	449 Employees	TAM + Shared Beliefs in Benefits	Corporate Environment
Benamati & Rajkamur, 2002	Outsourced System	IT Executives (sample size not reported)	Outsourcing Acceptance Model (PU, PEOU, Risk, Relations, Environment)	Corporate Environment
Briggs et al., 1999	Group Support System	U.S. Navy Personnel (sample size not reported)	Technology Transition Model	U.S. Navy Environment
Celuch et al., 2004	Web Insurance Portal	734 Insurance Staff	TRA + TPB + CSE	Corporate Environment
Chau, 1996	MS Excel & MS Word	192 Administrative Staff	TAM	Corporate Environment
Chau, 2001	MS Word	360 Students	TAM + CSE	University Environment
Chau & Hu, 2001	Telemedicine	408 Physicians	TAM + TPB + Decomposed TPB	Hospital Environment
Chen & Tan, 2004	Internet Shopping	253 Users	TAM + Compatibility, Trust, Service, Quality, Product Usability, Information	Home Environment
Colvin & Goh, 2005	Police Laptops	430 Police Officers	TAM + Information Quality, Timeliness of Data	Government/Police Environment
Davis, 1989	E-Mail, XEDIT, ChartMaster/PenDraw	109 Lab Workers 75 Lab Workers 40 Students	TAM TAM TAM	Corporate Environment Corporate Environment University Environment
Davis & Venkatesh, 1996	WordPerfect & Lotus 1-2-3	708 Students	TAM	University Environment
Dishaw & Strong, 1999	Programmer Tools	Programmers (sample size not reported)	TAM + Task Tech Fit, Tool Experience	Corporate Environment
Elbeltagi et al., 2005	Decision Support Systems	294 Managers	TAM + Characteristics, Support	Corporate Environment
Gefen et al., 2003	Internet Shopping	213 Students	TAM + Trust	University Environment
Hasan, 2006a	Unix	78 Students	CSE + PEOU, Anxiety, Far/Near Transfer Learning	University Environment
Hasan, 2006b	Text Editor	83 Students	TAM + CSE	University Environment
Hong, Thong, Wong, & Tam, 2002	Digital Library	585 Users	TAM + CSE, Domain Knowledge, Relevance, Terminology, Screen Design	University Environment
Hsu & Lu, 2004	Online Games	233 Users	TAM + Critical Mass, SN, Flow Experience	Home Environment
Hu et al., 1999	Telemedicine	408 Physicians	TAM	Hospital Environment
Huang & Chuang, 2007	Back-End system	223 Employees	TPB + Risk	Corporate Environment
Igbaria & Iivari, 1995	PCs	450 Users	TAM + CSE	Corporate Environment
Jackson, Chow, & Leitch, 1997	General IS	111 Professionals	TAM + User Involvement, Prior Use	Corporate Environment
Keil, Beranek, & Knsynski, 1995	CONFIG Software	118 Users	TAM	Corporate Environment
Lai & Li, 2005	Internet Banking	241 Students	TAM + Gender, Age, IT Competency	University Environment
Lederer, Maupin, Sena, & Zhuang, 2000	Web Sites	163 Users	TAM	Corporate Environment
Liaw, 2004	Search Engines	159 Students	TPB + Experience	University Environment

continued on following page

Table 1. continued

Author(s)	Target System(s)	Sample	Model	Environment
Lowry, 2002	Building Management System	58 Engineers	Relative Advantage, Compatibility, PEOU	Corporate Environment
Luarn & Lin, 2005	Mobile Banking	180 Users	TAM + CSE, Financial Cost, Credibility	Home Environment
Lucas & Spitler, 1999	Broker Workstations	107 Brokers	TAM + SN, System Quality	Corporate Environment
McCloskey, 2006	Internet Shopping	110 Users	TAM + Trust	Home Environment
McCoy et al., 2005	E-Mail	263 Students	TAM + PBC, SN	University Environment
McFarland & Hamilton, 2006	General Computer	108 Employees	TAM	Corporate Environment
Milchram, 2003	Risk Management System	494 Employees	TAM + System Trust	Corporate Environment
Moon & Kim, 2001	Internet	152 Students	TAM + Playfulness	University Environment
Morris & Venkatesh, 2000	Business Software	118 Users	TPB	Corporate Environment
Ndubisi & Jantan, 2003	General IS	177 Employees	TAM + Computing SKILL, Technical Background	Corporate Environment
Ngai, Poon, & Chai, 2007	Online Learning System (WebCT)	836 Students	TAM + Technical Support	University Environment
Ong, Lai, & Wang, 2004	Online Learning System	140 Engineers	TAM+ CSE, Credibility	Corporate Environment
Ong & Lai, 2006	Online Learning System	156 Tech Workers	TAM+ CSE	Corporate Environment
Pagani, 2004	Multimedia Mobile Services	1,000 Consumers	TAM + Price, Speed	Home Environment
Pavlou & Chai, 2002	E-Commerce	113 Users	TPB + Trust, Culture,	Corporate Environment
Pijpers, Bemelmans, Heemstra, & van Montfort, 2001	Executive IS	87 Executives	TAM	Corporate Environment
Roberts & Henderson, 2000	PCs	108 Government Employees	TAM + Fun, SN, Satisfaction, Anxiety	Government Environment
Rose & Straub, 1998	PCs	274 Employees	TAM	Corporate Environment
Saade & Bahli, 2005	Online Learning System	102 Students	TAM + Cognitive Absorption	University Environment
Simon & Paper, 2007	Navy Voice Recognition System	270 Sailors	TAM + SN	U.S. Navy Environment
Szajina, 1996	E-Mail	61 Students	TAM	University Environment
Taylor & Todd, 1995	Computer Resource Center	786 Students	TAM + TPB	University Environment
Thompson, Higgins, & Howell, 1991	PCs	212 Professionals	SN, Complexity, Job Fit, Long-Term	Corporate Environment
Thong, Hong, & Tam, 2002	Digital Libraries	397 Users	TAM + Organization, Interface Design	University Environment
Van der Heijden, 2003	Internet Shopping	828 Users	TAM + Enjoyment, Attractiveness	Home Environment
Venkatesh, 2000	Online Help Desk System Multimedia System Payroll Application	58 Employees 145 Employees 43 Employees	TAM + CSE, Intrinsic Motivation, Emotion	Corporate Environment Corporate Environment Corporate Environment
Venkatesh & Davis, 1996	General System	108 Students	TAM + CSE, Usability, Experience	University Environment
Venkatesh & Davis, 2000	Manufacture Schedule System MS Windows Accounting System Stock Portfolio Systems	38 Supervisors 39 Professionals 43 Professionals 36 Professionals	TAM TAM TAM TAM	Corporate Environment Corporate Environment Corporate Environment Corporate Environment
Wang, 2002	Electronic Tax Filing	260 Users	TAM + Credibility, CSE	Home Environment
Wang, Hsu, & Fang, 2005	Instant Messaging Service	437 Students	TAM + # of Users, Technology Utility	University Environment
Wixom & Todd, 2005	Data Warehouse	465 Users	TAM + Satisfaction	Corporate Environment
Wu, 2005	Mobile Commerce	310 Users	TAM + Risk, Cost, Compatibility	Corporate Environment
Yang & Yoo, 2004	Spreadsheet	211 Students	TAM (cognitive & affective attitude)	University Environment
Yi, Jackson, Park, & Probst, 2006	PDA's	222 Physicians	TAM + SN, PBC, Image, Innovativeness	Hospital Environment
Yu, Ha, Choi, & Rho, 2005	T-Commerce	1,001 Users	TAM + Trust, SN, Enjoyment	Corporate Environment

Figure 2. Conceptual map of the research model

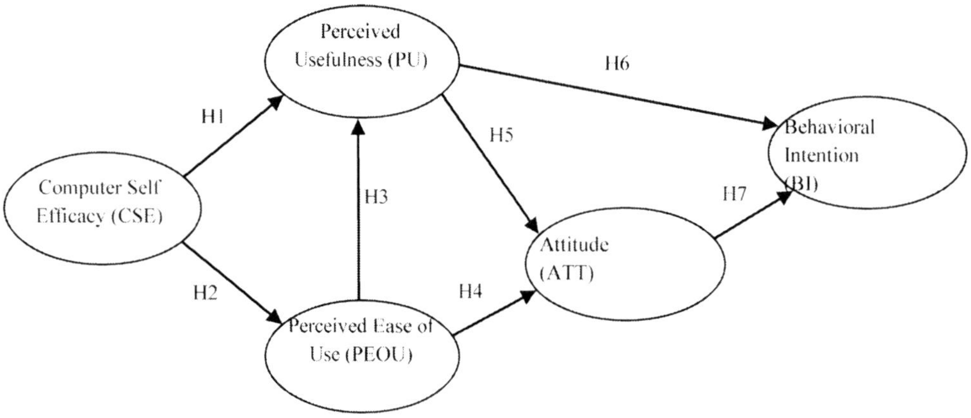

without the measure of actual system use. Additionally, more recent studies continue to show similar results of significant positive relation between BI and actual system use (Simon & Paper, 2007), while other recent studies continue to develop and test their models of technology acceptance without the measure of actual system use (Saade & Bahli, 2005; Thompson et al., 2006). Thus, consistent with such findings and due to the sensitivity of the system investigated in this study, actual use was not part of the model tested.

The seven hypotheses required for the model testing are:

H1: *Computer self-efficacy (CSE) of a U.S. Navy sailor will exert a positive influence on perceived usefulness (PU) of the combat IS.*

H2: *Computer self-efficacy (CSE) of a U.S. Navy sailor will exert a positive influence on perceived ease of use (PEOU) towards the combat IS.*

H3: *Perceived ease of use (PEOU) of a U.S. Navy sailor will exert a positive influence on perceived usefulness (PU) towards the combat IS.*

H4: *Perceived ease of use (PEOU) of a U.S. Navy sailor will exert a positive influence on attitude (ATT) towards the combat IS.*

H5: *Perceived usefulness (PU) of a U.S. Navy sailor will exert a positive influence on attitude (ATT) towards the combat IS.*

H6: *Perceived usefulness (PU) of a U.S. Navy sailor will exert a positive influence on behavioral intention (BI) towards the combat IS.*

H7: *Attitude (ATT) of a U.S. Navy sailor will exert a positive influence on behavioral intention (BI) towards the combat IS.*

A survey instrument was adapted from Chau and Hu (2001) which provides validated measures for the constructs relevant to PU, PEOU, attitude towards the system, and BI. The measures used by Chau and Hu (2001) were adapted from measures validated by Taylor and Todd (1995) as well as Davis (1989). PU, PEOU, and attitude towards the system were measured based on three items each, while BI was measured based on two items. CSE measures were adapted from Compeau and Higgins (1995). CSE was measured based on three items. All items were measured using a seven-point Likert-type scale. All measures for constructs (i.e., CSE, PU, PEOU, BI, and ATT) were adapted from their original sources noted above (Chau & Hu, 2001; Compeau & Higgins, 1995; Davis, 1989; Taylor & Todd, 1995) and were slightly modified to fit within the survey format or better relate to the system under study (i.e., a U.S. Navy's combat IS). This adaptation was accomplished by reviewing the survey instrument with subject matter experts experienced with the U.S. Navy's combat IS implementations onboard five U.S. Navy aircraft carriers. The results of the subject matter expert reviews were minor wording changes to clarify the intent of the questions for the U.S. Navy sailors. These minor modifications included changing the notation to the system's name from the generic notation of "combat IS" to the exact name of the system, particularly in the measures of the original TAM construct (i.e., PU, PEOU, ATT, and BI). The subject matter experts indicated that including the system's name may help reduce threats to internal validity (Table 2 provides the text of the survey items).

METHODOLOGY

This study used survey instrument methodology in order to empirically assess the aforementioned constructs (i.e., CSE, PU, PEOU, BI, and ATT) about sailors' perceptions of the Total Ship Information Management System (TSIMS) in the context of the U.S. Navy. The TSIMS is an information management system that provides situational awareness, equipment restoration, and maintenance management to combat systems personnel onboard U.S. Navy aircraft carriers (Green, 2003). It is specifically designed for the combat systems department onboard the carriers. The TSIMS was developed to help manage the maintenance, repair, and restoration of combat systems equipment. The system includes modules for 'smart drawings', power management, system status, and various system reports. The TSIMS reduces the time to accomplish administrative and operational tasks by providing a graphical interface of system and space diagrams. It helps shipboard sailors to research equipment status, enter work items, create trouble reports, and research ship valves and breakers alignments (Green, 2003).

The TSIMS was selected for this study as it is not mandatory, rather it is available to use at the discretion of the combat systems personnel. The TSIMS presents information in a graphical manner that allows sailors to determine the effects of equipment casualties on surrounding spaces and equipment by pointing-and-clicking on linked drawings. In contrast, the older legacy system requires sailors to perform text searches to access wiring or ventilation diagrams, and then to trace the diagrams by hand to determine the effects of an equipment casualty. Prior to this study the TSIMS program manager surveyed sailors and found that use of the TSIMS reduced the amount of time it took to locate critical information by 80% over the legacy system. However, the U.S. Navy had not mandated use of the TSIMS. Evidently and similar to the experience of Briggs et al. (1999), acceptance of the TSIMS was limited as some sailors used the system, while others used the legacy system still in place.

The survey instrument was distributed onboard five separate aircraft carriers while each carrier was at a U.S. Naval Station undergoing training and maintenance between deployments. The data collection took place over a six-month period in 2005. The survey instrument was distributed as paper based and was anonymously completed by the sailors. Responses were collated and entered into two separate spreadsheets by two separate individuals. The separate spreadsheets were then compared to assure that no data entry errors were made. Any difference in data was traced back to the original survey submitted, and the correct score was entered.

A total of five U.S. Navy aircraft carriers were represented in the sample, representing 42% of all U.S. Navy aircraft carriers. A total of 326 paper-based surveys were issued and 237 completed surveys were returned, a response rate of 73%. The survey response rate was high because the sample population was a captive audience. Each of the

Table 2. Descriptive statistics and analysis of instrument reliability (Cronbach's alpha)

Summary of Measurement Scales: (n=206)				
Construct	**Measure**	**Mean**	**SD**	**Cronbach's Alpha**
Computer Self Efficacy (CSE)				
CSE1	I am comfortable working with computers.	1.85	1.28	
CSE2	If I am given some training, I can learn to use most computer programs.	1.77	1.10	*0.77*
CSE3	I can learn to use most computer programs just by reading the manuals and help.	2.86	1.67	
Perceived Usefulness (PU)				
PU1	Using TSIMS will improve my support of casualty control, situational awareness, and logistical references.	2.54	1.53	
PU2	Using TSIMS will enhance my effectiveness in supporting combat operations.	2.27	1.27	*0.83*
PU3	I find TSIMS useful for my work on the ship.	2.54	1.29	
Perceived Ease of Use (PEOU)				
PEOU1	It was easy for me to learn to use TSIMS.	2.59	1.29	
PEOU2	It is easy for me to become skillful in TSIMS.	2.67	1.27	*0.91*
PEOU3	I find TSIMS easy to use.	2.72	1.36	
Attitude (ATT)				
ATT1	Using TSIMS is a good idea.	2.25	1.28	
ATT2	Using TSIMS is pleasant.	2.81	1.39	*0.65*
ATT3	Using TSIMS is beneficial to my ship.	2.20	1.27	
Behavioral Intention (BI)				
BI1	I intend to use TSIMS for casualty control, situational awareness, and logistical references as often as needed.	2.54	1.36	*0.89*
BI2	To the extent possible, I will use TSIMS in my work.	2.53	1.26	

237 returned surveys was checked for completeness and analyzed to determine if the participant had marked the same score for all items, which would suggest a response-set. Kerlinger and Lee (2000) noted that "response-set can be considered a mild threat to validity measures" (p. 713). They noted that scanning the data for response-set and removing those from final analysis helps with the overall validity of the results. Thus, the data were observed for response-sets, indicating 31 cases of sailors who just marked the whole survey on the same score. Such response-sets were eliminated, providing a total of 206 usable records for further analysis.

DATA ANALYSIS AND RESULTS

Analysis of Instrument Reliability

Table 2 provides the results of the analysis of instrument reliability. Results indicate that four out of the five constructs provided a very high reliability of 0.91, 0.89, 0.83, and 0.77 Cronbach's alpha for PEOU, BI, PU, and CSE, respectively, while Cronbach's alpha for ATT provided moderate reliability of 0.65. These results provide an indication that the survey instrument is reliable in its measurements and consistent with results found in prior literature such as Chau (2001).

Table 3. Analysis of overall goodness-of-fit

Goodness-of-Fit Measure (n=206)	Recommended Value*	Values from this Study	Chau (2001)
Chi-square (χ^2)		112.2	NR
Degrees of freedom (df)		70	NR
Chi-square/df	<3.00	1.61	2.09
Goodness-of-Fit Index (GFI)	>0.90	0.94	0.90
Adjusted Goodness-of-Fit Index (AGFI)	>0.80	0.90	0.88
Normalized Fit Index (NFI)	>0.90	0.94	0.94
Non-Normalized Fit Index (NNFI)	>0.90	0.97	0.91
Comparative Fit Index (CFI)	>0.90	0.98	0.94
Standardized Root Mean Square Residual (SRMSR)	<0.10	0.05	0.05

* Per Chau (2001)
NR – Not Reported

Model Testing Results

SPSS®'s AMOS™ statistical package was used to perform the model fit testing based on structural equation modeling (SEM). According to Simon and Paper (2007), SEM was documented in literature as an appropriate technique for model fit examination, superior to multiple regression analysis. The seven proposed hypotheses were tested using a model-fit analysis. Literature suggests seven common measures of model-fit analysis including Chi-square/degrees-of-freedom (Chi-square/df), goodness-of-fit index (GFI), adjusted goodness-of-fit index (AGFI), normed fit index (NFI), non-normed fit index (NNFI), comparative fit index (CFI), and standardized root mean square residual (SRMSR) (Chau, 2001; Chau & Hu, 2001; Simon & Paper, 2007; Somers, Nelson, & Karimi, 2003).

Within these seven model-fit measures, the literature provides specific guidelines for recommended values in order to indicate the performance of the model. Carmines and McIver (1981) recommended that a value of Chi-square/df less than 3 indicates good fit. Additionally, Somers et al. (2003) noted that Chi-square/df less than 2 indicates even "more restrictive [fit]" (p. 610) or a higher quality of model fit. Table 3 provides both the recommended values and the results of this study and results of a comparable published model by Chau (2001). Chi-square/df was found to be 1.6, which is much lower than both the recommended value (<3.00) and the restrictive fit (<2.00), indicating a good support for the model-data fit.

Two other common measures of model-fit analysis are GFI and AGFI. GFI measure is based on the amount of variance and covariance difference, while AGFI is similar to GFI but adjusted to the degrees of freedom relative to the number of variables in the model (Shumacker & Lomax, 2004). On both GFI and AGFI, 0 indicates no fit and 1 indicates perfect fit. Researchers suggested that values for GFI and AGFI above.90 and.80, respectively, indicate a good fit (Chau, 2001; Chau & Hu, 2001; Somers et al., 2003). Results of this study's model indicate support for the model fit, with GFI of.94 and AGFI of.90.

Additionally, three more common measures of model-fit analysis are NFI, NNFI, and CFI. For these three measures researchers suggested that values greater than.90 indicate support for the model fit (Chau, 2001; Chau & Hu, 2001; Somers et al., 2003). Based on these model-fit measures, results of this study's model indicate a near-perfect model fit, with NFI of.94, NNFI of.97, and CFI of.98 providing additional support for a good model-data fit. Mayers, Gamst, and Guarino (2006) suggested that SRMSR below.08 indicates good fit, between.08 and.10 indicates moderate fit, and above.10 indicates poor fit. Shumacker and Lomax (2004) also concur with these recommended model-fit values. Results of this study's model indicate SRMSR of.05, which additionally supports the fit of the model. Therefore, based on the results of this analysis that all seven model-fit measures were well within the specific guidelines for recommended values noted in literature, there is a strong support for the model's goodness-of-fit.

Following the justification for the overall model fit, examination for each of the seven specific hypotheses was done. Figure 3 indicates the results of the SEM analysis for the extended TAM and CSE model. Computer self-efficacy of U.S. Navy sailors exerted a positive influence on perceived usefulness, indicating support for the first hypothesis set by this study. This is consistent with the findings of Agarwal and Karahanna (2000), as well as Wang (2002). Moreover, computer self-efficacy has also exerted a positive influence on perceived ease of use. Thus, the second hypothesis set by this study appears to be supported also in the context of the U.S. Navy. This was also consistent with the results noted by Hasan (2006a), Igbaria and Iivari (1995), as well as Venkatesh and Davis (1996). Perceived ease of use of U.S. Navy sailors exerted a positive influence on perceived usefulness, indicating a support for the third hypothesis. According to Legris et al. (2003), 21 studies out of 28 studies in their review of TAM-related literature demonstrated similar results, while five studies found non-significant results and two studies did not test for such relationship (PEOU-PU). Perceived ease of use showed no significant influence on attitude, indicating a lack of support for the fourth hypothesis. Interestingly, only 10 studies out of the 28 reported by Legris et al. (2003) were found to have significant effect, while three studies found non-significant results and 15 studies did not test for such relationship (PEOU-ATT).

The fifth hypothesis was supported by the results of this study, where perceived usefulness of U.S. Navy sailors exerted a strong positive influence on attitude. Moreover, perceived usefulness exerted a strong positive influence on behavioral intention, indicating support for the sixth hypotheses. These findings indicates that one unit increase in sailor's perceived usefulness results in a.86 unit increase in their attitude towards the system and a.90 unit increase in their intention to use it. These results are consistent with the Hu et al. (1999) study. Finally, results of this study showed no significant influence of attitude on

Figure 3. Structural equation model testing results for extended TAM and CSE model

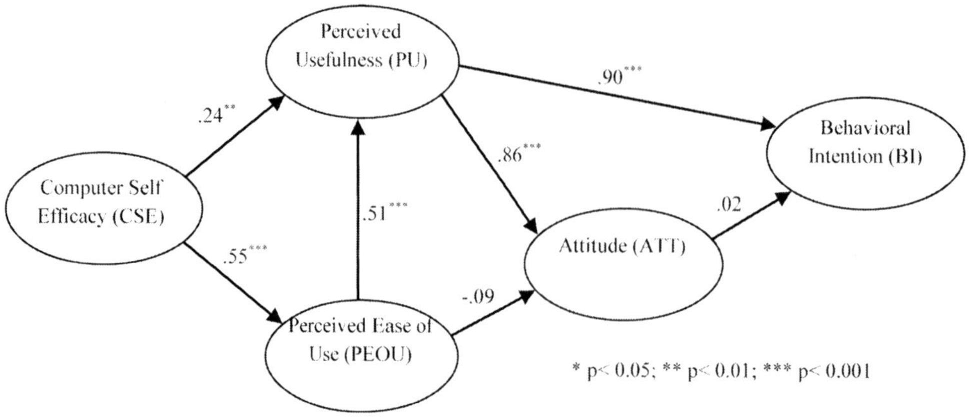

behavioral intention, indicating a lack of support for the seventh hypothesis. Legris et al.'s (2003) review also provided limited support in the literature on such an effect, with only seven out of the 28 studies indicating positive influence, four studies with no significant influences, and 17 studies that did not measure the influence of attitude on behavioral intention. Table 4 provides a summary of the hypotheses posed by this study with indication for the supported (or not) significant positive influences.

DISCUSSION

The TAM has long been a central model in IS research, with substantial numbers of studies validating it in various contexts. "However, very little attention has been given to factors that effect the acceptance of IS in the context of" military ISs, in particular when assessing IS that is used by combat personnel. Data collected from 206 sailors aboard five U.S. Navy aircraft carriers about combat IS provided empirical support for the extended TAM with computer self-efficacy. Analysis of instrument reliability indicated high Cronbach's alpha for four of the instrument constructs—computer self-efficacy, usefulness, ease of use, and behavioral intention—which is better than the recommended value for good reliability. The remaining construct (attitude) provided an acceptable reliability measure. These instrument reliability results appear to be consistent with other literature such as Thompson et al. (2006) and in the meta-analysis review of TAM studies by Legris et al. (2003).

In general, the results of the goodness-of-fit analysis obtained in this study are equally valid to those obtained by others with similar model (Chau, 2001). All seven measures of model-fit testing for the goodness-of-fit were found to be better than the accepted values noted in the literature. Moreover, five out of the seven hypotheses set for this study were supported. Results of this study show evidence that computer self-efficacy is a very reliable construct that provides a strong influence on usefulness and ease of use also in the context of military ISs. Moreover, the results of this study show a strong support for usefulness as the primary construct to influence intention-to-use, but it is affected by computer self-efficacy and ease of use. Usefulness is also found to be a strong construct to influence attitude towards the system. Additionally, ease of use was found to be less important than the usefulness of the system.

Two hypotheses that were not supported also demonstrated lack of support in the literature (Legris et al., 2003). The two relationships are between ease of use and attitude, as well as between attitude and behavioral intention. It appears that due to such lack of support, a substantial number of TAM-related studies have eliminated the measure of attitude altogether, compared to other TAM constructs (Legris et al., 2003). In the context of this study, sailors' attitudes towards the combat IS appear to have a limited role in the overall acceptance of such a system.

In general, the model tested in this study acknowledges the influences of computer self-efficacy on ease of use and usefulness, ease of use on usefulness, and usefulness on attitude and behavioral intention. Moreover, the results obtained by this study provide additional support for the validity and reliability of the constructs also

Table 4. Summary of hypotheses results

Hypothesis	Relations:	Sig. Positive Influence
H1:	CSE → PU	Yes
H2:	CSE → PEOU	Yes
H3:	PEOU → PU	Yes
H4:	PEOU → ATT	No
H5:	PU → ATT	Yes
H6:	PU → BI	Yes
H7:	ATT → BI	No

measured in the context of a specialized military system such as a U.S. Navy combat IS.

Implications to Research and Practice

There are several observed implications from this study to practice and research. For practitioners, such as U.S. Navy program managers, understanding the constructs that influence sailors' decisions to use combat IS is highly important. Development of a technology acceptance model for the U.S. Navy may lead to a better understanding of the key factors that need additional attention for future system developments. Furthermore, the results of this study are valuable to program managers who are required to make decisions on how to invest funds for additional IS improvements. This is especially critical for the U.S. Navy as it is the largest investor of IS development among all U.S. military branches. Moreover, this validated model can also be used as a tool to identify weaknesses in an implementation of U.S. Navy's ISs and help adjust the implementation approach.

For researchers, this study provides a number of interesting implications and opportunities for future investigation. First, this study provides additional support for the TAM augmented with computer self-efficacy for specialized professionals and when dealing with specialized systems. Researchers may wish to pursue further investigation of the antecedents of computer self-efficacy for specialized professionals. There are a number of studies that have investigated the effect of training on computer self-efficacy related to the Internet (Durndell & Haag, 2002; Torkzadeh, Chang, & Demirhan, 2006; Torkzadeh & Van Dyke, 2002), and researchers may wish to pursue validation of the effect of training on computer self-efficacy and the TAM in specialized environments, for example the U.S. Navy. Next, due to the lower reliability of the measure of attitude compared to the measures of the other constructs in this study and its limited influence on behavioral intention, researchers should consider investigation of attitude only of generic known types of systems, rather than specialized contexts.

Finally, although results of this study provide considerably good validation of the model-fit, such results must be taken in the specific context of combat IS in the U.S. Navy. Thus, additional research can investigate the acceptance of combat IS in other branches of the military. Specifically, researchers can investigate acceptance of various other types of systems such as handheld devices used by the U.S. Marines, night navigation systems used by the U.S. Army, and so forth. Additionally, researchers should explore similar model testing in other armies beyond the U.S. Specifically, researchers with access to soldiers from other countries, which are involved in combat deployment that use IS during such operations, can provide fertile insights into the constructs that significantly influence the acceptance of combat ISs by those soldiers.

Limitations

Several limitations can be observed for this study. First, examination of military ISs is largely unexplored territory. Although results of this study are valid as indicated by the analyses, additional measures should be explored in the context of military ISs. An observed limitation of this study deals with the high amount of response-sets collected. Although this study was able to collect a relatively high response rate (~73%) from the U.S. Navy sailors, there was a large number (~10%) of respondents who simply marked the survey with the same score on all measures in order to obey the request of completing the survey. Thus, by providing response-set, these sailors prevented assessment of their true perceptions and feelings about this U.S. Navy combat IS. This resulted in the need to eliminate these response-sets from the data prior to any analysis, giving a lower final response rate of 63%.

CONCLUSION

In summary, the results provided by this study indicate that the extended the TAM with computer self-efficacy is also valid in the specialized context of combat IS within the U.S. Navy. Managers concerned about user acceptance of their systems should understand the factors that influence system use. Based on findings of this study, developers, integrators, and program managers, specifically for U.S. Navy systems, should focus resources more on ensuring that systems help sailors achieve their goals and less on the ease of use of systems. Moreover, managers should also focus resources on ensuring that combat systems installed are useful because, consistent with previous TAM studies, perceived usefulness is the primary construct to influence behavioral intention. One of the reasons that a system may not be useful is that it is not aligned with the user's motivations and job goals (Malhotra & Galletta, 2004). A system may not be perceived as useful if the system addresses organizational goals that are abstract from the user's goals. Additionally, this study found that attitude was not a good influencing construct on intention to use the system. This finding indicates that the measures used in this study for attitude may not be as strongly needed for assessing the acceptance of combat IS. Consistent with Yang and Yoo (2004), this study reports the attitude construct had the lower reliability than the rest of the constructs measured. Future researchers may wish to further explore the measure for attitude when assessing constructs that influence acceptance of combat ISs.

This study found that computer self-efficacy significantly influences sailors' perceptions of system usefulness and ease of use. Sailors who are comfortable working with IS and learning to use them on their own are more likely intended to use such systems. It is evident that overall, the sailors indicated a high level of comfort with using ISs and high level of confidence using a new system if training is provided. However, evidences also suggest that these same sailors indicate a much lower level of comfort with using ISs if all they have been provided are ability to read the system manuals and help documentations. Thus, it appears that one of the important contributions of this study is not just that the model is valid in the U.S. Navy context, but that the implications of training are a critical success factor for the acceptance of combat ISs. It might be that due to the sensitivity of the system investigated and the fact that it is related to combat decisions, users without proper training may hesitate to use such a system. This is intuitive given the potential for political or lethal impacts from use of such a system. Therefore, managers and system integrators should ensure that users who are not comfortable working with ISs receive proper training in order to increase acceptance of such systems.

ACKNOWLEDGMENT

The authors would like to thank William "Doug" Faulkner for invaluable help administering the survey for this study and the sailors aboard the five U.S. Navy aircraft carriers for participating in this study. Moreover, the authors would like to thank the *JOEUC* editor-in-chief Dr. M. Adam Mahmood, the accepting associate editor, and the anonymous referees for their careful review and valuable suggestions.

REFERENCES

Adams, D. A., Nelson, R. R., & Todd, P. A. (1992). Perceived usefulness, ease of use, and usage of information technology: A replication. *Management Information Systems Quarterly*, *16*(2), 227–247. doi:10.2307/249577

Agarwal, R., & Karahanna, E. (2000). Time flies when you're having fun: Cognitive absorption and beliefs about information technology usage. *Management Information Systems Quarterly*, *24*(4), 665–694. doi:10.2307/3250951

Agarwal, R., & Prasad, J. (1999). Are individual differences germane to the acceptance of new information technologies? *Decision Sciences*, *30*(2), 361–391. doi:10.1111/j.1540-5915.1999.tb01614.x

Agarwal, R., Sambamurthy, V., & Stair, R. M. (2000). Research report: The evolving relationship between general and specific computer self-efficacy—an empirical assessment. *Information Systems Research*, *11*(4), 418–430. doi:10.1287/isre.11.4.418.11876

Ajzen, I., & Fishbein, M. (1975). *Belief, attitude, intension, and behavior: An introduction to theory and research*. Reading, MA: Addison-Wesley.

Al-Gahtani, S. S. (2001). The applicability of TAM outside North America: An empirical test in the United Kingdom. *Information Resources Management Journal*, *14*(3), 37–47. doi:10.4018/irmj.2001070104

Al-Gahtani, S. S., & King, M. (1999). Attitudes, satisfaction and usage: Factors contributing to each in the acceptance of information technology. *Behaviour & Information Technology*, *18*(4), 277–297. doi:10.1080/014492999119020

Amoako-Gyampah, K., & Salam, A. F. (2004). An extension of the technology acceptance model in an ERP implementation environment. *Information & Management*, *41*, 731–745. doi:10.1016/j.im.2003.08.010

Bandura, A. (1977). Self-efficacy: Toward a unifying theory of behavioral change. *Psychological Review*, *84*(2), 191–215. doi:10.1037/0033-295X.84.2.191

Bandura, A. (1982). Self-efficacy: Mechanism human agency. *The American Psychologist*, *37*(2), 122–147. doi:10.1037/0003-066X.37.2.122

Bandura, A. (1984). Recycling misconceptions of perceived self-efficacy. *Cognitive Therapy and Research*, *8*(3), 231–255. doi:10.1007/BF01172995

Benamati, J., & Rajkamur, T. M. (2002). The application development outsourcing decision: An application of the technology acceptance model. *Journal of Computer Information Systems*, *42*(4), 35–43.

Bisantz, A., Rothe, E., Brickman, B., Gosbee, L., Hettinger, L., & McKinney, J. (2003). Integrating cognitive analyses in a large-scale system design process. *International Journal of Human-Computer Studies*, *58*, 177–206. doi:10.1016/S1071-5819(02)00130-1

Briggs, R. O., Adkins, M., Kruse, J., Nunamaker, J. F., Mittleman, D., & Miller, S. (1999). Lessons learned using a technology transition model with the U.S. Navy. *Proceedings of the 32nd Hawaii International Conference on System Sciences* (pp. 1-10), Big Island, HI.

Carmines, E. G., & McIver, S. P. (1981). Analyzing models with unobserved variables: Analysis of covariance structures. In Bohrnstedt, G. W., & Borgatta, E. F. (Eds.), *Social measurement: Current issues*. Beverly Hills, CA: Sage.

Celuch, K., Taylor, S. A., & Goodwin, S. (2004). Understanding insurance salesperson Internet information management intentions: A test of competing models. *Journal of Insurance Issues*, *27*(1), 22–40.

Chau, P. Y. (1996). An empirical assessment of a modified technology acceptance model. *Journal of Management Information Systems*, *13*(2), 185–205.

Chau, P. Y. (2001). Influence of computer attitude and self-efficacy on IT usage behavior. *Journal of End User Computing*, *13*(1), 26–33. doi:10.4018/joeuc.2001010103

Chau, P. Y., & Hu, P. J. (2001). Information technology acceptance by individual professionals: A model comparison approach. *Decision Sciences*, *32*(4), 699–718. doi:10.1111/j.1540-5915.2001.tb00978.x

Chen, L. D., & Tan, J. (2004). Technology adaptation in e-commerce: Key determinants of virtual stores acceptance. *European Management Journal*, *22*(1), 74–84. doi:10.1016/j.emj.2003.11.014

Chung, S. H., Schwager, P. H., & Turner, D. E. (2002). An empirical of students' computer self-efficacy: Differences among four academic disciplines at a large university. *Journal of Computer Information Systems*, *42*(4), 1–6.

Colvin, C. A., & Goh, A. (2005). Validation of the technology acceptance model for police. *Journal of Criminal Justice*, *33*, 89–95. doi:10.1016/j.jcrimjus.2004.10.009

Compeau, D. R., & Higgins, C. A. (1995). Computer self-efficacy: Development of a measure and initial test. *Management Information Systems Quarterly*, *19*(2), 189–211. doi:10.2307/249688

Davis, F. D. (1989). Perceived usefulness, perceived ease-of-use, and user acceptance of information technology. *Management Information Systems Quarterly*, *13*(3), 319–340. doi:10.2307/249008

Davis, F. D., Bagozzi, R. P., & Warshaw, P. R. (1989). User acceptance of computer technology: A comparison of two theoretical models. *Management Science*, *35*(8), 982–1003. doi:10.1287/mnsc.35.8.982

Davis, F. D., & Venkatesh, V. (1996). A critical assessment of potential measurement biases in the technology acceptance model: Three experiments. *International Journal of Human-Computer Studies*, *45*, 19–45. doi:10.1006/ijhc.1996.0040

Dishaw, M. T., & Strong, D. M. (1999). Extending the technology acceptance model with task-technology fit constructs. *Information & Management*, *36*, 9–21. doi:10.1016/S0378-7206(98)00101-3

Elbeltagi, I., McBride, N., & Hardaker, G. (2005). Evaluating the factors affecting DSS usage by senior managers in local authorities in Egypt. *Journal of Global Information Management*, *13*(2), 42–65. doi:10.4018/jgim.2005040103

Gefen, D., Karahanna, E., & Straub, D. W. (2003). Trust and TAM in online shopping: An integrated model. *Management Information Systems Quarterly*, *27*(1), 51–90.

Green, B. D. (2003). Integration of TSIMS and ICAS for condition based maintenance. *Proceedings of the Intelligent Ship Symposium*, Philadelphia, PA.

Hasan, B. (2006). Effectiveness of computer training: The role of multilevel computer self-efficacy. *Journal of Organizational and End User Computing*, *18*(1), 50–68. doi:10.4018/joeuc.2006010103

Hasan, B. (2006). Delineating the effects of general and system-specific computer self-efficacy beliefs on IS acceptance. *Information & Management*, *43*, 565–571. doi:10.1016/j.im.2005.11.005

Hong, W., Thong, J. Y. L., Wong, W.-M., & Tam, K.-Y. (2001). Determinants of user acceptance of digital libraries: An empirical examination of individual differences and system characteristics. *Journal of Management Information Systems*, *18*(3), 97–124.

Hsu, C.-L., & Lu, H.-P. (2004). Why do people play on-line games? An extended TAM with social influences and flow experience. *Information & Management*, *41*(7), 853–868. doi:10.1016/j.im.2003.08.014

Hu, P. J., Chau, P. Y. K., Sheng, O. R. L., & Tam, K. Y. (1999). Examining the technology acceptance model using physician acceptance of telemedicine technology. *Journal of Management Information Systems*, *16*(2), 91–113.

Huang, E., & Chuang, M. H. (2007). Extending the theory of planned behavior as a model to explain post-merger employee behavior of IS use. *Computers in Human Behavior*, *23*, 240–257. doi:10.1016/j.chb.2004.10.010

Hutchins, S. G. (1996). *Principals for intelligent decision aiding* (Technical Report 1718). Retrieved March 23, 2007, from http://www.spawar.navy.mil/sti/publications/pubs/tr/1718/tr1718.pdf

Igbaria, M., & Iivari, J. (1995). The effects of self-efficacy on computer usage. *Omega*, *23*(6), 587–605. doi:10.1016/0305-0483(95)00035-6

Jackson, C. M., Chow, S., & Leitch, R. A. (1997). Toward an understanding of the behavioral intention to use an information system. *Decision Sciences*, *28*(2), 357–389. doi:10.1111/j.1540-5915.1997.tb01315.x

Keil, M., Beranek, P. M., & Knsynski, B. R. (1995). Usefulness and ease of use: Field study evidence regarding task considerations. *Decision Support Systems*, *13*, 75–91. doi:10.1016/0167-9236(94)E0032-M

Kerlinger, F. N., & Lee, H. B. (2000). *Foundations of behavioral research* (4th ed.). Toronto: Wadsworth Tomson Learning.

King, W. R., & He, J. (2006). A meta-analysis of the technology acceptance model. *Information & Management*, *43*, 740–755. doi:10.1016/j.im.2006.05.003

Lai, V. S., & Li, H. (2005). Technology acceptance model for Internet banking: An invariance analysis. *Information & Management*, *42*(2), 373–386. doi:10.1016/j.im.2004.01.007

Lederer, A. L., Maupin, D. J., Sena, M. P., & Zhuang, Y. (2000). The technology acceptance model and the World Wide Web. *Decision Support Systems*, *29*, 269–282. doi:10.1016/S0167-9236(00)00076-2

Legris, P., Ingham, J., & Collerette, P. (2003). Why do people use information technology? A critical review of the technology acceptance model. *Information & Management*, *40*, 191–204. doi:10.1016/S0378-7206(01)00143-4

Liaw, S.-S. (2004). The theory of planned behavior applied to search engines as a learning tool. *Journal of Computer Assisted Learning*, *20*, 283–291. doi:10.1111/j.1365-2729.2004.00087.x

Lowry, G. (2002). Modeling using acceptance of building management systems. *Automation in Construction*, *11*, 695–705. doi:10.1016/S0926-5805(02)00010-9

Luarn, P., & Lin, H.-H. (2005). Toward an understanding of the behavioral intention to use mobile banking. *Computers in Human Behavior*, *21*, 873–891. doi:10.1016/j.chb.2004.03.003

Lucas, H. C., & Spitler, V. K. (1999). Technology use and performance: A field study of broker workstations. *Decision Sciences*, *30*(2), 291–311. doi:10.1111/j.1540-5915.1999.tb01611.x

Ma, Q., & Liu, L. (2004). The technology acceptance model: A meta-analysis of empirical findings. *Journal of Organizational and End User Computing*, *16*(1), 59–72. doi:10.4018/joeuc.2004010104

Malhotra, Y., & Galletta, D. F. (2004). Building systems that users want to use. *Communications of the ACM*, *47*(12), 89–94. doi:10.1145/1035134.1035139

Marakas, G. M., Yi, M. Y., & Johnson, R. D. (1998). The multilevel and multifaceted character of computer self-efficacy: Toward clarification of the construct and an integrative framework for research. *Information Systems Research*, *9*(2), 126–153. doi:10.1287/isre.9.2.126

Mayers, L. S., Gamst, G., & Guarino, A. J. (2006). *Applied multivariate research. Design and interpretations*. Thousands Oaks, CA: Sage.

McCloskey, D. W. (2006). The importance of ease of use, usefulness, and trust to online consumers: An examination of the technology acceptance model with older consumers. *Journal of Organizational and End User Computing, 18*(3), 47–65. doi:10.4018/joeuc.2006070103

McCoy, S., Everard, A., & Jones, B. M. (2005). An examination of the technology acceptance model in Uruguay and the U.S.: A focus on culture. *Journal of Global Information Technology Management, 8*(2), 27–45.

McFarland, D. J., & Hamilton, D. (2006). Adding contextual specificity to the technology acceptance model. *Computers in Human Behavior, 22*, 427–447. doi:10.1016/j.chb.2004.09.009

Milchram, E. (2003). Modeling the acceptance of information technology: System trust, ease of use and usefulness. Fine tuning information strategies. *Proceedings of the 9th Annual Conference on Professional Information Resources,* Prague, Czech Republic.

Moon, J.-W., & Kim, Y.-G. (2001). Extending the TAM for a World Wide Web context. *Information & Management, 38*, 217–230. doi:10.1016/S0378-7206(00)00061-6

Morris, M. G., & Venkatesh, V. (2000). Age differences in technology adoption decisions: Implications for a changing work force. *Personnel Psychology, 53*(2), 375–403. doi:10.1111/j.1744-6570.2000.tb00206.x

Navy and Marines Lead Federal IT Spending. (2005, December 1)... *Aerospace Daily & Defense Report, 216*(42), 5.

Ndubisi, N. O., & Jantan, M. (2003). Evaluating IS usage in Malaysian small and medium-sized firms using the technology acceptance model. *Logistics Information Management, 16*(6), 440–450. doi:10.1108/09576050310503411

Ngai, E. W. T., Poon, J. K. L., & Chan, Y. H. C. (2007). Empirical examination of the adoption of WebCT using TAM. *Computers & Education, 48*(2), 250–267. doi:10.1016/j.compedu.2004.11.007

Ong, C.-S., & Lai, J.-Y. (2006). Gender differences in perceptions and relationships among dominant of e-learning acceptance. *Computers in Human Behavior, 22*, 816–829. doi:10.1016/j.chb.2004.03.006

Ong, C.-S., Lai, J.-Y., & Wang, Y.-S. (2004). Factors affecting engineers' acceptance of asynchronous e-learning systems in high tech companies. *Information & Management, 41*, 795–804. doi:10.1016/j.im.2003.08.012

Pagani, M. (2004). Determinants of adoption of third generation mobile multimedia services. *Journal of Interactive Marketing, 18*(3), 46–59. doi:10.1002/dir.20011

Pavlou, P. A., & Chai, L. (2002). What drives electronic commerce across cultures? A cross-cultural empirical investigation of the theory of planned behavior. *Journal of Electronic Commerce Research, 3*(4), 240–253.

Pijpers, G. G. M., Bemelmans, T. M. A., Heemstra, F. J., & van Montfort, K. A. G. M. (2001). Senior executives' use of information technology. *Information and Software Technology, 43*, 959–971. doi:10.1016/S0950-5849(01)00197-5

Roberts, P., & Henderson, R. (2000). Information technology acceptance in a sample of government employees: A test of the technology acceptance model. *Interacting with Computers, 12*, 427–443. doi:10.1016/S0953-5438(98)00068-X

Rose, G., & Straub, D. (1998). Predicting general IT use: Applying TAM to the Arabic world. *Journal of Global Information Management, 6*(3), 39–46.

Saade, R., & Bahli, B. (2005). The impact of cognitive absorption on perceived usefulness and perceived ease of use in on-line learning: An extension of the technology acceptance model. *Information & Management*, *42*, 317–327. doi:10.1016/j.im.2003.12.013

Sheng, Y. P., Pearson, J. M., & Crosby, L. (2003). Organizational culture and employees' computer self-efficacy: An empirical study. *Information Resources Management Journal*, *16*(3), 42–58. doi:10.4018/irmj.2003070103

Shumacker, R. E., & Lomax, R. G. (2004). *A beginner's guide to structural equation modeling* (2nd ed.). Mahwah, NJ: Lawrence Erlbaum.

Simon, S. J., & Paper, D. (2007). User acceptance of voice recognition technology: An empirical extension of the technology acceptance model. *Journal of Organizational and End User Computing*, *19*(1), 24–50. doi:10.4018/joeuc.2007010102

Somers, T. M., Nelson, K., & Karimi, J. (2003). Confirmatory factor analysis of the end-user computing satisfaction instrument: Replications within an ERP domain. *Decision Sciences*, *34*(3), 595–621. doi:10.1111/j.1540-5414.2003.02428.x

Stone, D., Arunachalam, N., & Chandler, V. (1996). Cross-cultural comparisons: An empirical investigation of knowledge, skill, self-efficacy and computer anxiety in accounting education. *Issues in Accounting Education*, *11*(2), 345–367.

Stone, R. W., & Henry, J. W. (2003). The roles of computer self-efficacy and outcome expectancy in influencing the computer end-user's organizational commitment. *Journal of End User Computing*, *15*(1), 38–53. doi:10.4018/joeuc.2003010103

Szajina, B. (1996). Empirical evaluation of the revised technology acceptance model. *Management Science*, *42*(1), 85–92. doi:10.1287/mnsc.42.1.85

Taylor, S., & Todd, P. (1995). Understanding information technology usage: A test of competing models. *Information Systems Research*, *6*(2), 144–176. doi:10.1287/isre.6.2.144

Thatcher, J. B., & Perrewe, P. L. (2002). An empirical examination of individual traits as antecedents to computer anxiety and computer self-efficacy. *Management Information Systems Quarterly*, *26*(4), 381–396. doi:10.2307/4132314

Thompson, R., Compeau, D., & Higgins, C. (2006). Intentions to use information technologies: An integrative model. *Journal of Organizational and End User Computing*, *18*(3), 25–46. doi:10.4018/joeuc.2006070102

Thompson, R. L., Higgins, C. A., & Howell, J. M. (1991). Personal computing: Toward a conceptual model of utilization. *Management Information Systems Quarterly*, *15*(1), 125–143. doi:10.2307/249443

Thong, J. Y. L., Hong, W., & Tam, K.-Y. (2002). Understanding user acceptance of digital libraries: What are the roles on interface characteristics, organizational context, and individual differences? *International Journal of Human-Computer Studies*, *57*, 215–242. doi:10.1016/S1071-5819(02)91024-4

Torkzadeh, G., Chang, J. C.-J., & Demirhan, D. (2006). A contingency model of computer and Internet self-efficacy. *Information & Management*, *43*(4), 541–550. doi:10.1016/j.im.2006.02.001

Torkzadeh, G., & Van Dyke, T. P. (2002). Effects of training on Internet self-efficacy and computer user attitudes. *Computers in Human Behavior*, *18*, 479–494. doi:10.1016/S0747-5632(02)00010-9

Van der Heijden, H. (2003). Factors influencing the usage of websites: The case of a generic portal in The Netherlands. *Information & Management*, *40*, 541–549. doi:10.1016/S0378-7206(02)00079-4

Venkatesh, V. (2000). Determinants of perceived ease of use: Integrating control, intrinsic motivation, and emotion into the technology acceptance model. *Information Systems Research*, *11*(4), 342–366. doi:10.1287/isre.11.4.342.11872

Venkatesh, V., & Davis, F. D. (1996). A model of the antecedents of perceived ease of use: Development and test. *Decision Sciences*, *27*(3), 451–481. doi:10.1111/j.1540-5915.1996.tb01822.x

Venkatesh, V., & Davis, F. D. (2000). A theoretical extension of the technology acceptance model: Four longitudinal field studies. *Management Science*, *46*(2), 186–204. doi:10.1287/mnsc.46.2.186.11926

Venkatesh, V., Morris, M. G., Davis, G. B., & Davis, F. D. (2003). User acceptance of information technology: Toward a unified view. *Management Information Systems Quarterly*, *27*(3), 425–478.

Wang, C.-C., Hsu, Y., & Fang, W. (2005). Acceptance of technology with network externalities: An empirical study of Internet instant messaging services. *Journal of Information Technology Theory and Application*, *6*(4), 15–29.

Wang, Y.-S. (2002). The adoption of electronic tax filing systems: An empirical study. *Government Information Quarterly*, *20*, 333–352. doi:10.1016/j.giq.2003.08.005

Wixom, B. H., & Todd, P. A. (2005). A theoretical integration of user satisfaction and technology acceptance. *Information Systems Research*, *16*(1), 85–102. doi:10.1287/isre.1050.0042

Wu, J.-H., & Wang, S.-C. (2005). What drives mobile commerce? An empirical evaluation of the revised technology acceptance model. *Information & Management*, *42*, 719–729. doi:10.1016/j.im.2004.07.001

Yang, H., & Yoo, Y. (2004). It's all about attitude: Revisiting the technology acceptance model. *Decision Support Systems*, *38*, 19–31. doi:10.1016/S0167-9236(03)00062-9

Yi, M. Y., & Im, K. S. (2004). Predicting computer task performance: Personal goal and self-efficacy. *Journal of Organizational and End User Computing*, *16*(2), 20–37. doi:10.4018/joeuc.2004040102

Yi, M. Y., Jackson, J. D., Park, J. S., & Probst, J. C. (2006). Understanding information technology acceptance by individual professionals: Toward an integrative view. *Information & Management*, *43*, 350–363. doi:10.1016/j.im.2005.08.006

Yu, J., Ha, I., Choi, M., & Rho, J. (2005). Extending the TAM for a t-commerce. *Information & Management*, *42*, 965–976. doi:10.1016/j.im.2004.11.001

This work was previously published in Journal of Organizational and End User Computing (JOEUC) 21(3), edited by Mo Adam Mahmood, pp. 1-23, copyright 2009 by IGI Publishing (an imprint of IGI Global).

Chapter 11
Errors in Operational Spreadsheets

Stephen G. Powell
Dartmouth College, USA

Kenneth R. Baker
Dartmouth College, USA

Barry Lawson
Dartmouth College, USA

ABSTRACT

Spreadsheets are used in almost all businesses, for applications ranging from the mundane to the mission-critical. Errors in the data, formulas, or manipulation of spreadsheets could be costly, even devastating. The received wisdom is that about 5% of all formulas in spreadsheets contain errors, and this rate is consistent across spreadsheets. However, this estimate is based on five studies, some of which are quite informal, and a total of only 43 spreadsheets. Our research was designed to deepen our understanding of spreadsheet errors. Specifically, we address three questions about errors in operational spreadsheets: what is the average cell error rate, how does it differ among spreadsheets, and what types of errors are most prevalent? We created a spreadsheet auditing protocol and applied it to 50 diverse operational spreadsheets. We found errors in 0.9% to 1.8% of all formula cells, depending on how errors are defined. We also found that the error rate differed widely from spreadsheet to spreadsheet.

INTRODUCTION

Errors in software have been a problem since the beginning of the computer era. The discipline of software engineering (Sommerville, 2004) was created in part to develop methods to minimize errors in software code. Professionally developed software is now generally created and debugged using disciplined approaches from software engineering.

DOI: 10.4018/978-1-60960-577-3.ch011

The advent of the personal computer in the 1980s increased by orders of magnitude the number of people who worked closely with computers. Just as professional programmers were learning to use disciplined approaches to programming, millions of so-called end-user programmers began to create their own programs in the form of spreadsheets. One of the appealing features of spreadsheet programming on a personal computer is that the end user can work independently of the constraints of a professional programmer or an MIS group. This allows the end user much more freedom and speed in completing the business task at hand. But very few end users have any training for the programming tasks they attempt, and many have little appreciation for the risks inherent in a casual approach to programming.

As spreadsheets have spread throughout business, they have increasingly been used for mission-critical applications (Croll, 2005; Grossman, Mehrotra, & Özluk, 2005). At the same time, evidence has accumulated that many spreadsheets have errors (Panko, 2005) and that sometimes these errors cost the organizations that use them millions of dollars (EUSPRIG, n.d.). End users and organizations that rely on spreadsheets generally do not fully recognize the risks of spreadsheet errors. In fact, spreadsheets tend to be somewhat invisible, both as corporate assets and as sources of risk.

Although the received wisdom holds that errors are prevalent in spreadsheets, our review of the literature suggests that this conclusion is based more on casual empiricism than solid research. In fact, researchers have produced only limited information on the types of errors that occur, how frequently they occur on average, and how the error rate varies from one spreadsheet to another.

The current study was designed to improve our understanding of spreadsheet errors by testing a large sample of spreadsheets in actual use by organizations. We developed a detailed auditing protocol and trained a group of researchers to apply it consistently. Using an explicit protocol is important for two reasons: (1) it allows other researchers to replicate and improve on our work; and (2) it contributes to the development of improved auditing procedures, which is important in its own right. The auditing procedure is described in detail in Powell, Baker, and Lawson (2008b).

We begin this article with a summary of previous work on spreadsheet errors which comes from field audits and laboratory experiments. Then we describe the design of our study and the sample of spreadsheets we audited. Our results are summarized in terms of *error instances* (the occurrence of a single type of error) and *error cells* (the number of cells affected by a single error instance). We also categorize the errors as to whether they generate wrong numerical results. We report the total number of errors we identified, as well as how they were distributed across error types and across spreadsheets. This is the first data on errors and their distribution to appear in the research literature that can be replicated with parallel studies using similar methods.

PREVIOUS WORK ON SPREADSHEET ERRORS

Since our interest in this article is primarily with the classification and frequency of errors, we will discuss only those questions here. In a related article (Powell, et al., 2008a), we provide a review of the literature on all aspects of spreadsheet errors.

Types of Errors

Before we can productively study spreadsheet errors, we need to define and classify the types of errors we seek. Classification is useful because it helps us to understand what is common among errors. It also allows us to compare different studies of errors, and eventually to understand the causes of errors and to develop cures.

At the outset, we make a distinction between errors in the *use* of a spreadsheet and errors in the *cells* of the spreadsheet itself. A spreadsheet can be perfectly correct but used to solve the wrong problem, or its results could be misinterpreted. More concretely, a correct spreadsheet can lead to an error if sorting is done improperly, or if formulas are overwritten, or if incorrect data were entered temporarily. All of these errors would be difficult or impossible to detect purely from examination of the spreadsheet itself.

Most classifications of spreadsheet errors have focused primarily on the spreadsheet itself, not on errors in use. Because spreadsheets essentially consist of data and formulas, an error in the spreadsheet must arise from erroneous data or erroneous formulas.

There is no generally accepted taxonomy of spreadsheet errors, possibly because different classifications are appropriate for different purposes. The first researchers who studied spreadsheet use simply listed examples of errors without attempting to classify them. Subsequent authors offered distinctions (but not complete taxonomies), such as that between *domain* errors (lack of knowledge of the application area) and *device* errors (misuse of the spreadsheet itself).

Panko and Halverson (1996) were the first to offer a real taxonomy of errors. They distinguished *qualitative* and *quantitative* errors, and further decomposed quantitative errors into *mechanical, logic,* and *omission* errors. Quantitative errors lead to wrong numbers in the current version of the spreadsheet. The three types were defined as follows:

- Mechanical errors arise from typing or pointing errors.
- Logic errors arise from choosing the wrong function or creating the wrong formula.
- Omission errors arise from misinterpretation of the situation to be modeled.

Qualitative errors do not lead to wrong numbers in the current version of the spreadsheet, but are risky practices that could lead to errors in subsequent use. This category includes practices such as hard-coding numbers into formulas. It can also include long formulas, poor physical layout, or lack of sufficient documentation.

Rajalingham, Chadwick, and Knight (2000) and Purser and Chadwick (2006) have developed the most elaborate taxonomy of errors available to date (see Table 1). The first distinction in this hierarchy is between *application-identified* errors and *developer/user-identified* errors. Excel has eight categories of errors that it displays in a cell when it cannot resolve a formula; these are application-identified errors. The remaining errors are developer/user-identified errors.

Although this taxonomy may be interesting from a theoretical perspective, it has limitations as a practical tool for auditing. First, its categories overlap. For example, an error caused by lack of domain knowledge could occur during insertion. Second, it may not be possible in practice to determine the cause of an error and therefore to properly categorize it. For example, a complex formula giving wrong results could be due to lack of domain knowledge, incorrect syntax, or an accidental typing mistake.

Powell et al. (2008a) summarized the literature on classification of errors as follows:

- Classifications are offered without specifying the contexts or purposes for which the classification is intended.

Table 1. Error taxonomy (Rajalingham et al., 2000; Purser & Chadwick, 2006)

1. Application-Identified Errors
2. Developer/User-Identified Errors
A. Qualitative Errors
I. Structural
a. Visible
b. Hidden
II. Temporal
B. Quantitative Errors
I. Reasoning
a. Domain Knowledge
i. Real-World Knowledge
ii. Mathematical Representation
b. Implementation
i. Syntax
ii. Logic
II. Accidental
a. Insertion
b. Update
i. Modification
ii. Deletion

- The existing classifications do not include sufficient examples of specific errors that satisfy each category.
- Classifications are not rigorously tested to demonstrate that multiple users can consistently classify actual errors into the proper categories.
- The boundary between quantitative errors and qualitative errors remains vague.
- No studies compare the types of errors by development stage.

Frequency of Errors

Research on the frequency of errors in spreadsheets comes from a variety of sources, mostly experiments in the laboratory. One approach is to observe subjects as they build spreadsheets and record the number of errors they make. Another approach is to ask subjects to build a spreadsheet from a written description and determine the frequency of errors in the finished product. However, the approach of most relevance to our research is the field audit, in which operational spreadsheets are examined for errors.

Panko (2005) summarized the results of seven field audits in which operational spreadsheets were examined, typically by an outsider to the organization. His results show that 94% of spreadsheets have errors and that the average cell error rate (the ratio of cells with errors to all cells with formulas) is 5.2%.

Table 2 summarizes the data behind these estimates. In total, 88 spreadsheets are represented in the table. For all 88, the weighted average percentage of spreadsheets with errors is 94%. Data on cell error rates were available on 43 of these spreadsheets, and the weighted average for this sample is 5.2%.

There are several reasons to question the reliability of these estimates. First, three of the seven sources are unpublished (Hicks, 1995; Lukasic, 1998; Butler, 1992). Second, the majority of the sources gave little or no information on their definition of errors or on the methods used to find errors. Third, Lawrence and Lee (2004), whose observations account for 70% of the sample used to estimate the cell error rate, did not actually report a cell error rate of 6.9% on *completed* spreadsheets. Rather, they reported that auditors had "issues" concerning 6.9% of the cells on the *initial review* of models that they subsequently discussed with the developers. The authors provided no details on the definition of an "issue" or its relation to an actual error. Moreover, the initial model version that was reviewed was revised an average of six times before the model was complete. Thus the estimate of a 6.9% error rate applies

Table 2. Spreadsheet error rates (Panko, 2005)

Source	Number Audited	Percent with Errors	Cell Error Rate (% of cells)
1. Coopers and Lybrand (1997)	23	91	N/A
2. KPMG (1998)	22	91	N/A
3. Hicks (1995)	1	100	1.2
4. Lukasic (1998)	2	100	2.2
5. Butler (2000)	7	86	0.4
6. Clermont (2002)	3	100	3.0
7. Lawrence and Lee (2004)	30	100	6.9
Average		**94***	**5.2****

*Weighted average of 88 spreadsheets in sources 1-7.
**Weighted average of 43 spreadsheets in sources 3-7.

only to issues raised by auditors on initial model versions, not to errors in completed spreadsheets. If, as seems warranted, we exclude this study from the calculation of the cell error rate, the average cell error rate decreases from 5.2% to 1.3% on a base of only 13 audited spreadsheets.

Our review of the literature on spreadsheet errors draws attention to several shortcomings. First, no generally accepted classification of errors exists. Second, the classifications that do exist are of more theoretical than practical value. Third, existing estimates of error rates are based on extremely limited data. Fourth, no studies of errors have fully revealed the sources of spreadsheets tested, how errors were defined, and the auditing methods that were used.

RESEARCH DESIGN

Our research into spreadsheet errors is predicated on several guiding principles or constraints. First, our interest is in errors in *completed, operational* spreadsheets, not errors made in a laboratory setting or errors made during the development of a spreadsheet. A second principle is that we conduct the audit using only the information in the spreadsheet itself, without relying on the developer. A third principle is that we use an explicit auditing protocol that any moderately experienced user of Excel can master.

These principles limit our study in certain ways. When we work without access to the spreadsheet developers, we are not able to check our understanding of a model with an expert. In practice, this means that at times we will accept a suspicious formula as correct because we cannot be *sure* that it is incorrect. It also means that we cannot hope to uncover errors in formulating the underlying problem or errors in interpreting spreadsheet results. Detecting these types of errors requires a much more time-intensive longitudinal study of how spreadsheets are used in the broader context of problem solving. Offsetting these limitations is the fact that we can audit a much larger volume of spreadsheets using our protocol than otherwise.

Our procedures almost certainly lead to an *underestimate* of the actual error rates in the spreadsheets we audit. We may occasionally classify a cell incorrectly as an error, but we have been conservative in limiting our definition of errors to cells for which we can have a high degree of confidence that our judgment is correct. On the other hand, there are entire classes of errors that we cannot hope to identify with the procedures used in this study. For example, most (but not all) errors in input data are beyond our scope.

Sample Spreadsheets

Our sample of 50 spreadsheets came from a wide variety of sources. Some were obtained during site visits to companies. We carried out site visits at two consulting companies, a bank, a college, a large energy company, and a state government agency. We also obtained spreadsheets from a variety of organizations through the alumni and faculty networks at the Tuck School of Business. No single source contributed more than five spreadsheets to the sample of 50 analyzed here.

We also obtained spreadsheets from various Web sites. Several software companies post spreadsheets on their Web site, either to illustrate how to use their software or to showcase the results that practitioners have had with their software. The Web site of Decisioneering Inc. (http://www.decisioneering.com), makers of the *Crystal Ball* add-in for Excel, is typical. This site lists hundreds of sample models used in industries ranging from aerospace to utilities. Each of these spreadsheets has been contributed by a practitioner, and it can be assumed that these spreadsheets are carefully engineered and tested by the time they appear on the Web site.

Our search for sample spreadsheets was not strictly random. We asked potential contributors to give us important spreadsheets that were completed and had been in use for some time.

We eliminated any spreadsheet that contained only data and no formulas. We also eliminated spreadsheets that contained a very small number of cells or that were too simple to warrant auditing (using only a couple of SUM functions, for example). We eliminated some spreadsheets that involved broken links to other spreadsheets. We also eliminated some that used complex macros. Thus our sample is by design not representative of the class of very small spreadsheets, which we believe are very common in practice. It is also not representative of the most elaborate spreadsheets in use. (Grossman et al. [2005] reported on some very large Excel models used in critical applications.)

While our sample is not strictly *random*, it is certainly *representative* of the general population of spreadsheets (with the caveats cited above). The sample includes spreadsheets from many different types of organizations, spreadsheets created by both novice and expert developers, and spreadsheets that span a broad range from small and simple to large and complex.

Auditing Software

When we began this research, we were aware of the auditing and error checking tools available in Excel, but we knew little about third-party auditing software. As we learned more, we realized that many auditing tools are available, and some research suggests that appropriate software can make auditing easier. Accordingly, we decided to include a small number of auditing tools in our protocol. From a list of roughly 50 such tools supplied by Roger Grinde of the University of New Hampshire, we selected 10 to review in some detail. Eventually we settled on two to use in our auditing protocol: *XL Analyst* (http://www.codematic.net/default.htm) and *Spreadsheet Professional* (http://www.spreadsheetinnovations.com/).

XL Analyst is an Excel add-in that evaluates 28 aspects of a spreadsheet, from "Formulas evaluating to an error" to "Use of SUMIF." *Spreadsheet Professional* is a collection of tools for building, testing, analyzing, and using spreadsheets. In our auditing protocol we made use of two features of this tool: maps and calculation tests. The mapping tool creates a coded version of each worksheet in a workbook. Each non-blank cell is coded as a label, a number, or a formula. It also shows which formulas have been copied from an original formula. The calculation test tool checks a workbook for 25 conditions such as "Blank cell referenced." For each of these categories it gives the number of cells involved and their cell addresses.

Selection and Training of Auditors

Our spreadsheet auditors were undergraduates, graduate students, or recent alumni from business or engineering schools. All had several years of experience with Excel, usually in a business setting. None were professional programmers or professional spreadsheet developers.

For an auditor, the first step in training was to study the auditing protocol, which describes in detail the stages an audit goes through and the data to be gathered at each stage. Then an auditor was given two or three spreadsheets to audit. The finished audited workbooks were then reviewed by the researchers for adherence to the auditing protocol and for the quality of the audit. In total, auditor training took an average of 10 hours.

Auditing Protocol

The auditing protocol we used in this research is a highly detailed document that specifies the steps to take in auditing a spreadsheet for size, complexity, several types of qualitative features, and errors. (A complete description of the protocol is available at http://mba.tuck.dartmouth.edu/spreadsheet/index.html.)

The auditing protocol involves the following 11 steps:

1. Run the two software tools *XLAnalyst* and *Spreadsheet Professional.*
2. Transfer selected results from the software tools to a data record sheet.
3. Record the purpose of the workbook and each worksheet.
4. Examine workbook for use of Excel functions.
5. Review the results of *XL Analyst* and use them to locate errors.
6. Review the *Spreadsheet Professional* maps and use them to locate errors.
7. Review the *Spreadsheet Professional* calculation tests and use them to locate errors.
8. Review all formulas not already reviewed for errors.
9. Conduct sensitivity analyses to uncover errors.
10. Rate the workbook on various aspects of spreadsheet design (e.g., use of modules).
11. Record the total time taken by the audit and record comments on any special situations encountered.

This particular sequence of steps evolved over several months of testing. During this time we trained auditors and tested the protocol ourselves and through our assistants on dozens of operational spreadsheets. More details on the auditing protocol are available in Powell et al. (2008b).

Error Taxonomy

One of the challenges of spreadsheet error research is how to categorize errors. As we pointed out earlier, many different error classifications have been offered. Most of these suffer from the same flaw: errors that arise from different causes cannot be distinguished by an auditor. For example, when we encounter an error in a formula, we rarely can determine whether the error was due to sloppy typing, lack of domain knowledge, lack of Excel knowledge, a subsequent user changing the formula, or some other cause. We can, however, easily detect some formulas that give the wrong result. With somewhat more effort we can sometimes identify formulas that would give a wrong result with a different set of numerical inputs. An example of the latter error is an IF formula whose True condition is active in the current version and is correct, but whose False condition can be activated with a different set of inputs and is incorrect. We can also identify many practices that are likely to cause errors as the spreadsheet is used or that simply will make it harder than necessary to use the spreadsheet productively. The most common of these poor practices is placing numerical inputs directly into formulas. Other poor practices include limited or nonexistent documentation, duplication of inputs, illogical physical layout, and so on. A fundamental question in spreadsheet error research is where to draw the line between errors and poor practices.

Initial Error Taxonomy

Recall that our study required our auditors to detect errors in the spreadsheets themselves, without access to external information or to the spreadsheet developer. Thus the types of errors we sought had to be *observable* by our auditors. A second requirement for our taxonomy was *consistency*: a single error must with high probability be placed in the same category by different auditors.

Our first attempt to define an operational taxonomy used three categories:

1. wrong result with current inputs,
2. wrong result with different but allowable inputs, and
3. poor practice.

After some experience with this classification, we discovered that the category of poor practices was so ill-defined that no two auditors could agree in specific instances. As a result we eliminated this category from our protocol. We also discovered that the second category, wrong result with different inputs, was ambiguous because it forced us to decide which numerical inputs were allowable or plausible. For example, most spreadsheets can be made to generate errors with unlikely inputs, such as text instead of numbers.

Interim Error Taxonomy

Eventually we settled on the following six error types that our experience with auditing suggested were well defined in theory and could be identified with high reliability in practice:

1. **Logic Error**: a formula is used incorrectly, leading to an incorrect result.
2. **Reference Error** a formula contains one or more incorrect references to other cells.
3. **Placing Numbers in a Formula:** one or more numbers appear in formulas.
4. **Copy/Paste Error:** a formula is wrong due to inaccurate use of copy/paste.
5. **Data Input Error:** an incorrect data input is used.
6. **Omission Error:** a formula is wrong because one or more of its input cells is blank.

More details on this taxonomy, including examples of situations in which a cell would or would not be classified as an error, are available in Powell et al. (2008b). Not surprisingly, we found that we had to test our categorization extensively before we could be confident that our auditors could implement it effectively. Even after auditing dozens of spreadsheets, we found it necessary for the senior researchers to review each audited workbook and to make judgments as to which of the errors cited would be included. (In the end, our overall inter-rater reliability was on the order of 90%).

Our experience has been that errors come in hundreds of subtle variations, many of which do not fit neatly into any classification scheme. If nothing else, this suggests that we should be skeptical of drawing firm conclusions from previous studies of errors in which both the errors themselves and the procedures used to find errors are not clearly spelled out.

Final Error Taxonomy

After completing our audits of 50 spreadsheets using the taxonomy described above, we returned to the question that motivated our initial taxonomy: which of these errors actually give wrong results and which are merely poor practices?

In order to investigate this distinction, we reviewed all the instances of errors we found and categorized each one as either a *wrong result* or a *poor practice.* While this distinction may appear to be objective, there are many subtle cases that require interpretation. For example, simply embedding a number in a formula is usually a poor practice, not a wrong result. However, we encountered situations in which one number was embedded in a formula and a related but *different* number was included elsewhere among inputs. For example, an input module might contain the number 4% next to the heading "Inflation," but the actual inflation rate used in a formula was 3.5%. We categorized this case as a wrong result, even though the actual spreadsheet may have been numerically correct. Again we stress that determining whether a particular cell is an error (or gives a wrong result) is not a purely objective task.

ERRORS FOUND DURING AUDITS

We audited 50 spreadsheet workbooks and in three of them were unable to find any errors of the types included in our auditing protocol. This implies a spreadsheet error rate of 94%, which is identical to the spreadsheet error rate estimated by Panko (2005).

In the remaining 47 spreadsheets, we found a total of 483 instances of errors involving a total of 4,855 error cells. (An error instance is a single occurrence of one of the six errors in our taxonomy.

Typically a single instance involves more than one cell.) Thus, on average each error instance involved 10.05 error cells. The average cell error rate over all 270,722 formulas audited was 1.79%. This is considerably lower than the 5.2% cell error rate cited by Panko (2005), although somewhat higher than the corrected estimate of 1.3% we derived earlier from Panko's data.

Table 3 shows how the error instances and error cells were distributed by error type.

Hard-coding errors were the most common (37.7% of instances and 43.5% of cells), followed by reference errors (32.9% of instances and 22.1% of cells) and logic errors (21.9% of instances and 28.6% of cells). The remaining three categories—copy/paste, omission, and data input errors—together accounted for less than 10% of instances and cells.

As explained earlier, not all of the 483 error instances we identified involved wrong results. In fact, roughly 40% of these were hard-coding errors, in which a number was included in a formula rather than a cell reference; most of these did not produce wrong results. In order to determine how many errors actually gave rise to wrong results, we categorized each instance as a wrong result or a poor practice. With this more restrictive definition, we found that 7 of the 50 spreadsheet workbooks we audited were error-free, for a spreadsheet error rate of 86%.

In the remaining 43 spreadsheets, we found a total of 281 instances of wrong results involving a total of 2,353 cells. Using this definition, the average cell error rate over all 270,722 formulas audited was 0.87%. This is, of course, substantially lower than the 1.79% cell error rate we estimated using our more inclusive definition of error, and much less than Panko's estimate of 5.2%.

Table 4 shows how wrong results break down by type of error. Most, but not all, hard-coding errors were categorized as poor practice. Most, but not all, of the other error categories were labeled wrong result. In total, 58% of error instances and 48% of error cells were categorized as wrong result.

Our results suggest that the average cell error rate across all spreadsheets is in the range of 1% when we use a restrictive definition and 2% when we use an inclusive definition. But the average error rate does not tell us how the error rate varies across spreadsheets. The received wisdom is that errors are unavoidable in spreadsheets, as they are in most facets of life. In fact, Panko (2005) cites an error rate of 5% as the norm for many

Table 3. Errors categorized by type

Error Type	Instances	Cells
Hard-Coding	182 (37.7% of total)	2,111 (43.5% of total)
Reference	159 (32.9%)	1,074 (22.1%)
Logic	106 (21.9%)	1,389 (28.6%)
Copy/Paste	17 (3.4%)	206 (4.2%)
Omission	13 (2.7%)	65 (1.3%)
Data Input	6 (1.2%)	10 (0.2%)
Total	**483**	**4,855**

Table 4. Wrong results and poor practices

Error Type	Wrong Results	Poor Practices
Instances		
Hard-Coding	31 (11.0% of total)	151 (74.8% of total)
Reference	137 (48.8%)	22 (10.9%)
Logic	89 (31.7%)	17 (8.4%)
Copy/Paste	14 (5.0%)	3 (1.5%)
Omission	7 (2.5%)	6 (3.0%)
Data Input	3 (1.1%)	3 (1.5%)
Totals	**281**	**202**
Cells		
Hard-Coding	191 (8.1% of total)	1,920 (76.7% of total)
Reference	857 (36.4%)	217 (8.7%)
Logic	1,073 (45.6%)	316 (12.6%)
Copy/Paste	203 (8.6%)	3 (0.1%)
Omission	26 (1.1%)	39 (1.6%)
Data Input	3 (0.1%)	7 (0.3%)
Totals	**2,353**	**2,502**

different activities. This suggests that we should expect most spreadsheets to have a cell error rate close to the average.

Figure 1 shows the distribution of cell error rates using our original, inclusive definition.

Using that definition, 46% of our sample spreadsheets had error rates below 2%; 70% had error rates below 5%. However, several spreadsheets had error rates above 10%; in fact one had a cell error rate of 28%. Figure 2 shows the distribution of cell error rates using the more restrictive definition. In this case 68% had cell error rates below 2% and 90% were below 5%. The highest single error rate was 17%.

We began this article by noting that the received wisdom on spreadsheet errors maintains that errors average 5% of cells and this rate is consistent across spreadsheets. Our results give a very different impression. The average cell error rate appears to be closer to 1% or 2%, depending on how errors are defined. Perhaps even more important, roughly half of the spreadsheets we tested had rates below these levels, although a few had astonishingly high rates. These results suggest that errors are not a constant factor, but presumably depend on the situation being modeled and the developer's skills. Finally, we document for the first time in the published literature the

Figure 1. Distribution of cell error rates across spreadsheets

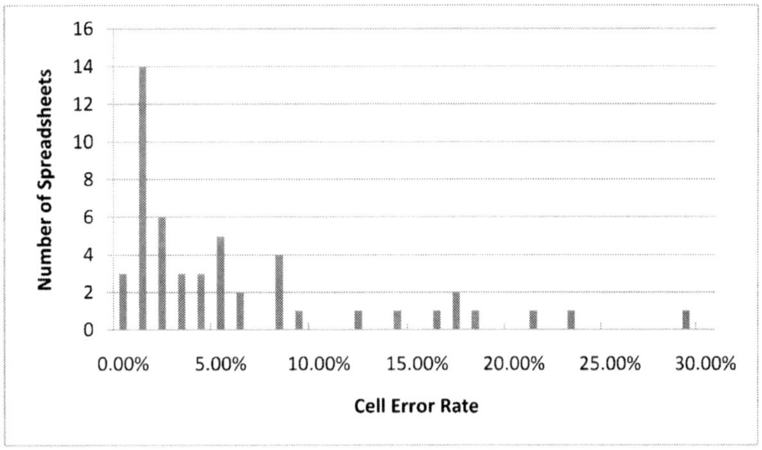

Figure 2. Distribution of cell error rates across spreadsheets (wrong results)

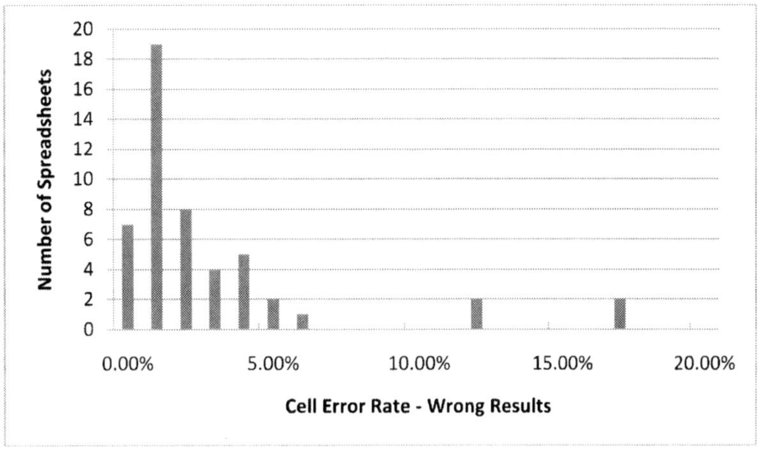

sources of errors. Thirty to forty percent of errors are due to embedding numbers in formulas. The next most common error type is reference errors, followed by logic errors. The remaining error types are far less common.

SUMMARY AND DIRECTIONS FOR FUTURE RESEARCH

We have audited 50 operational spreadsheet workbooks and discovered 483 error instances involving 1.79% of all formulas. This study is unique in several ways. First, this is the largest published sample of spreadsheets that has been audited for errors. In fact, our sample of 50 operational spreadsheets exceeds the *total* number of spreadsheets (43) cited in Panko's (2005) meta-study to estimate cell error rates. Second, we have been explicit about our definition of errors. Our work in this area has shown that errors manifest themselves in a wide variety of guises, so estimated cell error rates may be highly sensitive to how one defines errors. In fact, our own estimates range from 0.87 to 1.79% of cells, depending on the definition of error. Finally, the method we used to detect errors is fully documented and available to other researchers. In most previous studies the methods used to search for errors were not documented at all; in others only a brief summary of the methods is offered. Our study involves an explicit, detailed auditing protocol. It also used two types of auditing software to assist in the search for errors.

Our results confirm the general belief among those who have studied spreadsheets that errors are commonplace. The specific estimates we have made are somewhat lower than what has become received wisdom, but we note that previous studies of spreadsheet errors cannot easily be compared since they use different (and generally undocumented) auditing methods and definitions of errors. We now have sound evidence for the hypothesis that around 1% of all formulas in operational spreadsheets are in error.

Obtaining reliable estimates of cell error rates is only a first step toward understanding the fundamental question of the impact that spreadsheets have on the quality of decision making in organizations. Errors in formulas should be avoided, of course, but by themselves they do not necessarily translate into significant errors in the outcomes of spreadsheet use. The next step we envision in this line of research is to estimate the *numerical impact* of errors in spreadsheets. This investigation would require working closely with the developers of the spreadsheet to determine which outputs are most important and to determine the impact on those outputs of correcting errors.

Errors in spreadsheet data and formulas are not the only possible causes of errors in spreadsheet use. In fact, many of the press accounts reported by EUSPRIG involve *misuse* of spreadsheets. For example, spreadsheet results can be sorted incorrectly, or an out-of-date version of a spreadsheet may be used. More generally, poor decisions based on spreadsheet models can arise by modeling the wrong problem or by misinterpreting the results. These types of errors cannot be identified by auditing the data and formulas of the spreadsheet itself. To determine how frequent and damaging these types of errors are to decision making would involve a kind of ethnographic research, in which spreadsheet users were closely observed in their natural surroundings over months or years.

Finally, very little research (and none outside the laboratory) has been conducted to identify methods for avoiding or mitigating the impacts of errors in operational spreadsheets. One promising approach would be to audit a sample of spreadsheets from different organizations and attempt to correlate error rates with corporate or individual practices around spreadsheet use. Many practitioners have offered advice on what constitutes good spreadsheet practice, but there is no scientific evidence from the field yet to back up these claims.

ACKNOWLEDGMENT

This work was performed under the sponsorship of the U.S. Department of Commerce, National Institute of Standards and Technology. Reproduction of this article, with the customary credit to the source, is permitted.

REFERENCES

Butler, R. J. (1992). Personal communication to Ray Panko.

Clermont, J. M. (2002). A spreadsheet auditing tool evaluated in an industrial context. *Proceedings of the European Spreadsheet Risk Interest Group Annual Conference,* Cardiff, Wales.

Coopers and Lybrand. (1997). Retrieved from http://www.planningobjects.com/jungle1.htm

Croll, G. J. (2005). The importance and criticality of spreadsheets in the city of London. *Proceedings of the European Spreadsheet Risks Interest Group Conference,* Greenwich, UK.

EUSPRIG. (n.d.). European Spreadsheet Risks Interest Group stories. Retrieved from http://www.eusprig.org/stories.htm

Grossman, T. G., Mehrotra, V., & Özluk, Ö. (2005). *Spreadsheet information systems are essential to business.* Working paper, University of San Francisco, USA.

Hicks, L. (1995). Personal communication to Ray Panko.

KPMG. (1998). *Supporting the decision maker—a guide to the value of business modeling.* Retrieved from http://www.kpmg.co.uk/uk/services/manage/press/970605.html

Lawrence, R.J., & Lee, J. (2004). Financial modelling of project financing transactions. *Institute of Actuaries of Australia Financial Services Forum, 19.*

Lukasik, T. (1998). Personal communication to Ray Panko.

Panko, R. (2005). *What we know about spreadsheet errors.* Retrieved September 2, 2006, from http://panko.cba.hawaii.edu/ssr/Mypapers/whatknow.htm

Panko, R., & Halverson, R. (1996). Spreadsheets on trial: A survey of research on spreadsheet risks. *Proceedings of the 29th Annual Hawaii International Conference on Systems Sciences* (pp. 326-335).

Powell, S., Baker, K., & Lawson, B. (2008a). A critical review of the literature on spreadsheet errors. *Decision Support Systems, 46,* 128–138. doi:10.1016/j.dss.2008.06.001

Powell, S., Baker, K., & Lawson, B. (2008b). An auditing protocol for spreadsheet models. *Information & Management, 45*(5), 312–320. doi:10.1016/j.im.2008.03.004

Purser, M., & Chadwick, D. (2006). Does an awareness of differing types of spreadsheet errors aid end-users in identifying spreadsheet errors? *Proceedings of the European Spreadsheet Risk Interest Group Annual Conference* (pp. 185-204), Cambridge, UK.

Rajalingham, K., Chadwick, D., & Knight, B. (2000). Classification of spreadsheet errors. *Proceedings of the European Spreadsheet Risks Interest Group Annual Conference* (pp. 23-34), Greenwich, England.

Sommerville, K. (2004). *Software engineering* (7th ed.). Boston: Addison-Wesley.

This work was previously published in Journal of Organizational and End User Computing (JOEUC) 21(3), edited by Mo Adam Mahmood, pp. 24-36, copyright 2009 by IGI Publishing (an imprint of IGI Global).

Chapter 12
Organizational Factors and Information Technology Use:
Tying Perceptions of the Organization to Perceptions of IT

Riza Ergun Arsal
Istanbul Bilgi University, Turkey

Jason Thatcher
Clemson University, USA

Thomas Zagenczyk
Clemson University, USA

D. Harrison McKnight
Michigan State University, USA

Manju Ahuja
University of Louisville, USA

ABSTRACT

Studies of information technology (IT) use have focused on numerous antecedents to behavioral intent to use. Although some antecedents (such as subjective norms) reflect aspects of the organizational environment, most antecedents reflect beliefs or attitudes about the technology itself. Using TAM, social exchange theory, and social information processing theories as conceptual bases, we posit that general beliefs about the organizational environment influence IT use on the job. Specifically, we propose that affective commitment, autonomy, and team member trust will directly influence behavioral intent to use IT. However, TAM variables (perceived usefulness, subjective norm, and perceived ease of use) will mediate the effects of organizational variables on behavioral intent to use IT. The results provide initial evidence that organizational variables are related to behavioral intent to use IT, but only when IT is perceived to be useful and subjective norms favor its use. We suggest that when introducing IT, managers need to pay attention not only to technology-related issues, but also to the broader organizational environment in which IT will be used. Implications for researchers and practitioners are offered.

DOI: 10.4018/978-1-60960-577-3.ch012

INTRODUCTION

During the 1990s, organizations changed their technological and social infrastructures to encourage flexibility and responsiveness to global, hyper-competitive markets. In terms of technological change, organizations infused information technology (IT) into basic business processes in order to gain competitive advantage (Sambamurthy, 2000; Applegate et al., 2003). In terms of social change, when organizations restructured their business processes, they frequently engaged in activities such as outsourcing or job re-design, which changed the nature of their ties with employees (Iverson, 1996) and resulted in jobs that provided employees more autonomy over information technology use (Ahuja and Thatcher, 2005). As they emerged from the 1990s, organizations increasingly depended on IT and employee willingness to use IT applications. However, largely due to the lack of user commitment (Malhotra and Galletta, 2004), many IT implementation projects still failed.

Interestingly, the changes that occur in organizations that adopt new technologies may themselves discourage employees' future usage of IT. For instance, organizational researchers frequently note that changes in technology have contributed to the deteriorating relationship between employer and employee, because often changes in technology lead to changing work roles, restructuring, and even downsizing (Shore and Coyle-Shapiro, 2003). With this in mind, it is possible and even likely that employees' beliefs about the broader organizational environment may influence their use of workplace IT. Understanding how the broader organizational environment influences technology use is important because managers exert a direct influence on the work environment. Linking the organizational environment to beliefs about IT may help managers identify levers that encourage individual IT use. Hence, we examine the question: how do beliefs about the broader organizational environment influence technology use? Recent research raised concerns about the absence of detail on contextual and environmental factors that shape IT usage. In particular, Lamb and Kling (2003) argue that studies rooted in cognitive or social psychology do not pay sufficient attention to the organizational context as an influence on IT acceptance and use.

Accordingly, this study examines how the organizational environment influences IT usage. We examine three variables that, in a broad sense, capture employees' perceptions of important elements of the organizational environment: (1) affective organizational commitment (relationship with the organization itself); (2) job autonomy (characteristics of the job), and (3) team-member trust (interpersonal relationships with coworkers).

To develop theoretical arguments between these variables and IT usage, we integrate existing research on the technology acceptance model (TAM), social exchange theory (SET; Blau, 1964) and social information processing theory (SIP, Salancik and Pfeffer, 1978). Taken together, SET and SIP suggest that employees will tend to use IT to a greater extent when (1) they have favorable exchange relationships with their organizations (high levels of organizational commitment, high job autonomy) and (2) they trust team members who advocate the use of IT themselves. However, it is possible that these conditions exist, yet employees nonetheless refuse to use IT. TAM accounts for this possibility, as it suggests that when information technology has low perceived usefulness, low ease of use, and norms that disfavor its use, it will be used to a lesser extent. As a result, our proposed model suggests that organizational and technological factors will influence IT usage: favorable employer-employee and coworker-employee relationships will lead to IT use, but only to the extent that the technology is perceived to be useful and easy to use.

This chapter unfolds as follows; first, a theoretical justification is developed to link beliefs about the organizational environment to employees' technology use. Then the research model is introduced. Next, we present the data and method. We conclude with results, implications and directions for future research.

LITERATURE REVIEW AND HYPOTHESES DEVELOPMENT

In response to changing technologies and implementation problems, researchers direct substantial attention towards identifying beliefs about technology and technology development that influence employee use of IT. Because beliefs about IT have been consistently found to be essential antecedents to individual behaviors toward technology (e.g. Davis et al., 1989; Venkatesh and Davis, 2000), IS scholars have emphasized the importance of investigating the determinants of such beliefs (Agarwal and Prasad 1999; Venkatesh and Davis, 2000) as well as their formation process (Agarwal, 2000). Examining these attitudes and beliefs is particularly critical as the increased use of IT could positively affect job performance and decision-making performance of employees (e.g. Guimaraes and Igbaria, 1997; Torkzadeh and Doll, 1999).

Since the decision to use an IT is not only influenced by system and individual factors but also contextual factors (Mathieson, 1991), it is important to examine organizational factors in order to understand how to maximize utilization of IT. We argue that employees' beliefs about technology will not be driven solely by an evaluation of the usefulness of the IT itself, but instead are intertwined with their relationship with the organization and coworkers' beliefs about the appropriateness of IT use. Our argument is consistent with that of Orlikowski (2000), who suggests individual IT use behavior is strongly influenced by the organizational context within which the behavior is enacted. However, we extend the argument offered by Orlikowski (2000) by grounding our arguments about the effects of the organizational context on IT usage in social exchange theory (Blau, 1964), social information processing theory (Salancik & Pfeffer, 1978) and TAM (Davis, 1989). Taken together, these different theoretical perspectives suggest these potential antecedents of IT use: (1) employees' perception of their organization; (2) employee perceptions of their jobs; (3) employees' perceptions of their team members/coworkers; and (4) employees' perceptions of the usefulness and ease of use of technology.

In order to identify beliefs that directly influence IT use, we turn to TAM (Davis, 1989). TAM posits that two beliefs about a technology influence an individual's intention to use IT: perceived usefulness (PU) and perceived ease of use (PEOU). PEOU also influences PU. PU refers to the degree to which a person believes that using IT would enhance his or her job performance (Davis et al., 1989). PEOU refers to the belief that using IT will be relatively free of cognitive effort (Davis et al., 1989). PU and PEOU are individual beliefs about IT itself and do not capture perceptions about the organizational environment. TAM was extended to include other factors such as subjective norms (SN), which is defined as a focal individual's beliefs about how important others feel about the appropriateness of using IT and the focal individual's motivation to comply with their feelings. Research examining SN has found that perceptions of co-workers or peers frequently influence intention to use IT (Gallivan, 2001). While SN does assess a specific aspect of the social context, it would be misleading to suggest that SN captures the entirety of the effects that the work environment has on IT use. For instance, a focal employee may believe that important coworkers think that employee IT use is critical organizational success, but instead may choose behaviors which deviate from these beliefs under certain conditions.

Although TAM-based studies are the most dominant research paradigm in user acceptance (van der Heijden 2004), IS scholars still suggest exploring boundary conditions of TAM by examining the effects of different information systems and environments (Venkatesh, Davis, and Morris, 2007; Lucas, Swanson, and Zmud, 2007). While recent TAM-based research has extended user acceptance to incorporate the context, such as digital libraries (Thong et al. 2002) and online tax services (Wu and Chen 2005), our goal is to highlight the influence of perceptions of the organizational environment on the adoption of workplace information technologies. By integrating the influence of the organizational context on technology use, we contribute to a deeper understanding of why technologies succeed or fail within organizations.

Social exchange research in organizations is based on the premise that employees develop exchange relationships with the organizations for which they work. Levinson's (1965) seminal work argues that the actions of individuals who represent the organization are attributed to the intent of the organization itself. This is because (1) organizations are legally, financially and morally responsible for the actions of their agents; (2) organizational precedents, traditions, policies and norms provide continuity and prescribe role behaviors of organizational agents; and (3) the organization, through its agents, exerts power over individual employees.

Building on Levinson's work, Eisenberger et al. (1986) utilized social exchange theory (Blau, 1964) and the reciprocity norm (Gouldner, 1960), which obligates individuals to return help with help, to explain the give and take inherent in the employer-employee relationship. Social exchange relationships, according to Blau (1964), are based on the exchange of mutual support, much of which may be socioemotional in nature. Eisenberger and his colleagues (1986) proposed that the employee-organization connection is a social exchange relationship in which the organization offers employees rewards and favorable job conditions in exchange for loyalty and work effort. When employees believe that they are treated favorably by the organization, the reciprocity norm (Gouldner, 1960) obligates them to support the organization by helping it to achieve its goals and objectives. In this paper, we use social exchange theory to argue that affective organizational commitment and job autonomy will be positively related to intentions to use IT.

In addition to social exchange, we draw on social information processing theory to explain the effects of team-member trust on employees' IT usage. Salancik and Pfeffer (1978) argue that because organizations are complex and ambiguous environments, individuals utilize information that they obtain from other members when forming perceptions and evaluations concerning the organization and their jobs. Specifically, individuals use information they collect from others: (1) to learn to react to social cues; (2) to form perceptions by focusing attention on some aspects of the work environment but away from others; (3) to construct their interpretations of organizational events; and (4) to understand the requirements of their jobs. As IT becomes an increasingly important element of the jobs of today's employees, it stands to reason that information employees acquire informally through the social environment at work regarding their jobs will be increasingly concerned with technology.

Studies have demonstrated that social information processing results in similarity among attitudes, perceptions and behaviors of individuals who interact. For instance, Burkhardt (1994) found that employees' attitudes towards new technology were similar to the attitudes of individuals with whom they communicated frequently, while Zagenczyk, Scott, Gibney, Murrell and Thatcher (2010) demonstrated that employees' perceptions of the extent to which they were supported by their organization were similar to coworkers who occupied similar positions in organizational friendship and advice networks as well as to those of individuals with whom they maintained direct advice relationships. Overall, this research supports the idea that social information processing results in similarity among employees' attitudes, perceptions, and behaviors. In the context of this study, we use social information processing theory to argue that coworker/team-member trust will predict intentions to use IT.

Drawn from social exchange theory and social information processing, our research model (Figure 1) suggests affective commitment, autonomy, and trust will directly affect behavioral intent to use IT, but that these relationships will hold only when IT is believed to be useful, easy to use, and when subjective norms favor its use. That is, organizational variables will affect individuals' intent to use IT – as long as others are using IT, the IT is useful, and the IT is easy to use. The following present the logic behind the relationships in our research model.

Social Exchange Theory and Affective Commitment

Affective commitment refers to a "strong belief in and acceptance of the organization's goals and values [and] a willingness to exert considerable effort on behalf of the organization" (Porter et al., 1974: p. 604). Social exchange theory predicts that affective commitment is created when employees believe that their organization values their contributions and cares about their well-being. When employees believe that their organization is committed to them, they respond by being committed to the organization. Affective organizational commitment is critical to organizations because it is related to key employee beliefs and behavior, including turnover intentions (Mowday et al., 1982), work attitudes (Mowday et al., 1982), organizational citizenship (Meyer and Allen, 1991), and in-role performance (Near, 1989).

Consistent with past research that demonstrates that employees with high levels of affective commitment have higher in-role performance and are more likely to go above and beyond formal job duties to help the organization, we expect that employees with high levels of affective commitment

Figure 1. Theoretical and Research Model

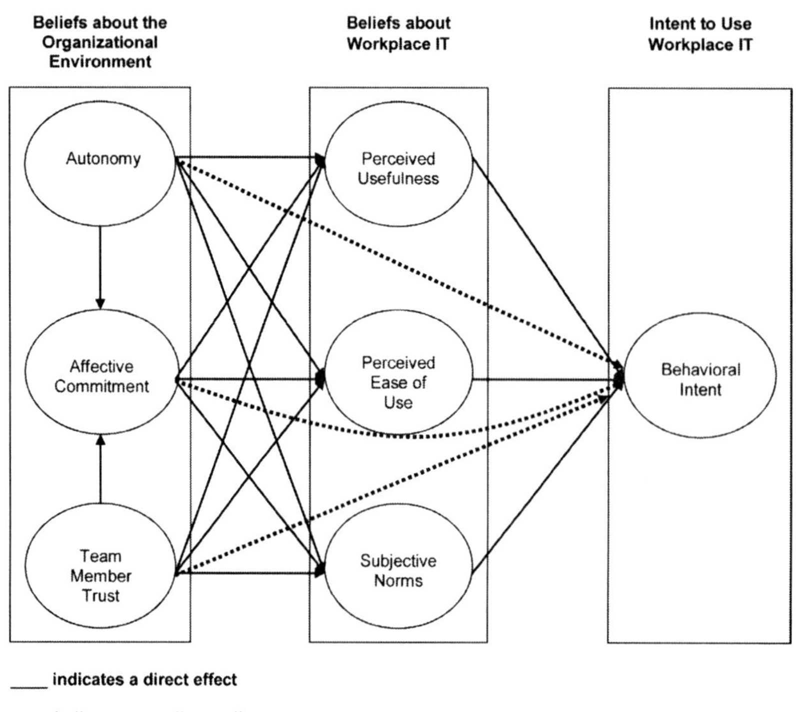

will also be more likely to use IT offered by the organization. From this perspective, employees may view IT usage as being "a favor" that they do for the organization to repay it for favorable treatment that it has provided. IT usage may also be viewed as an important part of the job; as a result, employees wishing to perform their jobs at a high level will be more apt to use IT offered by the organization in an effort to help the organization succeed.

Some past research provides a precedent for this claim. For instance, Malhotra and Galletta (2005) found that organizationally-committed users may believe that the use of the new system is the right thing to do. In a similar vein, Near (1989) found that when affective commitment increased, individuals used technology more effectively. Affectively committed employees are also likely to commit to working with computers resulting in more time and effort dedicated to learning to use new information technologies (Benkfoff, 1997). This existing research on the relationship between affective commitment and IT use is important, but provides little theoretical justification for the relationship between these variables. Our social exchange-based argument provides theoretical justification for the results of past research and drives our first hypotheses:

H1. Affective commitment will be positively associated with behavioral intentions to use IT.

Social Exchange Theory and Autonomy

Autonomy refers to beliefs about control over the task environment. Specifically, job autonomy reflects beliefs about "the degree to which the job provides substantial freedom, independence and discretion in scheduling the work and in determining the procedures to be used in carrying it out" (Hackman and Oldham, 1975: p. 162). Researchers have used social exchange theory to explain the effects of autonomy on workplace outcomes (e.g. Rhoades and Eisenberger, 2002). From this perspective, autonomy is viewed as a signal from the organization to employees that the organization trusts them to carry out tasks on their own, and that the contributions that they make benefit the organization. Employees with higher levels of autonomy, then, believe they are valued by the organization and will reciprocate by holding attitudes and behaving in a manner that helps the organization succeed. From a classic social exchange view, then, autonomy is expected to be related to affective organizational commitment. In addition, when employees are offered autonomy in their jobs, they will reciprocate with increased levels of in-role performance and citizenship behavior. We expect that employees with high levels of autonomy will also be more apt to use IT offered by the organization because this will be viewed as a "favor" to repay the organization for favorable treatment it has provided them.

H2a. Job autonomy will be positively associated with affective organizational commitment.

H2b. Job autonomy will be positively associated with behavioral intentions to use IT.

In jobs with high levels of autonomy, management may not directly observe employee work habits. Further, goals and other outcomes are likely to be relatively subjective in nature, rendering objective outcome controls hard to use (Kirsch, 1997; Sewell, 1998). Because of the uncertain framework for task evaluation, employees may turn to subjective norms as a means to determine when, and when not, to use IT. Through paying attention to social cues, an employee may appropriate and use technology as expected by top management. Hence, when working in high autonomy environments, employees may direct more attention to social norms for how to use IT. Hence,

H2c. Job autonomy will be positively associated with subjective norm towards information technology.

Trust

Trust has become a crucial factor for organizational commitment, coordination and performance, particularly due to recent changes in organizational dynamics (Tyler, 2003; Costa, 2003). Organizational structures have grown flatter and more team centered, and as a result, managers have adopted collaborative approaches that emphasize coordination, sharing of responsibilities and worker participation in decision processes (Keen, 1990 cf. Costa 2003). These changes, taken together with the increased autonomy inherent in many jobs, make organizations increasingly complex and ambiguous (Salancik & Pfeffer, 1978).

When employees trust peers to behave consistently, they are more likely to express commitment to the work unit and organization (Barling and Phillips, 1993). Kelloway and Barling (2000) suggest that employees' willingness to use their knowledge for organizational ends is a function of both their trust in the organization and their commitment to the organization. Beyond this, there is consistent data in the literature to suggest positive empirical relationships between trust and affective commitment. (e.g. Cook and Wall, 1980; Ruppel and Harrington, 2000).

H3a: Team member trust will be positively associated with affective commitment.

Some IT research has found that trust affects intent to use systems. Pavlou (2003) finds trust influences intent to transact with an e-vendor both directly and through risk and TAM variables. Gefen et al. (2003) finds trust directly influences intention to purchase from an e-vendor. Hence, trust is often a factor of use intentions. Salancik and Pfeffer (1978) argue that when the environment is complex and ambiguous, employees look for cues from others in order to help shape their perceptions of aspects of the organization. Burkhardt's (1994) longitudinal investigation of a federal agency responsible for collecting and disseminating information on nutrition revealed that employees' attitudes and behaviors towards a technological change were affected by individuals who held similar (or "structurally equivalent" positions) in the organization's social network, as opposed to individuals with whom they had direct interaction. A study of the student health services organization in a large university by Rice and Aydin (1991) showed that social information processing affected employees' perceptions of a new information system above and beyond the effects of employees' use of the system and occupational membership. Specifically, relationally and positionally proximate others (but not spatially proximate others) influenced employees' perceptions. Collectively, the results of these studies suggest that an employee's coworkers can affect their beliefs about new technology, particularly if those individuals hold similar positions in the organization's social network and interact with the same set of other employees. Logically then, it makes sense that coworkers who are on the same work team as a focal individual will influence beliefs about technology. Trust in one's team members suggests one feels a part of the unit. Arguably, one who feels part of the unit would be more willing to use the technology used in the unit. Trust in team members becomes a cue that tends to lead to intention to use. It is possible that team members would not want to use the technology, leading to a negative effect. But this is more the exception than the rule.

In this study, we build on the perspective presented by these researchers and suggest that the extent to which employees trust team members will be an important predictor of whether or not they intend to use technology. Therefore, we expect that:

H3b: Team member trust will be positively associated with behavioral intent to use information technology.

In addition, trust in peers should exert a positive influence on subjective norm towards technology use. In a study of information systems groups, Nelson and Cooprider (1996) found that mutual trust and mutual influence were related. As trust grew, peers exerted more influence on individuals' beliefs and behavior. Subjective norm represents peer influence. Therefore, the more one trusts peers, the more one allows them to influence one through subjective norm (Zand, 1972). This suggests that trust in peers will positively impact subjective norm towards IT use.

H3c. Team member trust will be positively associated with subjective norm towards information technology.

Full Mediation

In addition to the hypotheses above, the research model (Figure 1) suggests that TAM constructs fully mediate the effects of affective commitment, autonomy, and trust on behavioral intent to use technology. Consistent with TRA, recent TAM-based studies suggest that PU, EOU, and SN fully mediate the influence of external variables on behavioral intent to use (Leonard-Barton and Deschamps, 1988; Gefen and Keil, 1998; Venkatesh and Davis, 1996; Venkatesh and Davis, 2000). Essentially, what these researchers argue is that an employee may be committed to the organization, have a highly autonomous job, or have a high level of trust in team members – but if information technology is too difficult to use, is not useful, or is not advocated by peers, factors related to the organizational environment will not affect its use. Thus, in order to achieve the highest level of IT usage, managers must effectively manage employees' beliefs about the environment as well their beliefs about technology. This is likely because beliefs and norms about the technology itself are probably more salient to intentions about technology use than are context variables. Hence,

H4. Perceived usefulness, ease of use, and subjective norm will fully mediate the effects of affective commitment, autonomy and trust on behavioral intent to use information technology.

METHOD

Sample

The study was conducted at a public university in the Southeastern United States. The questionnaire was completed by employees of various organizations who were also enrolled in undergraduate business courses (total enrollment = 800) at a large public university in the Southeastern United States. Out of 635 respondents, 345 indicated that they currently held a job (54%). If respondents supplied inconsistent employment information or failed to complete construct measures, they were dropped from the final dataset. Overall, 263 (41%) of the responses were used. Basic sample characteristics are presented in Table 1. The use of student subjects, though sometimes criticized, seems appropriate in this case for several reasons. First, subjects were responding about technology use in their work. Second, these respondents had jobs in which they used technology during a significant portion of their work week (see Table 1; 3.3 below). Third, the sample represents educated young adults, a group of people who are likely to be making technology use decisions during their careers. Fourth, subjects were, on average, 24 years old, an age at which young adults tend to hold responsible jobs.

Measures. Indicators for each construct were distributed throughout a larger survey examining IT use. Items may be found in Appendix I. Affective commitment items were drawn from the

Organizational Commitment Questionnaire (Mowday et al., 1982). Autonomy items were drawn from Beehr (1976) and have been used in recent MIS research (Ahuja et al 2007). Trust in team members items were derived from the trust literature, reflecting general confidence or trust in the other, willingness to depend on others, and individual beliefs about co-worker competence, honesty, and benevolence. Finally, PU, PEOU, SN, and behavioral intent measures were adapted from the existing TAM literature (Davis, 1989). A pretest of the questionnaire indicated that the items were relatively clear and easy to complete, and the instrument design had no significant flaws.

Table 1. Sample Characteristics and Construct Averages

Total sample size	**263**	
Demographics	**Mean**	**Std. Dev.**
Age	24.3	7.6
Years of College Education	2.8	1.2
Years of Work Experience	3.2	3.9
Years in Current Job	2.5	2.9
Years of IT use	9.2	4.5
Weekly Hours of IT use at Work	16.3	13.7
Position in Organization	**Number**	**Percentage**
Executive	4	1.52%
Middle Management	21	7.98%
Supervisory	42	15.97%
Technical	18	6.84%
Administrative/Clerical	131	49.81%
Other	47	17.87%
Constructs	**Mean**	**Std. Dev.**
Ease of Use	4.9	1.1
Perceived Usefulness	5.2	1.3
Subjective Norm	4.9	1.2
Behavioral Intent	5.2	1.1
Affective Commitment	4.0	0.9
Autonomy	4.5	1.5
Team Member Trust	4.5	1.0

Preliminary Analysis. Preliminary analysis focused on response distributions and outlier influence. Although outliers did not represent a problem, histograms and scatter-plots indicated that item responses were not normally distributed (Tabachnick and Fidell, 1996). The sample average age (24.3) indicates that the sample has a relatively mature mix of student-employees. They averaged 3.2 years of work experience, including 2.5 years in their current job. This level of tenure would enable respondents to adequately develop autonomy, trust, and organizational commitment. Respondents had used IT for 9.2 years on average and used IT at work 16.3 hours a week, indicating that IT use is a significant part of their jobs. Based on these characteristics, we concluded that the grounding of these respondents in their jobs and in IT use was adequate for this study.

Data Analysis and Results

This study employs partial least squares (PLS), a structural equation modeling (SEM) technique. Because of its emphasis on predicting causality and variation, many methodologists (e.g. Joreskog and Wold, 1982) suggest PLS is well suited for analysis designed to test theoretically complex models.

Measurement Model

When evaluating the measurement model, researchers evaluate PLS item loadings, scale reliabilities and constructs' discriminant validity. From an initial confirmatory factor analysis, individual item loadings for most constructs were acceptable. However, because they did not load appropriately, affective commitment items 2 and 3 were dropped. Item 3 from the trust scale (loading of .59) was deemed sufficient to include in the final analysis as it is very close to the minimum level of .60 suggested by Chin (1998).

To assess reliability and convergent validity, we calculated each scale's internal composite reliability (ICR) and average variance extracted (AVE). ICR values over .70 reported in Table 2 demonstrate sufficient reliability for each construct (Fornell and Larcker, 1981). The AVE measures the variance captured by the indicators relative to measurement error, and should be greater than .50 (Chin, 1998). Table 2 reports that the AVEs are adequate to demonstrate valid measurement of the latent constructs. The lowest AVE was 0.58, for trust.

To test discriminant validity, Fornell and Larcker (1981) suggest that the square root of the AVE should be greater than the corresponding correlations among the latent variables. Table 2 shows that each construct demonstrates discriminant validity. A second way to evaluate discriminant validity is to examine the loadings and cross loadings of each indicator on the latent constructs (Chin, 1998). Each indicator should load higher on the construct of interest than on any other variable. Table 3 shows that this requirement is met, demonstrating that the observed indicators have adequate discriminant and convergent validity.

Structural Model

PLS structural model results may be interpreted like regression analysis. Each R^2 indicates the amount of variance explained in the latent construct (Chin, 1998). Path coefficients can be interpreted like standardized betas resulting from OLS regression. A bootstrapping procedure (samples = 120) was used to generate t-statistics (Chin, 1998) and test beta significance levels.

Evaluation of the structural model proceeded in a manner similar to stepwise regression (Tabachnick and Fidell, 1996). Separate structural models were estimated for the direct effects of autonomy, trust, and affective commitment on intent to use information technology (Figures 2-4). Then, relationships hypothesized by TAM were added to the model and tested, based on Figure 1 (Figure 5). Although many R-squares are relatively small, the findings for the separate structural models support the hypothesis that organizational factors will influence intent to use IT, but only when IT is perceived to be useful and subjective norms suggest that employees use IT. Hypothesis test results (based on Figure 5) may be found in Table 4. We now discuss the results.

Model 1: Affective Commitment

As is depicted in Figure 2, the model provides empirical support for the hypothesized relationship between affective commitment and behavioral intent to use IT (H1: $\beta = .36$, $p<.001$, $R^2=.13$).

*Table 2. Correlation of Constructs and Internal Composite Reliability**

Constructs		ICR	(1)	(2)	(3)	(4)	(5)	(6)	(7)
(1)	Ease of Use	0.89	0.86						
(2)	Perceived Usefulness	0.93	0.61	0.87					
(3)	Subjective Norm	0.95	0.44	0.58	0.88				
(4)	Behavioral Intent	0.97	0.48	0.63	0.57	0.91			
(5)	Commitment	0.89	0.18	0.28	0.30	0.27	0.76		
(6)	Autonomy	0.85	0.24	0.26	0.30	0.23	0.33	0.77	
(7)	Trust	0.90	0.14	0.21	0.21	0.19	0.64	0.22	0.76

* Diagonal elements in the 'correlation of constructs' matrix are the square root of the Average Variance Extracted. For adequate discriminant validity, diagonal elements should be greater than corresponding off-diagonal elements.

Table 3. Factor Loadings and Cross Loadings

	Ease of Use	Perceived Usefulness	Subjective Norm	Behavioral Intent	Commitment	Autonomy	Trust
EOU1	**0.89**	0.63	0.43	0.47	0.22	0.23	0.16
EOU2	**0.91**	0.65	0.43	0.45	0.20	0.26	0.13
PU1	0.64	**0.90**	0.54	0.54	0.28	0.27	0.18
PU2	0.64	**0.86**	0.54	0.53	0.24	0.26	0.15
SN1	0.38	0.55	**0.91**	0.52	0.26	0.28	0.19
SN2	0.43	0.54	**0.91**	0.52	0.29	0.26	0.19
INTENT1	0.39	0.56	0.50	**0.86**	0.21	0.20	0.16
INTENT2	0.44	0.63	0.51	**0.91**	0.24	0.24	0.18
COM1	0.09	0.14	0.12	0.18	**0.68**	0.16	0.50
COM4	0.15	0.16	0.24	0.19	**0.83**	0.32	0.51
COM5	0.15	0.18	0.26	0.16	**0.80**	0.36	0.49
COM6	0.21	0.30	0.26	0.23	**0.81**	0.31	0.47
COM7	0.03	0.01	0.09	0.05	**0.67**	0.15	0.57
AUTO1	0.27	0.27	0.28	0.22	0.25	**0.82**	0.13
AUTO2	0.16	0.16	0.20	0.13	0.34	**0.79**	0.24
AUTO3	0.14	0.19	0.22	0.18	0.27	**0.77**	0.15
AUTO4	0.22	0.23	0.24	0.19	0.26	**0.78**	0.18
TRUST1	0.14	0.23	0.20	0.20	0.53	0.19	**0.73**
TRUST2	0.06	0.14	0.15	0.16	0.47	0.15	**0.73**
TRUST3	0.10	0.12	0.11	0.09	0.34	0.22	**0.60**
TRUST4	0.10	0.10	0.16	0.14	0.53	0.17	**0.80**
TRUST5	0.15	0.17	0.17	0.16	0.53	0.17	**0.84**
TRUST6	0.16	0.18	0.16	0.14	0.50	0.14	**0.77**
TRUST7	0.14	0.15	0.15	0.12	0.57	0.16	**0.80**

Figure 2. Affective Commitment and Behavioral Intent

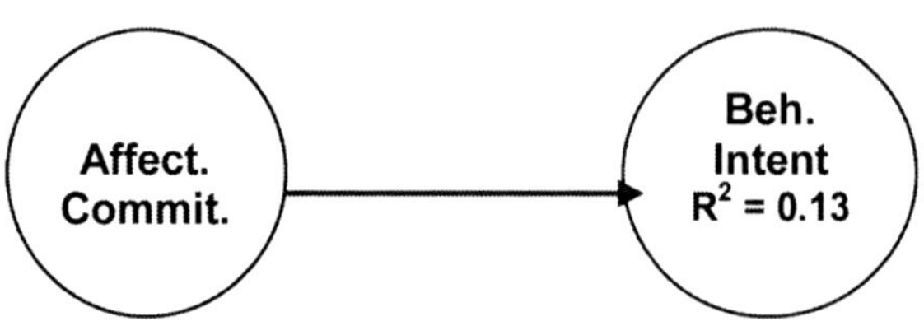

Model 2: Autonomy

Figure 3 depicts the relationships between autonomy and other variables. As hypothesized, autonomy demonstrated statistically significant relationships to affective organizational commitment ($H2a: \beta = .36, p<.001, R^2=.13$) and behavioral intent to use IT ($H2b: \beta = .26, p<.001, R^2=.05$). Inconsistent with expectations, autonomy was negatively related to SN ($H2c: \beta = -.30, p<.001,$

Table 4. Hypotheses and Results

Hypotheses		Support
Affective Commitment		
H1.	Affective commitment will be positively associated with behavioral intent to use IT.	Yes
Job Autonomy		
H2a.	Job autonomy will be positively associated with affective organizational commitment.	Yes
H2b.	Job autonomy will be positively associated with behavioral intentions to use IT.	Yes
H2c.	Job autonomy will be positively associated with subjective norm towards information technology.	No
Team Member Trust		
H3a.	Team member trust will be positively associated with affective commitment.	Yes
H3b.	Team member trust will be positively associated with behavioral intent to use IT.	Yes
H3c.	Team member trust will be positively associated with subjective norm towards information technology.	Yes
Full Mediation		
H4.	PU, PEOU, and SN will fully mediate the effects of autonomy, trust and affective commitment on behavioral intent to use IT.	Yes

Figure 3. Results of Hypotheses 2a, 2b, and 2c.

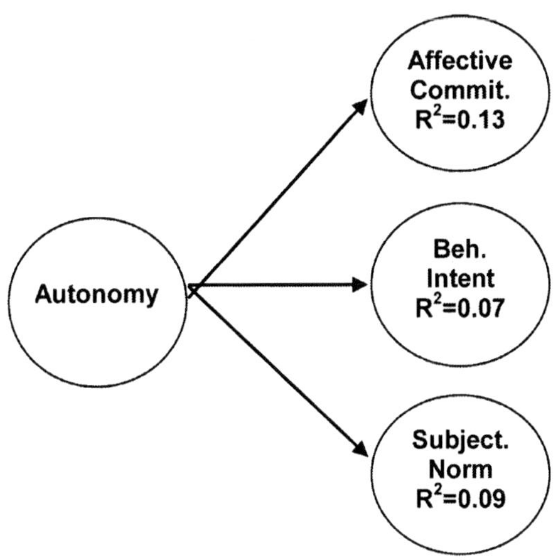

R^2=.09). Thus, autonomy was significantly associated with SN, but in the opposite direction than what we predicted.

Model 3: Team Member Trust

Trust was hypothesized to influence affective commitment, behavioral intent to use IT, and SN. Consistent with our hypotheses, trust was positively related to affective commitment (H3a: β = .67, p<.001, R^2=.45), behavioral intent to use IT (H3b: β = .19, p<.001, R^2=.04), and SN (H3c: β = .24, p<.01, R^2=.13) (see Figure 4).

Model 4: Affective Commitment, Autonomy, Trust, and TAM

In the final model (Figure 5), we tested the mediating effects of TAM variables on the relationship between organizational variables (affective commitment, job autonomy, and trust) on behavioral intent (H4). We tested for mediation using the steps proposed by Baron and Kenny (1986). The first requirement for mediation is that a significant association exists between the independent variable and the dependent variable. We tested for this relationship in H1, H2b, and H3b. Results of these hypotheses tests demonstrate that affective commitment (H1: β = .36, p<.001, R^2=.13), autonomy (H2b: β = .26, p<.001, R^2=.05), and team member trust (H3b: β = .19, p<.001, R^2=.04) were all positively and significantly associated with behavioral intent to use IT, meeting the criteria for step 1.

Figure 4. Results of hypotheses 3a, 3b, and 3c.

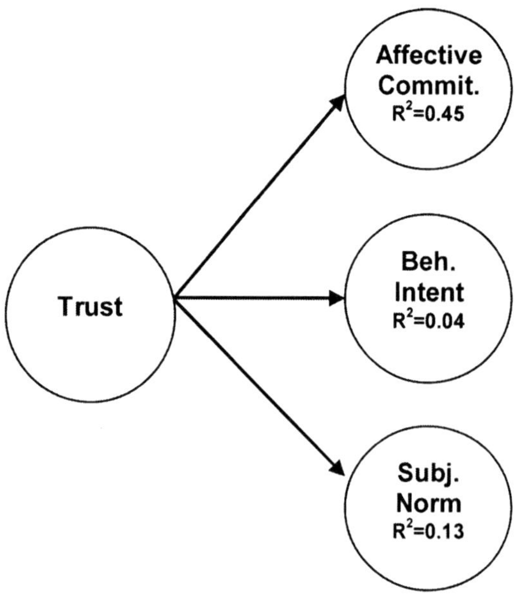

The second step in the Baron and Kenny approach is a significant relationship between the independent variable and the mediator variable. To test the relationships between organizational variables (IVs) and TAM variables (mediating variables), we ran separate models for organizational commitment, autonomy, and team member trust. Affective commitment exhibited positive significant relationships with perceived usefulness (β = .27, p<.001, R^2=.17), perceived ease of use (β = .25, p<.001, R^2=.10), and subjective norm (β=.30, p<.001, R^2=.14). Similarly, autonomy was positively and significantly related to perceived usefulness (β=.43, p<.001, R^2=.08) and perceived ease of use (β=.30, p<.001, R^2=.07); and negatively related to subjective norm (H2c: β = -.30, p<.001, R^2=.09). Finally, team member trust was

Figure 5. Summary of results

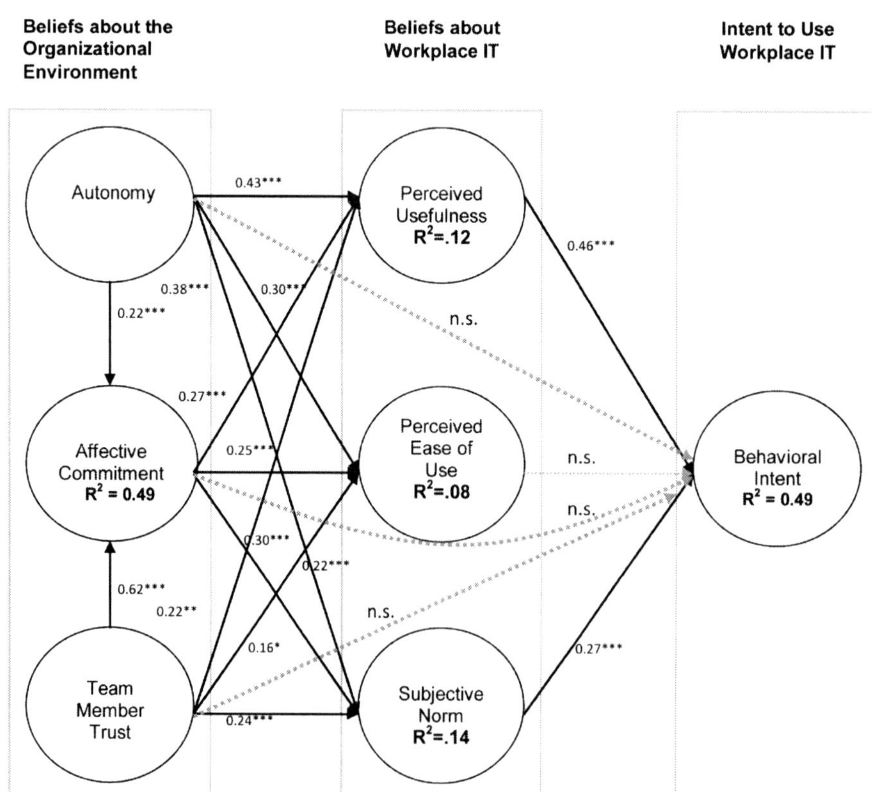

positively associated with subjective norm (H3c: β=.24, p<.001, R^2=.13), perceived ease of use (β=.16, p<.05, R^2=.03), and perceived usefulness (β=.22, p<.01, R^2=.05). Thus, we found support for the second step proposed by Baron and Kenny.

The third requirement for mediation proposed by Baron and Kenny (1986) is a significant relationship between the mediating variable and dependent variable. We ran models testing the relationships between perceived usefulness, perceived ease of use, and subjective norm and behavioral intent to use IT. Results of these hypotheses tests demonstrate that perceived usefulness (β= .47, p<.001) and SN (β=.27, p<.001) were positively and significantly associated with behavioral intent to use IT. However, ease of use was not significantly related to behavioral intent (β=.03, p>.05). Overall then, the third requirement for mediation was met for perceived usefulness and SN, but not ease of use.

The final step in Baron and Kenny's test for mediation is to assess the relationship between the independent variable and the dependent variable when the mediator variable is held constant. If the relationship between the independent variable and the dependent variable becomes insignificant and explains no significant additional variance beyond what is explained by the mediating variable, full mediation exists. We ran a model which tested the effects of both the independent (organizational) variables and the mediating (TAM) variables on the dependent variable, behavioral intent to use IT. When the TAM variables were included in the model, the relationships between affective commitment (β = .07, p>.05), autonomy (β = .01, p>.05), and team member trust (β = -.01, p>.05) all became insignificant. At the same time, perceived usefulness (β = .46, p<.001, R^2=.12) and SN (β =.27, p<.001, R^2=.14) demonstrated positive and significant relationships to behavioral intent to use IT. However, ease of use (β=.01, p>.05, R^2=.08) was not significantly associated with behavioral intent to use IT. Finally, direct links from the organizational variables (affective commitment, job autonomy, and trust) to behavioral intent explained an insignificant amount of incremental variance in behavioral intention (additional R^2 = 0.003, p>.05).

Overall, we found partial support for H4, as perceived usefulness and SN fully mediated the relationships between affective commitment, autonomy, and trust on behavioral intent to use IT. However, we did not find evidence of the predicted mediating effects of ease of use on the relationship between organizational variables and behavioral intent to use IT.

DISCUSSION

This study was motivated by a desire to understand how the organizational environment influences IT use. Our central thesis was that organizational variables would influence behavioral intent to use IT, but only when IT was perceived to be useful, easy to use, and when subjective norm favored IT usage. Specifically, we examined the direct effects of affective commitment, autonomy, and trust on behavioral intent to use IT. In addition, we tested the mediating effects of perceived usefulness of IT, perceived ease of use of IT, and subjective norm toward IT use on the relationship between organizational factors and behavioral intent to use IT. When considered separately, affective commitment, autonomy, and trust had positive, significant relationships with behavioral intent to use IT. When considered in unison with technology variables, we found evidence that perceived usefulness and subjective norm mediated the effects of affective commitment, job autonomy, and team-member trust on behavioral intent to use IT. In addition, our results showed that job autonomy and trust were positively and significantly related to affective commitment and subjective norms. The following paragraphs discuss the implications of the study's findings.

Affective Commitment

Consistent with Hypotheses 1, our results show that affective commitment is positively and significantly related to intent to use IT. This finding is consistent with social exchange theory, which suggests that positive treatment provided by the organization yields employee attitudes and behaviors which help the organization to reach its goals and objectives (Eisenberger et al., 1986). In this research, we show a link between employee attachment to the organization and employees' intent to use IT. This suggests that organizations that foster commitment among employees may not only lower absenteeism and turnover, but also more easily foster IT use. Second, when organizations seek to use IT to enable competitive advantage or restructuring, managers should pay careful attention to maintaining the relationship between employer and employee. Far too often, organizations have introduced new technologies in hopes of flattening organizational structures and letting go of employees (Beigbeder, 2000). Social exchange research shows that layoffs and restructuring in and of themselves damage the employer-employee relationship so severely that even remaining employees frequently report lower levels of commitment and motivation (Allen et al., 2001). Our results suggest that intent to use IT may in fact be enhanced when organizations carefully plan organizational change in such a manner that employees do not feel as if the organization does not care for them and does not value their contributions to its success.

Autonomy. To realize IT-enabled performance, managers may wish to grant employees more discretion over how they incorporate IT into their jobs (Ahuja and Thatcher, 2005). Findings regarding the relationship between autonomy and intent to use IT can also be explained through the lens of social exchange theory. From this perspective, autonomy is viewed as a favorable job condition that an organization provides for employees. Organizations that grant employees autonomy signal to employees that they are competent and valued (Wayne et al., 1997). As a result, such employees develop higher levels of affective commitment (Wayne et al., 1997). Indeed, we found a significant positive relationship between autonomy and commitment (H2a). Employees who have more autonomy in their jobs then "return the favor" to the organization by being more inclined to use IT on the job (H2b). In addition, our findings suggest that employees with autonomous jobs are less likely to respond to subjective norms towards IT use (H2c). Despite H2c results, these findings suggest that organizations may increase employee autonomy without fear of corresponding reductions in employee IT use, but instead that autonomy will increase employees' tendency to use IT.

Team Member Trust. The strong link from peer trust to affective commitment (H3a) suggests that building good relationships among team members may be a useful strategy for improving affective commitment and consequently increasing IT use. It is possible that trust in management or trust in the organization may have produced stronger results than trust in peers, because they more closely represent how one feels about the organization. However, by focusing on peers, we directed respondents' attention to the most immediate source of subjective norm in their organization. It means that employees who trust team members will be more apt to share information and adopt social norms in the organization (Krackhardt & Hansen, 1993). Certainly our results suggest that employees who trust team members endorse social norms towards IT to a greater extent (H3c). When considering general IT in the workplace, our findings suggest that trust in team members is a distal antecedent to beliefs about IT (H3b).

Mediating Effects of TAM Variables. While we expected that organizational variables such as affective commitment, autonomy, and team member trust would exert positive influence on behavioral intent to use IT, we did not expect that this relationship would occur if IT provided by the organization was not useful, if social norms did not prescribe the use of IT, or if IT was not easy to use. That is, we expected TAM variables to mediate the relationship between organizational variables and behavioral intent to use IT. Consistent with our expectations, we found that perceived usefulness and subjective norm toward information technology use fully mediated the relationship between organizational variables and behavioral intent to use IT. That is, although employees experience high-quality social exchange relationships with their organizations (through affective commitment and job autonomy) and trust team members, beliefs that IT is useful and what others say about IT are necessary preconditions for employees to have intentions to use IT offered by the organization. However, we did not find that perceived ease of use was a mediator of the relationship between organizational factors and intentions to use IT. This suggests that if favorable conditions in the organization exist, if IT is perceived to useful, and if others prescribe using technology, employees will do so regardless of whether or not it is easy to do. From a social exchange perspective, this finding is not all that surprising: employees will be more likely to endure IT-related difficulty to help the organization when they are attached to the organization because it helps them.

Study Limitations

The main limitation relates to the study sample. Sampling was limited to voluntary respondents enrolled in undergraduate classes in a business school. Therefore, there exists a possibility of sampling bias. However, we eliminated responses from students who were not working, thus providing a sample of organizational workers. In addition, we examined each case in terms of age, experience in the workplace, tenure in position, and position. When these indicators were incomplete or inconsistent, we dropped the case. While the sample is not representative of all technology users, it does represent a subset very likely to be involved in technology use in the future.

Another limitation of this study concerns self-reported measures. Self-report measures may suffer from common method variance that could inflate observed relationships among constructs. However, James et al. (1979) suggest that common method variance is a concern when there appears to be a systematic inflation in the correlation of constructs matrix. Although the TAM constructs were highly correlated, examination of the matrix in Table 3 demonstrates that correlations varied across TAM constructs and organizational constructs. This suggests that our respondents carefully read the questionnaire and assessed the distinct target objects (i.e., information technology or the organization) in a different light. Further, given the relatively small variance explained by autonomy, affective commitment, and trust, our analysis suggests that our findings are not a function of multicollinearity nor common method variance (Champoux and Peters, 1987; Evans, 1985). Thus, common method variance does not appear to explain our evidence of the relationship between the organizational context and perceptions of information technology.

Implications for Practice and Research

This research contributes to an understanding of how the organizational environment influences information technology use. For practitioners, this research has important implications for job design and managing the employer-employee relationship. When implementing technologies, managers need to consider how features of the task such as job autonomy influence employee perceptions of IT. After training, employers may want to give employees with less autonomous jobs more freedom to experiment with new IT. By doing so, they will increase individual sense of control, reducing the likelihood of overt resistance to the technology. Without autonomy, workers may perceive IT as a threat to their already limited control over their environment (Baba, 1999). Similarly, managers should promote a trusting environment that stimulates affective commitment in order to improve perceptions about technology. Through creating incentive systems that reward team performance, cooperation, and information sharing, managers may encourage trust between employees. Finally, careful management of the employer-employee relationship to foster organizational commitment can help managers to foster a sense of obligation within employees to help the organization reach its goals and objectives through IT use. By doing these things, employers may use IT to boost the productivity of autonomous and less-autonomous workers.

For scholars, this study provides preliminary evidence suggesting that integrating research from organizational behavior and management information systems may provide a clearer picture of how individuals develop beliefs about information technology. Specifically, we included measures of the employer-employee relationship (affective commitment), characteristics of employees' jobs (autonomy), and employee relationships with coworkers (team-member trust). We found that organizational variables influence employees' intentions to use IT – but only to the extent that IT is perceived to be useful and social norms support its use. When employees do not feel committed to their workplace, have lower job autonomy, or lack trust in peers, they will be less likely to form beliefs that lead to IT use. These findings suggest that scholars should take into account the environment's influence when studying volitional IT use in organizations. Other environmental factors should also be tested. For example, it may be that job security, perceived organizational support, or perceived fairness of the workplace may influence the level of commitment to the organization, which will in turn influence technology acceptance (Gallivan, 2001). In addition to autonomy, other job characteristics such as skill variety or task identify may influence IT use (Goodhue and Thompson, 1995). Job stress, job workload, or anxiety about the workplace may have negative or positive implications for IT use (Wastell and Newman, 1996). By examining a broader range of beliefs about the workplace, research may identify additional levers for managers to use to encourage IT acceptance.

Finally, it is important to note that our application of TAM differs from and extends prior research. In its initial conceptualization and subsequent empirical examinations, TAM constructs were measured when targeted on a specific technology within a specific context. Because of our interest in testing organizational environmental variables' influence on perceptions of workplace IT, items measured perceptions of workplace IT in general, rather than a target technology. This application is consistent with recent research which used TAM to examine intentions to use the WWW (see Agarwal and Karahanna, 2000). Also, to direct respondents' attention, we clearly defined workplace IT as information technologies such as computers, software applications or other computer-based technologies used to complete assigned work tasks. We suggest the strength of our findings provide further evidence that TAM may be used to examine broad classes of technologies. They suggest that TAM represents a parsimonious model useful for examining acceptance of categories of new IT.

CONCLUSION

This study articulates a parsimonious model that links beliefs about the organizational environment to beliefs about workplace information technology. It provides empirical evidence that affective commitment, job autonomy, and team-member trust have a direct effect on employees' intentions to use IT. However, this effect is mediated by perceived usefulness and social norms. As organizations continue to use IT to restructure organizations, these findings suggest that managers should carefully manage the employer-employee relationship as well as foster positive employee feelings towards their jobs and peers in order to increase IT acceptance. While the study provides only preliminary evidence of the broader organizational environments' influence, these results provide a foundation for future studies that link the organizational environment and IT acceptance.

REFERENCES

Agarwal, R. (2000). Individual acceptance of new information technologies . In Zmud, R. W. (Ed.), *Framing the Domains of IT Management Research: Glimpsing the Future through the Past* (pp. 85–104). Cincinnati, OH: Pinnaflex.

Agarwal, R., & Karahanna, E. (2000). Time flies when you're having fun: Cognitive absorption and beliefs about information technology usage. *Management Information Systems Quarterly*, *24*(4), 665–694. doi:10.2307/3250951

Agarwal, R., & Prasad, J. (1999). Are individual differences germane to the acceptance of information technologies? *Decision Sciences*, *30*, 361–391. doi:10.1111/j.1540-5915.1999.tb01614.x

Ahuja, M. K., Chudoba, K. M., Kacmar, C. J., McKnight, D. H., & George, J. F. (2007). IT road warriors: Balancing work-family conflict, job autonomy, and work overload to mitigate turnover intentions. *Management Information Systems Quarterly*, *31*(1), 1–17.

Ahuja, M. K., & Thatcher, J. B. (2005). Moving beyond intentions and toward the theory of trying: Effects of work environment and gender on post-adoption information technology use . *Management Information Systems Quarterly*, *29*, 427–459.

Allen, T. D., Freeman, D. M., Russell, J. A., & Reizenstein, R. C. (2001). Survivor reactions to organizational downsizing: Does time ease the pain? *Journal of Occupational and Organizational Psychology*, *74*, 145–165. doi:10.1348/096317901167299

Applegate, L. M., Austin, R. D., & McFarlan, W. (2003). *Corporate Information Strategy and Management: The Challenges of Managing in a Network Economy*. Boston: McGraw-Hill.

Baba, M., L. (1999). Dangerous liaisons: Trust, distrust, and information technology in American work organizations. *Human Organization*, *58*(3), 331–346.

Barling, J., & Phillips, M. (1993). Interactional, formal, and distributive justice in the workplace. *The Journal of Psychology*, *127*, 649–656. doi:10.1080/00223980.1993.9914904

Baron, R. M., & Kenny, D. A. (1986). The moderator-mediator distinction in social psychological research: Conceptual, strategic, and statistical considerations. *Journal of Personality and Social Psychology*, *51*, 1173–1182. doi:10.1037/0022-3514.51.6.1173

Beehr, T. (1976). Perceived situational moderators of the relationship between subjective role ambiguity and role strain. *The Journal of Applied Psychology*, *61*, 35–40. doi:10.1037/0021-9010.61.1.35

Beigbeder, S. (2000). Easing workforce reduction. *Risk Management*, *47*(5), 26–30.

Benkhoff, B. (1997). Ignoring commitment is costly: New approaches establish the missing link between commitment and performance. *Human Relations*, *50*(6), 701–726. doi:10.1177/001872679705000604

Blau, P. M. (1964). *Exchange and power in social life*. New York: Wiley.

Breaugh, J. A. (1985). The work autonomy scales: Validity evidence. *Human Relations*, *42*, 1033–1056. doi:10.1177/001872678904201105

Burkhardt, M. E. (1994). Social interaction effects following a technological change: A longitudinal investigation. *Academy of Management Journal*, *37*, 869–898. doi:10.2307/256603

Champoux, J. E., & Peters, W. S. (1987). Form, effect size, and power in moderated regression analysis. *Journal of Occupational Psychology*, *60*, 243–255.

Chin, W. W. (1998). The partial least squares approach to structural equation modeling . In Marcoulides, G. A. (Ed.), *Modern Methods for Business Research* (pp. 295–336). Mahway, New Jersey: Lawrence Erlbaum.

Chin, W. W., & Frye, T. (1996). *PLS Graph, 2.91.03.04 edition*. Calgary, Canada: University of Calgary.

Cook, J., & Wall, T. (1980). New work attitude measures of trust, organizational commitment and personal need non-fulfillment. *Journal of Occupational Psychology*, *53*, 39–52.

Costa, A. C. (2003). Work team trust and effectiveness. *Personnel Review*, *32*, 605–622. doi:10.1108/00483480310488360

Davis, F. D. (1989). Perceived usefulness, perceived ease of use, and user acceptance of information technology. *Management Information Systems Quarterly*, *13*(3), 319–340. doi:10.2307/249008

Davis, F. D., Bagozzi, R. P., & Warshaw, P. R. (1989). User acceptance of computer technology: A comparison of two theoretical models. *Management Science*, *35*(8), 982–1003. doi:10.1287/mnsc.35.8.982

Eisenberger, R., Huntington, R., Hutchison, S., & Sowa, D. (1986). Perceived organizational support. *The Journal of Applied Psychology*, *71*, 500–507. doi:10.1037/0021-9010.71.3.500

Evans, M. G. (1985). A Monte Carlo study of the effects of correlated method variance in moderated multiple regression analysis. *Organizational Behavior and Human Decision Processes*, *36*, 305–323. doi:10.1016/0749-5978(85)90002-0

Fornell, C., & Larcker, D. (1981). Evaluating structural equation models with unobservable variables and measurement error. *JMR, Journal of Marketing Research*, *18*(3), 39–50. doi:10.2307/3151312

Gallivan, M. (2001). Organizational adoption and assimilation of complex technological innovations: Development and application of a new framework. *The Data Base for Advances in Information Systems*, *32*(3), 51–85.

Gefen, D., Karahanna, E., & Straub, D. W. (2003). Inexperience and experience with online stores: The importance of TAM and trust' . *IEEE Transactions on Engineering Management*, *50*(3), 307–321. doi:10.1109/TEM.2003.817277

Gefen, D., & Keil, M. (1998). The impact of developer responsiveness on perceptions of usefulness and ease of use: An extension of the technology acceptance model. *The Data Base for Advances in Information Systems*, *29*(2), 35–49.

Gouldner, A. W. (1960). The norm of reciprocity: A preliminary statement. *American Sociological Review*, *25*, 161–178. doi:10.2307/2092623

Guimaraes, T., & Igbaria, M. (1997). Client/server system success: Exploring the human side. *Decision Sciences*, *28*, 851–876. doi:10.1111/j.1540-5915.1997.tb01334.x

Hackman, J., & Oldham, G. (1975). *Work redesign*. Reading, MA: Addison-Wesley.

Iverson, R. D. (1996). Employee acceptance of organizational change: The role of organizational commitment. *International Journal of Human Resource Management*, *7*(1), 122–149.

James, L. R., Gent, M. J., Hater, J. J., & Corey, K. E. (1979). Correlates of psychological influence: An illustration of the psychological climate approach to work environment perceptions. *Personnel Psychology*, *32*, 563–588. doi:10.1111/j.1744-6570.1979.tb02154.x

Joreskog, K. G., & Wold, H. (1982). The ML and PLS techniques for modeling latent variables: Historical and comparative aspects . In Joreskog, K. G., & Wold, H. (Eds.), *Systems under indirect observation: Causality, structure, prediction* (pp. 263–270). New York: North Holland.

Keen, P. (1990). *Shaping the Future: Business Design through Information Technology*. Cambridge, MA: Harvard Business School.

Kelloway, E. K., & Barling, J. B. (2000). Knowledge work as organizational behaviour. *International Journal of Management Reviews*, *2*, 287–304. doi:10.1111/1468-2370.00042

Kirsch, L. J. (1997). Portfolios of control modes and IS project management. *Information Systems Research*, *8*(3), 215–239. doi:10.1287/isre.8.3.215

Knoke, D. (1990). *Organizing for collective action: The political economies of associations.* de Gruyter, New York.

Krackhardt, D., & Hansen, J. R. (1993). Informal networks: The company behind the chart. *Harvard Business Review*, *71*, 104–111.

Lamb, R., & Kling, R. (2003). Reconceptualizing users as social actors in information systems research. *Management Information Systems Quarterly*, *27*(2).

Leonard-Barton, D., & Deschamps, I. (1988). Managerial influence on the implementation of new technology. *Management Science*, *34*(10), 1252–1265. doi:10.1287/mnsc.34.10.1252

Levinson, H. (1965). Reciprocation: The relationship between man and organization. *Administrative Science Quarterly*, *9*, 370–390. doi:10.2307/2391032

Lucas, H. C., Swanson, E. B., & Zmud, R. W. (2007). Implementation, innovation, and related themes over the years in information systems research. *Journal of the AIS*, *8*(4), 206–210.

Malhotra, Y., & Galletta, D. (2005). A multidimensional commitment model of volitional systems adoption and usage behavior. *Journal of Management Information Systems*, *22*, 117–151.

Malhotra, Y., & Galletta, D. F. (2004). Building systems that users want to use: Advancing beyond the rhetoric on "Does IT Matter". *Communications of the ACM*, *47*, 88–94. doi:10.1145/1035134.1035139

Mathieson, K. (1991). Predicting user intentions: Comparing the technology acceptance model with the theory of planned behavior. *Information Systems Research*, *2*(3), 173–191. doi:10.1287/isre.2.3.173

Meyer, J. P., & Allen, N. J. (1991). Development of organizational commitment. *Human Resource Management Review*, *1*, 61–89. doi:10.1016/1053-4822(91)90011-Z

Mowday, R. T., Porter, L. W., & Steers, R. M. (1982). *Employee-organization linkages: The psychology of commitment and absenteeism and turnover*. New York: Academic Press.

Near, J. P. (1989). Organizational commitment among Japanese and U.S. workers. *Organization Studies*, *10*(3), 281–301. doi:10.1177/017084068901000301

Nelson, K. M., & Cooprider, J. G. (1996). The Contribution of Shared Knowledge to IS Group Performance. *Management Information Systems Quarterly*, *20*(4), 409–432. doi:10.2307/249562

Orlikowski, W. J. (2000). Using technology and constituting structures: A practice lens for studying technology in organizations. *Organization Science*, *11*, 404–428. doi:10.1287/orsc.11.4.404.14600

Pavlou, P. (2003). Consumer Acceptance of Electronic Commerce: Integrating Trust and Risk with the Technology Acceptance Model . *International Journal of Electronic Commerce*, *7*(3), 101–134.

Porter, L. W., Steers, R. M., Mowday, R. T., & Boulian, P. (1974). Organizational commitment, job satisfaction and turnover among psychiatric technicians. *The Journal of Applied Psychology*, *59*(5), 603–609. doi:10.1037/h0037335

Rhoades, L., & Eisenberger, R. (2002). Perceived organizational support: A review of the literature. *The Journal of Applied Psychology*, *87*, 698–714. doi:10.1037/0021-9010.87.4.698

Rice, R. E., & Aydin, C. (1991). Attitudes toward new technology: Network proximity as a mechanism for social information processing. *Administrative Science Quarterly*, *36*, 219–244. doi:10.2307/2393354

Rousseau, D. M., Sitkin, S. B., Burt, R. S., & Camerer, C. (1998). Not so different after all: a cross-discipline view of trust. *Academy of Management Review*, *23*(3), 393–404.

Ruppel, C. P., & Harrington, S. J. (2000). The relationship of communication, ethical work climate, and trust to commitment and innovation. *Journal of Business Ethics*, *25*, 313–328. doi:10.1023/A:1006290432594

Salancik, G. R., & Pfeffer, J. (1978). A social information processing approach to job attitudes and task design. *Administrative Science Quarterly*, *23*, 224–253. doi:10.2307/2392563

Sambamurthy, V. (2000). Business strategy in hypercompetitive environments: Rethinking the logic of IT differentiation . In Zmud, R. W. (Ed.), *Framing the Domains of IT Management: Projecting the Future Through the Past* (pp. 65–104). Cincinnati, Ohio: Pinnaflex Educational Resources.

Sewell, G. (1998). The discipline of teams: The control of team-based industrial work through electronic and peer surveillance. *Administrative Science Quarterly*, *43*, 397–428. doi:10.2307/2393857

Shore, L. M., & Coyle-Shapiro, J. A. M. (2003). New developments in the employee-organization relationship. *Journal of Organizational Behavior*, *24*, 443–450. doi:10.1002/job.212

Tabachnick, B. G., & Fidell, L. S. (1996). *Using Multivariate Statistics* (3rd ed.). New York: HarperCollins.

Thong, J. Y. L., Hong, W. Y., & Tam, K. Y. (2002). Understanding user acceptance of digital libraries: what are the roles of interface characteristics, organizational context, and individual differences? *International Journal of Human-Computer Studies*, *57*(3), 215–242. doi:10.1016/S1071-5819(02)91024-4

Torkzadeh, G., Doll, W. J. (1999). The development of a tool for measuring the perceived impact of information technology on work. *Omega- International Journal of Management Science, 27*, 327-339.

Tyler, T. R. (2003). Trust within organisations. *Personnel Review*, *32*, 556–568. doi:10.1108/00483480310488333

van der Heijden, H. (2004). User acceptance of hedonic information systems. *Management Information Systems Quarterly*, *28*(4), 695–704.

Venkatesh, V., Davis, F., & Morris, M. (2007). Dead or Alive? The Development, Trajectory, and Future of Technology Adoption Research. *Journal of the Association for Information Systems*, *8*(4), 267–286.

Venkatesh, V., & Davis, F. D. (1996). A model of the antecedents of perceived ease of use: Development and test. *Decision Sciences*, *27*, 451–482. doi:10.1111/j.1540-5915.1996.tb01822.x

Venkatesh, V., & Davis, F. D. (2000). A theoretical extension of the technology acceptance model: Four longitudinal field studies. *Management Science*, *46*(4), 186–204. doi:10.1287/mnsc.46.2.186.11926

Wastell, D. G., & Newman, M. (1996). Stress, control and computer system design: A psychophysiological field study. *Behaviour & Information Technology*, *15*(3), 183–192. doi:10.1080/014492996120247

Wayne, S. J., Shore, L. M., & Liden, R. C. (1997). Perceived organizational support and leader-member exchange: A social exchange perspective. *Academy of Management Journal*, *40*, 82–111. doi:10.2307/257021

Wu, I. L., & Chen, E. L. (2005). An extension of Trust and TAM model with TPB in the initial adoption of on-line tax: An empirical study. *International Journal of Human-Computer Studies*, *62*(6), 784–808. doi:10.1016/j.ijhcs.2005.03.003

Zagenczyk, T. J., Scott, K. D., Gibney, R., Murrell, A. J., & Thatcher, J. B. (2010). Social influence and perceived organizational support: A social networks analysis. *Organizational Behavior and Human Decision Processes*, *111*(2), 127–138. doi:10.1016/j.obhdp.2009.11.004

Zand, D. E. (1972). Trust and managerial problem solving. *Administrative Science Quarterly*, *17*, 229–239. doi:10.2307/2393957

KEY TERMS AND DEFINITIONS

Affective Commitment: a "strong belief in and acceptance of the organization's goals and values [and] a willingness to exert considerable effort on behalf of the organization" (Porter et al., 1974: p. 604).

Trust: an individual's willingness towards vulnerability (Rousseau, Sitkin, Burt, and Camerer, 1998).

Autonomy: "the degree to which the job provides substantial freedom, independence and discretion in scheduling the work and in determining the procedures to be used in carrying it out" (Hackman and Oldham, 1975: p. 162).

Perceived Usefulness: "the degree to which a person believes that using a particular system would enhance his or her job performance" (Davis, 1989; p. 320).

Perceived Ease of Use: "the degree to which a person believes that using a particular system would be free from effort" (Davis, 1989, p. 320).

APPENDIX A

Stem: Think about your work environment, indicate the extent to which you agree or disagree with these statements.

Team Member Trust

1. We have confidence in one another in this workplace.
2. My co-workers are honest in their dealings with me.
3. Overall, my co-workers are capable and proficient.
4. Members of my workplace show a great deal of integrity.
5. I can rely on my co-workers.
6. If I required help, my co-workers would care enough to help me.
7. I feel I can depend on my co-workers on career-sensitive issues.

Stem: Indicate the extent to which these statements reflect your feelings about your current job.

Affective commitment

1. I am willing to put in effort beyond the norm for the success of the organization.
2. I am proud to tell others that I am part of this organization.*
3. For me this is the best of all possible organizations for which to work.*
4. I am extremely glad to have chosen this organization to work for over other organizations.
5. I would accept almost any type of job to keep working for this organization.
6. I talk up this organization to my friends as a great place to work for.
7. This organization inspires the very best in the way of job performance.

Stem: Indicate the extent to which these statements reflect your feelings about your current job.

Autonomy

1. I have a lot of freedom to decide how I perform assigned tasks.
2. I control the content of my job.
3. I have the authority to initiate projects at my job.
4. I set my own schedule for completing assigned tasks.

Stem: Indicate the extent to which these statements reflect how you interact with new workplace technologies.

Ease of Use

1. I find it easy to get IT applications to do what I want them to do.
2. Learning to operate information technology is easy for me.

Perceived Usefulness

1. Using IT enhances my effectiveness in completing projects.
2. When completing projects, I find IT useful.

Subjective Norm

1. People who are important to me think I should use IT.
2. People who influence my behavior think I should use information technologies.

Behavioral Intent

1. I intend to use new information technologies frequently at work.
2. I intend to use new IT to complete assigned tasks.

* Item dropped from final analysis

Chapter 13
Support and Facilitating Conditions to Computer Workers Who Dislike Working with Computers

Ranida Harris
Indiana University Southeast, USA

Kent Marett
Mississippi State University, USA

ABSTRACT

While the number of employees who primarily use computers to complete their work increases, a significant subset of those employees simply do not enjoy computer work. This dislike has an influence on work-related outcomes like perceived technology overload and job satisfaction. It is important to examine how work-related support from either supervisors or coworkers can minimize/buffer the negative outcomes related to an individual's disliking computer work. Using a sample of 225 workers from a range of businesses and industries, we investigated the influence of facilitating conditions on liking computer work. The results show that liking computer work is positively related to job satisfaction, and supervisor support helps moderate the relationships between liking computer work and the outcomes of job satisfaction and technology work overload. Implications for research and practice and directions for future research are offered.

INTRODUCTION

Computers seem to be omnipresent in today's society and the number of employees completing some, or all of their jobs on a computer continues to increase. However, not all individuals enjoy computer work as much as others. When employees who dislike computer work have to complete their jobs on a computer, they are likely to experience negative consequences (Compeau, Higgins, & Huff, 1999; Locke, 1976; Spector, 1997; Yi & Hwang, 2003). Two of these outcomes that we investigate in this study are job satisfaction, defined as a positive emotional state that results

DOI: 10.4018/978-1-60960-577-3.ch013

from how employees appraise their jobs and/or job experiences (Locke, 1976), and perceived technology work overload, defined as the extent to which perceptions of the technology related job performance required is excessive and feeling that computers have compounded the overall workload (Iverson, Deery, & Erwin, 1995). Not only are these outcomes important in and of themselves, but they have also been shown to be important predictors of other workplace consequences including turnover intentions, actual turnover, job performance, and health-related outcomes (e.g., Edmunds & Morris, 2000; Faragher, Cass, Cooper, 2005; Griffeth, Hom, & Gaertner, 2000; Judge, Thoresen, Bono, & Patton, 2001; Thatcher, Stepina, & Boyle, 2002) in a number of different samples including IT workers (e.g., Thatcher et al., 2002).

Although negative outcomes are likely to be associated with the dislike of computer work, there are factors in the workplace that may minimize or buffer (Ganster, Fusilier, & Mayes, 1986; Salanova, Peiro, & Schaufeli, 2002) these linkages. In particular, we examined how work-related support received from either the supervisor or an employee's coworkers will impact job satisfaction and perceived technology work overload. Both of these relationships are of considerable importance to computer workers, thus making the investigation of help received from these sources all the more necessary (e.g., Ferratt, Short, & Agarwal, 1993). Further, based on the social support framework (e.g., House, 1981; Viswesvaran, Sanchez, & Fisher, 1999) and the conservation of resources (COR) theory (Hobfoll, 1989), we expected that the dislike of computer work is related to job satisfaction and perceived technology work overload, and that receiving computer help from either the supervisor or coworkers will minimize these negative outcomes. Additionally, we hoped to determine whose (supervisor's or coworkers') support has a greater buffering impact. We explored these notions using a sample of 225 computer workers from a wide range of jobs, thus providing a more stringent test of these relationships across different workplaces and helping to establish the generalizability of our results.

LITERATURE REVIEW

Previous research has suggested and empirically shown that liking various aspects of one's work will be related to positive outcomes (e.g., Compeau et al., 1999; Shore, Newton, & Thornton, 2006; Spector, 1997). As is shown in Figure 1, we anticipate this to be especially true for computer workers and their like/dislike of computer work. We define "liking of computer work" as one's general affect toward all computer work rather than toward just one system (Sabherwal, Jayaraj, & Chowa, 2006). People who like computer work tend to be self-directed learners, seeking out new opportunities to innovate with technology, whereas people who dislike computer work tend not to engage in self-learning, and utilize less complex applications (Shaw, Lee-Partridge, & Ang, 2003). Although the like/dislike of computer work does not seem to directly influence the usage of a specific information system (Venkatesh, et al., 2003), if a computer worker enjoys his/her computer work, he/she is likely to be happy with the job and feel that the work he/she is performing is less overwhelming (e.g., Spector, 1997; Yi & Hwang, 2003). On the other hand, if a computer worker dislikes computer work, feelings of decreased job satisfaction and perceptions of computer-related work overload are likely to result (Hobfoll, 1989). We acknowledge that this notion has been tested in a number of different aspects of the work world, but this first set of hypotheses involve computer workers and their dislike of computer work, thus making these predictions unique. Additionally, these hypotheses lay the ground work for further predictions involving moderating factors, which is the more important contribution of this study. Based on all the above information, we predict that:

Figure 1. Theoretical Model of our Hypothesized Relationships

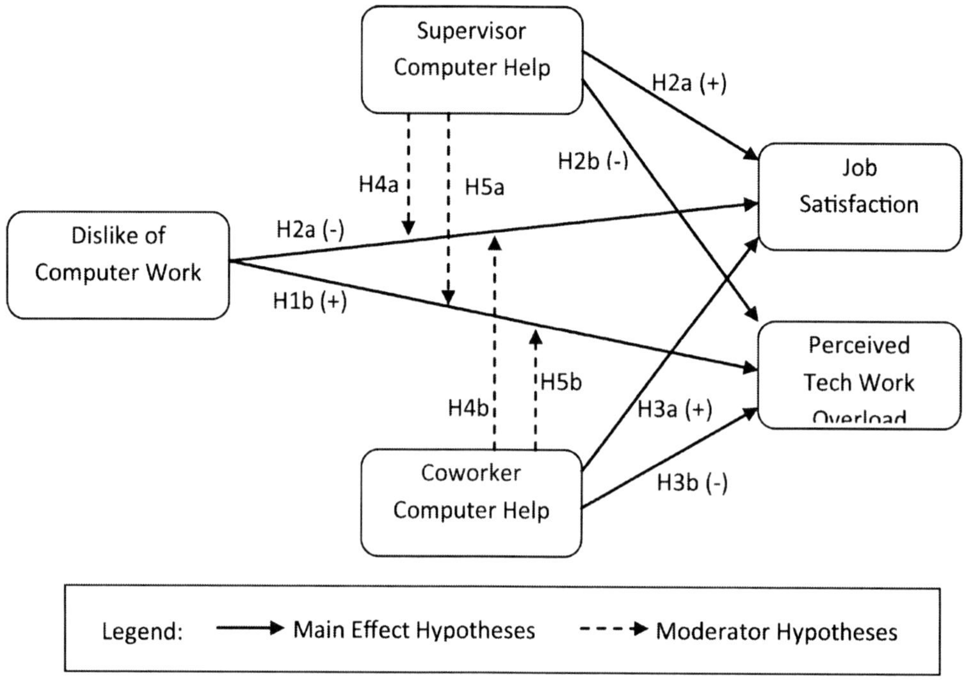

Hypothesis 1a: *Dislike of computer work is negatively associated with job satisfaction for individuals working more than 20 hours per week on a computer.*

Hypothesis 1b: *Dislike of computer work is positively associated with perceived technology work overload for individuals working more than 20 hours per week on a computer.*

Sources of Help on Computer Work

Although the amount an individual dislikes computer work is expected to be associated with job satisfaction and perceived technology work overload, situational variables also are likely to play a role in predicting these job outcomes. COR theory (Hobfoll, 1989, 2001) provides our framework for this prediction. The theory is based on the notion that individuals have valued resources that they seek to conserve and protect. In his 2001 publication, Hobfoll listed 74 COR resources that could be broken down into five overall categories: work resources (e.g., status or seniority at work), personal resources (e.g., feelings of achievement or optimism), material resources (e.g., financial stability), energy resources (e.g., time and effort), and interpersonal resources (e.g., companionship and feeling valuable to others). According to COR theory, when an individual's resources are threatened or are believed to be inadequate for handling a certain situation, negative outcomes (e.g., decreased job satisfaction and increased stress) are likely to result.

Following COR theory, we believe that personal and especially energy resources are likely to be threatened for workers who dislike computer work but are required to use information technology. However, computer help provided by others at the workplace is likely to provide individuals completing computer tasks with additional COR resources (e.g., time and energy, Hobfoll, 2001) and decrease the perceived threats from the dislike of computer work. Facilitating conditions, such as the availability of training programs, help desks, online assistance, and assistance from supervisors and coworkers, are a common source of help for computer workers.

Limayem and colleagues (2004) defined facilitating conditions in the realm of information technology as "those factors in the organization's environment that assist in the act of using a technology" (p.157). Prior research has linked the availability of facilitating conditions to user outcomes and perceptions, such as system usage, perceived ease-of-use, and perceived usefulness. For example, Venkatesh (2000) found that an employee's perceptions of facilitating conditions provided by his or her employer can help serve as a starting point for forming impressions of a system's ease of use, a point from which increasing experience with the system will eventually adjust those initial opinions of ease-of-use with more objective perceptions based on personal interaction. Likewise, the absence of facilitating conditions tends to make individuals aware of barriers to technology usage, as the resources for assistance are not available for users to draw from (Taylor & Todd, 1995). If a support network is available and is widely known to be offered, it should be of some importance to users, especially those who have just begun to use or intend to use the system. However, to our knowledge, prior research has not considered the influence of facilitating conditions on users who dislike working with technology. Thus, in the sections that follow, we examine the availability of computer help provided from two facilitating sources, an employee's supervisor and coworkers, as both direct predictors of job satisfaction and perceived technology work overload and as moderators of the dislike of computer work-outcome relationships.

Supervisor Computer Help

The supervisor-employee relationship is one of, if not the most important relationship an employee has in the workplace (Graen & Uhl-Bien, 1995; Manzoni & Barsoux, 2002). Supervisors often have considerable control over rewards, roles, assignments, and more (Yukl, 1989). Additionally, supervisors may be able and willing (or unwilling) to provide the work-related support that will help employees complete their jobs at a high level. COR theory suggests that receiving computer help with tasks at work, as well as support and understanding from a supervisor all provide employees with additional work resources (Hobfoll, 1989, 2001). As employees accumulate these resources, they are better able to handle stressful and challenging work events. Further, when an employee receives computer help from a supervisor, the individual expends less effort, time, and energy (all valued resources) (Hobfoll, 2001) in the process of completing work. Thus, for employees performing computer tasks, having access to computer help from a supervisor is likely to result in having greater amounts of resources and/or losing fewer resources, both of which will result in better outcomes (as shown in Figure 1). Thus, we predict that:

Hypothesis 2a: *Supervisor computer help is positively associated with job satisfaction for individuals working more than 20 hours per week on a computer.*

Hypothesis 2b: *Supervisor computer help is negatively associated with perceived technology work overload for individuals working more than 20 hours per week on a computer.*

Coworker Computer Help

Similar to the assistance provided by supervisors, positive associations are also expected when computer help is received from a coworker. The coworker provides a different source for computer related help. It is likely in many situations that coworkers, as opposed to supervisors, have a more intimate knowledge of the work being performed (e.g., Beehr, Jex, Stacy, & Murray, 2000). Additionally, individuals may not want to ask or let their supervisor know that they need assistance with computer related work (Deelstra, Peeters, & Zijlstra, 2003). Further, it may simply be more socially feasible to approach an expert coworker than to approach someone in a supervisory position (Spitler, 2005). For both of these reasons, employees who perceive their coworkers as a source of computer help are more likely to be satisfied with their jobs and less likely to experience perceived technology related work overload (as shown in Figure 1). Thus, we predict that:

Hypothesis 3a: *Coworker computer help is positively associated with job satisfaction for individuals working more than 20 hours per week on a computer.*

Hypothesis 3b: *Coworker computer help is negatively associated with perceived technology work overload for individuals working more than 20 hours per week on a computer.*

The Buffer Role of Receiving Computer Help for Those Who Dislike Computer Work

Although we suggest that the dislike of computer work and either supervisor or coworker computer help are independently associated with job satisfaction and perceived technology work overload, we also anticipate a synergistic (interactive) effect between the variables. A synergistic interaction occurs when "both predictors affect the (outcome) in the same direction, and together they produce a stronger than additive effect on the outcome" (Cohen, Cohen, West, & Aiken, 2003, p. 303). That is, it is not enough to simply like computer work or to have access to computer related help, but rather, it is the combination of the two that best predicts job satisfaction and perceived technology related overload. Additionally, as shown in Figure 1 we predict a buffering effect where computer help from either source can minimize the negative effects associated with the dislike of computer work. The specific nature of these interactions will be discussed in the section that follows.

Like/Dislike of Computer Work and Computer Help

In essence, the buffer hypothesis positions various kinds of support as moderators between stressors and work outcomes (i.e., individual strains) (Ganster et al., 1986; Parasuraman, Greenhaus, & Granrose, 1992; Salanova et al., 2002; Viswesvaran et al., 1999). In our study, the dislike of computer work, especially for a computer worker, can be viewed as a stressor. Thus, we suggest that computer help from either the supervisor or coworker will serve as a buffer for the negative outcomes associated with the dislike of computer work.

The COR theory (Hobfoll, 1989, 2001) can also be used as a lens for our predicted interaction. From a resource perspective, computer workers who dislike computer work will have to use more resources (energy, effort, time) and, as a result, the dislike of computer work is predicted to be negatively related to job satisfaction and positively related to perceived technology work overload. However, the availability of computer help (a facilitating condition) aids in offsetting the resource losses or actually helps to provide additional resources (Hobfoll & Freedy, 1993). As a result, we predict the most positive outcomes (highest job satisfaction and lowest perceived technology work overload) will result when the dislike of computer work is low and receiving computer work are both high, and that the negative relationships between the dislike of computer work and the positive outcomes will be weakest when employees receive computer help from either their supervisors or coworkers. Thus, we predict that:

Hypothesis 4a, 4b: *For individuals working more than 20 hours per week on a computer, supervisor*

(4a) or coworker (4b) computer help will moderate the negative relationship between dislike of computer work and job satisfaction, such that the negative relationship is weakest when computer help is highest.

Hypothesis 5a, 5b: *For individuals working more than 20 hours per week on a computer, supervisor (5a) or coworker (5b) computer help will moderate the positive relationship between dislike of computer work and perceived technology work overload such that positive relationship is strongest when computer help is lowest.*

Method

Sample and Procedure

The sample consisted of 225 full-time working individuals, each of whom worked at least 20 hours per week on a computer. These respondents worked in 133 different organizations. Respondents were recruited by members of a senior-level management class in a Midwestern university. Each student was given three surveys to distribute and have completed by individuals currently working full-time (at least 35 hours per week, and at least 20 of those hours had to be spent on a computer) in organizations with ten or more employees. In exchange for having the surveys completed by full-time employees, students received course credit. The respondents included a wide range of employees whose jobs require copious amounts of computer work, including lawyers, upper-levels managers, accountants, receptionists, service employees, teachers, and government workers.

This data collection technique and research design has been used successfully in a number of research efforts (e.g., Hochwarter, Kacmar, Perrewe, & Johnson, 2003; Rotondo, Carlson, & Kincaid, 2003; Treadway et al., 2004). Each survey contained a cover letter explaining that participants were being invited to participate in a study on workplace relationships, technology, and job attitudes. The respondents were required to provide the student's name on the first page of the survey and provide their phone numbers on the final page. To provide greater confidence in our findings, one of the authors randomly selected respondents to call and ask innocuous questions (e.g., "What section of the survey did you find to be the most interesting?"). Based on the responses to these questions, follow-up questions were asked about more objective information that was provided on the survey (i.e., "How many hours do you work per week?" or "How many coworkers do you regularly interact with?"), so that responses could be verified. Additionally, students were informed that if there were any questions or suspicions that the respondents did not complete the survey, no course credit would be given. This procedure did not reveal any instances of false responses. Although not foolproof, we believe that these measures helped to ensure the truthfulness of our responses.

In all, 303 surveys were distributed and we received complete data from 225 respondents (74% response rate), who worked in 133 different organizations. The demographic profile of our respondents is provided in Table 1. As can be seen, the sample was 39% male and 61% female, and the primary race of respondents was Caucasian (85.8%). The education levels varied, with the largest number (41.3%) of our respondents being college graduates. The average organizational tenure of our sample was 7.09 years, with the average job tenure of 4.90 years. The respondent ages ranged from 19 to 65 with a mean age of 37.12 years. On average, our respondents worked 41.4 hours per week, with 31.5 of those hours involving work on a computer.

Measures

Unless otherwise noted, responses to all of the items on the survey were provided by subjects using 5-point Likert scales. The anchors for the scales were "strongly disagree" (1) and "strongly

Table 1. Demographic Information of Respondents (N = 225)

		N	%
Gender	Male	88	39
	Female	137	61
Race	African-America	18	8.0
	Asian	1	0.4
	Caucasian	193	85.8
	Hispanic	8	3.6
	Other	5	2.2
Education	Some High School	0	0.0
	High School Graduate	29	12.9
	Some College	63	28.0
	College Graduate	93	41.3
	Graduate School	39	17.3
Organizational Tenure	Mean (SD)	7.09 (7.34)	
Job Tenure	Mean (SD)	4.90 (5.66)	
Age	Mean (SD)	37.12 (12.66)	
Computer Hours Worked Per Week	Mean (SD)	31.47 (10.00)	

agree" (5). The items in the scales were averaged to create an overall mean for each variable. The items were coded such that high values represent high levels of the constructs. A number of items, all of which are provided in the Appendix, in this study were specially developed for this research project, as scales did not exist to measure the desired variables.

- ***Like/dislike of computer work*.** To measure the like/dislike of computer work, we developed five items which are provided in the Appendix. A sample item was "Working on a computer is something I enjoy." The alpha reliability for this scale was.88. The scale was coded such that higher values represent higher levels of liking computer work.
- ***Supervisor computer help*.** To measure the perceived availability of supervisor computer help, we developed three items, all of which are shown in the Appendix. We were forced to develop these items after examining the extant literature on helping behaviors and found no scale that was intended for asking about or easily adapted to measure sources of computer help (e.g., Frenkel & Sanders, 2007; Van Dyne & Lepine, 1998). A sample item was "My supervisor will help me with any computer-related problems I have." The alpha reliability for this scale was.91.
- ***Coworker computer help*.** The same three-item scale used to examine supervisor computer help was used to examine the perceived availability of coworker computer help, with the word "coworkers" in place of the word "supervisor". These items are provided in the Appendix. The alpha reliability for this scale was.90.
- ***Job satisfaction*.** Cammann, Fichman, Jenkins, and Klesh's (1979) 3-item scale, which is provided in the Appendix, from the Organizational Assessment Questionnaire was used to measure job satisfaction. This scale has been used in

a considerable number of research studies in a number of different contexts. The extant research has found this measure to be a psychometrically sound measure of an employee's overall affective evaluation of his/her job. After the scale's development, it was validated in a series of studies that were administered to thousands of employees (Cook, Hepworth, Wall, & Warr, 1981). Although this scale was developed and validated many years ago, more recent research (e.g., Babette & Beehr, 2003) has shown this scale to be both reliable and valid. A sample item was "All in all, I am satisfied with my job. The alpha reliability for this scale was.94.

- ***Perceived technology work overload.*** Perceived technology work overload was measured with four items specially developed for this study. The Appendix shows all four of these items. A sample item was "Technology and computer-related information have increased my overall workload." The alpha reliability for this scale was.83.

To validate the measurement model, we first assessed the convergent validity of the five constructs. In addition to the inter-item reliabilities reported above, the average variance extracted, or AVE, values for each of the constructs were above 0.5, all of which provides evidence of convergent validity (Fornell & Larcker, 1981). Discriminant validity is determined by examining the square root of the AVE for each construct to compare with the inter-construct correlations, all of which are displayed in Table 3. The square roots of the AVE for each construct are larger than the correlations with other constructs, indicating the measurement model contained sufficient discriminant validity (Fornell & Larcker, 1981). Other evidence of measurement validity is provided by the factor loadings and cross-loadings produced by confirmatory factory analysis, which are displayed in Table 2. Each item loaded higher on the appropriate construct than on any other constructs, which further demonstrates convergent and discriminant validity (Chin, 1998). Finally, we checked for multicollinearity between the variables, and we determined there was none for two reasons. First, the largest correlation between two variables was 0.51 between supervisor help and coworker help, which is less than the level of concern, 0.70 (Tabachnick & Fidell, 1996). Second, the variance inflation factor (VIF) values for all the variables ranged between 1.098 and 1.397, well below the VIF level of 10.0 which hints at multicollinearity.

Control Variables

In this study we controlled for six variables. These variables were gender (males = 1, females = 2), organizational tenure (measured in years), age (measured in years), education, computer hours worked per week, and computer hours worked per week as a percentage of the whole (calculated by dividing computer hours worked per week by total hours worked per week). We controlled for these variables to help minimize or eliminate any spurious relationships with our outcomes, as these variables have been previously shown to be related to job satisfaction and/or perceptions of work overload (Spector, 1997).

Analysis Technique

Hierarchical moderated regression analyses were used to test the hypotheses. We conducted separate analyses for each of the two outcome variables and for each of the different sources of computer help. This resulted in four separate analyses. In the first step, we entered the control variables of gender, organizational tenure, age, education, computer hours worked per week, and computer hours worked per week as a percentage of the whole. The centered (Aiken & West, 1991) like/dislike of computer work term was entered in step 2 and it was in this step that we tested Hypotheses

Table 3. Means, Standard Deviations, and Correlations among the Study Variables

Variable	Mean	SD	1	2	3	4	5	6	7	8	9	10	11
1. Gender	1.61	.49	-										
2. Organizational Tenure	7.09	7.34	-.00	-									
3. Age	37.12	12.66	-.01	.60**	-								
4. Education	3.62	.92	-.11	-.13*	-.05	-							
5. Computer Hrs Worked Per Week	31.47	10.00	-.02	.02	-.07	.08	-						
6. Computer Hrs Out of Whole Hrs Worked	.76	.31	-.02	-.10	-.14*	-.03	.79**	-					
7. Liking of Computer Work	4.00	.73	-.02	-.04	-.04	-.03	.14*	.23**	**.82**				
8. Supervisor Computer Help	3.72	.92	.02	-.16**	-.21**	-.04	.08	.22**	.27**	**.88**			
9. Coworker Computer Help	3.88	.78	-.01	-.06	-.06	.05	.02	.17**	.26**	.51**	**.86**		
10. Job Satisfaction	4.04	.81	-.05	.03	.11	.13*	-.04	.03	.21**	.21**	.25**	**.92**	
11. Perc. Tec. Work Overload	3.37	.89	-.06	.14*	-.01	.05	.24**	.16**	-.05	-.03	-.10	-.09	**.81**

N = 225. Note: Hrs = Hours; * $p < .05$. ** $p < .01$. The bolded numbers in the diagonal are square roots of the average variance extracted (AVE).

1a and 1b. In step 3 in each of the analyses, we entered either the centered supervisor computer help (where we tested Hypotheses 2a and 2b) or the centered coworker computer help term (where we tested Hypotheses 3a and 3b). In the fourth and final step, we entered the interaction terms formed between the like of computer work and either of the sources of computer help. It was in this final step that we tested Hypotheses 4a, 4b, 5a, and 5b.

Results

Means, standard deviations, and correlations among the study variables are shown in Table 3. As can be seen, the control variables of gender, organizational tenure, age, and education were not significantly correlated with dislike of computer work. Additionally, we tested for any differences in dislike of computer work between the categorical variable of gender (males vs. females), as well as the ordinal variable of education. Our findings revealed no significant differences. As expected, the liking of computer work was significantly and positively correlated with job satisfaction, but surprisingly it was not negatively correlated with perceived technology work overload. These results point to the importance of examining an employee's like/dislike of computer work and potential moderating variables of the like/dislike of computer work-outcome associations.

Results of the hierarchical moderated regression analysis are presented in Table 4. There are four separate analyses, labeled Analysis 1-4, with steps 1 and 2 repeated for each outcome variable (i.e., steps 1 and 2 are the same in Analyses 1 and 3, and steps 1 and 2 are the same in Analyses 2 and 4), before new variables are introduced in steps 3 and 4. For this reason, when discussing steps 1 and 2, we will refer to Analyses 1 and 2. As the table indicates, the control variables in Analysis 1 step 1 explained 5% of the variance in job satisfaction and in Analysis 2 step 1 9% of the variance in perceived technology work

Table 2. Factor Analysis

	Computer Liking	Supervisor Help	Coworker Help	Job Satisfaction	Tech Overload
LIKE1	**.85**	.05	.06	.19	-.05
LIKE2	**.79**	.14	-.01	.03	.01
LIKE3	**.87**	.06	.05	.06	-.07
LIKE4	**.86**	.09	.11	.02	-.03
LIKE5	**.74**	.07	.19	.05	.07
SUPHELP1	.14	**.91**	.24	.03	-.02
SUPHELP2	.05	**.86**	.24	.12	-.01
SUPHELP3	.20	**.87**	.21	.10	-.01
COWHELP1	.09	.21	**.87**	.01	-.09
COWHELP2	.13	.24	**.87**	.21	-.02
COWHELP3	.14	.26	**.84**	.13	-.02
JOBSAT1	.09	.08	.13	**.94**	-.06
JOBSAT2	.07	.09	.14	**.93**	-.06
JOBSAT3	.12	.05	.04	**.91**	-.01
OVERLOAD1	.09	.05	-.03	.01	**.84**
OVERLOAD2	.03	-.01	-.06	-.02	**.86**
OVERLOAD3	-.13	-.01	-.06	-.06	**.72**
OVERLOAD4	-.04	-.08	.03	-.04	**.81**

overload. In Analysis 1 with job satisfaction as the dependent variable, gender, organizational tenure, and age were not significantly related to the outcome, but education, computer hours worked per week and computer hours worked per week as a percentage of the whole were significantly related. In particular, higher levels of education, working fewer hours per week on a computer, and completing more computer hours per week as a percentage of the whole workweek were all associated with higher levels of job satisfaction. In Analysis 2 with perceived technology work overload as the dependent variable, the only significant controls were organizational tenure and computer hours worked per week, which were both positively associated with higher levels of the outcome.

Step 2 in Analysis 1 shows that the dislike of computer work was negatively associated with job satisfaction (β =.26, p <.01, ΔR^2 =.04), but as shown in Analysis 2 step 2, it was not significantly associated with perceived technology work overload. These results provide support for Hypothesis 1a, but not 1b. The results from step 3 in Analysis 1 show that supervisor computer help was positively related to job satisfaction (β =.17, p <.01, ΔR^2 =.04), but step 3 in Analysis 2 shows it was not significantly related to perceived technology work overload. Thus, Hypothesis 2a was supported, but Hypothesis 2b was not. Also in step 3, Analysis 3 houses the results showing that coworker computer help was positively associated with job satisfaction (β =.21, p <.01, ΔR^2 =.04), Analysis 4 step 3 shows there was not a significant association with perceived technology work overload. These findings support Hypothesis 3a, but fail to support Hypothesis 3b.

Finally, step 4 provides the results for the interaction between the like of computer work and the different sources of computer help. Our results

Table 4. Hierarchical Moderated Regression Results for the Interaction of Liking Computer Work and Help from Different Sources

	Analysis 1			*Analysis 2*			*Analysis 3*			*Analysis 4*		
	Hypothesis 1a: Step 2 Hypothesis 2a: Step 3 Hypothesis 4a: Step 4			Hypothesis 1b: Step 2 Hypothesis 2b: Step 3 Hypothesis 5a: Step 4			Hypothesis 3a: Step 3 Hypothesis 4b: Step 4			Hypothesis 3b: Step 3 Hypothesis 5b: Step 4		
	DV = Job Satisfaction			*DV = Perceived Technology Work Overload*			*DV = Job Satisfaction*			*DV = Perceived Technology Work Overload*		
Variables	*B*	R^2	ΔR^2	*B*	R^2	ΔR^2	*B*	R^2	ΔR^2	*B*	R^2	ΔR^2
Step 1: Control Variables Gender Organizational Tenure Age Education Comp. Hrs/Week Comp. Hrs. of Whole	-.06 .00 .01 .14* -.01* .27*	.05	.05	-.10 .03* -.01 .05 .02* .03	.09	**.09****	-.06 .00 .01 .14* -.01* .27*	.05	.05	-.10 .03* -.01 .05 .02* .03	.09	**.09****
Step 2: Independent Variable LIKING (A)	.26**	.09	.04**	-.04	.10	**.01**	.26**	.09	.04**	-.04	.10	**.01**
Step 3: Moderator SUPHELP (B) COWHELP (C)	.17**	.13	.04**	-.02	.10	**.00**	.21**	.13	.04**	-.09	.11	**.01**
Step 4: Interaction A*B A*C	.21**	.17	.04**	.19*	.13	**.03***	.06	.13	.00	.12+	.12	**.01+**

N = 225. + p<.10. * *p*<.05. **p<.01. *Note:* Standardized regression coefficients from the last step.

Comp. Hrs/Week = Computer Hours Worked per Week, Comp. Hrs. of Whole = Computer Hours out of Whole Hours, LIKING = Liking of Computer Work, SUPHELP = Supervisor Computer Help, COWHELP = Coworker Computer Help.

showed that the like of computer work*supervisor computer help interaction term was a significant predictor in Analysis 1 of job satisfaction ($\beta = .21$, $p < .01$, $\Delta R^2 = .04$) and in Analysis 2 of perceived technology work overload ($\beta = .19$, $p < .05$, $\Delta R^2 = .03$). The term reflecting the interaction between the like of computer work and help from coworkers did not significantly predict job satisfaction in Analysis 3, but it was a moderately significant predictor of perceived technology work overload ($\beta = .12$, $p < .10$, $\Delta R^2 = .01$) in Analysis 4. Thus, we did not find support for Hypothesis 4b. To determine support for our significant interactions, we needed to graph the relationships. We did so by plotting two lines, one at one standard deviation (SD) above the mean and one at one SD below the mean (Stone & Hollenbeck, 1989). Figure 2 shows that the positive association between the like of computer work and job satisfaction was strongest when supervisor computer help was highest. These findings provide strong support for Hypothesis 4a. Figure 3 illustrates that the negative relationship between the like of computer work and perceived technology work overload was weakest when supervisor computer help was high. In fact, when supervisor computer help was high, the like of computer work-perceived technology work overload linkage was positive. This form of the interaction provides strong support for Hypothesis 5a. The final significant interaction is shown in Figure 4. This graph shows that the negative association between the like of computer work and perceived technology work overload was weakest when coworker computer help was highest. These results provide support for Hypothesis 5b.

DISCUSSION

This study had three purposes: to investigate the relations between the like of computer work and the outcomes of job satisfaction and perceived technology work overload, the associations between supervisor and coworker computer help on these same outcomes, and to examine either supervisor or coworker computer help as a moderator of the like of computer work – consequence relationships. Overall, we found that like/dislike of computer work and supervisor computer help were both related to job satisfaction. This finding is noteworthy as job satisfaction has been shown to be related to a number of important organizational outcomes including turnover and job performance (e.g., Griffeth, Hom, & Gaertner, 2000). In terms of the COR theory, when employees like computer work they are likely to expend fewer resources (Hobfoll, 1989) and as a result have increased job satisfaction. Similarly, when supervisors provide computer help (a facilitating condition), they are increasing the resource reservoirs for their subordinates, which ultimately leads to higher job satisfaction. An alternative explanation that is worth mentioning may be that job satisfaction levels can be inflated due to employees submitting socially-desirable responses when receiving increased attention from supervisors (i.e., the Hawthorne effect). It is unclear whether that occurred in this study, but either way, the increase in job satisfaction is an important finding that managers should be cognizant of. A further implication from our findings is the fact that supervisor computer help and not coworker computer help has a main effect on job satisfaction, as this result should help to guide organizational decisions in terms of training supervisors and making sure they are competent, able, and willing to provide help to their employees who work on computers.

Surprisingly, none of the main effects were significant predictors of perceived technology work overload. Some possible reasons for the non-significant findings might be that we need to examine not only main effects, but interactive effects to predict perceived technology work overload. For example, the amount of help received from a supervisor or coworker might not be associated with perceived technology work overload if the work is easy, an individual received considerable training (i.e., less help is needed),

Figure 2. Interaction between Liking of Computer Work and Supervisor Computer Help on Job Satisfaction

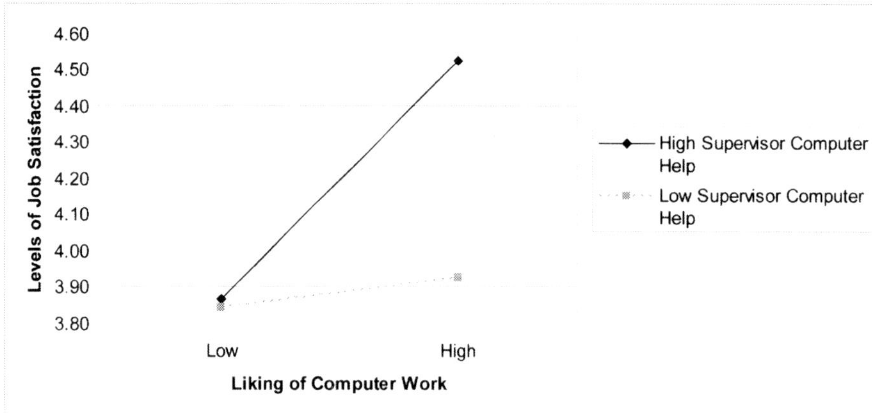

Figure 3. Interaction between Liking of Computer Work and Supervisor Computer Help on Perceived Technology Work Overload

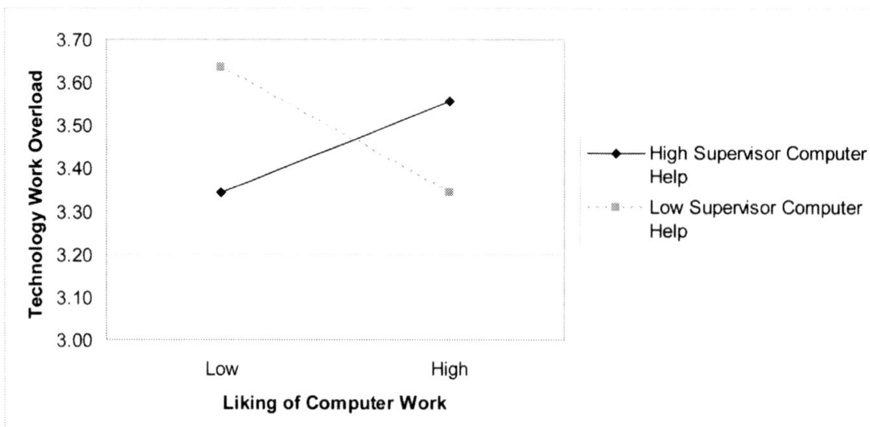

Figure 4. Interaction between Liking of Computer Work and Coworker Computer Help on Perceived Technology Work Overload

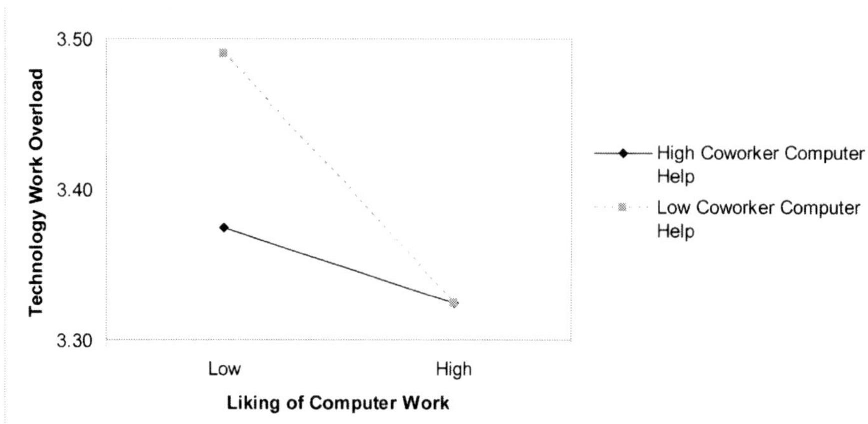

or he/she greatly enjoys computer work. These are all post hoc explanations that we hope future researchers will examine to help determine why we found these non-significant effects. With all that being said, it makes the examination of the interactions predicted in Hypotheses 4 and 5 all the more important.

To us, the more interesting findings from this study relate to the interactions between the like of computer work and the reception of computer help from either the supervisor or coworker. In terms of the like of computer work - job satisfaction relationship, coworker computer help was not a significant moderator, but supervisor computer help was. The form of this interaction showed that there were essentially no differences in job satisfaction levels when the like of computer work was low, but a synergistic effect (Cohen et al., 2003) when the like of computer work was high. In particular, the highest job satisfaction levels occurred when both the like of computer work and supervisor computer help were high. Thus, it is not enough to just like computer work, but an employee must also receive computer help from his/her supervisor to experience the highest job satisfaction levels. Recent work has speculated that managerial influence similar to that described in the current should facilitate improved computer user competency (Eschenbrenner & Nah, 2008). One could surmise that job satisfaction and task competency are likely to be highly correlated for workers who like using computers.

The interactions predicting perceived technology work overload show that high levels of either supervisor or coworker computer help are able to buffer (Ganster et al., 1986) the negative effects from the dislike of computer work. The nature of these interactions shows that the highest levels of perceived technology work overload (the worst outcome) result when the dislike of computer work is high and employees receive minimal computer help from either their supervisor or coworkers. On the flipside, when the dislike of computer work is high, but the reception of computer help is high, feelings of perceived technology work overload are considerably lower. These findings show that computer help from either source is able to buffer the negative effect from the dislike of computer work. From the COR perspective, receiving computer help from either source provides additional resources, resulting in the employee expending less time and energy and thus perceiving lower levels of perceived technology work overload (Hobfoll, 1989). These results are important for both theory and practical managerial behaviors, and lead to the question of how these interactions impact other outcome variables, as well as if other sources of computer help exhibit similar moderating effects. We will discuss both of these ideas in further detail in the directions for future research section.

Practical Implications

The findings from our study have practical implications for managers. One is the importance that employees who complete a majority of their work using computers actually liking computer work. This may seem basic, but when these individuals dislike computer work, their job satisfaction levels were significantly lower. Thus, managers should make every effort to increase the liking of computer work for those working on computers. Some potential ways to do this include providing computer training to increase computer self-efficacy (Torkzadeh, Pflughoeft, & Hall, 1999; Torkzadeh & Van Dyke, 2002), as well as positive feedback to employees after they work on their computers (Azevedo & Bernard, 1995). Additionally, managers should be cognizant of and, when possible, select employees to work on computers who enjoy working on computers.

Another practical application from our findings relates to the importance of receiving computer help from supervisors and coworkers at work. Our results showed that the availability of coworker computer help was valuable, but that supervisor computer help had a more powerful impact. Based on these findings, managers should be sure to inform supervisors of their vital role for computer workers. There is an abundance of research on the importance of supervisors communicating, providing clear expectations, listening, directing, being fair, and more (Yukl, 1989), but minimal research has shown the considerable help supervisors can provide to employees who work on computers. Additionally, not only should supervisors be informed of their important role, but they should also be able to facilitate helping employees when it does not take away from other aspects of their jobs, and they should seek training to continually improve their own computer skills, which would better enable them to help their employees (Sein, Bostrom, & Olfman, 1999).

Limitations and Suggestions for Future Research

Although this study has a number of strengths and makes a contribution to the extant literature, there are limitations that must be discussed to properly interpret the study's results. First, our research design was unable to test for causality, thus bringing about the potential that job satisfaction or perceived technology overload levels may actually lead to the like/dislike of computer work. However, we suggest that our predicted relationships are more in line with theory and existing research. Two other limitations relate to our data collection method and our research design. In the data collection process, we relied on students to help gather the data. To help ensure the truthfulness of responses, we employed certain techniques (see the Sample and Procedure section), but still must acknowledge that our reliance on students for data collection is a limitation of the study. The limitation related to our research design is that all of our data were collected from the same source, that is, the same individuals provided responses on the independent variables, moderators, and outcome variables. As a result, our results may have been influenced by common method variance (CMV) (Malhotra, Kim, & Patil, 2006; Podsakoff, MacKenzie, Lee, & Podsakoff, 2003). We acknowledge that this may be the case, but the relatively low correlations between our study variables suggest CMV was a minimal concern in this study (Spector, 2006). Additionally, previous research has shown that CMV actually decreases the probability of finding significant interaction effects (Wall, Jackson, Mullarkey, & Parker, 1996), which serves to strengthen our confidence in the significant interaction effects found in this study.

Another limitation is that our main effect and interaction findings did not explain large amounts of variance. Although small, we feel the results from our study are important, and previous research efforts have found that variance explained of less than 1% can still have considerable financial impacts for companies (e.g., Fichman, 1999). An additional limitation is that we did not examine the nature of computer work. In particular, the work completed on a computer, and the resulting outcomes, are likely to differ based on the industry (e.g., manufacturing vs. service) and the type of task being completed, such as if the tasks are transaction-based or decision-support based. Thus, we hope future researchers will extend our study's findings and examine these important potential contingency variables.

A final limitation relates to our sample, which had subjects from a wide range of industries and occupations, thus preventing us from "controlling" for more company specific information (top management effects, history of computers at the workplace, IT training classes, etc.). However, we view the range of our respondents as a strength, as the results are not specific to a certain company or industry, but relate to employees in general. That withstanding, one area for future research is to examine the variables and relationships hypothesized in this study in an organizational sample. In particular, samples from public, private, service, manufacturing, and military organizations would provide additional insights and help to establish the generalizability and/or boundary conditions of our results.

Another direction for future research is to investigate other outcome variables. In this study we examined job satisfaction and perceived technology work overload. However, some other interesting outcomes include desire to stay on the job, desire to remain with the organization, work-family conflict, and satisfaction with other aspects of the job (coworkers, supervisor, pay, technology, etc.) (Ahuja, Chudoba, Kacmar, McKnight, & George, 2007; Griffeth et al., 2000; Moore, 2000). Researchers should also examine other independent variables in predicting the outcomes in this research effort. This study examined the liking of computer work and accessible computer help from multiple sources, but there is a need to investigate personality and other individual difference variables that may help to explain the consequences examined (e.g., LeRouge, Nelson, & Blanton, 2006). Another avenue for future research would be to better determine if the computer work received was actually helpful. In our study, we made this assumption, but future studies employing either a qualitative or quantitative design could better determine if this is in fact the case. A final direction for future research is to examine other sources of computer help and facilitating conditions. Our investigation of supervisor and coworker computer help was important, as these are two proximal sources of help and they are important relationships for completing work. Nonetheless, research efforts examining computer help received from information technology staff, training centers, and other individuals would shed light on these relationships. Additionally, it may be fruitful to investigate the impacts of other factors involved in computer work, like formal and informal training programs (including e-training), the amount of autonomy workers have when using the computer, and the time and tenure workers have using the same computer system, to determine if these other variables exhibit moderating or mediating roles in the relationships examined in this study.

CONCLUSION

This study set out to examine how individuals like or dislike of computer work and help received from supervisors and coworkers were associated with the outcomes of job satisfaction and perceived technology work overload. We found that liking of computer work was associated with job satisfaction, and that computer help from a supervisor moderated the liking-outcome relationships. These findings are insightful, as they show the importance of receiving computer related help from a supervisor, and we hope will spur additional research on these topics.

REFERENCES

Ahuja, M., Chudoba, K. M., Kacmar, C., McKnight, D. H., & George, J. F. (2007). IT road warriors: Balancing work-family conflict, job autonomy, and work overload to mitigate turnover intention. *Management Information Systems Quarterly*, *31*(1), 1–17.

Aiken, L. S., & West, S. G. (1991). *Multiple regression: Testing and interpreting interactions*. Thousand Oaks: Sage.

Avezedo, R., & Bernard, R. M. (1995). A meta-analysis of the effects of feedback in computer-based instruction. *Journal of Educational Computing Research*, *13*, 111–127. doi:10.2190/9LMD-3U28-3A0G-FTQT

Babette, R., & Beehr, T. A. (2003). Formal mentoring versus supervisor and coworker relationships: differences in perceptions and impact. *Journal of Organizational Behavior*, *24*, 271–293. doi:10.1002/job.193

Beehr, T. A., Jex, S. M., Stacy, B. A., & Murray, M. A. (2000). Work stressors and coworker support as predictors of individual strain and job performance. *Journal of Organizational Behavior, 21*, 391–405. doi:10.1002/(SICI)1099-1379(200006)21:4<391::AID-JOB15>3.0.CO;2-9

Cammann, C., Fichman, M., Jenkins, D., & Klesh, J. (1979). *The Michigan organizational assessment questionnaire*. Ann Arbor, MI: University of Michigan.

Chin, W. W. (1998). The partial least squares approach to structural equation modeling. In G.A. Marcoulides (Ed.), Modern methods for business research: 295-336. Mahway, NJ: Lawrence Erlbaum Associates.

Cohen, J., Cohen, P., West, S., & Aiken, L. (2003). *Applied multiple regression/correlation analysis for the behavioral sciences* (3rd ed.). Hillsdale, NJ: Lawrence Erlbaum Associates.

Compeau, D., Higgins, C. A., & Huff, S. (1999). Social cognitive theory and individual reactions to computing technology: A longitudinal study. *Management Information Systems Quarterly, 23*, 145–158. doi:10.2307/249749

Cook, J. D., Hepworth, S. J., Wall, T. D., & Warr, P. B. (1981). *The experience of work*. New York: Academic Press.

Deelstra, J. T., Peeters, M. C., & Zijlstra, F. R. (2003). Receiving instrumental support at work: When help is not welcome. *The Journal of Applied Psychology, 88*(2), 324–331. doi:10.1037/0021-9010.88.2.324

Edmunds, A., & Morris, A. (2000). The problem of information overload in business organizations: A review of the literature. *International Journal of Information Management, 20*(1), 17–28. doi:10.1016/S0268-4012(99)00051-1

Eschenbrenner, B., & Nah, F. F. (2008). Understanding factors influencing proficient information systems usage. Proceedings of the 2008 Americas Conference on Information Systems, Toronto, ON.

Faragher, E. B., Cass, M., & Cooper, C. L. (2005). The relationship between job satisfaction and health: A meta-analysis. *Occupational and Environmental Medicine, 62*, 105–112. doi:10.1136/oem.2002.006734

Ferratt, T. W., Short, L. E., & Agarwal, R. (1993). Measuring the information systems supervisor's work-unit environment and demonstrated skill at supervising. *Journal of Management Information Systems, 9*(4), 121–144.

Fichman, M. (1999). Variance explained: Why size does not (always) matter. *Research in Organizational Behavior, 21*, 295–331.

Fornell, C., & Larcker, D. (1981). Structural equation models with unobservable variables and measurement errors. *JMR, Journal of Marketing Research, 18*(2), 39–50. doi:10.2307/3151312

Frenkel, S. J., & Sanders, K. (2007). Explaining variations in co-worker assistance in organizations. *Organization Studies, 28*, 797–823. doi:10.1177/0170840607073079

Ganster, D. C., Fusilier, M. R., & Mayes, B. T. (1986). Role of social support in the experience of stress at work. *The Journal of Applied Psychology, 71*, 102–110. doi:10.1037/0021-9010.71.1.102

Graen, G. B., & Uhl-Bien, M. (1995). Development of leader-member exchange (LMX) theory of leadership over 25 years: Applying a multi-level multi-domain perspective. *The Leadership Quarterly, 6*, 219–247. doi:10.1016/1048-9843(95)90036-5

Griffeth, R., Hom, P., & Gaertner, S. (2000). A meta-analysis of antecedents and correlates of employee turnover: Update, moderator tests, and research implications for the next millennium. *Journal of Management, 26*, 463–488. doi:10.1177/014920630002600305

Hobfoll, S., & Freedy, J. (1993). Conservation of resources: A general stress theory applied to burnout. In W. Schaufeli & C. Maslach & T. Marek (Eds.), Professional burnout: Recent developments in theory and practice: 115-129. Washington D.C.: Taylor & Francis.

Hobfoll, S. E. (1989). Conservation of resources: A new attempt at conceptualizing stress. *The American Psychologist*, *44*, 513–524. doi:10.1037/0003-066X.44.3.513

Hobfoll, S. E. (2001). The influence of culture, community, and the nested-self in the stress process: Advancing conservation of resources theory. *Applied Psychology: An International Review*, *50*, 337–421. doi:10.1111/1464-0597.00062

Hochwarter, W., Kacmar, C., Perrewe, P., & Johnson, D. (2003). Perceived organizational support as a mediator of the relationship between politics perceptions and work outcomes: A multi-level analysis. *Journal of Vocational Behavior*, *63*, 438–456. doi:10.1016/S0001-8791(02)00048-9

House, R. J. (1981). *Work stress and social support*. Reading, MA: Addison-Wesley.

Iverson, R. D., Deery, S. J., & Erwin, P. J. (1995). Absenteeism in the health services sector: A casual model and intervention strategies. In Riedel, P., & Preston, A. (Eds.), *Managing absenteeism: Analysing and preventing labour absence*. Canberra: AGPS.

Judge, T. A., Thoresen, C. J., Bono, J. E., & Patton, G. K. (2001). The job satisfaction-job performance relationship: A qualitative and quantitative review. *Psychological Bulletin*, *127*(3), 376–407. doi:10.1037/0033-2909.127.3.376

LeRouge, C., Nelson, A., & Blanton, J. E. (2006). The impact of role stress fit and self-esteem on the job attitudes of IT professionals. *Information & Management*, *43*, 928–938. doi:10.1016/j.im.2006.08.011

Limayem, M., Khalifa, M., & Chin, W. W. (2004). CASE tools usage and impact on system development performance. *Journal of Organizational Computing and Electronic Commerce*, *14*, 153–174. doi:10.1207/s15327744joce1403_01

Locke, E. A. (1976). The nature and causes of job satisfaction. In Dunnette, M. (Ed.), *The handbook of industrial/organizational psychology* (1st ed., pp. 1297–1349). Chicago: Rand McNally.

Malhotra, N. K., Kim, S. S., & Patil, A. (2006). Common method variance in IS research: A comparison of alternative approaches and a reanalysis of past research. *Management Science*, *52*, 1865–1883. doi:10.1287/mnsc.1060.0597

Manzoni, J., & Barsoux, J. (2002). *The set-up-to-fail syndrome. How good managers cause great people to fail.* Boston: Harvard Business School Press.

Moore, J. E. (2000). One road to turnover: An examination of work exhaustion in technology professionals. *Management Information Systems Quarterly*, *24*(1), 141–168. doi:10.2307/3250982

Parasuraman, S., Greenhaus, J. H., & Granrose, C. S. (1992). Role stressors, social support, and well-being among two-career couples. *Journal of Organizational Behavior*, *13*, 339–356. doi:10.1002/job.4030130403

Podsakoff, P. M., MacKenzie, S. B., Lee, J.-Y., & Podsakoff, N. P. (2003). Common method biases in behavioral research: A critical review of the literature and recommended remedies. *The Journal of Applied Psychology*, *88*, 879–903. doi:10.1037/0021-9010.88.5.879

Rotondo, D., Carlson, D., & Kincaid, J. (2003). Coping with multiple dimensions of work-family conflict. *Personnel Review*, *32*, 275–297. doi:10.1108/00483480310467606

Sabherwal, R., Jeyaraj, A., & Chowa, C. (2006). Information system success: Individual and organizational determinants. *Management Science*, *52*(12), 1849–1864. doi:10.1287/mnsc.1060.0583

Salanova, M., Peiro, J. M., & Schaufeli, W. B. (2002). Self-efficacy specificity and burnout among information technology workers: An extension of the job demand-control model. *European Journal of Work and Organizational Psychology*, *11*, 1–25. doi:10.1080/13594320143000735

Sein, M. K., Bostrom, R. P., & Olfman, L. (1999). Rethinking end-user training strategy: Applying a hierarchical knowledge-level model. *Journal of End User Computing*, *11*, 32–39.

Shaw, N., Lee-Partridge, J., & Ang, J. (2003). Understanding the hidden dissatisfaction of users toward end-user computing. *Journal of End User Computing*, *15*, 1–22. doi:10.4018/joeuc.2003040101

Shore, L. M., Newton, L. A., & Thornton, G. C. (2006). Job and organizational attitudes in relation to employee behavioral intentions. *Journal of Organizational Behavior*, *11*, 57–67. doi:10.1002/job.4030110108

Spector, P. (2006). Method variance in organizational research. *Organizational Research Methods*, *9*, 221–232. doi:10.1177/1094428105284955

Spector, P. E. (1997). *Job satisfaction*. Thousand Oaks, CA: Sage.

Spitler, V. (2005). Learning to use IT in the workplace: Mechanisms and masters. *Journal of Organizational and End User Computing*, *17*, 1–25. doi:10.4018/joeuc.2005040101

Stone, E. F., & Hollenbeck, J. R. (1989). Clarifying some controversial issues surrounding statistical procedures for detecting moderating variables: Empirical evidence and related matters. *The Journal of Applied Psychology*, *74*, 3–10. doi:10.1037/0021-9010.74.1.3

Tabachnick, B., & Fidell, L. (1996). *Using multivariate statistics*. New York: HarperCollins.

Taylor, S., & Todd, P. A. (1995). Understanding information technology usage – A test of competing models. *Information Systems Research*, *6*, 144–176. doi:10.1287/isre.6.2.144

Thatcher, J. B., Stepina, L. P., & Boyle, R. J. (2002). Turnover of information technology workers: Examining empirically the influence of attitudes, job characteristics, and external markets. *Journal of Management Information Systems*, *19*(3), 231–261.

Torkzadeh, G., & Van Dyke, T. P. (2002). Effects of training on internet self-efficacy and computer user attitudes. *Computers in Human Behavior*, *18*, 479–494. doi:10.1016/S0747-5632(02)00010-9

Torkzadeh, R., Pflughoeft, K., & Hall, L. (1999). Computer self-efficacy, training effectiveness, and user attitudes: An empirical study. *Behaviour & Information Technology*, *18*, 299–309. doi:10.1080/014492999119039

Treadway, D. C., Hochwarter, W., Ferris, G. R., Kacmar, C. J., Douglas, C., Ammeter, A. P., & Buckley, M. R. (2004). Leader political skill and employee reactions. *The Leadership Quarterly*, *15*, 493–513. doi:10.1016/j.leaqua.2004.05.004

Van Dyne, L., & Lepine, J. A. (1998). Helping and voice extra-role behaviors: Evidence of construct and predictive validity. *Academy of Management Journal*, *41*, 108–119. doi:10.2307/256902

Venkatesh, V. (2000). Determinants of perceived ease of use: Integrating control, intrinsic motivation, and emotion into the technology acceptance model. *Information Systems Research*, *11*, 342–365. doi:10.1287/isre.11.4.342.11872

Venkatesh, V., Morris, M., Davis, G. B., & Davis, F. D. (2003). User acceptance of information technology: Toward a unified view. *Management Information Systems Quarterly*, *27*(3), 425–478.

Viswesvaran, C., Sanchez, J. I., & Fisher, J. (1999). The role of social support in the process of work stress: A meta-analysis. *Journal of Vocational Behavior*, *54*, 314–334. doi:10.1006/jvbe.1998.1661

Wall, T. D., Jackson, P. R., Mullarkey, S., & Parker, S. K. (1996). The DC-model of job strain: A more specific test. *Journal of Occupational and Organizational Psychology*, *69*, 153–166.

Yi, M. Y., & Hwang, Y. (2003). Predicting the use of web-based information systems: Self-efficacy, enjoyment, learning goal orientation, and the technology acceptance model. *International Journal of Human-Computer Studies*, *59*, 431–449. doi:10.1016/S1071-5819(03)00114-9

Yukl, G. (1989). Managerial leadership: A review of theory and research. *Journal of Management*, *15*, 251–289. doi:10.1177/014920638901500207

Chapter 14

Analysis of User Involvement and Participation on the Quality of IS Planning Projects:

An Exploratory Study

Varadharajan Sridhar
Management Development Institute, India

Dhruv Nath
Management Development Institute, India

Amit Malik
Management Development Institute, India

ABSTRACT

The process of information systems planning is critically dependent on the users of the system. The involvement and participation of these users and its impact on the effectiveness of IS planning has not been studied in the literature. In this article we address the effect of user involvement and participation on the quality of IS planning projects. This was done through an exploratory quasi-experiment study conducted in an academic setting. We studied the effects of user involvement using two sets of teams doing IS planning exercises, one in which the user was involved as part of the project team and the other where the user was outside the project team, but was involved in interviews and reviews of project artifacts. We also measured the extent of user participation through a survey of participants engaged in the IS planning projects. Results indicate that user involvement has significant positive effect on user participation, as well as on the quality of IS planning projects. However the effect of user participation on the quality of projects is mixed and needs further research.

DOI: 10.4018/978-1-60960-577-3.ch014

INTRODUCTION

During the early days of computerization, several organizations had made major investments in hardware and software, but ended up with failed implementations. In many of these cases, the reasons for lack of success were not technical, but business related. Topmost among these was the fact that in many cases, there was no link between the business goals and strategies of an organization and the selection of information systems to be developed (McFarlan & Nolan, 1975; McFarlan, Nolan & Norton, 1973; Pyburn, 1983). In other words, an application would be identified not because it would have a major impact on the business strategies of the organization, but possibly because a competitor had implemented it, and the management felt they would be left behind if they did not follow suit. Or, some key manager had seen the application working wonders somewhere else and therefore assumed it would work the same wonders here as well. Quite naturally, even with the most highly skilled development team, such applications were less likely to impact the business strategy of the organization than those that were directly derived from the business strategy, by design. Teo and Yang (2001) pointed out that ignoring business goals or failing to translate these goals and strategies into action plans resulted in major problems during the information system (IS) plan development phase.

Similarly, not much attention was paid to how these applications, once selected, would be prioritized and ultimately sequenced. As a consequence, companies often went ahead and computerized applications that were doomed to fail, for a variety of reasons. For instance, the data they required might not be available. Or they might be dependent on other systems for which computerization had not yet been planned. In many cases, organizations faced political problems and strong opposing vested interests, which prevented certain applications from being successfully implemented.

This alarming failure rate led to the development of the discipline of IS planning (McFarlan & Nolan, 1975; McFarlan et al., 1973; NIIT, 1990). The IS planning has been described as a managerial process for integrating IS considerations into corporate planning process, linking IS applications to business goals, and determining information requirements necessary for meeting organizations' short- as well as long-term goals (Wang & Tai, 2003). Several researchers and consultants have created various methodologies and processes for IS planning such as IBM's business systems planning, strategy set transformation, critical success factors, business information characterization, portfolio management analysis, information engineering, and end/ means analysis as reported in Wang and Tai (2003). However, all of them have one critical common factor—namely, they all start with the business needs, goals and strategies of the organization, and then proceed to look at IS solutions to support these business needs (McFarlan & Nolan, 1975; Porter & Millar, 1985; Henderson, Rockart, & Sifonis, 1987; Peak, Guynes, & Kroon, 2005).

Despite the use of such methodologies in IS planning, there were many failures in the launching, development, and implementation phases of IS planning process as reported by Teo and Ang (2001). Earlier work by Earl (1993) provided taxonomy for IS planning problems including method, implementation, and process concerns, and pointed out that effective management of these concerns was a necessary condition for successful IS planning. However, Teo and Ang (2001) noted that the IS planning problems were rarely reported in the literature and were discussed only in candid, private conversations between associates engaged in systems work. It is in this context that we study an important IS planning problem that has not gained much attention of researchers.

There are three primary actors in the IS planning exercise. Firstly, the top management, who decide on the business goals and strategies, and also guide the entire process. Secondly, the users, who are middle- to senior-level managers, and who bring in details of critical success factors, information needs, processes in place, and so on. And finally, the consultants, who might be internal or external consultants, and who are responsible for carrying out the IS planning exercise.

Of these three categories, the role of the consultants and the top management is reasonably clearly understood (NIIT, 1990). Teo and Ang (2001) describe the many problems in IS planning and indicate that failing to secure top management support for the IS planning effort is the most serious one. However, several questions also exist regarding the role of the user in such an exercise. For instance: What is the impact of user involvement on the IS planning exercise? Does it impact the quality of the IS planning artifacts produced? An interesting practical question that can follow is: Should the user be an integral part of the IS planning team, or should the user work with the team as an outsider, sharing his or her requirements and views as needed?

Apart from user involvement, both practitioners as well as the research community consider "user participation" also to be critical in the system development process (Barki & Hartwick, 1994). To this end, this study was designed to look into the effect of user involvement and user participation on the quality of IS planning projects.

The rest of this article is organized as follows: In the next section, the literature on user involvement and user participation in IS projects are briefly reviewed. Then we discuss the IS planning process we used in this research. Following this, we present the hypotheses of our study and then discuss details of the research design and methodology. Finally, the research findings and possible areas for future research are presented.

USER INVOLVEMENT AND USER PARTICIPATION

In any IS planning project, the role of the user can have significant impact on the success of the project. However, it is important to examine this issue in more detail, and to look specifically at the impact of user involvement and participation on the quality of projects. Barki and Hartwick (1994) define "user involvement" as a psychological state reflecting the importance and personal relevance of the system to the user. They further categorize user involvement to reflect the two dimensions of importance and personal relevance. A survey of the literature indicates that the problem of user involvement has been studied extensively for software development projects. However, Cavaye (1995) pointed out that the results on causal relationship between user participation and project success were mixed. Ives and Olsen (1984) in their review of research pointed out that the benefits of user involvement were not strongly demonstrated due to the presence of other intervening and moderating variables such as user participation and outcome criteria. Tait and Vessey (1988) reported that system complexity and constraints on resources were the primary determinants of system success and not the user involvement. Corbin (1988), through a case study, looked at the positive impact of user involvement in planning for information resource management. In another empirical study, Foster and Franz (1999) demonstrated that the users and analysts did not agree on the amount of user involvement in IS projects. The users perceived themselves as being more involved than perceived by the analysts. They pointed out that the analysts and users also did not perceive the users' system acceptance to be the same. Schaik (1999) developed methods for involving users in the early stages of information system design projects and constructed models for evaluation. A study by Basu, Hartono, Lederer, and Sethi (2002) looked at the effect of organizational commitment, senior management involvement, and team involvement on the achievement of strategic IS planning objectives. They illustrated that the senior management involvement impacted the achievement of the objectives in a positive manner. Turban, McLean, and Wetherbe (2004) stressed the need for planners and end users to be involved in the planning process.

Barki (1989) was the first one to clearly point out the theoretical differentiation between user involvement and user participation. In a subsequent work, Barki and Hartwick (1994) reported "user participation" as a measure should include participative activities that were formal and informal, direct and indirect, active and passive, performed alone or with others, and that occurred both overall and in specific stages of the process. Later, comprehensive scales for measuring user involvement, user participation, and user attitude were developed by Barki and Hartwick (1994). Cavaye (1995) further refined the construct of user participation and established a framework for associating user participation and project success. Based on the constructs defined in Barki and Hartwick (1994), Hunton and Beeler (1997) examined the efficacy of user participation in developing an accounting application and enhanced the model of Barki and Hartwick (1994) by integrating theory from self-efficacy and procedural justice in to the research framework. Recently Lin and Shao (2000) reported an empirical work relating user participation and system success using a simultaneous contingency approach. They corroborate the positive link between user participation and user satisfaction, and provide evidence on the interplay between user attitude and user involvement.

Though the above definitions of user involvement and participation were defined in the context of software development process by Barki and Hartwick (1994), the concepts are in general applicable to the IS planning process itself.

Potentially, user involvement and participation could impact certain outcome variables, such as the quality of the project and the effectiveness of the project team. As indicated, several researchers have examined the effect of user involvement and participation, and their impact on project success in the IS development process. However, the effect of user involvement and participation in the IS planning process has rarely been addressed. In this exploratory experimental study conducted in academic settings, we analyze the causal relationships between user involvement and user participation on the quality of IS planning projects.

THE IS PLANNING PROCESS

Several approaches to IS planning have been discussed in the literature as followed by various IS consulting organizations. For instance, Earl (1989) identified five types of approaches for the IS planning process, namely business-led, method-driven, technology-based, administrative, and organizational. Of these, the business-led approach has been very commonly used in practice. In this approach, the IS plan is defined using the organization's business strategy as the starting point. Turban et al. (2004) also presents a four-stage planning model that involves strategic IS planning, information requirements analysis, resource allocation, and project planning. We describe below the four phases of IS planning that we used in this study along with the deliverables in each phase as identified in Earl (1989), NIIT (1990), and Turban et al. (2004) (refer to Figure 1).

Figure 1. Phases in the IS planning process

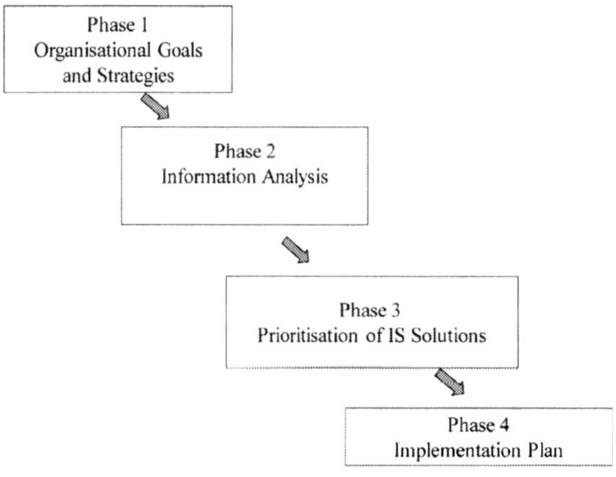

Phase 1: Organizational Goals and Strategies

This phase is the starting point for the IS plan, where the key goals or objectives of the organization are studied, along with the business strategies that the organization is pursuing in order to meet these goals. So far, this phase is simply a study of the business goals and strategies that have already been worked out by the organization, and therefore do not require any further analysis by the project team. However, beyond this, the team attempts to outline possible information technology (IT)-led strategies for the organization. In other words, strategies that had not already been identified by the management, but which could be implemented with the availability of IT were addressed. Clearly, these IT-led strategies require substantial additional analysis and brainstorming by the project team.

The following are the typical deliverables or artifacts in phase 1:

1. goals; and
2. strategies, including IT-led strategies.

Phase 2: Information Analysis

Having identified the business strategies, phase 2 now starts off by identifying the critical success factors (CSFs), which are critical in ensuring the success of these business strategies. Once these CSFs are known, we need to identify the critical information requirements (CIRs)—namely the information that is a key to managing these CSFs. At this point it is important to study the existing information systems in the organization, to see if this required information is already available.

Several different scenarios are possible here: First of all, in some cases the information might be fully available, accurate, as well as up to date. In such a case, nothing further needs to be done for this information. In other cases, the information might be incomplete, out of date, or even inaccurate. Or, the systems that provide this information might be slow, tough to maintain, or expensive to run. In either of these cases, the systems need to be developed (or perhaps bought out) afresh. In other words, a thorough analysis needs to be done of the existing information systems in the organization. In the process, we identify the systems that already exist and are working satisfactorily, and those that need to be modified or developed (or bought out) from scratch. We call this process "gap analysis"—in other words, the gap between the information provided by current systems and the critical information requirements. Clearly, based on this gap analysis, we are able to list out the information systems actually required as part of the IS plan.

The following are the deliverables in phase 2:

1. critical success factors,
2. critical information requirements,
3. evaluation of existing IS systems,
4. gap analysis, and
5. possible information system solutions describing the purpose and functionality of each system.

Phase 3: Prioritization of IS Solutions

Once the potential IS solutions have been identified in phase 2, they need to be prioritized, so as to sequence them in the appropriate order when developing or implementing them. The prioritization is done based on several factors. First of all, we use "value analysis," where we prioritize systems based on the value to the organization, as well as to its stakeholders. Ideally, IS systems that provide the highest value should be developed first and followed by those that provide less value. However, there are other factors that need to be considered in sequencing these systems. It is important to start with those systems where the probability of successful implementation is high. This creates success stories and provides a fillip to the IT implementation process in the organization. On the other hand, systems that provide high value but are likely to fail (for instance, due to lack of data or opposition from users) should be taken up later, once the organization has built up the maturity to live with failures and still proceed. Therefore the second stage in prioritization is "readiness analysis," which is used to determine how ready the organization is to implement each system. And finally, we do a "dependence analysis," where we look at the inter-linkages between the various systems. For instance, if system A creates most of the data that is used by system B, it makes sense to implement system A before system B. Based on these three kinds of analysis, the final sequencing of the IS systems is done.

Deliverables in Phase 3 include the following:

a. value analysis,
b. readiness analysis,
c. dependence analysis, and
d. final sequenced systems.

Phase 4: Implementation Plan

Finally, once the prioritized and sequenced IS solutions are available, we need to work out details of the implementation plan for developing/buying and implementing these IS solutions, as well as the underlying hardware and software required. This would include deciding whether to develop or buy the various systems, the underlying hardware, software, and architecture, a project plan for development and implementation, manpower and training requirements, and budgetary estimates.

As part of this research project, we focused on the first three phases. Phase 4 (the implementation plan) was left out because that required significant technical background among the participants which they did not possess. As indicated above, these are phases in which user involvement and participation are expected.

HYPOTHESIS DEVELOPMENT

User Involvement

There can be two models for user involvement in IS planning projects. One model is to make users an integral part of the project team and therefore equally responsible for creating the plan. We refer to this as the *user-inclusive model.* In the other model, users work with the project team as outsiders, but are not part of the team. We refer to this as the *user-exclusive model.* Clearly, there is a continuum between these two extreme scenarios. Without loss of generality, we focus on these two options in this research.

In the user-inclusive model, the user is expected to allot a fair amount of time from his or her busy schedule. He or she is equally responsible for delivering the final IS plan and for delivering it on time. In the process, project team meetings and interviews must be attended. Hence, the user-inclusive model evokes stronger user involvement. On the other hand, in the user-exclusive model, the user shares his or her views and requirements as appropriate, but as an outsider. The user is not required to join in all project meetings, but only those where the project team needs his or her involvement. The user-exclusive model thus requires less user involvement.

Based on the above models, the following hypothesis can be developed:

H1: *Quality of IS projects produced by user-inclusive teams will be better than that of the user-exclusive teams.*

If the above hypothesis is not proven to be true, then there is a possibility not to include the user as part of the team so that the user's precious time and resources can be used for other activities of higher priority.

User Participation

A user who is not an integral part of the team might be less committed than one who is fully integrated with the team, and hence the inputs that the project requires might not be forthcoming from the user. As an outsider, the user might not be willing to spare the kind of time required. The user might not get into the level of detail that he or she would, if his or her role included delivering a quality IS plan. In other words, user participation could vary depending on whether we use the user-inclusive or the user-exclusive approach. To find out whether there is any significant difference in user participation between the user-inclusive teams and the user-exclusive teams, the following hypothesis is constructed:

H2: *Participation of the users in user-inclusive teams will be better than that in user-exclusive teams.*

If the above hypothesis is not proven to be true, then even though the user has a stake in this project, he or she might not be participating and spending enough time in the project. If so, methods other than user involvement should be deployed to encourage the user to actively participate in the project.

User involvement and consequently user participation chosen become critical, both from the point of view of the quality of the IS plan and the fact that user management time is usually at a premium. Hence it is important to find out the effect of not only user involvement but also that of user participation on the quality of IS planning projects. To this end, the following hypothesis can be constructed and tested:

H3: *Consultants who perceived higher user participation will produce better IS planning projects compared to those that perceived lesser user participation.*

RESEARCH METHODOLOGY: CONTROLLED QUASI-EXPERIMENT WITH 2 × 1 FACTORIAL DESIGN SUBJECTS

In this exploratory research we study the problem of user involvement and participation in IS planning, by simulating it in an academic environment involving students enrolled in a graduate-level information systems courses at the Management Development Institute (MDI), India. The students were drawn from the regular MBA program as well as from the Executive MBA program; both were taught the core course on Management Information Systems in the same term. All the students were taught IS planning process and the preparation of the various artifacts as part of the course during the first three weeks of classes. Middle-level managers with several years of experience in a medium to large organization who were enrolled in the Executive MBA program were designated as *users*. There were nine such users who worked for diverse organizations in manufacturing, automotive, pharmaceuticals, chemicals, IT-enabled services, and the government, and had insights in to the organizations' IS needs. The rest of the participants were designated as the *consultants,* who were drawn from both the regular MBA program as well as the Executive MBA program so that there was a mix of participants with and without work experience.

Experiment Design

Consultants were then divided into two sets of teams (say A and B), with each set containing nine teams. Care was taken to ensure that the teams consisting of users and consultants were nearly homogenous. ANOVA results presented in Table 1 indicate that though age and years of experience of the consultants differ across the different teams, participants' work experience in IT did not differ significantly across the teams. Hence it was ensured to some extent that the IS

Table 1. Profile of the participating consultants

Variable	Mean	ANOVA on Means Across Teams
		F (p)
Age	25.56	1.86(0.03)
Total Years of Work Experience	3.63	1.98(0.02)
Years of Experience in IT	2.14	1.06(0.40)

Table 2. Design of the experiment

Teams	No. of Groups	Matching	Treatment
Set A: Control Group (user-inclusive)	9	IT experience	User part of the team
Set B: Experimental Group (user-exclusive)	9	IT experience	User not part of the team

planning skills were controlled across the teams. The average team size was 8.

Each of the nine users was allotted to one of the nine consultant teams in set A and was made part of the team. Thus users along with the consultants were then made responsible for the project deliverables and due dates. In the academic setting, engaging the users was ensured by making their grade in the course, dependent on the project delivery. These teams are referred to as user-inclusive teams. The nine consultant teams in set B are paired again with the same nine users. However, users were not made part of these teams and hence did not have any direct responsibility for the projects. Further, grades of the users were not dependent on the project delivered by teams in set B, and hence they were less engaged in the projects with these teams. These teams are referred to as user-exclusive teams. Thus there were nine user-inclusive teams that formed the control group and nine user-exclusive teams that formed the experiment group.

The experimental design is shown in Table 2. Figure 2 clearly illustrates the experimental set up.

Defining quasi-experimental designs, Campbell and Stanley (1966, pp. 34) state:

There are many natural settings in which a research person can introduce something like experimental design into his scheduling of data collection procedures (e.g., the when and to whom of measurement), even though he lacks the full control over the scheduling of experimental stimuli (the when and to whom of exposures) which makes a true experiment possible.

It is to be noted that in our research design the participants were not allotted randomly to teams. The teams were matched in terms of mean IT experience of the team members. Hence our research design adopts the quasi-experiment approach. Hence the limitations of quasi-experimentation as explained in Campbell and Stanley (1966) apply to our research setting as well.

Experiment Task

Both sets of teams were given the task of creating IS plans for the organization that the associated users worked for. The consultants elicited information from the corresponding users about organization goals and strategies, details about existing IS systems, and other project details to create their project deliverables. Table 3 gives details of the project deliverables along with the due dates. The project constituted about 15% of the course grade and lasted for about seven weeks. Hence the stakes were significant enough to warrant the participants' active involvement. It is to be noted that since the users and projects are the same for both the sets of teams, project complexity and scope were controlled across the two sets of user-inclusive and user-exclusive teams. Thus there were two distinct IS plans for each project,

Figure 2. Experimental set-up

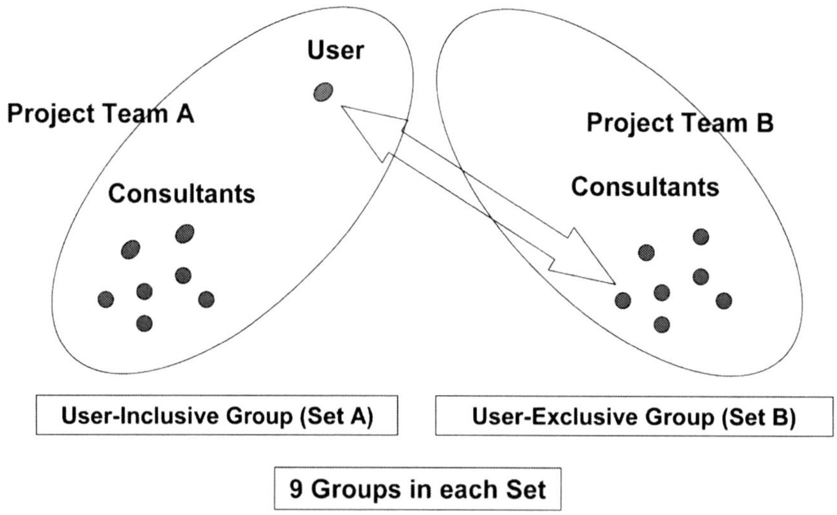

one by the user-inclusive team and the other by the user-exclusive team.

To minimize communication of the deliverables and ideas across the user-inclusive and user-exclusive teams that worked on the same projects, the students were informed that they would be heavily penalized, including possibly cancellation of the project and loss of grade, in case communication of this kind took place. There was, therefore, a reasonable likelihood that the projects executed by the two sets of teams were done independently.

Need for Experiment

A large amount of published research involving some form of laboratory experiments exists (Introna & Whitlei, 2000). Sangwan, Bass, Mullick, Paulish, and Kazmeier (2007) recommend that a way to advance the state of the practice in software development is through experimentation. They report findings of many software development projects from companies and the experiments conducted in collaboration with academic research community. They also argue that although the use of student teams does not exactly match the industrial environment, it is a useful simulation. For instance, students participating in the experimental project as a part of a course receive a grade rather than a salary and bonus. Nevertheless, they stress that researchers can get a good understanding of the underlying phenomenon through academic experiments. They also report that many of today's software engineering graduate students have some amount of industrial experience, and their skills profiles are not that much different from the staff at some companies. For example, students who participated as subjects in our experiment had work experience in large software companies in India such as Infosys Technologies, Tata Consultancy Services, IBM, and Aricent. MBA students similar to the ones that participated in our experiment were used as surrogate users in experiments conducted by Hazari (2005) and Briggs, Balthazard, and Dennis (1996).

A controlled experimental approach such as this makes available several teams that work in parallel thereby generating a large amount of data for drawing significant conclusions. It is to be noted that in our experiment, a total of 163 students participated, thus providing a rich dataset. This research also acknowledges the viewpoint

Table 3. Project deliverables and their timelines

Deliverables	Timeline
Phase 1: Goals and IT-Led Strategies	3 weeks
Phase 2: Information Analysis • Critical Success Factors • Critical Information Requirements • Critical Information Set • Critical Decision Set • Evaluation of Existing IS Systems • Systems Audit Grid • Gap Analysis • Possible Information System Solutions: A one-page description of the purpose and functionality of each system is required.	3 weeks
Phase 3: Prioritization • Value Analysis • Readiness Analysis • Dependence Analysis • Value Readiness Matrix • Final Sequenced Systems	1 week

of researchers arguing in favor of experimental research and believes that the biggest advantage of experimental projects is that there is no business risk associated with a failed project (Sangwan et al., 2007).

There are criticisms for the use of students in academic experiments as surrogates as well. However, Dipboye and Flanagan (1979) noted that students often represented a typical working professional and organizational member due to the variety of backgrounds and goals. In studies related to industrial organization psychology and organization behavior, results obtained from students were similar to those from managers (e.g., Locke, 1986). In a recent work, Kim (2006) argues that when training is given to ad hoc student groups, they seem to perform as well as established professional groups. In our experiment, the students were briefed about the project by the instructors and were given classroom training on the preparation of various IS planning artifacts before the start of the experiment. Given the above research support, we argue that simulating projects in a controlled academic setting could lead to conclusions that are valid in the real-world business setting.

DATA COLLECTION

User Participation

We measured perception of all the consultants engaged in both the user-inclusive and user-exclusive teams about the extent of user participation in the IS planning process. Items on user participation were adapted from Barki and Hartwick (1994), and the survey questionnaire was administered to all consultants at the end of the project. Responses were elicited in a seven-point Likert-type scale.

Quality of IS Planning Projects

We measured the quality of the IS planning projects produced by the consultant teams by:

1. evaluating the project artifacts produced by the teams, and
2. examining the perceptions of the team members about measures such as the quality of project artifacts and effectiveness of the teams in doing their projects.

We describe below the individual measures of project quality.

Assessed Quality of Project Artifacts

The IS planning project artifacts produced by the user-inclusive and user-exclusive teams involved in the exercise were evaluated for completeness. The artifacts were evaluated by an external expert well versed with the IS planning process and the corresponding artifacts. The expert compared each of the nine artifacts produced by user-inclusive team with the ones produced by the corresponding user-exclusive team and created a superset of components for each artifact for each project. Based on this superset, the expert evaluated each artifact submitted by the user-exclusive and user-inclusive team for each project on a Likert-type scale of 1-7 for completeness. The measure of

Figure 3. Model for analyzing user involvement in IS planning projects

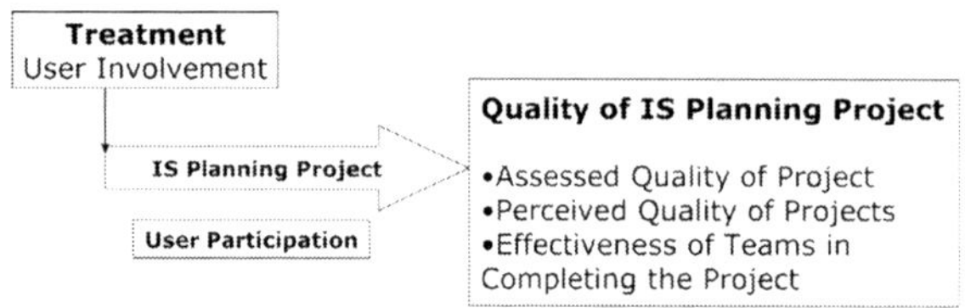

completeness as defined above is very similar to the one defined in Nath, Sridhar, Adya, and Malik (2006). The average of these evaluations across all artifacts for each project was taken as the assessed quality of the IS planning project completed by the team and hence a measure of team performance. By making the team assignments to the projects blind to the expert, we removed any possible subjective bias of the expert during the assessment. Based on the above measure of quality, we can further refine hypothesis H1 constructed in the previous section as follows:

H1a: *Assessed quality of project artifacts produced by the user-inclusive teams will be better than that produced by the user-exclusive teams.*

Perceived Quality and Effectiveness of Teams

Apart from the assessed quality of artifacts as mentioned above, we also measured the perceptions of consultants engaged in the project about the quality of project artifacts they developed, and the effectiveness with which they performed as a team using a survey questionnaire. Based on these perception measures, hypothesis H1 can be further classified as follows:

H1b: *The user-inclusive teams will perceive that quality of their project artifacts is better than that of the user-exclusive teams.*

H1c: *The user-inclusive teams will perceive that their teams are more effective in doing the projects compared to the user-exclusive teams.*

Further, based on the previously mentioned measure of user participation, hypothesis H3 can be further refined as follows:

H3a: *The consultants that perceive higher user participation will produce better quality artifacts compared to those that perceive lower levels of user participation.*

H3b: *The consultants that perceive higher user participation also will perceive that their projects are of better quality compared to those who perceive lower levels of user participation.*

H3c: *The consultants that perceive higher user participation also will perceive that their teams are more effective in completing the projects compared to those who perceive lower levels of user participation.*

The overall research model based on the above set of hypotheses is presented in Figure 3. It is to be noted from Figure 3 that user involvement was given as treatment at the beginning of the experiment. However, user participation occurred during the project and hence was measured at the end of the project.

Data Analysis

We performed statistical analysis on the survey data at the individual level rather than by teams. The larger sample size of $n = 163$ at the individual level minimizes the subjective bias in the outcome variables and reduces the chances of missing real relationships, compared to doing analysis on a

Table 4. Principal component analysis of the survey items (with Varimax rotation)

	Components		
Items	1	2	3
User Participation			
1	0.828	0.148	0.264
2	0.535	-0.150	0.290
3	0.844	0.184	0.197
4	0.872	0.249	0.145
5	0.722	0.168	0.109
6	0.680	0.236	0.328
7	0.851	0.265	0.173
8	0.579	0.456	0.148
Perceived Quality of Projects			
1	0.203	0.860	0.146
2	0.166	0.799	0.311
Effectiveness of Teams			
1	0.195	0.223	0.828
2	0.295	0.254	0.535
3	0.628	0.279	0.844

smaller sample size of 18 at the team level. Principal component analysis with Varimax rotation was performed on the items constructed for the above perception-based measures. The component matrix is given in Table 4. An examination of the rotated component matrix with the corresponding factor loadings clearly indicates that the items represent the associated constructs. Reliability of the constructs was further validated by computing reliability coefficients for each construct. The reliability statistics are given in Table 5. All the constructs have a Cronbach's alpha closer to or greater than 0.70 and hence prove construct validity. The final set of questions for each construct used for analysis is enclosed in the Appendix. High mean values of all the variables as shown in Table 5 indicate that the team members were positively oriented towards this experiment.

Pair-wise correlations between the different variables are presented in Table 6. The effect of user participation on all the outcome variables of

Table 5. Reliability analysis and descriptive statistics (n = 163)

Constructs (Number of Items)	Reliability Coefficient	Mean	Standard Deviation
Input Variable			
User Participation (8)	0.92	5.18	1.10
Output Variables			
Perceived Quality of Projects (2)	0.78	5.68	0.71
Effectiveness of Teams (3)	0.77	5.33	0.82

IS project success, except the assessed quality of projects, is as expected. All the outcome variables, except the assessed quality of projects, have significant positive correlations among each other, as expected. Though the associations of assessed quality of projects with the other variables are of expected sign, they are not statistically significant. Detailed analysis of these variables across user-inclusive and user-exclusive teams is presented in the next section.

FINDINGS AND DISCUSSIONS

Effect of User Involvement on Quality of Projects

Since there are multiple dependent variables in the model, a Multiple Analysis of Variance (MANOVA) test was carried out on the treatment variable, namely *user involvement.* MANOVA results presented in Table 7 clearly indicate that the dependent variables (assessed quality, perceived quality and effectiveness) do significantly differ across the user-inclusive and user-exclusive teams.

To further confirm this finding and to test hypotheses H1a-H1c, a one-way ANOVA test was performed on the three measures of performance

Table 6. Correlations of the variables (n =163)

Variable	User Participation	Assessed Quality of Projects	Perceived Quality of Projects	Effectiveness of Teams
User Participation		0.02	0.48 **	0.69 **
Assessed Quality of Projects			0.04	0.02
Perceived Quality of Projects				0.53 **

** Correlation is significant at 0.01 level (2-tailed)

Table 7. Results of MANOVA

Factor	Measure	F (p)
User Involvement	Pillai's Trace Wilk's Lambda	7.235 (0.00) 7.235 (0.00)
User Participation (coded as higher than average and lower than average)	Pillai's Trace Wilk's Lambda	19.026 (0.00) 19.026 (0.00)

between the user-inclusive and user-exclusive teams; the results are presented in Table 8.

A quick look at Table 8 indicates that all the outcome variables, including the assessed quality of the project artifacts, do vary significantly across the control (user-inclusive) and experimental (user-exclusive) groups. Hence hypotheses H1a-H1c cannot be rejected, indicating thereby that there are significant differences in assessed quality of project artifacts, quality as perceived by consultants, and team effectiveness across the two sets of teams. In other words, the user-inclusive teams that had a higher level of user involvement produced better IS planning projects compared to the user-exclusive teams.

Effect of User Involvement on User Participation

In order to find out whether user participation differs across the user-inclusive and user-exclusive groups, ANOVA was performed across the two sets of teams. The results are given in Table 9.

Table 8. ANOVA results for user involvement (n = 163)

Variable	Average		F-Value (p-value)
	User-Inclusive Teams	User-Exclusive Teams	
Assessed Quality of Project	6.0056	5.6696	14.2450 (0.000)
Perceived Quality of Project	5.7804	5.5000	5.883 (0.016)
Effectiveness of Teams	5.4285	5.1304	4.993 (0.027)

The results indicate there is indeed significant difference in user participation levels between the user-inclusive and user-exclusive teams. The more the user is involved in the project, the more is the perceived user participation, lending support to hypothesis H2.

Effect of User Participation on Quality of Projects

We computed mean values of perceived user participation as indicated by the consultants captured through the survey. We categorized the responses into two sets: (1) one in which the value of perceived user participation was above average, referred to as the "high perceived user participation" set; and (2) one in which the perceived user participation responses are below average, referred to as the "low perceived user participation" set. MANOVA tests on the four dependent

Table 9. ANOVA results for user involvement (n = 163)

Measure	Average		F-Value (p-value)
	User-Inclusive Teams	User-Exclusive Teams	
User Participation	5.4415	4.6720	20.2730 (0.000)

variables on the above categorization (see Table 7) indicate that these differ across groups having higher and lower perceived user participation. Further ANOVA was performed across these sets and the results are given in Table 10.

Results indicate that those that perceived higher user participation also perceived their project quality and effectiveness of their teams to be better, compared to those that perceived lower user participation levels. However, the quality of projects assessed by the expert does not differ across these two sets. This confirms the correlations presented in Table 6. This leads to the acceptance of hypotheses H3b and H3c and rejection of hypothesis H3a. A summary of hypotheses and their validity are presented in Table 11.

A look Table 11 indicates that there is a single discrepancy. The expert rated quality of projects produced by the user-inclusive team is better than that of user-exclusive teams. However, the expert's assessment of the project does not significantly vary across participants who perceived higher user participation, compared to those who perceived lower user participation. The high average of the assessment across these two groups indicates that those who perceived lower user participation also produced as good artifacts as the others. This implies that though user involvement clearly impacts positively the quality of the projects, user participation seems to have less effect. This needs to be studied further.

Table 10. ANOVA results for user participation (n = 163)

Measure	Average		F-Value (p-value)
	Higher User-Participation Set	Lower User-Participation Set	
Assessed Quality of Project	5.8837	5.8974	0.024 (0.877)
Perceived Quality of Project	5.9302	5.4091	25.039 (0.000)
Effectiveness of Team	5.7112	4.8960	53.247 (0.000)

Table 11. Summary of hypotheses testing

	User Involvement	User Participation
Assessed Quality of Project	UI > UE	-
Perceived Quality of Project	UI > UE	HUP > LUP
Effectiveness of Team	UI > UE	HUP > LUP

UI: User Inclusive Team;
UE: User Exclusive Team;
HUP: HIGHER perceived User Participation;
LUP: Lower Perceived User Participation

CONCLUSION AND FUTURE RESEARCH DIRECTIONS

In this article we have described an exploratory experimental study where real-world IS planning projects were simulated in an academic environment. The objective of our study was to establish the relationship between user involvement or participation and quality of IS planning projects. The results of the study indicate that user involvement does make significant difference on user participation as well as on the quality of IS planning projects. User participation does make significant difference on the perceived quality of IS projects and perceived effectiveness of the teams.

These results have important implications for organizations involved in IS planning projects. The quality of the planning process, which is one of the initial phases in the system development lifecycle, affects the rest of the projects. It is important to ensure active user involvement in the planning process for success of the projects. Getting the users to actively participate in the projects might not impact the assessed quality of deliverables, but might have a positive influence on other facets of team performance such as decision making and effectiveness. This research also extends the application of measures of user participation developed by Barki and Hartwick (1994) to IS planning projects.

Though the student subjects performing the roles of users and consultants in this exercise have experience in the industry, the limitations of using students as surrogate users apply to this experiment as well. An extension of the research would be to do an industry survey to validate the results of the academic experimental study. Since parameters such as age and work experience varied across teams, the effect of these on the results cannot be underestimated. A quasi-experiment strictly controlling all such variables, thus minimizing team heterogeneity, is warranted to confirm our research findings.

It would be interesting to see whether the findings of the study can also be extended to other similar projects—possibly beyond the IS planning domain—which involve intensive user interactions to draw out requirements.

REFERENCES

Barki, H. (1989). Rethinking the concept of user involvement. *Management Information Systems Quarterly*, *13*(1), 53–63. doi:10.2307/248700

Barki, H., & Hartwick, J. (1994). Measuring user attitude, user involvement and user attitude. *Management Information Systems Quarterly*, *18*(1), 59–82. doi:10.2307/249610

Basu, V., Hartono, E., Lederer, A., & Sethi, V. (2002). The impact of organizational commitment, senior management involvement and team involvement on strategic information systems planning. *Information & Management*, *39*(6), 513–524. doi:10.1016/S0378-7206(01)00115-X

Briggs, R. O., Balthazard, P. A., & Dennis, A. R. (1996). Graduate business students as surrogates for executives in the evaluation of technology. *Journal of End User Computing*, *8*(4), 11–17.

Campbell, D. T., & Stanley, J. C. (1966). *Experimental and quasi-experimental designs for research*. Chicago: Rand McNally.

Cavaye, A. (1995). User participation in system development revisited. *Information & Management*, *28*(5), 311–323. doi:10.1016/0378-7206(94)00053-L

Corbin, D. (1988). Strategic IRM plan: User involvement spells success. *Journal of Systems Management*, *39*(5), 12–16.

Dipboye, R. L., & Flanagan, M. F. (1979). Research setting in industrial and organization psychology: Are findings in the field more generalizable than in laboratory. *The American Psychologist*, *34*(2), 141–150. doi:10.1037/0003-066X.34.2.141

Earl, M. J. (1989). *Management strategies for information technology*. Englewood Cliffs, NJ: Prentice Hall.

Earl, M. J. (1993). Experiences in strategic information systems planning. *Management Information Systems Quarterly*, *17*(1), 1–24. doi:10.2307/249507

Foster, S., & Franz, C. (1999). User involvement in information systems development: A comparison of analyst and user perceptions of system acceptance. *Journal of Engineering and Technology Management*, *16*(3-4), 329–348. doi:10.1016/S0923-4748(99)00014-4

Hazari, S. I. (2005). Perceptions of end-users on the requirements in personal firewall software: An exploratory study. *Journal of Organizational and End User Computing*, *17*(3), 47–65. doi:10.4018/joeuc.2005070103

Henderson, J., Rockart, J., & Sifonis, J. (1987). A planning methodology for integrating management support systems into strategic information planning. *Journal of Management Information Systems*, *4*(1), 5–24.

Hunton, J., & Beeler, J. (1997). Effects of user participation in systems development: A longitudinal field experiment. *Management Information Systems Quarterly*, *21*(4), 359–388. doi:10.2307/249719

Introna, L., & Whitlei, E. (2000). About experiments and style: A critique of laboratory research in information systems. *Information Technology & People*, *13*(3), 161–173. doi:10.1108/09593840010377608

Ives, B., & Olson, M. H. (1984). User involvement and MIS success: A review of research. *Management Science*, *30*(5), 586–603. doi:10.1287/mnsc.30.5.586

Kim, Y. (2006). Supporting distributed groups with group support systems: A study of the effect of group leaders and communication modes on group performance. *Journal of Organizational and End User Computing*, *18*(2), 20–37. doi:10.4018/joeuc.2006040102

Lin, W., & Shao, B. (2000). A relationship between user participation and system success: A simultaneous contingency approach. *Information & Management*, *37*(6), 283–295. doi:10.1016/S0378-7206(99)00055-5

Locke, E. A. (1986). *Generalizing from laboratory to field setting: Research finding from industrial organization, organization behavior, and human resource management*. Lexington, MA: Lexington Books.

McFarlan, F. W., & Nolan, R. L. (1975). *The information systems handbook*. Homewood, IL: Down Jones-Irwin.

McFarlan, F. W., Nolan, R. L., & Norton, D. P. (1973). *Information systems administration*. New York: Holt, Rinehart and Winston.

Nath, D., Sridhar, V., Adya, M., & Malik, A. (2008). Project quality of off-shore virtual teams engaged in software requirements analysis: An exploratory comparative study. *Journal of Global Information Management*, *16*(4), 24–45. doi:10.4018/jgim.2008100102

NIIT. (1990). *CRISPLAN, version 1, release 2 (company internal note)*. New Delhi: Author.

Peak, D., Guynes, C. S., & Kroon, V. (2005). Information technology alignment planning—a case study. *Information & Management*, *42*(5), 635–649. doi:10.1016/j.im.2004.02.009

Porter, M. E., & Millar, V. E. (1985). How information technology gives you competitive advantage. *Harvard Business Review*, *63*(4), 149–160.

Pyburn, P. J. (1983). Linking the MIS plan with corporate strategy: An exploratory study. *Management Information Systems Quarterly*, *7*(2), 1–14. doi:10.2307/248909

Sangwan, R., Bass, M., Mullick, N., Paulish, D. J., & Kazmeier, J. (2007). *Global software development handbook*. Boca Raton, FL: Auerbach.

Schaik, P. (1999). Involving users in the specification of functionality using scenarios and model-based evaluation. *Behaviour & Information Technology*, *18*(6), 455–466. doi:10.1080/014492999118878

Tait, P., & Vessey, I. (1988). The effect of user involvement on system success: A contingency approach. *Management Information Systems Quarterly*, *12*(1), 91–108. doi:10.2307/248809

Teo, T., & Ang, J. (2001). An examination of major IS planning problems. *International Journal of Information Management*, *21*(6), 457–470. doi:10.1016/S0268-4012(01)00036-6

Turban, E., McLean, E., & Wetherbe, J. (2004). *Information technology for management.* Singapore: John Wiley & Sons (Asia).

Wang, E., & Tai, J. (2003). Factors affecting information systems planning effectiveness: Organizational contexts and planning systems dimensions. *Information & Management*, *40*(4), 287–303. doi:10.1016/S0378-7206(02)00011-3

APPENDIX: SURVEY ITEMS

Items for User Participation

1. The user spent adequate time on the project.
2. The user was a hindrance to the project deliverables (negative coded).
3. The user was available for project discussions.
4. The user was very much involved in the project.
5. The user clearly communicated business strategies, issues, and requirements.
6. We had healthy and useful discussions with the users during the project.
7. The user took sufficient interest in the project.
8. User involvement was useful in the preparation of goals, strategies, CSFs, and business issues.

Items for Perceived Quality of Projects

1. I think that our team produced high-quality project reports.
2. I think that the solutions/end deliverables of our project were of adequate quality.

Items for Team Effectiveness

1. We had an effective project team.
2. We were able to arrive at well-reasoned decisions during the project.
3. We effectively collaborated with the users in the project.

This work was previously published in Journal of Organizational and End User Computing (JOEUC) 21(3), edited by Mo Adam Mahmood, pp. 80-98, copyright 2009 by IGI Publishing (an imprint of IGI Global).

Section 4

Chapter 15
Knowledge Worker Productivity:
The Effects of Distraction and Task Complexity in Mobile Computing Environments

Darren Nicholson
Rowan University, USA

Jennifer Nicholson
Rowan University, USA

D. Parboteeah
Eastern New Mexico University, USA

Joseph Valacich
Washington State University, USA

ABSTRACT

Mobile wireless computing is changing the way in which people work, allowing work to occur in a broad range of environments on tasks that previously required fixed location-based, networked computing environments. Along with this greater work flexibility, it is also likely that these mobile work environments contain various types of distractions that could potentially affect the task performance of knowledge workers. Drawing on distraction-conflict theory, this research proposes a model of knowledge worker task performance within the context of a mobile wireless work environment. To test this model, a controlled laboratory experiment was conducted that contrasted task complexity and distraction levels on the task performance of individuals within a mobile wireless environment. Results indicate that regardless of task complexity, productivity losses will occur under both lower and higher levels of distraction. The implications of these results for future research and for the deployment of mobile technologies within organizations are discussed.

DOI: 10.4018/978-1-60960-577-3.ch015

1. INTRODUCTION

Mobile wireless computing is quickly growing in scope and popularity, and holds the promise of being the next major paradigm in personal computing (e.g., Barnes, 200; Ladd et al., 2010). Given that mobile wireless computing does not limit the personal movement of individuals, this anytime, anyplace computing will provide both benefits and challenges (Malladi & Agrawal, 2002; Philips, 2002). The ability to communicate anytime/anyplace offers new levels of flexibility and convenience (Looney, Jessup, & Valacich, 2004), opening up numerous possibilities within the realm of work. Tasks that have been traditionally undertaken in a fixed setting, such as an office, can now be performed virtually anywhere (Gorlenko & Merrick, 2003), liberating knowledge workers from their cubicle prisons ("Our Nomadic Future," 2008). Similarly, many types of field work can now benefit from any time/any place information accessibility and communications capabilities (Gorlenko & Merrick, 2003; Philips, 2002). It is believed that mobile wireless computing will "foster increased on-the-job productivity and promote the freedom to travel while working or playing" (Philips, 2002, p. 68).

Sherry and Salvador (2001) note, however, that the potential for disruptions to work and concentration can overshadow the productivity and efficiency benefits that mobile work appeared to offer. Additionally, the "always on" capabilities of many mobile devices have the potential to disrupt the work-life balance for many knowledge workers (Cousins and Varshney, 2009). As more organizations are moving toward a mobile workforce, understanding the potential undesirable effects of mobile computing is becoming a particularly vital area of research. In fact, International Data Corporation (IDC) (2010) reported that the US mobile workforce is expected to exceed 119.7 million workers, or 75.5% of the US workforce, by 2013 and will exceed a billion worldwide by year's end. A review of current literature on mobile wireless computing however reveals that little is known about how mobile wireless technologies can be systematically integrated into organizational activities and how this will impact day-to-day processes and overall productivity (Ladd et al., 2010).

Prior research on mobile wireless computing can be classified into three general categories. The first category, which has been the focus of several studies, deals with the acceptance of these new technologies (e.g., Abraham, 2001; Lu, Liu, Yu, & Yao, 2003; Okoli, Ives, Jessup, & Valacich, 2002; Sarker & Wells, 2003; Wakefield & Whitten, 2006). For example, Okoli *et al.* (2002) describe the challenges that are associated with deploying mobile wireless computing technologies within the realm of professional conferences. Second, the technical design aspects of the technology have been examined (e.g., Andersson, 2008; Boncella, 2002; Dekleva, Shim, Varshney & Knoerzer, 2007; Lee & Shin, 2005; Shim, Varshney, Dekleva, & Knoerzer, 2002; Viehland & Hughes, 2002). For example, Boncella (2002) provided an overview of how a secure channel can be established in a wireless environment. Third, the implications of mobile commerce or m-commerce have been studied extensively (e.g., Balasubramanian, Peterson, & Jarvenpaa, 2002; Jarvenpaa, Lang, Takeda, & Tuunainen, 2003; Lee, 2005; Ngai & Gunasekaran, 2005; Stafford & Gillenson, 2003; Urbaczewski, Valacich, & Jessup, 2003). For instance, Jarvenpaa and colleagues (2003) reported that mobile technologies provide not only greater freedoms and connectedness, but also manage the pressure between the two.

In addition to these relatively more established areas, a new stream of research is emerging which focuses on the examination of mobile wireless computing within organizational settings. However, only a few studies were found to investigate such phenomenon (e.g., Beulen & Streng, 2002; Gebauer, Shaw & Gribbins, 2010; Shen & Jones, 2003). For example, Beulen and Streng (2002) reported a field experiment that tested the hypothesis that mobile workers benefit from a specific kind of wireless application protocol (WAP) technology. They found that workers had a positive attitude towards WAP if, when mobile, their working environment was available. Additionally, Shen and Jones (2003) described a field study of knowledge sharing in mobile work settings and examined how rich data capture 'in situ' can be utilized to improve knowledge management practices. This study enhances the understanding of how future mobile multimedia messaging technology can be used in the design of organizational knowledge management systems. Chen and Nath (2006) examined the impact of wireless local area networks (WLAN) on organizational users. Survey results revealed that overall "users felt that WLAN improved their quality of work life, enhanced work efficiency and effectiveness, and led to better collaboration and communication" (p. 77). More recently, Gebauer et al., (2009) developed a task-technology fit profile for designing mobile information systems that support organizational processes. Specifically, they present a three-step conceptual model to derive fit between managerial tasks, mobile information systems, and the mobile use context. Other studies have cited additional benefits of wireless computing, including improved mobility, flexibility, and timeliness of information (Cantwell, 2003; Gopal, Compeau, Marcon, & Olivera, 2006; Jessup & Robey, 2002; Keane, 2002; Looney, Jessup, & Valacich, 2004; Prasopoulou, Pouloudi & Panteli, 2006).

In addition to the purported positive impacts of mobile technologies, there is also the possibility that such anytime/anyplace computing can have unforeseen negative consequences (e.g., Cousins & Varshney, 2009; Davis, 2002). For example, mobile wireless work environments harbor a host of shortcomings, such as unstable connectivity, poor ergonomics, and potential distractions that, under the right conditions, may influence individual productivity. Further, with mobile computing, the boundaries between personal and business activities become blurred, resulting in challenges of achieving work-life balance.

While the aforementioned studies add to our knowledge about individual's perceptions of the effects of mobile wireless computing, a recent analysis of trends in mobile computing research by Ladd et al., (2010) revealed a dearth of understanding regarding the effects of mobile technologies on both individual and organizational performance outcomes. In particular, one area of study yet to be examined is the affect of mobile wireless computing on knowledge worker productivity (e.g., Zhang & Li, 2005).

Knowledge work is defined as being more cognitive than physical in nature (Davis, 1999). According to Davis (2002), knowledge work is "human mental work performed to generate useful information and knowledge." Since a vast proportion of the work performed in an organization can be categorized as knowledge work, the productivity of knowledge workers is of great importance to an organization (Drucker, 1969). Knowledge work requires a considerable amount of concentration and attention; hence, to be productive, a knowledge worker must be able to successfully manage his/her time, attention, and motivation (Davis, 2002). This may be difficult to do when the knowledge worker is conducting work from outside the organizational boundaries in a mobile wireless environment that may be host to a number of interruptions and distractions. Davis (2002) provides an overview of the possible effects of mobile computing on the productivity of knowledge workers, which includes a decrease in productivity due to interruptions and distractions, however, no empirical evidence was provided for these propositions

The goal of this research is to gain an understanding of the effects of various levels of distraction and task complexity on an individual knowledge worker's performance in a mobile wireless work environment. Based on the distraction-conflict theory, a research model is proposed to elucidate how different levels of external distractions and task complexity affect the performance of individuals in a mobile wireless work setting. An experimental study has been designed to empirically test the model. The empirical findings provide insights for understanding the performance of individuals in mobile wireless computing environments.

The paper is organized as follows. First, the research model, as well as specific hypotheses, are presented. Next, the research methodology utilized to empirically test the research model is presented. This is followed by a brief presentation of the results of a laboratory experiment. The paper concludes by outlining the contributions, limitations and implications of this study for practice and future research.

2. THEORETICAL FRAMEWORK AND RESEARCH MODEL

A distraction is any stimuli which is irrelevant to a person's primary task (Sanders, Baron, & Moore, 1978); the primary task being that activity on which the person is focusing all his/her attention. The distraction can differ in its nature. It can be social or nonsocial; an external stimulus or an internal thought; imposed by a second party or created by the individual himself (Sanders et al., 1978).

To fully understand what a distraction is, it is essential to differentiate between interruptions and distractions. Speier, Vessey and Valacich (2003) explain this difference with reference to the primary task. According to Speier et al. (2003), the similarity between interruptions and distractions is that they both occur when the individual is performing a primary task. The main difference lies in the manner in which interruptions and distractions are detected. Interruptions are detected by the same sensory channel as the primary task (Speier et al., 2003), which is the main reason why the individual cannot ignore them (Baron, 1986). In other words, an interruption requires the necessary and complete shift of one's core, task-related sensory channels and cognitive resources away from the primary task at hand. In contrast, a distraction is often detected by a different sensory channel than that involved in the primary task and as a result, the distraction can be ignored or processed at the same time as the primary task (Groff, Baron, & Moore, 1983).

For instance, a phone call, depending on the context of the call (e.g., importance, caller, involvement, etc.) and the sensory channels or cognitive resources required to meaningfully participate in the primary task, can either be considered a distraction or an interruption. The phone call is considered an interruption any time the phone call and the primary task require the same sensory channels (i.e., if you are engaged in a face-to-face conversation and at the same time, receive a phone call) and when the call requires an individual's full cognitive resources (i.e., one needs to make a critical, timely decision with great uncertainty). In contrast, the phone call is considered a distraction any time the phone call and the primary task require different sensory channels (i.e., reading an email while listening to a routine inquiry from a subordinate) and when the call requires very little cognitive resources (e.g., a routine response).

Distraction-conflict theory has been used to explain how a particular distraction, specifically the presence of others, can affect an individual's performance on the primary task. It postulates that the presence of others distracts an individual, causing an attentional conflict (Sanders et al., 1978). Attentional conflict refers to the situation where the individual feels the tendency, desire, or obligation to allocate attention to these two (or more) exclusive inputs (i.e., the distraction and the primary task) (Baron, 1986; Sanders et al., 1978). This also includes the effort that it takes to ignore a distraction. Empirical evidence indicates that the mental process of ignoring something requires cognitive effort, that is, individuals must constantly remind themselves of what it is that they are trying to ignore in order to expend the effort to ignore it (Kunda, 2001). Essentially, choosing to attend to or ignore a stimulus, whether internal or external, can elevate stress, arousal, and drive in an individual and may lead to cognitive overload (Baron, 1986), thereby leaving an individual with less cognitive resources for completing the primary task. This increased stress may not have a detrimental effect on simple or well-learned tasks, where irrelevant cues may just be dismissed or excluded. However, it can have a disruptive effect on more complex or novel tasks that are associated with an increase in information cues, as an individual may not have the excess cognitive capacity to process relevant cues. This contradictory effect is known as social facilitation (Zajonc, 1965). In order to better understand the distraction-conflict theory, it is important to further review the concepts that underlie the theory, specifically working memory and cognitive load, task complexity, as well as social facilitation.

2.1. Working Memory and Cognitive Load

Working memory, as defined by cognitive psychologists, refers to "a system for the temporary holding and manipulation of information during the performance of a range of cognitive tasks such as comprehension, learning and reasoning" (Baddeley, 1986, pp. 34). Working memory is intimately related to where and how we direct our attention to think, or to process information.

The biggest limitation of working memory is its capacity to deal with no more than about seven elements (plus or minus two) of information simultaneously (Miller, 1956). With this limitation in mind, Baddeley (1986) discusses the concept of *displacement/interference* in working memory. Displacement/interference refers to the repercussions involved when additional new items enter an individual's working memory. As a result, existing items tend to become harder to access, can become displaced by new information, and can cause decreased cognitive efficiency. The displacement or interference of additional new items can be conceptualized as placing an additional cognitive load on working memory. Cognitive load refers to the total amount of mental activity imposed on working memory at an instance in time (Sweller, 1988, 1994). The major factor that contributes to cognitive load is the number of distinct information elements or chunks (Miller, 1956) that needs to be attended to. Complex tasks, which require the processing of more distinct information elements, are one of many culprits that can lead to cognitive overload (Wood, 1986).

2.2. Task Complexity

Wood (1986) attributes increases in the component complexity of a task to the occurrence of more information cues to process, more acts to execute, or increased interdependence between the cues and acts. Simpler tasks are associated with lower cognitive load while tasks that are highly complex result in excessive cognitive load, which produces negative effects on performance, learning, and motivation (Sweller, vanMerrienboer, & Paas, 1998).

Support for these propositions has been found in prior research. For instance, Kahneman (1973) found that harder or more difficult tasks, as opposed to easier tasks, place greater demands on an individual's mental or cognitive capacity. Furthermore, Easterbrook (1959) found that reduced performance occurred when individuals performed complex tasks in combination with high arousal states, such as high emotionality or anxiety. The findings above suggest that a distraction, such as the presence of others, can act as a cognitive load, or can add to the existing cognitive load, on working memory, resulting in reduced performance on tasks requiring all of a person's cognitive capacity (Eysenck, 1984; Kahneman, 1973).

Figure 1. Research model

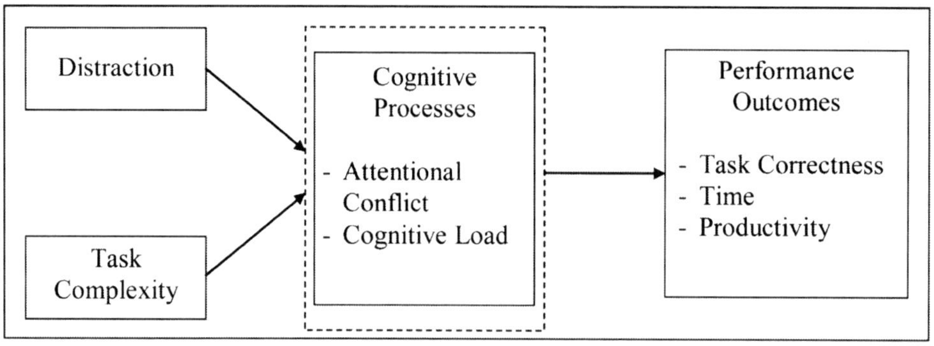

2.3. Social Facilitation

Triplett (1898) conducted the first study that documented the enhancement of an individual's performance when others are present. This phenomenon was later coined *Social Facilitation* by Allport (1920). Essentially, a U-shaped relationship emerged where initial levels of stimuli (i.e., the presence of others) improved performance but did so only up to a critical point where increasing stimulus levels resulted in degradation in performance. Subsequent studies in the area of social facilitation resulted in mixed findings. While some researchers found an increase in performance when others were present, performance decreases were also reported. It was hence apparent that there was more to this effect than could be explained by the mere presence of others.

In an effort to integrate these divergent results, Zajonc (1965) theorized that an individual's performance was linked to a physiological arousal state, which may be affected by the task as well as the presence of others. In other words, if others are present, and we are asked to perform an easy task (either simple or well-learned), then social facilitation occurs and the dominant response would be to perform well. The reason being that a simple task is associated with fewer cues (e.g., pieces of information) (Payne, 1982) than a difficult task and thus places less demand on an individual's mental or cognitive capacity (Kahneman, 1973). Therefore, even in the presence of a distraction, an individual will perform well at an easy task because he/she has ample cognitive resources to use in processing information (Speier et al., 2003). On the other hand, if an individual is asked to perform a difficult task (either complex or unfamiliar to the individual), both the distraction and the complexity of the task may lead to the depletion of cognitive resources. In this case, the individual tries to minimize this depletion by ignoring important cues from the task, which affects overall performance (Baron, 1986). Thus, the increased arousal state, or cognitive load, that is created by both the distraction and the complexity of the task negatively affects the individual's performance. High arousal, or cognitive load, affects performance by reducing an individual's attentional control, accuracy, short-term memory (working memory), and retrieval efficiency (Eysenck, 1984).

2.4. Proposed Model

Our research model (see Figure 1) extends distraction-conflict theory to examine the effects of mobile wireless computing on individual performance. We propose that various types of prolonged, external distractions will lead to attentional conflict. The attentional conflict created by the distraction, coupled with the cognitive load created by the complexity of the task, will affect an individual's performance on the task. We develop specific hypotheses below.

According to the concept of social facilitation, an individual's performance on a task will vary depending on the task complexity and the type of distraction (Zajonc, 1965). Highly complex tasks are associated with excessive cognitive load (Sweller et al., 1998). In fact, complex tasks, as compared to easier tasks, place greater demands on an individual's cognitive capacity (Kahneman, 1973), which can have negative effects on performance (Sweller et al., 1998). In the presence of a high distraction, the individual experiences attentional conflict, which is the condition where the individual feels the obligation to allocate attention to both the primary task and the distraction (Baron, 1986; Sanders et al., 1978). At the same time, the individual expends cognitive effort to try to ignore the distraction (Kunda, 2001). Therefore, both the distraction and the complex task lead to the depletion of cognitive resources. To minimize this depletion, the individual may ignore important cues from the task, which negatively impacts task performance (Baron, 1986). Therefore, we propose that the presence of a distraction will lower performance on a complex task.

Hypothesis 1a: *For a complex task, individuals in the no distraction condition will outperform those in the low distraction condition.*

Hypothesis 1b: *For a complex task, individuals in the low distraction condition will outperform those in the high distraction condition.*

Simple tasks are associated with lower cognitive load (Sweller et al., 1998). These tasks do not place a great demand on an individual's cognitive capacity. Therefore, the task alone will not deplete the individual's cognitive resources, and should not impact task performance. In other words, if there is no distraction, the individual will have ample cognitive resources to perform the simple task (Speier et al., 2003).

However, in the presence of a high distraction, the individual will experience attentional conflict (Baron, 1986; Sanders et al., 1978), which will leave the individual with less cognitive resources to complete the task at hand. At the same time, the individual will expend cognitive effort to try and ignore the distraction (Kunda, 2001). Therefore, in the presence of high distraction, an individual's performance at a simple task will be worse than that of an individual in a no distraction condition. Therefore, we propose that for a simple task, the task and the distraction will not create enough of a cognitive load to negatively affect performance, unless the distraction is high.

Hypothesis 2a: *For a simple task, there will be no difference in performance between individuals in the no distraction condition and those in a low distraction condition.*

Hypothesis 2b: *For a simple task, individuals in the no and low distraction conditions will outperform those in the high distraction condition.*

3. METHODOLOGY

3.1. Research Design

A laboratory experiment with a 3 X 2 full factorial design was employed to mitigate the potential that individual factors would confound the hypothesized relationships under investigation (e.g., Campbell & Stanley, 1966; Cook & Campbell, 1979). Subjects were presented with two different computer-based tasks – simple (S) and complex (C) – under three different conditions – no distraction (ND), low distraction (LD) and high distraction (HD). Subjects were randomly assigned to one of six treatments – S/ND, S/LD, S/HD, C/ND, C/LD, and C/HD.

3.2. Subjects

A post hoc power analysis performed on pilot data (Nunnally & Bernstein, 1994) indicated a strong effect size (Cohen's d = 0.97) suggesting a sample size of 48. Nevertheless, given that subjects were voluntarily recruited from a junior-level information systems course, a sample size of 81 was obtained (66% male and 34% female). The average age of subjects was 22. No significant difference was found between groups on gender or Microsoft Excel experience, which was measured using a 7-point scale asking students to self-report their prior experience using Excel. While differences were found between subjects on computer self-efficacy, these differences were only found in the S/ND and S/LD groups, both of which outperformed the HD group on all dimensions.

The experiment was conducted in a controlled computer laboratory at a large state university in the United States. Subjects received credit for this scheduled research only if they completed the study in a conscientious and responsible manner. No additional incentives were provided. All subjects received course-based training on necessary task-relevant software prior to participating in the experiment.

3.3. Factors Investigated

3.3.1. Distraction

For the no-distraction condition, there were no purposeful distractions. For the low-level distraction subjects, a taping of the world news was played. For the high-level distraction, a gender-balanced social distraction was used. A conversation between four college-aged students discussing "college life" was video taped and played in the presence of subjects in the high-distraction condition. The actors and subject matter were chosen based on Similarity-Attraction Theory (Byrne & Griffitt, 1969), which posits that individuals will be more attracted to others who exhibit similar characteristics (personality traits, interests, etc.). Since the subjects exhibit similar characteristics to the individuals in the video tape, they should be interested in listening to the conversation. In other words, a level of attraction to the distraction in the study would provide a realistic and conscious shift in cognitive resources, as opposed to a purposeful shift in work location. Given the nomadic nature of wireless mobile computing, one would expect an individual to remain in the presence of an interesting or enjoyable high-level distraction, whereas an annoying high-level distraction may not result in the same behavior – an individual would remove himself/herself from the nuisance. We expect that a low-level distraction will simply be ignored. However, as identified in the pilot tests, as well as being supported by the extant working memory and social cognition literature, ignoring a stimulus will unknowingly increase cognitive load and therefore lead to impaired performance (e.g., Kunda, 2001).

A manipulation check, which asked subjects to what extent they were distracted during the task (a 7-point scale was used where 1 was "not at all" and 7 was "to a great extent"), revealed a significant difference between distraction levels ($F(2, 78) = 33.661$, $p < .001$). A follow-up test using Tukey HSD revealed a significant difference between the high and low distraction groups ($p < .001$), and the low and no distraction groups ($p < .005$) in the direction theorized.

3.3.2. Task Complexity

Individuals were randomly assigned to one of two tasks – simple or complex. A manipulation check was not performed on task complexity; rather, perceived mental effort was used as a proxy for measuring the perceived complexity of the task. The manipulation check revealed a significant difference between complexity treatments ($t(77) = 3.135$, $p < .001$) on perceived mental effort. In other words, those subjects in the more complex condition perceived the task to require much more mental effort than those subjects in the less complex condition.

To simulate a typical business-related event, subjects were told that their boss had just emailed them with a request and that they were expected to evaluate and respond to the request in a timely manner. The web-based email messages differed only with respect to the corresponding treatments (i.e., the complex condition contained more information cues); all other features were identical. The web-based email application was specifically developed for this study. The body of the email contained a brief message, including a detailed list of the desired data analysis and an attached Microsoft Excel file. The complex and simple tasks (see Appendix A) asked users to perform the same type of calculations (e.g., sum and difference); however, the complex task asked users to work with more data. In the complex condition, subjects were forced to expend additional cognitive resources as they were required to keep track of more data, develop more complicated formulas, and account for a larger number of information cues.

3.4. Performance Outcomes

Three aspects of performance are of major importance to this research – task correctness, time, and overall productivity. *Task correctness* compares each subject's answer to the optimal answer and indicates a subject's ability to perform the task correctly. Scores for the task correctness were calculated as the percentage of correct answers obtained. As such, a higher score represents a higher number of correct answers. *Time* (in minutes) is the time it took a subject to complete a particular task. This measure is an indication of speed, which represents how fast the subject completed the task. *Overall productivity* (correctness/time) combines these two components into one measure, the value of which depends both on task correctness and the time taken to complete the task. This measure reveals a different and interesting aspect of performance. In an organizational setting, where time is money, it is desirable to have employees who, in addition to completing a task correctly, can complete the task in a timely manner. The productivity measure hence emphasizes efficiency (Hiltz, 1988) and therefore is a more comprehensive measure of performance (Ives, 1994). Consequently, overall productivity is used as our dependent measure for hypothesis testing.

3.5. Procedure

Subjects entered a wireless computing laboratory and were evenly dispersed throughout the room. While subjects were free to move about the room, so as to distance themselves from the distraction during the experiment, no one chose to do so. The lab was equipped with two large RGB projectors, equally positioned across one wall. Researchers introduced themselves and gave specific instructions to subjects. Subjects were then given a brief tutorial on how to use simple formulas in Excel (e.g., sum and difference). Following this, each subject, using their student identification number, logged into the research application on a wireless laptop computer. All phases of the study were automated from within this application. Additionally, because the research application was located on a local server, latency and bandwidth issues were equivalent. The first screen was a home location from which the students were able to invoke questionnaires and launch their web-based email. After completing an initial set of questionnaires (e.g., demographics, prior computer experience, prior excel experience, and computer self-efficacy), the subjects' homepages were automatically reconfigured. The updated configuration contained a text-based message informing subjects that their boss had just emailed them with a request and that they could retrieve it by clicking the "open email" button. Once selected, a web-based email application was launched with a text-only request corresponding to their treatment group. Upon task completion, subjects submitted their solutions in

Table 1. Descriptive statistics (simple task)

		Simple Task					
		ND	LD	HD	Total	X^2 / F	Sig.
Gender	Male	11	6	10	27	3.93	0.200
	Female	5	7	2	14		
Average Age		21.06 (1.48)	23.38 (4.36)	23.08 (4.69)	22.51	1.762	0.185
Excel Experience		5.37 (.719)	5.46 (.519)	5.42 (.793)	5.42	0.057	0.945
Computer Self Efficacy		7.12 (1.84)	7.05 (1.44)	8.65 (.954)	7.61	4.561	0.017 **
Correctness (percentage)		.969 (.125)	.923 (.277)	.958 (.144)	0.95	0.217	0.806
Time (minutes)		4.21 (1.36)	8.28 (3.74)	11.28 (3.09)	7.92	22.24	0.001 **
Productivity (c/t)		.2494 (.0753)	.1314 (.0575)	.0932 (.0393)	0.158	25.54	0.001 **

Key: ND = No Distraction; LD = Low Distraction; HD = High Distraction.

Table 2. Descriptive statistics (complex task)

		Complex Task					
		ND	LD	HD	Total	X^2 / F	Sig.
Gender	Male	12	6	8	26	5.77	0.100
	Female	1	5	7	13		
Average Age		21.93 (5.16)	22.0 (2.14)	21.8 (1.32)	21.91	0.012	0.988
Excel Experience		5.36 (.929)	5.64 (.809)	5.40 (.986)	5.47	0.319	0.729
Computer Self Efficacy		7.28 (1.95)	8.01 (1.59)	7.34 (1.52)	7.54	0.674	0.514
Correctness (percentage)		.943 (.094)	.873 (.185)	.693 (.212)	0.836	8.157	0.001 **
Time (minutes)		14.56 (2.63)	21.11 (2.93)	22.87 (6.89)	19.51	11.87	0.001 **
Productivity (c/t)		.0667 (.0137)	.0425 (.0126	.0326 (.0115)	0.047	27.43	0.001 **

Key: ND = No Distraction; LD = Low Distraction; HD = High Distraction.

an email response. Following the submission, subjects' home pages were reconfigured with a new message and link requesting that they complete a final questionnaire, which included manipulation checks for complexity and distraction.

5. RESULTS

Planned contrasts were used in order to test the hypotheses. Two major advantages of the contrast approach to data analysis are "that it can provide relatively clear and direct evaluations of theoretically-driven predictions" (Furr & Rosenthal, 2003, p. 48), while at the same time providing greater statistical power (Rosenthal & Rosnow, 1991). Contrasts provide a simple and efficient technique to analyze focused questions in which specific predictions can be evaluated by examining the extent to which the observed pattern of data matches the pattern of data implied by theory (Furr & Rosenthal, 2003; Rosenthal & Rosnow, 1991). Planned comparisons do, however, increase the probability of making a type I error. Hence, a Bonferroni adjustment was made ($\alpha = 0.025$). Descriptive statistics are provided in Table 1 and Table 2.

Figure 2. Results for simple and complex tasks

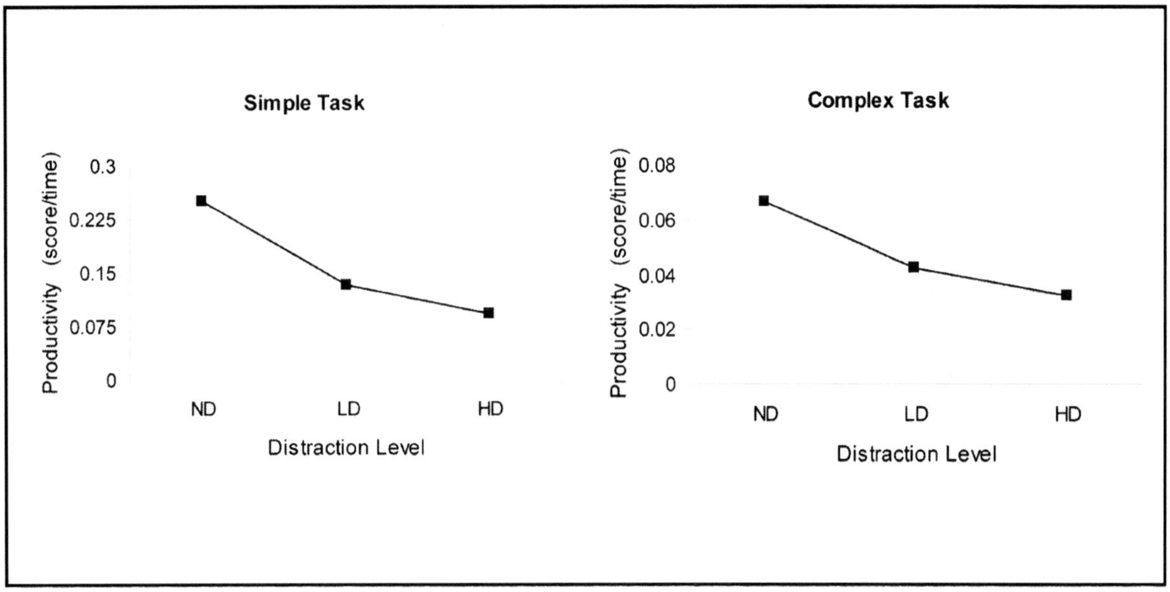

5.1. Complex Task

H1a and H1b predict that for a complex task, the cognitive load generated by both the task and the distraction will have a negative effect on performance. More specifically, H1a predicts that subjects in the no distraction condition will outperform those in the low distraction condition (i.e., ND > LD). The results indicate that task correctness for subjects in the low distraction condition was equivalent to the no distraction condition ($t(23) = 1.949$, $p = 0.030$), however, subjects in the low distraction condition took longer than those in the no distraction condition to complete the task ($t(23) = 3.313$, $p = .001$). Hence, when examining overall productivity, results indicate that subjects in the no distraction condition outperformed those in the low distraction condition ($t(23) = 3.535$, $p = .001$), providing support for H1a (see Figure 2).

Hypothesis 1b predicts that subjects in the low distraction condition will outperform those in the high distraction condition for complex tasks (i.e., LD > HD). The results indicate that task correctness for subjects in the low distraction condition was higher than the high distraction condition ($t(26) = 2.247$, $p = 0.015$), while subjects in the low and high distraction conditions took the same time to complete the task ($t(26) = 1.415$, $p = 0.084$). Hence, when examining overall productivity, subjects in the low distraction condition outperformed those in the high distraction condition ($t(26) = 2.735$, $p = 0.005$), providing support for H1b (see Figure 2).

5.2. Simple Task

H2a and H2b predict that the task and the distraction will not create enough of a cognitive load to negatively affect performance unless the distraction is high. More specifically, H2a predicts that subjects in the no distraction condition will not outperform those in the low distraction condition (i.e., ND = LD). The results indicate that task correctness for subjects in the low distraction condition were equal to those in the no distraction condition ($t(27) = 0.591$, $p = 0.280$), however, those in the no distraction condition took less time to complete the task than those in the low distraction condition ($t(27) = 4.044$, $p = 0.002$). As a result, contrary to H2a, subjects in the no

Table 3. Hypothesis testing summary table

	Support		
	Correctness	**Time**	**Overall Productivity**
Complex Tasks			
H1a: ND > LD	ND = LD	ND < LD	√
H1b: LD > HD	LD > HD	LD = HD	√
Simple Tasks			
H2a: ND = LD	ND = LD	ND < LD	×
H2b: LD > HD	LD = HD	LD < HD	√

distraction condition outperformed those in the low distraction condition on overall productivity (t(27) = 4.651, p <.001) (see Figure 2).

Hypothesis 2b predicts that subjects in the two lower distraction conditions – no/low – should outperform those in the high distraction condition (i.e., ND/LD > HD). The results indicate that task correctness for subjects in the high distraction condition were the same as those in the lower (i.e., no/low) distraction conditions (t(23) = 0.393., p = 0.249). However, subjects in the lower distraction conditions finished the task in significantly less time than subjects in the high distraction condition (t(39) = 4.659, p <.001). Hence, when examining overall productivity, subjects in the lower distraction conditions – no/low – outperformed those in the high distraction condition (t(39) = 5.131, p <.001), finding support for H2b (see Figure 2). Table 3 provides a summary of results of hypothesis testing.

6. DISCUSSION

Our findings indicate that regardless of task complexity, the no distraction group outperformed the low distraction group and the low distraction group outperformed the high distraction group. These findings are in accordance with the distraction-conflict theory. According to this theory, the presence of others, which creates a distraction, can affect the performance of an individual as he/she is forced to allocate his/her attention to two or more inputs (Sanders et al., 1978). Therefore, as the level of distraction increases, overall performance decreases.

The social facilitation literature, however, also suggests that it is not just the mere presence of others that will affect performance, but also the psychological arousal created by the task (Zajonc, 1965). Hence, based on both the distraction-conflict theory and the social facilitation literature, we also expected a significant performance difference between each of the distraction levels for the complex task and between the high and low/no distraction levels for the simple task. As predicted, we found that when performing a complex task subjects in the no distraction group outperformed those in the low distraction group and subjects in the low distraction group outperformed those in the high distraction group. In other words, as the distraction level increased, the arousal created by both the distraction and the complexity of the task had a negative effect on performance.

Similarly, the findings for the simple task indicate that subjects in the lower distraction conditions significantly outperformed those in the high distraction condition. Hence it appears that even though the task was simple, the psychological arousal created by the high distraction condition alone created enough psychological arousal to negatively affect performance. Contrary to what we predicted, subjects in the no distraction condition outperformed those in the low distraction condition. Interestingly, had we only examined correctness for both the no and low distraction groups, there would have been no significant difference. In other words, the no and low distraction groups scored very similarly on the task. However, it is not practical to look at task correctness alone, especially when it may have taken one person 10 minutes to complete the task and another person 20 minutes. Thus, when we take correctness and time into consideration to get overall productivity, there is a significant difference between the no and low distraction groups.

A possible explanation for these unanticipated results may be that the simple task may not have been simple enough. Had the task been simpler, individuals in the low distraction group may have had enough cognitive capacity to deal with the distraction and the task without it affecting their performance. We do not believe, however, that the simplicity, or lack thereof, of the task led to these results. Rather, a more plausible explanation for these findings is that it did not matter whether an individual was attending to or ignoring a distraction, his/her cognitive capacity was still being loaded by a set of non-task related cognitions (Kunda, 2001) to the point of creating enough arousal to impair performance. In other words, the distraction level alone was enough to affect overall performance.

Another interesting observation is that rather than move away from a perceived distraction, subjects chose to remain in the presence of the distraction. For the high distraction condition, we attribute this to Similarity-Attraction Theory in that subjects found the individuals and content in the high-distraction video interesting rather than annoying and thus chose not to remove themselves from the distracting environment. With respect to the low-level distraction, we believe subjects most likely did not perceive the distraction to be at a level that would adversely affect completing the task. Hence, they chose to remain in the environment and ignore or block out external stimuli, which as Kunda (2001) points out can increase cognitive load and impair performance.

7. LIMITATIONS, IMPLICATIONS, FUTURE RESEARCH, AND CONCLUSION

Inherent with any study are limitations that can potentially affect the findings. Here, we specifically address the limitations of this study. First, using homogenous student subjects can lead to issues regarding the generalizability of the results. When conducting experiments, however, there is a tradeoff between generalizability and precision (McGrath, Martin, & Kulka, 1984). In early studies of an emerging phenomenon, it is important to focus on precision to isolate the effects of the treatment. Hence, despite using homogenous subjects, we believe that the tasks used in this study would certainly be relevant to those working in a business environment. Second, the distraction, while being highly salient for college-aged students, may not be salient for other populations. In other words, a high-level distraction for one person may be a low-level distraction for another. However, we would argue that regardless of the type of distraction, the outcomes for no, low, and high levels would be very similar to those observed in this study. Additionally, it is likely that different types of distractions will have differing effects on task performance. For example, a "distraction" of enjoyable and user controlled music would likely have less deleterious impacts than random, uncontrolled annoyances. It is also likely that the type of task being performed will interplay with the type of distraction. Here we utilized a spreadsheet type task that focused on "left brain" analytical processes. However, had the task been more of a subjective, "right brain" task, the results could be different. Additionally, any of these impacts are also likely to be influenced by the personal characteristics of each individual (e.g., mood). Lastly, our study was cross sectional and can in no way predict the influence of distractions on individual performance over time. Clearly, each of these limitations provides opportunities for future research (discussed below).

In terms of theoretical contributions, this study conducted a test of the distraction-conflict theory within the context of mobile wireless environments. As a result, this study extends the distraction-conflict theory by illustrating that any type of prolonged distraction, not just a distraction created by the presence of others, will increase an individual's arousal. Additionally, we draw on social facilitation literature from psychology to further guide our exploration into the effects of various levels of distractions given certain task types. The results of the study show that no matter how complex a task an individual is working on, any type of distraction will affect their performance on that task.

We believe that our findings have serious implications for organizations which may be considering a mobile wireless initiative for their employees. In accordance with this study, the belief that mobile wireless devices will result in productivity gains may be more of an illusion than a reality. While today's mobile technologies enable knowledge workers to perform their work from anyplace at anytime, this does not necessarily mean that they should do so. As indicated previously, knowledge work is characterized by high levels of attention and concentration. Based on our findings, however, knowledge workers may not be able to concentrate, or focus their attention, on their work if a distraction is present. Our results indicate that being in an environment where there are moderate to high levels of distractions can impair the performance of an individual, even if they are working on a simple or well-learned task. As would be expected, our findings also indicate that if an individual is trying to complete a task in a distracting environment, they did better on a simple task than a complex task.

Hence, if an organization is considering moving toward a mobile wireless initiative, they may first want to consider the type of work that their mobile workforce will be performing, as well as the environment in which that work may be performed. If the work to be performed requires a significant amount of attention and/or the work environment is believed to contain too many opportunities for distraction, the organization may need to consider retaining a more traditional work environment. An alternative solution, as suggested by Davis (2002), would be to provide training and mentoring on self-management from others who have learned to work productively in a distracting environment. Moreover, it is quite plausible that as the effects of distractions on performance become more salient to knowledge workers, they may themselves seek out optimal work conditions. Although not specifically tested in the current study, the efficacy of such longitudinal effects clearly provides an opportunity for future research.

Future research may want to focus on improving the generalizability of the study by replicating the study across different populations and in more natural settings. Further, the effects of individual differences, such as culture, gender, and personality traits, on how people respond to different types of distractions should be examined. The effects of different types of distractions on different types of tasks need investigation. For instance, researchers may want to investigate the effects of distractions on performance for wireless mobile collaboration tasks at the individual and group levels as well as investigate welcomed versus unwelcomed distractions. Another area of future research that could be explored is an examination of how, why, and under what conditions distracting work environments influence individual performance longitudinally as well as the mix and magnitude to which the combinations of different wireless devices (e.g., BlackBerry vs. notebook) affect performance Additionally, with the push for wireless computing in academic settings, we believe that our findings can be extrapolated and applied to this environment as well and that it offers fertile ground for further investigating the effects of distractions on productivity.

Mobile wireless computing is opening up numerous possibilities in the realm of knowledge work. According to Work Design Collaborative, a small think-tank, knowledge workers spend about one-third of their working time in public places such as cafes, libraries or parks ("Labour Movement," 2008). Little is known, however, about the impact of mobile wireless technologies on the productivity of knowledge workers (e.g., Andersson, 2008; Ladd et al., 2010). Moreover, very little is actually known about the effects of mobility on society in general and organization metrics more specifically (e.g., Ladd et al., 2010). The research reported in this study provides an understanding of how task complexity and varying levels of distraction influence the performance of individuals within a mobile wireless environment. It was found that regardless of task complexity, a knowledge worker's performance is negatively affected when he/she is working in an environment where there are moderate to high levels of distractions. While future research is necessary in order to fully understand this phenomenon, the results herein provide both important and interesting insights into productivity considerations for mobile, wireless work environments.

REFERENCES

Abraham, D. L. (2001). Mobile Enterprise Computing and the Diffusion of Mobile Enterprise Business Applications in Organizations. *Proceedings of 2001 Americas Conference on Information Systems (AMCIS 2001)*, Boston, MA, 461-464.

Allport, F. H. (1920). The Influence of the Group Upon Association and Thought. *Journal of Experimental Psychology, 3*, 159–182. doi:10.1037/h0067891

Andersson, B. (2008). Mobile Computing from a Developer's Perspective: A 10-Year Review, 1999-2008. *Business Information Processing, 24*(5), 220–233.

Baddeley, A. D. (1986). *Working Memory*. London: Oxford University Press.

Balasubramanian, S., Peterson, R. A., & Jarvenpaa, S. L. (2002). Exploring the Implications of M-Commerce for Markets and Marketing. *Journal of the Academy of Marketing Science, 30*(4), 348–361. doi:10.1177/009207002236910

Barnes, S. J. (2001). Big in Japan - iMode and the Mobile Internet. *Journal of Information Technology Theory and Application, 3*(4), 27–32.

Baron, R. S. (1986). Distraction-Conflict Theory: Progress and Problems. In Berkowitz, L. (Ed.), *Advances in Experimental Social Psychology (Vol. 19*, pp. 1–40). New York: Academic Press.

Beulen, E., & Streng, R. (2002). The Impact of Online Mobile Office Applications on the Effectiveness and Efficiency of Mobile Workers' Behavior. *Proceedings of the 2002 International Conference on Information Systems (ICIS 2002)*, Barcelona, Spain, 629-640.

Boncella, R. J. (2002). Wireless Security: An Overview. *Proceedings of 2002 Americas Conference on Information Systems (AMCIS 2002)*, Dallas, TX, 2381-2386.

Byrne, D., & Griffitt, W. (1969). Similarity and Awareness of Similarity of Personality Characteristics as Determinants of Attraction. *Journal of Experimental Research in Personality, 3*, 179–186.

Cambell, D. T., & Stanley, J. C. (1966). *Experimental and Quasi-Experimental Designs for Research*. Chicago, IL: Rand McNally.

Cantwell, E. (2003). In-building Wireless: How to Keep a Signal When You're Indoors. *Wireless Business & Technology, 3*(3), 12–14.

Chen, L., & Nath, R. (2006). Impact of Wireless Local Area Networks on Organization of Users. *Journal of Electronic Commerce in Organizations, 4*(2), 62–81. doi:10.4018/jeco.2006040104

Cook, T. D., & Campbell, D. T. (1979). *Quasi-Experimentation: Design and analysis issues for field settings*. Chicago, IL: Rand McNally.

Cousins, K. C., & Varshney, U. (2009). Designing Ubiquitous Computing Environments to Support Work Life Balance. *Communications of the ACM, 52*(5), 117–123. doi:10.1145/1506409.1506438

Davis, G. B. (1999). A Research Perspective for Information Systems and Example of Emerging Area of Research. *Information Systems Frontiers, 1*(3), 195–203. doi:10.1023/A:1010094126762

Davis, G. B. (2002). Anytime/Anyplace Computing and the Future of Knowledge Work. *Communications of the ACM, 45*(12), 67–73. doi:10.1145/585597.585617

Dekleva, S. M., Shim, J. P., Varshney, U., & Knoerzer, G. (2007). Evolution and Emerging Issues in Mobile Wireless Networks. *Communications of the ACM, 50*(6), 38–43. doi:10.1145/1247001.1247003

Drucker, P. F. (1969). *The Age of Discontinuity*. New York: Harper & Row.

Easterbrook, J. A. (1959). The Effect of Emotion on Cue Utilization and the Organization of Behavior. *Psychological Bulletin, 66*, 183–201.

Eysenck, M. W. (1984). *A Handbook of Cognition Psychology*. London: Lawrence Erlbaum Associates, Ltd.

Furr, R. M., & Rosenthal, R. (2003). Evaluating Theories Efficiently: The Nuts and Bolts of Contrast Analysis. *Understanding Statistics, 2*(1), 45–67. doi:10.1207/S15328031US0201_03

Gebauer, J., Shaw, M. J., & Gribbins, M. L. (2010). Task-Technology Fit for Mobile Information Systems. *Journal of Information Technology, 25*(3), 259–272. doi:10.1057/jit.2010.10

Gopal, A., Compeau, D., Marcon, T., & Olivera, F. (2006). Learning with Laptops: Information Technology and the Transformation of an MBA Program. *Proceedings of the 39th Annual Hawaii International Conference on System Sciences (HICSS)*, 1-10.

Gorlenko, L., & Merrick, R. (2003). No Wires Attached: Usability Challenges in the Connected Mobile World. *IBM Systems Journal, 42*(4), 639–651. doi:10.1147/sj.424.0639

Groff, B. D., Baron, R. S., & Moore, D. L. (1983). Distraction, Attentional Conflict, and Drive-like Behavior. *Journal of Experimental Social Psychology, 19*(4), 359–380. doi:10.1016/0022-1031(83)90028-8

Hiltz, S. R. (1988). Productivity Enhancement from Computer-Mediated Communication: A Systems Contingency Approach. *Communications of the ACM, 31*(12), 1438–1454. doi:10.1145/53580.53583

Ives, B. (1994). Probing the Productivity Paradox (Editorial Comment). *Management Information Systems Quarterly, 18*(2), XXI–XXIV.

Jarvenpaa, S. L., Lang, K. R., Takeda, Y., & Tuunainen, V. K. (2003). Mobile Commerce at Crossroads. *Communications of the ACM, 46*(12), 41–44. doi:10.1145/953460.953485

Jessup, L. M., & Robey, D. (2002). The Relevance of Social Issues in Ubiquitous Computing Environments. *Communications of the ACM, 45*(12), 88–91. doi:10.1145/585597.585621

Kahneman, D. (1973). *Attention and Effort*. Englewood Cliffs: Prentice Hall.

Keane, B. (2002). Lowering Health Care Costs Out-Of-The-Box. *Wireless Business & Technology, 2*(2), 36–38.

Kunda, Z. (2001). *Social Cognition: Making Sense of People*. Cambridge, MA: MIT Press.

Labour Movement. (2008, April 12). *The Economist, 387*(8575), 5-8.

Ladd, D. A., Datta, A., Sarker, S., & Yu, Y. (2010). Trends in Mobile Computing within the IS Discipline: A Ten-Year Retrospective. *Communications of the AIS, 27*, 285–306.

Lee, T. (2005). The Impact of Perceptions of Interactivity on Customer Trust and Transaction Intentions in Mobile Commerce. *Journal of Electronic Commerce Research, 6*(3), 165–181.

Lee, Y. J., & Shin, D. C. (2005). Performance of Caching Strategies for Pull-Based Data Broadcast Systems in Mobile Computing Environments. *Journal of Computer Information Systems, 45*(4), 102–115.

Looney, C. A., Jessup, L. M., & Valacich, J. S. (2004). Emerging Business Models for Mobile Brokerage Services. *Communications of the ACM, 47*(6), 71–77. doi:10.1145/990680.990683

Lu, J., Liu, C., Yu, C., & Yao, J. E. (2003). Acceptance of Wireless Internet via Mobile Technology in China. *Proceedings of 2003 Americas Conference on Information Systems (AMCIS 2003)*, Tampa, FL, 1165-1173.

Malladi, R., & Agrawal, D. P. (2002). Current and Future Applications of Mobile and Wireless Networks. *Communications of the ACM, 45*(10), 144–146. doi:10.1145/570907.570947

McGrath, J. E., Martin, J., & Kulka, R. (1984). *Judgment Calls in Research*. Beverly Hills, CA: Sage Publications.

Miller, G. A. (1956). The Magical Number Seven, Plus or Minus Two: Some Limits on Our Capacity for Processing Information. *Psychological Review, 63*, 81–97. doi:10.1037/h0043158

More than a Billion Mobile Workers Worldwide by Year's End. (2010). *IDC Press Release*. Retrieved from http://www.idc.com/getdoc.jsp?containerId=prUS22214110

Ngai, E. W. T., & Gunasekaran, A. (2005). A Review for Mobile Commerce Research and Applications. *Decision Support Systems, 43*, 3–15. doi:10.1016/j.dss.2005.05.003

Nunnally, J. C., & Bernstein, I. H. (1994). *Psychometric Theory* (3rd ed.). New York: McGraw-Hill, Inc.

Okoli, C., Ives, B., Jessup, L. M., & Valacich, J. S. (2002) The Mobile Conference Information System: Unwiring Academic Conferences with Wireless Mobile Computing. *Communications of the AIS,* 9, 180-206.

Our Nomadic Future. (2008, April 12). *The Economist.* 387(8575), 16-16.

Payne, J. W. (1982). Contingent Decision Behavior. *Psychological Bulletin, 92*(2), 382–402. doi:10.1037/0033-2909.92.2.382

Philips, J. T. (2002). Welcome to the New Wireless Culture. *Information Management Journal, 36*(1), 64–68.

Prasopoulou, E., Pouloudi, A., & Panteli, N. (2006). Enacting New Temporal Boundaries: The Role of Mobile Phones. *European Journal of Information Systems, 15*(3), 227–284. doi:10.1057/palgrave.ejis.3000617

Rosenthal, R., & Rosnow, R. L. (1991). *Essentials of Behavioral Research: Methods and Data Analysis* (2nd ed.). Boston, MA: McGraw-Hill.

Sanders, G. S., Baron, R. S., & Moore, D. L. (1978). Distraction and Social Comparison as Mediators of Social Facilitation Effects. *Journal of Experimental Social Psychology, 14*(3), 291–303. doi:10.1016/0022-1031(78)90017-3

Sarker, S., & Wells, J. D. (2003). Understanding Mobile Handheld Device Use and Adoption. *Communications of the ACM, 46*(12), 35–40. doi:10.1145/953460.953484

Shen, J., & Jones, Q. (2003). *In Situ* Data Capture and Mobile Knowledge Management: Helping Technicians Share Case Stories. *Proceedings of 2003 Americas Conference on Information Systems (AMCIS 2003)*, Tampa, FL, 2231-2236.

Sherry, J., & Salvador, T. (2001). Running and Grimacing: The Struggle for Balance in Mobile Work. In Brown, B., Harper, R., & Green, N. (Eds.), *Wireless World: Social and Interactive Aspects of the Mobile Age* (pp. 108–120). New York: Springer Verlag.

Shim, J. P., Varshney, U., Dekleva, S. M., & Knoerzer, G. (2002). Mobile Wireless Technology and Services: Evolution and Outlook. *Proceedings of 2002 Americas Conference on Information Systems (AMCIS 2002)*, Dallas, TX, 1998-1999.

Speier, C., Vessey, I., & Valacich, J. S. (2003). The Effects of Interruptions, Task Complexity, and Information Presentation on Computer-Supported Decision-Making Performance. *Decision Sciences*, *34*(4), 771–797. doi:10.1111/j.1540-5414.2003.02292.x

Stafford, T. F., & Gillenson, M. L. (2003). Mobile Commerce: What it Is and What it Could be. *Communications of the ACM*, *46*(12), 33–34. doi:10.1145/953460.953483

Sweller, J. (1988). Cognitive Load during Problem Solving: Effects on Learning. *Cognitive Science*, *12*, 257–285. doi:10.1207/s15516709cog1202_4

Sweller, J. (1994). Load Theory, Learning Difficulty and Instructional Design. *Learning and Instruction*, *4*, 295–312. doi:10.1016/0959-4752(94)90003-5

Sweller, J., vanMerrienboer, J. J. G., & Paas, F. G. W. C. (1998). Cognitive Architecture and Instructional Design. *Educational Psychology Review*, *10*, 251–296. doi:10.1023/A:1022193728205

Triplett, N. (1898). The Dynamogenic Factors in Pacemaking and Competition. *The American Journal of Psychology*, *9*, 507–533. doi:10.2307/1412188

Urbaczewski, A., Valacich, J. S., & Jessup, L. M. (2003). Mobile Commerce: Opportunities and Challenges. *Communications of the ACM*, *46*(12), 31–32.

Viehland, D., & Hughes, J. (2002). The Future of Wireless Application Protocol. *Proceedings of 2002 Americas Conference on Information Systems (AMCIS 2002)*, Dallas, TX, 1883-1891.

Wakefield, R. L., & Whitten, D. (2006). Mobile Computing: A User Study on Hedonic/Utilitarian Mobile Device Usage. *European Journal of Information Systems*, *15*(1), 292–300. doi:10.1057/palgrave.ejis.3000619

Wood, R. (1986). Task complexity: Definition of the Construct. *Organizational Behavior and Human Decision Processes*, *37*(1), 60–82. doi:10.1016/0749-5978(86)90044-0

Zajonc, R. B. (1965). Social Facilitation. *Science*, *149*, 269–274. doi:10.1126/science.149.3681.269

Zhang, P., & Li, N. (2005). The Intellectual Development of Human-Computer Interaction Research: A Critical Assessment of the MIS Literature (1990 - 2000). *Journal of the Association for Information Systems*, *6*(1), 227–291.

APPENDIX A

Simple Task

I would like you to review the overall sales for each of the four regions for the years 2002 and 2003 and report the following information next to the corresponding answer at the top of the spreadsheet:

1. What were the total sales for the year 2003.
2. What were the total sales for the year 2002.
3. What was the difference in sales for North America from 2002 to 2003.
4. What was the difference in sales between the year 2003 and 2002.

Table 4.

Wholesale Distributors Incorporated			
Regional Sales for the Years 2002 and 2003			
Region	**Year 2003**	**Year 2002**	**Change**
North America	447305	436849	
South America	408680	398549	
Australia	274521	254900	
Europe	325482	285504	
Total			

Complex Task

I would like you to review the sales for each of the four quarters of the year 2003 and report the following information next to the corresponding answer at the top of the spreadsheet.

1. Which appliance had the highest total sales for the year.
2. Which region had the highest total sales for the year.
3. What was the difference in total sales of microwaves between the fourth and first quarters.
4. What were the total sales for the year for refrigerators in Europe.
5. What was the difference in sales of washers and dryers combined between the second and third quarters for Australia.

Table 5.

Wholesale Distributors Incorporated						
Year 2003						
First Quarter						
Region	**Washers**	**Dryers**	**Refrigerators**	**Stoves**	**Microwaves**	**All Appliances**
NorthAmerica	447305	436849	542857	499239	684112	
SouthAmerica	408680	398549	482739	380560	429184	
Australia	274521	254900	394827	355932	398201	
Europe	325482	285504	487928	397100	432039	
Total						
Second Quarter						
Region	**Washers**	**Dryers**	**Refrigerators**	**Stoves**	**Microwaves**	**All Appliances**
NorthAmerica	4529484	472947	529473	4728437	648217	
SouthAmerica	449822	439482	498484	382948	437582	
Australia	278721	264732	385717	365734	401930	
Europe	324283	265483	467211	403920	438274	
Total						
Third Quarter						
Region	**Washers**	**Dryers**	**Refrigerators**	**Stoves**	**Microwaves**	**All Appliances**
NorthAmerica	402918	400198	520192	502247	621298	
SouthAmerica	401389	403221	472888	388929	419281	
Australia	288490	264726	387298	366100	400293	
Europe	243529	235423	472323	388182	428829	
Total						
Fourth Quarter						
Region	**Washers**	**Dryers**	**Refrigerators**	**Stoves**	**Microwaves**	**All Appliances**
NorthAmerica	463737	465002	563292	500143	698928	
SouthAmerica	402473	402238	472110	385765	433020	
Australia	265699	257718	396382	359111	401219	
Europe	309837	294812	468802	403339	443902	
Total						

Chapter 16
Assessing the Dimension of Magnitude in Computer Self-Efficacy:
An Empirical Comparison of Task-Based and Levels of Assistance-Based Methodologies

James Downey
University of Central Arkansas, USA

R. Rainer Jr.
Auburn University, USA

ABSTRACT

Computer Self-efficacy (CSE) has been used in many studies as a predictor of individual competence or performance, usage behavior, and a variety of attitudes. Although CSE has been effective in explaining a variety of human computing interactions, there have been a number of studies in which the relationship was weak or nonexistent. One reason for such findings concerns how CSE is operationalized in extant instruments. Many (if not most) leading cognitive theorists (Bandura, 1997; Gist & Mitchell, 1992; Marakas et al., 1998) rather emphatically state that actual tasks must be used to most accurately determine an individual's perception of ability (i.e., self-efficacy) for some task or domain. They suggest that using tasks, of incremental difficulty level within the intended domain, most accurately presents an individual's self-efficacy and leads to stronger relationships with outcomes such as competence or performance. Yet one of the most utilized measures of self-efficacy uses levels of assistance (GCSE of Compeau & Higgins, 1995a), and not specific tasks. This study examines which methodology provides a stronger relationship with competence and performance. Using a sample of 610, self-efficacy (using both

DOI: 10.4018/978-1-60960-577-3.ch016

methodologies) and competence or performance were measured for six different computer application domains. Results indicate that for domains in which individual's had lower ability, actual tasks were superior. For domains of higher ability, however, levels of assistance yielded stronger relationships. This study clarifies the relationship between self-efficacy and performance as an individual moves from low to high ability in a computing domain as a result of training or experience. Implications and suggestions for further study are included.

INTRODUCTION

Computer Self-efficacy (CSE) has long been a construct of interest to the IT community of practitioners and researchers. CSE remains a strong predictor of computer performance and a variety of computer related activities, attitudes and beliefs. Computer Self-efficacy is defined as an individual judgment of one's capability to use a computer (Compeau & Higgins, 1995a). Self-efficacy serves as a motivator of action and is influenced by experience (Igbaria & Iivari, 1995) and training (Yi & Davis, 2003). In studies, Computer Self-efficacy has had significant relationships with enhanced attitudes toward computing (Harrison & Rainer, 1992), higher performance (Compeau & Higgins, 1995b), increased computer usage (Compeau, Higgins, & Huff, 1999), and improved computer skills development (Martocchio & Webster, 1992).

Despite previous results, using CSE to help explain behavior and predict performance has not always yielded consistent results, blurring its value in both IT research and usage in organizations. Despite successes noted by researchers, there have been other studies in which the results were either weak or baffling (Chau, 2001; Hasan, 2006; Henry & Martinko, 1997; Martocchio & Webster, 1992; Yi & Im, 2004). These inconsistencies, covered in more detail in the next section, suggest that the relationship between self-efficacy and related constructs is not always as predictable or as strong as expected. While weak or insignificant results may be due to problematic theory or poor research design, instrumentation issues can also affect results (Bandura, 1997; Gist 1987; Marakas, Yi, & Johnson, 1998). An instrument that measures Computer Self-efficacy should *accurately* capture a respondent's perception of their ability for the given computing domain. To the extent that a self-efficacy (SE) instrument does not represent an individual's true perception of ability in the domain, subsequent relationships with key outcomes or antecedents may be insignificant or distorted.

This study examines one important instrumentation issue which can affect results. There are the two common methodologies extant CSE instruments use in capturing an individual's perception of ability for a computing domain, one based on actual domain tasks and the other based on levels of assistance in completing tasks. Using a sample of 610, this study compares these two methodologies to determine if one is statistically better than the other in the relationship with common outcomes of self-efficacy, including computing competence (in four different domains) and computer performance (two domains). We suggest that the methodology used in measuring an individual's perception of ability impacts how accurately the domain is captured, and therefore influences its relationship with key outcomes.

This is an important conceptual and empirical consideration and there is no known study which examines this issue. We believe that some of the problems noted in the relationship between self-efficacy and its related constructs may be due to the inability of some instruments to sufficiently capture the intended computing domain. Accurately determining an individual's "true" perception of ability for a domain will enhance our conceptual knowledge of CSE and provide a more precise description of self-efficacy relationships with related constructs. It appears that most researchers and practitioners use extant CSE instruments without an appreciation of the consequences of its instrumentation methodology. It is the goal of this study to empirically compare the two CSE methodologies, task-based and levels of assistance-based, to determine significant differences between the two and under what circumstances each is more appropriate.

THE STRUCTURE OF CSE AND THE MAGNITUDE DIMENSION

Self-efficacy stems from the work of Bandura and his Social Cognitive Theory (1986, 1997). According to this theory, grounded by impressive empirical research (see Marakas et al., 1998, for a summary), human behavior is predictable and reciprocally influenced by both environmental and cognitive factors. Self-efficacy, one of the most important of the cognitive factors, is an individual's confidence that he or she can successfully accomplish a given task. Bandura maintains that self-efficacy is not merely a "passive foreteller" of one's ability level (1997, p. 39), it also helps govern and stimulates the motivation necessary to conduct the behavior. Whether the judgment is accurate or not, self-efficacy helps determine what activities an individual engages in, the effort in pursuing that activity, and the persistence in the face of adversity (Murphy, Coover & Owens, 1989).

Computer self-efficacy, or the judgment of ability to use a computer, is a multileveled construct. That is, one can judge their computing ability at multiple levels, including the application-specific level (for example, spreadsheet or database CSE) and at a general level which is a judgment of the entire computing domain, called general CSE or GCSE (Marakas et al., 1998). Self-efficacy has three distinct but related dimensions, including strength, generality, and magnitude (Bandura, 1997; Compeau & Higgins, 1995a; Gist & Mitchell, 1992).

- **Strength:** Strength is an assessment of confidence in successfully completing a given task. It is the level of conviction about the self-efficacy judgment. Those with higher self-efficacy have more confidence in their ability to carry out the task. To measure strength, instruments generally use a ten point response scale that ranges from 1 to 10 (or 10 to 100), as recommended (Bandura, 1986, 1997; Gist & Mitchell, 1992).
- **Generality:** Generality refers to the extent that a self-efficacy judgment in one area applies (generalizes) to a judgment in another area. Bandura recognized that SE judgments are rarely made with no beginning information; rather they are formed based on previous experiences, particularly in related domains (1997).
- **Magnitude:** Magnitude refers to the difficulty level of a given task an individual believes he/she can accomplish. Individuals with higher self-efficacy believe they can accomplish more difficult tasks. In the IT field, magnitude represents levels of task difficulty within the intended domain, such as databases, spreadsheets, or the full computing domain. All domains inherently include tasks of different levels of difficulty. In order to effectively measure an individual's perception of ability for the intended domain, all levels of difficulty should be included (Bandura, 1997). Magnitude is operationalized using either tasks or levels of assistance.

Magnitude is the instrumentation issue that is the focus of this study. Cognitive theorists maintain that self-efficacy instruments *should* capture the entire intended domain for an instrument to possess validity (Bandura, 1997; Compeau & Higgins, 1995a; Gist and Mitchell, 1992; Marakas et al., 1998). For example, if the domain is spreadsheets, the CSE instrument should allow the respondent to give a judgment of ability for the entire spreadsheet domain, including tasks covering all difficulty levels within the domain. Excluding difficulty levels within a domain yields a reduced range of scores, may not distinguish a ceiling or floor effect (the most or least difficult task that a respondent believes he/she can perform), and may not distinguish between individuals who have similar but not the same self-efficacy beliefs (Bandura, 1997).

While both theory and previous research confirm that self-efficacy is a strong predictor of performance, there have been several studies where the findings have been puzzling. In some of these studies, instrumentation issues appear to distort or confound results. For example, one study found the relationship between application-specific spreadsheet CSE and performance (using actual spreadsheet tasks) not significant (Yi & Im, 2004). In the study, the authors selected only five of the original ten items from the task-based spreadsheet CSE instrument (Johnson & Marakas, 2000), including *only the simpler tasks*, while excluding those items that dealt with more difficult tasks, such as applying formulas, graphing and cell referencing. The performance test, on the other hand, included more sophisticated tasks, such as macro programming, pivot table analysis, and advanced filtering. Therefore a plausible reason for this insignificant finding is that the CSE instrument did not adequately measure spreadsheet self-efficacy because it did not provide sufficient task differentiation levels. In another recent study (Hasan, 2006), the relationship between self-efficacy (measured two ways), performance (declarative knowledge items) and perceived ease of use was not significant. One scale, measuring general SE (GCSE), included ten points (1-10), anchored by "Not at all confident" and "Totally confident" (as recommended by Bandura, 1997). The other CSE scale was a seven-point Likert-type scale anchored by "Strongly disagree" and "Strongly agree". The item construction methodology of this instrument and the scaling differences may have introduced bias and/or respondent confusion, confounding the findings. Martocchio and Webster (1992) found that the relationship between training and the acquisition of declarative knowledge was not moderated as expected by Computer self-efficacy. Still another study found that CSE was significant *but in the opposite direction* to perceived usefulness (Chau, 2001). Finally, one study found the relationship between CSE and effort was not significant (Henry & Martinko, 1997). CSE was operationalized using only a four-point Likert scale (0-3), with anchors of "Always true" and "Always false". We suspect that a probable cause of the non-significant finding was that instrument's inability to accurately capture respondent's self-efficacy for the domain. Four point scales do not provide sufficient granularity (Bandura, 1997) and using the term "Always" as anchors (items 0 and 3) seems counter-productive, in effect leaving only two choices (1-2) to measure CSE (when is anyone "always" confident?).

Task-Based and Assistance-Based Methodologies

How well an instrument captures perception of ability for the intended domain is a critical consideration and one that may help explain some puzzling results. CSE instruments typically use two different methodologies in assessing this. Most cognitive theorists agree that the best approach in instrumentation is to use "task-focused" instruments (Compeau & Higgins, 1995a, p. 193). But how an instrument does this best is a matter of some debate. Task-based instruments rely on actual tasks in the domain to be measured, optimally including tasks representing all difficulty levels. The idea is that using representative tasks (simple to more complex) within a computing domain allows full coverage of domain content and provides the most accurate measure of self-efficacy for that domain. Many (if not most) cognitive theorists have ascribed to this position (Bandura, 1997; Gist & Mitchell, 1992; Marakas et al., 1998). The spreadsheet instrument of Johnson and Marakas (2000), for example, includes ten tasks, ranging from simple to more complex (see Appendix A).

The other type of instrument uses levels of assistance and includes arguably the most utilized CSE instrument in the IT field, that of Compeau and Higgins (1995a). This instrument asks respondents their perception of ability to complete an unnamed job using an unfamiliar software package, with various levels of assistance. It uses the following base: "I could complete the job using the software package", followed by ten levels of assistance. The assistance levels include items such as "…if I had never used a package like this before" and "…if I had seen someone else using it before trying it myself". These levels of assistance provide levels of task difficulty (magnitude) in that the levels range from almost no assistance to greater amounts of assistance. This type of instrument does not rely on component skills (like task-based instruments) but rather "it incorporates judgments of the ability to apply those skills to broader tasks", such as "analyzing financial data" (Compeau & Higgins, 1995a, p. 192). Levels of assistance instruments have been used successfully in many studies, including in an earlier instrument by Gist, Schwoerer, and Rosen (1989). While this type of instrument has been generally used to measure CSE for the entire computing domain (i.e., GCSE), it has been modified and used for individual applications (by the authors Compeau and Higgins themselves) by modifying the stem as such: "I could complete the job using the WORD PROCESSING, SPREADSHEET, DATABASE, etc. package…" with the same ten levels of assistance as the GCSE instrument (Compeau and Higgins, 1995b).

The question for this paper is which of these two methodologies provides a more accurate representation of an individual's self-efficacy, given the domains to be measured? Will different domains yield different results? This study examines both task- and assistance-based methodologies, measured for six computing domains (email applications, word processing (WP), spreadsheets (SS), graphic programs, such as PowerPoint (GP), databases (DB), and web design applications), in its relationship with the outcomes of performance and competence.

Outcomes of CSE

The relationship between CSE and its related outcomes (and antecedents) is well-researched (Bandura, 1997; see Marakas et al., 1998 for an IT review). Common outcomes of CSE include attitudes, such as anxiety or affect, beliefs, such as perceived usefulness, and usage. However one of the strongest and most important outcomes of CSE is performance. Individuals with higher self-efficacy tend to perform better at domain tasks and have higher competence (Bandura, 1986, 1997; Compeau & Higgins, 1995b; Munro, Huff, Marcolin, and Compeau, 1997). This study includes outcomes of competence and performance, but it should be noted that there is a distinction between the two; competence is antecedent to performance. To perform a task correctly, requisite skills or competencies are required (Adams, 1987; Attewell, 1990). For example, in order to implement a new database (performance task), one must be competent in database design, table creation, keys, etc.

In accordance with past research, self-efficacy is predicted to significantly influence both competence and performance. That said, we make no a priori hypothesis on which methodology is better or even whether the strength of the relationships will differ by domain. Figure 1 provides the research model. Competence was assessed in four domains (GP, DB, web, email) and performance was assessed in word processing and spreadsheets. Self-efficacy was assessed for the same six domains using both a task-based and level of assistance methodology (each respondent received one or the other). The six domains selected were those which we thought were the most common for the population of interest.

Figure 1. Research model

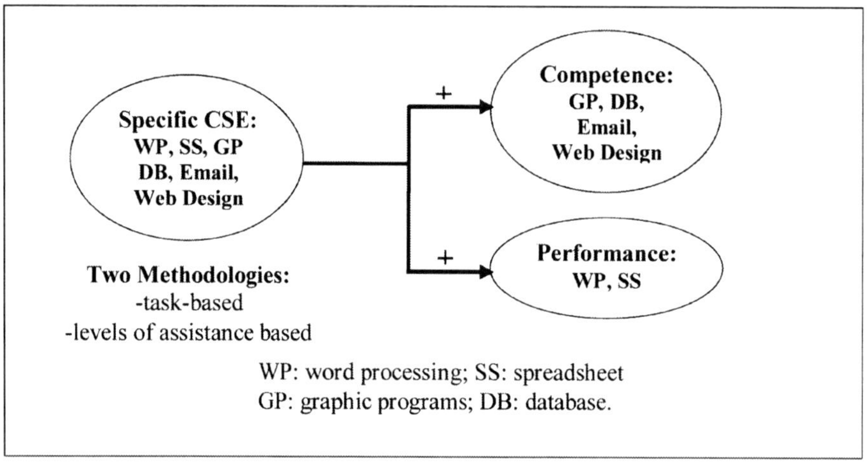

We chose to evaluate performance for only two domains because of survey length considerations (in fact, we made the performance tests optional). We chose the domains of word processing and spreadsheets for the performance tests for several reasons. Most importantly, we wanted domains that had sufficient numbers of respondents throughout the entire range of competence. The domains of databases and web design were rejected because we thought most respondents would be in the little to no competence range, limiting the range of scores in a performance test. Likewise, we suspected that respondents in the domain of email programs would be at the upper end of competency. This left word processing, spreadsheets, and graphic programs, and we eliminated graphic programs only because we were not as confident that many respondents would have much experience in that domain. The domains of word processing and spreadsheets were expected to have the most variation in ability level, from novice to expert, which would provide a more complete analysis of the relationship between CSE and performance.

This research design avoids "specificity matching" problems, in that all CSE measures and outcomes are measured at the same domain level, in this case at the computer application level (Chen et al., 2001, p. 65). Many contend that predictability is greatest and most accurate when self-efficacy and related constructs are measured at the same level of specificity (Bandura, 1997; Chen et al.; 2001).

RESEARCH METHODOLOGY

Participants and Methodology

The population chosen for this study was Midshipmen in the U.S. Navy's commissioning program. This was part of an ongoing study to examine the effectiveness of technology training in universities for newly commissioned officers in the U.S. Navy and Marine Corps. Thirteen universities with Navy ROTC (NROTC) programs were chosen at random (from 57 total) to participate, as well as the US Naval Academy (with the largest number of Midshipmen). Several schools were used in order to gain a cross-section from across the US. Each NROTC university was sent 48 surveys, while the Naval Academy received 128. Of the 751 sent out, 630 were returned (86%), of which 610 were usable (81%). The list of universities, with the number of returned surveys in parentheses, includes US Naval Academy (125), South Florida (48), Florida

(48), Missouri (45), Kansas (44), Minnesota (42), South Carolina (42), Penn State (40), Idaho (40), Ohio State (35), Washington (30), Purdue (30), Oregon State (29), and Vanderbilt (12).

Two different versions of the surveys were used for this study, differing only in the way CSEs were measured for the six applications. One version, the "task-based" version, measured all six application-specific CSEs using actual tasks within the domain. The other version, labeled "assistance-based", measured the six application-specific CSEs using levels of assistance. Of the returned surveys, approximately half were task-based (308) and half assistance-based (302). Each university *received exactly half of each of the two types*, the surveys interleaved evenly in the packet to ensure randomness.

On average, respondents were 21.1 years of age (sd = 2.78), 84% were male and 16% female. Respondents on average had 2.4 years of college (sd =.99), evenly spread from freshman through seniors. The respondents' majors included liberal arts (30%), engineering but not computer science (19%), IT/MIS (14%), math or science (12%), business but not MIS (12%), computer science (6%), and others (7%).

Study Measures

Many of the measures in this study utilized previously reported and validated instruments. Appendix A presents selected scales.

Self-Efficacy Measures

- **Assistance-based CSE:** All six of the levels of assistance scales were derived from the GCSE instrument of Compeau and Higgins (1995a). The instruments use the same item stem as the GCSE scale, but add the application: "I could complete the job using the WORD PROCESSING, SPREADSHEET, DATABASE, etc. package..." with the same ten levels of assistance as the GCSE instrument. The authors themselves used this type of instrument for the two domains of word processing and spreadsheets (Compeau & Higgins, 1995b). Following the recommendation of Bandura (1986, 1997), each application-specific CSE included both magnitude (task difficulty) and strength (confidence in that ability). Magnitude was measured by a "Yes" or "No"; strength was measured based on the respondent's confidence level to complete each task on a scale of 1-10. Following the recommendation of Lee and Bobko (1994), each application CSE score was derived from averaging the strength of only those tasks that the respondent believed they could accomplish (by answering "Yes").
- **Task-based CSE:** All of the survey items in each of the six application-domain scales in this version of the survey were task-based. In order to adequately cover each application domain, the tasks ranged from relatively simple ones to those more complex. All start with the same stem, "I believe I have the ability to...", followed by the actual task within the domain. The scoring was done exactly the same as the CSEs in the assistance-based group.

The spreadsheet instrument was developed and validated by Johnson and Marakas (2000) (also validated by Yi & Davis, 2003). The other five task-based scales were self-developed, but similar in scope and design to the spreadsheet scale. Particular attention was placed on this development, and followed an iterative process in keeping with standard practices (Churchill, 1979; Straub, 1989). First we examined domain content for each of the five domains (WP, GP, DB, email, and web). This included examining and listing the skills required for common application packages, such as Word, WordPerfect (for word processing),

PowerPoint, Harvard Graphics (for graphical programs), Oracle, Access, DB2 (for databases), basic html, FrontPage, Dreamweaver (for web design) and GroupWise, Outlook (and many others for email programs). We used actual packages, package documentation, and online information to examine tasks required. For each domain, this process yielded a list of between twenty and forty tasks/skills (less for email programs). We next presented this list to both faculty and students (five faculty and ten students) who were asked to individually examine each domain and examine potential missing skills. This yielded several tasks not included in the previous list, such as inserting frames in web pages and using slide templates in PowerPoint. These were added. The tasks for each domain were then loosely ranked from simple to the more difficult. Because we wanted to maintain approximately ten for each domain, in keeping with the spreadsheet instrument of Johnson and Marakas (2000), the next task involved culling the list to representative tasks that included all difficulty levels. This culling process was done in a group context that included the researchers, three other faculty members, and nine students. The tasks which remained consisted of approximately twelve to fifteen for most of the domains and eight for email. We pilot tested these scales using 135 respondents, purifying them using factor analyses in a process similar to that described in the results section below of this study. This resulted in some items being eliminated due to cross-loads. Attention was paid to ensure each domain included tasks of different difficulty level. The resulting scales, used in this study, included the following number of items: WP 12, SS 10 (from Johnson & Marakas, 2000), DB 10, GP 9, Web 8, and email 6.

- ***Computing Competence***. Computer competence was measured using an instrument from Munro et al. (1997). Competence in the four domains was measured based on number of different packages previously used in that application domain (e.g., the number of different databases, spreadsheet packages, etc. used), number of academic or training courses taken in the application, and thoroughness of current knowledge of the domain (on a scale of 0 = "No Knowledge", to 7 = "Complete Knowledge").
- ***Performance Tests***. Performance tests of fourteen questions each were developed for this study, consisting of declarative knowledge items in a multiple choice format. The tests were specific to Microsoft's Word and Excel (both 2003 versions) and the process of determining the questions was conducted in a similar manner as developing the new task-based CSEs discussed above. These tests were included in the results only for those who indicated that Word and Excel were the word processing/spreadsheet applications they "know best", in order to avoid a potential confound for those respondents who were skilled in a non-Microsoft applications.

ANALYSES OF FINDINGS

Because respondents received either a task-based or an assistance-based survey, same-group analyses were not appropriate. In order to compare the results from these two separate groups, first we had to establish that the groups themselves were not statistically different. Using t-tests, results indicated that the two groups were **not significantly different** in all the following areas (t-test results in parentheses): age ($t = 1.1$, ns), ratio of male/female ($t = .61$, ns), class in college ($t = .70$, ns), major ($t = .67$, ns), and college attended (each college returned about the same number of task-based and assistance-based surveys; $t = .14$, ns). Additionally, there was no difference in average scores in most competencies (GP: $t = .10$, ns; DB: $t = .84$, ns; email: $t = .99$, ns) or either performance

Table 1. Descriptive statistics for task-based CSEs

Task-based	Mean	SD	α	Correlations and AVE					
				(1)	(2)	(3)	(4)	(5)	(6)
(1) CSE (WP)	9.14	1.35	.94	**.88**					
(2) CSE (email)	8.89	2.00	.92	.56	**.89**				
(3) CSE (GP)	8.82	1.82	.95	.61	.48	**.88**			
(4) CSE (SS)	7.49	2.58	.97	.43	.32	.55	**.90**		
(5) CSE (web)	5.30	3.60	.97	.30	.31	.25	.40	**.91**	
(6) CSE (DB)	3.61	3.23	.99	.11*	.18	.19	.40	.49	**.95**

n = 308. Bolded elements along diagonal represent the square root of the variance shared between constructs and their measures. Off diagonal elements are correlations. For discriminant validity, diagonal elements should be larger than correlations. All correlations significant at p <.01 except one indicated by * (significant at p <.05)

tests (word processing: t =.09, ns; spreadsheet: t =.25, ns). The only area in which there was a significant difference was web design competence, where the difference in means was 2.84 (task) versus 2.46 (level), t = 2.69, p <.01. Despite this solitary difference, the tests suggest that the two groups were for the most part not different in any significant way, and that any difference in the CSE/outcome relationship was likely a result of the difference in how CSE was measured (task or level-based).

Two separate models were created, based on how CSE was measured. To test each model, we used confirmatory factor analysis and regression.

- **Self-efficacy measures:** Each respondent had six application-specific self-efficacy scores. Self-efficacy constructs were first factor analyzed separately and reliability tested. Secondly, all CSE measures were factor analyzed simultaneously, to test discriminant and convergent validity.

Task-Based Scales

When each task-based CSE measure was factor analyzed independently; all six constructs were unidimensional. To assess convergent and discriminant validity of the full measurement model, the six CSE scales were factor analyzed simultaneously. Discriminant validity is indicated if each item loads highest on its own construct, which was the case. However, seven items were eliminated due to high cross loads (three from WP, one from SS, two from GP, and one from email). The resulting six scales, which are used throughout the rest of the study, included the following number of items: WP (9), SS (9), GP (7), DB (10), email (5), and web design (8). This factor analysis is presented in Appendix B. Correlations between all CSEs were significant, ranging from.11 to.61. Table 1 presents descriptive statistics and correlations of all task-based scales.

A second way to assess discriminant validity is by computing average variance extracted (AVE). The AVE of a scale is its variance divided by its standard error. AVE should be greater than.50 to justify using a construct. For discriminant validity, AVE should be greater than other construct correlations (Fornell & Larcker, 1981; Netemeyer, Bearden, & Sharma, 2003). Results are presented in Table 3; on the diagonal in bold-face is AVE. These results indicate adequate discriminant validity.

Levels of Assistance-Based Scales

The same methodology was used in the second measurement model, where all CSEs were assistance-based. When factor analyzed separately, all

Table 3. Descriptive statistics for competence

Competence	Mean	SD	1	2	3	4
1. Email	7.76	2.3	1.0			
2. GP	5.50	2.1	.50	1.0		
3. Web	2.66	3.1	.34	.34	1.0	
4. DB	2.11	2.4	.23	.31	.44	1.0

n = 610. All correlations significant at p <.01

Table 2. Descriptive statistics for level of assistance CSEs

	Mean	SD	Reliability	Correlations and AVE					
Level of Asst.			**α**	**(1)**	**(2)**	**(3)**	**(4)**	**(5)**	**(6)**
(1) CSE (email)	8.62	1.63	.97	**.89**					
(2) CSE (WP)	8.37	1.82	.94	.65	**.89**				
(3) CSE (GP)	7.55	2.00	.96	.56	.58	**.87**			
(4) CSE (SS)	7.54	2.11	.96	.58	.61	.69	**.85**		
(5) CSE (web)	6.18	2.61	.96	.42	.41	.55	.54	**.87**	
(6) CSE (DB)	5.95	2.50	.97	.42	.41	.62	.70	.68	**.88**

n = 302. Bolded elements along diagonal represent the square root of the variance shared between constructs and their measures. Off diagonal elements are correlations. For discriminant validity, diagonal elements should be larger than correlations. All correlations significant at p <.01.

six AS-CSEs were unidimensional. However when the CSE scales were factor analyzed simultaneously, there were some high cross-loads in most scales. In order to maintain one-dimensional constructs, an iterative process was employed to purify the scales, where a single item (with high cross-loads) was eliminated and the composite factor analysis re-run. First, for example, item #1 of the Word Processing scale "if there was no one around to tell me what to do as I go", loaded highly on WP (.552) as well as GP (.486) and email (.481). This item was eliminated from the WP scale and the composite factor analysis rerun. Then another factor with high cross loads was eliminated, etc. The scales which resulted from this process were one-dimensional and varied in length from six to ten items: WP: 6, SS: 6, GP: 8, DB: 7, email: 10, web: 7.

Descriptive statistics and correlations are provided in Table 4. Although the resulting composite factor analysis (with six variables) had higher cross-loads than the task-based structure, each item loaded highest on its respective factor, indicating satisfactory discriminant validity, as did AVE.

Competence and Performance Measures

Computing competence was calculated for all respondents in four domains, while performance was assessed in two domains. Respondents had the highest competency in email, followed by graphic programs; they were least competent in web design and databases. Descriptive statistics and correlations are presented in Table 3.

In addition to the competence measures above, a single performance test was included in each survey, for either word processing or spreadsheets. Although they were actually optional, a total of 404 tests were received (66%), including 209 WP tests and 195 SS tests. There was no statistical

Table 4. Descriptive statistics for performance tests

	WP Test			SS Test		
	n	Mean	SD	n	Mean	SD
Task Survey	105	7.80	2.48	99	9.49	3.73
Level Survey	104	7.77	2.47	96	9.62	3.23
Full Sample	209	7.79	2.48	195	9.55	3.48

Table 5. Regression of CSE and competencies/performance

	SS Test		DB		Web		GP		WP Test		Email	
	R^2	β	R^2	β	R^2	β	R^2	β	R^2	β	R^2	β
Task	.39	.63	.38	.62	.42	.65	.23	.48	.14	.39	.14	.38
Level	.09	.32	.20	.45	.24	.49	.33	.57	.18	.44	.18	.43
Diff.	Task (4.3)		Task (1.9)		Task (1.8)		Level (1.4)		Level (1.3)		Level (1.3)	

All β are standardized and significant at $p < .01$. In parenthesis is the difference in variance explained between task and assistance-based instruments

difference in the returned tests from the group that filled out the task-based survey from those that filled out the assistance-based survey in terms of test means or demographics. Descriptive statistics for the performance tests are presented in Table 4.

Model Testing

Given satisfactory constructs (measurement model), the next step involved testing using regression analyses. There were six competence/performance outcomes: four domain competencies (GP, DB, email, and web) and two performance tests (WP and SS). The relationship between CSE and these outcomes were tested with simple regression. In determining which methodology (task or level) provides the stronger relationship with these outcomes, we examined R^2, which is proportion of variability in the dependent variable that is explained by the independent variable (i.e., CSEs). This statistic is the most useful one in examining differences in strength of predictors (Cohen & Cohen, 1983). We also included the regression standardized β, which represent the change in competence or performance resulting from a change of one standard deviation of each CSE. Because all units are the same scale (1-10), standardized β provides another effective measure of comparison.

Results are presented in Table 5. As expected, all CSEs significantly and positively predicted every competency outcome at $p < .01$. Some of the relationships were quite strong, explaining over 40% of the variance in the outcome. In general, in those domains where respondents had less competence (database, web design, and spreadsheets), the task-based CSE explained a greater portion of the variance. Level of assistance CSEs explained more variance for email, graphic programs, and the word processing domains. Examining the standardized betas, which allows a direct comparison of strength, reveals the same results. For domains in which respondents had higher competence or performance, the level of assistance instrument had higher standardized betas. For those domains where competence/performance was lower, the task-based methodology was higher. Interestingly, for those domains where the task-based instrument was better, the difference between the two instrument types was striking. In the spreadsheet domain, the task-based instrument accounted for 4.3 times as much variance in spreadsheet performance as the assistance-based instrument (indicated in parenthesis in Table 5, last row). For both databases and web design domains, it was almost twice as much variance explained. In the other three domains, where the assistance-based instrument was better, the difference was much smaller, either 1.3 or 1.4 times as much variance explained

RESULTS, IMPLICATIONS AND RECOMMENDATIONS

The goal of this study was to empirically determine whether the methodology used to operationalize the magnitude dimension made any difference in the strength of the CSE-outcome relationship. Specifically, we wished to examine whether task-based or levels of assistance-based methodologies provided a more accurate assessment of individual CSE for six common computing applications. Both theory and previous research suggests that the more accurate this assessment is, the stronger its relationship with competence and performance in those domains. The findings of this study suggest that the choice of methodology does make a difference. These findings are summarized below:

Task-Based vs. Levels of Assistance-Based

-Assessing CSE using task-based instruments is beneficial when the domain(s) of interest is one where respondents have less competence. This includes domains that may be new to the individual, or where the individual has little or no experience. This type of instrument presents respondents with tasks they don't know how to accomplish, providing a more accurate assessment of CSE for that domain. This supports previous research, which suggests actual tasks, of various difficulty levels, provide a more accurate estimation of ability and stronger relationships with actual performance (Bandura, 1997; Marakas et al., 1998). For these types of domains, task-based instruments are superior.

Task-based instruments are not always best! Despite determined contentions that actual tasks always provide the strongest relationship (Bandura, 1997; Marakas et al., 1998), this study indicates that for some domains, this is simply not the case. In domains where individuals had higher competence or ability, using levels of assistance to assess CSE provided stronger relationships with competence and performance. This suggests that self-efficacy judgments do not necessarily have to include actual tasks. As competence in domains increases (and even approaches mastery), using levels of assistance to assess one's perception of ability provided a stronger relationship with competence and performance.

Reexamining the CSE/ Performance Relationship

The results of this study suggest that the relationship between CSE and performance or competence changes as an individual's ability increases. When ability in the domain is low, the relationship is strong and positive. Standardized betas and the amount of variance explained for domains of less competence are higher than for the domains of greater competence or performance. This was true for both the task-based and assistance-based instruments (though the difference is more noticeable for the former). This supports some previous research. For example, in a study of repeated trials in an academic setting, Mone (1994) found that the relationship between SE and performance decreased over time as performance improved.

Examining the differences between the two instrument types may provide a key reason for this finding. Levels of assistance instruments appear to focus respondent's attention on the *process* of accomplishing tasks, rather than the actual tasks. Successful accomplishment of the task may depend more on the perceived effect of processes involved, including enablers (e.g., help along the way) or obstacles (missing software manuals, lack of time). Therefore, as mastery in a domain occurs, the individual relies less on actual tasks and more on other factors in task accomplishment. Kanfer and Ackerman (1989) found that learning new tasks (low competence) is accompanied by increased attentional resources, such as cognitive processing. Similarly, when individuals with low competence make a self-efficacy judgment, the process involves considerable cognitive effort, including assessments of task difficulty, constraints, time, etc. During this phase, actual tasks aid in this assessment. But as competence improves, other factors gain in importance. Bandura (1997) and others (Gist & Mitchell, 1992) maintain that the most important cue in a self-efficacy judgment is prior experience, which is only available as competence increases. In a study of multiple trials of a complex computer task (air traffic control), Gist and Mitchell (1992) found that though self-efficacy significantly influenced performance in each trial, its ability to predict diminished with improved performance. They also found that while past performance was consistently the most important factor of a CSE judgment, the importance of other factors changed significantly. Early in the trials (when competence was low), assessments of task difficulty and complexity were very important in determining CSE, while in the later trials factors reflecting momentary internal states were more important, such as level of alertness, physical comfort, and desire. This study supports such findings which suggest that as competence in domain increases, self-efficacy as a predictor decreases.

Implications

These results suggest that choice of CSE instrument makes a difference in findings. Both researchers and practitioners should utilize the appropriate instrument in order to maximize the benefits of testing an individual's perceived ability in computer domains. This research suggests that for domains of lesser competence, task-based instruments are clearly better. But for domains in which competence is higher, the better choice is a level of assistance instrument. Where the dividing line is in competence level is unclear and requires further study.

This study raises a legitimate question concerning one of the most utilized CSE instruments, that of Compeau & Higgins (1995a), which provided the basis for the levels of assistance instruments used in this study. In its more utilized form, the instrument measures an individual's self-efficacy for the entire computing domain (and is labeled general CSE, or GCSE). Because it uses the same levels of assistance, it can be argued that it should have the same limitations as noted in this study. Accordingly, we submit that this GCSE instrument should be used with caution when the respondents' computer ability level is low. It is likely that the resulting self-efficacy score will be artificially lower and its relationships with outcomes (and possibly antecedents) will be weaker. On the other hand, if respondents have considerable computer competence, GCSE should provide accurate results. It should be noted that there is no a task-based instrument that measures CSE of the entire computing domain.

Limitations

There are several limitations which should be addressed. This population is one in a Navy commissioning program and may be different from the American population at large or even a university student population. However there are studies which suggest this population is no different from other student groups (Carlson & Grabowski, 1992; Neiberg, 2000). As with most military groups, there are more men than women, and this sample was no different. Although a gender effect could be present, t-tests were run which indicated there were no significant differences between the two groups, suggesting such an effect was minimal.

As with any cross-sectional instrument, common method variance and other related limitations arise. Although reliabilities were high, anytime all measures are collected simultaneously validity may suffer. However this is routinely practiced in academic settings, particularly when the variables of interest must be self-reported (such as self-efficacy, which is a personal judgment of ability). Attempts were made to reduce the influence by including performance tests which provided objective outcomes to this study in which most other variables were self-reported.

Although this study examined how instruments capture a computing domain, by task-based tasks or by levels of assistance, there are other instrumentation issues which can affect results. One in particular is a limitation. Are the differences noted in this study a result of the difference between task and assistance based instruments, or could the differences be a result of inadequate coverage of task difficulty? The degree to which an instrument covers simple to complex (or easy to difficult) tasks determines its effectiveness in covering the entire domain. For both task and assistance-based methodologies, it is difficult to assess the how successfully the instrument was in covering all task difficulty levels. In particular the assistance "levels" (of the levels of assistance instrument) do not seem to include much coverage for "lots of assistance". Perhaps this is why this methodology was weaker for domains where competence was less. While we recognize this as a limitation, all results were statistically significant, some quite strong, suggesting that there was adequate coverage of difficulty levels.

Directions for Further Research and Conclusion

The results from this study suggest that the methodology used to capture an individual's perception of ability for a computing domain reflects its accuracy or validity and influences the actual SE score and its relationship with other constructs. Generalizing these findings to other populations and with other domains is an important first step. In particular, the full computing domain should be examined; unfortunately, there is not as yet a real task-based instrument that measures CSE for that domain (which includes all applications, environments, etc.). Further examining differences in strength of the relationship between self-efficacy and performance as competence improves is also important. The results of this study (and other studies) suggest that as an individual masters a computing domain, the ability of CSE to predict performance diminishes. This raises an interesting question: does this mean that CSE is less important as a motivator of performance? Does one's perception of ability (i.e., their self efficacy) for a mastered domain influence performance at all? Does it influence other important factors in task accomplishment (such as attitudes or perceived usefulness)? The factors that affect performance, including self-efficacy, from attempting new and difficult tasks through mastery requires clarification. Clearly, if CSE has only a small direct effect on individuals who have mastered a domain, organizations should focus more attention on those factors which do influence performance. And if this is the case, at what point does this occur? These questions require further study. On a similar note, given that competence is antecedent to performance, in what way, if any, does competence mediate the CSE-performance relationship?

Straub (1989) recommended improved IT instruments (vis-à-vis validity) to promote co-operative research efforts, to triangulate results, and to bring greater clarity to the formulation and interpretation of research questions. We concur and suggest that understanding the impact of instrument characteristics, such as how magnitude is operationalized, helps fulfill this imperative. It also provides clarity in understanding human-computer interaction. The domain of computing is rapidly changing. Twenty years ago computer operators were likely programmers, while today end users function on many levels. If organizations are to maximize the potential, proficiency, and efficiency of end users, a clear and concise understanding of the process of learning new competencies is essential. Therefore all factors, including self-efficacy, which synergize this learning process, from learning a new technology to being highly proficient, are critical to understand.

REFERENCES

Adams, J. A. (1987). Historical review and appraisal of research on the learning, retention, and transfer of human motor skills. *Psychological Bulletin, 101*, 41–74. doi:10.1037/0033-2909.101.1.41

Attewell, P. (1990). What is skill? *Work and Occupations, 17*, 422–448. doi:10.1177/0730888490017004003

Bandura, A. (1986). *Social foundations of thought and actions*. Englewood Cliffs, N.J.: Prentice-Hall.

Bandura, A. (1997). *Self-efficacy: the exercise of control*. New York: W.H. Freeman and Company.

Carlson, R., & Grabowski, B. (1992). The effects of Computer Self-efficacy on direction-following behavior in computer-assisted instruction. *Journal of Computer-Based Instruction, 19*(1), 6–11.

Chau, P. Y. (2001). Influence of computer attitude and self-efficacy on IT usage behavior. *Journal of End User Computing, 13*(1), 26–33. doi:10.4018/joeuc.2001010103

Chen, G., Gully, S. M., & Eden, D. (2001). Validation of a new general self-efficacy scale. *Organizational Research Methods, 4*(1), 62–84. doi:10.1177/109442810141004

Churchill, G. A. (1979). A paradigm for developing better measures of marketing constructs. *JMR, Journal of Marketing Research, 16*, 64–73. doi:10.2307/3150876

Cohen, J., & Cohen, P. (1983). *Applied regression/correlation analysis for the behavioral sciences*. Hillsdale, N.J.: Lawrence Erlbaum Associates.

Compeau, D., Higgins, C. A., & Huff, S. (1999). Social cognitive theory and individual reactions to computing technology: A longitudinal study. *Management Information Systems Quarterly, 23*(2), 145–158. doi:10.2307/249749

Compeau, D. R., & Higgins, C. A. (1995a). Computer Self-efficacy: Development of a measure and initial test. *Management Information Systems Quarterly, 19*(2), 189–202. doi:10.2307/249688

Compeau, D. R., & Higgins, C. A. (1995b). Application of social cognitive theory to training for computer skills. *Information Systems Research, 6*(2), 118–143. doi:10.1287/isre.6.2.118

Fornell, C., & Larcker, D. F. (1981). Evaluating structural equation models with unobservable variables and measurement error. *JMR, Journal of Marketing Research, 18*(1), 39–50. doi:10.2307/3151312

Gist, M. E. (1987). Self-efficacy: Implications for organizational behavior and human resource management. *Academy of Management Review, 12*(3), 472–485. doi:10.2307/258514

Gist, M. E., & Mitchell, T. R. (1992). Self-efficacy: a theoretical analysis of its determinants and malleability. *Academy of Management Review, 17*(2), 183–211. doi:10.2307/258770

Gist, M. E., Schwoerer, C., & Rosen, B. (1989). Effects of alternative training methods on self-efficacy and performance in computer software training. *The Journal of Applied Psychology, 74*(5), 884–891. doi:10.1037/0021-9010.74.6.884

Harrison, A. W., & Rainer, R. K. (1992). The influence of individual differences on skill in end-user computing. *Journal of Management Information Systems*, *9*(1), 93–111.

Hasan, B. (2006). Effectiveness of computer training: The role of multilevel Computer Self-efficacy. *Journal of Organizational and End User Computing*, *18*(1), 50–68. doi:10.4018/joeuc.2006010103

Henry, J. W., & Martinko, M. J. (1997). An attributional analysis of the rejection of information technology. *Journal of End User Computing*, *9*(4), 3–17.

Igbaria, M., & Iivari, J. (1995). The effects of self-efficacy on computer usage. *Omega*, *23*(6), 587–605. doi:10.1016/0305-0483(95)00035-6

Johnson, R. D., & Marakas, G. M. (2000). Research report: The role of behavioral modeling and computer skills acquisition-toward refinement of the model. *Information Systems Research*, *11*(4), 402–417. doi:10.1287/isre.11.4.402.11869

Kanfer, R., & Ackerman, P. L. (1989). Motivation and cognitive abilities: An integrative/aptitude-treatment interaction approach to skill acquisition. *The Journal of Applied Psychology*, *74*(4), 657–690. doi:10.1037/0021-9010.74.4.657

Lee, C., & Bobko, P. (1994). Self-efficacy beliefs: Comparison of five measures. *The Journal of Applied Psychology*, *79*(3), 364–369. doi:10.1037/0021-9010.79.3.364

Marakas, G. M., Yi, M. Y., & Johnson, R. D. (1998). The multilevel and multifaceted character of Computer Self-efficacy: Toward clarification of the construct and an integrative framework for research. *Information Systems Research*, *9*(2), 126–163. doi:10.1287/isre.9.2.126

Martocchio, J. J., & Webster, J. (1992). Effects of feedback and cognitive playfulness on performance in microcomputer software training. *Personnel Psychology*, *45*, 553–578. doi:10.1111/j.1744-6570.1992.tb00860.x

Mone, M. A. (1994). Comparative validity of two measures of self-efficacy in predicting academic goals and performance. *Educational and Psychological Measurement*, *54*(2), 516–529. doi:10.1177/0013164494054002026

Munro, M. C., Huff, S. L., Marcolin, B. L., & Compeau, D. R. (1997). Understanding and measuring user competence. *Information & Management*, *33*, 45–57. doi:10.1016/S0378-7206(97)00035-9

Murphy, C. A., Coover, D., & Owen, S. V. (1989). Development and validation of the Computer Self-efficacy scale. *Educational and Psychological Measurement*, *49*(2), 893–899. doi:10.1177/001316448904900412

Neiberg, M. S. (2000). *Making Citizen Soldiers: ROTC*. Cambridge, MA: Harvard University Press.

Netemeyer, R. G., Bearden, W. O., & Sharma, S. (2003). *Scaling Procedures Issues and Applications*. Thousand Oaks, CA: Sage Publications.

Straub, D. W. (1989). Validating instruments in MIS research. *Management Information Systems Quarterly*, *10*(2), 147–169. doi:10.2307/248922

Yi, M. Y., & Davis, F. D. (2003). Developing and validating an observational learning model of computer software training and skill acquisition. *Information Systems Research*, *14*(2), 146–169. doi:10.1287/isre.14.2.146.16016

Yi, M. Y., & Im, K. S. (2004). Predicting computer task performance: Personal goal and self-efficacy. *Journal of Organizational and End User Computing*, *16*(2), 20–37. doi:10.4018/joeuc.2004040102

APPENDIX A. SELECTED SURVEY ITEMS

Task-Based CSE Scales

All scales included Yes/No (for magnitude) and levels of confidence for "yes" answers, on a ten point scale (1-10), with anchors at "Not at all Confident" to "Totally Confident". All start with the stem "I believe I have the ability…".

Word Processing CSE

...to *effectively* use different fonts, including colors and sizes, in a word processing file.
…to apply character (letter) effects such as bolding, italicizing, or subscripting in a word processing document.
…to cut, copy and paste in a word processing document.
…to add symbols (such as foreign letters or yen symbol) to a document.
…to insert and manipulate endnotes or footnotes in a word processing program.
…to efficiently set different margins in a word processing document.
…to set page or section breaks in a word processing file.
…to effectively add bulletized (or numbered) lists to a word processing document.
…to add pictures, graphics, or objects into a word processing document.

Spreadsheet CSE (from Johnson & Marakas, 2000)

…to manipulate the way a number appears in a spreadsheet.
…to use and understand the cell references in a spreadsheet.
…to use a spreadsheet to communicate numeric information to others.
…to use a spreadsheet to assist me in making decisions.
…to manipulate data using formulas that come with a spreadsheet program.
…to write a simple formula in a spreadsheet to perform math calculations.
…to summarize numeric information using a spreadsheet.
…to use a spreadsheet to share numeric information with others.
…to use a spreadsheet to display numbers as graphs.

Graphic Programs CSE

…to copy or delete slides from a graphic slide presentation.
…to copy an individual slide from one graphic slide presentation to another.
…to import text from another application (e.g., word processor) to a slide.
…to use a graphic presentation program (e.g., PowerPoint) to convey information to others.
…to manipulate objects on a slide (align, tilt, rotate, etc.).
…to add color to words or objects on a slide.
…to use a slide template to create a new graphic slide presentation.

Database CSE

...to create a new database using a database application.
...to create and work with database tables in a database application.
...to modify field properties in a database application.
...to import or export data from one database to another.
...to use primary keys in a database application.
...to use a database to assist in making decisions.
...to sort or filter records in a database application.
...to use a database application to display information.
...to create forms to input data into a database application.
...to design queries to manipulate and access information in a database.

Email Programs CSE

...to build, update, and manage a personal address book for email.
...to reply to individual and multiple recipients.
...to check email from multiple computers or locations.
...to set up groups (such as all those in a particular class), in order to send mass emails.
...to effectively attach other documents to an email.

Web Design CSE

...to design a simple web page using an editor (e.g. FrontPage or Dreamweaver).
...to design a simple web page using html.
...to insert an image into a webpage.
...to create a hyperlink in a webpage
...to create and use tables in designing webpages.
...to insert frames in a web page.
...to insert forms into a webpage.
...to publish a webpage to a web server.

Levels of Assistance-Based Scales

All scales use some or all of the ten levels of assistance given below. The stem for all items is: "I could complete the job using the [word processing, spreadsheet, etc.] package ...". The items used for each individual scale follow and are indicated by level of assistance number. **Levels of assistance include**:

1...if there was no one around to tell me what to do as I go.
2...if I had never used a package like it before.
3...if I had only the software manuals for reference.
4...if I had seen someone else using it before trying it myself.
5...if I could call someone for help if I got stuck.

6...if someone else had helped me get started.
7...if I had a lot of time to complete the job for which the software was provided.
8...if I had just the built-in help facility for assistance.
9...if someone showed me how to do it first
10..if I had used similar packages before this one to do the same job.

WP Scale SS Scale GP Scale

1, 4, 5, 6, 7, 8 4, 5, 6, 7, 9, 10 1, 4, 5, 6, 7, 8, 9, 10
DB Scale Email Scale Web Design Scale
4, 5, 6, 7, 8, 9, 10 1, 2, 3, 4, 5, 6, 7, 8, 9, 10 4, 5, 6, 7, 8, 9, 10

APPENDIX B. FACTOR ANALYSES

Table 6. Task-based CSEs

	1	2	3	4	5	6
WP1	-.04	.07	.08	**.78**	.29	.21
WP2	-.05	.07	.02	**.81**	.24	.26
WP3	-08	.04	.02	**.81**	.28	.25
WP4	.03	.22	.15	**.75**	.14	.14
WP5	.05	.27	.16	**.73**	.09	.17
WP6	.01	.20	.12	**.81**	.17	.15
WP7	.13	.19	.15	**.73**	.15	.09
WP8	.05	.18	.11	**.80**	.24	.15
WP9	-.02	.15	.13	**.76**	.30	.17
SS1	.19	**.77**	.19	.24	.13	.04
SS2	.17	**.82**	.14	.21	.10	.06
SS3	.14	**.83**	.09	.16	.27	.11
SS4	.21	**.86**	.17	.17	.17	.04
SS5	.18	**.84**	.21	.12	.18	.01
SS6	.20	**.87**	.13	.12	.19	.06
SS7	.18	**.86**	.11	.16	.24	.12
SS8	.18	**.83**	.10	.14	.22	.06
SS9	.20	**.77**	.16	.11	.19	.14
GP1	.01	.26	.01	.34	**.81**	.09
GP2	.09	.23	.07	.29	**.80**	.07
GP3	.10	.33	.09	.28	**.74**	.13
GP4	-.01	.19	.01	.36	**.80**	.23
GP5	.09	.26	.09	.29	**.79**	.16
GP6	.04	.19	.10	.21	**.80**	.19

continued on following page

Table 6. contnued

	1	2	3	4	5	6
GP7	.12	.34	.07	.22	**.67**	.20
DB1	**.90**	.20	.19	.06	.06	.03
DB2	**.92**	.20	.18	.03	.06	.04
DB3	**.93**	.19	.17	.03	.04	.04
DB4	**.92**	.17	.21	.01	.06	.04
DB5	**.90**	.13	.24	.01	.01	.01
DB6	**.89**	.19	.21	-.02	.05	.06
DB7	**.93**	.14	.18	-.01	.05	.04
DB8	**.93**	.14	.19	.02	.07	.04
DB9	**.93**	.12	.22	-.01	.04	.03
DB10	**.92**	.12	.25	.01	.03	.03
EM1	.09	.13	.12	.29	.22	**.72**
EM2	.06	.05	.11	.25	.16	**.86**
EM3	.01	.05	.09	.30	.15	**.83**
EM4	.13	.21	.19	.22	.15	**.74**
EM5	.01	.06	.09	.29	.17	**.84**
Web1	.21	.16	**.86**	.14	.06	.13
Web2	.23	.14	**.85**	.12	.03	.07
Web3	.22	.15	**.88**	.15	.07	.09
Web4	.24	.16	**.86**	.12	.10	.13
Web5	.24	.18	**.89**	.11	.05	.09
Web6	.27	.12	**.88**	.10	.06	.05
Web7	.29	.11	**.86**	.10	.03	.05
Web8	.24	.15	**.86**	.05	.06	.07

Table 7. Level of Assistance-based CSEs

	1	2	3	4	5	6
WP1	.27	.22	.07	.12	**.75**	.08
WP4	.35	.19	.17	.07	**.73**	.28
WP5	.34	.16	.11	.13	**.79**	.17
WP6	.38	.20	.11	.09	**.77**	.20
WP7	.35	.22	.11	.12	**.76**	.16
WP8	.34	.26	.20	.06	**.67**	.21
SS4	.28	.26	.24	.35	.28	**.65**
SS5	.25	.27	.24	.34	.29	**.69**
SS6	.29	.30	.18	.35	.27	**.68**
SS7	.25	.25	.22	.31	.28	**.67**
SS9	.25	.30	.19	.28	.24	**.74**

continued on following page

Table 7. contnued

	1	2	3	4	5	6
SS10	.26	.34	.12	.31	.15	**.73**
GP1	.20	**.73**	.17	.17	.23	.01
GP4	.26	**.78**	.21	.24	.24	.19
GP5	.24	**.76**	.20	.26	.20	.22
GP6	.26	**.81**	.20	.22	.18	.24
GP7	.22	**.79**	.20	.23	.18	.18
GP8	.19	**.77**	.23	.21	.21	.15
GP9	.24	**.77**	.18	.23	.17	.28
GP10	.25	**.76**	.19	.19	.11	.29
DB4	.13	.18	.32	**.82**	.12	.16
DB5	.15	.22	.30	**.82**	.12	.19
DB6	.15	.23	.30	**.82**	.10	.24
DB7	.17	.24	.28	**.81**	.10	.19
DB8	.10	.20	.32	**.79**	.12	.16
DB9	.17	.30	.32	**.74**	.07	.27
DB10	.13	.30	.31	**.70**	.04	.27
EM1	**.83**	.18	.13	.13	.19	.08
EM2	**.80**	.18	.15	.11	.14	.08
EM3	**.83**	.16	.10	.10	.22	.05
EM4	**.87**	.14	.14	.13	.24	.15
EM5	**.86**	.15	.15	.12	.20	.13
EM6	**.85**	.19	.10	.12	.18	.20
EM7	**.85**	.17	.12	.10	.21	.15
EM8	**.78**	.20	.15	.14	.28	.16
EM9	**.76**	.21	.15	.13	.25	.22
EM10	**.81**	.25	.14	.10	.20	.21
Web4	.16	.14	**.83**	.30	.14	.12
Web5	.16	.18	**.82**	.30	.17	.17
Web6	.18	.16	**.87**	.30	.07	.12
Web7	.19	.20	**.83**	.27	.09	.10
Web8	.17	.19	**.81**	.33	.16	.09
Web9	.11	.21	**.73**	.13	.07	.11
Web10	.13	.23	**.82**	.25	.08	.14

Chapter 17
A Theoretical Investigation and Extension of a Model of Information Technology Architecture Maturity

Randy V. Bradley
The University of Tennessee, USA

Terry Anthony Byrd
Auburn University, USA

ABSTRACT

Organizations that lack a coherent strategy for managing and evolving their IT platform and resources end up with fragmentation within the organization. Because the need for data sharing and systems integration is not always limited to the internal organization, the boundaries between the organization and its customers, vendors, suppliers, and partners are often blurred. It appears to be evident that organizations must have a clear idea of where they stand in regards to their own Information Technology Architecture (ITA) before preparing to adopt a new, shared ITA. This paper applies the reach and range concept and theory associated with strategic information systems planning to conceptually position ITA as a concept that provides convergence of a variety of frameworks related to IT and business alignment.

INTRODUCTION

IT resources must be managed in an orderly, effective manner to successfully implement the IT strategy[1] (Bradley & Byrd, 2007; Earl, 1989). This management can be facilitated by the development and utilization of an organizational architecture, specifically an Information Technology Architecture[2] (ITA). ITA is a plan or model that guides the identification and utilization of the technical and human IT resources at the disposal of an organization (Curle, 1993; Hildebrand, 2000) that enable the organization to successfully accomplish its business objectives. Most IT functions see the development of an ITA "as an urgent priority if the organization's needs are to be met efficiently and effectively most of the time" (Earl, 1989, p. 37). An ITA should provide organizations with

DOI: 10.4018/978-1-60960-577-3.ch017

the knowledge to utilize dynamic capabilities that would enable them to quickly adapt to changes in technology, their respective organization, their inter-organizational relationships and alliances, and their respective industry (Allen & Boynton, 1991). By exploiting the usefulness of an ITA, the occurrence of organization's independent, mission critical systems and applications caught in a quagmire of inflexibility and "rigid business processes" (Hagel & Brown, 2001), which makes it difficult for an organization to adapt quickly to changes in the marketplace and strategic restructurings, can be minimized, if not avoided. The process of developing a more mature ITA is dynamic in nature, requiring continuous change (Henderson & Venkatraman, 1995). Such a task requires organizations to develop an even more sophisticated planning process that facilitates organizational learning and architectural competency as they evolve their ITA.

The purpose of this paper is to theoretically examine and conceptually extend Ross' (2003) four-stage model of ITA competency and maturity. The four stages consist of the business silo stage, standardized technology stage, optimized core stage, and business modularity stage. Our examination and extension of her model highlights its intra-organizational scope of an ITA, and extends her model to include inter-organizational collaboration and communication, thus looking outside the organization. Presenting the ITA in such a manner contributes to answering Segars and Grover's (1998) call for research to provide valuable insight into the evolutionary path of strategic information systems planning (SISP), in terms of the type of systems developed and implemented within particular evolutionary stages, and motivations for moving between stages. This evolutionary perspective of the ITA sets it apart from previous studies by expanding the scope of the ITA to include resources and relationships external to the organization. It is also our motive to present the proposed added benefits that come as a result of the development and implementation of an ITA grounded in the latter stages of ITA competency. This is accomplished by investigating ITA through Keen's (1991) concept of reach and range and Segars and Grover's (1998) strategic information systems planning (SISP) model. We use the concept of reach and range and each construct of the SISP model as theoretical lenses to view conceptually the intricacies of the latter stages of enterprise IT competency.

LITERATURE REVIEW

Prior research related to organizational architectures focused on subject areas closely related to ITA (i.e. IT infrastructure, information architecture, and information systems architecture) but very little on the subject itself. For instance, a review of the academic literature indicates that a considerable amount of research exists in the subject areas of IT infrastructure (Broadbent, 1999; Byrd, Lewis, & Bradley, 2006; Byrd & Turner, 2000; Duncan, 1995), information architecture (IA) (Allen & Boynton, 1991; Evernden & Evernden, 2003; Farnum, 2002; Niederman, Brancheau, & Wetherbe, 1991; Periasamy & Feeny, 1997; Pervan, 1998), and information systems architecture (ISA) (Brown et al., 2000; Gifford, 1992; Hackathorn & Karimi, 1988; Sowa & Zachman, 1992), whereas only Curle (1993), Gibson (1994), and more recently Ross (2003), Ross, Weill, & Robertson (2006), and Bradley & Byrd (2007) focus primarily on ITA.

The focus of Curle's (1993) research of ITA was limited to the development of an ITA. Gibson's (1994) research of ITA centered around the empirical testing and validation of four generic architectural types. The generic architectural types discussed by Gibson (1994) were not treated as linear growth stages, rather he suggested that a single architectural type is most appropriate for a given situation. The information provided by Curle (1993) and Gibson (1994), though vital, does not appear to provide insight as to the value of the ITA to the organization, nor does their research consider the architectural competency and organizational learning necessary to move between ITA stages.

Ross (2003) takes a learning-in-stages approach to discuss the ITA. Her study focuses more on the development of the competency to create such organizational architectures. Similar to the previously mentioned studies, her unit of analysis seems to be the internal organization. Building upon her theory that the byproduct of each stage is a type of ITA and that the ITA continues to mature as organizations move between stages, so as to guide the IT planning, policies and security issues for the entire organization, we further contend that the stages identified by Ross (2003) also depict the maturation process of the organization. As organizations go through this process of maturation (organizational learning), they are better able to develop, implement, and effectively utilize the ITA. In other words, in agreeing with Ross (2003) that the ITA matures from stage to stage and that the architectural byproduct of each stage is, in the sense of the ITA, reflective, we further suggest that the organization also undergoes a maturation process, which enables the development of a more mature ITA.

Bradley & Byrd (2007) focus more on the governance of IT resources within the organization and they theoretically analyze the ITA's ability to yield a competitive advantage through the mediation of various IT resources. Furthermore, they establish the ITA as competitive advantage-yielding IT resource by applying the theories of complementarity and resource-based view. Their propositions are in line with our thoughts and help to shape our extension to Ross' (2003) four-stage model of ITA competency.

In light of the limited attention given to ITA in the academic setting, and the increased interest in organizational architectures by practitioners, it is necessary to investigate theoretically ITA and its value to organizations. Our investigation provides many opportunities for us to further refine and extend ITA theories identified in prior studies. The next section discusses the lenses used to investigate ITA and its value to organizations.

RESEARCH LENSES

Reach and Range

Keen (1991) introduced the reach and range concept as a means of defining the business functionality of the IT infrastructure. Reach and range have also been referenced in the literature as connectivity and compatibility, respectively (Byrd & Turner, 2000). The ideology behind reach and range is to be able to connect anyone anywhere and that any transaction message or document generated by one system can be used in another system, regardless of the hardware or software base (see Figure 1).

Strategic Information Systems Planning Model

Segars and Grover's (1998), after an extensive literature review, a series of discussions and interviews, and a survey targeting CIOs, grouped 28 objectives of fulfillment into four dimensions of SISP (alignment, analysis, cooperation, and improvement in capabilities). The unit of analysis in their study was limited to the internal organization. Since it is our intent to show that an ITA adds inter-organizational value, in addition to intra-organizational value, our proposed model's units of analyses include departmental units, functional units, and intra- and inter-organizational units. We will now define each lens in the context and order in which they will be applied to each stage.

DEFINITIONS

We extend the application of the dimensions, developed by Segars and Grover (1998), to an inter-

Figure 1. The Reach and Range of the IT Platform (adapted from Keen, 1991)

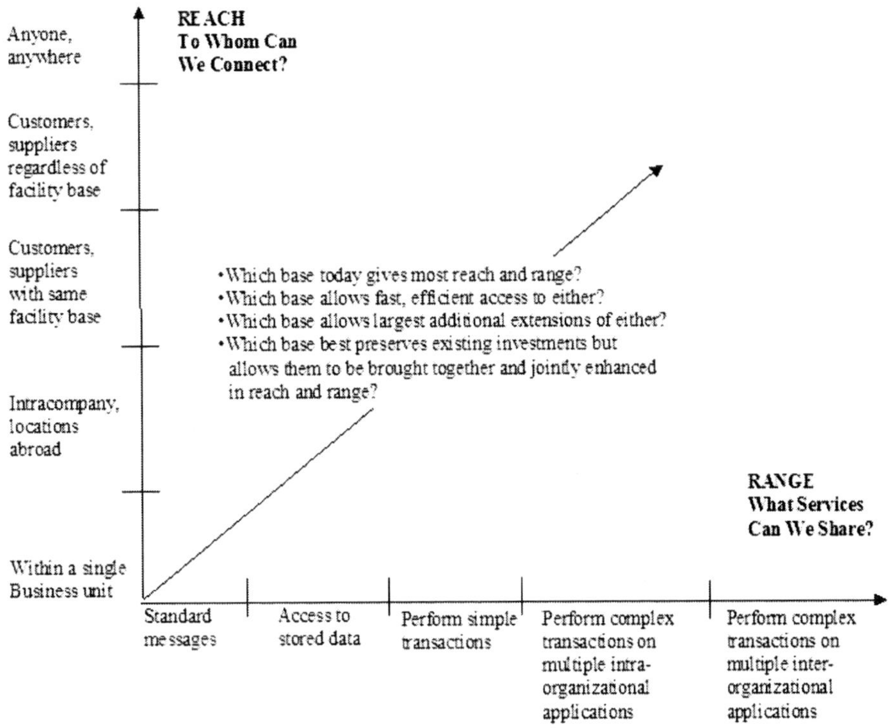

organizational aspect, in addition to the current intra-organizational aspects of the constructs. We discuss the dimensions in the order presented in our study, and we define the first three constructs of the SISP model as follows:

- **Alignment:** the coupling of the IT strategies and the business strategies of the department, functional unit, or organizational unit of the firm.
- **Analysis:** the process used by organizations to find ways to operate and compete with technology in an effort to provide an understanding of how information is used within and outside the organization and to uncover critical development areas that will lead to integrated applications and databases throughout the firm.
- **Cooperation:** the degree of communication between various levels of management, user groups, and information systems in an effort to build internal and external coalitions to facilitate a general level of agreement on development priorities, implementation schedules, and managerial responsibilities. This includes IT management, the planning, coordination and organization of the strategy, investment, deployment and utilization of IT components, activities, and resources (both human and technical), and governance of IT resources, locus of decision-making as it pertains to IT resources, standard setting and funding processes.

We define reach and range, as follows:

- **Reach:** the degree of connectivity, "the ability of any technology component to attach to any of the other components inside and outside the organizational environment," (Byrd & Turner, 2000, p. 171) of the IT platform.

- **Range:** the degree to which any type of information can be shared across any technology component, system, or service.

Lastly, we define the fourth construct in the SISP model as follows:

- **Improvement in Capabilities:** the value added by identifying the IT capabilities provided and the strategic opportunities they present to the organization through increased organizational learning, which better enables the organization to adapt to unexpected changes in its internal and external environments.

In the subsequent sections, we briefly discuss Ross' (2003) four-stage model of ITA competency and apply our theoretical lenses to each stage of her model.

STAGES OF ITA COMPETENCY AND MATURITY

In examining ITA in organizations, Ross (2003) and Ross et al. (2006) intimate that four distinct stages of organizational maturation[3] and ITA competency are evident as organizations evolve their ITA. Ross (2003) and Ross et al. (2006) identify the four stages of ITA competency and maturity as the (1) application silo, which Ross et al. (2006) later referred to as business silo, (2) standardized technology, (3) rationalized data, which Ross et al. (2006) later referred to as optimized core, and (4) modular, which Ross et al. (2006) later referred to as business modularity. Table 1 lists some of the attributable characteristics of each stage and representative organizations. Firms in the business silo stage focus their resources on developing individual applications (Ross, 2003; Ross et al., 2006). Firms in the standardized technology stage focus their efforts and resources on the development of a shared infrastructure (Ross, 2003; Ross et al., 2006). Firms in the optimized core stage focus their efforts and resources on data management and infrastructure development (Ross, 2003; Ross et al., 2006). Firms in the business modularity stage focus efforts and resources on attaining strategic agility (Ross, 2003; Ross et al., 2006).

Each of the aforementioned stages has implications for the types of systems that organizations develop and/or purchase and implement. As such, it is important that organizations have a proper view and understanding of what an IS is not. This is important because an organization's view and understanding of an IS (whether it is flawed or not) greatly affects their use of the IS.

Weill (1992) states that an IS is not necessarily a homogeneous entity. He attributes this to the fact that different systems exist for different management objectives. The different types most likely consist of very different IS applications with many varying characteristics. There is also some evidence that separating technology into different types can help in predicting firm effectiveness (Bradley, 2006). Furthermore, the use of IS and the impact and intent of their use is commonly separated into three levels – operational, tactical/managerial, and strategic (Bradley, Pridmore, & Byrd, 2006; Weill, 1992). The intent of IS at the operational level focuses on directing resource use and the performance of tasks to yield labor productivity (Weill, 1992). The intent of IS at the tactical level focuses on allocating resources and monitoring the performance of subunits, divisions, and departments. The intent of IS at the strategic level focuses on overall organizational goals, strategies, policies, and objectives.

The use and impact of IS at any of these three levels is dependent upon the intent/objective(s) of the organization for a particular system or set of systems. Ross' current model of ITA maturity does not enable us to see clearly these distinctions because her model is positioned from the perspective of developing competency to implement an ITA of sufficient maturity. Her approach can be referred to as taking an architecture perspective because the focus is on the resulting ITA stage. Whereas, there is nothing wrong with her approach, it does provide an opportunity and need for the discussion and extension of her model so that it captures, and is representative of, any shifts/changes in an organization's focus. This latter approach can be referred to as an organizational perspective because the focus is on what is happening within and outside of the organization (as it pertains to our research lenses) as the organization moves from one stage of ITA maturity to another. Because the objective of our study is better accomplished by taking an organizational perspective rather than an architecture perspective, this is the perspective we take when considering the stages of Ross' ITA maturity model.

THEORETICAL APPLICATION OF RESEARCH LENSES

Up to this point we have discussed the four stages of Ross' (2003) model and have provided some insights within each stage as it pertains to shifts and changes in organizations' focus. We also

Table 1. Attributable Characteristics of the ITA Stage

ITA Stage	Attributable Characteristics	Representative Organizations	Rationale for Inclusion
Business Silo	• IT investments primarily focus on delivering systems/solutions unique to problems or opportunities in local business units (Ross et al., 2006) • Governance (i.e., business and IT decisions) resides with business unit managers (Ross, 2003; Ross et al., 2006) • Shared infrastructure services (e.g. data centers) accommodate the needs of local business units only (Ross et al., 2006) • Little to no reliance on established technology standards (Ross et al., 2006) • Integration and standardization of business processes are obstructed by legacy systems that cannot talk to each other (Ross et al., 2006)	Dow Corning (circa 1992... prior to their maturation to the Standardized Technology stage)	Overwhelmed by legacy systems that couldn't talk to each other (Ross, 2003)
Standardized Technology	• IT management concerns shift from the functionality of applications to the cost-effectiveness and reliability of systems (Ross et al., 2006) • IT efficiencies through technology standardization and infrastructure sharing (Ross, 2003; Ross et al., 2006) • Informed decisions are made by lower level organizational units (Goodhue et al., 1992; Kim & Everest, 1994) • Systems and their data fit into the organization's enterprise IS plan (Kim & Everest, 1994) • Establishment of standard setting, exception, and funding processes (Ross, 2003; Ross et al., 2006)	• Guardian Life • Johnson & Johnson • Pfizer	• All three have achieved cost savings and reliability through their technology standardization efforts (Ross et al., 2006)

continued on following page

Table 1. continued

ITA Stage	Attributable Characteristics	Representative Organizations	Rationale for Inclusion
Optimized Core	• Business unit managers lose discretion over core business processes (Ross et al., 2006) • Local decision-making patterns are disrupted by enterprise-wide data and process standards (Ross et al., 2006) • Ownership of data resides with business managers and process owners, not IT (Ross, 2003) • IT capabilities respond to business strategy (Ross, 2003; Ross et al., 2006) • Predictable processes and greater data transparency (Ross et al., 2006)	• Air Products and Chemicals (APC) • Nestle USA • UPS • Delta Airlines • Citibank Asia Pacific	• APC and Nestle digitized their supply chains using ERP systems to provide a set of predictable core processes and reusable data; they defined their business rules and wired those rules into their ERP system so that data automatically flowed to related processes (Ross, 2003; Ross et al., 2006) • UPS uses a single source of data to support its package delivery (Ross, 2003; Ross et al., 2006) • Delta determined their two core processes, identified the data they rely on, recognized how they share data with other processes, and created middleware that would notify relevant processes when a piece of data changed (Ross, 2003; Ross et al., 2006) • Citibank Asia Pacific established a core set standard processes for personal and commercial banking that could be replicated as they acquired or opened new banks (Ross, 2003; Ross et al., 2006)
Business Modularity	• IT investments primarily focus on attaining strategic agility (Ross, 2003; Ross et al., 2006) • Governance resides with top management (Ross, 2003; Ross et al., 2006) • Standardized business core (i.e., processes and data) with allowances for local customization via reusable modules (Ross et al., 2006) • The role of IT is to provide seamless linkages among core business process modules (Ross et al., 2006) • Ability to leverage ITA competencies and strategic agility to forge and better manage external relationships (Bradley, 2006)	• ING DIRECT • MeadWestvaco	• ING DIRECT affords local managers the latitude to adjust the modules they use to respond to local regulations and requirements (Ross et al., 2006) • MeadWestvaco gave local managers greater control over marketing decision by building modules on its ERP system, while maintaining the standardization of manufacturing decisions (Ross et al., 2006)

presented our reason for extending the scope of the business modularity stage. We now apply our research lenses to all four stages. We use each dimension of the Segars and Grover's (1998) SISP model and Keen's (1991) model of reach and range as lenses to assess the value of each stage to the organization.

Business Silo Stage

It is common for firms in the first stage to focus their IT resources on developing functional systems. Most often, these systems are developed to address specific business needs, and usually lead to highly developed systems. Nevertheless, since most systems tend to be created independent of the needs of other systems and functional areas that would use similar (if not the same) data, this stage results in the development of systems whose processes are limited to a single functional area or geography (Goodhue, Kirsch, Quillard, & Wybo, 1992; Ross, 2003). We now view this stage through the lens of our underlying research model.

Alignment

Since the business silo is at a more functional level, alignment in this stage refers to business unit alignment, and is quite important to organizations that operate in this stage. We define business unit alignment as the linkage between the IT infrastructure domain and an individual business unit

(Blaize Horner Reich & Benbasat, 2000). In this definition, alignment is viewed as an outcome, in which the mission of the IT domain supports the mission and objectives of the individual business unit (Chan, Huff, Copeland, & Barclay, 1997; B.H. Reich & Benbasat, 1996). Furthermore, business unit alignment appears to be evident in this stage when there exist a set of interrelated IT and business plans within the business unit (Blaize Horner Reich & Benbasat, 2000).

Alignment is believed to be driven by planning and communication (Blaize Horner Reich & Benbasat, 2000), which we refer to as analysis and cooperation. Although we expect business unit alignment to exist in this stage, there are a number of factors that could potentially affect the degree of this alignment. One contributing factor is that the depth of planning and analysis is limited to a specific business unit, totally ignoring the needs of other business units. In addition, communication between the IT domain and users within the business units, as well as the communication between middle and senior managers, tend to be, at best, intermittent (Goodhue et al., 1992). Based on the premise that analysis and cooperation are determinants of alignment (Blaize Horner Reich & Benbasat, 2000), we would expect the degree of business unit alignment in this stage to be in proportion to the level of communication and the depth of planning.

Analysis

In the business silo stage, analysis is viewed as the process used within a business unit to identify ways to compete with technology. Firms that operate in this stage seek to identify critical development areas that will lead to highly developed applications and databases that support the aims of the business unit. This objective is facilitated by the utilization of the set of interrelated IT and business plans within the business unit.

Cooperation

There is very little boundary crossing in terms of communication in the business silo stage, Departments tend to be segregated by functions and rarely share resources of any type. This lack of cooperation is further complicated due to feelings of provincialism by departments and functional units that control the data (Goodhue et al., 1992). Although the emphasis of this stage is on systems development, there is minimal interaction between developers and end-users of the systems. In addition, there is little communication between senior management and middle management in terms of decision-making (Goodhue et al., 1992). Often times this lack of communication makes it difficult to reach a general level of agreement on development priorities, implementation schedules, and managerial responsibilities. It is also evident that, in this stage, IT governance and locus of control of IT resources rests at the departmental and business unit level (Ross et al., 2006).

Reach and Range

Systems communications are constrained by geography or functionality in the business silo stage. This is often the case because applications are developed or purchased to address specific business needs. These business needs are often needs voiced by individual departments and business units. This usually leads to the development of systems that define their own data and rarely manage this data apart from their simple and localized transactions (Gibson, 1994; Ross, 2003). Thus, the reach and range of applications and systems developed in this stage are limited to sending and receiving standard messages from the same platform, access to locally stored data, and performing simple transactions, all within a single business unit.

Improvement in Capabilities

With the business silo stage being the first stage in the evolution, it serves as the baseline for comparing the other stages. As such, it would be premature (and possibly flawed) to refer to improvement in capabilities. However, it is worth noting that firms can generate business value at each stage if they are able to capitalize on the proposed benefits inherit to each stage. Some of the proposed benefits to organizations in the business silo stage include the ability to identify opportunities for improvement within the IS department (Goodhue et al., 1992) and better management of systems development projects. A major milestone that helps firms realize the proposed benefits and prepares the firms in this stage for the next stage is an in-depth understanding of the data requirements and technology requirements of the organization. This knowledge of standards and guidelines for new systems developed within a particular business unit (Goodhue et al., 1992; Zachman, 1982), will better enable the organization to standardize the technology platform across the enterprise.

Standardized Technology Stage

The standardized technology stage, which primarily focuses on IT management and management of the internal organization, is more easily attained by addressing and improving upon some of the inherent limitations of organizations in the business silo stage. A major limitation of the business silo stage is that it appears to place more emphasis on IS segregation, departmental-wise, rather than corporate integration of IS. In addition, organizations in the business silo stage fail to recognize the need to share information across business units and throughout the organization. This suggests that the primary focus of the business silo stage is systems development, not IT management or management of the organization. Although these limitations are serious, recognition of these limitations and the improvement upon them positions organizations to be able to move to the next stage of EA maturity, the standardized technology stage. It is in the standardized technology stage that organizations recognize the lack of systems integration and data sharing within the organization and attempt to remedy the problem. We now view this stage through the lens of our underlying research model.

Alignment

Since the standardized technology stage centers on IT management and management of the internal organizations, it calls for a definition of alignment that transcends the boundaries of individual business units. Therefore, in this stage, we define alignment as the linkage between the IT infrastructure domain and all business units. Similar to the definition of alignment in the business silo stage, this definition of alignment is viewed as an outcome, in which the mission of the IT domain supports the mission and objectives of all business units. This further allows the organization to take advantage of IT opportunities and capabilities (Blaize Horner Reich & Benbasat, 2000). Furthermore, since organizations that operate in the standardized technology stage are more focused on data and systems integration, attainment of alignment can be viewed as a major milestone that will serve as a catalyst for data and systems integration across business units.

Analysis

Organizations that operate in the standardized technology stage proceed to correct the inability or unwillingness to share data. They also endeavor to resolve issues and problems of IS segregation and disjointedness by identifying the data needs and resources throughout the organization. This identification of data needs and resources are made possible by employing the appropriate systems planning methodology/methodologies within the organization.

Cooperation

Systems and communication boundaries are removed in the standardized technology stage. Senior managers and middle managers, in an effort to control IT expenditures, begin to collaborate more (Brown et al., 2000). As the focus shifts to data sharing and systems integration, end-users begin to play a vital role in the system development process. This is due in part to improved communications between end-users and top managers (Goodhue et al., 1992). Additionally, as organizations implement technology standards and begin to move towards a centralized, shared infrastructure, communication among business units increases. With this increase in communication at various levels, it is now feasible to reach a general level of agreement on development priorities, implementation schedules, and managerial responsibilities. It is also evident that, in this stage, IT governance and locus of control of IT resources begin to shift from the departmental and functional unit level to middle management.

Reach and Range

Due to the emphasis on technology standards in the standardized technology stage, applications and systems developed or purchased by organizations are capable of connecting to, communicating with, and sharing data with other systems within the organization. The accomplishment of systems integration and a centralized data repository makes this possible regardless of business unit or geographical boundaries. However, in this stage, systems communications are still somewhat constrained by geography and functionality.

Systems in the standardized technology stage, like those in the business silo stage, are capable of performing simple transactions, but, in contrast, are not limited to a single business unit. In addition to performing simple transactions, the implementation of a shared infrastructure positions organizations in the standardized technology stage to be able to make the shift to performing complex transactions on multiple intra-organizational applications. These organizations are now primed to begin communicating with their vendors' and customers' systems that operate on the same IT platform.

Improvement in Capabilities

Organizations in the standardized technology stage have one major improvement over organizations in the business silo stage -- IT efficiency. This efficiency can be measured in terms of several improved capabilities: data sharing, linking of systems across business unit boundaries, and the ability to perform complex transactions on multiple intra-organizational applications. Another major improvement in capabilities is the ability of middle and senior managers to overcome communication barriers in order to agree on technology standards. This standardization effort, while reducing complexity, leads to increases in IT maintainability, reliability, and security. This is possible because of the organizational learning that takes place, which fundamentally changes organizations' approaches to solutions delivery (Ross, 2003).

Organizations that reach the standardized technology stage face numerous proposed benefits. For instance, proposed benefits to organizations in this stage include improved data consistency (Goodhue et al., 1992; Goodhue, Quillard, & Rockart, 1988), development of systems that are easier to integrate (Goodhue et al., 1992; Goodhue et al., 1988), better understanding of the data by those involved in the systems planning process (Goodhue et al., 1992; Goodhue et al., 1988), and a constant flow of information to all facets of internal operations (Stein, 1999). These proposed benefits, whether directly or indirectly, are related to the organizational learning that has taken place in the process of maturing from the business silo stage operating effectively in the standardized technology stage.

Optimized Core Stage

The optimized core stage is the third stage of the ITA competency and maturity model. Attainment of this stage is more easily accomplished by improving upon the limitations of the standardized technology stage. A major limitation of the standardized technology stage is the lack of cohesiveness between firms IT strategies and priorities and their business strategies and priorities. This lack of cohesiveness is sometimes evident by the mindset that IT or business strategy alone "drives" the organization (Ross, 2003; Ross et al., 2006). That is to say, a lack of shared domain knowledge can affect strategic alignment (Blaize Horner Reich & Benbasat, 2000).

Organizations in the optimized core stage primarily focus on the linkage or alignment between their IT strategy and business strategy. Organizations that operate in this stage anticipate that this alignment will enable the acquisition and deployment of IT resources that are congruent with the organizations' competitive needs rather than existing patterns of usage within the organizations (Richardson & Jackson, 1990; Segars & Grover, 1998). We now apply the research lenses to the optimized core stage.

Alignment

Whereas the alignment of the IT strategy and business strategy was once considered a luxury for most organizations, it is now considered a necessity for those organizations that wish to keep pace and remain competitive in today's fast changing environment (Johnston & Carrico, 1988; Johnston & Vitale, 1988; Sabherwal & Chan, 2001). It has been suggested that the stature of the IT resources is heightened by such an alignment, thus facilitating the financial and managerial support necessary to effectively implement innovative systems (Richardson & Jackson, 1990; Segars & Grover, 1998). In addition to this, once strategic alignment has been achieved, organizations are better positioned to embed core business processes in their IT infrastructure (Butler, 2001; Gibson, 1994; Ross, 2003). This means creating and utilizing new technologies or modifying existing technologies so that core business processes are automated. The technological solution deemed appropriate for the organization to accomplish this task should be evaluated with respect to cost, speed, business functionality, synergy, and standardization (Richardson & Jackson, 1990). Upon attaining strategic alignment and embedding core business functionality in the IT infrastructure, a firm can be classified in McFarlan's (1984) strategic quadrant and can be expected to seek IT opportunities to achieve the flexibility needed to take advantage of competitive situations and adapt to new, dynamic environments (Gibson, 1994; Richardson & Jackson, 1990).

Analysis

The optimized core stage requires executives, both IT and business, to fundamentally change their thinking about the role of IT in organizational transformation (Henderson & Venkatraman, 1999; Richardson & Jackson, 1990). Executives must begin to see the strategic role and value of IT to the firm– the potential to support chosen business strategies and shape new business strategies (Richardson & Jackson, 1990). This change in thinking also requires "an understanding of the critical components of the IT strategy and the role of the IT strategy in supporting and shaping the business strategy decisions" (Henderson & Venkatraman, 1999). It is important for firms to meet both requirements if they are to be able to deliver a sustained competitive advantage, which is obtained through its capability to exploit continuously IT functionality throughout the organization (Henderson & Venkatraman, 1999; G. S. Kearns & Lederer, 2000; Porter & Millar, 1985). Thus, organizations in this stage may now be able to see that strategic alignment is not a single state, or event, that is easily attained, nor is it a destination that is easily reached. Rather, strategic alignment is a process of continuous adaptation and change, hence a dynamic capability (Henderson & Venkatraman, 1999).

Cooperation

In the optimized core stage, we begin to see the dissipation of communication boundaries between senior business and IT managers. Senior business and IT managers, in an effort to align their respective strategies, begin to collaborate more (Richardson & Jackson, 1990). As the focus shifts from a myriad of diverse groups of senior managers, each group with its own ideas of which and what type of strategy is best for the organization, to a virtually seamless and more focused unit of senior managers whose sole purpose is to work together to help make the organization increasingly competitive, the alignment of the IT strategy and business strategy, which is so desperately needed, becomes a reality. With this increase in communication between senior business and IT managers, it is now feasible for both sides to reach a general level of agreement as to what joint business and IT decisions and resources will and will not lend themselves to enabling the organization to accomplish its overall objectives. This increase in communication and collaboration between the two parties provides a perfect opportunity for one group to better understand and appreciate the priorities and managerial responsibilities of the other group (Richardson & Jackson, 1990). In other words, the senior IT managers get a lesson in business while the senior business managers learn to appreciate the capabilities IT provide. The relationship between the two groups of managers becomes harmonious when both groups understand that neither strategy alone will facilitate competitive advantage. It is also evident that, in this stage, IT governance and the locus of control of data and core processes shifts from middle (local) management to senior management, while the locus of control of IT resources remains with middle (local) management.

Reach and Range

Due to the emphasis on strategic alignment and the embedding of core business functionality[4] in the IT infrastructure, and as technology standards are further refined, data standardization continues to be a primary concern for organizations in the optimized core stage (Richardson & Jackson, 1990). The continued refinement of technology standardization and the accomplishment of data standardization, systems integration, and a centralized data repository enable organizations in the optimized core stage to extend the reach of their IT platform. In this stage, systems communications are not as constrained by geography and functionality, as it relates to the internal organization. The range of these systems is the same as those in the standardized technology stage in that they are capable of performing complex transactions on multiple intra-organizational applications. However, in contrast to the systems in the standardized technology stage whose reach was limited to customers and suppliers with the same facility base, the reach of systems in the optimized core stage enables organizations to connect to their customers and suppliers, regardless of their facility base. These organizations are now primed to begin communicating with the systems of their vendors and customers, whose IT platforms are the same or different from their own IT platform.

This is made possible since the ITA, in this stage, is a plan or set of plans developed independently of information systems. If constructed and implemented in a consistent manner, the ITA will allow for the utilization of data by wider audiences and systems. The process, which will create the potential for greater compatibility between applications and databases, will also facilitate the portability of applications" (Keen, 1991; Richardson & Jackson, 1990).

Improvement in Capabilities

Organizations in the optimized core stage have several major improvements over organizations in the previous stages, including the alignment of the IT strategy and business strategy. Although it may appear that this improvement in capabilities is minute, the strategic value of this stage, as seen in the implications of this major improvement in capabilities, is enormous. For instance, this alignment can be seen in a more balanced strategy that facilitates an organization's increasing competitiveness. Additionally, the implications of this newfound "strategic balance" can be measured in terms of several improved capabilities: improved data sharing, the ability to link systems across business unit and geographical boundaries, and the ability to perform complex transactions on multiple intra-organizational applications.

Another major improvement in capabilities is the ability of senior business and IT managers to overcome communication barriers in order to agree on data standards and refinements of previously established technology standards. These standardization efforts help organizations to identify and define core business processes and the data on which they rely (Ross, 2003). This is possible because in this stage the ITA is tightly coupled with the corporate business plan. The coupling of the ITA and the corporate business plan suggests that the role of IT in the organization is to support "the business mission, objectives, and strategies, as outlined in the business plan" (Grover S. Kearns & Lederer, 1997) – hence strategic alignment is attained.

Once strategic alignment has been attained, organizations in the optimized core stage have the additional proposed benefit of being able to embed their core business functionality in the organization's IT infrastructure (Butler, 2001; Gibson, 1994; Ross, 2003). Although Butler (2001) urges against embedding core business functionality in the IT infrastructure for fear of difficulty in managing the core business processes, others hold true to their belief that by embedding core business functionality in the IT infrastructure, organizations position their IT platform for innovation (Gibson, 1994; Ross, 2003). Butler (2001) makes a case for using Web Services to handle the core business functionality of an organization (see Hagel and Brown, 2001, for more on using Web Services). This approach to automating core business functionality is designed to help prevent organizations from falling into the trap of having core business processes "locked away" in legacy systems (Butler, 2001).

The optimized core stage has an enormous number of other proposed benefits to the organization. The proposed benefits include the ability to articulate the strategy to define IT capabilities (Ross, 2003), utilization of the ITA as an educational tool for new employees (Curle, 1993), improved ability to provide planning for migration of aging and new technology (Curle, 1993), and increased flexibility of the organization in dealing with external changes that affect the competitiveness of the organization (Kim & Everest, 1994). These proposed benefits make the optimized core stage a vast improvement over the preceding stages.

Business Modularity Stage

The business modularity stage, the fourth and final stage of our proposed model, enables organizations to extend their reach to anyone anywhere and their range to encompass performing multiple complex transactions on inter-organizational systems (see Figure 2). However, there are limitations inherent to the optimized core stage that should be improved upon to make a successful transition to the business modularity stage. The major limitation of organizations in the optimized core stage is their inability to overcome geographical and technical constraints fully. This is to say that even though organizations are able to attain strategic balance in this stage, they still lack the ability to extend their reach to anyone anywhere and their range

Figure 2. The Reach and Range of the ITA Stages of Evolution

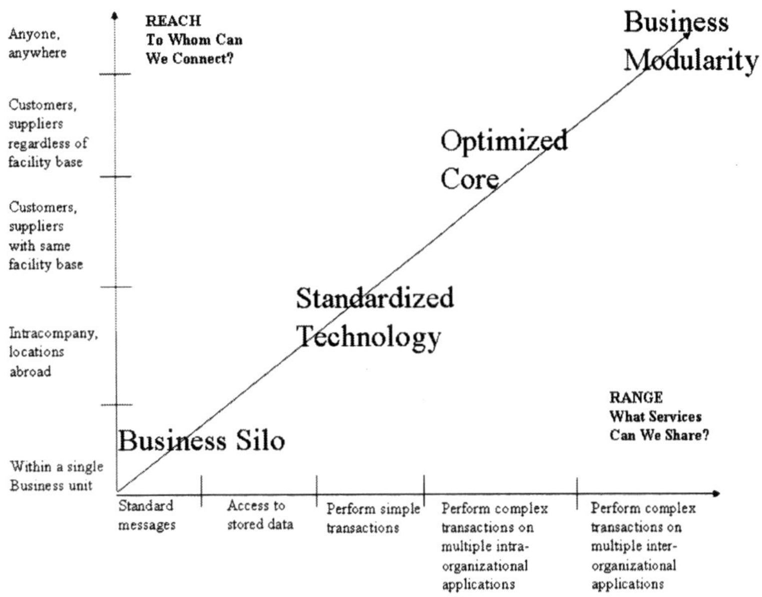

to systems beyond the scope of their enterprise and internal customer/supplier relationships. The inability of organizations in the optimized core stage to fully overcome geographical and technological constraints, may be due in part to several reasons: (a) organizations lack the technology or technical competency available to allow for "true" inter-organizational transactions, (b) organizations lack the "total fulfillment" of both technology and data standardization and integration, (c) organizations lack the depth and breadth of knowledge about their own data and IT platform required to overcome such constraints, (d) organizations lack the business and technical competency necessary to accomplish the formation of strategic alliances, and (e) potential alliance partners lack the organizational and architectural maturity to complete the strategic alliance.

The business modularity stage ignores neither the success of organizations in the three previous stages nor the value of those stages to the organizations that operate in them. Rather, this stage represents organizations that are able to overcome the geographical and technical boundaries that limited organizations in the three preceding stages. The extension of the ITA of the three previous stages to include the management and integration of inter-organizational relationships and systems is due, in part, to efforts to overcome the limitations and constraints of the previous stages.

In the business modularity stage, companies typically move away from developing their own proprietary hardware and software applications and begin to take advantage of the savings offered by outside organizations specializing in such things. For those that choose to maintain their hosts of independent applications, they tend to make use of Web services or some other form of middleware that enables the independent applications to communicate and share data (Ross et al., 2006). One of the more difficult parts in the formulation of strategic alliances and partnerships is the integration of the organizations' systems (Gadiesh, Buchanan, Daniell, & Ormiston, 2002). Therefore it should be no surprise that as the number of inter-organizational alliances has increased (Gadiesh et al., 2002; Gordon, Kruger, & Helman, 2002; Lubove, 2002; Rubinfeld & Singer, 2001), implementing an ITA has become a priority (Bradley, 2006; Hagel & Brown, 2001; Ross, 2003; Ross et al., 2006). In recent years, an ITA has become of particular value since more organizations are abandoning the traditional way of doing business that restricts data sharing and strategic alignment to the internal organization. Organizations have now started to embrace the concept of data sharing, systems integration, and strategic alignment with external organizations.

The business modularity stage requires complex and sophisticated planning, not to mention an enormous amount of financial and human resources. As such, few organizations (i.e., 4-5%) have attained or are on the verge of attaining this stage (Ross, 2003; Ross et al., 2006). Therefore, we are merely proposing it as means to generate interest within the IS research community and to stimulate thoughts and ideas about potential avenues of research within the domain of ITA. We also do not intend to insinuate that the business modularity stage is the final stage of ITA competency and maturity. Rather, it is meant to serve as the latter stage of our proposed model at this point in time. Furthermore, Ross et al (2006) suggest that the inter-organizational aspect of the business modularity stage can be split into a fifth stage, which they refer to as the dynamic venturing stage. We now apply the research lenses to the business modularity stage.

Alignment

In the previous stages, alignment has been viewed as the close linkage between the IT strategy and business strategy. In this stage, alignment takes on two different views -- strategic inter-organizational alignment and strategic alliance alignment. Herein, we will briefly discuss both views.

The first view is merely the extension of the traditional view to include the alignment or linkage between two organizations. By this, we mean the close linkage between the IT strategy and business strategy in one organization is aligned with the close linkage between the IT strategy and business strategy in another, external organization. As can be seen in the application of the "cooperation" lens below, this inter-organizational alignment requires intense collaboration and communication on the part of top IT and business strategic planners within and across both organizations. The second view is the alignment between the business strategy and the alliance strategy (Parise & Henderson, 2001). The alliance strategy contains the rationale for attempting the formation of a strategic alliance. The rationale, contained in the alliance strategy, helps to identify the right target ally and set boundaries for negotiations (Gadiesh et al., 2002). These boundaries include the responsibilities of each partner as well as which party will retain control of certain intellectual or tangible byproduct(s) of the alliance. Thus, each organization must ensure that its alliance strategy will facilitate the accomplishment of organizational objectives, hence matching or aligning with the organization's business strategy.

Analysis

Apart from forming strategic alliances, organizations in this stage also seek strategic agility. Strategic agility is made possible through customization and modularity of the IT platform. By modularity, we mean the creation of reusable modules that are available for selection by various business units and partners. Modularity provides a means for organizations to give business units and partners greater discretion in their local processes (Byrd & Turner, 2000; Ross, 2003). Although the degree of discretion allows for local customization, it does not negate the need for standardization.

In the business modularity stage, such standardization efforts are a byproduct of a shared ITA. The shared ITA makes inter-organizational communications between systems possible. With the addition of newer technologies, specifically Web services, a shared ITA also enables connections between applications, both within and across organizations, to be managed automatically.

Cooperation

In the business modularity stage, we begin to see the dissipation of communication boundaries between collaborating organizations. Senior business and IT managers, in an effort to align their respective ITA with the ITA of potential allied organizations begin to collaborate more. In this stage, the focus shifts from diverse organizations, each with its own technology and data standards, IT and business strategy, and IT platform(s) to a distributed, yet virtually seamless, conglomerate whose sole purpose is to work together to help make each allied organization increasingly competitive. This increase in competitiveness hinges on the alignment of the business strategy and alliance strategy (Parise & Henderson, 2001) within each organization. This task requires and facilitates increased collaboration within and among business and IT executives of the potential allied organizations. With an increase in collaboration between business and IT executives of allied organizations, it is now feasible for both sides to reach a general level of agreement as to what type of joint venture(s) and resources will and will not lend themselves to enabling the allied organizations to accomplish their respective business objectives. Additionally, this increase in communication and collaboration among the allied organizations provides a perfect opportunity for each to better understand and appreciate the priorities and core competencies of the other. This provides an extended, yet different view of shared domain knowledge.

Reach and Range

Since the focus of the business modularity stage is on strategic agility, the reach and range of the organizational systems in this stage are no longer limited by geographical and technological boundaries. Due to this stage's emphasis on reusability, modularity, componentization, and customization at the local level, organizations in this stage are able to obtain the flexibility in their IT infrastructure necessary to help promote strategic agility (Byrd & Turner, 2000; Ross, 2003). It should be noted that the amount of customization should be limited and should be guided by the shared ITA to prevent local customization from having an adverse effect on the standardization efforts that have taken place. Following the guidelines of the ITA should make certain that the limitations placed on customization efforts in no way impacts strategic agility. Strategic agility is evident in the extension of the reach and range of the IT platform. In this stage, systems communications are no longer constrained by geography and functionality in any sense. The reach of these systems enables an organization to connect to anyone, anywhere. Likewise, the range of these systems enables an organization to share all services, making it possible to perform complex transactions on multiple inter-organizational applications. The reach and range of this stage represents the distant future for most organizations and the near future for some.

Improvement in Capabilities

In today's era of alliances, it is not enough to understand the internal organization, but one must also understand the organizational structure and IT platform of potential allies. This has become increasingly important and viable with the emergence and availability of technologies such as "Web services", ".Net", "network services", and the "open network environment" (Hagel & Brown, 2001). In addition to the improvement in IT, organizations in the business modularity stage have several major improvements over organizations in the previous stages. These improvements include inter-organizational communications between systems, more efficient means of automatically managing the inter-organizational connection between applications, strategic agility, and a shared ITA.

Furthermore, the majority of these improvements in capabilities and the proposed benefits to organizations in the business modularity stage are mostly attributable to the successful attainment of strategic agility. Strategic agility affords organizations the dynamic capabilities that make it easier to shift operations and various alliances in response to market and competitive stimuli (Bradley, 2006; Hagel & Brown, 2001). Technologies like web services, due to their loose couplings, allow organizations to be more flexible when integrating a diverse set of applications that reside within most organizations (Hagel & Brown, 2001; Ross et al., 2006). At the same time, web services make these seemingly integrated applications available to strategic allies (Hagel & Brown, 2001). The ITA in this stage, which is sometimes referred to as a web services architecture (WSA) and service-oriented architecture (SOA), does several things for organizations: (1) reduces the chance that organizations will end up using obsolete technologies, (2) makes it easier for organizations to outsource activities and processes at any time, and (3) supports more flexible collaboration among organizations' business units and between its allies (Butler, 2001; Hagel & Brown, 2001).

CONCLUSION

Organizations that lack a coherent strategy for managing and evolving their IT platform and resources end up with fragmentation within the organization. In this paper, we theoretically examined and conceptually extended Ross' (2003) four-stage model of ITA competency and maturity. Our examination and extension of her model highlights its intra-organizational scope of an ITA, and extends her model to include inter-organizational collaboration and communication, thus looking outside the organization. We also applied our underlying research model to the two latter stages of Ross' (2003) model to provide some insight as to how an ITA can add strategic value an organization.

Figure 3 summarizes the paper as it depicts the organizational maturity and learning that takes place as organizations move between stages. The degree of organizational maturity and learning is indicative of an organization's architectural competency. Figure 3 also shows how the aggregate themes of the proposed benefits and the strategic value of IT to the organization accumulate as organizations advance through the four stages. As part of a separate study on enterprise IT capabilities and ITA maturity in healthcare organizations, in which we surveyed 140 CIOs of US hospitals, we received comments and feedback about the nature and status of ITA initiatives in US hospitals (Bradley, 2006). Nearly 60% of the represented hospitals are medium- to large-sized hospitals with annual total operating revenues in excess of $45 million. We used the comments and feedback (provided via the survey that we administered to them), in addition to the results of our theoretical analysis to develop Figure 3 and provide support for our arguments. Given that very few organizations have reached the business modularity stage, we received no useable feedback and comments about this stage from the CIOs.

In the business silo stage, the sole focus is on systems development. Business and IT personnel define strategy and make recommendations without input from one another. The value of this stage to the organization lies in its provision of standards and guidelines for systems development. Though the development of such functional systems limits their usefulness within the enterprise, the process of developing standards and guidelines for these systems provides a basis for starting a dialogue between IT and business managers about IT value. Such dialogue can lead to organiza-

Figure 3. Aggregated Themes of the ITA Maturity and the Strategic Value to the Organization

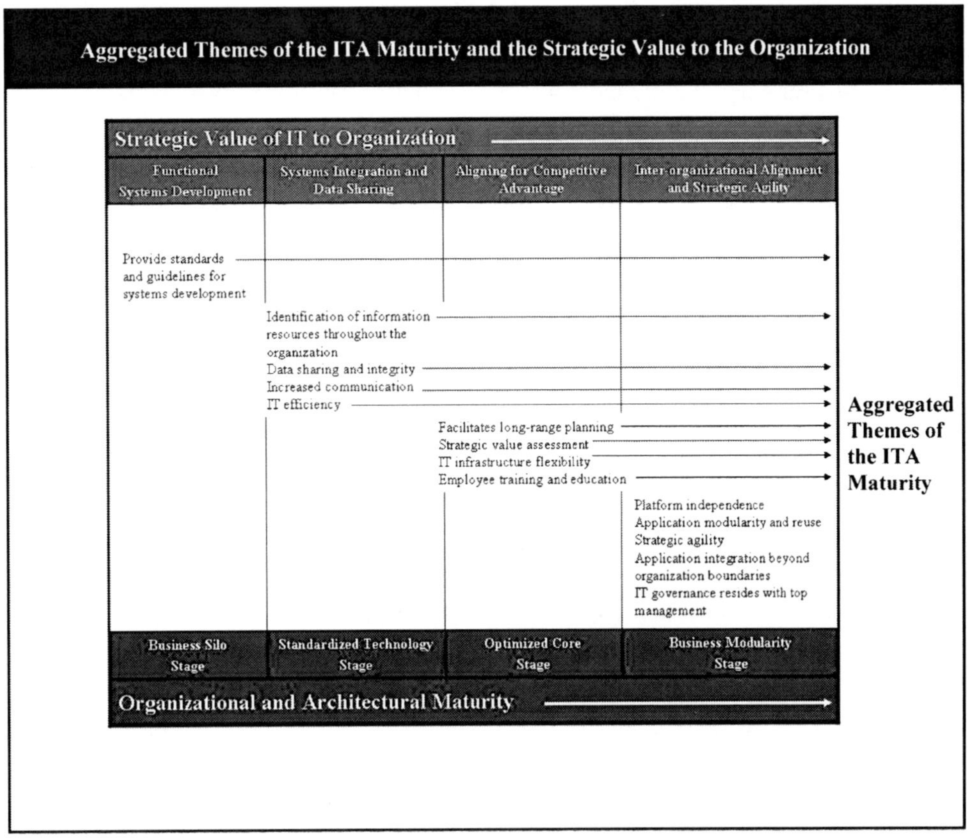

tional learning that not only generates value to organizations in the in this stage but also positions them for subsequent stages. The comments and feedback we received from aforementioned hospital CIOs, whose organizations' ITA maturity is equivalent to the business silo stage, support our arguments. Samplings of the comments are as follows:

- "[We have] many free standing programs that do not interface with current platforms."
- "[We have take a] silo approach for each functional area with no common data infrastructure."
- "[It is a problem] to get Steering Committee participation with an emphasis of the organization as a whole as opposed to individual business units."

The standardized technology stage builds on the communication between IT and business managers, regarding the value of IT to the organization. Together, business and IT managers are able to identify information resources within the organization. The strategic value of IT to the organization is in the identification of these resources, which leads to the notion of data sharing and systems integration. With the identification of information resources comes the issue of control and decision-making authority (i.e., governance). This issue prompts the development of decision-making structures to control information resources, thus making it feasible for IT and business managers to reach a general level of agreement on development priorities, implementation schedules, and managerial responsibilities. The development of these decision-making structures foster communication between business and IT mangers and provides organizational learning that will enable organizations to be more efficient in subsequent stages. The comments and feedback we received from the abovementioned hospital CIOs, whose organizations' ITA maturity is equivalent to the business silo stage, support our arguments. Samplings of the comments are as follows:

- "[We have a] flexible and robust IT architecture...[but] our IT governance process lacks consistent support by senior management and business unit leaders...[there is] resistance by some of [the] senior management due to cost and perception of [IT] value [and] reluctance of senior management to participate in assessment, evaluation, of IT needs and strategic plan."
- "[Our] current architecture is a hodgepodge of pieced together technology implemented with little future thought and to meet individual needs...there is a current commitment to planning and fixing/straightening out the current architecture. The applications purchased are now done through a strategy of primarily a single vender approach."
- "Standardization of support capability has increased since architecture guidelines established and put into force."

In the optimized core stage, organizations are focused on aligning for competitive advantage. This includes the alignment of the IT strategy and business strategy and the embedding of core processes in the IT platform. The increased collaboration and communication between senior business and IT managers enable them to articulate their intended strategy, critical IT capabilities and opportunities, and the target ITA clearly. Assessments of the strategic value of IT and the identification of core processes and the data that drives those processes contribute greatly to the education and training of new and existing employees about the strategic intent of the organization. Additionally, organizations are able to leverage their accumulated learning about standards to standardize data and processes and further refine technology standards. These standardization efforts provide organizations with the IT infrastructure flexibility needed to adapt to changes in the business and IT strategy and the architectural core competency necessary to be successful in the current stage and to begin the journey to the business modularity stage easily. The comments and feedback we received from the previously mentioned hospital CIOs, whose organizations' ITA maturity is equivalent to the business silo stage, support our arguments. Samplings of the comments are as follows:

- "Because we empower users and include them in all of our planning processes, IT technology, for the most part, is being pulled through the organization, rather than pushed by IT...IT systems are no longer considered IT projects, but are 'owned' by the business units, and IT acts as a facilitator."
- "We outsourced the technology infrastructure which allowed us to focus on IT applications and enterprise processes."
- "[We have] a deeper understanding of business alignment and IT projects through improved governance procedures...[but there are some] differences of opinion and knowledge as to what constitutes an IT Architecture."
- "We've adopted a standard for just about everything to keep things simple. Senior management backs up the policies as well."
- "Excellent governance model includes Senior Executives, Business Unit leaders, and physicians/clinicians. [Our] firm funds IT at a level that is balanced with IT staff

technology, infrastructure, applications, and support requirements."

The business modularity stage provides an architecture that embodies inter-organizational alignment and strategic agility. This stage promotes platform independence, application modularity, reusability and customization, inter-organizational systems integration, and an IT decision-making structure that resides with top management. Because the need for data sharing is not always limited to the internal organization, the boundaries between the organization and its customers, vendors, suppliers, and allies are often blurred (Nolan, 2001). It appears to be evident that organizations must have a clear idea of where they stand in regards to their own ITA before preparing to adopt a new, shared ITA.

This study contributes to the literature in several ways. One contribution is that we attempt to combine two theories – reach and range and SISP – that have typically been applied separately. Another contribution is applying the combined theories holistically to an established maturity model to provide greater insights about the stages of ITA maturity. Another unique aspect of this paper is explaining how the internally oriented maturity model can be extended to include inter-organizational relationships, an aspect that is virtually nonexistent in other studies related to ITA.

FUTURE RESEARCH

Since no cohesive measurement instrument currently exists to identify where organizations fall on the proposed four-stage continuum, future research could make a major contribution in this area by developing such an instrument. The development of an instrument to accurately perform the aforementioned task, as well as assess the successfulness of organizations at each given stage (including cross-stage comparisons) could also prove to be of great value to the IS community. Future research could also investigate the relationship between an organization's level of architectural and organizational maturity to a particular systems planning approach within and across stages. Future research could also empirically assess the nature of the relationship between the ITA stages and the three IT outsourcing arrangements identified by Ross and Beath (2006). Finally, given the increase in communication and collaboration between those responsible for the development of an ITA, an investigation into the role of those who participate in the development effort and the medium(s) used to communicate and collaborate might provide valuable insights into a long, difficult, and often tedious process.

REFERENCES

Allen, B. R., & Boynton, A. C. (1991). Information Architecture: In Search of Efficient Flexibility. *MIS Quarterly*, *15*(4), 435–445. doi:10.2307/249447

Bradley, R. V. (2006). Strategic Valuation of Enterprise Information Technology Architecture in Healthcare Organizations. Unpublished Ph.D. Dissertation, Auburn University, Auburn.

Bradley, R. V., & Byrd, T. A. (2007). Information Technology Architecture as a Competitive Advantage-yielding Resource: A Theoretical Perspective. *International Journal of Networking and Virtual Organisations*, *4*(1), 1–19. doi:10.1504/IJNVO.2007.012079

Bradley, R. V., Pridmore, J., & Byrd, T. A. (2006). Information Systems Success in the Context of Different Corporate Cultural Types: An Empirical Investigation. *Journal of Management Information Systems*, *23*(2), 267–294. doi:10.2753/MIS0742-1222230211

Broadbent, M., Weill, P., & St. Clair, D. (1999). The Implications of Information Technology Infrastructure for Business Process Redesign. *MIS Quarterly*, *23*(2), 159–182. doi:10.2307/249750

Brown, G., Fisher, M., Stoll, N., Beeksma, D., Black, M., & Taylor, R. (2000). Using the Lessons of Y2K to Improve Information Systems Architecture. *Communications of the ACM*, *43*(10), 90–97. doi:10.1145/352183.352210

Butler, M. (2001, December 6, 2001). Best of Both Worlds. Retrieved December 22, 2003, from http://www.computerweekly.com/Article108572.htm

Byrd, T. A., Lewis, B., & Bradley, R. V. (2006). IS Infrastructure: The Influence of Senior IT Leadership and Strategic Information Systems Planning. *Journal of Computer Information Systems*, *47*(1), 101–113.

Byrd, T. A., & Turner, D. E. (2000). Measuring the Flexibility of Information Technology Infrastructure: Exploratory Analysis of a Construct. *Journal of Management Information Systems*, *17*(1), 167–208.

Chan, Y. E., Huff, S. L., Copeland, D. G., & Barclay, D. W. (1997). Business Strategic Orientation, Information Systems Strategic Orientation and Strategic Alignment. *Information Systems Research*, *8*(2), 125–150. doi:10.1287/isre.8.2.125

Curle, H. A. J. (1993). Supporting Strategic Objectives: Building a Corporate Information Technology Architecture. *Information Strategy: The Executive's Journal*, *10*(1), 5–12.

Duncan, N. B. (1995). Capturing Flexibility of Information Technology Infrastructure: A Study of Resource Characteristics and Their Measure. *Journal of Management Information Systems*, *12*(2), 37–57.

Earl, M. J. (1989). Management Strategies for Information Technology. London: Prentice Hall.

Evernden, R., & Evernden, E. (2003). Third Generation Information Architecture. *Communications of the ACM*, *46*(3), 95–98. doi:10.1145/636772.636777

Farnum, C. (2002). Information Architecture: Five Things Information Managers Need to Know. *Information Management Journal*, *36*(5), 33–39.

Gadiesh, O., Buchanan, R., Daniell, M., & Ormiston, C. (2002). The Leadership Testing Ground. *The Journal of Business Strategy*, *23*(2), 12–17. doi:10.1108/eb040230

Gibson, R. (1994). Global Information Technology Architectures. *Journal of Global Information Management*, *2*(1), 28–38.

Gifford, R. (1992). Implementing the IS Architecture. *Information Systems Management*, *9*(4), 41–47. doi:10.1080/10580539208906898

Goodhue, D. L., Kirsch, L. J., Quillard, J. A., & Wybo, M. D. (1992). Strategic Data Planning: Lessons from the Field. *MIS Quarterly*, *16*(1), 11–34. doi:10.2307/249699

Goodhue, D. L., Quillard, J. A., & Rockart, J. F. (1988). Managing The Data Resource: A Contingency Perspective. *MIS Quarterly*, *12*(3), 11–34. doi:10.2307/249204

Gordon, J., Kruger, D., & Helman, C. (2002, February 18). Streetwalker. *Forbes*, *169*, 108.

Hackathorn, R. D., & Karimi, J. (1988). A Framework for Comparing Information Engineering Methods. *MIS Quarterly*, *12*(2), 202–220. doi:10.2307/248845

Hagel, J. I., & Brown, J. S. (2001). Your Next IT Strategy. *Harvard Business Review*, *79*(9), 105–113.

Henderson, J. C., & Venkatraman, N. (1995). Strategic Alignment: A Model for Organisational Transformation Via Information Technology. In T. J. Allen & M. S. S. Morton (Eds.), Information Technology and the Corporation of the 1990s: Research Studies (pp. 202-220). Oxford: Oxford University Press.

Henderson, J. C., & Venkatraman, N. (1999). Strategic Alignment: Leveraging Information Technology for Transforming Organizations. *IBM Systems Journal*, *38*(2/3), 472–484.

Hildebrand, C. (2000). What is Infrastructure? Retrieved January 18, 2002, from http://www.darwinmag.com

Johnston, H. R., & Carrico, S. R. (1988). Developing Capabilities to Use Information Strategically. *MIS Quarterly*, *12*(1), 37–48. doi:10.2307/248801

Johnston, H. R., & Vitale, M. R. (1988). Creating Competitive Advantage with Interorganizational Information Systems. *MIS Quarterly*, *12*(2), 152–165. doi:10.2307/248839

Kearns, G. S., & Lederer, A. L. (1997). Alignment of Information Systems Plans with Business Plans: The Impact on Competitive Advantage. Paper presented at the Proceedings of the Second Americas Conference on Information Systems, Indianapolis.

Kearns, G. S., & Lederer, A. L. (2000). The Effect of Strategic Alignment on the Use of IS-based Resources for Competitive Advantage. *The Journal of Strategic Information Systems*, *9*(4), 265–293. doi:10.1016/S0963-8687(00)00049-4

Keen, P. G. W. (1991). Shaping the Future: Business Design through Information Technology. Cambridge, MA: Harvard Business School Press.

Kim, Y., & Everest, G. C. (1994). Building an IS Architecture. *Information & Management*, *26*(1), 1–11. doi:10.1016/0378-7206(94)90002-7

Lubove, S. (2002). Do Oil and Data Mix? *Forbes*, *169*, 76–77.

McFarlan, F. W. (1984). Information Technology Changes the Way You Compete. *Harvard Business Review*, *62*(3), 98–103.

Niederman, F., Brancheau, J. C., & Wetherbe, J. C. (1991). Information Systems Management Issues for the 1990s. *MIS Quarterly*, *15*(4), 474–500. doi:10.2307/249452

Nolan, R. L. (2001). Information Technology Management from 1960-2000 (pp. 1-31). Cambridge: Harvard Business School.

Parise, S., & Henderson, J. C. (2001). Knowledge Resource Exchange in Strategic Alliances. *IBM Systems Journal*, *40*(4), 908–924.

Periasamy, K. P., & Feeny, D. F. (1997). Information Architecture Practice: Research-Based Recommendations for the Practitioner. *Journal of Information Technology*, *12*(3), 197–205. doi:10.1080/026839697345062

Pervan, G. (1998). How Chief Executive Officers in Large Organizations View The Management of Their Information Systems. *Journal of Information Technology*, *13*(2), 95–109. doi:10.1080/026839698344882

Porter, M. E., & Millar, V. E. (1985). How Information Gives You a Competitive Advantage. *Harvard Business Review*, *63*(4), 149–160.

Raghu-Nathan, B., Ragu-Nathan, T. S., Tu, Q., & Shi, Z. (2001). Information Management (IM) Strategy: The Construct and Its Measure. *The Journal of Strategic Information Systems*, *10*(4), 265–289. doi:10.1016/S0963-8687(01)00053-1

Reich, B. H., & Benbasat, I. (1996). Measuring the linkage between business and information technology objectives. *MIS Quarterly*, *20*(1), 55–81. doi:10.2307/249542

Reich, B. H., & Benbasat, I. (2000). Factors That Influence the Social Dimension of Alignment between Business and Information Technology Objectives. *MIS Quarterly*, *24*(1), 81–113. doi:10.2307/3250980

Richardson, G. L., & Jackson, B. M. (1990). A Principles-Based Enterprise Architecture: Lessons Learned from Texaco and Star Enterprise. *MIS Quarterly*, *14*(4), 385–403. doi:10.2307/249787

Ross, J. W. (2003). Creating a Strategic IT Architecture Competence: Learning in Stages. *MIS Quarterly Executive*, *2*(1), 31–43.

Ross, J. W., & Beath, C. M. (2006). Sustainable IT Outsourcing Success: Let Enterprise Architecture be Your Guide. *MIS Quarterly Executive*, *5*(4), 181–192.

Ross, J. W., Weill, P., & Robertson, D. (2006). Enterprise Architecture As Strategy: Creating a Foundation for Business Execution. Boston: Harvard Business School Press.

Rubinfeld, D. L., & Singer, H. J. (2001). Vertical Foreclosure in Broadband Access? *The Journal of Industrial Economics*, *49*(3), 299–318.

Sabherwal, R., & Chan, Y. E. (2001). Alignment between Business and IS Strategies: A Study of Prospectors, Analyzers, and Defenders. *Information Systems Research*, *12*(1), 11–33. doi:10.1287/isre.12.1.11.9714

Segars, A. H., & Grover, V. (1998). Strategic Information Systems Planning Success: An Investigation of the Construct and its Measurement. *MIS Quarterly*, *22*(2), 139–163. doi:10.2307/249393

Sowa, J. F., & Zachman, J. A. (1992). Extending and Formalizing the Framework for Information Systems Architecture. *IBM Systems Journal*, *31*(3), 590–616.

Stein, T. (1999, April 12). Liz Claiborne Gets New IT Architecture. Information Week.

Weill, P. (1992). The Relationship Between Investment in Information Technology and Firm Performance: A Study of the Valve Manufacturing Sector. *Information Systems Research*, *3*(4), 307–333. doi:10.1287/isre.3.4.307

Zachman, J. A. (1982). Business Systems Planning and Business Information Control Study: A Comparison. *IBM Systems Journal*, *21*(1), 31–53.

ENDNOTES

1. Earl (1989) states that there exists three levels of strategy as it relates to IS, information Management (IS) strategy, IS strategy, IT strategy. This paper focuses on the two latter strategies, and in order to avoid confusion, which exists "partly because of loose terminology of planning and strategy in discourse and literature…and partly because senior management tends to be concerned about both technology policy issues and business needs and about both planning information resources and controlling them," (Earl, 1989, cited in Raghu-Nathan, Ragu-Nathan, Tu, & Shi, 2001, pp., p. 268), we delineate between IS strategy and IT strategy. IS strategy in this study, in accordance with previous research (Earl, 1989; Raghu-Nathan et al., 2001), is primarily concerned with aligning IS development with business needs and with seeking strategic advantage from IS applications developed with IT. Likewise, IT strategy is primarily concerned with technology policies, including questions about architecture, risk attitudes, security, vendor policies, and technical standards. In this paper we follow the same school of thought in delineating between IS and IT strategy.
2. The terms planning and plan have not been clearly distinguished in past literature, and are often used interchangeably. In an effort to alleviate the ongoing cycle of ambiguity, as well as the ambiguity that could arise in this paper if the terms are not delineated, we thought it necessary to provide such delineation between the two terms. Our usage of the term planning is indicative of an ongoing

process of some type that leads to an end product, whereas our usage of the term plan is indicative of the artifact that comes as a byproduct of planning. This artifact may later be used in planning to bring about another artifact, which could quite possibly be a new and improved version of the original artifact. In the context of this paper, we consider the process of developing the ITA to be planning, while the ITA itself is the plan (artifact).

3 The term maturation is not meant to insinuate that an organization needs to go through each stage. For instance, it is possible for an organization to start in the standardized technology stage or optimized core stage. It is worth noting that in the event that an organization starts in the operational stage, it is highly likely that the organization will proceed to the standardized technology stage. Bypassing stages, though permissive, may not be in the best interest of the organization since the organizational learning that takes place at each stage helps organizations to understand how to realize the proposed benefits of each stage and how to prepare for movement to the next stage of the ITA competency model (Ross, 2003).

4 Embedding core business functionality into the IT infrastructure refers having a stable core by hardwiring core processes into a foundation for execution. Such a foundation provides greater agility and efficiency (see Ross et al. 2006 for more information on hardwiring/embedding core processes).

This work was previously published in Journal of Organizational and End User Computing (JOEUC) 21(4), edited by Mo Adam Mahmood, pp. 41-62, copyright 2009 by IGI Publishing (an imprint of IGI Global).

Chapter 18
Friend or Foe?
Leveraging – and Mitigating – the Access and Immediacy of Social Media and Information Technologies

Linda Brennan
Mercer University, USA

ABSTRACT

While many organizations and individuals use social media and information technologies (IT) to overcome the limitations of time and space, they often experience unintended consequences from increased immediacy and access. How can they achieve the desirable changes and address the negative effects that can result? This article presents a systematic framework that managers can use to proactively identify ways to either leverage or mitigate the increased immediacy and access. Specific examples are used as illustrations to demonstrate how these issues can be anticipated and used for competitive advantage. They are not offered as specific "prescriptions" for any one organization. Rather, they show how the framework can inform managers as they evaluate proposals for, and implementation plans of, new information systems in their organizations.

INTRODUCTION

Anyone who has said "IT doesn't matter," must not have a wireless personal digital assistant (PDA). For people connected to communications and information systems, IT (information technology) can have a profound – and not always positive – effect. Many years ago, *The Academy of Management Executive* published a survey (Veiga & Dechant, 1997, p. 77) describing the "wired world woes" of 350 executives from major corporations. The study revealed several common frustrations, with more than half expressing concern that:

- IT has not made their lives better, just busier
- IT wastes as much time as it saves
- IT has caused work relationships to deteriorate
- IT means serious information redundancy and overload
- IT means my office is always with me 24 hours a day.

DOI: 10.4018/978-1-60960-577-3.ch018

In today's wireless world, these concerns resonate even more loudly. Conference rooms and private offices are no longer safe havens for meetings; they are continually interrupted with a barrage of buzzing messages. Privacy and courtesy are victims of access and immediacy. *The Wall Street Journal* coined the term "surfer's voice," to describe the inattention evident in a person's voice while talking on the telephone and communicating electronically (Berman, 2003), and recently noted the "Twitter headaches" of immediacy (Needleman, 2009) and the "Blackberry jam" of people walking along the streets of New York checking email and text messages and frequently bumping into one another (Noonan, 2010).

This goes beyond inconvenience to questions of corporate governance. With the increasing use of the Internet, the availability of information has raised the awareness – if not the execution – of corporations' activities. Environmental practices, fiscal integrity, international performance and philanthropic work are easily scrutinized and questioned with the broad access afforded by networks. Customer satisfaction complaints may be widely discussed online by users before the company even realizes there is a problem.

In addition, the reliance of individuals and organizations on IT makes them vulnerable to system failures. This vulnerability is heightened by broad access. Consider the pharmaceutical company sending an e-mail message to users of an anti-depressant, essentially publishing the names of these patients (Federal Trade Commission, 2002; Rothfeder, 2006). The ripple effect of such a problem is hard to overcome.

These issues are exacerbated when one considers the prevalence of social media and pervasive computing in personal and professional lives. The categorical term, "social media," generally encompasses Internet-enabled applications for which the content is user generated and modified in a participatory and collaborative fashion. This includes collaborative projects, blogs, content communities, social networking sites, virtual game worlds, and virtual social worlds (Kaplan and Haenlein, 2010, p.60). Consider the multitude of ways in which an average individual can be reached: home, cellular, and office telephone; personal and professional email; personal and professional social networks; and, just maybe – in person. This does not factor in the information the individual might seek for personal or professional purposes, e.g., the weather, the news, various blogs, and online services. Immediacy barely describes the situation.

Pervasive computing seems to be more hardware-based, whereby "ubiquitous and mobile systems interact seamlessly in everyday life (Soares, 2002)." The computer chip embedded in your garment's care tag will give care instructions to your washing machine, while your refrigerator will manage the inventory of its contents and the energy consumption of your home. The grocery cart will tempt you with advertisements that change as you walk through the aisles of the store – pervasive means anytime, anywhere. Supermarkets already know what you buy and when you shop. At what point does pervasive become invasive? Intrusive? Inconvenient? Vulnerable?

Of course, these technologies enable positive change and can be transformational. Examples of improvements in productivity, cost structures, value propositions, and customer relations abound. As (Clark, 2006) points out, handheld devices and wearable technologies can improve processes: "Data accessibility, immediate processing, and virtual office capabilities provide positive returns." Shih (2009) describes how online social networks can be used to build better products, reach new markets, engage customers, and recruit employees. This is why such technologies are adopted. The challenge is to find ways to achieve such desirable changes and address the negative effects that can result.

One useful framework distinguishes between the direct, easily anticipated, first-level productivity effects and the second-level social system effects which are harder to measure and are generally more profound (Sproull & Keisler, 1991). The social system results arise when the ways in which people interact are changed. By transcending the limitations of time to achieve immediacy and overcoming the boundaries of space to provide access, social media, pervasive computing and similar applications can make a significant difference in the way people live and work.

USING SOCIAL SYSTEM CHANGES TO ADVANTAGE

The problem is to anticipate the social system changes so that they can be used to advantage and prevent them from becoming issues. This can be done with a common technique used in strategic management. "SWOT" analysis helps an organization evaluate its internal strengths (S) and weaknesses (W) vis-à-vis its competition, as well as the external opportunities (O) and threats (T) perceived in the organization's environment. Often the evaluation stops with a list that is summarized as bullet points in a presentation. A better approach poses strengths and weaknesses against opportunities and threats in a matrix (Khalil, 2000). In this format, the analyst is encouraged to consider strategies which:

- Leverage strengths to pursue opportunities
- Mitigate weaknesses to pursue opportunities
- Leverage strengths to neutralize threats
- Mitigate weaknesses to neutralize threats.

A similar strategic approach might be useful in identifying social system effects introduced by IT, as simply:

- Access that can be leveraged (e.g., to apply flexibility or promote innovation)
- Immediacy that can be leveraged (e.g., to emphasize responsiveness or accelerate business cycles)
- Access that could be mitigated (e.g., to prevent overuse or address overload)
- Immediacy that could be mitigated (e.g., to assure quality control or protect users).

Table 1 Matrix of opportunities and threats of access and immediacy

	Leverage	Mitigate
Anywhere Access (vs. location-dependence)	How can anywhere access help?	Are there circumstances that should be avoided with anywhere access?
Immediacy (vs. time-delayed)	How can immediacy provide additional benefits?	In what cases is immediacy a problem?

This is summarized by Table 1.

Fundamentally, this approach challenges executives to consider the social system effects in an explicit, procedural way that is proactive – perhaps even strategic – for the organization. As (Fowler & Horan, 2007) note, the impact can be different, depending on when the impact is evaluated and at which level it is anticipated. In this way, questions like "How can we leverage access to promote innovation in developing countries," "How can we leverage immediacy to emphasize responsiveness in the distribution centers," "How can we insulate our premier customer users from access to prevent overuse," and "How can we mitigate immediacy to assure quality control in this division?" are considered proactively. This method may not only help with an organization's wired – and wireless – world woes, it may also uncover ways to create or sustain a competitive advantage.

Ignoring these possibilities can magnify the unintended consequences. Customers may become irritated with intrusive, or impolite, computing such as pop-up windows and spam. Whitworth (2005, p. 357) suggests that "polite computing" respects user choices, discloses access explicitly, offers useful choices, and remembers past choices.

Users who view the systems as invasive will adopt coping behaviors – which may work at cross-purposes with the information system. Beaudry and Pinsonneault (2005) suggest that users cope with disruptions in a way that depends on their appraisal of the situation (p. 495):

"Problem-focused coping aims at managing the disruptive issue itself. It is oriented toward dealing with the specific aspects of the situation by changing the environment (e.g., altering or alleviating environmental pressures, barriers, resources, or procedures) or changing one's self… Emotion-focused coping change one's perception of the situation, but does not alter the situation itself. It aims at… minimizing the consequences of threats."

It seems that, without a proactive organizational approach, individuals will resort to personal coping methods which may not be in the best interests of the organization.

ILLUSTRATIONS

The following examples are offered as illustrations of proactive implementations. Each individual cell of the matrix will be illustrated with a variety of applications. The matrix as a whole will then be illustrated with a single case in point, customer relationship management.

Examples were gathered with a systematic search of popular business (e.g., *The Wall Street Journal, FORTUNE, BusinessWeek)* and technology management publications (e.g., *Computerworld, CIO, Business 2.0)*. Specifically, the same sets of key words were used in each publication's search engine; the results were then subjected to content analysis for relevance. The resulting articles were then used as the basis for these examples of effective leverage or mitigation. There is no evidence that the organizations used the recommended framework; rather these examples are intended to further explicate the framework, based on secondary sources.

Leveraging Access

There are really two ways in which to leverage access; the first is being able to reach anywhere and the second is making location irrelevant. A key technology in the first case is the global positioning system (GPS), satellite signals made available by the United States Department of Defense. Savings from navigation systems, in terms of time and fuel costs are significant first-level savings. More advanced applications are used to reduce labor costs and improve yield by providing automated guidance systems in agriculture and mining.

To really leverage GPS, consider how tracking position information could change people's behavior. Transportation companies can keep track of vehicles and loads. For example, "geo-fencing" software sends alerts when a company vehicle is speeding or entering unauthorized territory, limiting liability. Parents also use GPS for safety purposes, tracking the location of their children (Maier, 2005).

In a more localized application of leveraging access, the Boston Marathon implemented a radio frequency identification system, using a "ChampionChip" attached to the runner's shoe or wheelchair. These chips track the runners by location and time at several points throughout the race. Using this technology increased the accuracy of the timed results, deterred deviations (i.e., short cuts) from the course, and delivered automatic updates of the runners' progress to family and friends (Cassavoy, 2008).

In the second approach, where location is irrelevant, benefits are being realized by companies using virtual teams, i.e., groups of people who collaborate without actually being co-located (and in fact, may never have met). This provides access to expertise that might otherwise be unavailable or more costly. A similar example is e-mentoring, where protégés and mentors communicate electronically, without actually meeting. This can provide options with more diverse pairings and greater flexibility for communication, as well as greater access to knowledge (Hamilton & Scandura, 2003). Such collaboration may rely simply on electronic mail exchanges, or more formally, on knowledge management systems. Within this spectrum of formality lies wiki software:

"The latest player in the collaborative technology game harnesses any group's collaborative energy and takes it to the next level... it succeeds because, under the right circumstances, spontaneous and largely unsupervised collaboration gets the job done... With global competition ... companies are exploring ways to encourage greater collaboration among employees, suppliers, and customers. Wiki is one mechanism that makes that possible (Evans, 2006, p. 8) ..."

One such example is the internal wiki used by the Geek Squad at Best Buy. In face of the concerns that it would lower staff productivity by being a distraction, it actually increased staff productivity as more pages were added and specialists shared knowledge with one another (Powell, 2009).

Other social system effects are evidenced when organizations extend their reach to increase revenues. Dell Computer used a combination of social media in its "Digital Nomads" campaign to promote its products by illustrating different ways in which their laptop computers enable a mobile workforce (Kaplan and Haenlein, 2010). In a different domain, *The Wall Street Journal* reported that, "Rock band Widespread Panic played to a sold-out crowd... at Atlanta's Fox Theatre. At the same time, the group also performed in Houston, Pittsburgh, and Denver. It was a simulcast performance in 100 movie theatres around the country – and part of a new wave of virtual concert-going that is changing the live-music industry" (Jurgensen, 2006). While location is not exactly irrelevant in this example, because of the technologies involved, the social system impact is evident.

Product developers and market researchers can use the social graph (i.e., the network of people interconnected by social media) to gather ideas for new opportunities or solutions to existing problems. Generally referred to as "crowdsourcing," this practice reaches out to leverage talent outside of an organization. For example, a gold-mining company challenged geologists all over the world. In giving them the company's data about mining regions, they were asking for suggestions as to where best to dig for gold. Awarding prizes worth a combined total of 575 million USD, the company netted more than 3 billion USD (Powell, 2009).

The key to leveraging access is to change the impact of location – i.e., can you add value by using the knowledge of where your customer or driver or salesperson is, or can you make location superfluous, delivering service or information anywhere?

Leveraging Immediacy

Similarly, to take advantage of instantaneous capabilities, the challenge is to determine how to add value immediately. One way in which this has been manifest is in online shopping. With more people using e-commerce to purchase goods, the technological sophistication of the typical customer is declining. This means shoppers get frustrated more easily and are more inclined to abandon their "shopping cart." Using software that alerts the vendor to a potential problem, the customer service agents can proactively offer help by inviting the customer to chat (Prince, 2005).

Of course, proactive service can seem "pushy" or intrusive to some people. In these cases, simply being promptly reactive can be of value to customers. One new venture in North Carolina is applying wireless technology to full-service restaurants, to improve waiters' responsiveness. By wearing a wrist device, the waiter can be alerted to new arrivals, summoned to a table, notified by the kitchen, and communicate with the busboy (Russo, 2007). Plans are to extend this application to hospitals.

Health care represents a huge opportunity to leverage immediacy, where saving time is not only a matter of saving money, but could also mean saving lives. With "... networked software,.... nurses use wireless laptops on wheels to log in to [a] system to record patients' symptoms and get all the information they need to shuttle patients through their stay. Doctors tap into the network... to order prescriptions and lab tests. Everything else is linked into the system... eliminating the need for most faxes, phone calls, and administrative hassles (Mullaney & Weintraub, 2005, p. 77)." Productivity improvements are common first-level effects when a hospital invests in IT. As the wealth of knowledge in medicine grows, important second-level effects are realized, impacting the quality of care. For example, physicians can be alerted to potential drug interactions as they enter a prescription into a system that references a drug knowledge base and the patient's record. The doctor can be assured of up-to-date information on which to base his treatment. "The power of knowledge-based order-entry, referral, computerized medical-record, and event-detection systems is that they operate in real time (Davenport & Glaser, 2002)." In this way, IT impacts how doctors provide care to patients (Gruman, 2003).

In other industries, time is a source of competitive advantage. One recent phenomenon is a new application for arbitrage, a practice traditionally used in the financial markets to take advantage of short-term price disparities, "Drop catchers" watch for Internet domain names to expire (approximately 20,000 per day), register them, and then resell them to the original owners who neglected to renew them (Kesmodel, 2006).

Savvy marketers can also use the Internet opportunistically, especially in combination with other media, turning a minor or even non-event into a news story. By creating a "buzz," or what Kevin Kelly (1998) termed a "swarm" of users, interest and enthusiasm (and most importantly, Web traffic) can increase exponentially. This viral phenomenon is evidenced in consumer products (Fuscaldo, 2003), political campaigns (Heilemann, 2004), and investor relations (Mucha, 2003).

Entrepreneurs and small businesses have used the immediacy of Twitter messages, i.e., "tweets," to their advantage. Needleman (2009b) reported one company used the service to notify followers of a server crash caused by a surge of traffic prompted by a segment on a cable television news program. Another company used it to respond when its site was hacked so visitors were greeted with pornography. Not just useful in emergencies, Twitter might be used for a "limited time only" promotional sale.

To leverage immediacy, then, is to consider where time is of the essence to your prospective customers/patients/clients. Are there windows of opportunity that would open if information were available faster?

Mitigating Access

There are two primary issues with the extensive access that technology provides. The first is overload, with the abundance of information that becomes available with increased access. The second is inappropriate use of that access.

Eppler and Mengis (2004, p. 326) report that research on overload indicates that performance of an individual correlates positively with the amount of information available – up to a point. After that point, "the burden of a heavy information load will confused the individual, affect his or her ability to set priorities, and make prior information harder to recall. Reported countermeasures include focus on creating value-added information, establish rules for information and communication design, and schedule uninterrupted blocks of time for completing critical work" (p. 335).

The focus on creating value-added information has led to an interesting change in the social system with the emergence of new kinds of intermediaries who collect and broker the information to make it more useful. Sawhney et.al. (2003, p. 78) distinguish between two types of intermediaries on the Internet: infomediaries and innomediaries. "Infomediaries gather and organize information ... for individuals who are considering a purchase; they also organize communities of customers on the basis of common interests or specific industries... to facilitate transactions in a way that complements a company's direct e-commerce channels... While infomediaries focus on aggregating product- and company-related information, innomediaries concentrate on aggregating and disseminating customer-generated knowledge." This means an organization has new "middlemen" with which to work and through which it much market its products competitively. It can also mean, in the case of innomediaries, tremendous insight about customer buying behavior, such as comparison shopping, navigation paths, and click-through patterns. As a result, organizations are encouraged to innovate based on customer preferences – and innomediaries are adding value to both the customer (by mitigating access) and the organization (by providing customer data).

For companies using social media to increase their access to current and prospective customers, there is a risk of over-exposure. One way to reduce the potential annoyance this access can cause is to use already available access. "It may make sense to join an existing social media application and benefit from its popularity and user base..., especially given that Social media show positive network externalities in the sense that they get more attractive to join the more participants they have" (Kaplan and Haenlein, 2010, p. 65).

Technologically, increased access can mean increased vulnerability. As networks and their applications grow, there are more potential points of failure – and more opportunities for unauthorized use. It is important to understand this exposure and address it. Technological solutions such as spyware detectors, firewalls, encryption tools, and virus software can be part of the solution for "leaky" corporations (Poulsen, 2007). Policy and procedural changes may also be needed. More and more organizations are finding that it is helpful to develop and practice plans for the business continuity of key applications and for safeguarding critical data (Croy, 2004).

Mitigating Immediacy

Like access, immediacy can be both an opportunity and a threat. Perhaps this is most evident in the personal lives of professionals. As *Wall Street Journal* columnist Carol Hymowitz (2003) explained:

"The 10-hour work day now typical at many companies increasingly means having to blend professional and personal tasks... Since [managers] now expect employees to be accessible 24/7 on e-mail and cell phone, they also must give the freedom to handle personal chores during regular office hours."

More recently, another columnist reflected that (Vascellaro, 2009):

"Years ago, we were frustrated if it took a few days for a letter to arrive. A couple of years ago, we'd complain about a half-hour delay in getting an email. Today, we gripe about it taking an extra few seconds for a text message to go through. In a few months, we may be complaining that our cell phones aren't automatically able to send messages to friends within a certain distance, letting them know we're nearby. (A number of services already do this.)"

The increasing volume of instantaneous information, much of it generated with little thought and/or effort makes the signal-to-noise ratio diminish. It becomes more difficult to identify the important messages. Technological solutions such as filtering incoming messages and tagging (i.e., categorizing) outgoing ones can help, but do require effort on the users' part.

Having the flexibility to see a child's ballgame or go to a doctor's appointment is very appealing. However, it also makes it possible for the office to intrude on a family dinner or vacation. The best way to mitigate this immediacy is to set expectations; companies should have explicit policies about personal time on the job, and employees should set limits on when they are and are not available.

Even if the employee is "on the job" at the office, he or she may still need to mitigate the immediacy that tweets, instant messages (IMs) and e-mail afford. These instantaneous technologies can be very efficient communications tools or extremely distracting interruptions. Henricks (2005) cites "... a 2004 study by the ePolicy Institute and the American Management Association found that 10% of employees reported more than half the day is spent on e-mail, up from 8% in 2003.... A staggering 90% of employees spend up to 90 minutes per day sending IMs." More recently, Crovitzthe (2008) found that, not only did knowledge workers change activities every three minutes with frequent distractions; it then took nearly 30 minutes to get back to the task once attention is lost. A study commissioned by a large high technology company indicated that the IQ scores of knowledge workers distracted by incoming communications decreased 10 points" (Hemp, 2009, p.84). Arguably, the new generation entering the workforce has a gift for multitasking and "hypersocializing" may not reduce productivity (although a study done at Covenant College found that it could be related to lower grades and weaker study habits) (Zaslow, 2009). While technology is available to notify senders that a recipient is not available, with a "Do not disturb" setting, it still requires the individual's willingness to establish limits.

The problem of overload exists even when the information is generated by computers. The instantaneous ability that pervasive computing and radio frequency identification (RFID) applications provide generates data for real-time tracking in businesses. The volume of data generated can be staggering. Summary tools such as dashboards or learning tools that synthesize the data can reduce the fog (Wailgum, 2006). Otherwise, more information does not mean better decisions. Overload lowers productivity and leads to stress from not being able to process information as fast as it arrives, as well as concern about not having all of the relevant information needed for a task or project.

It is important to note that although technology may create problems of invasive access and immediacy, the way to limit these social system problems tends to be as much behavioral as technological. If technology is being used to transcend the limitations of time and space, where should the new boundaries lie? At what point does the impact become detrimental?

THE MATRIX AS A WHOLE

The social system effects of an information system are likely to be multi-faceted and complex, when broad-based enterprise-wide applications are used. One such application is Customer Relationship Management (CRM), an information-based system that provides a deep (detailed) and broad (integrated) view of an organization's customers, with the intent of building stronger relationships. As Wailgum (2007) explains:

"The idea of CRM is that it helps businesses use technology and human resources to gain insight into the behavior of customers and the value of those customers. With an effective CRM strategy a business can increase revenues by: providing services and products that are exactly what your customers want; offering better customer service; cross-selling products more effectively; helping sales staff close deals faster; retaining existing customers and discovering new ones."

Table 2. Matrix of opportunities and threats in field service

	Leverage	Mitigate
Anywhere Access (vs. location-dependence)	How can anywhere access help improve service? What information can make the service representatives better prepared? How can knowing where the service representatives are improve dispatching? How can we use local expertise across the system? What other applications do the service representatives use that can be made mobile?	Are there circumstances that should be avoided with anywhere access? At what point would the field representatives experience overload? What controls are needed to ensure proprietary data are handled correctly? What are the risks if the mobile device is lost or stolen?
Immediacy (vs. time-delayed)	How can immediacy provide additional benefits? Where in the service process are there opportunities to improve response times? Resolution times? Can we be more precise in our guarantees of service times? Can we improve the profitability of our service level agreements?	In what cases is immediacy a problem? How can we avoid priority conflicts among customer calls? How can we limit interruptions during a service call? What policies should be established for non-business uses of the technology? For the responsiveness of the service representative to incoming messages?

According to global management consultancy Accenture (CIO, 2007), CRM technologies should ensure a consistent experience for customers, enable an organization to distinguish itself with branded customer experiences, and gain insight into customer preferences and profitability.

For many businesses, an important part of the customer relationship is field service, i.e., the maintenance and repair of purchased equipment. By combining CRM with mobile computing, an organization can greatly improve the effectiveness of its field service, with greater access and immediacy. Using the strategic approach suggested here, the field service executive and the chief information officer (CIO) might ask the types of questions presented in Table 2.

A case in point is Pitney Bowes (Sacco, 2008):

"a global provider of physical and digital mailing products and services, [whose] drivers and service representatives rely on mobile applications to get them to their next job sites, ensure they've got the proper parts and inventory within their vans, access client service histories... [and] compare best practices."

After a pilot test of the application, Pitney Bowes gradually implemented it across the United States, Europe and Canada. They report first-level savings of time and money resulting from a reduction in return visits to customers (i.e., "callbacks"), and reductions in repair parts inventory, and increased throughput of service calls. Second-level effects include improved customer service and field technicians' effectiveness, as a result of real-time progress reports and the capability to distinguish priorities of incoming calls.

With the use of social networks for CRM, corporations can engage existing and prospective customers. It is important to first find out what social media are being used in unsanctioned forums. According to Shih (2009, p. 148):

"What you learn might surprise you. For instance, Victoria's Secret executives were pleasantly surprised to learn over 500 unofficial groups had sprung up around their brand on Facebook... It's important to tie the input from these unofficial mediums [sic] back to your overall social networking strategy... You can then decide whether it makes sense or not to respond."

Online retailer Threadless, with annual revenues of approximately 30 million USD, uses its customer relationships for 'customer cocreation" of its T-shirts (Powell, 2009, p. 101):

"Seasoned designers and novices alike submit more than 1,000 new T-shirt designs a week to the Threadless Web site. Users then have a seven-day window in which they vote on and rate the submissions. The company... chooses... from the top-scoring submissions to be printed in limited quantities of 1,500. Invariably, every single design sells out."

This process engages the designers and their friends and prior customers in the voting; buyers earn purchase credits by inviting friends to the site; wearers who are photographed can also earn credits; and more visitors are drawn into the process as a result.

DISCUSSION

While acknowledging the potential benefits of information systems that provide greater access and immediacy, businesses tend to focus on the technical challenges of the implementation and on the first-level effects of the improvements. The second-level social system effects are harder to anticipate and can have unintended consequences.

As IT becomes more pervasive, it is clear that the management of it can no longer be solely the responsibility of IT managers (Kanter 2004). Social system effects should be the domain of professionals and business executives, as the technology enables increased access and immediacy to them and their organizations. It can be of critical importance to proactively lead the changes, instead of passively accepting the consequences.

A Generalized Framework

Using the specific cases to inductively create a more generalized framework, as presented in Table 3, can be a starting point for proactively anticipating the social system effects of real-time systems. The actions identified in this generalized framework suggest specific actions to consider for a strategic approach.

Table 3. A generalized framework to leverage and mitigate access and immediacy

	Leverage	Mitigate
Anywhere Access (vs. location-dependence)	Reach new users Engage existing customers Make location irrelevant Add location-specific value Track key resources	Use infomediaries Secure points of access Use existing relationships
Immediacy (vs. time-delayed)	Use alerts to avert problems Increase throughput Lower response time Improve data usability Accelerate awareness	Set expectations Allow uninterrupted times Apply filters and tags

The examples in the article illustrate how this strategic approach is feasible and can even leverage a competitive advantage from IT-enabled access and immediacy. They are not offered as specific "prescriptions" for any one organization. Rather, they show how the framework can inform managers as they evaluate proposals for and implementation plans of new information systems in their organizations.

RESEARCH IMPLICATIONS

The generalized model has been developed inductively, using current examples. The approach is grounded in the theory of the social system effects of information technology. The next step is for the model to be validated *a priori* with business practitioners. Another interesting line of inquiry would be to survey businesses about their current practices in anticipating social system effects.

REFERENCES

Beaudry, A., & Pinsonneault, A. (2005). Understanding user adaptation behaviors: A coping acts model. *Management Information Systems Quarterly*, *3*(29), 493–524.

Berman, D. K. (2003, November 10). Technology has us so plugged into data, we have turned off. *The Wall Street Journal,* p. B1.

Cassavoy, L. (2008, April 21). Boston marathon gets wired. *PC World*. Retrieved September 1, 2008, from http://www.cio.com/article/print/338615.

CIO. (2007, January 2). CRM: Challenges and advice for CIOs in 2007. *CIO.* Retrieved September 1, 2008, from http://www.cio.com/article/print/27802.

Clark, C. (2006). End user computing ergonomics: Facts or fads? *Journal of Organizational and End User Computing, 18*(3), 66. doi:10.4018/joeuc.2006070104

Crovitzthe, L. G. (2008). Unloading immediacy. *The Wall Street Journal*, July 7, 2008. Retrieved February 8, 2010, fromhttp://online.wsj.com.

Croy, M. (2004, May 4). Six tips for IT in planning a business continuity strategy. *Computerworld.* Retrieved August 18, 2005, fromwww.computerworld.com/printhis/2004/0,4814,92872,00.html.

Davenport, T. H., & Glaser, J. (2002). Just-in-Time delivery comes to knowledge management. *Harvard Business Review*, (July): 107–111.

Eppler, M. J., & Mengis, J. (2004). The concept of immediacy: A review of literature from organization science, accounting marketing MIS, and related disciplines. *The Information Society, 20*, 325–344. doi:10.1080/01972240490507974

Evans, P. (2006). The Wiki Factor. *BizEd*, January/February 2006, 28-32.

Federal Trade Commission. (2002, January 18). Eli Lilly settles FTC charges concerning security breach. Retrieved May 20, 2007, from http://www.ftc.gov/opa/2002/01/elililly.shtm.

Fowler, J. J., & Horan, P. (2007). Are information systems' success and failure factors related? An exploratory study. *Journal of Organizational and End User Computing, 19*(2), 1. doi:10.4018/joeuc.2007040101

Fuscaldo, D. (2003, September 15). The best way to create a buzz for your product. *The Wall Street Journal,* p. R6.

Gruman, G. (2003, August 1, 2003). Wireless: Just what the doctor ordered. *CIO.* Retrieved August 18, 2005, from http://www.cio.com/article/print/29587.

Hamilton, B. A., & Scandura, T. A. (2003). E-Mentoring: Implications for organizational learning and development in a wired world. *Organizational Dynamics, 31*(4), 388–402. doi:10.1016/S0090-2616(02)00128-6

Heilemann, J. (2004). The $100 million dinosaur. *Business 2.0*, 60-62.

Hemp, P. (2009). Death by immediacy. *Harvard Business Review*, September 2009, 83-89. Reprint #R0909J.

Henricks, M. (2005). Falling behind. *Entrepreneur,* February 2005, 19-20.

Hymowitz, C. (2003, October 28). More managers allow workers to multitask as job and home blur. *The Wall Street Journal,* B1.

Jurgensen, J. (2006, 6-3-2006). The "virtual" concert tour. *The Wall Street Journal,* p. 1.

Kanter, J. (2004). An IT manifesto for business managers. *Information Strategy: The Executive's Journal*, *20*(3), 6–12.

Kaplan, A. M., & Haenlein, M. (2010). Users of the world, unite! The challenges and opportunities of Social media. *Business Horizons*, *53*, 59–68. doi:10.1016/j.bushor.2009.09.003

Kelly, K. (1998). *New Rules for the New Economy: 10 Radical Strategies for a Networked World*. New York, NY: Viking Press.

Kesmodel, D. (2006, February 22). 'Drop catchers' buy and sell web names others let slip. *The Wall Street Journal,* p. B12.

Khalil, T. (2000). *Management of Technology*. New York, NY: McGraw-Hill.

Maier, M. (2005). Mobile technology-finding profits in the GPS economy. *Business 2.0*, 21-22.

Mucha, T. (2003, May 1). We're in trouble.com: Got bad news? Use the web to spill it. Fast. *Business 2.0* Retrieved June 15, 2004, from www.business2.com.

Mullaney, T. J., & Weintraub, A. (2005, March 28). The digital hospital: How info tech saves lives and money at one medical center. Is this the future of health care? *BusinessWeek*, 77-84.

Needleman, S. E. (2009a, September 14). Relief for Twitter headaches. *The Wall Street Journal.* Retrieved 7 October, 2010 from http://online.wsj.com.

Needleman, S. E. (2009b, September 15). Entrepreneurs 'tweet' their way through crises. *The Wall Street Journal*. Retrieved 7 October, 2010 from http://online.wsj.com.

Noonan, P. (2010, August 20). Immediacy is nothing new. *The Wall Street Journal.* Retrieved 7 October, 2010 from http://online.wsj.com.

Pennington, R., & Tuttle, B. (2007). The effects of immediacy on software project risk assessment. *Decision Sciences*, *38*(3), 489–526. doi:10.1111/j.1540-5915.2007.00167.x

Poulsen, K. (2007). Patching up the leaky corporation. *Business 2.0.* Retrieved 20 May, 2007 from http://money.cnn.com.

Powell, J. (2009). *33 Million People in the Room.* Upper Saddle River, NJ: FT Press.

Prince, M. (2005, March 21). Help (may be) on the way. *The Wall Street Journal,* pp. R13-14.

Rothfeder, J. (2006, September 5). The death of privacy. *CIO Insight*. Retrieved 20 May, 2007, from http://www.cioinsight.com/c/a/Past-News/The-Death-of-Privacy/2/.

Russo, F. (2007, May 1). Taking the 'wait' out of 'Waiter!' *Business 2.0,* 31.

Sacco, A. (2008, April 28). Inside Pitney Bowes choice for a mobile CRM/ERP solution. *CIO.* Retrieved September 1, 2008, from http://www.cio.com/article/print/342763.

Sawhney, M., Prandelli, E., & Verona, G. (2003). The power of innomediation. *MIT Sloan Management Review* (Winter 2003), 77-82.

Shih, C. (2009). *The Facebook Era*. Upper Saddle River, NJ: Prentice-Hall.

Soares, S. (2002). Forecast for a multimodal future. *Communique Newsletter*, *39*(9), 26.

Sproull, L., & Kiesler, S. (1991). *Connections: New Ways of Working in the Networked Organization*. Cambridge, MA: MIT Press.

Vascellaro, J. E. (2009, October 12). Why email no longer rules… *The Wall Street Journal*. Retrieved October 7, 2010 from http://online.wsj.com.

Veiga, J. F., & Dechant, K. (1997). Wired world woes: www.help. *The Academy of Management Executive*, *11*(3), 73–78.

Wailgum, T. (2006). more. *CIO.* November 15, 2006, 58-65.

Wailgum, T. (2007, March 6). ABC: An introduction to CRM. *CIO.* Retrieved September 1, 2008, from http:///www.cio.com/article/print/40295.

Whitworth, B. (2005). Polite computing. *Behaviour & Information Technology, 24*(5), 353–363. doi:10.1080/01449290512331333700

Zaslow, J. (2009, November 5). The greatest generation (of networkers). *The Wall Street Journal.* Retrieved October 7, 2010 from http://online.wsj.com.

Compilation of References

Aaker, D. (1996). *Building strong brands*. New York: Free Press.

Aaker, D. (2000). *Brand leadership*. New York: Free Press.

Aaker, J. (1997). Dimensions of brand personality. *JMR, Journal of Marketing Research, 34*(3), 347–357. doi:10.2307/3151897

Abbasi, A., Zhang, Z., Zimbra, D., Chen, H., & Nunamaker, J. F. (2010). Detecting fake websites: The contribution of statistical learning theory. *Management Information Systems Quarterly, 34*(3), 435–461.

Abels, S., Brehm, N., Hahn, A., & Gomez, J. (2006). Change management issues in federated ERP systems: An approach for identifying requirements and possible solutions. *International Journal of Information Systems and Change Management, 1*(3), 318–335. doi:10.1504/IJISCM.2006.011202

Abraham, D. L. (2001). Mobile Enterprise Computing and the Diffusion of Mobile Enterprise Business Applications in Organizations. *Proceedings of 2001 Americas Conference on Information Systems (AMCIS 2001)*, Boston, MA, 461-464.

Adams, B., Berner, E. S., & Rousse, J. (2004). Applying strategies to overcome user resistance in a group of clinical managers to a business software applications: A case study. *Journal of Organizational and End User Computing, 16*(4), 55–64. doi:10.4018/joeuc.2004100104

Adams, D. A., Nelson, R. R., & Todd, P. A. (1992). Perceived usefulness, ease of use, and usage of information technology: A replication. *Management Information Systems Quarterly, 16*(2), 227–247. doi:10.2307/249577

Adams, J. A. (1987). Historical review and appraisal of research on the learning, retention, and transfer of human motor skills. *Psychological Bulletin, 101*, 41–74. doi:10.1037/0033-2909.101.1.41

Agarwal, R., Sambamurthy, V., & Stair, R. (2000). Research report: The evolving relationship between general and special computer self-efficacy--An empirical assessment. *Information Systems Research, 11*(4), 418–430. doi:10.1287/isre.11.4.418.11876

Agarwal, R., & Karahanna, E. (2000). Time flies when you're having fun: Cognitive absorption and beliefs about information technology usage. *Management Information Systems Quarterly, 24*(4), 665–694. doi:10.2307/3250951

Agarwal, R., & Venkatesh, V. (2002). Assessing a firm's web presence: A heuristic evaluation procedure for the measurement of usability. *Information Systems Research, 13*(2), 168–186. doi:10.1287/isre.13.2.168.84

Agarwal, R., & Prasad, J. (1999). Are individual differences germane to the acceptance of new information technologies? *Decision Sciences, 30*(2), 361–391. doi:10.1111/j.1540-5915.1999.tb01614.x

Agarwal, R., Sambamurthy, V., & Stair, R. M. (2000). Research report: The evolving relationship between general and specific computer self-efficacy—an empirical assessment. *Information Systems Research, 11*(4), 418–430. doi:10.1287/isre.11.4.418.11876

Agarwal, R., & Prasad, J. (1999). Are individual differences germane to the acceptance of information technologies? *Decision Sciences, 30*, 361–391. doi:10.1111/j.1540-5915.1999.tb01614.x

Agarwal, R. (2000). Individual acceptance of new information technologies. In Zmud, R. W. (Ed.), *Framing the Domains of IT Management Research: Glimpsing the Future through the Past* (pp. 85–104). Cincinnati, OH: Pinnaflex.

Agerfalk, P., & Goldkuhl, G. (2001). Business action and information modeling – The task of the new millenium. In Rossi, M., & Siau, K. (Eds.), *Information Modeling in the New Millenium* (pp. 110–137). Hershey, PA: Idea Group Publishing. doi:10.4018/9781878289773.ch007

Ahuja, M. K., Chudoba, K. M., Kacmar, C. J., McKnight, D. H., & George, J. F. (2007). IT road warriors: Balancing work-family conflict, job autonomy, and work overload to mitigate turnover intentions. *Management Information Systems Quarterly*, *31*(1), 1–17.

Ahuja, M. K., & Thatcher, J. B. (2005). Moving beyond intentions and toward the theory of trying: Effects of work environment and gender on post-adoption information technology use. *Management Information Systems Quarterly*, *29*, 427–459.

Aiken, L. S., & West, S. G. (1991). *Multiple regression: Testing and interpreting interactions*. Thousand Oaks: Sage.

Ajzen, I. (2002). Perceived behavioral control, self-efficacy, locus of control, and the theory of planned behavior. *Journal of Applied Social Psychology*, *32*, 1–20. doi:10.1111/j.1559-1816.2002.tb00236.x

Ajzen, I. (1975). *Belief, attitude, intention, and behavior: An introduction to theory and research*. Reading, MA: Addison-Wesley.

Ajzen, I. (1985). From intentions to actions: A theory of planned behavior in J. K. J. Beckmann (Ed.), *Action-control: From Congnition to Behavior* (pp. 11-39). Heidelberg: Springer.

Aladwani, A. M. (2002). Organizational actions, computer attitudes, and end-user satisfaction in public organizations: An empirical study. *Journal of End User Computing*, *14*(1), 42–49. doi:10.4018/joeuc.2002010104

Alexander, B., Friend, L., Godwin, B., & Babis, P. (2006). Learning to trust e-tailers: Strategies used by consumers. *Journal of Research for Consumers*, *10*, 1–9.

Al-Gahtani, S. S. (2001). The applicability of TAM outside North America: An empirical test in the United Kingdom. *Information Resources Management Journal*, *14*(3), 37–47. doi:10.4018/irmj.2001070104

Al-Gahtani, S. S., & King, M. (1999). Attitudes, satisfaction and usage: Factors contributing to each in the acceptance of information technology. *Behaviour & Information Technology*, *18*(4), 277–297. doi:10.1080/014492999119020

Aljukhadar, M. (2010). Can the media richness of a privacy disclosure enhance outcome? A multifaceted view of trust in rich media environments. *International Journal of Electronic Commerce*, *14*(4), 103–126. doi:10.2753/JEC1086-4415140404

Allen, T. D., Freeman, D. M., Russell, J. A., & Reizenstein, R. C. (2001). Survivor reactions to organizational downsizing: Does time ease the pain? *Journal of Occupational and Organizational Psychology*, *74*, 145–165. doi:10.1348/096317901167299

Allen, B. R., & Boynton, A. C. (1991). Information Architecture: In Search of Efficient Flexibility. *MIS Quarterly*, *15*(4), 435–445. doi:10.2307/249447

Allport, F. H. (1920). The Influence of the Group Upon Association and Thought. *Journal of Experimental Psychology*, *3*, 159–182. doi:10.1037/h0067891

Alpert, S., Karat, J., Karat, C.-M., Brodie, C., & Vergo, J. (2003). User attitudes regarding a user-adaptive e-commerce Web site. *User Modeling and User-Adapted Interaction*, *13*(4), 373–396. doi:10.1023/A:1026201108015

Altman, I., & Taylor, D. (1973). *The development of interpersonal relationships*. New York: Holt, Rinehart & Winston.

Amoako-Gyampah, K., & Salam, A. F. (2004). An extension of the technology acceptance model in an ERP implementation environment. *Information & Management*, *41*, 731–745. doi:10.1016/j.im.2003.08.010

Anderson, E., & Weitz, B. (1989). Determinants of continuity in conventional industrial dyads. *Marketing Science*, *8*(4), 310–323. doi:10.1287/mksc.8.4.310

Anderson, L. M., & Bateman, T. S. (1997). Cynicism in the workplace: Some causes and effects. *Journal of Organizational Behavior*, *18*, 449–469. doi:10.1002/(SICI)1099-1379(199709)18:5<449::AID-JOB808>3.0.CO;2-O

Andersson, B. (2008). Mobile Computing from a Developer's Perspective: A 10-Year Review, 1999-2008. *Business Information Processing*, *24*(5), 220–233.

Applegate, L. M., Austin, R. D., & McFarlan, W. (2003). *Corporate Information Strategy and Management: The Challenges of Managing in a Network Economy*. Boston: McGraw-Hill.

Armstrong J. S. & Overton, T. S. (1977). Estimating nonresponse bias in mail surveys. *ournal of Marketing Research, 14*(3), 396-402.

Attewell, P. (1990). What is skill? *Work and Occupations*, *17*, 422–448. doi:10.1177/0730888490017004003

Auster, E. (1989). Task characteristics as a bridge between macro and micro research on salary inequality between men and women. *Academy of Management Review*, *14*(2), 173–193. doi:10.2307/258415

Avezedo, R., & Bernard, R. M. (1995). A meta-analysis of the effects of feedback in computer-based instruction. *Journal of Educational Computing Research*, *13*, 111–127. doi:10.2190/9LMD-3U28-3A0G-FTQT

Ba, S., Whinston, A., & Zhang, H. (2003). Building trust in online auction markets through an economic incentive mechanism. *Decision Support Systems*, *35*(3), 273–286. doi:10.1016/S0167-9236(02)00074-X

Ba, S., & Pavlou, P. (2002). Evidence of the effect of trust building technologies in electronic markets: Price premiums and buyer behavior. *Management Information Systems Quarterly*, *26*(3), 243–268. doi:10.2307/4132332

Ba, S. (2001). Establishing online trust through a community responsibility system. *Decision Support Systems*, *31*(3), 323–336. doi:10.1016/S0167-9236(00)00144-5

Baba, M., L. (1999). Dangerous liaisons: Trust, distrust, and information technology in American work organizations. *Human Organization*, *58*(3), 331–346.

Babette, R., & Beehr, T. A. (2003). Formal mentoring versus supervisor and coworker relationships: differences in perceptions and impact. *Journal of Organizational Behavior*, *24*, 271–293. doi:10.1002/job.193

Baddeley, A. D. (1986). *Working Memory*. London: Oxford University Press.

Bagozzi, R. P., Yi, Y., & Phillips, L. W. (1991). Assessing construct validity in organizational research. *Administrative Science Quarterly*, *36*(3), 421–458. doi:10.2307/2393203

Bailey, A. A. (2005). Consumer awareness and use of product review websites. *Journal of Interactive Advertising*, *6*(1), 90–108.

Balasubramanian, S., Peterson, R. A., & Jarvenpaa, S. L. (2002). Exploring the Implications of M-Commerce for Markets and Marketing. *Journal of the Academy of Marketing Science*, *30*(4), 348–361. doi:10.1177/009207002236910

Bandura, A. (1982). Self-Efficacy mechanism in human agency. *The American Psychologist*, *37*, 122–147. doi:10.1037/0003-066X.37.2.122

Bandura, A. (1986). *Social foundations of thought and action: A social cognitive theory*. Englewood Cliffs, NJ: Prentice Hall.

Bandura, A. (1991). Social cognitive theory of self-regulation. *Organizational Behavior and Human Decision Processes*, *50*, 248–287. doi:10.1016/0749-5978(91)90022-L

Bandura, A. (1997). *Self-efficacy: The exercise of control*. New York: Freeman.

Bandura, A. (1977). *Social learning theory*. Englewood Cliffs, NJ: Prentice-Hall.

Bandura, A. (1977). Self-efficacy: Toward a unifying theory of behavioral change. *Psychological Review*, *84*(2), 191–215. doi:10.1037/0033-295X.84.2.191

Bandura, A. (1984). Recycling misconceptions of perceived self-efficacy. *Cognitive Therapy and Research*, *8*(3), 231–255. doi:10.1007/BF01172995

Bandura, A. (1986). *Social foundations of thought and actions*. Englewood Cliffs, N.J.: Prentice-Hall.

Bandura, A. (1997). *Self-efficacy: the exercise of control*. New York: W.H. Freeman and Company.

Barber, B. (1983). *The logic and limits of trust*. New Brunswick, NJ: Rutgers University Press.

Barclay, D., Higgins, C., & Thompson, R. (1995). The partial least squares approach to causal modeling: Personal computer adoption and use as an illustration. *Technology Studies*, *2*(2), 285–309.

Barki, H. (1989). Rethinking the concept of user involvement. *Management Information Systems Quarterly*, *13*(1), 53–63. doi:10.2307/248700

Barki, H., & Hartwick, J. (1994). Measuring user attitude, user involvement and user attitude. *Management Information Systems Quarterly*, *18*(1), 59–82. doi:10.2307/249610

Barling, J., & Phillips, M. (1993). Interactional, formal, and distributive justice in the workplace. *The Journal of Psychology*, *127*, 649–656. doi:10.1080/00223980.1993.9914904

Barnes, S. J. (2001). Big in Japan - iMode and the Mobile Internet. *Journal of Information Technology Theory and Application*, *3*(4), 27–32.

Barney, J. B., & Hansen, M. H. (1994). Trustworthiness as a source of competitive advantage. *Strategic Management Journal*, *15*, 175–190. doi:10.1002/smj.4250150912

Baron, R. M., & Kenny, D. A. (1986). The moderator-mediator variable distinction in social psychological research: Conceptual, strategic, and statistical considerations. *Journal of Personality and Social Psychology*, *51*, 1173–1182. doi:10.1037/0022-3514.51.6.1173

Baron, R. S. (1986). Distraction-Conflict Theory: Progress and Problems. In Berkowitz, L. (Ed.), *Advances in Experimental Social Psychology* (*Vol. 19*, pp. 1–40). New York: Academic Press.

Bartunek, J. M. (1984). Changing interpretive schemes and organizational restructuring: The example of a religious order. *Administrative Science Quarterly*, *29*, 355–372. doi:10.2307/2393029

Baskerville, R. (1991). Practitioner autonomy and the bias of methods and tools. In H.E. Nissen., H. K. Klein., & R. Hirschheim (Eds.), *Information systems research: Contemporary approaches and emergent traditions*, Amsterdam: North-Holland, 673-697.

Basu, V., Hartono, E., Lederer, A., & Sethi, V. (2002). The impact of organizational commitment, senior management involvement and team involvement on strategic information systems planning. *Information & Management*, *39*(6), 513–524. doi:10.1016/S0378-7206(01)00115-X

Bauer, H. H. (2002). Customer relations through the internet. *Journal of Relationship Marketing*, *1*(2), 39. doi:10.1300/J366v01n02_03

Beaty, R., & Williams, C. (2006). ERP II: Best practices for successfully implementing an ERP upgrade. *Communications of the ACM*, *49*(3), 105–109.

Beaudry, A., & Pinsonneault, A. (2005). Understanding user adaptation behaviors: A coping acts model. *Management Information Systems Quarterly*, *3*(29), 493–524.

Beehr, T. (1976). Perceived situational moderators of the relationship between subjective role ambiguity and role strain. *The Journal of Applied Psychology*, *61*, 35–40. doi:10.1037/0021-9010.61.1.35

Beehr, T. A., Jex, S. M., Stacy, B. A., & Murray, M. A. (2000). Work stressors and coworker support as predictors of individual strain and job performance. *Journal of Organizational Behavior*, *21*, 391–405. doi:10.1002/(SICI)1099-1379(200006)21:4<391::AID-JOB15>3.0.CO;2-9

Beigbeder, S. (2000). Easing workforce reduction. *Risk Management*, *47*(5), 26–30.

Bem, D. J. (1972). Self-perception theory. In Berkowits, L. (Ed.), *Advances in Experimental Social Psychology* (pp. 1–62). New York: Academic Press.

Benamati, J., & Rajkamur, T. M. (2002). The application development outsourcing decision: An application of the technology acceptance model. *Journal of Computer Information Systems*, *42*(4), 35–43.

Benassi, P. (1999). TRUSTe: An online privacy seal program; Association for computing machinery. *Communications of the ACM*, *42*(2), 56–58. doi:10.1145/293411.293461

Benkhoff, B. (1997). Ignoring commitment is costly: New approaches establish the missing link between commitment and performance. *Human Relations*, *50*(6), 701–726. doi:10.1177/001872679705000604

Bentler, P. M., & Bonnet, D. G. (1980). Significance tests and goodness of fit in the analysis of covariance structures. *Psychological Bulletin*, *88*, 588–606. doi:10.1037/0033-2909.88.3.588

Berlanger, F., Hiller, J. S., & Smith, W. J. (2002). Trustworthiness in electronic commerce: The role of privacy, security, and site attributes. *The Journal of Strategic Information Systems*, *11*, 245–270. doi:10.1016/S0963-8687(02)00018-5

Berman, D. K. (2003, November 10). Technology has us so plugged into data, we have turned off. *The Wall Street Journal,* p. B1.

Beulen, E., & Streng, R. (2002). The Impact of Online Mobile Office Applications on the Effectiveness and Efficiency of Mobile Workers' Behavior. *Proceedings of the 2002 International Conference on Information Systems (ICIS 2002)*, Barcelona, Spain, 629-640.

Bevin, N. (2000). Usability issues in web site design. In *Proceedings of 6m Interactive Publishing*, Serco Usability Services (pp. 1-7).

Bhatnagar, A., Misra, S., & Rao, H. R. (2000). On risk, convenience and Internet shopping behavior. *Communications of the ACM*, *43*, 98–108. doi:10.1145/353360.353371

Bhattacharya, R., Devinney, T. M., & Pillutla, M. M. (1998). A formal model of trust based on outcomes. *Academy of Management Review*, *23*, 459–472. doi:10.2307/259289

Bhattacherjee, A. (2002). Individual trust in online firms: Scale development and initial test. *Journal of Management Information Systems*, *19*(1), 211–241.

Bhattacherjee, A. (2001). Understanding Information Systems Continuance: An Expectation-Confirmation Model. *Management Information Systems Quarterly*, *25*(3), 51–370. doi:10.2307/3250921

Bhattacherjee, A. (2002). Individual trust in online firms: Scale development and initial test. *Journal of Management Information Systems*, *19*(1), 211–241.

Bisantz, A., Rothe, E., Brickman, B., Gosbee, L., Hettinger, L., & McKinney, J. (2003). Integrating cognitive analyses in a large-scale system design process. *International Journal of Human-Computer Studies*, *58*, 177–206. doi:10.1016/S1071-5819(02)00130-1

Blau, P. M. (1964). *Exchange and power in social life*. New York: John Wiley & Sons.

Bloomfield, B. P., & Coombs, R. (1992). Information technology, control and power: The centralization and decentralization debate revisited. *Journal of Management Studies*, *29*(4), 459–484. doi:10.1111/j.1467-6486.1992.tb00674.x

Boland, R. J., & Greenberg, R. H. (1992). Method and metaphor in organizational analysis. *Accounting. Management and Information Technology*, *2*(2), 117–141. doi:10.1016/0959-8022(92)90004-C

Bolton, G., Katok, E., & Ockenfels, A. (2004). How effective are electronic reputation mechanisms? An experimental investigation. *Management Science*, *50*(11), 1587–1602. doi:10.1287/mnsc.1030.0199

Boncella, R. J. (2002). Wireless Security: An Overview. *Proceedings of 2002 Americas Conference on Information Systems (AMCIS 2002)*, Dallas, TX, 2381-2386.

Bosco, A., Longoni, A. M., & Vecchi, T. (2004). Gender effects in spatial orientation: Cognitive profiles and mental strategies. *Applied Cognitive Psychology*, *18*(5), 519–532. doi:10.1002/acp.1000

Bosscher, R., & Smit, J. H. (1998). Confirmatory factor analysis of the general self-efficacy scale. *Behaviour Research and Therapy*, *36*, 339–343. doi:10.1016/S0005-7967(98)00025-4

Bradley, R. V., & Byrd, T. A. (2007). Information Technology Architecture as a Competitive Advantage-yielding Resource: A Theoretical Perspective. *International Journal of Networking and Virtual Organisations*, *4*(1), 1–19. doi:10.1504/IJNVO.2007.012079

Bradley, R. V., Pridmore, J., & Byrd, T. A. (2006). Information Systems Success in the Context of Different Corporate Cultural Types: An Empirical Investigation. *Journal of Management Information Systems*, *23*(2), 267–294. doi:10.2753/MIS0742-1222230211

Bradley, R. V. (2006). Strategic Valuation of Enterprise Information Technology Architecture in Healthcare Organizations. Unpublished Ph.D. Dissertation, Auburn University, Auburn.

Breaugh, J. A. (1985). The work autonomy scales: Validity evidence. *Human Relations*, *42*, 1033–1056. doi:10.1177/001872678904201105

Brehm, J., & Cole, A. (1966). Effect of a favor which reduces freedom. *Journal of Personality and Social Psychology*, *3*(4), 420–426. doi:10.1037/h0023034

Brehm, S., & Brehm, J. (1981). *Psychological reactance: A theory of freedom and control*. New York, NY: Academic Press.

Briggs, R. O., Balthazard, P. A., & Dennis, A. R. (1996). Graduate business students as surrogates for executives in the evaluation of technology. *Journal of End User Computing*, *8*(4), 11–17.

Briggs, R. O., Adkins, M., Kruse, J., Nunamaker, J. F., Mittleman, D., & Miller, S. (1999). Lessons learned using a technology transition model with the U.S. Navy. *Proceedings of the 32nd Hawaii International Conference on System Sciences* (pp. 1-10), Big Island, HI.

Broadbent, M., Weill, P., & St. Clair, D. (1999). The Implications of Information Technology Infrastructure for Business Process Redesign. *MIS Quarterly*, *23*(2), 159–182. doi:10.2307/249750

Brown, E. (2006). Online shopping is only 3% of all retail sales. Gary Marino knows what's holding it back. *Forbes*, *178*(12).

Brown, G., Fisher, M., Stoll, N., Beeksma, D., Black, M., & Taylor, R. (2000). Using the Lessons of Y2K to Improve Information Systems Architecture. *Communications of the ACM*, *43*(10), 90–97. doi:10.1145/352183.352210

Bryant, J. (1993). OR Enactment: The theatrical metaphor as an analytical framework. *The Journal of the Operational Research Society*, *44*(6), 551–561.

Bryman, A. (2001). *Social research methods*. Oxford: Oxford University Press.

Brynjolfsson, E., & Smith, M. (2000). Frictionless commerce? A comparison of internet and conventional retailers. *Management Science*, *46*(4), 563–585. doi:10.1287/mnsc.46.4.563.12061

Burke, R. (2002). Technology and the customer interface: What consumers want in the physical and virtual store. *Journal of the Academy of Marketing Science*, *30*(4), 411–432. doi:10.1177/009207002236914

Burkhardt, M. E. (1994). Social interaction effects following a technological change: A longitudinal investigation. *Academy of Management Journal*, *37*, 869–898. doi:10.2307/256603

Burns, J., Winstead, W., & Hayworth, B. (1989). Semantic nets as paradigms for both causal and judgmental knowledge representation. *IEEE Transactions on Systems, Man, and Cybernetics*, *SMC-19*(1), 58–68. doi:10.1109/21.24531

Burrell, G., & Morgan, G. (1979). *Sociological paradigms and organizational analysis*. London: Heinemann.

Butler, J., & Cantrell, R. (1984). A behavioral decision theory approach to modeling dyadic trust in superiors and subordinates. *Psychological Reports*, *55*, 19–28.

Butler, J. K. (1991). Toward understanding and measuring conditions of trust: Evolution of conditions of trust inventory. *Journal of Management*, *17*(3), 643–663. doi:10.1177/014920639101700307

Butler, T., & Fitzgerald, B. (2001). The relationship between user participation and the management of change surrounding the development of information systems: A European perspective. *Journal of End User Computing*, *13*(1), 12–25. doi:10.4018/joeuc.2001010102

Butler, M. (2001, December 6, 2001). Best of Both Worlds. Retrieved December 22, 2003, from http://www.computerweekly.com/Article108572.htm

Byrd, T. A., Lewis, B., & Bradley, R. V. (2006). IS Infrastructure: The Influence of Senior IT Leadership and Strategic Information Systems Planning. *Journal of Computer Information Systems*, *47*(1), 101–113.

Byrd, T. A., & Turner, D. E. (2000). Measuring the Flexibility of Information Technology Infrastructure: Exploratory Analysis of a Construct. *Journal of Management Information Systems*, *17*(1), 167–208.

Byrne, B. M. (2001). *Structural equation modeling with AMOS: basic concepts, applications, and programming*. Mahwah, N.J.: Lawrence Erlbaum Associate.

Byrne, D., & Griffitt, W. (1969). Similarity and Awareness of Similarity of Personality Characteristics as Determinants of Attraction. *Journal of Experimental Research in Personality*, *3*, 179–186.

Calder, B., Phillips, L., & Tybout, A. (1981). Designing research for application. *The Journal of Consumer Research*, *8*(September), 197–207. doi:10.1086/208856

Cambell, D. T., & Stanley, J. C. (1966). *Experimental and Quasi-Experimental Designs for Research*. Chicago, IL: Rand McNally.

Cammann, C., Fichman, M., Jenkins, D., & Klesh, J. (1979). *The Michigan organizational assessment questionnaire*. Ann Arbor, MI: University of Michigan.

Campbell, D. T., & Stanley, J. C. (1966). *Experimental and quasi-experimental designs for research*. Chicago: Rand McNally.

Cannon, J., & Doney, P. (1997). An examination of the nature of trust in buyer-seller relationships. *Journal of Marketing*, *61*(2), 35–51. doi:10.2307/1251829

Cantwell, E. (2003). In-building Wireless: How to Keep a Signal When You're Indoors. *Wireless Business & Technology*, *3*(3), 12–14.

Carlson, R., & Grabowski, B. (1992). The effects of Computer Self-efficacy on direction-following behavior in computer-assisted instruction. *Journal of Computer-Based Instruction*, *19*(1), 6–11.

Carmines, E. G., & Zeller, R. A. (1979). *Reliability and validity assessment*. Beverly Hills, CA: Sage.

Carmines, E. G., & McIver, S. P. (1981). Analyzing models with unobserved variables: Analysis of covariance structures. In Bohrnstedt, G. W., & Borgatta, E. F. (Eds.), *Social measurement: Current issues*. Beverly Hills, CA: Sage.

Carr, M., & Jessup, D. L. (1997). Gender differences in first-grade mathematics strategies: Social and metacognitive influences. *Journal of Educational Psychology*, *89*(2), 318–328. doi:10.1037/0022-0663.89.2.318

Cassavoy, L. (2008, April 21). Boston marathon gets wired. *PC World*. Retrieved September 1, 2008, from http://www.cio.com/article/print/338615.

Cavaye, A. (1995). User participation in system development revisited. *Information & Management*, *28*(5), 311–323. doi:10.1016/0378-7206(94)00053-L

Cegielski, C., Hall, D., & Rebman, C. (2006). Enterprise resource planning systems implementation success. *International Journal of Information Systems and Change Management*, *1*(3), 301–317. doi:10.1504/IJISCM.2006.011201

Celuch, K., Taylor, S. A., & Goodwin, S. (2004). Understanding insurance salesperson Internet information management intentions: A test of competing models. *Journal of Insurance Issues*, *27*(1), 22–40.

Champoux, J. E., & Peters, W. S. (1987). Form, effect size, and power in moderated regression analysis. *Journal of Occupational Psychology*, *60*, 243–255.

Chan, Y. E., Huff, S. L., Copeland, D. G., & Barclay, D. W. (1997). Business Strategic Orientation, Information Systems Strategic Orientation and Strategic Alignment. *Information Systems Research*, *8*(2), 125–150. doi:10.1287/isre.8.2.125

Chau, P. Y. K. (2001). Influence of computer attitude and self-efficacy on it usage behavior. *Journal of End User Computing*, *13*(1), 26–33. doi:10.4018/joeuc.2001010103

Chau, P. Y. K., Au, G., & Tam, K. Y. (1995). Impact of information presentation models on online shopping: An empirical evaluation of a broadband interactive shopping service. *Journal of Organizational Computing and Electronic Commerce*, *10*(1), 1–22.

Chau, P. Y. (1996). An empirical assessment of a modified technology acceptance model. *Journal of Management Information Systems*, *13*(2), 185–205.

Chau, P. Y., & Hu, P. J. (2001). Information technology acceptance by individual professionals: A model comparison approach. *Decision Sciences*, *32*(4), 699–718. doi:10.1111/j.1540-5915.2001.tb00978.x

Chaudhuri, A., & Holbrook, M. (2001). The chain of effects from brand trust and brand affect to brand performance: The role of brand loyalty. *Journal of Marketing*, *65*(2), 81–93. doi:10.1509/jmkg.65.2.81.18255

Chen, C. C., Chen, X. P., & Meindl, J. R. (1998). How can cooperation be fostered? The cultural effects of individualism-collectivism. *Academy of Management Review*, *23*(2), 285–304. doi:10.2307/259375

Chen, G., Gully, S. M., & Eden, D. (2001). Validation of a new general self-efficacy scale. *Organizational Research Methods*, *4*(1), 62–84. doi:10.1177/109442810141004

Chen, Y., & Barnes, S. (2007). Initial trust and online buyer behavior. *Industrial Management & Data Systems*, *107*(1), 21–36. doi:10.1108/02635570710719034

Chen, L. D., & Tan, J. (2004). Technology adaptation in e-commerce: Key determinants of virtual stores acceptance. *European Management Journal*, *22*(1), 74–84. doi:10.1016/j.emj.2003.11.014

Chen, L., & Nath, R. (2006). Impact of Wireless Local Area Networks on Organization of Users. *Journal of Electronic Commerce in Organizations*, *4*(2), 62–81. doi:10.4018/jeco.2006040104

Chen, G., Gully, S. M., & Eden, D. (2001). Validation of a new general self-efficacy scale. *Organizational Research Methods*, *4*(1), 62–84. doi:10.1177/109442810141004

Cheung, M. K., & Lee, M. K. O. (2001). Trust in Internet shopping: Instrument development and validation through classical and modern approaches. *Journal of Global Information Management*, *9*(3), 23–35. doi:10.4018/jgim.2001070103

Chidambaram, L., Bostrom, R., & Wynne, B. (1990). A longitudinal study of the impact of group decision support systems on group development. *Journal of Management Information Systems*, *7*(3), 7–25.

Chin, W. (1998). Issues and opinion on structural equation modeling. *Management Information Systems Quarterly*, *22*(1), vii–xvi.

Chin, W. W., Marcolin, B. L., & Newsted, P. R. (2003). A partial least squares latent variable modeling approach for measuring interaction effects: Results from a Monte Carlo simulation study and an electronic-mail emotion/adoption study. *Information Systems Research*, *14*(2), 189–217. doi:10.1287/isre.14.2.189.16018

Chin, W. W., & Frye, T. (1996). *PLS Graph, 2.91.03.04 edition*. Calgary, Canada: University of Calgary.

Chin, W. W. (1998). The partial least squares approach to structural equation modeling. In Marcoulides, G. A. (Ed.), *Modern methods for business research* (pp. 295–336). Mahway, New Jersey: Lawrence Erlbaum.

Chung, S. H., Schwager, P. H., & Turner, D. E. (2002). An empirical of students' computer self-efficacy: Differences among four academic disciplines at a large university. *Journal of Computer Information Systems*, *42*(4), 1–6.

Churchill, G. A. (1979). A paradigm for developing better measures of marketing constructs. *JMR, Journal of Marketing Research*, *16*, 64–73. doi:10.2307/3150876

Chwelos, P., Benbasat, I., & Dexter, A. S. (2001). Research report: Empirical test of an EDI adoption model. *Information Systems Research*, *12*(3), 304–321. doi:10.1287/isre.12.3.304.9708

CIO. (2007, January 2). CRM: Challenges and advice for CIOs in 2007. *CIO*. Retrieved September 1, 2008, from http://www.cio.com/article/print/27802.

Clark, C. (2006). End user computing ergonomics: Facts or fads? *Journal of Organizational and End User Computing*, *18*(3), 66. doi:10.4018/joeuc.2006070104

Clee, M., & Wicklund, R. (1980). Consumer behavior and psychological reactance. *The Journal of Consumer Research*, *6*(4), 389–405. doi:10.1086/208782

Clermont, J. M. (2002). A spreadsheet auditing tool evaluated in an industrial context. *Proceedings of the European Spreadsheet Risk Interest Group Annual Conference*, Cardiff, Wales.

Cleveland, M., Babin, B. J., Laroche, M., Ward, P., & Bergeron, J. (2003). Information search patterns for gift purchases: A cross-national examination of gender differences. *Journal of Consumer Behaviour*, *3*(1), 20–47. doi:10.1002/cb.120

Cochran, K. F., & Wheatley, G. H. (1989). Ability and sex-related differences in cognitive strategies on spatial tasks. *The Journal of General Psychology*, *116*(1), 43–55. doi:10.1080/00221309.1989.9711109

Cohen, J., Cohen, P., West, S. G., & Aiken, L. S. (2003). *Applied multiple regression/correlation analysis for the behavioral sciences* (3rd ed.). Mahwah, NJ: Lawrence Erlbaum.

Cohen, J., & Cohen, P. (1983). *Applied regression/correlation analysis for the behavioral sciences*. Hillsdale, N.J.: Lawrence Erlbaum Associates.

Cole, S. J. (1998). Testimony before the Subcommittee on Telecommunications, Trade, and Consumer Protection Committee on Commerce, U.S. House of Representatives. Retrieved on August 27, 2010, from Better Business Bureau website: www.bbb.org/alerts/cole.asp.

Collier, J., & Bienstock, C. (2006). How do customers judge quality in an e-tailer? *MIT Sloan Management Review*, *48*(1), 35–40.

Colvin, C. A., & Goh, A. (2005). Validation of the technology acceptance model for police. *Journal of Criminal Justice*, *33*, 89–95. doi:10.1016/j.jcrimjus.2004.10.009

Compeau, D., Higgins, C., & Huff, S. (1999). Social cognitive theory and individual reactions to computing technology: A longitudinal study. *Management Information Systems Quarterly*, *23*(2), 145–158. doi:10.2307/249749

Compeau, D. R., & Higgins, C. A. (1995). Computer self-efficacy: Development of a measure and initial Test. *Management Information Systems Quarterly*, *19*(2), 189–211. doi:10.2307/249688

Compeau, D., Higgins, C. A., & Huff, S. (1999). Social cognitive theory and individual reactions to computing technology: A longitudinal study. *Management Information Systems Quarterly*, *23*(2), 145–158. doi:10.2307/249749

Coner, A. (2003). Personalization and customization in financial portals. *Journal of American Academy of Business*, *2*(2), 498–504.

Constantinides, E. (2004). Influencing the online consumer's behavior: the Web experience. *Internet Research*, *4*(2), 111–126. doi:10.1108/10662240410530835

Constantinides, P., & Barrett, M. (2006). Large-Scale ICT innovation, power, and organizational change: The case of a regional health information network. *The Journal of Applied Behavioral Science*, *42*(1), 76–90. doi:10.1177/0021886305284291

Cook, T. D., & Campbell, D. T. (1979). *Quasi-experimentation: Design & analysis issues for field settings*. Boston, MA: Houghton Mifflin Co.

Cook, J., & Wall, T. (1980). New work attitude measures of trust, organizational commitment and personal need non-fulfillment. *Journal of Occupational Psychology*, *53*, 39–52.

Cook, J. D., Hepworth, S. J., Wall, T. D., & Warr, P. B. (1981). *The experience of work*. New York: Academic Press.

Coopers and Lybrand. (1997). Retrieved from http://www.planningobjects.com/jungle1.htm

Corbin, D. (1988). Strategic IRM plan: User involvement spells success. *Journal of Systems Management*, *39*(5), 12–16.

Corbitt, B. J., Thanasankit, T., & Yi, H. (2003). Trust and e-commerce: A study of consumer perceptions. *Electronic Commerce Research and Applications*, *2*, 203–215. doi:10.1016/S1567-4223(03)00024-3

Cost, K., & Slaughter, K. (1997). *Best Business: Spanning the boundaries of business and IT. Vanenburg*. Putten, The Netherlands: Baan Institute Press.

Costa, A. C. (2003). Work team trust and effectiveness. *Personnel Review*, *32*, 605–622. doi:10.1108/00483480310488360

Couger, J. D., Higgins, L. F., & McIntyre, S. C. (1993). (Un)Structured creativity in information systems organizations. *Management Information Systems Quarterly*, *17*(4), 375–397. doi:10.2307/249584

Coursaris, C., Hassanein, K., & Head, M. (2003). M-commerce in Canada: An interaction framework for wireless privacy. *Canadian Journal of Administrative Sciences*, *20*, 54–73. doi:10.1111/j.1936-4490.2003.tb00305.x

Cousins, K. C., & Varshney, U. (2009). Designing Ubiquitous Computing Environments to Support Work Life Balance. *Communications of the ACM*, *52*(5), 117–123. doi:10.1145/1506409.1506438

Crain, R. (2006). Czech advertising business lacks a footbridge to the future, *Advertising Age*, September 17, 14.

Crego, E. T. J., & Schiffrin, P. D. (1995). *Customer-centered reengineering: remapping for total customer value*. Burr Ridge, IL: Irwin.

Cremer, D. D., Snyder, M., & Dewitte, S. (2001). The less I trust, the less I contribute (or not)?: The effects of trust, accountability, and self-monitoring in social dilemmas. *European Journal of Social Psychology*, *31*, 93–107. doi:10.1002/ejsp.34

Croll, G. J. (2005). The importance and criticality of spreadsheets in the city of London. *Proceedings of the European Spreadsheet Risks Interest Group Conference*, Greenwich, UK.

Cronbach, L. (1951). Coefficient alpha and the internal structure of tests. *Psychometrika*, *16*, 297–335. doi:10.1007/BF02310555

Crovitzthe, L. G. (2008). Unloading immediacy. *The Wall Street Journal*, July 7, 2008. Retrieved February 8, 2010, fromhttp://online.wsj.com.

Croy, M. (2004, May 4). Six tips for IT in planning a business continuity strategy. *Computerworld.* Retrieved August 18, 2005, fromwww.computerworld.com/printhis/2004/0,4814,92872,00.html.

Cummings, L. L., & Bromiley, P. (1996). The organizational trust inventory (OTI): Development and validation. In Kramer, R. M., & Tyler, T. R. (Eds.), *Trust in organizations* (pp. 302–330). Thousand Oaks, CA: Sage.

Curle, H. A. J. (1993). Supporting Strategic Objectives: Building a Corporate Information Technology Architecture. *Information Strategy: The Executive's Journal*, *10*(1), 5–12.

Curran, T., & Keller, G. (1998). *SAP R/3 business blueprint*. Upper Saddle River, NJ: Prentice Hall.

Cyr, D., & Bonanni, C. (2005). Gender and website design in e-business. *International Journal of Electronic Business*, *3*(6), 565–582. doi:10.1504/IJEB.2005.008536

Cyr, D. (2008). Modeling Web site design across cultures: Relationships to trust, satisfaction, and e-loyalty. *Journal of Management Information Systems*, *24*(4), 47–72. doi:10.2753/MIS0742-1222240402

Dabolkar, P. A., Shepard, C. D., & Thorpe, D. I. (2000). A comprehensive framework for service quality: An investigation of critical conceptual and measurement issues through a longitudinal study. *Journal of Retailing*, *76*(2), 139–173. doi:10.1016/S0022-4359(00)00029-4

Dasgupta, P. (2000). Trust as a commodity, in Gambetta, Diego (ed.) *Trust: Making and Breaking Cooperative Relations*, electronic edition, Department of Sociology, University of Oxford, Chapter 4, <http://www.sociology.ox.ac.uk/papers/dasgupta49-72.pdf>: 49-72.

Davenport, T. H., & Glaser, J. (2002). Just-in-Time delivery comes to knowledge management. *Harvard Business Review*, (July): 107–111.

David, G. (1989). Perceived usefulness, perceived ease of use and user acceptance of information technology. *Management Information Systems Quarterly*, *13*(3), 319–339. doi:10.2307/249008

David, P., Song, M., Hayes, A., & Fredin, E. S. (2007). A cyclic model of information seeking in hyperlinked environments: The role of goals, self-efficacy, and intrinsic motivation. *International Journal of Human-Computer Studies*, *65*(2), 170–182. doi:10.1016/j.ijhcs.2006.09.004

Davidson, E. (2006). A technological frames perspective on information technology and organizational change. *The Journal of Applied Behavioral Science*, *42*(1), 23–39. doi:10.1177/0021886305285126

Davis, F. D., Bagozzi, R. P., & Warshaw, P. R. (1989). User acceptance of computer technology: A comparison of two theoretical models. *Management Science*, *35*(8), 982–1003. doi:10.1287/mnsc.35.8.982

Davis, F. D. (1989). Perceived usefulness, perceived ease-of-use, and user acceptance of information technology. *Management Information Systems Quarterly*, *13*(3), 319–340. doi:10.2307/249008

Davis, F. D., & Venkatesh, V. (1996). A critical assessment of potential measurement biases in the technology acceptance model: Three experiments. *International Journal of Human-Computer Studies*, *45*, 19–45. doi:10.1006/ijhc.1996.0040

Davis, G. B. (1999). A Research Perspective for Information Systems and Example of Emerging Area of Research. *Information Systems Frontiers*, *1*(3), 195 203. doi:10.1023/A:1010094126762

Davis, G. B. (2002). Anytime/Anyplace Computing and the Future of Knowledge Work. *Communications of the ACM*, *45*(12), 67–73. doi:10.1145/585597.585617

Debevoise, T. (2005). *Business process management with a business rules approach: Implementing the service oriented architecture*. Canada: Business Knowledge Architects, Arbor Books.

Debreceny, R., Putterill, M., Tung, L., & Gilbert, A. L. (2003). New tools for the determination of e-commerce inhibitors. *Decision Support Systems*, *34*(2), 177–195. doi:10.1016/S0167-9236(02)00080-5

Deelstra, J. T., Peeters, M. C., & Zijlstra, F. R. (2003). Receiving instrumental support at work: When help is not welcome. *The Journal of Applied Psychology*, *88*(2), 324–331. doi:10.1037/0021-9010.88.2.324

Dekleva, S. M., Shim, J. P., Varshney, U., & Knoerzer, G. (2007). Evolution and Emerging Issues in Mobile Wireless Networks. *Communications of the ACM*, *50*(6), 38–43. doi:10.1145/1247001.1247003

DeSanctis, G. (1983). Expectancy theory as an explanation of voluntary use of a decision support system. *Psychological Reports*, *52*, 247–260.

Deutsch, M. (1958). Trust and suspicion. *The Journal of Conflict Resolution*, *2*, 265–279. doi:10.1177/002200275800200401

Dindia, K., & Duck, S. (2000). *Communication and personal relationships*. Chichester, England: Wiley.

Dinev, T., & Hart, P. (2006). An extended privacy calculus model for e-commerce transactions. *Information Systems Research*, *17*(1), 61–80. doi:10.1287/isre.1060.0080

Dipboye, R. L., & Flanagan, M. F. (1979). Research setting in industrial and organization psychology: Are findings in the field more generalizable than in laboratory. *The American Psychologist*, *34*(2), 141–150. doi:10.1037/0003-066X.34.2.141

Dishaw, M. T., & Strong, D. M. (1999). Extending the technology acceptance model with task-technology fit constructs. *Information & Management*, *36*, 9–21. doi:10.1016/S0378-7206(98)00101-3

Doherty, N. F., & King, M. (1998). The importance of organizational issues in systems development. *Information Technology & People*, *11*(2), 104–123. doi:10.1108/09593849810218300

Doney, P. M., & Cannon, J. P. (1997). An examination of the nature of trust in buyer-supplier relationships. *Journal of Marketing*, *61*(2), 35–51. doi:10.2307/1251829

DoubleClick. (2004). [*Ad Serving Trend Report*: Doubleclick.com.]. *DoubleClick*, *Q3*, 2004.

Drucker, P. F. (1969). *The Age of Discontinuity*. New York: Harper & Row.

Duncan, C., & Nelson, J. (1985). Effects of humor in radio advertising Experiment. *Journal of Advertising*, *14*(2), 33–40.

Duncan, N. B. (1995). Capturing Flexibility of Information Technology Infrastructure: A Study of Resource Characteristics and Their Measure. *Journal of Management Information Systems*, *12*(2), 37–57.

Dwyer, C. (2010) The effect of behavioral targeting on trust in e-commerce. Available at http://csis.pace.edu/~dwyer/research/

Earl, M. J. (1989). *Management strategies for information technology*. Englewood Cliffs, NJ: Prentice Hall.

Earl, M. J. (1993). Experiences in strategic information systems planning. *Management Information Systems Quarterly*, *17*(1), 1–24. doi:10.2307/249507

Easterbrook, J. A. (1959). The Effect of Emotion on Cue Utilization and the Organization of Behavior. *Psychological Bulletin*, *66*, 183–201.

Eastin, M. S., & LaRose, R. (2000). Internet self-efficacy and the psychology of the digital divide. *Journal of Computer-mediated Communication, 6*, 1. Retrieved on May 16, 2008 from http://www.ascusc.org/jcmc/vol6/issue1/eastin.html.

Eastin, M. S., & Robert, L. L. (2000). Internet self efficacy and the psychology of the digital divide. *Journal of Computer Mediated Communication, 6*(1). Retrieved November 4, 2008, from http://www.ascusc.org/jcmc/vol6/issue1/eastin.html

Eden, D. (1988). Pygmalion, goal setting, and expectancy: Compatible ways to raise productivity. *Academy of Management Review*, *13*(4), 639–652. doi:10.2307/258381

Eden, D., & Zuk, Y. (1995). Seasickness as a self-fulfilling prophecy: Raising self-efficacy to boost performance at sea. *The Journal of Applied Psychology*, *80*, 628–635. doi:10.1037/0021-9010.80.5.628

Edmunds, A., & Morris, A. (2000). The problem of information overload in business organizations: A review of the literature. *International Journal of Information Management*, *20*(1), 17–28. doi:10.1016/S0268-4012(99)00051-1

Edwards, S., Hairong, L., & Lee, J. (2002). Forced exposure and psychological reactance: Antecedents and consequences of the perceived Intrusiveness of pop-up Ads. *Journal of Advertising*, *31*(3), 83–95.

Eisenberger, R., Huntington, R., Hutchison, S., & Sowa, D. (1986). Perceived organizational support. *The Journal of Applied Psychology*, *71*, 500–507. doi:10.1037/0021-9010.71.3.500

Eisenhardt, K. M. (1989). Building theories from case study research. *Academy of Management Review*, *14*(4), 532–550. doi:10.2307/258557

Elbeltagi, I., McBride, N., & Hardaker, G. (2005). Evaluating the factors affecting DSS usage by senior managers in local authorities in Egypt. *Journal of Global Information Management*, *13*(2), 42–65. doi:10.4018/jgim.2005040103

Elliott, M., & Speck, P. (2005). Factors that affect attitude toward a retail website. *Journal of Marketing Theory and Practice*, *13*(1), 40–51.

Eppler, M. J., & Mengis, J. (2004). The concept of immediacy: A review of literature from organization science, accounting marketing MIS, and related disciplines. *The Information Society*, *20*, 325–344. doi:10.1080/01972240490507974

Eschenbrenner, B., & Nah, F. F. (2008). Understanding factors influencing proficient information systems usage. Proceedings of the 2008 Americas Conference on Information Systems, Toronto, ON.

Esper, T., Jensen, T., Turnipseed, F., & Burton, S. (2003). The last mile: An examination of effects of online retail delivery strategies on consumers. *Journal of Business Logistics*, *24*(2), 177–203.

Etezadi-Amoli, J., & Farhoomand, A. F. (1996). A structural model of end user computing satisfaction and user performance. *Information & Management*, *30*(2), 65–73. doi:10.1016/0378-7206(95)00052-6

EUSPRIG. (n.d.). European Spreadsheet Risks Interest Group stories. Retrieved from http://www.eusprig.org/stories.htm

Evans, M. G. (1985). A Monte Carlo study of the effects of correlated method variance in moderated multiple regression analysis. *Organizational Behavior and Human Decision Processes*, *36*, 305–323. doi:10.1016/0749-5978(85)90002-0

Evans, P. (2006). The Wiki Factor. *BizEd*, January/February 2006, 28-32.

Evernden, R., & Evernden, E. (2003). Third Generation Information Architecture. *Communications of the ACM*, *46*(3), 95–98. doi:10.1145/636772.636777

Eysenck, M. W. (1984). *A Handbook of Cognition Psychology*. London: Lawrence Erlbaum Associates, Ltd.

Fan, H., & Poole, M. S. (2006). What is personalization? Perspectives on the design and implementation of personalization in information systems. *Journal of Organizational Computing and Electronic Commerce*, *16*(3), 179–202. doi:10.1207/s15327744joce1603&4_2

Faragher, E. B., Cass, M., & Cooper, C. L. (2005). The relationship between job satisfaction and health: A meta-analysis. *Occupational and Environmental Medicine*, *62*, 105–112. doi:10.1136/oem.2002.006734

Farnum, C. (2002). Information Architecture: Five Things Information Managers Need to Know. *Information Management Journal*, *36*(5), 33–39.

Featherman, M. S., & Pavlou, P. A. (2003). Predicting e-services adoption: A perceived risk facets perspective. *International Journal of Human-Computer Studies*, *59*(4), 451–474. doi:10.1016/S1071-5819(03)00111-3

Federal Trade Commission. (2002, January 18). Eli Lilly settles FTC charges concerning security breach. Retrieved May 20, 2007, from http://www.ftc.gov/opa/2002/01/elililly.shtm.

Fernandes, A. D. (2001). Risking "trust" in a public key infrastructure: Old techniques of managing risk applied to new technology. *Decision Support Systems, 31*(3), 303–322. doi:10.1016/S0167-9236(00)00139-1

Ferratt, T. W., Short, L. E., & Agarwal, R. (1993). Measuring the information systems supervisor's work-unit environment and demonstrated skill at supervising. *Journal of Management Information Systems, 9*(4), 121–144.

Festinger, L. A. (1957). *A theory of cognitive dissonance*. Evanston, IL: Row and Peterson.

Fichman, M. (1999). Variance explained: Why size does not (always) matter. *Research in Organizational Behavior, 21*, 295–331.

Fischer, E., & Arnold, S. J. (1994). Sex, gender identity, gender role attitudes, and consumer behavior. *Psychology &. Marketing, 11*(2), 163–182.

Fishbein, M., & Ajzen, I. (1975). *Belief, attitude, intention and behavior: An introduction to theory and research*. MA: Addison-Wesley Publishing Company.

Fogg, B., & Tseng, H. (1999). The elements of computer credibility. In proceedings of CHI'99 (Pittsburgh, May 15-20). ACM Press, New York, 80-87.

Fornell, C., & Larcker, D. (1981). Evaluating structural equation models with unobservable variables and measurement error. *JMR, Journal of Marketing Research, 18*, 39–50. doi:10.2307/3151312

Fornell, C., & Lacker, D. F. (1981). Evaluating structural equation with unobservable variables and measurement error. *JMR, Journal of Marketing Research, 18*(2), 39–50. doi:10.2307/3151312

Fornell, C., & Larcker, D. (1981). Structural equation models with unobservable variables and measurement errors. *JMR, Journal of Marketing Research, 18*(2), 39–50. doi:10.2307/3151312

Fornell, C., & Larcker, D. F. (1981). Evaluating structural equation models with unobservable variables and measurement error. *JMR, Journal of Marketing Research, 18*(1), 39–50. doi:10.2307/3151312

Foster, S., & Franz, C. (1999). User involvement in information systems development: A comparison of analyst and user perceptions of system acceptance. *Journal of Engineering and Technology Management, 16*(3-4), 329–348. doi:10.1016/S0923-4748(99)00014-4

Fowler, J. J., & Horan, P. (2007). Are information systems' success and failure factors related? An exploratory study. *Journal of Organizational and End User Computing, 19*(2), 1. doi:10.4018/joeuc.2007040101

Frayne, C. A., & Latham, G. P. (1987). Application of social learning theory to employee self-management of attendance. *The Journal of Applied Psychology, 72*, 387–392. doi:10.1037/0021-9010.72.3.387

Frenkel, S. J., & Sanders, K. (2007). Explaining variations in co-worker assistance in organizations. *Organization Studies, 28*, 797–823. doi:10.1177/0170840607073079

Friedman, B., Kahn, P. K., & Howe, D. C. (2000). Trust online. *Communications of the ACM, 43*(12), 34–40. doi:10.1145/355112.355120

Fukuyama, F. (1995). *Trust: The social virtues and the creation of prosperity*. New York: The Free Press.

Fung, R. K. K., & Lee, M. K. O. (1999). EC-Trust (Trust in electronic commerce): Exploring the antecedent factors. *Proceedings of the Fifth Americas Conference on Information Systems*, Miwaukee, Wisconsin, 517-519.

Furr, R. M., & Rosenthal, R. (2003). Evaluating Theories Efficiently: The Nuts and Bolts of Contrast Analysis. *Understanding Statistics, 2*(1), 45–67. doi:10.1207/S15328031US0201_03

Fuscaldo, D. (2003, September 15). The best way to create a buzz for your product. *The Wall Street Journal,* p. R6.

Gabarro, J. J. (1978). The development of trust influence and expectations. In Athos, A. G., & Gabarro, J. J. (Eds.), *Interpersonal behavior: Communication and understanding in relationships* (pp. 290–303). Upper Saddle River, NJ: Prentice Hall.

Gadiesh, O., Buchanan, R., Daniell, M., & Ormiston, C. (2002). The Leadership Testing Ground. *The Journal of Business Strategy, 23*(2), 12–17. doi:10.1108/eb040230

Gale, T., & Eldred, J. (1996). *Getting results with the object-oriented models*. New York: SIG Books.

Gallant, S. I. (1993). *Neural network learning and expert systems*. Cambridge: MIT Press.

Galleta, D., Henry, R., McCoy, S., & Polak, P. (2006). When the Wait Isn't So Bad: The Interacting Effects of Web Site Speed, Familiarity, and Breadth. *Information Systems Research*, *17*(1), 20–37. doi:10.1287/isre.1050.0073

Gallivan, M. (2001). Organizational adoption and assimilation of complex technological innovations: Development and application of a new framework. *The Data Base for Advances in Information Systems*, *32*(3), 51–85.

Gambetta, D. (1988). *Trust: Making and breaking cooperative relations*. Oxford, UK: Basil Blackwell.

Ganesan, S. (1994). Determinants of long-term orientation in buyer-seller relationships. *Journal of Marketing*, *58*(2), 1–19. doi:10.2307/1252265

Ganster, D. C., Fusilier, M. R., & Mayes, B. T. (1986). Role of social support in the experience of stress at work. *The Journal of Applied Psychology*, *71*, 102–110. doi:10.1037/0021-9010.71.1.102

Gattiker, T., & Goodhue, D. (2002). Software-driven changes to business processes: An empirical study of impacts of enterprise resource planning (ERP) systems at the local level. *International Journal of Production Research*, *37*(9), 2093–2108.

Gebauer, J., Shaw, M. J., & Gribbins, M. L. (2010). Task-Technology Fit for Mobile Information Systems. *Journal of Information Technology*, *25*(3), 259–272. doi:10.1057/jit.2010.10

Gefen, D. (2000). E-commerce: The role of familiarity and trust. *Omega: The International Journal of Management Science*, *28*, 725–737. doi:10.1016/S0305-0483(00)00021-9

Gefen, D., Karahanna, E., & Straub, D. W. (2003). Trust and TAM in online shopping: An integrated model. *Management Information Systems Quarterly*, *27*(1), 51.

Gefen, D., & Straub, D. (2000). The relative importance of perceived ease-of-use in IS adoption: A study of e-commerce adoption. *Journal of the Association for Information Systems*, *1*(8), 1–30.

Gefen, D., & Straub, D. (2003). Trust and TAM in online shopping: An integrated model. *Management Information Systems Quarterly*, *27*(1), 51–90.

Gefen, D. (2000). E-commerce: the role of familiarity and trust. *Omega: The International Journal of Management Science*, *28*(6), 725–737. doi:10.1016/S0305-0483(00)00021-9

Gefen, D. (2002). Reflections on the dimensions of trust and trustworthiness among online consumers. *ACM SIGMIS Database*, *33*(3), 38–53. doi:10.1145/569905.569910

Gefen, D. (2002). Customer loyalty in e-commerce. *Journal of the Association for Information Systems*, *3*, 27–51.

Gefen, D., & Straub, D. W. (2004). Consumer trust in B2C e-commerce and the importance of social presence: experiments in e-products and e-services. *Omega*, *32*, 407–424. doi:10.1016/j.omega.2004.01.006

Gefen, D., Karahanna, E., & Straub, D. W. (2003). Trust and TAM in online shopping: An integrated model. *Management Information Systems Quarterly*, *27*(1), 51–90.

Gefen, D., & Straub, D. W. (1997). Gender differences in the perception and use of e-mail: An extension of the technology acceptance model. *Management Information Systems Quarterly*, *21*, 389–400. doi:10.2307/249720

Gefen, D., Karahanna, E., & Straub, D. W. (2003). Inexperience and experience with online stores: The importance of TAM and trust'. *IEEE Transactions on Engineering Management*, *50*(3), 307–321. doi:10.1109/TEM.2003.817277

Gefen, D., & Keil, M. (1998). The impact of developer responsiveness on perceptions of usefulness and ease of use: An extension of the technology acceptance model. *The Data Base for Advances in Information Systems*, *29*(2), 35–49.

Gefen, D., & Devine, P. (2001). Customer loyalty to an online store: The meaning of online service quality. *Proceedings of the International Conference on Information Systems*, New Orleans, Louisiana, 613-617.

Gefen, D., & Straub, D. W. (2003). Managing user trust in B2C e-services. e-Service Journal, 2, 7-24.

Gefen, D., Rao, V. S., & Tractinsky, N. (2003b). *The conceptualization of trust, risk and their relationship in electronic commerce: The need for clarifications.* Paper presented at the 36th Hawaii International Conference on System Sciences, Big island, Hawaii.

Gibson, C. B., & Zellmer-Bruhn, M. E. (2001). Metaphors and meaning: An intercultural analysis of the concept of teamwork. *Administrative Science Quarterly*, *46*(2), 274–303. doi:10.2307/2667088

Gibson, R. (1994). Global Information Technology Architectures. *Journal of Global Information Management*, *2*(1), 28–38.

Giddens, A. (1990). *The consequences of modernity.* Oxford: Polity Press.

Gifford, R. (1992). Implementing the IS Architecture. *Information Systems Management*, *9*(4), 41–47. doi:10.1080/10580539208906898

Gist, M. E., & Mitchell, T. R. (1992). Self-efficacy:A theoretical analysis of its determinants and malleability. *Academy of Management Review*, *17*(2), 183–211. doi:10.2307/258770

Gist, M. E., Schwoerer, C., & Rosen, B. (1989). Effects of alternative training methods on self-efficacy and performance in computer software training. *The Journal of Applied Psychology*, *74*, 884–891. doi:10.1037/0021-9010.74.6.884

Gist, M. E. (1987). Self-efficacy: Implications for organizational behavior and human resource management. *Academy of Management Review*, *12*(3), 472–485. doi:10.2307/258514

Gist, M. E., & Mitchell, T. R. (1992). Self-efficacy: a theoretical analysis of its determinants and malleability. *Academy of Management Review*, *17*(2), 183–211. doi:10.2307/258770

Gist, M. E., Schwoerer, C., & Rosen, B. (1989). Effects of alternative training methods on self-efficacy and performance in computer software training. *The Journal of Applied Psychology*, *74*(5), 884–891. doi:10.1037/0021-9010.74.6.884

Golden-Biddle, K., & Locke, K. (1993). Appealing work: An investigation of how ethnographic texts convince. *Organization Science*, *4*, 595–616. doi:10.1287/orsc.4.4.595

Goodhue, D. L., Kirsch, L. J., Quillard, J. A., & Wybo, M. D. (1992). Strategic Data Planning: Lessons from the Field. *MIS Quarterly*, *16*(1), 11–34. doi:10.2307/249699

Goodhue, D. L., Quillard, J. A., & Rockart, J. F. (1988). Managing The Data Resource: A Contingency Perspective. *MIS Quarterly*, *12*(3), 11–34. doi:10.2307/249204

Goodwin, N. (1996). *Economic meanings of trust and responsibility.* Ann Arbor, MI: The University of Michigan Press.

Gopal, A., Compeau, D., Marcon, T., & Olivera, F. (2006). Learning with Laptops: Information Technology and the Transformation of an MBA Program. *Proceedings of the 39th Annual Hawaii International Conference on System Sciences (HICSS)*, 1-10.

Gordon, J., Kruger, D., & Helman, C. (2002, February 18). Streetwalker. *Forbes*, *169*, 108.

Gorlenko, L., & Merrick, R. (2003). No Wires Attached: Usability Challenges in the Connected Mobile World. *IBM Systems Journal*, *42*(4), 639–651. doi:10.1147/sj.424.0639

Gouldner, A. W. (1960). The norm of reciprocity: A preliminary statement. *American Sociological Review*, *25*, 161–178. doi:10.2307/2092623

Gounaris, K. M., & Prout, M. F. (2009). Repairing relationships and restoring trust: Behavioral finance and the economic crisis. *Journal of Financial Service Professionals*, *63*(4), 75–84.

Grabner-Kraeuter, S. (2002). The role of consumers' trust in online shopping. *Journal of Business Ethics*, *39*, 43–51. doi:10.1023/A:1016323815802

Graen, G. B., & Uhl-Bien, M. (1995). Development of leader-member exchange (LMX) theory of leadership over 25 years: Applying a multi-level multi-domain perspective. *The Leadership Quarterly*, *6*, 219–247. doi:10.1016/1048-9843(95)90036-5

Granovetter, M. (1985). Economic action and social structure: The problem of embeddedness. *American Journal of Sociology*, *91*, 481–510. doi:10.1086/228311

Green, B. D. (2003). Integration of TSIMS and ICAS for condition based maintenance. *Proceedings of the Intelligent Ship Symposium*, Philadelphia, PA.

Greene, C. N., & Organ, D. W. (1973). An evaluation of causal models linking the received role with job satisfaction. *Administrative Science Quarterly, 18*, 95–103. doi:10.2307/2391931

Gregg, D. G., & Scott, J. E. (2006). The role of reputation systems in reducing online auction fraud. *International Journal of Electronic Commerce, 10*(3), 95–120. doi:10.2753/JEC1086-4415100304

Griffeth, R., Hom, P., & Gaertner, S. (2000). A meta-analysis of antecedents and correlates of employee turnover: Update, moderator tests, and research implications for the next millennium. *Journal of Management, 26*, 463–488. doi:10.1177/014920630002600305

Groff, B. D., Baron, R. S., & Moore, D. L. (1983). Distraction, Attentional Conflict, and Drivelike Behavior. *Journal of Experimental Social Psychology, 19*(4), 359–380. doi:10.1016/0022-1031(83)90028-8

Grossman, T. G., Mehrotra, V., & Özluk, Ö. (2005). *Spreadsheet information systems are essential to business.* Working paper, University of San Francisco, USA.

Gruman, G. (2003, August 1, 2003). Wireless: Just what the doctor ordered. *CIO.* Retrieved August 18, 2005, from http://www.cio.com/article/print/29587.

Guerin, B. (1993). *Social facilitation*. Cambridge, Great Britain: Cambridge University Press. doi:10.1017/CBO9780511628214

Guimaraes, T., & Igbaria, M. (1997). Client/server system success: Exploring the human side. *Decision Sciences, 28*, 851–876. doi:10.1111/j.1540-5915.1997.tb01334.x

Gulati, R. (1995). Does familiarity breed trust? The implications of repeated ties for contractual choices in alliances. *Academy of Management Journal, 38*(1), 85–112. doi:10.2307/256729

Gupta, P., Yadav, M. S., & Varadarajan, R. (2010). How task-facilitative interactive tools foster buyers' trust in online retailers: A process view of trust development in the electronic marketplace. *Journal of Retailing, 85*(2), 159–176. doi:10.1016/j.jretai.2009.02.001

Ha, H. (2004). Factors influencing consumer perceptions of brand trust online. *Journal of Product and Brand Management, 13*(5), 329–442. doi:10.1108/10610420410554412

Hackathorn, R. D., & Karimi, J. (1988). A Framework for Comparing Information Engineering Methods. *MIS Quarterly, 12*(2), 202–220. doi:10.2307/248845

Hackbarth, G., Grover, V., & Yi, M. Y. (2003). Computer playfulness and anxiety: positive and negative mediators of the system experience effect on perceived ease of use. *Information & Management, 40*, 221–232. doi:10.1016/S0378-7206(02)00006-X

Hackman, J., & Oldham, G. (1975). *Work redesign*. Reading, MA: Addison-Wesley.

Hagel, J. I., & Brown, J. S. (2001). Your Next IT Strategy. *Harvard Business Review, 79*(9), 105–113.

Hair, J., Anderson, R., Tatham, R., & Black, W. (1998). *Multivariate data analysis*. Upper Saddle River: Prentice Hall.

Hair, J. F., Anderson, R. E., Tatham, R. L., & Black, W. C. (1998). *Multivariate data analysis*. Upper Saddle River, NJ: Prentice-Hall.

Hamilton, B. A., & Scandura, T. A. (2003). E-Mentoring: Implications for organizational learning and development in a wired world. *Organizational Dynamics, 31*(4), 388–402. doi:10.1016/S0090-2616(02)00128-6

Hammer, M., & Champy, J. (1993). *Reengineering the corporation: A manifesto for business revolution*. New York: Harper.

Hanai, T., & Oguchi, T. (2009). How do consumers perceive the reliability of online shops? Cyberpsychology. *Journal of Psychosocial Research on Cyberspace, 3*(2), 1–9.

Harary, H., Norman, Z., & Cartwright, D. (1965). *Structural models: An introduction to the theory of directed graphs*. New York: Wiley.

Harley, B., Wright, C., Hall, R., & Dery, K. (2006). Management reactions to technological change: The example of enterprise resource planning. *The Journal of Applied Behavioral Science, 42*(1), 58–75. doi:10.1177/0021886305284857

Harridge-March, S. (2006). Can the building of trust overcome consumer perceived risk online? *Marketing Intelligence & Planning, 24*(7), 746–761. doi:10.1108/02634500610711897

Harris, R. W. (2000). Schools of thought in research into end-user computing success. *Journal of End User Computing, 12*(1), 24–34. doi:10.4018/joeuc.2000010103

Harrison, A. W., & Rainer, R. K. (1992). The influence of individual differences on skill in end-user computing. *Journal of Management Information Systems, 9*(1), 93–111.

Hart, P., & Saunders, C. (1997). Power and trust: Critical factors in the adoption and use of electronic data interchange. *Organization Science, 8*(1), 23–42. doi:10.1287/orsc.8.1.23

Hasan, B. (2007). Examining the effects of Computer self-efficacy and system complexity on technology acceptance. *Information Resources Management Journal, 20*(3), 76–88. doi:10.4018/irmj.2007070106

Hasan, B. (2006). Effectiveness of computer training: The role of multilevel computer self-efficacy. *Journal of Organizational and End User Computing, 18*(1), 50–68. doi:10.4018/joeuc.2006010103

Hasan, B. (2006). Delineating the effects of general and system-specific computer self-efficacy beliefs on IS acceptance. *Information & Management, 43*, 565–571. doi:10.1016/j.im.2005.11.005

Hayduk, L. A. (1987). *Structural equation modeling with LISREL: Essentials and advances*. Baltimore, MD: The Johns Hopkins University Press.

Hazari, S. I. (2005). Perceptions of end-users on the requirements in personal firewall software: An exploratory study. *Journal of Organizational and End User Computing, 17*(3), 47–65. doi:10.4018/joeuc.2005070103

Heijden, H., Tibert, V., & Creemers, M. (2003). Understanding online purchase intentions: contributions from technology and trust perspectives. *European Journal of Information Systems, 12*(1), 41–48. doi:10.1057/palgrave.ejis.3000445

Heilemann, J. (2004). The $100 million dinosaur. *Business 2.0*, 60-62.

Heiskanen, A. (1993). Organizational metaphors and information systems practice: a case example of implementation strategy formulation. In Avison, D., Kendall, J. E., & DeGross, J. I. (Eds.), *Human, organizational, and social dimensions of information systems development* (pp. 399–417). Amsterdam: North-Holland.

Hemp, P. (2009). Death by immediacy. *Harvard Business Review*, September 2009, 83-89. Reprint #R0909J.

Henderson, J., Rockart, J., & Sifonis, J. (1987). A planning methodology for integrating management support systems into strategic information planning. *Journal of Management Information Systems, 4*(1), 5–24.

Henderson, J. C., & Venkatraman, N. (1999). Strategic Alignment: Leveraging Information Technology for Transforming Organizations. *IBM Systems Journal, 38*(2/3), 472–484.

Henderson, J. C., & Venkatraman, N. (1995). Strategic Alignment: A Model for Organisational Transformation Via Information Technology. In T. J. Allen & M. S. S. Morton (Eds.), Information Technology and the Corporation of the 1990s: Research Studies (pp. 202-220). Oxford: Oxford University Press.

Hendricks, K., Singhal, V., & Stratman, J. (2007). The impact of enterprise systems on corporate performance: A study of ERP, SCM, and CRM system implementations. *Journal of Operations Management, 25*(1), 65–82. doi:10.1016/j.jom.2006.02.002

Henricks, M. (2005). Falling behind. *Entrepreneur*, February 2005, 19-20.

Henry, J. W., & Martinko, M. J. (1997). An attributional analysis of the rejection of information technology. *Journal of End User Computing, 9*(4), 3–17.

Heracleous, L. (2001). An ethnographic study of culture in the context of organizational change. *The Journal of Applied Behavioral Science, 37*(4), 426–446. doi:10.1177/0021886301374003

Herche, J., & Engelland, B. (1989). Reverse-polarity items and scale unidimensionality. *Journal of the Academy of Marketing Science, 24*, 366–374. doi:10.1177/0092070396244007

Hicks, L. (1995). Personal communication to Ray Panko.

Hildebrand, C. (2000). What is Infrastructure? Retrieved January 18, 2002, from http://www.darwinmag.com

Hill, J. R., & Hannafin, M. J. (1997). Cognitive strategies and learning from the world wide web. *Educational Technology Research and Development, 45*(4), 37–64. doi:10.1007/BF02299682

Hill, T., Smith, N. D., & Mann, M. F. (1997). Role of efficacy expectations in predicting the decision to use advanced technologies: The case of computers. *The Journal of Applied Psychology*, *72*(2), 307–313. doi:10.1037/0021-9010.72.2.307

Hiltz, S. R. (1988). Productivity Enhancement from Computer-Mediated Communication: A Systems Contingency Approach. *Communications of the ACM*, *31*(12), 1438–1454. doi:10.1145/53580.53583

Hirschheim, R., Klein, H. K., & Lyytinen, K. (1995). *Information systems development and data modeling*. Chichester: Cambridge University Press.

Hirschheim, R., & Newman, M. (1991). Symbolism and information systems development: myth, metaphor and magic. *Information Systems Research*, *2*(1), 29–62. doi:10.1287/isre.2.1.29

Hobfoll, S. E. (1989). Conservation of resources: A new attempt at conceptualizing stress. *The American Psychologist*, *44*, 513–524. doi:10.1037/0003-066X.44.3.513

Hobfoll, S. E. (2001). The influence of culture, community, and the nested-self in the stress process: Advancing conservation of resources theory. *Applied Psychology: An International Review*, *50*, 337–421. doi:10.1111/1464-0597.00062

Hobfoll, S., & Freedy, J. (1993). Conservation of resources: A general stress theory applied to burnout. In W. Schaufeli & C. Maslach & T. Marek (Eds.), Professional burnout: Recent developments in theory and practice: 115-129. Washington D.C.: Taylor & Francis.

Hochwarter, W., Kacmar, C., Perrewe, P., & Johnson, D. (2003). Perceived organizational support as a mediator of the relationship between politics perceptions and work outcomes: A multi-level analysis. *Journal of Vocational Behavior*, *63*, 438–456. doi:10.1016/S0001-8791(02)00048-9

Hoffman, D. L., Novak, T. P., & Peralta, M. (1999). Building consumer trust online; Association for computing machinery. *Communications of the ACM*, *42*, 480–486.

Hofstede, G. (1980). *Culture's consequences: International Differences in Work Related Values*. London: Sage.

Hollingshead, A., McGrath, J., & O'Connor, K. (1993). Group task performance and communication technology: A longitudinal study of computer-mediated vs. face-to-face work groups. *Small Group Research*, *24*(3), 307–333. doi:10.1177/1046496493243003

Holsapple, C. & Whinston, M. (1996). Decision support systems: A knowledge-based approach. St. Paul, MN: West Publishing company. *Implementation of an Enterprise Resource Planning system with Focus on end-User Training*, (2007) [http://www.diplomica.com/db/diplomarbeiten1906.html], April.

Hong, W., Thong, J. Y. L., Wong, W.-M., & Tam, K.-Y. (2001). Determinants of user acceptance of digital libraries: An empirical examination of individual differences and system characteristics. *Journal of Management Information Systems*, *18*(3), 97–124.

Hosmer, L. T. (1995). Trust: The connecting link between organizational theory and philosophical ethics. *Academy of Management Review*, *20*(2), 379–403. doi:10.2307/258851

House, R. J. (1981). *Work stress and social support*. Reading, MA: Addison-Wesley.

Hsu, C.-L., & Lu, H.-P. (2004). Why do people play online games? An extended TAM with social influences and flow experience. *Information & Management*, *41*(7), 853–868. doi:10.1016/j.im.2003.08.014

Hsu, Yu-chang. (2006). Better educational website interface design: The implications from gender-specific preferences in graduate students. *British Journal of Educational Technology*, *37*(2), 233-242.

Hu, P. J., Chau, P. Y. K., Sheng, O. R. L., & Tam, K. Y. (1999). Examining the technology acceptance model using physician acceptance of telemedicine technology. *Journal of Management Information Systems*, *16*(2), 91–113.

Huang, E., & Chuang, M. H. (2007). Extending the theory of planned behavior as a model to explain post-merger employee behavior of IS use. *Computers in Human Behavior*, *23*, 240–257. doi:10.1016/j.chb.2004.10.010

Huff, L., & Kelley, L. (2003). Levels of organizational trust in individualist versus collectivist societies. *Organization Science*, *14*(1), 81–90. doi:10.1287/orsc.14.1.81.12807

Huizingh, E. (2000). The content and design of Websites: An empirical study. *Information & Management, 37*, 123–134. doi:10.1016/S0378-7206(99)00044-0

Hunton, J., & Beeler, J. (1997). Effects of user participation in systems development: A longitudinal field experiment. *Management Information Systems Quarterly, 21*(4), 359–388. doi:10.2307/249719

Hussain, Z., & Taylor, A. (2007). Evaluating the Behaviour of Information Systems Developers: The relevance and utility of paradigms. *Behaviour & Information Technology, 26*(3), 221–236. doi:10.1080/01449290600877413

Hutchins, S. G. (1996). *Principals for intelligent decision aiding* (Technical Report 1718). Retrieved March 23, 2007, from http://www.spawar.navy.mil/sti/publications/pubs/tr/1718/tr1718.pdf

Hymowitz, C. (2003, October 28). More managers allow workers to multitask as job and home blur. *The Wall Street Journal,* B1.

Igbaria, M., & Iivari, J. (1995). The effects of self-efficacy on computer usage. *Omega, 23*(6), 587–605. doi:10.1016/0305-0483(95)00035-6

Imhof, M., Vollmeyer, R., & Beierlein, C. (2007). Computer use and the gender gap: The issue of access, use, motivation, and performance. *Computers in Human Behavior, 23*(6), 2823–2837. doi:10.1016/j.chb.2006.05.007

Introna, L., & Whitlei, E. (2000). About experiments and style: A critique of laboratory research in information systems. *Information Technology & People, 13*(3), 161–173. doi:10.1108/09593840010377608

Iverson, R. D. (1996). Employee acceptance of organizational change: The role of organizational commitment. *International Journal of Human Resource Management, 7*(1), 122–149.

Iverson, R. D., Deery, S. J., & Erwin, P. J. (1995). Absenteeism in the health services sector: A casual model and intervention strategies. In Riedel, P., & Preston, A. (Eds.), *Managing absenteeism: Analysing and preventing labour absence*. Canberra: AGPS.

Ives, B., & Olson, M. H. (1984). User involvement and MIS success: A review of research. *Management Science, 30*(5), 586–603. doi:10.1287/mnsc.30.5.586

Ives, B. (1994). Probing the Productivity Paradox (Editorial Comment). *Management Information Systems Quarterly, 18*(2), XXI–XXIV.

Jackson, L. A., Ervin, K. S., Gardner, P. D., & Schmitt, N. (2001). Gender and the Internet: Women communicating and men searching. *Sex Roles, 44*(5/6), 363–379. doi:10.1023/A:1010937901821

Jackson, C. M., Chow, S., & Leitch, R. A. (1997). Toward an understanding of the behavioral intention to use an information system. *Decision Sciences, 28*(2), 357–389. doi:10.1111/j.1540-5915.1997.tb01315.x

Jacobs, F., & Weston, F. (2007). Enterprise resource planning (ERP)—A brief history. *Journal of Operations Management, 25*, 357–363. doi:10.1016/j.jom.2006.11.005

James, L. R., Gent, M. J., Hater, J. J., & Corey, K. E. (1979). Correlates of psychological influence: An illustration of the psychological climate approach to work environment perceptions. *Personnel Psychology, 32*, 563–588. doi:10.1111/j.1744-6570.1979.tb02154.x

Jameson, A., & Schwarzkopf, E. (2002). Pros and cons of controllability: an empirical study. Adaptive Hypermedia 2002. *Lecture Notes in Computer Science, 2347*, 193–202. doi:10.1007/3-540-47952-X_21

Jarvenpaa, S. L., Knoll, K., & Leidner, D. E. (1998). Is anybody out there? Antecedents of trust in global virtual teams. *Journal of Management Information Systems, 14*(4), 26–64.

Jarvenpaa, S. L., & Todd, P. A. (1996). Consumer reactions to electronic shopping on the World Wide Web. *International Journal of Electronic Commerce, 1*(2), 59–88.

Jarvenpaa, S. L., & Tractinsky, N. (1999). Consumer trust in an Internet store. *Information Technology Management, 5*(2), 1–35.

Jarvenpaa, S. L., Tractinsky, N., & Vitale, M. (2000). Consumer trust in an Internet store. *Information Technology Management, 1*(1-2), 45–71. doi:10.1023/A:1019104520776

Jarvenpaa, S. L., Knoll, K., & Keidner, D. E. (1998). Is anybody out there? Antecedents of trust in global virtual teams. *Journal of Management Information Systems, 14*(4), 29–64.

Jarvenpaa, S. L., & Leidner, D. E. (1999). Communication and Trust in Global Virtual Teams. *Organization Science, 10*(6), 791–815. doi:10.1287/orsc.10.6.791

Jarvenpaa, S., & Todd, P. (2004). Consumer reactions to electronic shopping on the World Wide Web. *International Journal of Electronic Commerce, 1*(2), 59–88.

Jarvenpaa, S. L., Lang, K. R., Takeda, Y., & Tuunainen, V. K. (2003). Mobile Commerce at Crossroads. *Communications of the ACM, 46*(12), 41–44. doi:10.1145/953460.953485

Jayaratna, N. (1996). Choice of a methodology for information systems development! *Proceedings of the Fourth Conference of the British Computer Society Information Systems Methodologies Specialist Group*, 12-14 September. Cork, Ireland, 23-28.

Jessup, L. M., & Robey, D. (2002). The Relevance of Social Issues in Ubiquitous Computing Environments. *Communications of the ACM, 45*(12), 88–91. doi:10.1145/585597.585621

Jevons, C. Gabbott, M., & de Chernatony. L. (2001). A taxonomy of brand linkages: the brand-relationship-interaction (BRI) matrix, http://business.bham.ac.uk/business/papers/taxonomy.htm.

Johnson, R. D., & Marakas, G. M. (2000). Research report: The role of behavioral modeling and computer skills acquisition-toward refinement of the model. *Information Systems Research, 11*(4), 402–417. doi:10.1287/isre.11.4.402.11869

Johnston, H. R., & Carrico, S. R. (1988). Developing Capabilities to Use Information Strategically. *MIS Quarterly, 12*(1), 37–48. doi:10.2307/248801

Johnston, H. R., & Vitale, M. R. (1988). Creating Competitive Advantage with Interorganizational Information Systems. *MIS Quarterly, 12*(2), 152–165. doi:10.2307/248839

Jones, E., & Archer, R. (1976). Are there special effects of personalistic self-disclosure? *Journal of Experimental Social Psychology, 12*, 180–193. doi:10.1016/0022-1031(76)90069-X

Jones, M., & Price, R. (2004). Organizational knowledge sharing in ERP implementation: Lessons from industry. *Journal of Organizational and End User Computing, 16*(1), 21–41. doi:10.4018/joeuc.2004010102

Jones, N., & Kochtanek, T. (2004). Success factors in the implementation of a collaborative technology and resulting productivity improvements in a small business: An exploratory study. *Journal of Organizational and End User Computing, 16*(1), 1–20. doi:10.4018/joeuc.2004010101

Jonkers, H., & Franken, H. (1996). Quantitative modeling and analysis of business processes. In *Proceedings of 8th European Simulation Systems: Simulation in Industry*, Vol. 1, 175-179.

Joreskog, K. G., & Wold, H. (1981). The ML and PLS techniques for modeling with latent variables: Historical and comparative aspects. In Joreskog, H. W. A. K. (Ed.), *System under indirect observation: Causality, structure and prediction* (pp. 263–270). Amsterdam: North-Holland.

Jourard, S. (1973). *Transparent self.* New York: Van Nostrand Reinhold Company.

Judge, T. A., Erez, A., & Bono, J. A. (1998). The power of being positive: The relation between positive self-concept and job performance. *Human Performance, 11*, 167–187. doi:10.1207/s15327043hup1102&3_4

Judge, T. A., Thoresen, C. J., Bono, J. E., & Patton, G. K. (2001). The job satisfaction-job performance relationship: A qualitative and quantitative review. *Psychological Bulletin, 127*(3), 376–407. doi:10.1037/0033-2909.127.3.376

Jung, D., & Burns, J. (1993). Connectionist approaches to inexact reasoning and learning systems for executive and decision support. *Decision Support Systems, 10*, 37–66. doi:10.1016/0167-9236(93)90004-M

Jung, D. (1990). *Design of inexact reasoning systems for managerial problem diagnosis.* Unpublished doctoral dissertation, Texas Tech University, Lubbock, TX.

Jurgensen, J. (2006, 6-3-2006). The "virtual" concert tour. *The Wall Street Journal*, p. 1.

Kaarst-Brown, M. L., & Robey, D. (1999). More on myth, magic and metaphor: Cultural insights into the management of information technology in organizations. *Information Technology & People, 12*(2), 192–217. doi:10.1108/09593849910267251

Kafetsios, K. (2004). Attachment and emotional intelligence abilities across the life course. *Personality and Individual Differences, 37*(1), 129–146. doi:10.1016/j.paid.2003.08.006

Kahneman, D. (1973). *Attention and Effort*. Englewood Cliffs: Prentice Hall.

Kanfer, R., & Ackerman, P. L. (1989). Motivation and cognitive abilities: An integrative/aptitude-treatment interaction approach to skill acquisition. *The Journal of Applied Psychology*, *74*(4), 657–690. doi:10.1037/0021-9010.74.4.657

Kanter, J. (2004). An IT manifesto for business managers. *Information Strategy: The Executive's Journal*, *20*(3), 6–12.

Kaplan, A. M., & Haenlein, M. (2010). Users of the world, unite! The challenges and opportunities of Social media. *Business Horizons*, *53*, 59–68. doi:10.1016/j.bushor.2009.09.003

Karacapilidis, N., & Moraïtis, P. (2001). Building an agent-mediated electronic commerce system with decision analysis features. *Decision Support Systems*, *32*(1), 53–69. doi:10.1016/S0167-9236(01)00100-2

Karahanna, E., Straub, D. W., & Chervany, N. L. (1999). Information technology adoption across time: A cross-sectional comparison of pre-adoption and post-adoption beliefs. *Management Information Systems Quarterly*, *23*(2), 183–213. doi:10.2307/249751

Katerattanakul, P., & Siau, K. (1999). Measuring information quality of web sites: Development of an instrument. In *Proceedings of the Twentieth International Conference on Information Systems* (pp. 279-285), Charlotte, North Carolina.

Kathryn, M. K., & Mary, M. (2002). Third-party assurance: Mapping the road to trust in e-retailing. *Journal of Information Technology Theory and Application*, *4*(2), 63–82.

Keane, B. (2002). Lowering Health Care Costs Out-Of-The-Box. *Wireless Business & Technology*, *2*(2), 36–38.

Kearns, G. S., & Lederer, A. L. (2000). The Effect of Strategic Alignment on the Use of IS-based Resources for Competitive Advantage. *The Journal of Strategic Information Systems*, *9*(4), 265–293. doi:10.1016/S0963-8687(00)00049-4

Kearns, G. S., & Lederer, A. L. (1997). Alignment of Information Systems Plans with Business Plans: The Impact on Competitive Advantage. Paper presented at the Proceedings of the Second Americas Conference on Information Systems, Indianapolis.

Kee, H. W., & Knox, R. E. (1970). Conceptual and methodological considerations in the study of trust and suspicion. *The Journal of Conflict Resolution*, *14*(3), 357–366. doi:10.1177/002200277001400307

Keen, P. (1990). *Shaping the Future: Business Design through Information Technology*. Cambridge, MA: Harvard Business School.

Keen, P. G. W. (1991). Shaping the Future: Business Design through Information Technology. Cambridge, MA: Harvard Business School Press.

Keil, M., Beranek, P. M., & Knsynski, B. R. (1995). Usefulness and ease of use: Field study evidence regarding task considerations. *Decision Support Systems*, *13*, 75–91. doi:10.1016/0167-9236(94)E0032-M

Keller, K., Heckler, S., & Houston, M. (1998). The effects of brand name suggestiveness on advertising recall. *Journal of Marketing*, *62*, 48–57. doi:10.2307/1251802

Keller, K. L., & Moorthi, Y. L. R. (2003). Branding in developing markets. *Business Horizons*, *46*(3), 49–59. doi:10.1016/S0007-6813(03)00029-6

Kelloway, E. K., & Barling, J. B. (2000). Knowledge work as organizational behaviour. *International Journal of Management Reviews*, *2*, 287–304. doi:10.1111/1468-2370.00042

Kelly, A. (2002). *The psychology of secrets*. New York: Kluwer Academic Plenum Publishers.

Kelly, K. (1998). *New Rules for the New Economy: 10 Radical Strategies for a Networked World*. New York, NY: Viking Press.

Kendall, J. E., & Kendall, K. E. (1993). Metaphors and methodologies: Living beyond the systems machine. *Management Information Systems Quarterly*, *17*(2), 149–168. doi:10.2307/249799

Kerlinger, F. N., & Lee, H. B. (2000). *Foundations of behavioral research* (4th ed.). Toronto: Wadsworth Tomson Learning.

Kesmodel, D. (2006, February 22). 'Drop catchers' buy and sell web names others let slip. *The Wall Street Journal*, p. B12.

Kettinger, W., & Grover, V. (1995). Toward a theory of business process change management. *Journal of Management Information Systems*, *12*(18), 9–12.

Keys, P. (1991). Operational research in organizations: A metaphorical analysis. *Journal of Res. Soc*, *42*(6), 435–446.

Khalil, T. (2000). *Management of Technology*. New York, NY: McGraw-Hill.

Kim, D. (2008). Self-perception-based versus transference-based trust determinants in computer-mediated transactions: A cross-cultural comparison study. *Journal of Management Information Systems*, *24*(4), 13–45. doi:10.2753/MIS0742-1222240401

Kim, D., & Benbasat, I. (2006). The effects of Trust-assuring arguments on consumer trust in Internet stores: Application of Toulmin's model of argumentation. *Information Systems Research*, *17*(3), 286–300. doi:10.1287/isre.1060.0093

Kim, D., & Benbasat, I. (2009-10). Trust-assuring arguments in b2c e-commerce: Impact of content, source, and price on trust. *Journal of Management Information Systems*, *26*(3), 175–206. doi:10.2753/MIS0742-1222260306

Kim, D. J., Ferrin, D. L., & Rao, H. R. (2008). A trust-based consumer decision making model in electronic commerce: The role of trust, perceived risk, and their antecedents. *Decision Support Systems*, *44*, 544–564. doi:10.1016/j.dss.2007.07.001

Kim, D. J., Sivasailam, N., & Rao, H. R. (2004). Information assurance in B2C websites for information goods/services. *Electronic Markets*, *14*, 344–359. doi:10.1080/10196780412331311784

Kim, D. J., Song, Y. I., Braynov, S. B., & Rao, H. R. (2005). A multi-dimensional trust formation model in B-to-C e-commerce: A conceptual framework and content analyses of academia/practitioner perspective. *Decision Support Systems*, *40*(2), 143–165. doi:10.1016/j.dss.2004.01.006

Kim, D., & Benbasat, I. (2006). The effect of trust-assuring arguments on consumer trust in internet stores: Application of Toulmin's model of argumentation. *Information Systems Research*, *17*(3), 286–300. doi:10.1287/isre.1060.0093

Kim, D., & Benbasat, I. (2010). Designs for effective implementation of trust assurance in internet stores. *Communications of the ACM*, *53*(2), 121–126. doi:10.1145/1646353.1646386

Kim, E. Y., & Kim, Y. (2004). Predicting online purchase intentions for clothing products. *European Journal of Marketing*, *38*(7), 883–907. doi:10.1108/03090560410539302

Kim, Y. (2006). Supporting distributed groups with group support systems: A study of the effect of group leaders and communication modes on group performance. *Journal of Organizational and End User Computing*, *18*(2), 20–37. doi:10.4018/joeuc.2006040102

Kim, Y., & Everest, G. C. (1994). Building an IS Architecture. *Information & Management*, *26*(1), 1–11. doi:10.1016/0378-7206(94)90002-7

Kim, D., & Benbasat, I. (2009) Trust-assuring arguments in B2C e-commerce: Impact of content, source, and price on trust. *Journal of Management Information Systems, Winter, 26*(3), 175-206.

Kimery, K. M., & McCord, M. (2002). Third-party assurances: Mapping the road to trust in e-retailing. *JITTA: Journal of Information Technology Theory and Application*, *4*(2), 63–83.

King, W. R., & He, J. (2006). A meta-analysis of the technology acceptance model. *Information & Management*, *43*, 740–755. doi:10.1016/j.im.2006.05.003

Kirk, R. (1995). *Experimental design: Procedures for the behavioral sciences* (3rd ed.). Pacific Grove, CA: Brooks/Cole Publishing Company.

Kirsch, L. J. (1997). Portfolios of control modes and IS project management. *Information Systems Research*, *8*(3), 215–239. doi:10.1287/isre.8.3.215

Klaus, H., Roseman, M., & Gable, G. (2000). What is ERP. *Information Systems Frontiers*, *2*(2), 141–162. doi:10.1023/A:1026543906354

Klein, B., & Leffler, K. (1981). The role of market forces in assuring contractual performance. *The Journal of Political Economy*, *89*(4), 615–641. doi:10.1086/260996

Klein, H. K., & Myers, M. D. (1999). A set of principles for conducting and evaluating interpretive field studies in information systems. *Management Information Systems Quarterly*, *23*(1), 67–93. doi:10.2307/249410

Kling, R. (1978). Automated welfare client-tracking and service integration: the political economy of computing. *Communications of the ACM, 21*(6), 484–493. doi:10.1145/359511.359528

Kling, R. (1980). Social analyses of computing: Theoretical perspectives in recent empirical research. *ACM Computing Surveys, 12*(1), 61–110. doi:10.1145/356802.356806

Kling, R., & Iacono, S. (1984). The control of information systems developments after implementation. *Communications of the ACM, 24*(12), 1218–1226. doi:10.1145/2135.358307

Knoke, D. (1990). *Organizing for collective action: The political economies of associations*. de Gruyter, New York.

Koufaris, M., & Hampton-Sosa, W. (2004). The development of initial trust in an online company by new customers. *Information & Management, 41*, 377–397. doi:10.1016/j.im.2003.08.004

Koulopoulos, T. (1995). *The workflow imperative*. New York: Van Nostrand Reinhold.

KPMG. (1998). *Supporting the decision maker—a guide to the value of business modeling.* Retrieved from http://www.kpmg.co.uk/uk/services/manage/press/970605.html

Kracher, B., Corritore, C. L., & Wiedenbeck, S. (2005). A foundation for understanding online trust in electronic commerce. *Information. Communications and Ethics in Society, 3*(3), 131–141. doi:10.1108/14779960580000267

Krackhardt, D., & Hansen, J. R. (1993). Informal networks: The company behind the chart. *Harvard Business Review, 71*, 104–111.

Kunda, Z. (2001). *Social Cognition: Making Sense of People*. Cambridge, MA: MIT Press.

Labour Movement. (2008, April 12). *The Economist, 387*(8575), 5-8.

Ladd, D. A., Datta, A., Sarker, S., & Yu, Y. (2010). Trends in Mobile Computing within the IS Discipline: A Ten-Year Retrospective. *Communications of the AIS, 27*, 285–306.

Lai, V. S., & Li, H. (2005). Technology acceptance model for Internet banking: An invariance analysis. *Information & Management, 42*(2), 373–386. doi:10.1016/j.im.2004.01.007

Lakoff, G., & Johnson, M. (1980). *Metaphors we live by*. Chicago: University of Chicago Press.

Lamb, R., & Kling, R. (2003). Reconceptualizing users as social actors in information systems research. *Management Information Systems Quarterly, 27*(2).

Larwood, L., Gutek, B. A., & Gattiker, U. E. (1984). Perspective on institutional discrimination and resistance to change. *Group and Organizational Studies, 9*, 333–352. doi:10.1177/105960118400900303

Lau, F., & Herbert, M. (2001). Experiences from health information system implementation projects reported in Canada between 1991 and 1997. *Journal of End User Computing, 13*(4), 17–25. doi:10.4018/joeuc.2001100102

Lawrence, R.J., & Lee, J. (2004). Financial modelling of project financing transactions. *Institute of Actuaries of Australia Financial Services Forum, 19.*

Lederer, A. L., Maupin, D. J., Sena, M. P., & Zhuang, Y. (2000). The technology acceptance model and the World Wide Web. *Decision Support Systems, 29*, 269–282. doi:10.1016/S0167-9236(00)00076-2

Lee, C., & Bobko, P. (1994). Self-efficacy beliefs: Comparison of five measures. *The Journal of Applied Psychology, 79*(3), 364–369. doi:10.1037/0021-9010.79.3.364

Lee, B. C., Ang, L., & Dubelaar, C. (2005). Lemons on the web: A signaling approach to the problem of trust in internet commerce. *Journal of Economic Psychology, 2*(5), 607–623. doi:10.1016/j.joep.2005.01.001

Lee, Z., & Lee, S. J. (2006). The effect of buyer feedback scores on internet auction prices. *Journal of Organizational Computing and Electronic Commerce, 16*(1), 51–64. doi:10.1080/10919390609540290

Lee, M. K. O., & Turban, E. (2001). A trust model for consumer internet shopping. *International Journal of Electronic Commerce, 6*(1), 75–91.

Lee, T. (2005). The Impact of Perceptions of Interactivity on Customer Trust and Transaction Intentions in Mobile Commerce. *Journal of Electronic Commerce Research, 6*(3), 165–181.

Lee, Y. J., & Shin, D. C. (2005). Performance of Caching Strategies for Pull-Based Data Broadcast Systems in Mobile Computing Environments. *Journal of Computer Information Systems*, *45*(4), 102–115.

Lee, C., & Bobko, P. (1994). Self-efficacy beliefs: Comparison of five measures. *The Journal of Applied Psychology*, *79*(3), 364–369. doi:10.1037/0021-9010.79.3.364

Legris, P., Ingham, J., & Collerette, P. (2003). Why do people use information technology? A critical review of the technology acceptance model. *Information & Management*, *40*, 191–204. doi:10.1016/S0378-7206(01)00143-4

Leonard-Barton, D., & Deschamps, I. (1988). Managerial influence on the implementation of new technology. *Management Science*, *34*(10), 1252–1265. doi:10.1287/mnsc.34.10.1252

LeRouge, C., Nelson, A., & Blanton, J. E. (2006). The impact of role stress fit and self-esteem on the job attitudes of IT professionals. *Information & Management*, *43*, 928–938. doi:10.1016/j.im.2006.08.011

Leuthesser, L. (2003). 2+2=5? A framework for using co-branding to leverage a brand. *Brand Management*, *11*(1), 35–47. doi:10.1057/palgrave.bm.2540146

Levinson, H. (1965). Reciprocation: The relationship between man and organization. *Administrative Science Quarterly*, *9*, 370–390. doi:10.2307/2391032

Lewicki, R., & Bunker, B. (1995). Trust in relationship. In Bunker, B., & Rubin, J. (Eds.), *Conflict, cooperation, and justice* (pp. 133–169). San Francisco, CA: Jossey-Bass Inc.

Lewicki, R., & Bunker, B. (1996). Developing and maintaining trust in work relationships. In Kramer, R., & Tyler, T. (Eds.), *Trust in organizations: Frontiers of theory and research* (pp. 114–139). Thousand Oaks, CA: Sage.

Lewicki, R. J., & Bunker, B. B. (1996). Developing and maintaining trust in work relationships. In Kramer, R. M., & Tyler, T. (Eds.), *Trust in organizations: Frontiers of theory and research* (pp. 114–139). Thousand Oaks, CA: Sage.

Lewis, J., & Weigert, A. (1985). Trust as a social reality. *Social Forces*, *63*, 967–985. doi:10.2307/2578601

Lewis, C. (1985). An exploratory study of the influences of self efficacy on the personal computer learner. *Dissertation Abstracts International*.

Liaw, S.-S. (2004). The theory of planned behavior applied to search engines as a learning tool. *Journal of Computer Assisted Learning*, *20*, 283–291. doi:10.1111/j.1365-2729.2004.00087.x

Lillibridge, J., & Lundstedt, S. (1967). Some initial evidence for an interpersonal risk theory. *The Journal of Psychology*, *66*, 119–128.

Limayem, M., Khalifa, M., & Chin, W. W. (2004). CASE tools usage and impact on system development performance. *Journal of Organizational Computing and Electronic Commerce*, *14*, 153–174. doi:10.1207/s15327744joce1403_01

Lin, W., & Shao, B. (2000). A relationship between user participation and system success: A simultaneous contingency approach. *Information & Management*, *37*(6), 283–295. doi:10.1016/S0378-7206(99)00055-5

Liu, C., Marchewka, J. T., Lu, J., & Yu, C. S. (2005). Beyond concern - A privacy-trust-behavioral intention model of electronic commerce. *Information & Management*, *42*, 289–304. doi:10.1016/j.im.2004.01.003

Locke, E. A. (1986). *Generalizing from laboratory to field setting: Research finding from industrial organization, organization behavior, and human resource management*. Lexington, MA: Lexington Books.

Locke, E. A. (1976). The nature and causes of job satisfaction. In Dunnette, M. (Ed.), *The handbook of industrial/organizational psychology* (1st ed., pp. 1297–1349). Chicago: Rand McNally.

Lohtia, R., Bello, D., & Porter, C. (2009). Building trust in US-Japanese business relationships: Mediating role of cultural sensitivity. *Industrial Marketing Management*, *38*(3), 239–252. doi:10.1016/j.indmarman.2007.06.016

Lonzinsky, S. (1998). *Enterprise-wide software solutions: Integration strategies and practices*. Reading, MA: Addison Wesley.

Looney, C. A., Jessup, L. M., & Valacich, J. S. (2004). Emerging Business Models for Mobile Brokerage Services. *Communications of the ACM*, *47*(6), 71–77. doi:10.1145/990680.990683

Lowry, P. B., Vance, A., Moody, G., Beckman, B., & Read, A. (2008). Explaining and predicting the impacts of brand alliances and web site quality on initial consumer trust of e-commerce web sites. *Journal of Management Information Systems*, *24*(4), 199–224. doi:10.2753/MIS0742-1222240408

Lowry, G. (2002). Modeling using acceptance of building management systems. *Automation in Construction*, *11*, 695–705. doi:10.1016/S0926-5805(02)00010-9

Lu, J., Liu, C., Yu, C., & Yao, J. E. (2003). Acceptance of Wireless Internet via Mobile Technology in China. *Proceedings of 2003 Americas Conference on Information Systems (AMCIS 2003)*, Tampa, FL, 1165-1173.

Luarn, P., & Lin, H.-H. (2005). Toward an understanding of the behavioral intention to use mobile banking. *Computers in Human Behavior*, *21*, 873–891. doi:10.1016/j.chb.2004.03.003

Lubove, S. (2002). Do Oil and Data Mix? *Forbes*, *169*, 76–77.

Lucas, H. C., & Spitler, V. K. (1999). Technology use and performance: A field study of broker workstations. *Decision Sciences*, *30*(2), 291–311. doi:10.1111/j.1540-5915.1999.tb01611.x

Lucas, H. C., Swanson, E. B., & Zmud, R. W. (2007). Implementation, innovation, and related themes over the years in information systems research. *Journal of the AIS*, *8*(4), 206–210.

Luhmann, N. (1979). *Trust and power*. Chichester, UK: Wiley.

Luhmann, N. (1988). Familiarity, confidence, trust: Problems and alternatives. In Gambetta, D. G. (Ed.), *Trust* (pp. 94–107). New York: Basil Blackwell.

Luo, X., Li, H., Zhang, J., & Shim, J. P. (2010). Examining multi-dimensional trust and multi-faceted risk in initial acceptance of emerging technologies: An empirical study of mobile banking services. *Decision Support Systems*, *49*, 222–234. doi:10.1016/j.dss.2010.02.008

Ma, Q., & Liu, L. (2004). The technology acceptance model: A meta-analysis of empirical findings. *Journal of Organizational and End User Computing*, *16*(1), 59–72. doi:10.4018/joeuc.2004010104

Maccoby, E., & Jacklin, C. (1994). *The psychology of sex differences*. New York: University Press.

Maddux, J. E., & Stanley, M. A. (1986). Self efficacy theory in contemporary psychology. *Journal of Social and Clinical Psychology*, *4*(3), 347–382. doi:10.1521/jscp.1986.4.3.249

Madsen, K. H. (1989). Breakthrough by breakdown: metaphors and structured domains. In H.K. Klein., & K. Kumar (Eds.), *Systems development for human progress*. Amsterdam: North-Holland, 41-53.

Maheswaranam, D., Mackie, D., & Chaiken, S. (1992). Brand name as a heuristic cue: The effects of task importance and expectancy confirmation on consumer judgments. *Journal of Consumer Psychology*, *1*(4), 317–336. doi:10.1016/S1057-7408(08)80058-7

Maier, M. (2005). Mobile technology-finding profits in the GPS economy. *Business 2.0*, 21-22.

Malhotra, N. K., Kim, S. S., & Agarwal, J. (2004). Internet Users' Information Privacy Concerns (IUIPC): The Construct, the Scale, and a Causal Model. *Information Systems Research*, *15*(4), 336–355. doi:10.1287/isre.1040.0032

Malhotra, Y., & Galletta, D. (2005). A multidimensional commitment model of volitional systems adoption and usage behavior. *Journal of Management Information Systems*, *22*, 117–151.

Malhotra, Y., & Galletta, D. F. (2004). Building systems that users want to use: Advancing beyond the rhetoric on "Does IT Matter". *Communications of the ACM*, *47*, 88–94. doi:10.1145/1035134.1035139

Malhotra, N. K., Kim, S. S., & Patil, A. (2006). Common method variance in IS research: A comparison of alternative approaches and a reanalysis of past research. *Management Science*, *52*, 1865–1883. doi:10.1287/mnsc.1060.0597

Malladi, R., & Agrawal, D. P. (2002). Current and Future Applications of Mobile and Wireless Networks. *Communications of the ACM*, *45*(10), 144–146. doi:10.1145/570907.570947

Manzoni, J., & Barsoux, J. (2002). *The set-up-to-fail syndrome. How good managers cause great people to fail*. Boston: Harvard Business School Press.

Marakas, G. M., Yi, M. Y., & Johnson, R. D. (1998). The multilevel and multifaceted character of computer self-efficacy: Toward clarification of the construct and an integrative framework for reason. *Information Systems Research*, *9*(2), 126–163. doi:10.1287/isre.9.2.126

Marakas, G. M., Johnson, R. D., & Clay, P. F. (2007). The evolving nature of the computer self-efficacy construct: An empirical investigation of measurement construction, validity, reliability and stability over time. *Journal of the Association for Information Systems*, *8*(1), 15–46.

Marakas, G. M., Yi, M. Y., & Johnson, R. D. (1998). The multilevel and multifaceted character of computer self-efficacy: Toward clarification of the construct and an integrative framework for research. *Information Systems Research*, *9*(2), 126–153. doi:10.1287/isre.9.2.126

Martin, J. (1993). *Principles of object-oriented analysis and design*. Upper Saddle River, NJ: Prentice-Hall.

Martocchio, J. J., & Webster, J. (1992). Effects of feedback and cognitive playfulness on performance in microcomputer software training. *Personnel Psychology*, *45*, 553–578. doi:10.1111/j.1744-6570.1992.tb00860.x

Mathieson, K. (1991). Predicting user intentions: Comparing the technology acceptance model with the theory of planned behavior. *Information Systems Research*, *2*(3), 173–191. doi:10.1287/isre.2.3.173

Mayer, R. C., Davis, J. H., & Schoorman, F. D. (1995). An integrative model of organizational trust. *Academy of Management Review*, *20*(3), 709–735. doi:10.2307/258792

Mayers, L. S., Gamst, G., & Guarino, A. J. (2006). *Applied multivariate research. Design and interpretations*. Thousands Oaks, CA: Sage.

Mazis, M., Settle, R., & Leslie, D. (1973). Elimination of phosphate detergents and psychological reactance. *JMR, Journal of Marketing Research*, *X*, 390–395. doi:10.2307/3149386

McAllister, D. J. (1995). Affect- and cognition-based trust as foundations for interpersonal cooperation in organizations. *Academy of Management Journal*, *38*(1), 24–59. doi:10.2307/256727

McClindon, A. (2001). Strong on-line brands enhance sales, http://www.enn.ie/news.html?code=4236914.

McCloskey, D. W. (2006). The importance of ease of use, usefulness, and trust to online consumers: An examination of the technology acceptance model with older consumers. *Journal of Organizational and End User Computing*, *18*(3), 47–65. doi:10.4018/joeuc.2006070103

McClure, C. R., Wyman, S. K., Beachboard, J. B., & Eschenfelder, K. R. (1997). Developing system-based and user-based criteria for assessing federal websites. *Journal of the American Society for Information Science American Society for Information Science*, *34*, 78–88.

McCormick, M., & Martinko, M. J. (2004). Social cognitive theory and leadership research: Toward a causal reasoning perspective. *Proceedings of the Southern Management Association*.

McCourt, W. (1997). Discussion note: using metaphors to understand and to change organizations: A critique of Gareth Morgan's approach. *Organization Studies*, *18*(3), 511–522. doi:10.1177/017084069701800307

McCoy, S., Everard, A., & Jones, B. M. (2005). An examination of the technology acceptance model in Uruguay and the U.S.: A focus on culture. *Journal of Global Information Technology Management*, *8*(2), 27–45.

McFarlan, F. W., & Nolan, R. L. (1975). *The information systems handbook*. Homewood, IL: Down Jones-Irwin.

McFarlan, F. W., Nolan, R. L., & Norton, D. P. (1973). *Information systems administration*. New York: Holt, Rinehart and Winston.

McFarlan, F. W. (1984). Information Technology Changes the Way You Compete. *Harvard Business Review*, *62*(3), 98–103.

McFarland, D. J., & Hamilton, D. (2006). Adding contextual specificity to the technology acceptance model. *Computers in Human Behavior*, *22*, 427–447. doi:10.1016/j.chb.2004.09.009

McGee, M. (1979). Human spatial abilities, psychometric studies and environmental, genetic, hormonal, and neurological influences. *Psychological Bulletin*, *86*, 889–918. doi:10.1037/0033-2909.86.5.889

McGill, T. (2004). The effect of end user development on end user success. *Journal of Organizational and End User Computing*, *16*(1), 41–58. doi:10.4018/joeuc.2004010103

McGrath, J. E., Martin, J., & Kulka, R. (1984). *Judgment Calls in Research*. Beverly Hills, CA: Sage Publications.

Mcknight, D. H., Kacmar, C. J., & Choudhury, V. (2004). Shifting factors and the ineffectiveness of third party assurance seals: A two-stage model of initial trust in a web business. *Electronic Markets*, *14*(1), 252–266. doi:10.1080/10196780420000245263

McKnight, D., Choudhury, V., & Kacmar, C. (2002). The impact of initial consumer trust on intentions to transact with a Web site: a trust building model. *The Journal of Strategic Information Systems*, *11*(3-4), 297–323. doi:10.1016/S0963-8687(02)00020-3

McKnight, D., Cummings, L., & Chervany, N. (1998). Initial trust formation in new organizational relationships. *Academy of Management Review*, *23*(3), 473–490. doi:10.2307/259290

McKnight, D. H., & Chervany, N. L. (2001). What trust means in e-commerce customer relationships: An interdisciplinary conceptual typology. *International Journal of Electronic Commerce*, *6*(2), 35–59.

McKnight, D. H., Choudhury, V., & Kacmar, C. (2002). Developing and validating trust measures for e-commerce: An integrative typology. *Information Systems Research*, *13*(3), 334–359. doi:10.1287/isre.13.3.334.81

McKnight, D. H., Cummings, L. L., & Chervany, N. L. (1998). Initial trust formation in new organizational relationships. *Academy of Management Review*, *23*(3), 473–490. doi:10.2307/259290

McKnight, D. H., Kacmar, C., & Choudhury, V. (2004). Shifting factors and the Ineffectiveness of third party assurance seals: A two-stage model of initial trust in a web business. *Electronic Markets*, *14*(3), 252–266. doi:10.1080/10196780420000245263

McKnight, D. H., & Chervany, N. L. (2001-2002). What trust means in e-commerce customer relationships: an interdisciplinary conceptual typology. *International Journal of Electronic Commerce*, *6*, 235–260.

McNight, D. H., Kacmar, C. J., & Choudhury, V. (2004). Shifting factors and the ineffectiveness of third party assurance seals: A two-stage model of initial trust in a Web business. *Electronic Markets*, *14*(3), 252–266. doi:10.1080/10196780420000245263

Merrilees, B., & Fry, M. (2003). E-trust the influence of perceived interactivity on e-retailing uses. *Marketing Intelligence & Planning*, *21*(2), 123–128. doi:10.1108/02634500310465461

Meyer, J. P., & Allen, N. J. (1991). Development of organizational commitment. *Human Resource Management Review*, *1*, 61–89. doi:10.1016/1053-4822(91)90011-Z

Meyers-Levy, J., & Maheswaran, D. (1991). Exploring differences in males' and females' processing strategies. *The Journal of Consumer Research*, *18*(1), 63–70. doi:10.1086/209241

Meyers-Levy, J., & Sternthal, B. (1991). Gender differences in the use of message cues and judgments. *JMR, Journal of Marketing Research*, *28*(1), 84–96. doi:10.2307/3172728

Meyerson, D., Weick, K. E., & Kramer, R. M. (1996). Swift trust and temporary groups. In Kramer, R. M., & Tyler, T. R. (Eds.), *Trust in Organizations: Frontiers of Theory and Research* (pp. 166–195). Thousand Oaks, CA: Sage Publications.

Milam, M. (2008). The rise of brandjacking against major brands. *Computer Fraud & Security*, (October): 10–13. doi:10.1016/S1361-3723(08)70149-0

Milchram, E. (2003). Modeling the acceptance of information technology: System trust, ease of use and usefulness. Fine tuning information strategies. *Proceedings of the 9th Annual Conference on Professional Information Resources,* Prague, Czech Republic.

Millan, E., & Mittal, B. (2010). Advertising's new audiences: Consumer response in the new free market economies of central and eastern Europe-The case of the Czech republic. *Journal of Advertising*, *39*(3), 81–98. doi:10.2753/JOA0091-3367390300

Miller, G. A. (1956). The Magical Number Seven, Plus or Minus Two: Some Limits on Our Capacity for Processing Information. *Psychological Review*, *63*, 81–97. doi:10.1037/h0043158

Miranda, S., & Bostrom, R. (1993). The impact of group support systems on group conflict and conflict management. *Journal of Management Information Systems*, *10*(3), 63–95.

Mishra, A. K. (1996). Organizational responses to crisis: The centrality of trust. In Kramer, R. M., & Tyler, T. (Eds.), *Trust in Organizations* (pp. 261–287). Newbury Park, CA: Sage Publications.

Mitchell, T. R., Hopper, H., Daniels, D., George-Falvy, J., & James, L. R. (1994). Predicting self-efficacy and performance during skill acquisition. *The Journal of Applied Psychology*, *79*, 506–517. doi:10.1037/0021-9010.79.4.506

Miyazaki, A. D., & Fernandez, A. (2001). Consumer perceptions of privacy and security risks for online shopping. *The Journal of Consumer Affairs*, *35*(1), 27–45. doi:10.1111/j.1745-6606.2001.tb00101.x

Miyazaki, A. D., & Fernandez, A. (2000). Internet privacy and security: An examination of online retailer disclosures. *Journal of Public Policy & Marketing*, *19*(1), 54–61. doi:10.1509/jppm.19.1.54.16942

Mone, M. A. (1994). Comparative validity of two measures of self-efficacy in predicting academic goals and performance. *Educational and Psychological Measurement*, *54*(2), 516–529. doi:10.1177/0013164494054002026

Money, R. B., Gilly, M. C., & Granham, J. L. (1998). Explorations of national culture and word-of-mouth referral behavior in the purchase of industrial services in the United States and Japan. *Journal of Marketing*, *62*, 76–87. doi:10.2307/1252288

Montgomery, A., & Smith, M. D. (2008) Prospects for personalization on the internet. Available at SSRN: http://ssrn.com/abstract=1169874

Moon, J.-W., & Kim, Y.-G. (2001). Extending the TAM for a World Wide Web context. *Information & Management*, *38*, 217–230. doi:10.1016/S0378-7206(00)00061-6

Moore, J. E. (2000). One road to turnover: An examination of work exhaustion in technology professionals. *Management Information Systems Quarterly*, *24*(1), 141–168. doi:10.2307/3250982

More than a Billion Mobile Workers Worldwide by Year's End. (2010). *IDC Press Release*. Retrieved from http://www.idc.com/getdoc.jsp?containerId=prUS22214110

Morgan, G. (1980). Paradigms, metaphors and puzzle solving in organization theory. *Administrative Science Quarterly*, *25*(4), 605–622. doi:10.2307/2392283

Morgan, G. (1997). *Images of organization. New edition*. USA: Sage Publications.

Morris, M. G., & Venkatesh, V. (2000). Age differences in technology adoption decisions: Implications for a changing workforce. *Personnel Psychology*, *53*(2), 375–403. doi:10.1111/j.1744-6570.2000.tb00206.x

Morrison, D. E., & Firmstone, J. (2000). The social function of trust and implications for e-commerce. *International Journal of Advertising*, *19*(5), 599–624.

Mowday, R. T., Porter, L. W., & Steers, R. M. (1982). *Employee-organization linkages: The psychology of commitment and absenteeism and turnover*. New York: Academic Press.

Mucha, T. (2003, May 1). We're in trouble.com: Got bad news? Use the web to spill it. Fast. *Business 2.0* Retrieved June 15, 2004, from www.business2.com.

Mullaney, T. J., & Weintraub, A. (2005, March 28). The digital hospital: How info tech saves lives and money at one medical center. Is this the future of health care? *BusinessWeek*, 77-84.

Multon, K. D., Brown, S. D., & Lent, R. W. (1991). Relation of self efficacy beliefs to academic outcomes: A meta-analytic investigation. *Journal of Counseling Psychology*, *38*, 30–38. doi:10.1037/0022-0167.38.1.30

Mumford, E., & Weir, M. (1979). *Computer systems in work design: The ETHICS method*. New York: Wiley.

Munro, M. C., Huff, S. L., Marcolin, B. L., & Compeau, D. R. (1997). Understanding and measuring user competence. *Information & Management*, *33*, 45–57. doi:10.1016/S0378-7206(97)00035-9

Murphy, C. A., Coover, D., & Owen, S. V. (1989). Development and validation of the Computer Self-efficacy scale. *Educational and Psychological Measurement*, *49*(2), 893–899. doi:10.1177/001316448904900412

Nadan, R. K. (1997). *The dialectic of management control: The Case of the Fiji Development Bank*, PhD Thesis. UK: Bristol University, 1997.

Nadkarni, S., & Gupta, R. (2007). A Task-Based Model of Perceived Website Complexity. *Management Information Systems Quarterly*, *31*(3), 501–524.

Nahl, D., & Tenopir, C. (1996). Affective and cognitive searching behavior of novice end-users of a full-text database. *Journal of the American Society for Information Science American Society for Information Science, 47*(4), 276–286. doi:10.1002/(SICI)1097-4571(199604)47:4<276::AID-ASI3>3.0.CO;2-U

Nan Si, S., & Murthy, V. (2003). *Architecture issues of Web-enabled electronic business*. Hershey, PA: Idea Group Publishing.

Nath, D., Sridhar, V., Adya, M., & Malik, A. (2008). Project quality of off-shore virtual teams engaged in software requirements analysis: An exploratory comparative study. *Journal of Global Information Management, 16*(4), 24–45. doi:10.4018/jgim.2008100102

Navy and Marines Lead Federal IT Spending. (2005, December 1)... *Aerospace Daily & Defense Report, 216*(42), 5.

Ndubisi, N. O., & Jantan, M. (2003). Evaluating IS usage in Malaysian small and medium-sized firms using the technology acceptance model. *Logistics Information Management, 16*(6), 440–450. doi:10.1108/09576050310503411

Near, J. P. (1989). Organizational commitment among Japanese and U.S. workers. *Organization Studies, 10*(3), 281–301. doi:10.1177/017084068901000301

Neiberg, M. S. (2000). *Making Citizen Soldiers: ROTC*. Cambridge, MA: Harvard University Press.

Nelson, P. (1974). Advertising as information. *The Journal of Political Economy, 82*(4), 729–754. doi:10.1086/260231

Nelson, K. M., & Cooprider, J. G. (1996). The Contribution of Shared Knowledge to IS Group Performance. *Management Information Systems Quarterly, 20*(4), 409–432. doi:10.2307/249562

Netemeyer, R. G., Bearden, W. O., & Sharma, S. (2003). *Scaling Procedures Issues and Applications*. Thousand Oaks, CA: Sage Publications.

Ngai, E. W. T., Poon, J. K. L., & Chan, Y. H. C. (2007). Empirical examination of the adoption of WebCT using TAM. *Computers & Education, 48*(2), 250–267. doi:10.1016/j.compedu.2004.11.007

Ngai, E. W. T., & Gunasekaran, A. (2005). A Review for Mobile Commerce Research and Applications. *Decision Support Systems, 43*, 3–15. doi:10.1016/j.dss.2005.05.003

Niederman, F., Brancheau, J. C., & Wetherbe, J. C. (1991). Information Systems Management Issues for the 1990s. *MIS Quarterly, 15*(4), 474–500. doi:10.2307/249452

Nielsen, J. (2000). *Design web usability*. Indianapolis, IN: New Riders Publishing.

NIIT. (1990). *CRISPLAN, version 1, release 2 (company internal note)*. New Delhi: Author.

Nolan, R. L. (2001). Information Technology Management from 1960-2000 (pp. 1-31). Cambridge: Harvard Business School.

Noonan, P. (2010, August 20). Immediacy is nothing new. *The Wall Street Journal*. Retrieved 7 October, 2010 from http://online.wsj.com.

Nunnally, J. C., & Bernstein, I. H. (1994). *Psychometric Theory* (3rd ed.). New York: McGraw-Hill, Inc.

Oates, B. J., & Fitzgerald, B. (2007). Multi-metaphor method: organizational metaphors in information systems development. *Information Systems Journal, 17*(4), 421–449. doi:10.1111/j.1365-2575.2007.00266.x

Okoli, C., Ives, B., Jessup, L. M., & Valacich, J. S. (2002) The Mobile Conference Information System: Unwiring Academic Conferences with Wireless Mobile Computing. *Communications of the AIS*, 9, 180-206.

Oliver, R. L. (1980). A cognitive model for the antecedents and consequences of satisfaction. *JMR, Journal of Marketing Research, 17*, 460–469. doi:10.2307/3150499

Oliver, R. L. (1981). Measurement and evaluation of satisfaction processes in retail settings. *Journal of Retailing, 57*(3), 25–48.

Oliver, R. L. (1993). Cognitive, affective, and attitude bases of the satisfaction response. *The Journal of Consumer Research, 20*, 418–430. doi:10.1086/209358

Oliver, T. A., & Shapiro, F. (1993). Self efficacy and computers. *Journal of Computer-Based Interactions, 20*, 81–85.

Ong, C.-S., & Lai, J.-Y. (2006). Gender differences in perceptions and relationships among dominant of e-learning acceptance. *Computers in Human Behavior, 22*, 816–829. doi:10.1016/j.chb.2004.03.006

Ong, C.-S., Lai, J.-Y., & Wang, Y.-S. (2004). Factors affecting engineers' acceptance of asynchronous e-learning systems in high tech companies. *Information & Management, 41*, 795–804. doi:10.1016/j.im.2003.08.012

Orlikowski, W. J., & Baroudi, J. J. (1991). Studying information technology in organizations: research approaches and assumptions. *Information Systems Research*, (2): 1–28. doi:10.1287/isre.2.1.1

Orlikowski, W. J., & Gash, D. C. (1994). Technological frames: Making sense of information technology in organizations. *ACM Transactions on Information Systems, 12*(2), 174–207. doi:10.1145/196734.196745

Orlikowski, W. J. (2000). Using technology and constituting structures: A practice lens for studying technology in organizations. *Organization Science, 11*, 404–428. doi:10.1287/orsc.11.4.404.14600

Ortony, A. (1975). Why metaphors are necessary and not just nice. *Educational Theory, 25*, 45–53. doi:10.1111/j.1741-5446.1975.tb00666.x

Oswick, C., & Grant, D. (1996). *Organisation development - metaphorical exploration*. London: Pitman.

Oudan, R. (2010). Strategic decision-making in the emerging field of e-Commerce, International. *Journal of Management Information Systems, 14*(2), 19–26.

Our Nomadic Future. (2008, April 12). *The Economist*. 387(8575), 16-16.

Ozkan, S., Bindusara, G., & Hackney, R. (2010). Facilitating the adoption of e-payment systems: Theoretical constructs and empirical analysis. *Journal of Enterprise Information Management, 23*(3), 305–325. doi:10.1108/17410391011036085

Pagani, M. (2004). Determinants of adoption of third generation mobile multimedia services. *Journal of Interactive Marketing, 18*(3), 46–59. doi:10.1002/dir.20011

Panko, R. (2005). *What we know about spreadsheet errors.* Retrieved September 2, 2006, from http://panko.cba.hawaii.edu/ssr/Mypapers/whatknow.htm

Panko, R., & Halverson, R. (1996). Spreadsheets on trial: A survey of research on spreadsheet risks. *Proceedings of the 29th Annual Hawaii International Conference on Systems Sciences* (pp. 326-335).

Parasuraman, S., Greenhaus, J. H., & Granrose, C. S. (1992). Role stressors, social support, and well-being among two-career couples. *Journal of Organizational Behavior, 13*, 339–356. doi:10.1002/job.4030130403

Parise, S., & Henderson, J. C. (2001). Knowledge Resource Exchange in Strategic Alliances. *IBM Systems Journal, 40*(4), 908–924.

Parks, M., & Floyd, K. (1996). Making friends in cyberspace. *The Journal of Communication, 46*(1), 80–98. doi:10.1111/j.1460-2466.1996.tb01462.x

Pavlou, P. A., & Chai, L. (2002). What drives electronic commerce across cultures? A cross-cultural empirical investigation of the theory of planned behavior. *Journal of Electronic Commerce Research, 3*(4), 240–253.

Pavlou, P. A., & Gefen, D. (2004). Building effective online marketplaces with institution-based trust. *Information Systems Research, 15*(1), 37–59. doi:10.1287/isre.1040.0015

Pavlou, P. A. (2003). Consumer acceptance of electronic commerce: Integrating trust and risk with the technology acceptance model. *International Journal of Electronic Commerce, 7*(3), 101–134.

Pavlou, P. A., & Fygenson, M. (2006). Understanding and predicting electronic commerce adoption: An extension of the theory of planned behavior. *Management Information Systems Quarterly, 30*(1), 115–143.

Pavlou, P. A., & Gefen, D. (2004). Building effective online marketplaces with institution-based trust. *Information Systems Research, 15*(1), 37–59. doi:10.1287/isre.1040.0015

Pavlou, P. A., & Chai, L. (2002). What drives electronic commerce across cultures? A cross-cultural empirical investigation of the theory of planned behavior. *Journal of Electronic Commerce Research, 3*(4), 240–253.

Pavlou, P. A., & Chellappa, R. K. (2001). The role of perceived privacy and perceived security in the development of trust in electronic commerce transaction. Unpublished Working paper.

Payne, J. W. (1982). Contingent Decision Behavior. *Psychological Bulletin, 92*(2), 382–402. doi:10.1037/0033-2909.92.2.382

Peak, D., Guynes, C. S., & Kroon, V. (2005). Information technology alignment planning—a case study. *Information & Management, 42*(5), 635–649. doi:10.1016/j.im.2004.02.009

Pennanen, K. (2006). How consumers build trust in e-commerce: Towards a trust formation model. *Advances in Consumer Research-Latin American Conference Proceedings, 1*, 38-43.

Pennington, R., Wilcox, H. D., & Grover, V. (2003). The role of system trust in business-to-consumer transactions. *Journal of Management Information Systems, 20*(3), 197–226.

Pennington, R., & Tuttle, B. (2007). The effects of immediacy on software project risk assessment. *Decision Sciences, 38*(3), 489–526. doi:10.1111/j.1540-5915.2007.00167.x

Pepper, S. (1942). *World Hypotheses: a study in evidence*. California: University of California Press.

Periasamy, K. P., & Feeny, D. F. (1997). Information Architecture Practice: Research-Based Recommendations for the Practitioner. *Journal of Information Technology, 12*(3), 197–205. doi:10.1080/026839697345062

Pervan, G. (1998). How Chief Executive Officers in Large Organizations View The Management of Their Information Systems. *Journal of Information Technology, 13*(2), 95–109. doi:10.1080/026839698344882

Peter, M. (1995). Spatial ability, student gender, and academic performance. *Journal of Engineering Education, 84*(1), 69–73.

Peterson, R., & Ross, I. (1972). How to name new brands. *Journal of Advertising, 12*(6), 29–34.

Petrides, K. V., Furnham, A., & Martin, G. N. (2004). Estimates of emotional and psychometric intelligence. *The Journal of Social Psychology, 144*(2), 149–162. doi:10.3200/SOCP.144.2.149-162

Philips, J. T. (2002). Welcome to the New Wireless Culture. *Information Management Journal, 36*(1), 64–68.

Pijpers, G. G. M., Bemelmans, T. M. A., Heemstra, F. J., & van Montfort, K. A. G. M. (2001). Senior executives' use of information technology. *Information and Software Technology, 43*, 959–971. doi:10.1016/S0950-5849(01)00197-5

Podsakoff, P. M., MacKenzie, S. B., Lee, J.-Y., & Podsakoff, N. P. (2003). Common method biases in behavioral research: A critical review of the literature and recommended remedies. *The Journal of Applied Psychology, 88*, 879–903. doi:10.1037/0021-9010.88.5.879

Polley, D. (1997). Turbulence in organizations: New metaphors for organizational research. *Organization Science, 8*(5), 445–457. doi:10.1287/orsc.8.5.445

Porra, J., Hirschheim, R., & Parks, M. S. (2005). The history of Texaco's corporate information technology function: A general systems theoretical interpretation. *Management Information Systems Quarterly, 29*, 721–746.

Porter, L. W., Steers, R. M., Mowday, R. T., & Boulian, P. (1974). Organizational commitment, job satisfaction and turnover among psychiatric technicians. *The Journal of Applied Psychology, 59*(5), 603–609. doi:10.1037/h0037335

Porter, M. E., & Millar, V. E. (1985). How information technology gives you competitive advantage. *Harvard Business Review, 63*(4), 149–160.

Poulsen, K. (2007). Patching up the leaky corporation. *Business 2.0*. Retrieved 20 May, 2007 from http://money.cnn.com.

Powell, J. (2009). *33 Million People in the Room*. Upper Saddle River, NJ: FT Press.

Prasopoulou, E., Pouloudi, A., & Panteli, N. (2006). Enacting New Temporal Boundaries: The Role of Mobile Phones. *European Journal of Information Systems, 15*(3), 227–284. doi:10.1057/palgrave.ejis.3000617

Prince, M. (2005, March 21). Help (may be) on the way. *The Wall Street Journal*, pp. R13-14.

Purser, M., & Chadwick, D. (2006). Does an awareness of differing types of spreadsheet errors aid end-users in identifying spreadsheet errors? *Proceedings of the European Spreadsheet Risk Interest Group Annual Conference* (pp. 185-204), Cambridge, UK.

Pyburn, P. J. (1983). Linking the MIS plan with corporate strategy: An exploratory study. *Management Information Systems Quarterly*, *7*(2), 1–14. doi:10.2307/248909

Raghu-Nathan, B., Ragu-Nathan, T. S., Tu, Q., & Shi, Z. (2001). Information Management (IM) Strategy: The Construct and Its Measure. *The Journal of Strategic Information Systems*, *10*(4), 265–289. doi:10.1016/S0963-8687(01)00053-1

Rajalingham, K., Chadwick, D., & Knight, B. (2000). Classification of spreadsheet errors. *Proceedings of the European Spreadsheet Risks Interest Group Annual Conference* (pp. 23-34), Greenwich, England.

Ranganathan, C., & Ganapathy, S. (2002). Key dimensions of business-to-consumer web sites. *Information & Management*, *39*(6), 457–465. doi:10.1016/S0378-7206(01)00112-4

Rather, J., & Grose, E. M. (1996). Characterization and assessment of HTML style guides. *CHI*, *96*, 115–116.

Reed, W. M., & Oughton, J. M. (1997). Computer experience and interval-based hypermedia navigation. *Journal of Research on Computing in Education*, *30*(1), 38–42.

Reich, B. H., & Benbasat, I. (1996). Measuring the linkage between business and information technology objectives. *MIS Quarterly*, *20*(1), 55–81. doi:10.2307/249542

Reich, B. H., & Benbasat, I. (2000). Factors That Influence the Social Dimension of Alignment between Business and Information Technology Objectives. *MIS Quarterly*, *24*(1), 81–113. doi:10.2307/3250980

Reichheld, F. F., & Schefter, P. (2000). E-loyalty: Your secret weapon on the Web. *Harvard Business Review*, *78*(4), 105–113.

Rempel, J. K., Holmes, J. G., & Zanna, M. P. (1985). Trust in close relationships? *Journal of Personality and Social Psychology*, *49*(1), 95–112. doi:10.1037/0022-3514.49.1.95

Ren, (2000). Library instruction and college student self-sufficiency in electronic information searching. *Journal of Academic Librarianship*, *26*(5), 323-328.

Rhoades, L., & Eisenberger, R. (2002). Perceived organizational support: A review of the literature. *The Journal of Applied Psychology*, *87*, 698–714. doi:10.1037/0021-9010.87.4.698

Rice, R. E., & Aydin, C. (1991). Attitudes toward new technology: Network proximity as a mechanism for social information processing. *Administrative Science Quarterly*, *36*, 219–244. doi:10.2307/2393354

Richardson, G. L., & Jackson, B. M. (1990). A Principles-Based Enterprise Architecture: Lessons Learned from Texaco and Star Enterprise. *MIS Quarterly*, *14*(4), 385–403. doi:10.2307/249787

Ricoeur, P. (1978). The metaphorical process as cognition, imagination and feeling. In Sacks, S. (Ed.), *On metaphors*. Chicago: University of Chicago Press.

Ridings, C. M., Gefen, D., & Arinze, B. (2002). Some antecedents and effects of trust in virtual communities. *The Journal of Strategic Information Systems*, *11*(3), 271–295. doi:10.1016/S0963-8687(02)00021-5

Riedl, R., Hubert, M., & Kenning, P. (2010). Are there neural gender differences in online trust? An fMRI Study on the Perceived Trustworthiness of eBay Offers. *Management Information Systems Quarterly*, *34*(2), 397–428.

Ring, P., & Van de Ven, A. (1994). Developmental processes of cooperative interorganizational relationships. *Academy of Management Review*, *19*, 90–118. doi:10.2307/258836

Roberts, P., & Henderson, R. (2000). Information technology acceptance in a sample of government employees: A test of the technology acceptance model. *Interacting with Computers*, *12*, 427–443. doi:10.1016/S0953-5438(98)00068-X

Rohloff, M. (1996). Reference model and object oriented approach for business process design and workflow management. In *Proceedings of IEEE*.

Rose, G., Khoo, H., & Straub, D. W. (1999). Current technological impediments to business-to-consumer electronic commerce. *Communications of the AIS*, *1*(16), 1–74.

Rose, G., & Straub, D. (1998). Predicting general IT use: Applying TAM to the Arabic world. *Journal of Global Information Management*, *6*(3), 39–46.

Rosen, D. E., & Purinton, E. (2004). Website design: Viewing the web as a cognitive landscape. *Journal of Business Research*, *57*(7), 787–794. doi:10.1016/S0148-2963(02)00353-3

Rosenthal, R., & Rosnow, R. L. (1991). *Essentials of Behavioral Research: Methods and Data Analysis* (2nd ed.). Boston, MA: McGraw-Hill.

Ross, J. W. (2003). Creating a Strategic IT Architecture Competence: Learning in Stages. *MIS Quarterly Executive*, *2*(1), 31–43.

Ross, J. W., & Beath, C. M. (2006). Sustainable IT Outsourcing Success: Let Enterprise Architecture be Your Guide. *MIS Quarterly Executive*, *5*(4), 181–192.

Ross, J. W., Weill, P., & Robertson, D. (2006). Enterprise Architecture As Strategy: Creating a Foundation for Business Execution. Boston: Harvard Business School Press.

Rothfeder, J. (2006, September 5). The death of privacy. *CIO Insight*. Retrieved 20 May, 2007, from http://www.cioinsight.com/c/a/Past-News/The-Death-of-Privacy/2/.

Rotondo, D., Carlson, D., & Kincaid, J. (2003). Coping with multiple dimensions of work-family conflict. *Personnel Review*, *32*, 275–297. doi:10.1108/00483480310467606

Rotter, J. (1971). Generalized expectancies for interpersonal trust. *The American Psychologist*, *26*(5), 443–452. doi:10.1037/h0031464

Rotter, J. (1980). Interpersonal trust, trustworthiness, and gullibility. *The American Psychologist*, *35*(1), 1–7. doi:10.1037/0003-066X.35.1.1

Rotter, J., Hamsher, J., & Geller, J. (1968). Interpersonal trust, internal-external control, and the Warren commission report. *Journal of Personality and Social Psychology*, *9*, 210–215. doi:10.1037/h0025900

Rotter, J. B. (1971). Generalized expectancies for interpersonal trust. *The American Psychologist*, *26*, 443–452. doi:10.1037/h0031464

Rousseau, D. M., Sitkin, S. B., Burt, R. S., & Camerer, C. (1998). Not so different after all: a cross-discipline view of trust. *Academy of Management Review*, *23*(3), 393–404.

Rubin, Z., & Shenker, S. (1978). Friendship, proximity, and self-disclosure. *Journal of Personality*, *46*, 1–23. doi:10.1111/j.1467-6494.1978.tb00599.x

Rubinfeld, D. L., & Singer, H. J. (2001). Vertical Foreclosure in Broadband Access? *The Journal of Industrial Economics*, *49*(3), 299–318.

Rumelhart, D., Widrow, B., & Lehr, M. A. (1994). The basic ideas in neural networks. *Communications of the ACM*, *37*(3), 87–92. doi:10.1145/175247.175256

Rumelhart, D. & McClelland, J. & PDP Research Group (1986). *Parallel distributed processing: Explorations in the microstructure of cognition* (Vol. 1)*: Foundations*. Cambridge: MIT Press.

Ruparelia, N., White, L., & Hughes, K. (2010). Drivers of brand trust in internet retailing. *Journal of Product and Brand Management*, *19*(4), 250–260. doi:10.1108/10610421011059577

Ruppel, C. P., & Harrington, S. J. (2000). The relationship of communication, ethical work climate, and trust to commitment and innovation. *Journal of Business Ethics*, *25*, 313–328. doi:10.1023/A:1006290432594

Russo, F. (2007, May 1). Taking the 'wait' out of 'Waiter!' *Business 2.0*, 31.

Ruth, J., & Simonin, B. (2003). Brought to You by brand A and brand B. *Journal of Advertising*, *32*(3), 19–30.

Ruyter, K. D., Moorman, L., & Lemmink, J. (2001). Antecedents of commitment and trust in customer–supplier relationships in high technology markets. *Industrial Marketing Management*, *30*, 271–286. doi:10.1016/S0019-8501(99)00091-7

Saade, R., & Bahli, B. (2005). The impact of cognitive absorption on perceived usefulness and perceived ease of use in on-line learning: An extension of the technology acceptance model. *Information & Management*, *42*, 317–327. doi:10.1016/j.im.2003.12.013

Sabherwal, R., Jeyaraj, A., & Chowa, C. (2006). Information system success: Individual and organizational determinants. *Management Science*, *52*(12), 1849–1864. doi:10.1287/mnsc.1060.0583

Sabherwal, R., & Chan, Y. E. (2001). Alignment between Business and IS Strategies: A Study of Prospectors, Analyzers, and Defenders. *Information Systems Research*, *12*(1), 11–33. doi:10.1287/isre.12.1.11.9714

Sacco, A. (2008, April 28). Inside Pitney Bowes choice for a mobile CRM/ERP solution. *CIO.* Retrieved September 1, 2008, from http://www.cio.com/article/print/342763.

Sacks, S. (Ed.). (1978). *On metaphors*. Chicago: University of Chicago Press.

Salancik, G. R., & Pfeffer, J. (1978). A social information processing approach to job attitudes and task design. *Administrative Science Quarterly*, *23*, 224–253. doi:10.2307/2392563

Salanova, M., Peiro, J. M., & Schaufeli, W. B. (2002). Self-efficacy specificity and burnout among information technology workers: An extension of the job demand-control model. *European Journal of Work and Organizational Psychology*, *11*, 1–25. doi:10.1080/13594320143000735

Salisbury, D. W., Pearson, R. A., Pearson, A. W., & Miller, D. W. (2001). Perceived security and World Wide Web purchase. *Industrial Management & Data Systems*, *101*(3/4), 165–176. doi:10.1108/02635570110390071

Sambamurthy, V. (2000). Business strategy in hypercompetitive environments: Rethinking the logic of IT differentiation. In Zmud, R. W. (Ed.), *Framing the Domains of IT Management: Projecting the Future Through the Past* (pp. 65–104). Cincinnati, Ohio: Pinnaflex Educational Resources.

San Martin, S., & Camarero, C. (2008). Consumer trust to a website: Moderating effect of attitudes toward online shopping. *Cyberpsychology & Behavior*, *11*(5), 549–554. doi:10.1089/cpb.2007.0097

Sanders, G. S., Baron, R. S., & Moore, D. L. (1978). Distraction and Social Comparison as Mediators of Social Facilitation Effects. *Journal of Experimental Social Psychology*, *14*(3), 291–303. doi:10.1016/0022-1031(78)90017-3

Sangwan, R., Bass, M., Mullick, N., Paulish, D. J., & Kazmeier, J. (2007). *Global software development handbook*. Boca Raton, FL: Auerbach.

Sarker, S., & Wells, J. D. (2003). Understanding Mobile Handheld Device Use and Adoption. *Communications of the ACM*, *46*(12), 35–40. doi:10.1145/953460.953484

Sawhney, M., Prandelli, E., & Verona, G. (2003). The power of innomediation. *MIT Sloan Management Review* (Winter 2003), 77-82.

Schaik, P. (1999). Involving users in the specification of functionality using scenarios and model-based evaluation. *Behaviour & Information Technology*, *18*(6), 455–466. doi:10.1080/014492999118878

Scharl, A., & Bauer, C. (1999). Explorative analysis and evaluation of commercial web information systems. In *Proceedings of the Twentieth International Conference on Information Systems* (pp. 534-539), Charlotte, North Carolina.

Scheer, A. (1989). *Enterprise-wide data modeling: Information systems in industry*. Berlin, Germany: Springer-Verlag.

Scheer, A. (1992). *Architecture of integrated information systems: Foundations of enterprise-modeling*. Berlin, Germany: Springer-Verlag.

Scheer, A. (1994). *Business process engineering: Reference models for industrial enterprises* (2nd ed.). Berlin, Germany: Springer-Verlag.

Schoder, D., & Haenlein, M. (2004). The relative importance of different trust constructs for sellers in the online world. *Electronic Markets*, *14*(1), 48–57. doi:10.1080/10196780420001752 98

Schoenbachler, D. D., & Gordon, G. L. (2002). Trust and customer willingness to provide information in database-driven relationship marketing. *Journal of Interactive Marketing*, *16*(3), 2–16. doi:10.1002/dir.10033

Schonberg, T. R., Hoch, M., Podlaseck, M., & Spraragen, S. (2000). Measuring success. *Communications of the ACM*, *43*(8), 53–57. doi:10.1145/345124.345142

Schuette, D. (2000). Turning e-business barriers into strengths. *Information Systems Management*, *17*(4), 20–25. doi:10.1201/1078/43193.17.4.20000901/31248.4

Schurr, P. H., & Ozanne, J. L. (1985). Influences on exchange processes: Buyer's preconceptions of a seller's trustworthiness and bargaining toughness. *The Journal of Consumer Research*, *11*(4), 939–953. doi:10.1086/209028

Scroggins, W. A. (2006). Managing meaning for strategic change: The role of perception and meaning congruence. *Journal of Health and Human Services Administration*, *29*(1), 83–103.

Segars, A. H., & Grover, V. (1998). Strategic Information Systems Planning Success: An Investigation of the Construct and its Measurement. *MIS Quarterly*, *22*(2), 139–163. doi:10.2307/249393

Sein, M. K., Bostrom, R. P., & Olfman, L. (1999). Rethinking end-user training strategy: Applying a hierarchical knowledge-level model. *Journal of End User Computing*, *11*, 32–39.

Selnes, F. (1998). Antecedents and consequences of trust and satisfaction in buyer-seller relationships. *European Journal of Marketing*, *32*(3/4), 305–322. doi:10.1108/03090569810204580

Sen, R., King, R. C., & Shaw, M. J. (2006). Buyers' choice of online search strategy and its managerial implications. *Journal of Management Information Systems*, *23*(1), 211–238. doi:10.2753/MIS0742-1222230107

Senge, P. (1990). *The fifth discipline: The art & practice of the learning organization*. New York: Doubleday Currency.

Sewell, G. (1998). The discipline of teams: The control of team-based industrial work through electronic and peer surveillance. *Administrative Science Quarterly*, *43*, 397–428. doi:10.2307/2393857

Shapiro, D., Shepard, B., & Cheraskin, L. (1992). Business on a handshake. *Negotiation Journal*, *8*, 365–377. doi:10.1111/j.1571-9979.1992.tb00679.x

Shapiro, S. (1987). The social control of impersonal trust. *American Journal of Sociology*, *93*(3), 623–658. doi:10.1086/228791

Sharma, S., Durand, R. M., & Gurarie, O. (1981). Identification and analysis of moderator variables. *JMR, Journal of Marketing Research*, *18*(3), 291–300. doi:10.2307/3150970

Shaw, N., & Lee-Partidge, J.-E. (2003). Understanding the hidden dissatisfaction of users towards end-user computing. *Journal of End User Computing*, *15*(2), 1–22. doi:10.4018/joeuc.2003040101

Sheikh, K. (2004). Predicting risk among non-respondents in prospective studies. *European Journal of Epidemiology*, *2*(1), 39–43. doi:10.1007/BF00152716

Shelton, S. H. (1990). Developing the construct of general self-efficacy. *Psychological Reports*, *66*, 987–994.

Shen, J., & Jones, Q. (2003). *In Situ* Data Capture and Mobile Knowledge Management: Helping Technicians Share Case Stories. *Proceedings of 2003 Americas Conference on Information Systems (AMCIS 2003)*, Tampa, FL, 2231-2236.

Sheng, Y. P., Pearson, J. M., & Crosby, L. (2003). Organizational culture and employees' computer self-efficacy: An empirical study. *Information Resources Management Journal*, *16*(3), 42–58. doi:10.4018/irmj.2003070103

Sherer, M., Maddux, J. E., Mercandante, B., Prentice-Dunn, S., Jacobs, B., & Rogers, R. W. (1982). The self-efficacy scale: Construction and validation. *Psychological Reports*, *51*, 663–671.

Sherry, J., & Salvador, T. (2001). Running and Grimacing: The Struggle for Balance in Mobile Work. In Brown, B., Harper, R., & Green, N. (Eds.), *Wireless World: Social and Interactive Aspects of the Mobile Age* (pp. 108–120). New York: Springer Verlag.

Shih, C. (2009). *The Facebook Era*. Upper Saddle River, NJ: Prentice-Hall.

Shim, S. B., Shin, Y. B., & Nottingham, L. (2002). Retailer web site influence on customer shopping: An exploratory study on key factors of customer satisfaction. *Journal of the Association for Information Systems*, *3*, 53–76.

Shim, J. P., Varshney, U., Dekleva, S. M., & Knoerzer, G. (2002). Mobile Wireless Technology and Services: Evolution and Outlook. *Proceedings of 2002 Americas Conference on Information Systems (AMCIS 2002)*, Dallas, TX, 1998-1999.

Shneiderman, B. (2000). Designing trust into online experiences. *Communications of the ACM*, *43*(1), 57–59. doi:10.1145/355112.355124

Shore, L. M., & Coyle-Shapiro, J. A. M. (2003). New developments in the employee-organization relationship. *Journal of Organizational Behavior*, *24*, 443–450. doi:10.1002/job.212

Shore, L. M., Newton, L. A., & Thornton, G. C. (2006). Job and organizational attitudes in relation to employee behavioral intentions. *Journal of Organizational Behavior*, *11*, 57–67. doi:10.1002/job.4030110108

Shumacker, R. E., & Lomax, R. G. (2004). *A beginner's guide to structural equation modeling* (2nd ed.). Mahwah, NJ: Lawrence Erlbaum.

Siau, K., & Shen, Z. X. (2003). Building customer trust in mobile commerce. *Communications of the ACM*, *46*(4), 91–94. doi:10.1145/641205.641211

Simon, S. J., & Peppas, S. (2005). Attitudes towards product website design: A study of the effects of gender. *Journal of Marketing Communications*, *11*(2), 129–144. doi:10.1080/1352726042000286507

Simon, S. J., & Paper, D. (2007). User acceptance of voice recognition technology: An empirical extension of the technology acceptance model. *Journal of Organizational and End User Computing*, *19*(1), 24–50. doi:10.4018/joeuc.2007010102

Smith, H. J., Milberg, S. J., & Burke, S. J. (1996). Information privacy: Measuring individuals' concerns about organizational practices. *Management Information Systems Quarterly*, *20*(2), 167–196. doi:10.2307/249477

Smith, K. K., & Simmons, V. M. (1983). A rumpelstiltskin organization: Metaphors or metaphors in field research. *Administrative Science Quarterly*, *28*(3), 377–392. doi:10.2307/2392248

Soares, S. (2002). Forecast for a multimodal future. *Communique Newsletter*, *39*(9), 26.

Somers, T. M., Nelson, K., & Karimi, J. (2003). Confirmatory factor analysis of the end-user computing satisfaction instrument: Replications within an ERP domain. *Decision Sciences*, *34*(3), 595–621. doi:10.1111/j.1540-5414.2003.02428.x

Sommerville, K. (2004). *Software engineering* (7th ed.). Boston: Addison-Wesley.

Sowa, J. F., & Zachman, J. A. (1992). Extending and Formalizing the Framework for Information Systems Architecture. *IBM Systems Journal*, *31*(3), 590–616.

Spector, P. (2006). Method variance in organizational research. *Organizational Research Methods*, *9*, 221–232. doi:10.1177/1094428105284955

Spector, P. E. (1997). *Job satisfaction*. Thousand Oaks, CA: Sage.

Speier, C., Vessey, I., & Valacich, J. S. (2003). The Effects of Interruptions, Task Complexity, and Information Presentation on Computer-Supported Decision-Making Performance. *Decision Sciences*, *34*(4), 771–797. doi:10.1111/j.1540-5414.2003.02292.x

Spitler, V. (2005). Learning to use IT in the workplace: Mechanisms and masters. *Journal of Organizational and End User Computing*, *17*, 1–25. doi:10.4018/joeuc.2005040101

Spreng, R. A., & Olshavsky, R. W. (1993). A desires congruency model of consumer satisfaction. *Journal of the Academy of Marketing Science*, *21*(3), 169–177. doi:10.1177/0092070393213001

Sproull, L., & Kiesler, S. (1991). *Connections: New Ways of Working in the Networked Organization*. Cambridge, MA: MIT Press.

Srinivasan, S. (2004). Role of trust in e-business success. *Information Management & Computer Security*, *12*(1), 66–72. doi:10.1108/09685220410518838

Stafford, T. F., & Gillenson, M. L. (2003). Mobile Commerce: What it Is and What it Could be. *Communications of the ACM*, *46*(12), 33–34. doi:10.1145/953460.953483

Stajkovic, A. D., & Luthans, F. (1998). Self-efficacy and work-related performance: A metaanalysis. *Psychological Bulletin*, *124*(2), 240–261. doi:10.1037/0033-2909.124.2.240

Stanley, K. D., & Murphy, M. D. (1997). A comparison of general self-efficacy with self-esteem. *Genetic, Social, and General Psychology Monographs*, *123*, 79–100.

Stein, E. W., & Vandenbosch, B. (1996). Organizational learning during advanced systems development: Opportunities. *Journal of Management Information Systems*, *13*(2), 115–136.

Stein, T. (1999, April 12). Liz Claiborne Gets New IT Architecture. Information Week.

Sterman, J. (2000). *Business dynamics: Systems thinking and modeling for a complex world.* Boston: Irwin McGraw-Hill.

Stewart, K. J. (2003). Trust transfer on the World Wide Web. *Organization Science, 14*(1), 5–17. doi:10.1287/orsc.14.1.5.12810

Stewart, K. (2003). Trust transfer on the world wide web. *Organization Science, 14*(1), 5–17. doi:10.1287/orsc.14.1.5.12810

Stewart, K. (2006). How hypertext links influence consumer perceptions to build and degrade trust online. *Journal of Management Information Systems, 23*(1), 183–210. doi:10.2753/MIS0742-1222230106

Stone, R. W., & Henry, J. W. (2003). The roles of computer self-efficacy and outcome expectancy in influencing the computer end-users' organizational Commitment. *Journal of End User Computing, 15*(1), 38–53. doi:10.4018/joeuc.2003010103

Stone, D., Arunachalam, N., & Chandler, V. (1996). Cross-cultural comparisons: An empirical investigation of knowledge, skill, self-efficacy and computer anxiety in accounting education. *Issues in Accounting Education, 11*(2), 345–367.

Stone, E. F., & Hollenbeck, J. R. (1989). Clarifying some controversial issues surrounding statistical procedures for detecting moderating variables: Empirical evidence and related matters. *The Journal of Applied Psychology, 74*, 3–10. doi:10.1037/0021-9010.74.1.3

Straub, D. W., Hoffman, D. L., Weber, B. W., & Steinfield, C. (2002). Measuring e-commerce in net-enabled organizations: An introduction to the special issue. *Information Systems Research, 13*(2), 115–124. doi:10.1287/isre.13.2.115.86

Straub, D. W. (1989). Validating instruments in MIS research. *Management Information Systems Quarterly, 10*(2), 147–169. doi:10.2307/248922

Suh, B., & Han, I. (2002). Effect of trust on customer acceptance of Internet banking. *Electronic Commerce Research and Applications, 1*, 247–263. doi:10.1016/S1567-4223(02)00017-0

Suh, K. S., & Lee, Y. E. (2005). The effects of virtual reality on consumer learning: An empirical investigation. *Management Information Systems Quarterly, 29*(4), 673–697.

Sushil. (2001). Flexibility metaphors. Systems Research and Behavioural Science, 18, 569-575.

Sweller, J. (1988). Cognitive Load during Problem Solving: Effects on Learning. *Cognitive Science, 12*, 257–285. doi:10.1207/s15516709cog1202_4

Sweller, J. (1994). Load Theory, Learning Difficulty and Instructional Design. *Learning and Instruction, 4*, 295–312. doi:10.1016/0959-4752(94)90003-5

Sweller, J., vanMerrienboer, J. J. G., & Paas, F. G. W. C. (1998). Cognitive Architecture and Instructional Design. *Educational Psychology Review, 10*, 251–296. doi:10.1023/A:1022193728205

Szajina, B. (1996). Empirical evaluation of the revised technology acceptance model. *Management Science, 42*(1), 85–92. doi:10.1287/mnsc.42.1.85

Tabachnick, B. G., & Fidell, L. S. (1996). *Using Multivariate Statistics* (3rd ed.). New York: HarperCollins.

Tait, P., & Vessey, I. (1988). The effect of user involvement on system success: A contingency approach. *Management Information Systems Quarterly, 12*(1), 91–108. doi:10.2307/248809

Tan, M., & Teo, T. S. H. (2000). Factors influencing the adoption of internet banking. *Journal of the AIS, 1*(5), 1–5.

Tan, Y., & Thoen, W. (2002). Formal aspects of a generic model of trust for electronic commerce. *Decision Support Systems, 33*(3), 233–246. doi:10.1016/S0167-9236(02)00014-3

Taylor, S., & Todd, P. A. (1995). Understanding information technology usage: A test of competing models. *Information Systems Research, 6*(2), 144–176. doi:10.1287/isre.6.2.144

Taylor, D. (1996). *Business engineering with object technology*. New York: Wiley.

Taylor, S., & Todd, P. (1995). Understanding information technology usage: A test of competing models. *Information Systems Research, 6*(2), 144–176. doi:10.1287/isre.6.2.144

Taylor, D., & Altman, I. (1987). Social penetration processes. In Roloff, M., & Miller, G. (Eds.), *Interpersonal processes: New directions in communication research* (*Vol. 14*). New York: Sage Publications.

Teo, T. S. H., & Lim, V. K. G. (2000). Gender differences in Internet usage and task preferences. *Behaviour & Information Technology*, *19*(4), 283–295. doi:10.1080/01449290050086390

Teo, T., & Ang, J. (2001). An examination of major IS planning problems. *International Journal of Information Management*, *21*(6), 457–470. doi:10.1016/S0268-4012(01)00036-6

Thatcher, J. B., & George, J. F. (2004). Commitment, trust, and social involvement: An exploratory study of antecedents to web shopper loyalty. *Journal of Organizational Computing and Electronic Commerce*, *14*(4), 243–268. doi:10.1207/s15327744joce1404_2

Thatcher, J. B., & Perrewe, P. L. (2002). An empirical examination of individual traits as antecedents to computer anxiety and computer self-efficacy. *Management Information Systems Quarterly*, *26*(4), 381–396. doi:10.2307/4132314

Thatcher, J. B., Stepina, L. P., & Boyle, R. J. (2002). Turnover of information technology workers: Examining empirically the influence of attitudes, job characteristics, and external markets. *Journal of Management Information Systems*, *19*(3), 231–261.

Thompson, R., Compeau, D., & Higgins, C. (2006). Intentions to use information technologies: An integrative model. *Journal of Organizational and End User Computing*, *18*(3), 25–46. doi:10.4018/joeuc.2006070102

Thompson, R. L., Higgins, C. A., & Howell, J. M. (1991). Personal computing: Toward a conceptual model of utilization. *Management Information Systems Quarterly*, *15*(1), 125–143. doi:10.2307/249443

Thong, J. Y. L., Hong, W., & Tam, W. Y. (2004). What leads to user acceptance Of digital libraries? *Communications of the ACM*, *47*(11), 78–83. doi:10.1145/1029496.1029498

Thong, J. Y. L., Hong, W. Y., & Tam, K. Y. (2002). Understanding user acceptance of digital libraries: what are the roles of interface characteristics, organizational context, and individual differences? *International Journal of Human-Computer Studies*, *57*(3), 215–242. doi:10.1016/S1071-5819(02)91024-4

Tiwana, A., & McLean, E. R. (2005). Expertise integration and creativity in information systems development. *Journal of Management Information Systems*, *22*(1), 13–44.

Togo, D. F., & Hood, J. N. (1992). Quantitative information presentation and gender: An interaction effect. *The Journal of General Psychology*, *119*(2), 161–167. doi:10.1080/00221309.1992.9921169

Tomlinson, E. C., & Lewicki, R. J. (2004). *The Effects of Reputation and Post Violation Communication on Trust and Distrust*. Social Science Electronic Publishing, Inc.

Torkzadeh, G., Chang, J. C.-J., & Demirhan, D. (2006). A contingency model of computer and Internet self-efficacy. *Information & Management*, *43*(4), 541–550. doi:10.1016/j.im.2006.02.001

Torkzadeh, G., & Van Dyke, T. P. (2002). Effects of training on internet self-efficacy and computer user attitudes. *Computers in Human Behavior*, *18*, 479–494. doi:10.1016/S0747-5632(02)00010-9

Torkzadeh, R., Pflughoeft, K., & Hall, L. (1999). Computer self-efficacy, training effectiveness, and user attitudes: An empirical study. *Behaviour & Information Technology*, *18*, 299–309. doi:10.1080/014492999119039

Torkzadeh, G., Doll, W. J. (1999). The development of a tool for measuring the perceived impact of information technology on work. *Omega- International Journal of Management Science, 27*, 327-339.

Treadway, D. C., Hochwarter, W., Ferris, G. R., Kacmar, C. J., Douglas, C., Ammeter, A. P., & Buckley, M. R. (2004). Leader political skill and employee reactions. *The Leadership Quarterly*, *15*, 493–513. doi:10.1016/j.lcaqua.2004.05.004

Triplett, N. (1898). The Dynamogenic Factors in Pacemaking and Competition. *The American Journal of Psychology*, *9*, 507–533. doi:10.2307/1412188

Turban, E., McLean, E., & Wetherbe, J. (2004). *Information technology for management*. Singapore: John Wiley & Sons (Asia).

Tyler, T. R. (2003). Trust within organisations. *Personnel Review*, *32*, 556–568. doi:10.1108/00483480310488333

Urbaczewski, A., Valacich, J. S., & Jessup, L. M. (2003). Mobile Commerce: Opportunities and Challenges. *Communications of the ACM*, *46*(12), 31–32.

Utz, S., Matzat, U., & Snijders, C. (2009). On-line reputation systems: The effect of feedback comments and reactions on building and rebuilding trust in on-line auctions. *International Journal of Electronic Commerce*, *13*(3), 95–118. doi:10.2753/JEC1086-4415130304

van der Heijden, H., Verhagen, T., & Creemers, M. (2003). Understanding online purchase intentions: Contributions from technology and trust perspectives. *European Journal of Information Systems*, *12*, 41–48. doi:10.1057/palgrave.ejis.3000445

van der Heijden, H. (2004). User acceptance of hedonic information systems. *Management Information Systems Quarterly*, *28*(4), 695–704.

Van der Heijden, H. (2003). Factors influencing the usage of websites: The case of a generic portal in The Netherlands. *Information & Management*, *40*, 541–549. doi:10.1016/S0378-7206(02)00079-4

Van Dyne, L., & Lepine, J. A. (1998). Helping and voice extra-role behaviors: Evidence of construct and predictive validity. *Academy of Management Journal*, *41*, 108–119. doi:10.2307/256902

van Es, R., & Post, R. (1996). *Dynamic enterprise modeling: A paradigm shift in software implementation*. Baan Business Innovation.

Van Slyke, C., Shim, J. T., Johnson, R., & Jiang, J. (2006). Concern for information privacy and online consumer purchasing. *Journal of the Association for Information Systems*, *7*(6), 415–443.

Van Slyke, C., Belanger, F., & Comunale, C. L. (2004). Factors influencing the adoption of web-based shopping: the impact of trust. *ACM SIGMIS Database*, *35*(2), 32–49. doi:10.1145/1007965.1007969

Vascellaro, J. E. (2009, October 12). Why email no longer rules... *The Wall Street Journal*. Retrieved October 7, 2010 from http://online.wsj.com.

Veiga, J. F., & Dechant, K. (1997). Wired world woes: www.help. *The Academy of Management Executive*, *11*(3), 73–78.

Venkatesh, V. (2000). Determinants of perceived ease of use: Integrating control, intrinsic motivation, and emotion into the technology acceptance model. *Information Systems Research*, *11*(4), 342–365. doi:10.1287/isre.11.4.342.11872

Venkatesh, V., & Davis, F. D. (1996). A model of the antecedents of perceived ease of use: Development and test. *Decision Sciences*, *27*(3), 451–481. doi:10.1111/j.1540-5915.1996.tb01822.x

Venkatesh, V., & Davis, F. D. (2000). A theoretical extension of the technology acceptance model: Four longitudinal field studies. *Management Science*, *46*(2), 186–204. doi:10.1287/mnsc.46.2.186.11926

Venkatesh, V., Morris, M., Davis, G., & Davis, F. D. (2003). User acceptance of information technology: toward a unified view. *Management Information Systems Quarterly*, *27*(3), 425–478.

Venkatesh, V., Morris, M., & Ackerman, P. (2000). A longitudinal field investigation of gender differences in individual technology adoption decision-making processes. *Organizational Behavior and Human Decision Processes*, *83*, 33–60. doi:10.1006/obhd.2000.2896

Venkatesh, V., & Morris, M. G. (2000). Why don't men ever stop to ask for directions? Gender, social influence, and their role in technology acceptance and usage behavior. *Management Information Systems Quarterly*, *24*(1), 115–139. doi:10.2307/3250981

Venkatesh, V., Davis, F., & Morris, M. (2007). Dead or Alive? The Development, Trajectory, and Future of Technology Adoption Research. *Journal of the Association for Information Systems*, *8*(4), 267–286.

Vesanen, J. (2007). What is personalization? A conceptual framework. *European Journal of Marketing*, *41*(5/6), 409–418. doi:10.1108/03090560710737534

Viehland, D., & Hughes, J. (2002). The Future of Wireless Application Protocol. *Proceedings of 2002 Americas Conference on Information Systems (AMCIS 2002)*, Dallas, TX, 1883-1891.

Viswesvaran, C., Sanchez, J. I., & Fisher, J. (1999). The role of social support in the process of work stress: A meta-analysis. *Journal of Vocational Behavior*, *54*, 314–334. doi:10.1006/jvbe.1998.1661

Von Halle, B., Goldberg, L., & Zachman, J. (2006). *Business rule revolution: Running business the right way*. Silicon Valley, CA: Happy About.

Votolato, N., & Unnava, H. (2006). Spillover of negative information on brand alliances. *Journal of Consumer Psychology*, *16*(2), 192–202.

Wagner, C. (2000). End user as expert developer? *Journal of End User Computing*, *12*(3), 3–13. doi:10.4018/joeuc.2000070101

Wagner, E. L., & Newell, S. (2006). Repairing ERP: Producing social order to create a working information system. *The Journal of Applied Behavioral Science*, *42*(1), 40–57. doi:10.1177/0021886305284290

Wailgum, T. (2006). more. *CIO.* November 15, 2006, 58-65.

Wailgum, T. (2007, March 6). ABC: An introduction to CRM. *CIO.* Retrieved September 1, 2008, from http:///www.cio.com/article/print/40295.

Wakefield, R. J., Stocks, M. H., & Wilder, W. M. (2004). The role of website characteristics in initial trust formation. *Journal of Computer Information Systems*, *45*(1), 94–103.

Wakefield, R., & Whitten, D. (2006). Examining user perceptions of third-party organization credibility and trust in an e-tailer. *Journal of Organizational and End User Computing*, *18*(2), 1–19. doi:10.4018/joeuc.2006040101

Wakefield, R. L., & Whitten, D. (2006). Mobile Computing: A User Study on Hedonic/Utilitarian Mobile Device Usage. *European Journal of Information Systems*, *15*(1), 292–300. doi:10.1057/palgrave.ejis.3000619

Wall, T. D., Jackson, P. R., Mullarkey, S., & Parker, S. K. (1996). The DC-model of job strain: A more specific test. *Journal of Occupational and Organizational Psychology*, *69*, 153–166.

Walsham, G. (1991). Organizational metaphors and information systems research. *European Journal of Information Systems*, *1*(2), 83–94. doi:10.1057/ejis.1991.16

Walsham, G. (1993). *Interpreting information systems in organizations*. Chichester: John Wiley & Sons.

Walther, J. (1992). Interpersonal effects in computer-mediated interaction: A relational perspective. *Communication Research*, *19*, 52–90. doi:10.1177/009365092019001003

Walther, J. (1993). Impression development in computer-mediated interaction. *Western Journal of Communication*, *57*, 381–398.

Walther, J., Anderson, J., & Park, D. (1994). Interpersonal effects in computer-mediated interaction: A meta-analysis of social and antisocial communication. *Communication Research*, *21*, 460–487. doi:10.1177/009365094021004002

Walther, J., & Burgoon, J. (1992). Relational communication in computer-mediated interaction. *Human Communication Research*, *19*, 50–88. doi:10.1111/j.1468-2958.1992.tb00295.x

Waltz, D., & Feldman, J. (1988). *Connectionist models and their implications: Readings from cognitive science*. Norwood, New Jersey: Ablex Publishing Corp.

Wang, T. D., & Emurian, H. H. (2005). An overview of online trust: Concepts, elements, and implications. *Computers in Human Behavior*, *21*, 105–125. doi:10.1016/j.chb.2003.11.008

Wang, R. Y., & Strong, D. M. (1997). Beyond accuracy: What data quality means to data consumers. *Journal of Management Information Systems*, *12*(4), 5–34.

Wang, W., & Benbasat, I. (2005). Trust in and adoption of online recommendation agents. *Journal of the Association for Information Systems*, *6*(3), 72–101.

Wang, C.-C., Hsu, Y., & Fang, W. (2005). Acceptance of technology with network externalities: An empirical study of Internet instant messaging services. *Journal of Information Technology Theory and Application*, *6*(4), 15–29.

Wang, Y.-S. (2002). The adoption of electronic tax filing systems: An empirical study. *Government Information Quarterly*, *20*, 333–352. doi:10.1016/j.giq.2003.08.005

Wang, E., & Tai, J. (2003). Factors affecting information systems planning effectiveness: Organizational contexts and planning systems dimensions. *Information & Management*, *40*(4), 287–303. doi:10.1016/S0378-7206(02)00011-3

Ward, M., & Lee, M. (1999). Internet shopping, consumer search, and product branding. *Journal of Product and Brand Management*, *9*(1), 6–20. doi:10.1108/10610420010316302

Washburn, J., Till, B., & Priluck, R. (2000). Co-branding: brand equity and trial effects. *Journal of Consumer Marketing*, *17*(7), 591–604. doi:10.1108/07363760010357796

Wastell, D. G., & Newman, M. (1996). Stress, control and computer system design: A psychophysiological field study. *Behaviour & Information Technology*, *15*(3), 183–192. doi:10.1080/014492996120247

Wayne, S. J., Shore, L. M., & Liden, R. C. (1997). Perceived organizational support and leader-member exchange: A social exchange perspective. *Academy of Management Journal*, *40*, 82–111. doi:10.2307/257021

Weick, K. (1995). *Sensemaking in organizations*. Thousand Oaks, CA: Sage Publications.

Weill, P. (1992). The Relationship Between Investment in Information Technology and Firm Performance: A Study of the Valve Manufacturing Sector. *Information Systems Research*, *3*(4), 307–333. doi:10.1287/isre.3.4.307

Whitworth, B. (2005). Polite computing. *Behaviour & Information Technology*, *24*(5), 353–363. doi:10.1080/01449290512331333700

Wikipedia (2006). *Business process management*. Retrieved November 5, 2008, from wikipedia.org/wiki/Business_Process_Management

Wikipedia (2006). *Product life cycle management*. Retrieved November 5, 2008, from en.wikipeida.org/wiki/Product_Lifecycle_Management

Williamson, O. (1993). Calculativeness, trust, and economic organization. *The Journal of Law & Economics*, *36*, 453–486. doi:10.1086/467284

Wilson, F. A. (1994). Computer-based systems and organizational structures: designing the ghost in the machine. In R. Baskerville., O. Ngwenyama., S. Smithson., & J.I. DeGross, (Eds.), *Transforming organizations with information technology.* Amsterdam: North-Holland, 343-355.

Wixom, B. H., & Todd, P. A. (2005). A theoretical integration of user satisfaction and technology acceptance. *Information Systems Research*, *16*(1), 85–102. doi:10.1287/isre.1050.0042

Wood, R., & Bandura, A. (1989). Impact of conceptions of ability on self-regulatory mechanisms and complex decision making. *Journal of Personality and Social Psychology*, *56*, 407–415. doi:10.1037/0022-3514.56.3.407

Wood, R. (1986). Task complexity: Definition of the Construct. *Organizational Behavior and Human Decision Processes*, *37*(1), 60–82. doi:10.1016/0749-5978(86)90044-0

Wu, J.-H., & Wang, S.-C. (2005). What drives mobile commerce? An empirical evaluation of the revised technology acceptance model. *Information & Management*, *42*, 719–729. doi:10.1016/j.im.2004.07.001

Wu, I. L., & Chen, E. L. (2005). An extension of Trust and TAM model with TPB in the initial adoption of on-line tax: An empirical study. *International Journal of Human-Computer Studies*, *62*(6), 784–808. doi:10.1016/j.ijhcs.2005.03.003

Wu, D., Im, I., Tremaine, M., Instone, K., & Turoff, M. (2002). A framework for classifying personalization scheme used on e-commerce websites. *Proceedings of the 36th Hawaii International Conference on Systems Sciences*, 12 pp., doi: 10.1109/HICSS.2003.1174586; http://ieeexplore.ieee.org/stamp/stamp.jsp?tp=&arnumber=1174586&isnumber=26341.

Xia, W., & Lee, G. (2005). Complexity of information systems development projects: conceptualization and measurement development. *Journal of Management Information Systems*, *22*(1), 45–83.

Yang, M., Chandlrees, N., Lin, B., & Chao, H. (2009). The effect of perceived ethical performance of shopping websites on consumer trust. *Journal of Computer Information Systems*, *50*(1), 15–24.

Yang, Z. L., & Jun, M. J. (2002). Consumer perception of e-service quality: From Internet purchaser and non-purchaser perspectives. *The Journal of Business Strategy*, *19*(1), 19–41.

Yang, H., & Yoo, Y. (2004). It's all about attitude: Revisiting the technology acceptance model. *Decision Support Systems*, *38*, 19–31. doi:10.1016/S0167-9236(03)00062-9

Yavas, U. (1994). Research note: Students as subjects in advertising and marketing. *International Marketing Review*, *11*(Winter), 35–44. doi:10.1108/02651339410069236

Yi, M. J., & Hwang, Y. (2003). Predicting the use of web-based information systems: Self-efficacy, enjoyment, learning goal orientation and the technology acceptance model. *International Journal of Human-Computer Studies*, *59*, 431–449. doi:10.1016/S1071-5819(03)00114-9

Yi, M. Y., & Im, K. S. (2004). Predicting computer task performance: Personal goal and self-efficacy. *Journal of Organizational and End User Computing*, *16*(2), 20–37. doi:10.4018/joeuc.2004040102

Yi, M. Y., Jackson, J. D., Park, J. S., & Probst, J. C. (2006). Understanding information technology acceptance by individual professionals: Toward an integrative view. *Information & Management*, *43*, 350–363. doi:10.1016/j.im.2005.08.006

Yi, M. Y., & Davis, F. D. (2003). Developing and validating an observational learning model of computer software training and skill acquisition. *Information Systems Research*, *14*(2), 146–169. doi:10.1287/isre.14.2.146.16016

Yoon, S. (2002). The antecedents and consequences of trust in online-purchase decisions. *Journal of Interactive Marketing*, *16*(2), 47. doi:10.1002/dir.10008

Young, L., & Albaum, G. (2003). Measurement of trust in salesperson-customer relationships in direct selling. *Journal of Personal Selling & Sales Management*, *23*(3), 253–264.

Yu, J., Ha, I., Choi, M., & Rho, J. (2005). Extending the TAM for a t-commerce. *Information & Management*, *42*, 965–976. doi:10.1016/j.im.2004.11.001

Yukl, G. (1989). Managerial leadership: A review of theory and research. *Journal of Management*, *15*, 251–289. doi:10.1177/014920638901500207

Zachman, J. A. (1982). Business Systems Planning and Business Information Control Study: A Comparison. *IBM Systems Journal*, *21*(1), 31–53.

Zagenczyk, T. J., Scott, K. D., Gibney, R., Murrell, A. J., & Thatcher, J. B. (2010). Social influence and perceived organizational support: A social networks analysis. *Organizational Behavior and Human Decision Processes*, *111*(2), 127–138. doi:10.1016/j.obhdp.2009.11.004

Zaheer, A., McEvily, B., & Vincenzo, P. (1998). Does trust matter? Exploring the effects of interorganizational and interpersonal trust on performance. *Organization Science*, *9*(2), 141–159. doi:10.1287/orsc.9.2.141

Zajonc, R. B. (1965). Social Facilitation. *Science*, *149*, 269–274. doi:10.1126/science.149.3681.269

Zand, D. E. (1972). Trust and managerial problem solving. *Administrative Science Quarterly*, *17*, 229–239. doi:10.2307/2393957

Zaslow, J. (2009, November 5). The greatest generation (of networkers). *The Wall Street Journal*. Retrieved October 7, 2010 from http://online.wsj.com.

Zeithaml, V. (1988). Consumer perceptions of price, quality and value: A means-end model and synthesis of evidence. *Journal of Marketing*, *52*(3), 2–22. doi:10.2307/1251446

Zeithaml, V. A. (1985). The new demographics and market fragmentation. *Journal of Marketing*, *49*(3), 64–75. doi:10.2307/1251616

Zhang, P., & Li, N. (2005). The Intellectual Development of Human-Computer Interaction Research: A Critical Assessment of the MIS Literature (1990 - 2000). *Journal of the Association for Information Systems*, *6*(1), 227–291.

Zhang, P., von Dran, G. M., Small, R. V., & Barcellos, S. (1999). *Websites that satisfy users: A theoretical framework for Web user interface design and evaluation.* Paper presented at the the 32nd Hawaii International Conference on System Sciences, Maui, HI.

Zhang, X., Keeling, K., & Pavur, R. (2000). Information quality of commercial web site: An explorative analysis. In *Proceedings of the International Conference on Information Systems (ICIS)*, Brisbane, Australia.

Zhou, L., Dai, L., & Zhang, D. (2007). Online Shopping Acceptance Model - A Critical Survey of Consumer Factors in Online Shopping. *Journal of Electronic Commerce Research*, *8*(1), 41–62.

Zucker, L.-G. (1986). Production of trust: Institutional sources of economic structure, 1840-1920. *Research in Organizational Behavior*, *8*, 53–111.

Zucker, L. (1986). Production of trust: Institutional sources of economic structure, 1840-1920. *Research in Organizational Behavior*, *8*, 53–111.

About the Contributors

Steve Clarke received a BSc in Economics from The University of Kingston Upon Hull, an MBA from the Putteridge Bury Management Centre, The University of Luton, and a PhD in human centred approaches to information systems development from Brunel University – all in the United Kingdom. He is Professor of Information Systems in the University of Hull Business School. Steve has extensive experience in management systems and information systems consultancy and research, focusing primarily on the identification and satisfaction of user needs and issues connected with knowledge management. His research interests include: social theory and information systems practice; strategic planning; and the impact of user involvement in the development of management systems. Major current research is focused on approaches informed by critical social theory.

Ashish Dwivedi commenced his career in the financial services industry and then moved to academia where he is currently a Lecturer at the Hull University Business School. Ashish is also associated with the management of the high-tech Management Learning Laboratory (MLL) and is the programme leader for a newly-created Masters in Knowledge Management. Ashish has previously taught and researched at Coventry University and the University of Northampton.

* * *

Manju Ahuja is Professor of CIS at the University of Louisville. She has previously held faculty positions at the Kelley School of Business, Indiana University, Florida State University, and Pennsylvania State University. She is currently an Associate Editor at MIS Quarterly, and has recently served in this role at Information Systems Research. Her publications have appeared in journals such as MIS Quarterly, Management Science, Information Systems Research, Organization Science, Communications ofthe ACM, Journal of Management, European Journal of Information Systems, Journalof MIS, Journal of AIS, Small Group Research, and other outlets. She has been consistently ranked among top100 IS researcher worldwide by a variety of sources (e.g., Gallivan and Benbunan-Fich, 2006; http://www.vvenkatesh.com/ISranking).

Riza Ergun Arsal is a PhD candidate in the Department of Management at Clemson University. His research interests include individual adoption and use of Information technologies, and behavioral issues in online settings. His work has been accepted into journals such as Information & Management, Decision Support Systems, IEEE Transactions on Engineering Management and Journal of Organizational and End User Computing.

Ken Baker is a faculty member at Dartmouth College. He is currently Nathaniel Leverone Professor of Management at the Tuck School of Business and also adjunct professor at the Thayer School of Engineering. At Dartmouth, he has taught courses relating to decision science, manufacturing management, and environmental management. Over the years, much of his teaching and research has dealt with production planning and control, and he is widely known for his textbook Elements of Sequencing and Scheduling, in addition to a variety of technical articles. He has served as the Tuck School's associate dean and directed the Tuck School's management development programs in the manufacturing area. In 2001 he was named a Fellow of INFORMS's Manufacturing and Service Operations Management (MSOM) Society, and in 2004 a Fellow of INFORMS. He is the co-author with Stephen Powell of The Art of Modeling with Spreadsheets (Wiley, 2004).

Linda Brennan is a professor of management at Mercer University in Macon. Her teaching portfolio includes graduate and undergraduate courses in operations management, leadership, international business and strategy. She conducts research and consults in the areas of technology impact assessment, process and project management, and instructional effectiveness. Brennan has been published in scholarly and practitioner-oriented journals such as International Journal of Quality and Reliability Management, Engineering Management Journal, The Journal of Management in Engineering, IEEE Technology and Society, and Corporate Governance. Two of her books, Computer-Mediated Relationships and Trust: Organizational and Managerial Implications and The Social, Ethical, and Policy Implications of Information Systems, were co-edited with Dr. Victoria Johnson and published by IGI Global. Her most recent book, Operations Management, was published by McGraw-Hill in 2010. Dr. Brennan's prior work experience includes management positions at The Quaker Oats Company and marketing and systems engineering experience with the IBM Corporation. A licensed professional engineer, she received her Ph.D. in industrial engineering from Northwestern University, her MBA in policy studies from the University of Chicago, and her B.I.E. in industrial engineering from the Georgia Institute of Technology.

James R. Burns is a Professor of Information Technology and Operations Management in the Rawls College of Business Administration at Texas Tech University. He received a BS from the University of Colorado and an MS and a PhD from Purdue University, respectively. He teaches courses in project management, operations management, information technology and management science. His research is currently focused on new developments in project/process management, the use of system dynamics to redesign supply chains and energy/economic modeling based on system dynamics. He is the author/co-author of 100 journal papers and publications on subjects as diverse as knowledge management to design of decision support systems. He is also the author/coauthor of several textbooks on subjects ranging from information technology to management science.

Michelle Carter is a PhD candidate in the Department of Management at Clemson University, majoring in Information Systems. Her research focuses on how adoption and diffusion of information technologies changes organizational practices, as well as individuals' social and work lives. Her research has appeared in the proceedings of the AMCIS, SAIS, DIGIT, SIGHCI and IFIP WG.8.2.

James P. Downey is an associate professor in the MIS Department in the College of Business at the University of Central Arkansas. He received his Ph.D. in Management Information Systems at Auburn

University. He spent 25 years as an active duty US Naval officer, including a tour in the Computer Science Department at the U.S. Naval Academy, before leaving the Navy in November 2004. His current research interests include project management, database management, individual differences in behavior in human-computer interactions, the elderly and IT, and IT curriculum issues. He has been published in several journals, including Journal or Organizational and End User Computing, Interacting with Computers, Journal of Information Technology Education, Journal of Quantitative Analysis in Sports, Journal of Information Systems Education, and International Journal of Training and Development.

Bruce D. Green is the COO and Director of Technology Programs for The GBS Group a business and technical services consultancy headquartered in Virginia Beach, VA. Mr. Green provides technology consulting to corporations in defense and transportation sectors as well as to the U.S. Navy. Prior to co-founding The GBS Group, he spent 18 years with the Naval Surface Warfare Center in various engineering and management positions that directly affected the design, development, installation, and maintenance of shipboard technologies. His responsibilities included acting as Principal Software Support Agent for major shore-side and shipboard systems and guiding a major software program to achieve Capability Maturity Model (CMM) Level 3 assessment. He received his Bachelor of Science in Mechanical Engineering and his Master of Science in Information Systems from Drexel University in Philadelphia. He has been published in proceeding for Information Resources Management Association (IRMA) International, American Society of Naval Engineers (ASNE), and Joint Technical Rail conferences. He is currently a doctoral student in Information Systems at Nova Southeastern University with research interests in technical project management and user acceptance of technology.

Anil Gurung is an Assistant Professor of Management Information Systems in Lewis College of Business at Marshall University. He received his Ph.D. from the University of Texas at Arlington. Current research interests are in the areas of IT adoption, information security and privacy, ecommerce, and cultural and social aspects of business computing. He has published in various journals and conference proceedings.

Ranida B. Harris is an Associate Professor of Management Information Systems at Indiana University Southeast. She received her Ph.D. in Management Information Systems from Florida State University. Her research interests include the effects of computer technologies on communication, performance, and decision making. Her publications appear in Journal of Applied Social Psychology, Journal of Social Psychology, Journal of Managerial Issues, Journal of Behavioral and Applied Management, Information Systems Education Journal, and other journals. Dr. Harris's teaching interests include business computer applications, systems analysis and design, and database management systems.

Charles M. "Chuck" Hermans is an Associate Professor in Marketing at Missouri State University. His research interests include, Cross-cultural comparisons in consumer behavior, international diffusion models and segmentation, Internet marketing, and international e-commerce. Dr. Hermans teaches International Marketing, International Logistics, and Marketing Research at MSU. He has been published in Journal of Current Issues and Research in Advertising, International Journal of Bank Marketing, Journal of Fashion Marketing and Management, International Journal of Consumer Studies, Marketing

Management Journal, Journal of Business and Behavioral Sciences, International Journal of Business Disciplines, Journal of Foodservice Business Research, Marketing Education Review and others.

James J. Hoffman is a full professor and a member of the area of Information Systems and Quantitative Sciences in the College of Business at Texas Tech University. Dr. Hoffman is Associate Dean for MBA Programs and Executive Education at the Rawls College of Business. Dr. Hoffman is also one of the founding co-editors of the Journal of Business Valuation and Economic Loss Analysis. He holds a Ph.D. from the College of Business Administration at the University of Nebraska-Lincoln. Dr. Hoffman's research interests are in the areas of business valuation, operations management, business strategy, and the management of health care organizations. He has published in top academic journals such as the European Journal of Operational Research, International Journal of Operations and Production Management, Journal of Engineering and Technology Management, Journal of High Technology Management Research, Academy of Management Journal, Strategic Management Journal, Journal of Management, and Organization Studies. Dr. Hoffman has also won numerous teaching awards.

Robert Hooker, Ph.D. is a graduate of the College of Business at Florida State University. Rob's research focuses on the convergence of MIS, marketing, and supply chain management. His work has been published or accepted for publication in various journals, books, and academic conferences including the Journal of Supply Chain Management, MIS Quarterly Executive, DSI, and the International Conference on Information Systems. Rob's research has been highlighted by various media outlets around the world, and he has also spoken at executive forums. Prior to academia, Rob worked in corporate marketing, finance, and consulting.

Don G. Jung is a full professor in the Department of Information and Knowledge Management at MyongJi University in Seoul, Korea. He received his PhD in information systems from Texas Tech University. He teaches courses in information systems and knowledge management. He has had a continuing research interest in enterprise resource planning systems, business process redesign, and connectionist modeling. His dissertation focused on the use of dynamic connectionist models to understand economic systems. He has published many journal articles in both Korean and American journals. His dissertation was published in Decision Support Systems.

Young Hoon Kim is a doctoral student in the School of Communication and Information at Rutgers University. He earned his M.A. from the department of Telecommunication, Information, & Media Studies at Michigan State University. His research interests center on the relationship between people's communicative behaviors and their use of information and communication technologies. Currently, his research interests focus on the interaction taking place among computer-mediated group participants in organizational settings. In addition, he is also interested in exploring the impact of anonymity/deindividuation on an individual's communicative behaviors in computer-mediated communication. His work has been published in Journal of Organizational and End User Computing.

Dan J. Kim is an Associate Professor of Computer Information Systems at University of Houston-Clear Lake (UHCL). Before joining the UHCL, he was an Assistant Professor at Michigan State University. He earned his Ph.D. in MIS from SUNY at Buffalo. He also holds a MBA degree with management science concentration and MS degree in computer science. His research interests are in multidisciplinary areas such as electronic commerce, mobile commerce, information security and assurance. Recently he has focused on trust in electronic commerce, wireless and mobile commerce, and information security and assurance. His research work has been published or in forthcoming more than 85 papers in refereed journals and conference proceedings including ISR, JMIS, CACM, CAIS, DSS, IJHCI, JOEUC, IEEE-TPC, Electronic Market, IEEE IT Professional, JGIM, IJMC, ICIS, HICSS, AMCIS, INFORMS, ICEC, ICA, and so on. He received an Emerald Literati Network 2009 - Outstanding Paper Award, the best-paper runner-up award at the International Conference on Information Systems (ICIS) 2003 and the best research paper award at Americas Conference on Information Systems (AMCIS) 2005. He was ranked at top 22 worldwide in terms of research productivity in the area of information systems from year 2007 to 2009 based on top three leading IS journals: ISR, MISQ and JMIS.

Barry Lawson is a research associate at the Tuck School of Business at Dartmouth and is also a visiting scholar in the geography department of the college. He founded and has served as president of Barry Lawson Associates, a consulting firm, since 1978. As visiting scholar, he coordinates the development of an atlas of the upper Connecticut River Watershed in New Hampshire and Vermont. As research associate at Tuck he serves as the program manager for the Tuck Spreadsheet Engineering Research Project. Lawson has taught in graduate programs at Boston University and Wayne State University as well as in short courses at Bentley College. He has moderated a host of public hearings for local, state and federal governments on controversial environmental and energy- and waste-related projects, and has considerable experience in group facilitation, conflict resolution and simulation design.

Yair Levy is an associate professor of Information Systems (IS) at the Graduate School of Computer and Information Sciences at Nova Southeastern University. During the mid to late 1990s, Dr. Levy helped NASA develop e-learning platforms as well as managing Internet and Web infrastructures. He earned his Bachelor's degree in Aerospace Engineering from the Technion, Israel Institute of Technology. He received his MBA with MIS concentration and Ph.D. in Management Information Systems from Florida International University. His current research interests include cognitive value of information systems, cognitive value of online learning systems, effectiveness of IS and online learning, as well as IS education. Dr. Levy is the author of the book titled Assessing the Value of e-Learning Systems. His research publications appear in the IS journals, conference proceedings, invited book chapters, and encyclopedias. Dr. Levy's research publications have been acknowledged internationally for outstanding quality, with recognitions such as Editor's Award of Excellence and Best Paper Awards. Additionally, he has chaired and co-chaired multiple sessions/tracks of his research area in recognized scientific conferences. Dr. Levy is the editor-in-chief for the journal of doctoral studies (IJDS). He is also serving as an associate editor for the International Journal of Web-based Learning and Teaching Technologies. He also serves as a member of the academic review board and a referee research reviewer for numerous national and international scientific journals, conference proceedings, and MIS and Information Security textbooks. In addition, he is a frequent speaker at national and international meetings on MIS and online learning topics. To find out more about Dr. Levy, please visit his site: http://scis.nova.edu/~levyy/.

Qinyu Liao is an Assistant Professor of Management Information Systems at the University of Texas at Brownsville. She holds a Ph.D. in Management Information Systems from Mississippi State University.

Her current research interests are in consumer behavior in electronic commerce, cross-cultural Influences of IT adoption and web-based education. She has published articles in the Journal of Internet Banking and Commerce, Journal of Computer Information Systems, Information Management and Computer Security, Journal of Organizational and End User Computing, Information System Security, International Journal of Information Systems and Change Management etc.

Xin (Lucie) Li is an associate professor of Information Technology Management in the School of Business at the University of North Carolina at Pembroke. She received a PhD in Management Information Systems (MIS) and MBA concentrating in MIS from Washington State University. Her research interests include trust in Information Systems (IS), e-Commerce, IS in organization, IS security and privacy, IS personnel, E-learning and Collaborative IS, and cultural issues in IS. She has published her research in such outlets as the Data Base for Advances in Information Systems, Journal of Strategic Information Systems, and Journal of Organizational and End User Computing.

Xin Luo is an Assistant Professor of Management Information Systems in Anderson School of Management at The University of New Mexico. He received his Ph.D. in Information Systems from Mississippi State University. His research interests center around information security, E-commerce/M-commerce, and global IT adoption and management. His research articles have appeared in Journal of Association for Information Systems, European Journal of Information Systems, Decision Support Systems, Communications of the ACM, Communications of Association for Information Systems, Cross Cultural Management, Information Systems Security, Journal of Information Security and Privacy, International Journal of Information Security and Privacy, and Journal of Internet Banking and Commerce, etc.

Amit Malik is a doctoral candidate in Information Management at the Management Development Institute, India. He has done bachelors in Computer Engineering from National Institute of Technology, India. He has over 3 years of professional experience in software design and development, process designing and implementation. His research interests include virtual teams, software development offshoring, and knowledge management.

Kent Marett is an Assistant Professor of Business Information Systems at Mississippi State University. He received his Ph.D. in Management Information Systems from Florida State University. His research is primarily focused on online deceptive communication, information security, the use of technology by work groups, and human-computer interaction. His research has been published in several leading journals, including Journal of Management Information Systems, Journal of the AIS, and Journal of Organizational and End User Computing.

D. Harrison McKnight is an Associate Professor in the Accounting and Information Systems department of The Eli Broad College of Business at Michigan State University. He received a Ph.D. in Management Information Systems from the University of Minnesota. Before obtaining a Ph.D., he pursued an 11-year corporate career, including ten years at American Airlines' SABRE Computer Services division. His research interests include trust building within e-commerce and information systems settings and the retention and motivation of information systems professionals. His work has been published at such journals as Information Systems Research, MIS Quarterly, IEEE-Transactions on Engineering Management, and the Academy of Management Review.

Dhruv Nath is Professor and Chairman of the Doctoral Program at the Management Development Institute (MDI), Gurgaon, India. Earlier, he was Senior Vice President at NIIT Ltd, a leading software and education company. Prof. Nath holds a B Tech in Electrical Engineering and a PhD in the area of Computer Science, both from IIT Delhi. He has conducted Top Management Workshops in IT and has been a consultant in the area to several organizations such as Glaxo, Unilever, Gillette, Nestle, etc. He has published research papers in International Journals such as the IEEE transactions on Computers, and has written two books on Managing IT Technologies.

Darren B. Nicholson is an Associate Professor in MIS at Rowan University. He received his Ph.D. in Business Administration, with a specialization in Information Systems from Washington State University. His research interests include virtual teams, human-computer interaction, e-business, and distance education. His research has been published in outlets such as IEEE Transactions on Professional Communication (IEEE), Journal of Information Technology Theory and Application (JITTA), Journal of Information Technology Education (JITE), Journal of Organizational and End User Computing (JOEUC), and the proceedings of many national and international conferences.

Jennifer A. Nicholson is an Associate Professor in MIS at Rowan University. She received her Ph.D. in Business Administration, with a specialization in Information Systems from Washington State University. Her research interests include computer-mediated learning, human-computer interaction, and mobile technologies. She has published articles in Informing Science Journal (ISJ), Journal of Information Technology Education (JITE), Journal of Organizational and End User Computing (JOEUC), and the proceedings of many national and international conferences.

David Paradice is the Sprint Professor of MIS and Associate Dean for Undergraduate Programs in the College of Business at Florida State University. He has worked as a programmer analyst and consultant. Dr. Paradice has published numerous articles focusing on the use of information systems in business contexts. His publications appear in Journal of MIS, IEEE Transactions on Systems, Man & Cybernetics, Decision Sciences, Communications of the ACM, Decision Support Systems, Annals of Operations Research, Journal of Business Ethics, and other journals. His research also appears as chapters in several books.

D. Veena Parboteeah is an Assistant Professor of Information Systems at Eastern New Mexico University. She received her Ph.D. from Washington State University in 2005. Her research focuses on the design of human-computer interface and the effect of culture on IT adoption. Her research has appeared in journals, such as the Communications of the ACM, the Journal of Global Information Technology Management, Information Systems Research, and Journal of Organizational and End User Computing, as well as conferences, such as the Decision Sciences Institute Annual Meeting, the European Conference on Information Systems, the Global Information Technology Management World Conference, and the Hawaii International Conference on System Sciences.

Robert Pavur is a Professor of Information Technology and Decision Sciences at the University of North Texas. He received his PhD in Statistics from Texas Tech University. He has held several officer positions within the Decision Sciences Institute including the position of President of Southwest Region of Decision Sciences. He has published in such journals as the Annals of Operations Research, IEEE Transactions on Reliability, European Journal of Operational Research, Journal of the Operational Research Society, and International Journal of Operations and Quantitative Management. He is a co-author of the textbook Introduction to Business Statistics: A Computer Integrated, Data Analysis Approach published by Thomson Learning Company.

Steve Powell is a Professor at the Tuck School of Business at Dartmouth. His primary research interest lies in modeling production and services processes, but he has also been active in research in energy economics, marketing, and operations. At Tuck, he has developed a variety of courses in management science, including the core Decision Science course and electives in the Art of Modeling, Business Process Redesign, and Applications of Simulation. He originated the Teacher's Forum column in Interfaces, and has written a number of articles on teaching modeling to practitioners. He is the academic director of the INFORMS Annual Teaching of Management Science Workshop. In 2001 he was awarded the INFORMS Prize for the Teaching of Operations Research/Management Science Practice. He is the co-author with Kenneth Baker of The Art of Modeling with Spreadsheets (Wiley, 2004).

Victor R. Prybutok is a Regents Professor of Decision Sciences in the Information Technology and Decision Sciences Department and Director of the Center for Quality and Productivity in the College of Business Administration at the University of North Texas. He received, from Drexel University, his B.S. with High Honors in 1974, a M.S. in Bio-Mathematics in 1976, a M.S. in Environmental Health in 1980, and a Ph.D. in Environmental Analysis and Applied Statistics in 1984. He is a senior member of the American Society for Quality (ASQ) and active in the American Statistical Association, Decision Sciences Institute, Institute of Electrical and Electronic Engineers, and Operations Research Society of America. Dr. Prybutok is an ASQ certified quality engineer, certified quality auditor, certified quality manager, and served as a Texas Quality Award Examiner in 1993. Journals where his published articles have appeared include The American Statistician, Communications of the ACM, Communications in Statistics, Data Base, Decision Sciences, European Journal of Operational Research, IEEE Transactions on Engineering Management, MIS Quarterly, OMEGA: The International Journal of Management Science, and Operations Research. In addition, he is in Who's Who in American Education and Who's Who in America, and Who's Who in the South and Southwest.

R. Kelly Rainer, Jr. is the George Phillips Privett Professor in the Department of Management in the College of Business at Auburn University. He received his Ph.D. in MIS from the University of Georgia. Prior to his studies in MIS, he was a dentist in the US Army. He is the author of numerous articles and books, his current research interests are information security, psychometrics, and end user computing.

Guang Rong is a PhD candidate in the Department of Management at Clemson University, majoring in Information Systems. Her research focuses on knowledge management, project management, trust in online environment, and technology adoption. Her research has been published in Information and

Management, Journal of Organizational and End User Computing, Communications of the Association for Information Systems, and in book chapters.

Sherry D. Ryan is an Associate Professor of Information Technology and Decision Sciences at the University of North Texas. She received her Ph.D. in IS from the University of Texas at Arlington and an MBA from the University of Southern California. Prior to returning to academia she worked for IBM, teaching courses and speaking at national conferences. Her research interests include knowledge management, IT training and human resource issues, and IT investment decisions. Her work has appeared in journals including Journal of Management Information Systems, Decision Support Systems, Information and Management, and DATA BASE.

Kevin J. Shanahan (PhD, New Mexico State University) is an Assistant Professor of Marketing at Mississippi State University. Prior to joining Mississippi State, he was an Associate Professor of Marketing at The University of Texas at Tyler. Dr. Shanahan's research interests include online consumer behavior, advertising strategy, non-profit marketing and ethics and social responsibility. His articles have been published in Journal of Advertising, the Journal of the Academy of Marketing Science, Journal of Business Research, Journal of Public Policy and Marketing, Journal of Business Ethics, Journal of Current Issues and Research in Advertising and numerous other academic journals.

Varadharajan Sridhar is Professor in Information Management at the Management Development Institute, India. He received his Ph.D. from the University of Iowa, U.S.A. Dr. Sridhar's primary research interests are in the area of telecommunication management and policy and Global Software Development. He has published his research work in European Journal of Operational Research, Telecommunication Systems, International Journal of Business Data Communications and Networking, Applied Econometrics and International Development, Information Resource Management Journal, Journal of Global Information Management, Journal of Regional Analysis and Policy, and Journal of Information System Security. He was the recipient of the Nokia Visiting Fellowship awarded by the Nokia Research Foundation. He is Associate Editor of International Journal of Business Data Communications and Networking and is on the editorial board of the Journal of Global Information Management.

Catharina Stoecklin-Serino (deceased) received her PhD in Business Administration (MIS) from Florida State University.

Jason Bennett Thatcher is an Associate Professor in the College of Business and Behavioral Sciences at Clemson University. He received his Ph.D. in Management Information Systems from the College of Business at Florida State University. His work has appeared in MIS Quarterly, Journal of Management Information Systems, Journal of Applied Psychology, and Organizational Behavior and Human Decision Processes.

Joseph S. Valacich is the Hubman Distinguished Professor of MIS at Washington State University. His primary research interests include technology-mediated collaboration, human-computer interaction, mobile and emerging technologies, e-business, and distance education. He is a prolific researcher, with more than 70 journal publications in numerous prestigious journals including MIS Quarterly, Information Systems Research, Management Science, Academy of Management Journal, Communications of the ACM, Decision Science, Journal of MIS, Journal of Applied Psychology, and many others.

Barbara Ross Wooldridge (PhD, Louisiana State University) is an Associate Professor of Marketing at the University of Texas at Tyler. She has been a marketing and sales manager for Universal Safari Tours in Nairobi, Kenya, and a director of marketing for Seychelles Hotels in Mahe, Seychelles. Her research interests are consumer behavior, acceptance of technology, and service quality. She has published in such journals as the Journal of Marketing Channels, The Journal of Consumer Marketing, Marketing Education Review, Corporate Communications, and The Cornell Quarterly.

Thomas J. Zagenczyk (PhD, University of Pittsburgh, 2006) is an Assistant Professor in the Department of Management at Clemson University. Tom's research interests include the employer-employee relationship (psychological contracts and perceived organizational support), abusive supervision, and social influence/social networks in organizations. His work has appeared in or is forthcoming in journals including the Journal of Applied Psychology, Organizational Behavior and Human Decision Processes, Industrial Relations, Journal of Management Studies, Group and Organization Management, Journal of Research in Personality, Journal of Cross-Cultural Psychology, Journal of Applied Social Psychology, Journal of Business and Psychology, and Human Resource Management Journal, among others. Tom has also presented more than 20 papers at regional, national, and international conferences and is a member of the editorial board of the Journal of Business and Psychology.

Xiaoni Zhang is an Associate Professor of Business Informatics at the Northern Kentucky University. She received her Ph.D. in Business Computer Information Systems from the University of North Texas in 2001. Her research interests include business intelligence, Web usability, e-commerce systems, enterprise systems and mobile technology. She is a member of Decision Science Institute and Association for Information System. Her publications appear in IEEE Transactions on Engineering Management, Communications of the ACM, International Conference of Information Systems, and Information & Management.

Index

A

B

C

L

M

N

O

P

Q

R

S

T

U

V

W

X

Breinigsville, PA USA
07 April 2011
259405BV00008B/1-62/P

9 781609 605773